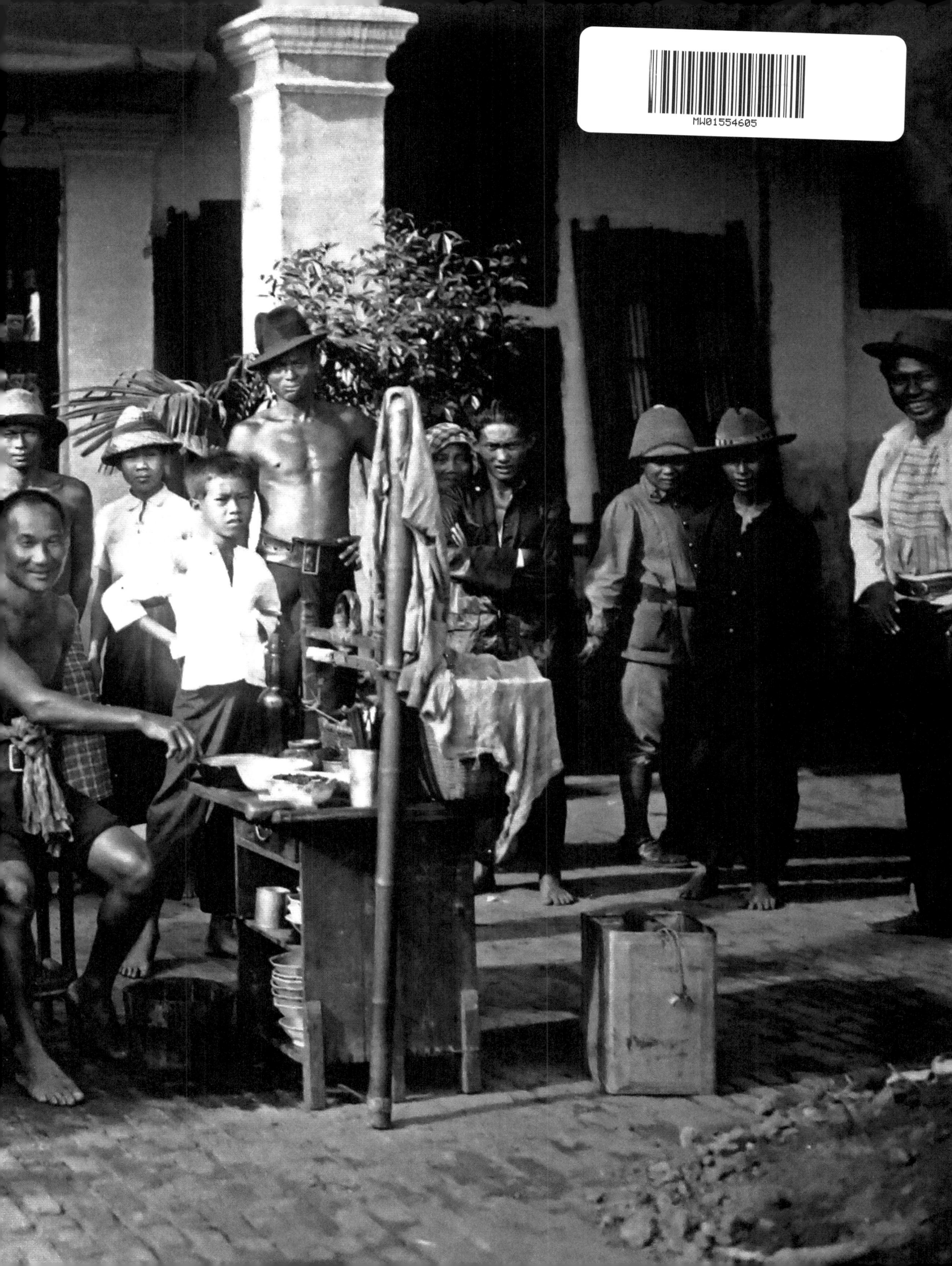

"I know many people will think I'm weird—I'm just a young adult. Why [am I] so interested in old things from many years ago that many teenagers aren't interested in? I think it's my personality and my hobby, as well.... Yes, I like the past—I don't know why. It's hard to explain."

Srin Sokmean. Conversation with Rosa Ellen.
"Let's Say I'm Conservative." 7 Days. *Phnom Penh Post*. August 23, 2013.

"With the joy of a world-wanderer who has at last discovered something picturesque, I unslung the battered relic of a camera which I had purchased in Saigon. Immediately, as though I had unslung a machine gun, every man, woman, and child in Pailin fled for cover."

A Beachcomber in the Orient. Harry L. Foster. John Lane,
The Bodley Head. London. 1923.

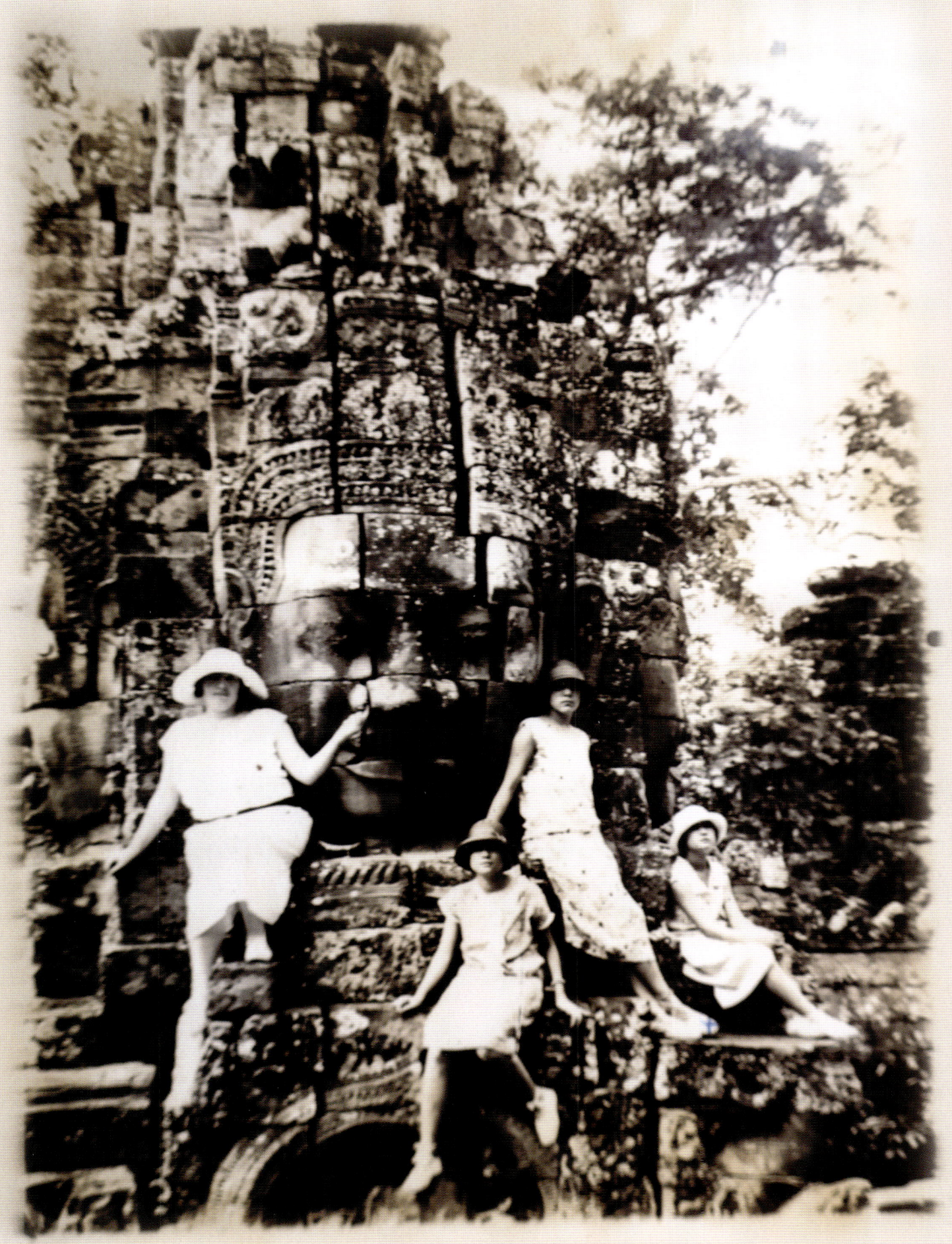

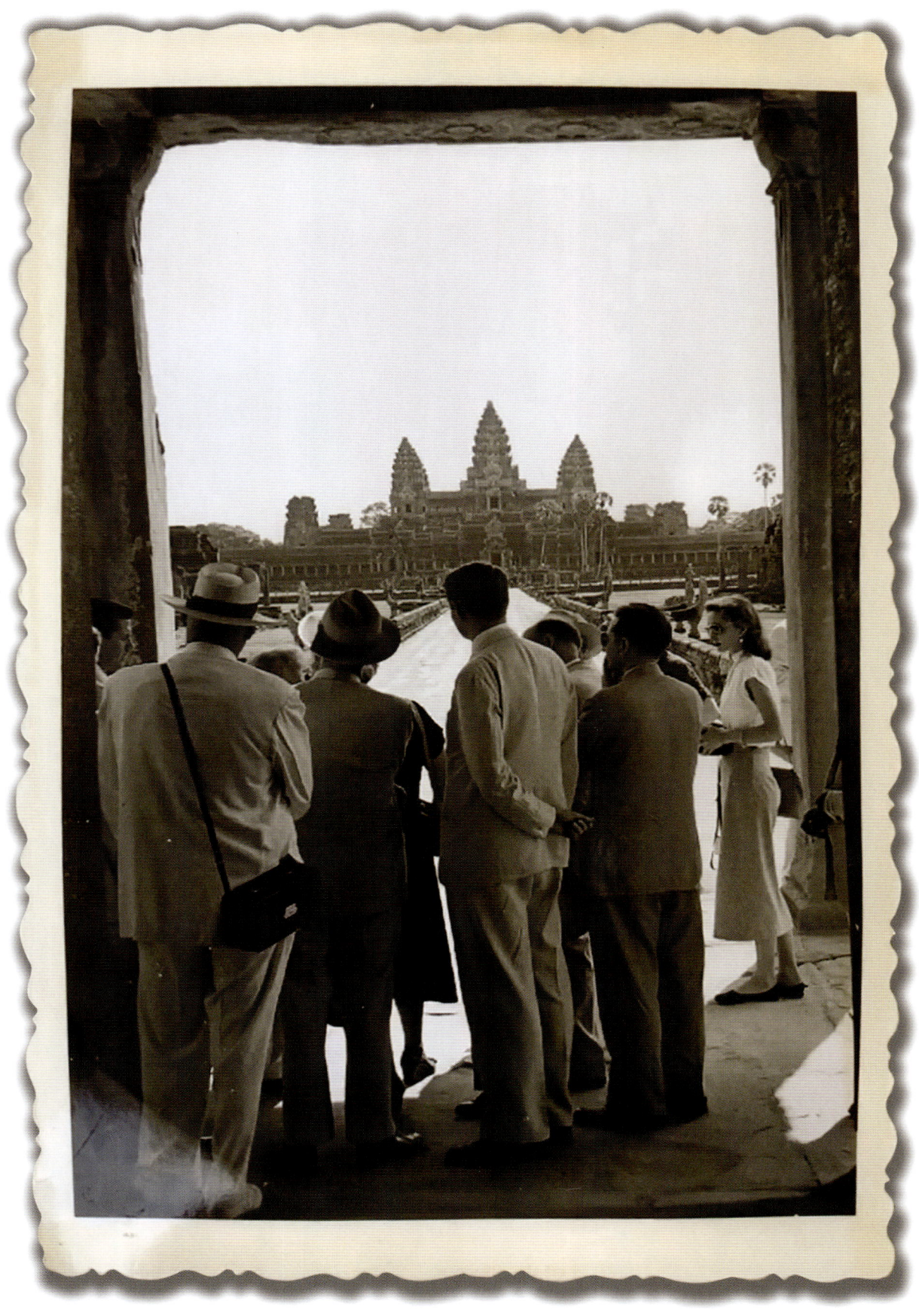

ABOVE: **An unknown group visiting Angkor Wat.** Siem Reap. ca. 1959. Photographer unknown. Author's Collection.

PAGE 1: **Four women at the Bayon temple.** Siem Reap. 1928. Photographer unknown. Philippe Damas Collection, Singapore.

PHOTOGRAPHY *in* CAMBODIA

1866 to the Present

NICHOLAS COFFILL

TUTTLE Publishing

Tokyo | Rutland, Vermont | Singapore

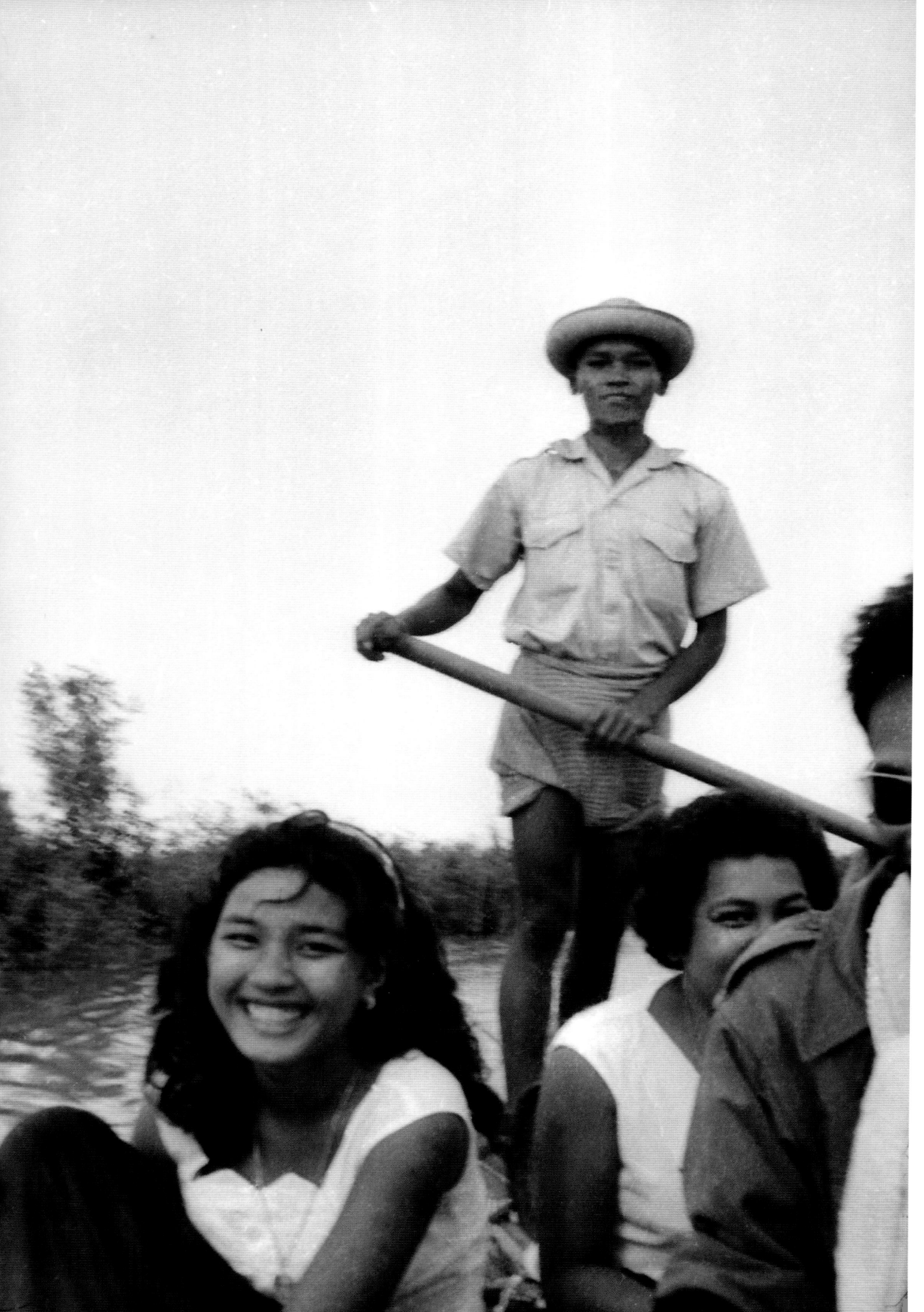

contents

The Theater of Photography	6
Cambodia Seen Through the Photographer's Eye	10
1860–1906 The Reign of King Norodom	24
1906–1927 The Reign of King Sisowath	52
1927–1941 The Reign of King Monivong	76
1941–1955 The Reign of King Sihanouk	94
1955–1970 The People's Socialist Community	112
1970–1975 Lon Nol's Khmer Republic	146
1975–1979 Democratic Kampuchea and the Khmer Rouge	174
1979–2000 The Republic, the United Nations, and the Kingdom	188
2000–2020 King Sihamoni and the Age of Plenitude	210
Cambodian Photographers: Where Were They?	240
The Photographers	244
The Collections	246
Acknowledgments	249
Index	252

OPPOSITE: **Friends on a boat.**
Battambang. 1961. Michael Vickery.

The Theater of Photography

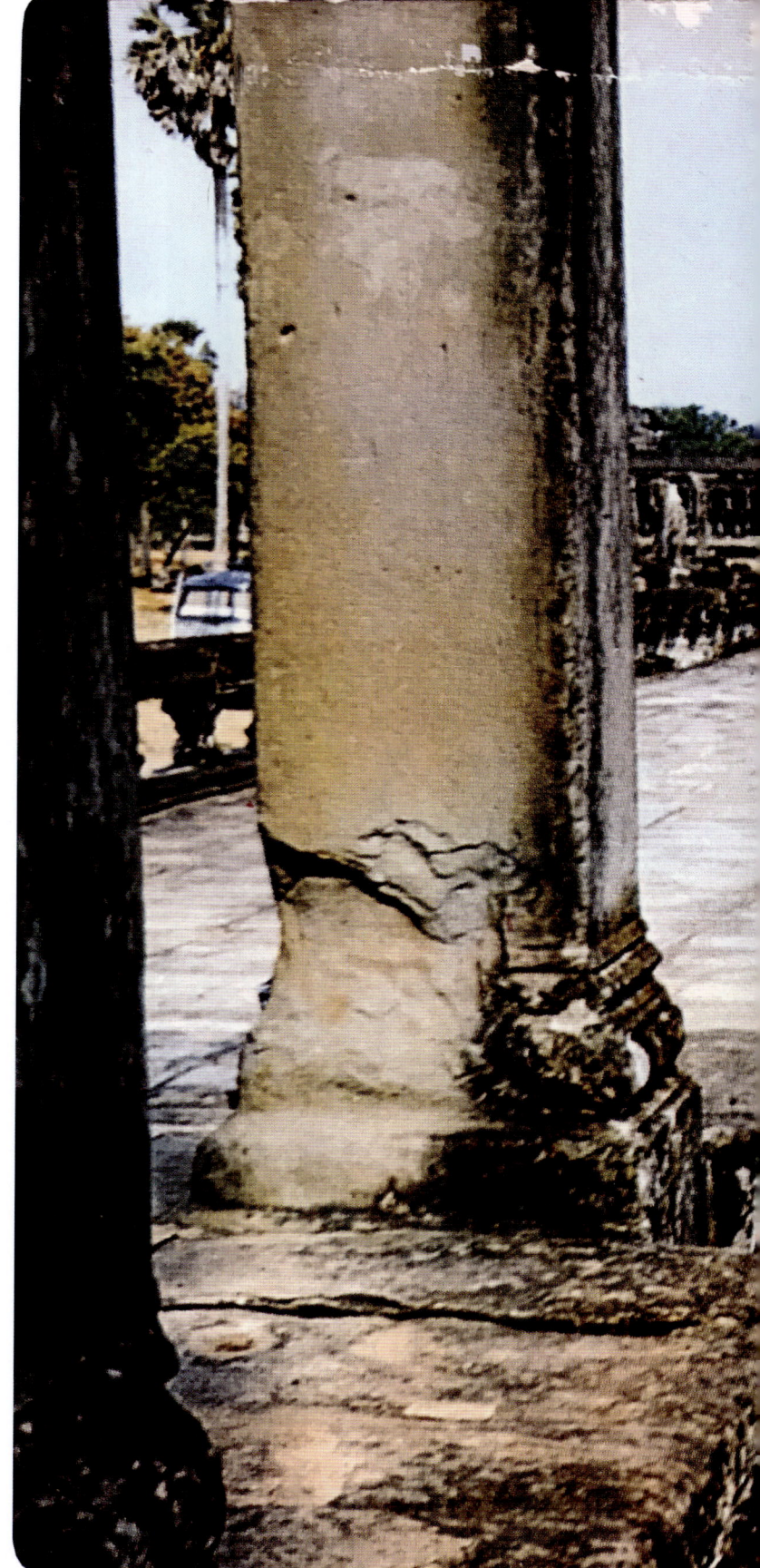

There have been many books written about the history of Cambodia. One popular genre focuses on the country's classical past, where plans of the various Angkorian monuments combined with lavish illustrations are presented either as engaging "coffee table" books or smaller, handy tourist guides revealing the latest archaeological discoveries. They encourage constant updating and reprinting. Another genre focuses on Cambodia's modern history, where the personalities of monarchs and ministers, generals and dictators predominate, as they wrestle with shifting geopolitical circumstances and local rivalries in their attempts to shape their country's future. The later body of work focuses on popular culture or everyday life, and this is precisely where the photographic record comes to the fore. Most photographs, no matter how well "managed," contain enthralling details and oddities and multiple ways of "reading" their content. A studio portrait not only captures the likeness of its sitter but is also a source of further information obtained by observing and understanding the choice of the clothes they are wearing, their jewelry, hairstyles, and hats, and the array of furniture, backdrops, and props that are equally a part of the display. And then there is the pose, which, whether intentionally or not, often reveals a great deal about the sitter's aspirations, social status, occupation, and indeed Cambodian society in general. Ultimately, it is photography's very accessibility—a photograph can be looked at by anyone, either cursorily within the blink of

Dancers performing inside Angkor Wat. Detail of postcard. ca. 1960. Photographer unknown. Darryl Collins Collection, Siem Reap.

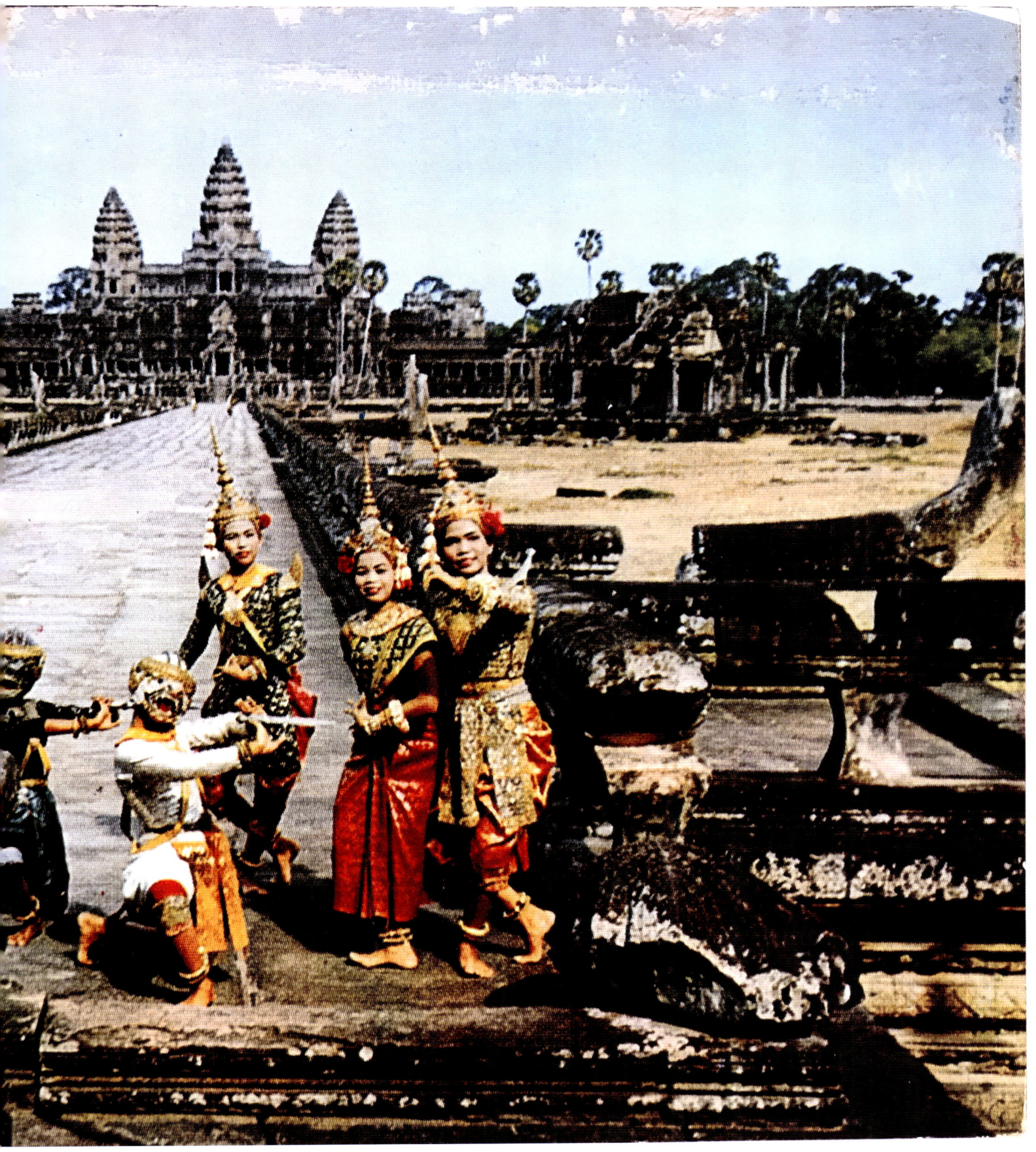

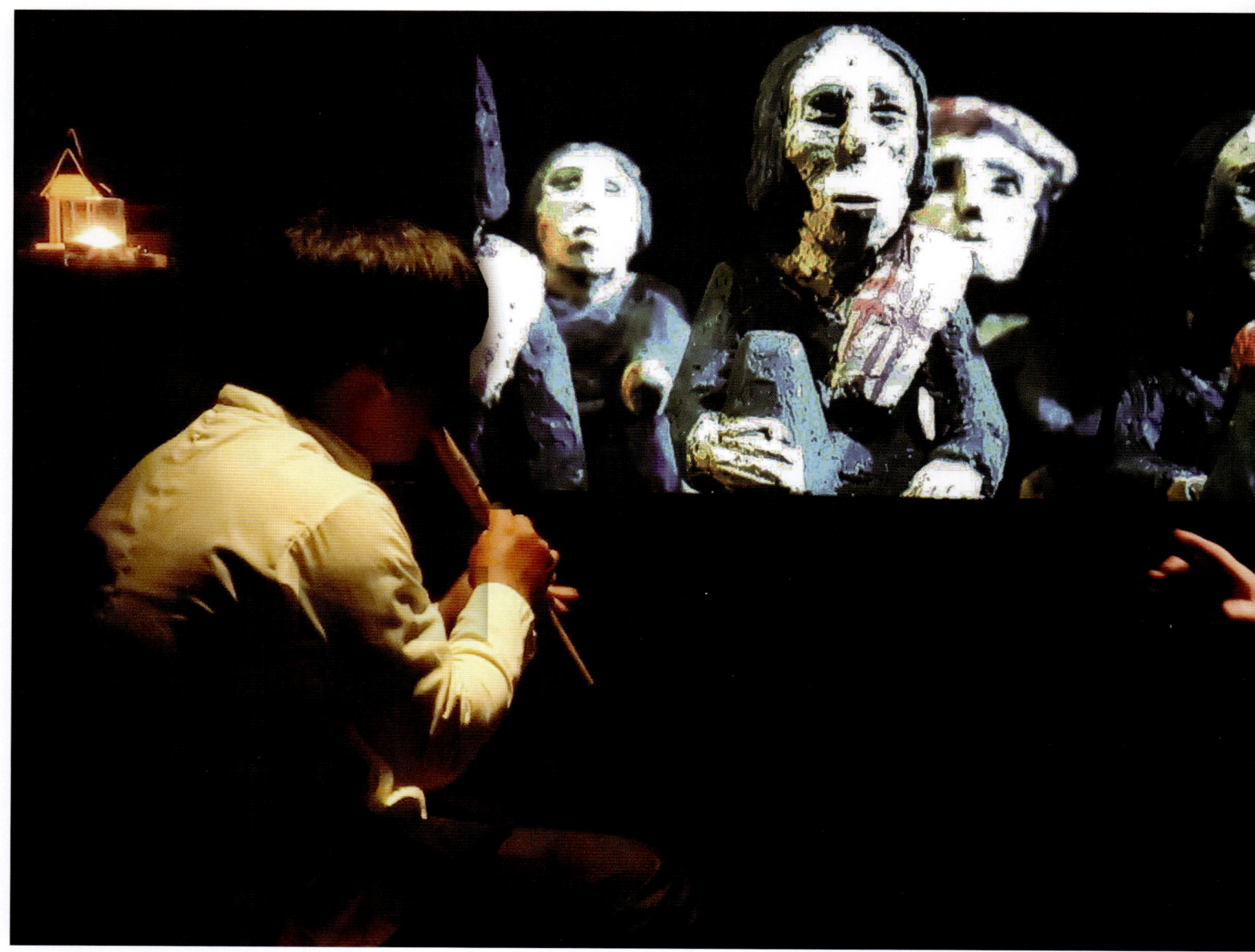

an eye, or with detailed forensic obsession, that makes it such a seductive medium to introduce and explore Cambodia's past and present in an appealing and insightful manner.

The project began six years ago when I was working in Cambodia with my business partner Jon de Rule. Both of us came from a theater background, with Jon later working in events while I branched into museums. With the strategic advice of Bhavna Soni Shivpuri, we established a for-profit theater company in Siem Reap supported by a wide investor pool from across Asia. Our focus was the creation of a compelling repertoire of mixed media and shadow and spoken theater—theatrical TED Talks if you will—creating stories about the Angkorian monuments and Cambodia's modern history. For the shadow theater, we created a traditional *sbaek touch* leather puppet troupe under the leadership of a local puppeteer Sorn Soran. Serendipitously, I was browsing through the local Monument bookstore when I discovered Jim Mizerski's *Cambodian Captured*, which presented the extensive black-and-white photographs of the pioneering explorer-photographers John Thomson and Emile Gsell, dating back to the 1860s. I asked Jon if he thought these could make the basis of a creative work, and he instantly gave the idea his full support.

For the next six months, I visited the library of the Center for Khmer Studies in the beautiful grounds of Wat Damnak, where I found a wealth of archival material in academic journals, photocopies of doctoral dissertations, old magazines, and beautiful art books. I was lucky, too, that the 10th Angkor Photo Festival and Workshops was in full swing, with outdoor exhibitions, nightly projections, and engaging workshops. Combined with online research and the constant advice and direction from the art historian and Khmerophile Darryl Collins, within months I had accumulated enough material about individual photographers and events in Cambodia's modern history to create an engaging one-hour show.

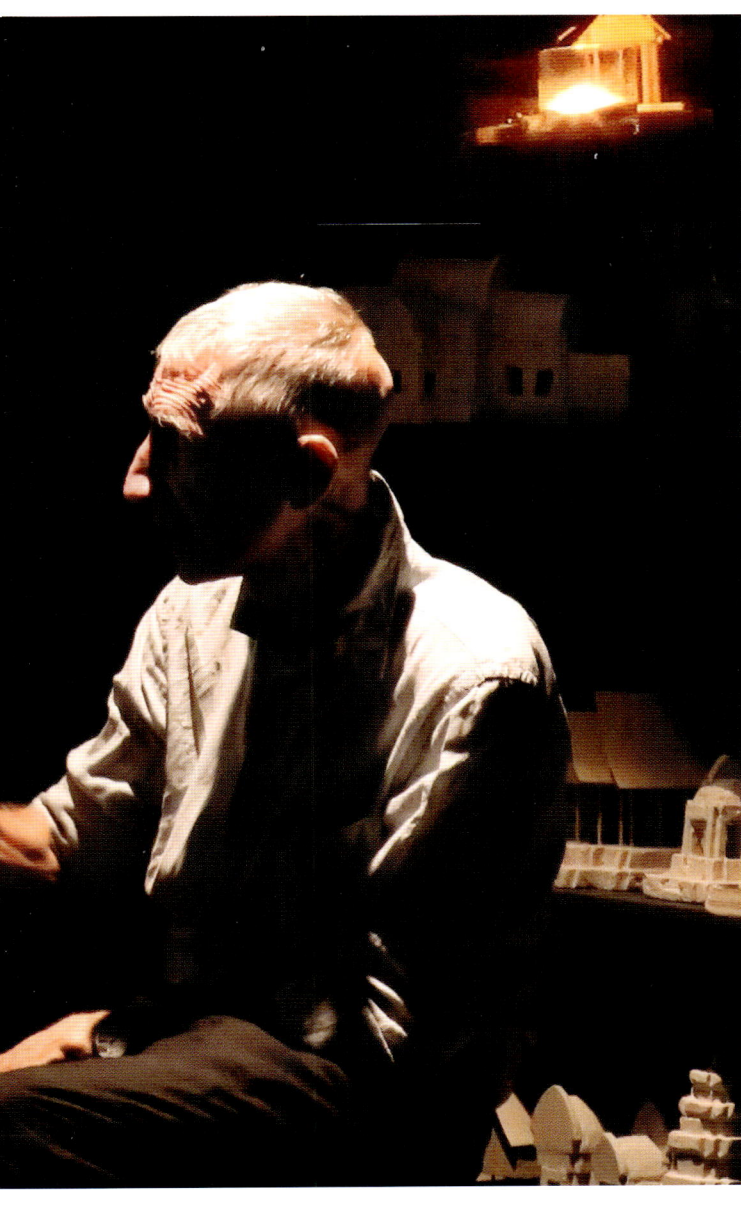

Performance of *Snap! 150 Years of Photography in Cambodia*. Bambu Stage, Siem Reap. March 2017. Ros Ray. (far left, flautist Nem Sengheang).

Turning that compilation of photographs into an evening's entertainment was Jon's great skill, and with the mechanical and carpentry talents of Chen Pheakdey and the adroit handling of the light-and-sound mixing desk by Paoem Bunsang, a show began to take form. We experimented with different presentation techniques using projection cloths of different textures and translucency, as well as *kabuki* drops, raised cut-outs, and an old-fashioned epidiascope to add visual intrigue. The final layer was to add live sound effects, and ultimately, the masterful playing of a handmade bamboo flute by Nem Sengheang. His haunting tunes, played to photographs of Panh Rithy and Mak Remissa's take on the Khmer Rouge, added great emotional impact to the evening.

So, this book is, in many ways, a memorial to those theatrical days at Bambu Stage, but it is not a mere transcription of the evening. Research over the following years has revealed the complexities and richness of Cambodian photography that I had not discovered. Even thirty one-hour-long shows could do no justice to its epic range and complexity.

A Way of Selecting

In putting together this book, I have focused my research on materials available online from international public libraries and archives, as well as private collections across Southeast Asia. I also traveled to Phnom Penh many times, spending numerous hours at the National Archives of Cambodia, the National Museum of Cambodia, and the Documentation Center of Cambodia (D-Cam). The theater-show had eight scenes, with each segment presenting images that enabled us to build an overarching dramatic narrative. Transposing the show into a book format has enabled the inclusion of a wider range of photographers, though each photographer is now represented by fewer images, sometimes just the one. I have also created a stronger chronological format. Whether some photographers are "the best" to include, I cannot say, but I do believe that the selection reflects the changing historical and social influences that have driven Cambodia's modern history, a history that began, coincidently, 150 years ago, in the 1860s, with the simultaneous expansion of French colonialism across Indochina and the introduction of the new craft of photography. Ultimately, the legacy of the Bambu Stage show lingers, and the idiosyncrasy of theater abounds. That explains, sprinkled through the selection of photographs, a fin de siècle chocolate box card, a burst of images by women photographers in the 1950s and 1960s, and the decision, in the final section relating to the twenty-first century, to include a montage of a chirpy youngster against the backdrop of a Dutch windmill and a panoramic dental X-ray. The choice, quite literally, is mine.

Cambodia Seen Through the Photographer's Eye

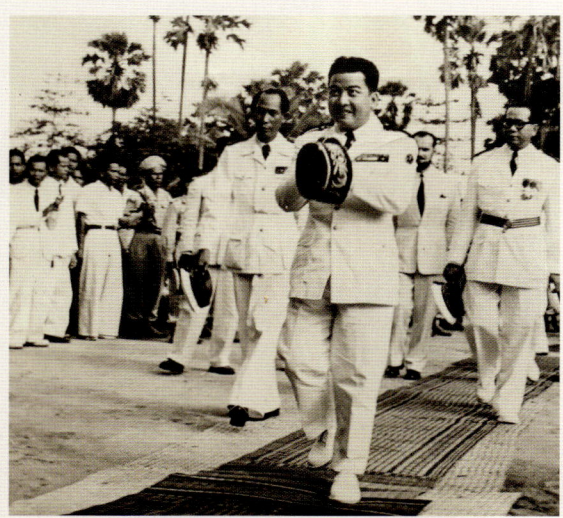

Sihanouk as democrat. 1952.

To begin to understand Cambodia's photographic story, it is best to look at it through the complex geopolitical forces that shaped the country's modern history. Contrary to popular opinion, Cambodia was anything but an isolated backwater during the period we are considering. Many important global issues of the past 150 years have affected the country: the waning power of hereditary monarchy; the expansionist forces of nineteenth-century European colonialism; the period of decolonization after World War II and the attendant effervescence of national independence; destabilizing Cold War rivalries between Western capitalist alliances and their communist counterparts from the 1950s through to 1989; the intervention of the United Nations in the early 1990s, which for a brief period "normalized" Cambodia's fractious political environment; and, finally, the digital revolution and the re-emergence of Chinese influence through its economic power. *Photography in Cambodia* is both a documentation of these transformative global forces, reflecting in tone and content their localized impact, while also allowing a more intimate glimpse of everyday life as seen through a uniquely Cambodian lens.

Cambodia's Political Periods

From 1860 through to the beginning of World War II, Cambodia was ruled by three consecutive kings who represented a conservative kingdom that accepted French colonial control of their affairs, initially with reluctance, but with growing acquiescence. The symbolic spiritual center of the kingdom, the magnificent temple of Angkor Wat and its surrounding monuments, was appropriated by the French as a jewel in their "civilized" empire, while becoming an alluring destination for foreign adventurers, archaeologists, writers, itinerants, and thieves. They brought their cameras to record their journey and "capture" the prized temple.

World War II disrupted both the geopolitical and regional status quo. During these times of change, there was one eighteen-year-old man, a timid prince, who came of age after his coronation, and through deft political maneuvring brought the colony to peaceful independence in 1953 (see "Sihanouk as democrat," 1952; above left). The young King Sihanouk's exuberant character and ability to lead rather than reject modernity and change, was a startling departure from previous kings, and a perfect fit for a new nation looking to embrace the spirit of independence in the postwar era of decolonization and nation building. Photography was the medium of the age, and Sihanouk played to the lens. As cameras and film went through a technological revolution, they allowed different kinds of photographs to be taken. Lighter cameras and more responsive films gave photographers an "agility" they previously did not have, and with it there was a changing attitude to camera craft and the types of photographs that were taken. If we take, for example, the photographs of two teachers, Michael Vickery and Marie-Françoise Châtel, both working in Cambodia as the country transitioned through independence in the 1950s and early 1960s (see Marie-Françoise Châtel, "Chhay and friend," 1963; right), one notices they were using close-ups and spontaneous interaction with their subjects to capture naturally "awkward" poses. There is a sense that their cameras were moving with their subjects, reflecting both the capability of new camera technology and new ways of thinking about how a camera could be used to engage with the world around them.

These technological advances and shifting perspectives do not mean that Cambodian photography is necessarily any "better" after independence. Each photograph is an image bound within the cultural, social, and technological constraints and opportunities of its time. Even the most creative photographers working today are not automatically making better photographs than their predecessors; camera skills, personality, and "the moment" are still the prerequisites for producing a memorable image. But while architecture and the arts flourished during Sihanouk's reign, the country's nascent democracy was sorely tested by factionalism and political infighting, a microcosm of the larger geopolitical struggles of the Cold War. In neighboring Vietnam, the French were fighting a rear-guard action against a communist-led insurgency, with America stepping in, initially to stem the losses but subsequently taking up the fight when the French withdrew from Vietnam in 1954. The "American War" was an "open" war, with journalists, photographers, and television crews given cover by the American military to document the confrontation between East and West. As the conflict spilled over into Cambodia, local photographers answered the call (see Kuoy Sarun, "Cambodian solders carry a wounded comrade past a machine gun post," 1974; lower right).

In April 1975, both Phnom Penh and Saigon fell to communist forces, but while the Khmer Rouge were fiercely Maoist, the newly liberated Vietnamese followed a Soviet ideology. They did not make good neighbors. The Khmer Rouge abolished all aspects of modern Cambodian life and the infrastructure that supported it. Photography still played a role, however, to promote the achievements of the revolution. The Khmer Rouge's meticulous use of photography to document the prisoners in the secret Toul Sleng (S-21) prison is one of the regime's most disturbing material legacies (see page 186).

After the 1979 liberation of the country by the Vietnamese army, Cambodia was destitute, and since cameras were generally unaffordable we see the return of small-scale commercial studio photography. A few NGOs were allowed into the country but most were clustered along the Thai border managing the major refugee exodus. There were, however, photographers present within Cambodia to record the struggle of its people for survival.

With the collapse of the Soviet Union in 1989, funding for Vietnamese liberation dried up and the country moved to a market-driven economy. It was an historic occasion when the 1991 Paris Peace Agreement was signed and the United Nations stepped in to manage refugee resettlement and multiparty elections—the first free election in over forty years. Travelers started to trickle back. Photography thrived as journalists returned to the country to cover the complex sociopolitical maneuvers, and tourism, with its attendant holiday snapshots, slowly began to recover. Over the next thirty years, Cambodia's economy flourished and photography expanded in breadth of technique, application, and style.

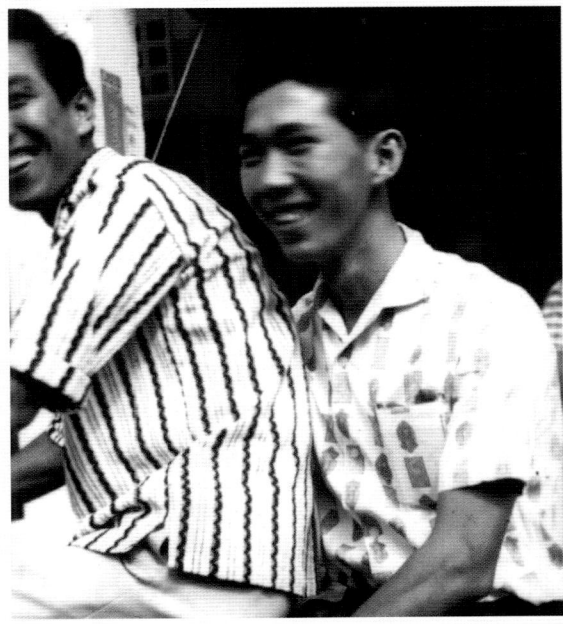

Chhay and friend. 1963. Marie-Françoise Châtel.

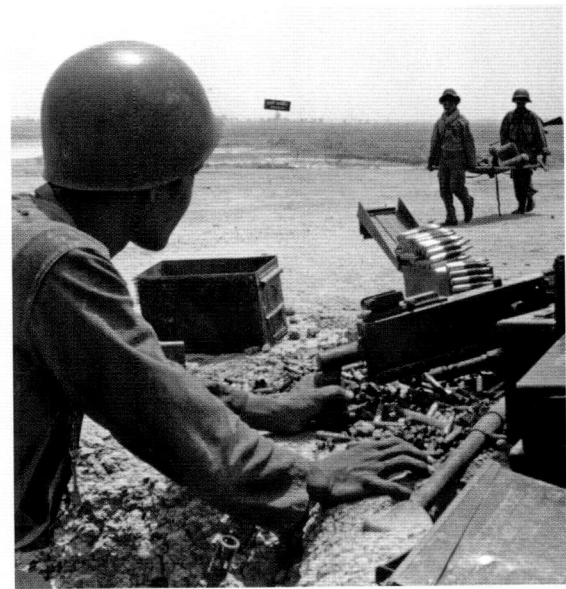

Cambodian solders carry a wounded comrade past a machine gun post. 1974. Kuoy Sarun.

Photographers and Their Work

It is also important to note that the different types of photographers—explorers, colonial adminstrators, military photographers, writers, archaeologists, news photographers, expatriates, and private travelers—did not always focus on their "expected" subject matter in predetermined ways. This is what makes their work so difficult to represent, since it often goes against the flow of contemporary events and the larger geopolitical circumstances of the day. But it is also what makes this body of work so revealing to explore. While each chapter of this book begins with a short historical introduction, readers are still in a position to make their own observations about pictorial similarities and differences across decades, even centuries, of social, political, and cultural change in Cambodia.

Which brings us to the different genres of photography that occur in this book, particularly "peoplescapes," landscapes, portraiture, still life, and photojournalism. Finally, I want to reflect on how three subjects in particular—the monument of Angkor Wat, Khmer Rouge identity photographs, and the presentation of Cambodian royalty—have weighed heavily on the consciousness of a uniquely Cambodian photographic identity.

Peoplescapes

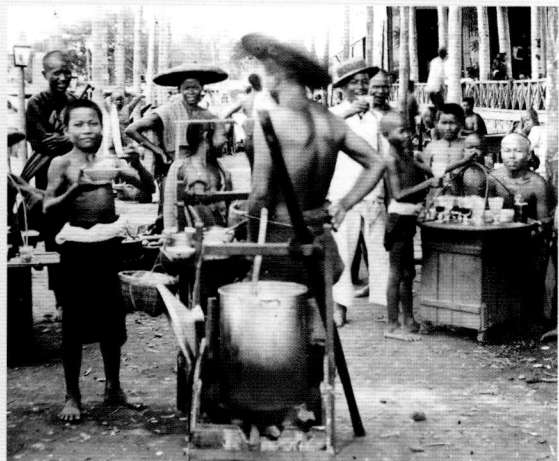

Food hawkers at the Pochani Pavilion. Detail. ca. 1912.

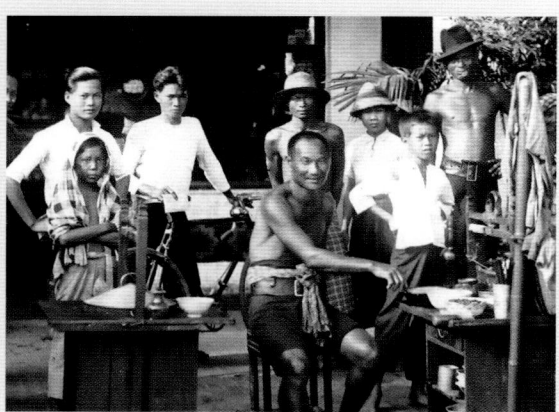

Chinese food hawker. Detail. 1924. George Groslier.

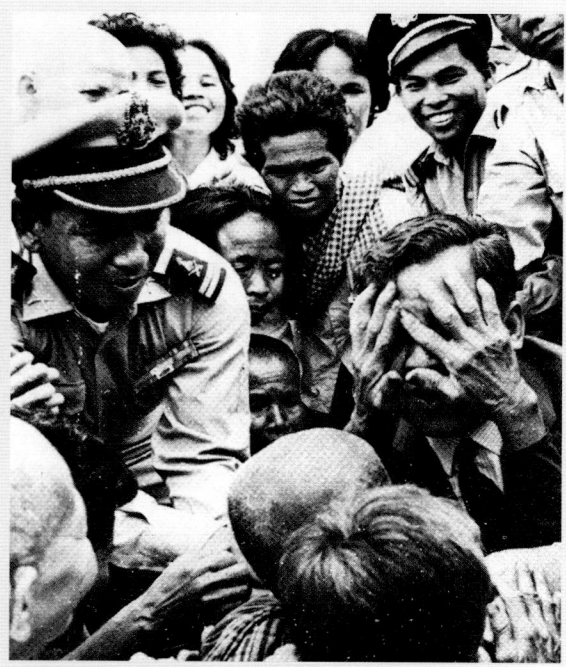

"When the eye-sight is failing...." 1968.

Unlike impressionism in French painting, where a mass of individuals disappear into a blur of rapid painterly brushstrokes, photography stilled the moment, capturing the crowd as a conglomerate of individuals, each pursuing their path through life. The young, the skinny, the poor, the government servant, the street vendor, and the itinerant rural worker—all are given space, facial expressions, and clothes that we can scrutinize, including hats, equipment, and the tools of their trade. Some are aware of the photographer, some are not. Framing this hub of activity is the structure of the built environment—streetlights, roadside stalls, commercial signage, shopfronts, and telegraph wires—which collectively constitute the diverse elements we call a cityscape.

The anonymously photographed "Food hawkers at the Pochani Pavilion" (ca. 1912; see top left) and George Groslier's "Chinese food hawker" (1924; see middle left), appear outwardly similar, but if we look at the clothing and hats that the people are wearing, we see they are worlds apart, separated by the tumultuous events of World War I (1914–18).

Massed street crowds that were drawn out to witness royal funerary and coronation parades and important Cambodian religious festivals are common subject matter, where the focus is centered either on the monarch or the Buddha. A similar line could extend to the enormous output of photo-documentation during the Sangkum period—a kind of Cambodian form of nationalist socialism which lasted from 1955 to 1970. Prince Sihanouk engineered huge rallies where crowds assembled in their masses to see him open glittering new additions to the infrastructure of Phnom Penh—sports complexes, theaters, universities, and concert halls. With "When the eye-sight is failing" (1968; see lower left), Prince Sihanouk's magnetism has pulled both people and camera towards him. The crowds are willing participants of the photographed spectacle, while the photographer's low, close framing completely obscures any contextual environment. It is pure cinema.

A decade later, after the Khmer Rouge had seized power, we come across a group photograph of an army unit of "child soldiers" (1977; see page 180). No doubt a propaganda photograph, we can nevertheless see in every face the burden of an oppressed and war-weary childhood.

Then again, in 2010, surging crowds at the Phnom Penh Water Festival turned into a deadly stampede. Hundreds were killed on the bottleneck of the narrow Ko Pich bridge across the Tonlé Sap. While there were many images posted on social media of compressed, trapped youth, Pha Lina's "Remnants of Koh Pich bridge" (2010; see page 218), taken some hours later, shows the curved deck of the suspension bridge littered with shoes and discarded plastic water bottles as police and civilians walk through the sobering scene. The festive crowd is absent, but knowing the tragic circumstances, the photograph is no less compelling.

Landscape Photography

Photographs of peasants toiling away, either transplanting seedlings in verdant rice fields or harvesting abundant grain from yellow pastures, is the ubiquitous fodder of tourist postcards. It is good for business and for political propaganda, too, as with the Khmer Rouge's "Happy and proud" (1977; see page 177). There is, however, a more complex view of Cambodia's landscape to be discovered beyond this innocuous imagery.

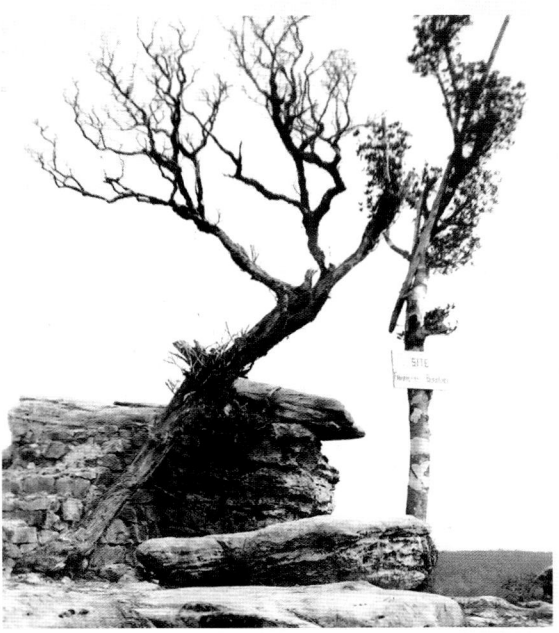

Bokor lookout, Kampot. ca. 1923–24. George Groslier.

For nineteenth-century colonial photographers, rural scenes of the Cambodian countryside do not appear to have been of particular concern. Perhaps the mercantile spirit of the colonial enterprise and an unfamiliar climate clouded a more thoughtful contemplation of an agrarian lifestyle that supported the vast majority of Cambodia's population. In 1920, George Groslier succeeded in designing and building a new museum in Phnom Penh. It was opened with suitable festive pride by the governor-general, Albert Sarraut. Four years later, building on his achievements, Groslier was touring the country, capturing with his camera all manner of aspects of Cambodian life. Venturing into the mountainous south of the country, he photographed "Bokor lookout, Kampot" (ca. 1923–24; see top right). The rickety wooden bridge and the small sign nailed to the tree trunk do not attenuate the impact of the unknown precipice beyond. The tortuous shape of the windblown tree and its sublime aspect pushes the boundaries of Groslier's interests in all things cultured and authentically Khmer. He captured in this landscape a metaphor for the spirit of Cambodia, something more dynamic and perilous than the usual colonial trope, which typically projected an image of Cambodians as a "docile and lazy race." In the same decade, Martin Hurlimann's "Forest in west Cambodia" (1929; see page 91) continues this darker, more threatening theme. The tracks of the photographer's automobile are clearly marked on the forest's dusty road and draw us back upon the journey just taken. It is the end of the dry season, the trees are losing their leaves, the oppressive, searing heat palpable through the naked branches.

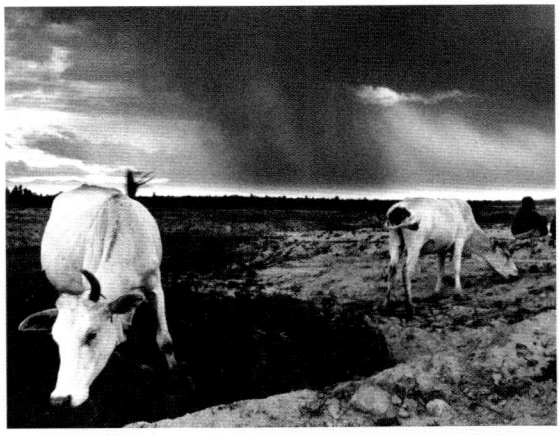

Storm approaching, Poipet. 1972. Colin Grafton.

Moving forward a half century, Colin Grafton's "Storm approaching, Poipet" (1972; see right), holds a dual tension between humanity and landscape. In the foreground is a pastoral idyll as beasts graze, minded by their resting cowgirls. They watch the tempestuous monsoon storm as it sweeps across the distant horizon, a powerful metaphor for the decade of crippling war engulfing the country.

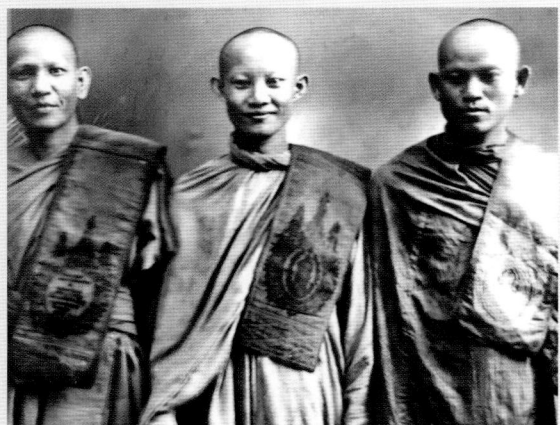

Three monks. 1924. George Groslier.

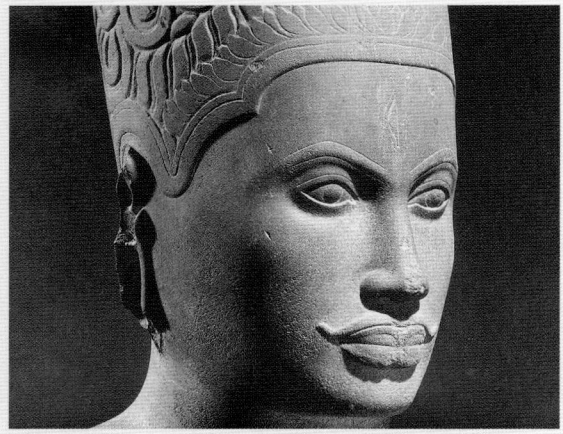

Harihara. 1965. Photographer unknown.

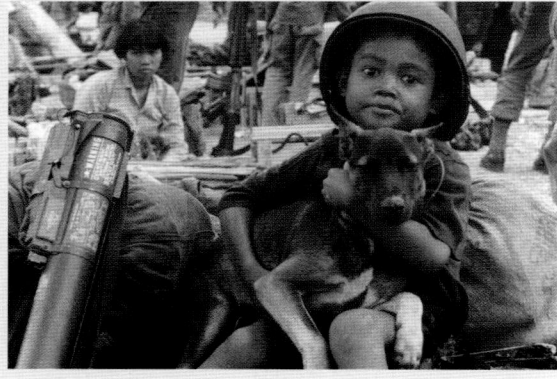

A boy and his pet. 1975. Thong Veasna.

Portraiture

When the first two photographers in Cambodia, John Thomson and Emile Gsell, passed through Phnom Penh, they took numerous images of the extended royal family. While the subjects were shot within the secluded confines of the palace, both photographers sought to emulate prevailing studio techniques by appropriating available furnishings, such as chairs and side tables, to steady the subjects for the long exposure times. Textiles were also used to create a sense of luxury, and royal regalia was used as props to represent their subjects' entitlement. A "social distance" is evident, with the subjects most often in full figure view and a generous space left between them and the edge of the photographic frame. It was all very "salon" and academic. Gsell's "Portrait of Chhun" (1866–73; see page 38), however, is a startling departure, not only because it tightly frames his head and shoulders but because Gsell was prepared to accept Chhun's demonstratively less than compliant demeanor. In contrast, sixty years later, George Groslier's enchanting "Three monks" (1924; see above left), is unique in capturing a cheerful expression from a profession known for its outward appearance of reserve and reflection. Groslier, the first Frenchman to be born in Cambodia, was a cultural advisor to many a French administrator and was renowned for his affinity with, and support for, the Cambodian people.

In the aftermath of World War II, the stand-up "formalism" of the prewar colonial era gave way to a more informal engagement between photographer and subject, no doubt facilitated by the availability of lighter roll-film cameras and the youthfulness of the photographers. When we look at the wildly candid photographs in the early 1960s by Michael Vickery and Marie-Françoise Châtel, as mentioned previously, we cannot but be overwhelmed by the vivacity and persuasive affection between the photographers and their student companions, something only hinted at in Groslier's portrait thirty-five years earlier.

By contrast, the careful illumination that highlights the facial features of "Harihara" (1965; see middle left), by an unknown École française d'Extrême-Orient (EFEO) photographer, makes this one of the great formal portraits of Cambodian photography. The careful modulation of light across the neck and cheeks gives a sensuous human quality, while the sharper shadows beneath the eyebrows, nostrils, and lower lip highlight the original sculptor's skill in carving an idealized yet living image. The camera's slightly upwards point of view accentuates the stature of the god while adding an authoritative weight to the towering miter of entangled locks.

During the first half of the 1970s, the Khmer Republic's war footing was documented by a host of Cambodian and international photographers, all of whom worked in a dangerous and unpredictable environment. War photojournalism was at its zenith. Therefore, Thong Veasna's "A boy and his pet" (1975; see left) stands out with its aching vulnerability as the child cuddles his pet surrounded by military activity. Over his shoulder, mid-distance, the young girl echoes their helplessness. By contrast, Pierre Toutain-Dorbec's "Laughing Khmer Serai soldier" (1981; see page 193) caught a rebel soldier who had just stolen rice rations from a refugee camp. The bravado of his laugh is tinged with a cynical disregard for the plight of his fellow Cambodians, dispossessed of their homes and livelihood.

A quintessential aspect of Cambodian photography is the small family studio serving mainly Cambodian clients for rites-of-passage photography, particularly weddings. Archives like the Documentation Center of Cambodia (DC-Cam), and projects such as the Reyum Institute of Arts and Culture's *Seams of Change* exhibition and Charles Fox's "Found Cambodia" digital archives, have discovered an unending flow of private collections. These caches have miraculously survived the widespread devastation of war and the social convulsions of the 1970s. The diversity of imagery, the age range and fashion styles reflect wildly differing responses to the camera, from the conservative formality of rural folk in front of a painted backdrop of an idealized home, such as "Ros Sithat and her husband Nhem Noeun's marriage photograph" (ca. 1970; see page 1670), to photographs taken prior to 1975 by Khmer Rouge cadres depicting families wearing the ubiquitous uniform of the revolution in "liberated" zones where small photo businesses must have still been running to develop and print the film. A more optimistic note is struck by urban youth confidently posing in the latest fashions, as in "Yanny in denim" (1989; see above right). The tenacity of these small photo studios to survive and then to re-emerge so quickly after the fall of the Khmer Rouge reflects the emotional and commemorative value of a photographic keepsake, a sentiment that is still present today.

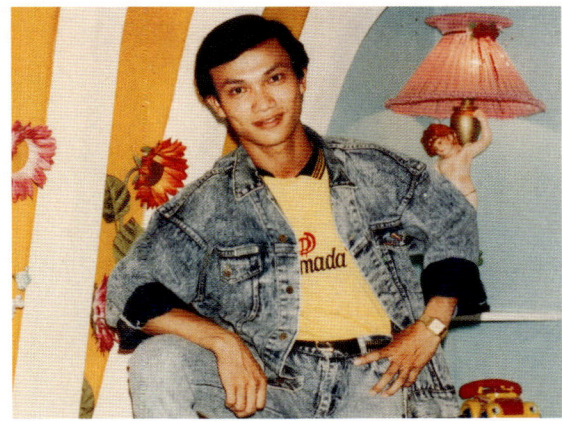

Yanny in denim. 1989.

In its original condition, Dani Planas Labad's image of a defaced photograph of Son Sen, "The defacing of Son Sen's photograph" (2007; see right), displayed at the infamous Toul Sleng (S-21) prison, would have been a straightforward portrait. The image gains resonance through its wilful vandalizing by multiple visitors who were seeking some form of retribution. Could not this "new" image now be considered an object with multiple authors?

Later, in the twenty-first century, a young Cambodian photographer struggles with the shifting daylight as he tries to reproduce the Italian Amendeo Modigliani's post-impressionist painting *The Boy* from 1910. Pech Sophea's nonchalant "Self-portrait" (2016; see page 230) captures not just the structure and mood of Modigliani's famous portrait but bathes it with the melancholy of his nation's past.

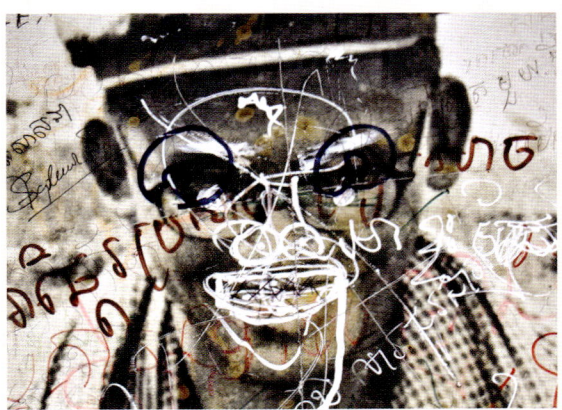

The defacing of Son Sen's photograph. 2007. Dani Planas Labad.

Still Life

Considering the thousands of archaeological artifacts that make up their collections, photographs of "things" could properly be considered the domain of the École française d'Extrême-Orient (EFEO) and the National Museum. But if we were to put aside the act of photography as a means of neutrally recording and cataloging the quotidian, then still life has a slim, but diverse representation in Cambodia's photographic record.

Adhémard Leclère's "Office of the mayor" (1889–1903; see page 41), is a dark meditation on colonial administration. By placing his camera on a sideboard, or similar, Leclère offers us an unusual "furniture's point of view," lower than a human's standing perspective. After World War II, as Mimijac Palgen was traveling on Highway 6 between Phnom Penh and Siem Reap, she stopped off at Skuon and took two photographs of a tabletop display of the township's infamous local delicacy, "Street café serving fried spiders" (1946–62; see right). Both an object of fascination and repulsion for travelers unfamiliar with the local cuisine, Palgen has nonetheless

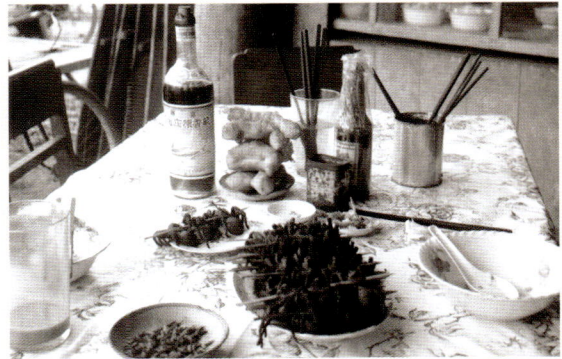

Street café serving fried spiders. 1946–62. Mimijac Palgen. MimiJac Palgen Memorial Collection, Distinctive Collections, Arizona State University Library.

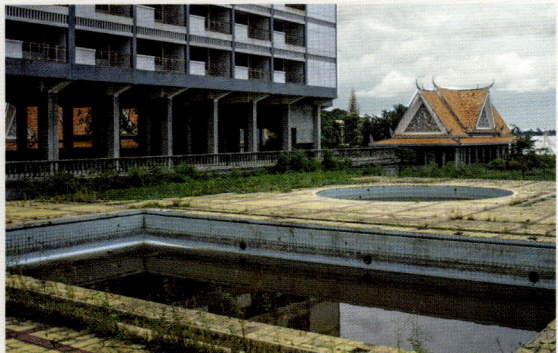

Hotel Cambodiana. 1984. Jean-Noel Wetterwald.

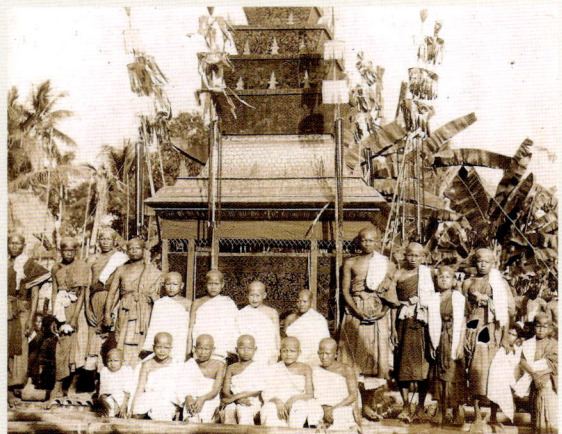

A funerary procession in Strung-Treng. 1903. Albert Tajasque.

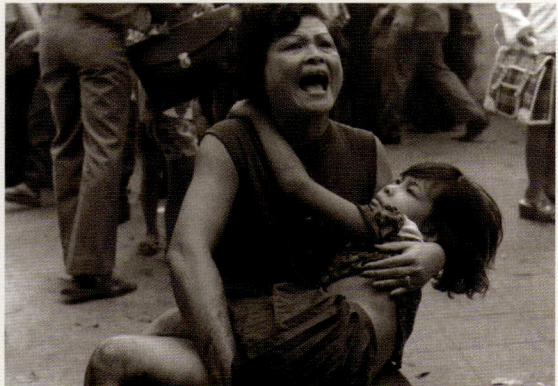

Mother holding her dying child. 1975. Sou Vichith.

framed the spiders within a complete culinary and cultural context, including cutlery, crockery, and condiments, a finished glass of milky tea, and glimpses of the restaurant's furniture and views to the street beyond.

By contrast, "Cadeau de Joie Bijoux Mekong" (1966; see page 137) is pure advertising photography, where the product, an expensive woman's bracelet and pearl necklaces, are given "social value" with the addition of the little ribbon-wrapped box at the apex of the cascade. Now the message is clear: this is an act of gift-giving, of seduction, and the intended audience is not the woman wearer but the giver, the potential male buyer. The soft fabric backdrop subtly enhances the temptation. Finally, Jean-Noel Wetterwald's "Hotel Cambodiana" (1984; see above left) is not a meditation on things but on place, and the very absence of all those things—deck chairs, umbrellas, bamboo-clad poolside bar, and hotel guests in swimming costumes—that during the Khmer Rouge's five-year rule denoted the depravity of foreign luxury. Although photographed four years after the Khmer Rouge had been ousted from the capital, the hotel's neglect highlights the fact that for a traumatized population the necessities of basic sanitation, adequate food, and survival were more important than a poolside cocktail.

Photojournalism

Albert Tajasque's "A funerary procession in Strung-Treng" (1903; see left) is a unique suite of eight glass-plate photographs documenting the burial of a provincial elder in Stung-Treng. It is the earliest and most complete sequence of photographs by a photographer that focuses on a singular event, from setting the scene with the principal characters through to the preparations and then final burning of the funeral pyre. By the time Cambodia gained independence some fifty years later, in 1953, photojournalism had come into its own. The postwar Japanese domination of refined, interchangeable lenses on lighter 35 mm cameras enabled photojournalists to become more actively engaged with their stories. They took compelling images under the most difficult of circumstances. This had unintended consequences, as many cameramen and journalists were killed across the multiple fronts of a war that engulfed the region.

On the domestic front, Cambodian photographers working for the Royal Cambodian Armed Forces (FARK) used their vantage point to get the best shots of the mutual admiration between Prince Sihanouk and his subjects as he toured the country. They also recorded the army's military bases and campaigns against antiroyalist and communist insurgents. The Cold War and its proxy battlefronts in Vietnam, Laos, and Cambodia, was to have a devastating impact on the country. As Lon Nol ousted Sihanouk as head of state and formed a new republic in 1970, these incursions of foreign fighters working with local Khmer Rouge insurgents escalated into full-blown warfare.

Photographers, both foreign and local, recorded the trajectory of unfolding events: the wanton destruction of the civil war and acts of almost nihilistic violence and unimaginable cruelty. Cambodian photographers became war photographers. Many images captured the civilian toll, such as Sou Vichith's "Mother holding her dying child" (1975; see left). Other images by photographers Pen, Kuoy Sarun, and Chhor Vuthi focused on the frontlines of combat. A raft of international journalists and photographers worked alongside their Cambodian colleagues. Often they had previously covered the adjacent Vietnam War and other regional conflicts. They brought their previous experience as war photographers with them and shared this with their local comrades.

After the collapse of Lon Nol's republic, the Khmer Rouge placed an almost total ban on foreign journalists coming into the country. Pro-Maoist photographers were allowed, but on highly scripted tours. A similar policy was adopted by the People's Republic, which succeeded the Khmer Rouge, but photographers like Craig Buck and Pierre Tourtain-Dorbec managed to slip across the Thai border to photograph the various factional fighters, such as "Laughing Khmer Serei soldier" (1981; see right). After the collapse of the Soviet Union in 1989 and the reconstitution of the republic into a market-orientated State of Cambodia, the occupying Vietnamese army returned home, leaving the Cambodian People's Armed Forces (CPAF) in control. These events were photographed by Jeff Widener, while Bruce Sharp covered the slow socioeconomic recovery of Cambodia as the country embraced an open economy.

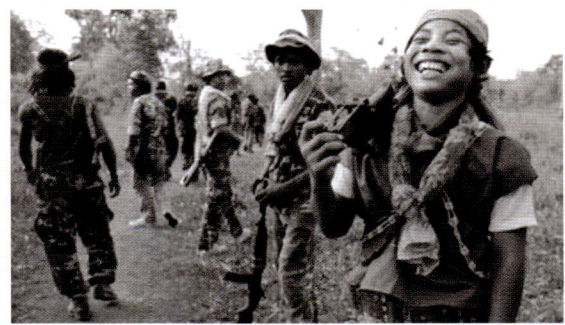

Laughing Khmer Serei soldier. 1981. Pierre Tourtain-Dorbec.

Meanwhile, the Paris Peace Agreement of 1991, brokered between proxies of the warring parties, enabled the United Nations to move in, managing its largest ever and most comprehensive endeavor in nation building. Tim Page was there to cover the events. In his photograph "Helicopter dust" (1993; see right), the cowering crowds are protecting themselves from swirling dust kicked up by the ascending helicopter containing the politician Prince Norodom Ranariddh (son of Sihanouk), a reminder of the traditional power distances that are embedded in the country to this day.

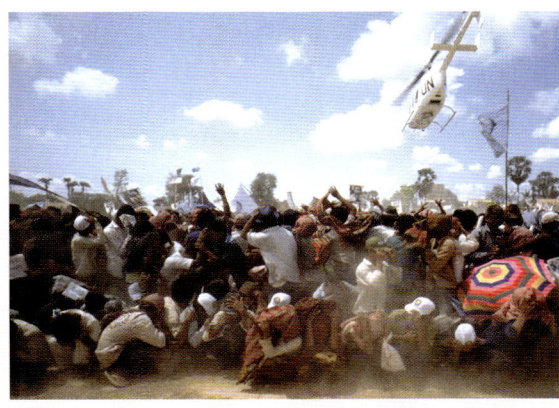

Helicopter dust. 1993. Tim Page.

As the complicated urban politics of the 1990s played out, with different factions jostling for power and legitimacy, the original leader of the Khmer Rouge, the ageing Pol Pot, was under house arrest, having been deposed by his own lieutenants. When he died of illness, David Longstreath was there to record his makeshift funeral (see "The body of Pol Pot," 1998; page 209). It marked a symbolic conclusion to a tumultuous century of Cambodia's history.

In the 1990s, the media was unshackled from socialist control, allowing photographers like Pha Lina, Meng Kimlong, and John Vink to focus on domestic issues, which became the hallmark for an emerging demand for basic human rights; the symbolism of Page's "helicopter" photograph was never so prescient.

National Identity

Within the history of photography there are iconic images. Some have earned their status by recording breathtaking human achievements or catastrophic events. Others have focused on powerful political figures or those of the entertainment world with their sparkling celebrity status. Sometimes a photograph can capture "the spirit of the time" simply by observing the common man as he goes about his daily business; his pose, the clothes he is wearing, or even the hat on his head can become an iconic representation of a era. Or it might be an accessory like a walking stick, a cigarette, or a handgun—they all have a story to tell.

If we consider images that are emblematic of Cambodia, it would surely be a view of the 900-year-old Angkorian monument Angkor Wat, backlit at sunrise. Annually, millions of tourists take almost identical photographs of this scene, which are then uploaded onto various social media platforms. In complete contrast to this enduring architectural wonder as a symbol of national identity, would be the thousands of individual black-and-white photographs of Khmer Rouge prisoners taken in the late 1970s, showing them trussed and stunned, unaware of their imminent execution. It is only natural that impressive monuments from a classical past or spectacular landscapes become identified as symbols, or cultural signifiers, of a country's national identity. That something as ephemeral as a collection of identity photographs has become so closely linked to a representation of the country in the public imagination is highly unusual. In this respect, Cambodia is unique in that two iconic representations of the country should be so opposite in their materiality and emotional tenor.

The Khmer Rouge Photographs

When the Khmer Rouge fighters took Phnom Penh in April 1975, a Democratic Kampuchea was proclaimed. It was, however, to be anything but. According to party ideology, a thousand years earlier it was exploited peasants who had heroically built the great city of Angkor. The elite had polluted that dream, causing Angkor's downfall. Now was the time to wipe the slate clean, to start afresh, so Angkar—the secretive political wing behind the Khmer Rouge army—divided Cambodian society into the lionized "old people," comprising mainly the rural peasantry, and the detested "new people," the educated and Western-influenced urban population. The new people were relocated by truck and train to the countryside and used as forced labor to rebuild Angkar's vision of Cambodia as an agricultural utopia. In April 1975, within weeks of taking the capital, Angkar set up a secret prison inside the abandoned Chao Ponhea Yat High School at Toul Sleng, in the outer southwest of the city. In typical Angkar manner, proper names that referred to familiar geographical locations were erased, and the prison was anonymously codenamed S-21. In 1976, a group of young Khmer Rouge cadres were sent by boat to Shanghai for training in mapping, surveying, and photography. Upon their return, some were assigned to S-21.

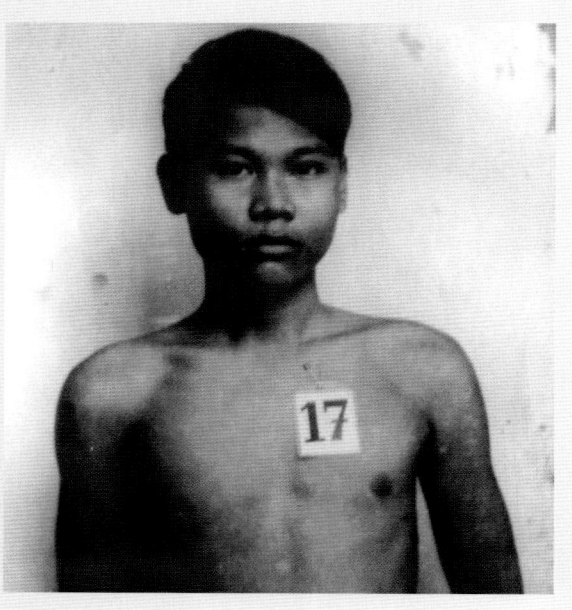

Prisoner 17. 1978.

In the first few years, S-21 prisoners were mostly the urbanized "new people"—white-collar professionals, teachers, government servants, artists and musicians, and ex-republican soldiers. The prisoners were interrogated, tagged with an identity number, and photographed, mostly framed as a full head-and-shoulder shot (see "Prisoner 17," 1978; left), but occasionally a profile image, an iron brace being sometimes used to steady their heads. Some photographs capture a prisoner fully standing, while in others shackles, ropes, or ties can be seen securing the subject. The young photographers did their job silently and diligently. To make mistakes in their work or to talk to prisoners—even to ones they may have recognized—would have meant a terrible retribution by their camp commander, Brother Duch, alias Kaing Guek Eav (1942–2020). The photographers unloaded the film from the cameras at the end of the day, developed the negatives, and made prints to show to Brother Duch to prove the process of confession had been completed. The size of the prints varied. As materials were in short supply, the photographer Nhem En cycled around Phnom Penh, ransacking abandoned commercial studios for film, photographic chemicals, and paper. After being photographed, the prisoners were again blindfolded and returned to their cells for further interrogation or else trucked under the cover of dark to the nearby rice fields to be bludgeoned to death, their bodies thrown into large pits and buried.

In 1978, Angkar became increasingly paranoid about both the United States Central Intelligence agency (CIA) and Soviet spies infiltrating Cambodia, a situation that was exacerbated by continual border disputes with the People's Army of Vietnam (PAVN). Information from previous interrogations, whether truthful or not, was used in an ever-increasing wave of purges. Top political cadres down to extended village families were caught in the distrustful net, along with anyone from the eastern provinces who was suspected of being tarnished by Vietnamese influences.

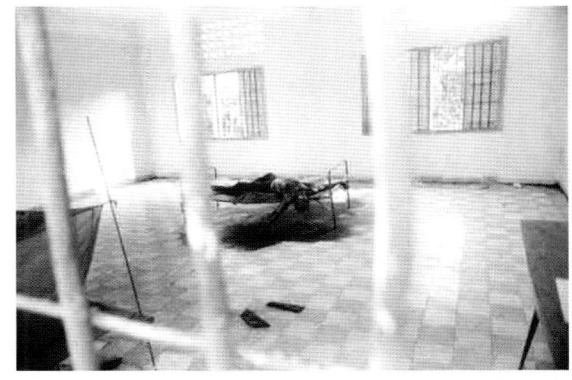

S-21 prison. 1975. Ho Van Tay.

When the Vietnamese army finally overran Phnom Penh in January 1979, they came across the recently abandoned prison. Two photographers embedded in the army, Ho Van Tay and Dinh Fong, took photographs of the ghastly remains (see "S-21 prison," 1975; above right). The new authorities set about turning the prison into a memorial. The identity photographs were reproduced and pinned to large boards. By March 1979, they guided foreign delegations through the site, and from July 1980 they allowed ordinary Cambodians to enter, searching for lost family members, loved ones, and friends. Over time, photographs of Khmer Rouge prison guards and officials accumulated a stream of scribbled and scratched graffiti, gouges, and defacement.

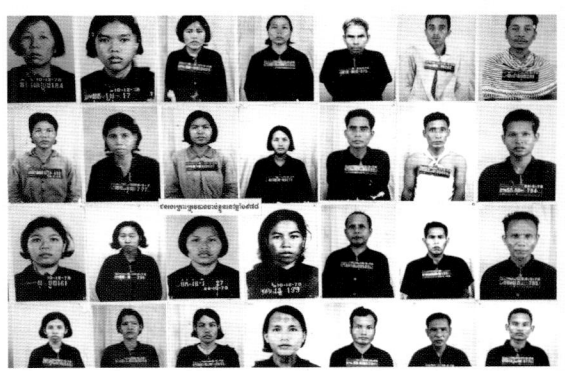

S-21 prisoner ID photographs. 1985.

For both Cambodians and tourists, a visit to the S-21 prison, officially known as the Tuol Sleng Genocide Museum, is a significant rite of passage. On private and government websites, the prison museum is invariably featured on the list of the top ten "things to do" for visitors exploring the capital. Viewing the massed ranks of the identity photographs of political violence is a sobering and riveting experience. Over 5,000 photographs of the genocide have survived (see "S-21 prisoner ID photographs," 1985; right). In 2009, the archives were recognized as a world documentary heritage of international significance and were inscribed on the UNESCO Memory of the World (MOW) Register.

Cambodia's photographs from the Khmer Rouge period simultaneously belong to a number of overlapping genres: the "neutral" category of identity photography, compounded with the darker genre of execution photography, and analytical police mugshots employed to identify suspects of crime (the first use of photography to methodically record prisoners in Cambodia was by Joseph Ferdinand Perrot in 1923). The photographs can also be the material evidence of a national memory and memorialization process to inform younger generations who have no recollection of these dark times. Lastly, they are portraits. We can see individual personalities and observe distinctive details—the characters of "real people," as it were—looking directly through the lens towards us. But they are not willing participants; they are fearful, bewildered, confused, and violated.

Above all, the Khmer Rouge images provide forensic evidence of heinous crimes and murderous deeds. Since 1992, D-Cam has collected and digitized the photographs and other documents of the regime, and

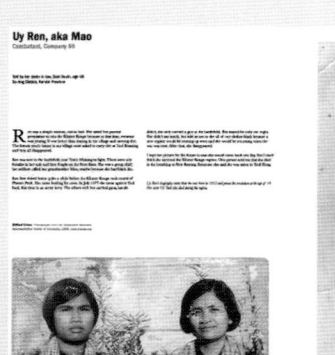

Uy Ren aka Mao. DC-Cam.

passed them on as evidence to the United Nations-sponsored Extraordinary Chambers in the Courts of Cambodia (ECCC). From 2009 to 2015, the evidence was used to prosecute leading Angkar cadres of crimes against humanity. During the long trial period, DC-Cam organized tours to Phnom Penh by various villagers from the countryside to view the proceedings of the trials and gave explanatory lectures about the trials' complicated proceedings. Temporary free-standing display panels of photographs were assembled, with substantial explanatory notes in the Khmer language, inviting the villagers to review and make comments about their own experiences during those troubled times. DC-Cam also designed photo essays. One of them tells "the stories of men and women who joined the Khmer Rouge revolution in the 1960s and early 1970s, [showing] that they and their families faced the same struggles and hardships as their victims, [while] pointing to our common humanity" (see "Uy Ren aka Mao," DC-Cam (above left). The photographs continue to follow their own trajectory. In 2018, DC-Cam issued a series of interactive audiovisual CDs with accompanying booklets that were sent to schools and libraries across the country, hoping to inform a younger generation with no direct experience of the Democratic Kampuchea regime.

Angkor Wat

The monument of Angkor Wat is a representation of the kingdom's glorious past and a symbol of national identity. Dedicated to the Hindu god Vishnu, work on the temple began during the reign of King Suravarman II (r. 1113–50) and was completed in 1220. Being the symbolic center of an idealized Hindu mandala state, the temple is admired for its massive scale, the astronomical codes embedded in its elegant proportions, and the grand mythological and historical stories carved along its sandstone galleries. For centuries, successive Cambodian kings made pilgrimages to Angkor Wat to acquire a divine legitimacy to their rule. In later years, they were accompanied by the French résident-supérieur of the day, seeking their own endorsement from this mystical site.

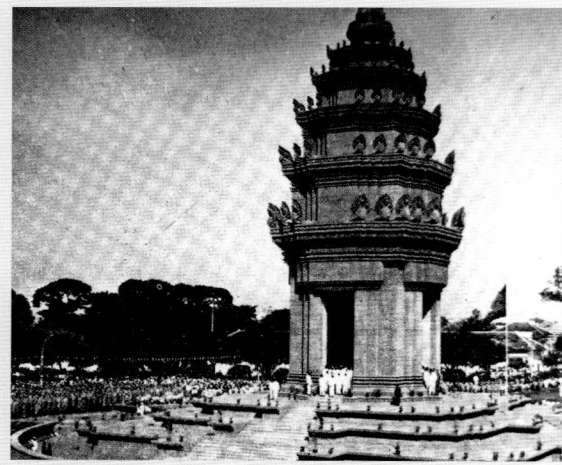

A crowd ... around the monument. 1967.

After Cambodia gained its independence from France in 1953, King Sihanouk commissioned a monument to celebrate the achievement. Designed by the architect Van Molyvann, it was a massive tiered concrete tower based on the proportions of Angkor, and sited in the middle of a wide, tree-lined boulevard in Phnom Penh. It opened to great fanfare in 1962 and quickly became a favorite photographic backdrop for young couples and families visiting the capital (see "A crowd ... around the monument," 1967; left).

Sihanouk traveled to Angkor multiple times in the 1950s and 1960s, escorting visiting dignitaries on personalized tours, motorcading around various Angkor monuments, and in the evenings watching performances of classical ballet and sparkling fireworks ignited from the monument's elevated terraces. His favored guests included the French president, Charles de Gaulle, who visited in 1966, and the international icon of style, Jacqueline (Jackie) Kennedy, in 1967.

In between these celebrity highlights were the regular visits by ordinary Cambodians, who bussed or shared motorbikes with their families to the temples. Their visits typically culminated with informal picnics on the grass under the shade of the surrounding forest or eating at small open-air cafés. While souvenir stalls catered to the need for a memento, few Cambodians could afford a camera, so when they returned to the nearby Siem Reap or their hometown, a studio group portrait in front of a painted backdrop of the temple was the solution.

During the postindependence years, a logo of Angkor Wat was used in advertising to promote almost any kind of product from beer to matchboxes. It also appeared on the record sleeves of popular singers and was used on official postage stamps and paper currency. A place of pilgrimage for kings and commoners alike, Angkor appeals across the political divide, with the temple appearing in silhouette on the country's flag since 1863 as a symbol of national identity that has been embraced by political partisans of every hue, from royalist autocracies, right-wing republics, and parliamentary democracies, to the staunch communist regime of the Khmer Rouge.

During the tumultuous first year of the Khmer Republic (1970–75), the September 1971 edition of the eponymous *Khmer Republic Illustrated Monthly Magazine* published a six-page article on the temples. The article began with an aerial view of Angkor Wat followed by these words about their mortal enemy: "The Cambodian government sadly announces to its people and the world at large that the Vietcong C-40 front had occupied the temples of Angkor Wat on June 11, 1970." The article included four photographs taken by Lai Dat Huong, a defector from the Vietnamese army, with two colleagues nonchalantly relaxing in front of the monument (see "Lai Dat Huong," 1971; above right). From a propaganda perspective, it seems unusual that the military-controlled republic would release such damning evidence of the fact that they had lost the nation's most valued icon. Perhaps the unthreatening posture of the soldiers in the photograph ameliorated the republic's concerns for the safe custody of the ruins. Or perhaps they thought that advertising their loss would galvanize their own troops to rally to the cause and repel the invaders. In a following edition, a photograph of a headless guardian figure, "One of the prasats on the Bakheng" (1972; see middle right), was accompanied with a more belligerent headline, "Angkor Wat Must Be Saved!"

When the communist Khmer Rouge won full control of the country in 1975, the temple ruins were not demolished, but rather were held in great esteem by the secretive Communist Party. Seen through their eyes, the temples were a potent symbol of how the Cambodian masses could be marshalled into building reservoirs and canals to create verdant rice fields and abundant harvests just as they had supposedly done in Cambodia's ancient and illustrious past. One simply had to substitute the temples with modern socialist factories to bring the narrative up to date.

After the Vietnamese ousted the Chinese-backed Khmer Rouge and installed their own government, the temple ruins remained closed to uninvited outsiders for another decade. In the interim, the image of Angkor Wat was appropriated by family-run photography studios and montaged into the background of clients' portraits. This would have been done in the darkroom rather than physical cutting together two separate photographs. The temple, in this instance, is repossessed as a symbol of recovery and the longing for a renewed national identity. A more blatant use of Angkor is a photograph titled "Unity Under the Flag of the National Liberation Front" on the cover of the new republic's picture magazine, *People's Republic of Kampuchea*, in which six heroic figures representing a cross-section of

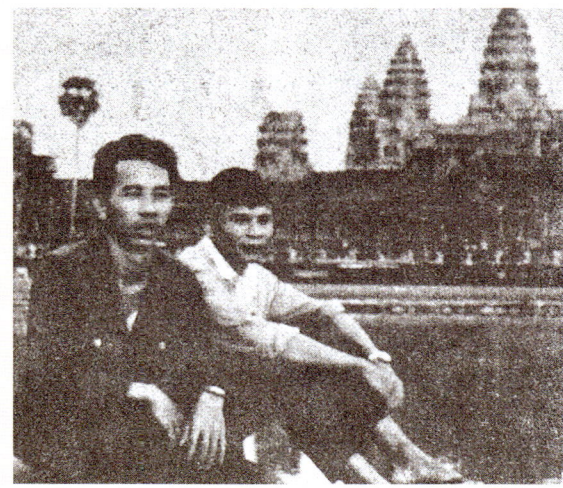

Lai Dat Huong. 1971.

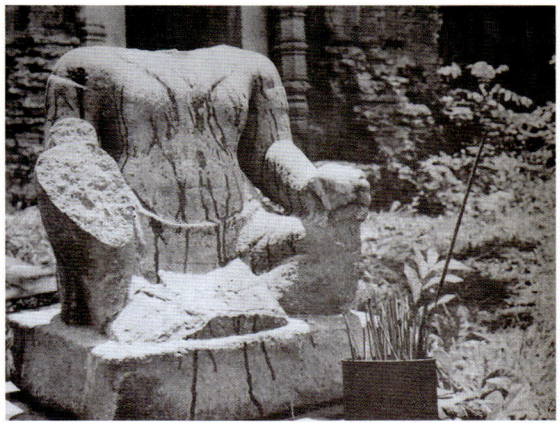

One of the prasats on the Bakheng. 1972.

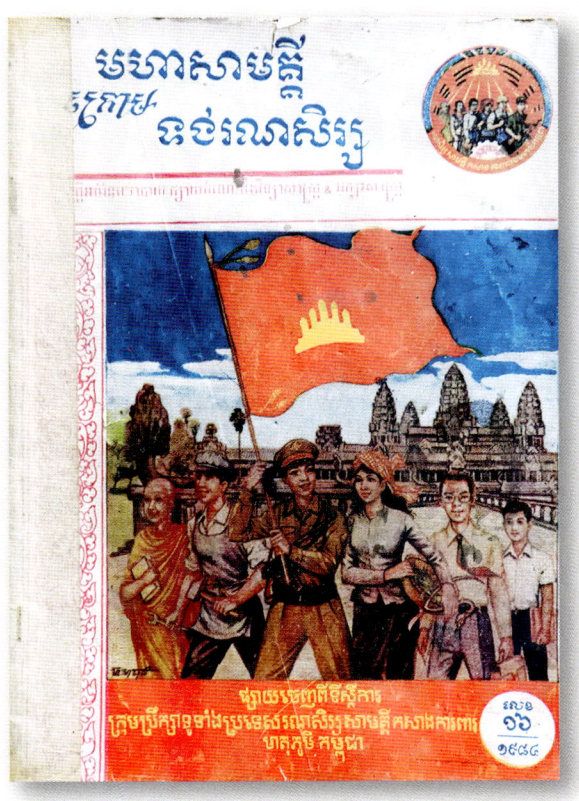

People's Republic of Kampuchea. Magazine cover. 1978.

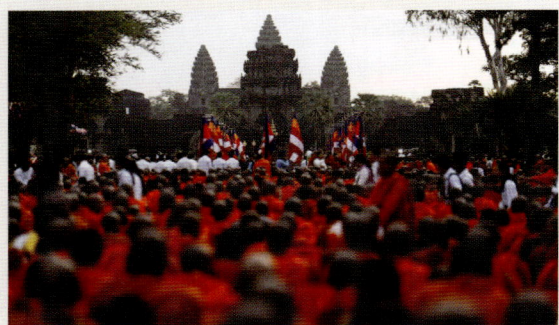

Hun Sen prays at Angkor Wat. Samrang Pring. 2017.

Cambodia's new society, stride forth arm in arm along Angkor's causeway carrying the republic's new flag (see previous page, lower right).

From 1992 to 1993, when the United Nations was mandated to take temporary control of Cambodia, things began to open up. The economy moved to a free market, mobile telephony connected the kingdom, and the listing by UNESCO of the temple complex as an endangered World Heritage site in 1992, ignited a surge in tourism, and then a boom. As myriads of hotels and guesthouses were built, they used the "Angkor" name to add appeal to their establishments. It is not until the end of the twentieth century, when peace has returned and the Angkorian monuments have been disencumbered from military authority, that John McDermott's "Panorama of Angkor Wat" (1995; see page 205) restores a cosmological majesty to the temple.

A major televised event occurred in 2017. At sunrise on December 7, Hun Sen, prime minister of Cambodia since 1985, knelt before the temple with 5,000 orange-clad Buddhist monks to pray for peace and stability in the country. Photographic banners of the prime minister, clad in white robes rather than his preferred khaki military uniform or Western business suit, lined the boulevards of Phnom Penh. Many ordinary Cambodians were impressed by this extravagant display of piety (see "Hun Sen prays at Angkor Wat," 2017; above left).

Conclusion

In our intensely shared twenty-first century, the digital age of relative peace in the region has coincided with a flowering of photography in Cambodia. Private studios are once again flourishing, infused with the scent of wedding glamor. Digital news channels upload images of the latest political scandal, a busted drug ring, or bloody family feuds. Cheap inkjet printing on large plastic banners has enabled businesses to plaster their shopfronts with 20-foot (6-meter)-high images of consumer products and services, obliterating the architecture beneath. The tree-lined boulevards of the 1960s are now lined with digital signboards, all too often broken, the heat, dust, and monsoon rain playing havoc with their less than robust electronics. Art galleries host fashionable openings featuring the work of trending photographers.

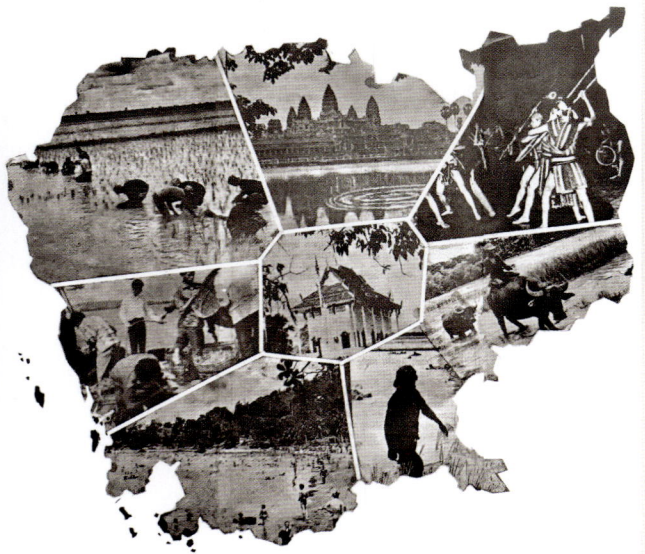

ABOVE: **Montaged map of Cambodia.** Khmer Republic Illustrated Monthly Magazine. 1971.

OPPOSITE: **Climbing the sugar palm.** Location unknown. 1946–62. Photographer unknown. Mimijac Palgen Memorial Collection, Arizona State University Library.

The brave photographer's friend appears to ascend the rickety bamboo pole used to access the sweet sap high in the crown of the sugar palm.

The "thumbnail" photographs that have been cropped in this introduction can be seen in their original form in the relevant book chapters. Captions have also been abbreviated. All photographs reproduced in this book were sourced from the photographer or his/her heirs, unless otherwise stated.

This same period has witnessed the rapid expansion of government bureaucracy and their attendant entanglements. A national identity card system is in place, with photographs required for land titles, vehicle licenses, work permits, business and tax registration, student IDs, bank accounts, even mobile phone SIM cards [registered mobile phone subscriptions reached saturation point in 2018]. By contrast, the shattered geometry of the photo-map of Cambodia, created during Lon Nol's republic in 1971, has a comforting handmade quality compared to this age of plenitude (see "Montaged map of Cambodia," 1971; left).

In return, the digital world has enabled this present selection of photographs to be compiled from online collections housed in long-established museums and international archives, as well as individual blogs and galleries. Without these archives, this record of the photographic history of Cambodia could not have been assembled, and neither this book, nor the Bambu Stage theater show that preceded it, could have existed.

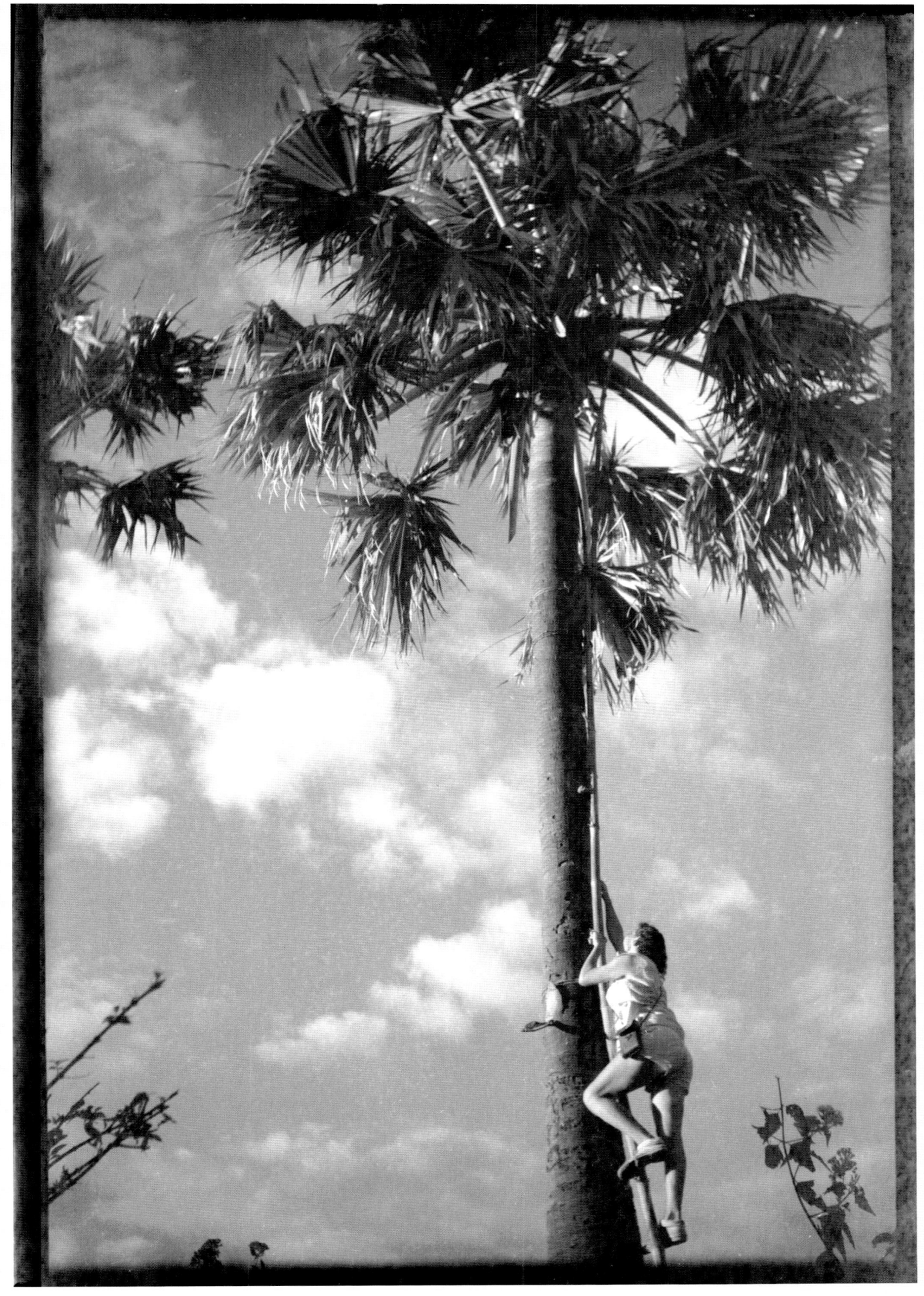

1860–1906
The Reign of King Norodom

The 1868 coronation of King Norodom (1834–1904), which was largely orchestrated by the French, symbolically marked the beginning of their influence in Cambodia. For the next forty-one years, Norodom deflected, ignored, then finally acquiesced to French intervention in the Cambodian court and its patronage network of nobles and provincial mandarins. The romantic allure of Angkor's great temples, the economic possibilities of a flourishing Mekong waterway, and the fear of British expansion from Burma, drove the French to gain greater control, both political and economic, over their newly acquired colonial possession.

From Europe the new technological marvel that combined glass lenses, chemistry, and timber craftsmanship—the camera and its photograph—was perfectly timed to document French ambitions. Cumbersome, yet fragile at the same time, the heavy wooden cameras and their delicate glass plates and toxic chemicals had to be carefully crated by explorers and carted by elephants and oxcarts across the country, and by sailing boats and steam launches up the inland waterways. From the original large-glass negatives, silvery paper contact prints were made. They were then presented in albums to their political patrons, Parisian-based scientific societies, and friends back home.

The earliest photographers to visit Cambodia were participants in expeditions of exploration and discovery, or self-funded curiosity, most notably the Scotsman John Thomson (1837–1921) and the Saigon-based Emile Gsell (1838–79), who accompanied the French Mekong Expedition in 1866. There were also professionals in other fields who took time out to use the camera as gifted amateurs, such as the director of the River Shipping Company of Cochinchina (Messageries Fluviales de Cochinchine) Fernan Blanchet (1853–1914?) and the respected linguist Father Marie-Joseph Guedson (1852–1939).

Well-heeled private adventurers like Jules Agostini (1859–1930) or explorers such as Auguste Jean-Marie Paive (1847–1925) played their part, while many late nineteenth-century French administrators like Adhémard Leclère (1853–1917) and the elegant Albert Tajasque (1877–1959) were also avid photographers. André Salles (1860–1929), as inspector of the colonies between 1896 and 1898, used his camera as a professional asset to document the peoples of Cambodia and their activities.

Across Europe, grand colonial exhibitions fueled the desire of an emerging bourgeoisie to view the curiosities of their colonial possessions in startling photographic detail. The images revealed rugged adventurers in front of towering stone temples; cascading waterfalls; seminaked indigenous people; courtly dancers in rich attire; and breezy colonial bungalows with louvered shutters. Hundreds of photographers had visited Cambodia by the end of the nineteenth century. Their works, now preserved in multiple archives, also reveal that commercial studios were operating in the capital, Phnom Penh. The fingerprint of actual Cambodian photographers, however, even those of royal family members who had direct access to the new technology, are nowhere to be found.

King Norodom in a French field marshal uniform. Phnom Penh. 1866. John Thomson. Wellcome Collection, London.

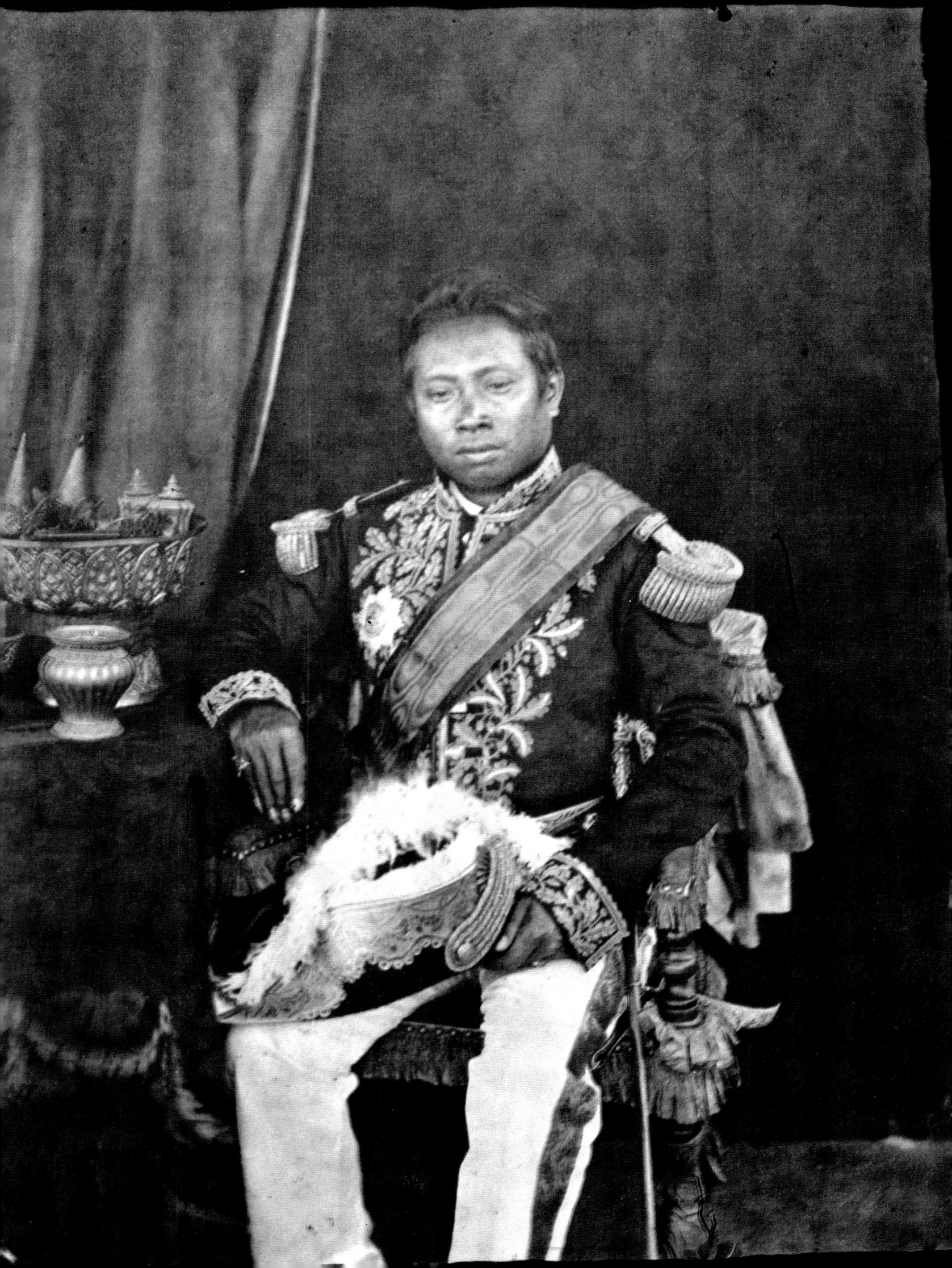

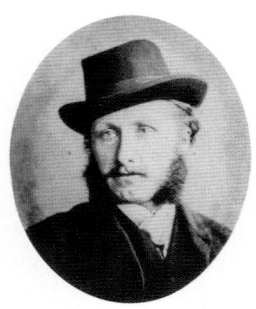

The First Photographer at Angkor

In the hot, dusty February of 1866, John THOMSON (1837–1921) and a retinue of Thai and Khmer porters traveled on lumbering elephants through the northern Cambodian jungle. Dry leaves crackled under foot. Thomson was equipped with the latest hefty wood and brass camera equipment, along with wooden boxes of page-sized glass plates and jars of dangerous chemicals, to capture an image of the fabled temples. The adventurous Scot set to work to assemble his contraption, cloaked himself in a dark cloth to cut out the light, and took the very first photographs of the monuments of Angkor. Thomson was an astute businessman. He traveled widely and included Singapore, Siam, and China in his itinerary. But while it was the photographs he published of the Middle Kingdom that established his reputation, for photography in Cambodia it was Thomson's images of Angkor's ruined temples that signaled an important beginning.

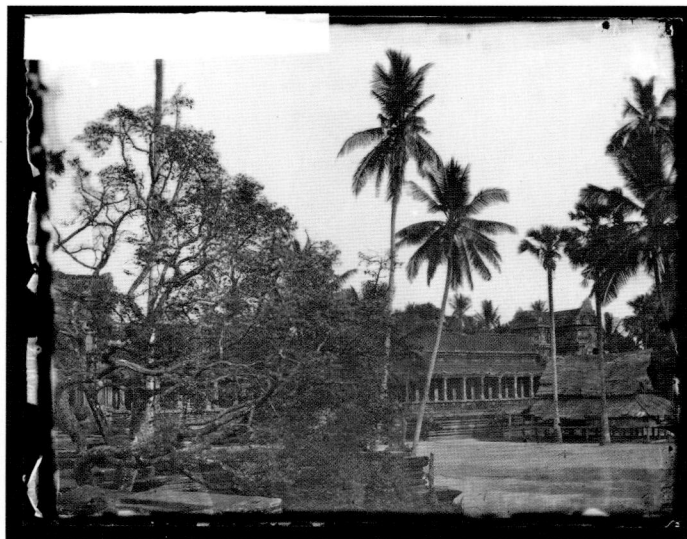

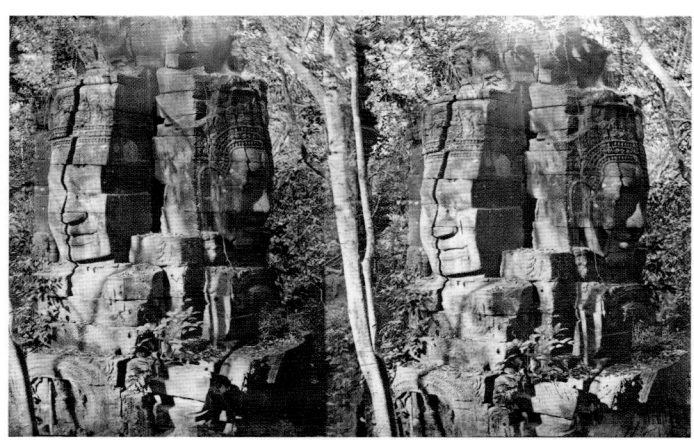

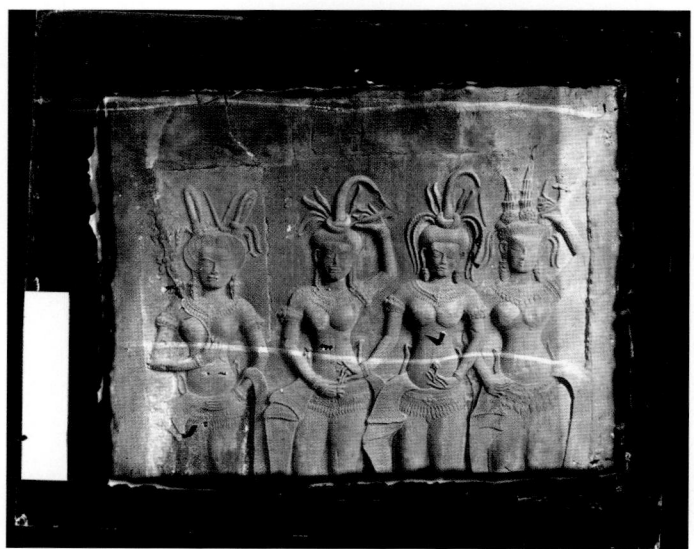

TOP LEFT, CLOCKWISE: **Portrait of Thomson.** Photographer unknown.

View of Angkor Wat. Siem Reap.

Angkor Thom gateway. Siem Reap.

Detail of dancer and three attendants. Bayon temple, Siem Reap.

Photographs: John Thomson. Wellcome Collection, London.

RIGHT: **Elephants and their mahouts in the precinct of Angkor Wat.** Siem Reap. 1866. John Thomson. Wellcome Collection, London.

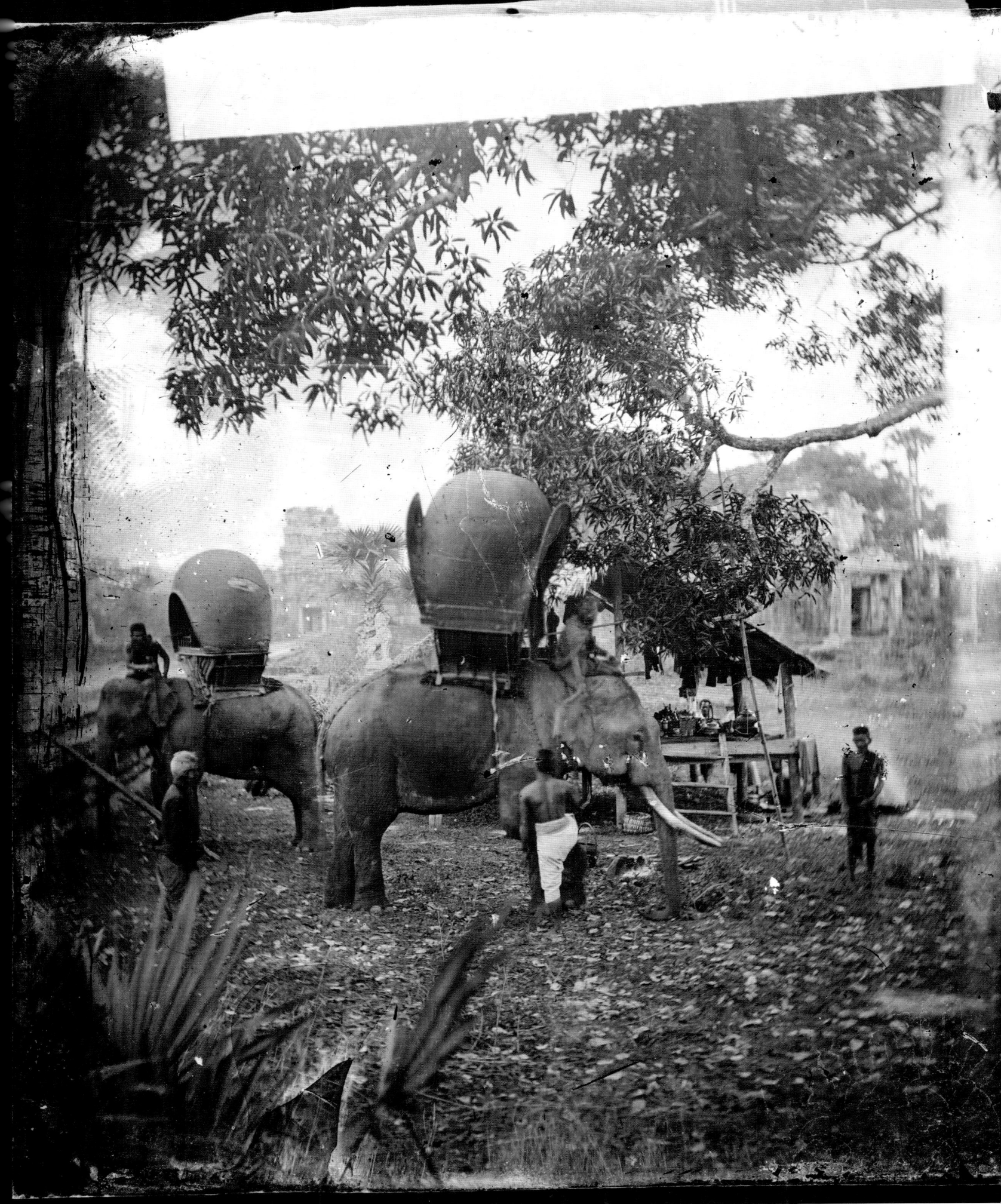

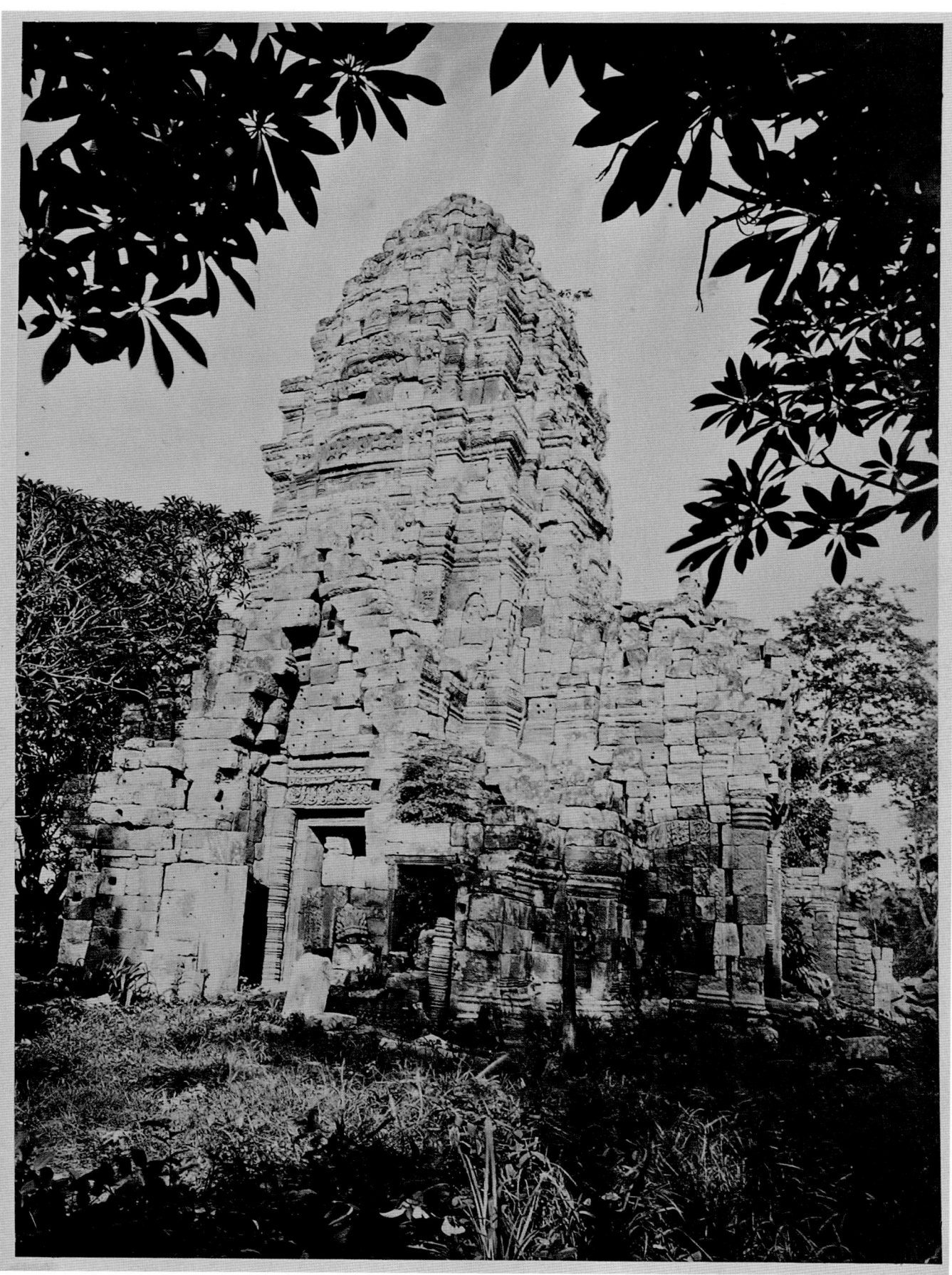

RIGHT: **Monks, Angkor Wat.** Siem Reap. ca. 1866. Archives nationales d'outre-mer, Paris.

FAR RIGHT: **Houses of the monks, Angkor Wat.** Siem Reap. ca. 1866. Metropolitan Museum of Art, New York.

BELOW: **View of the central towers, Angkor Wat.** Siem Reap. 1866. Metropolitan Museum of Art, New York.

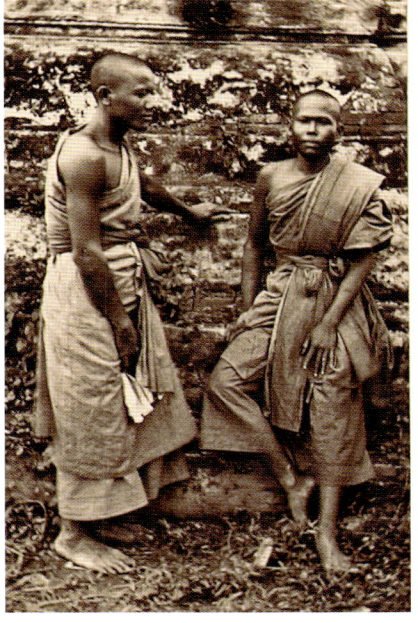

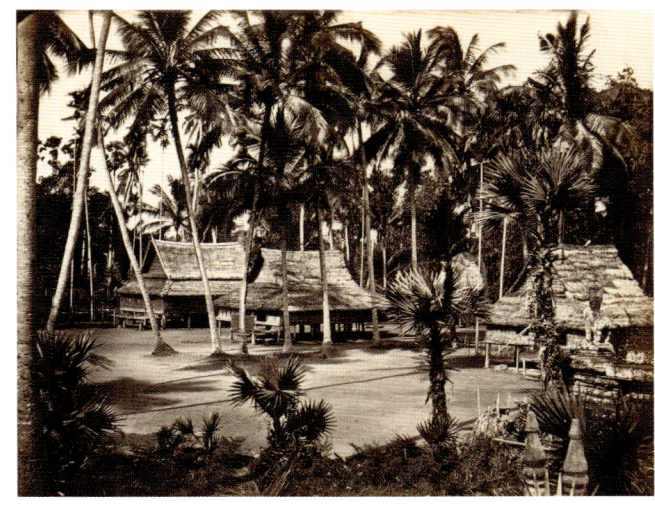

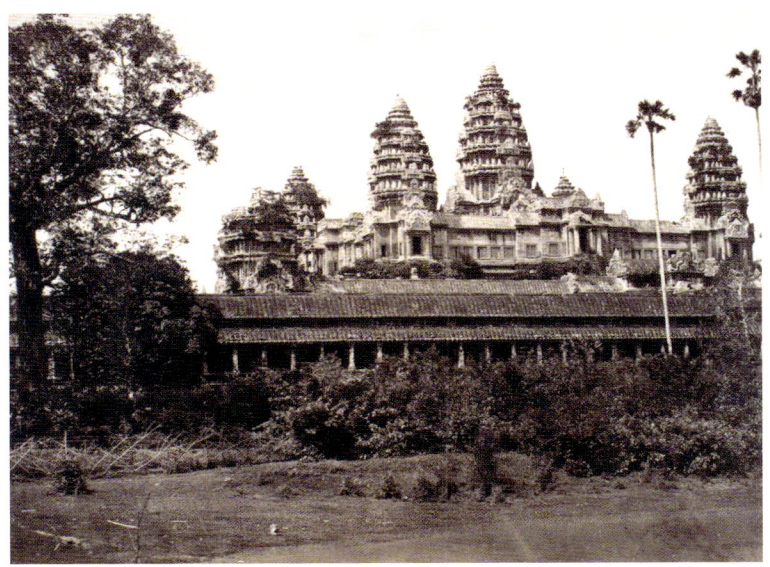

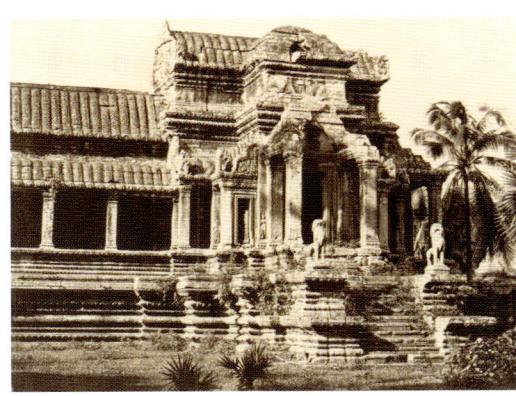

ABOVE: **Main portico to the Grand Gallery, Angkor Wat.** Siem Reap. 1870–75. Metropolitan Museum of Art, New York.

LEFT: **Banan temple.** Battambang. 1866. Archives nationales d'outre-mer, Paris.

Photographs: Emile Gsell.

The French Mekong Expedition

Emile GSELL (1838–79) had just started his photographic practice in Saigon when he was fortuitously invited to join the French Mekong Expedition commanded by the naval officer Ernest Doudart de Lagrée. A photographic survey and archaeological exploration of Angkorian temples was their first major task. When they arrived in June 1866, three months after Thomson's earlier visit, the monsoon had broken and the landscape was flourishing. The following year, Gsell's photographs were bound into a lavish album and presented to Empress Eugénie as a record of the successes of the French Second Republic in gaining Indochina as a prized colonial possession. Gsell was to return regularly to Cambodia, expanding his photographic portfolio in geographic breadth well beyond Thomson's pioneering visit. Early photography had a problem with exposure. If you pointed the camera towards the skies while capturing those magnificent towers, the skies tended to be bleached white. With this photograph of the Angkor-period temple of Wat Banan, near Battambang, Gsell cleverly uses the hanging branches of trees to mask out the sky, thereby overcoming these technical limitations.

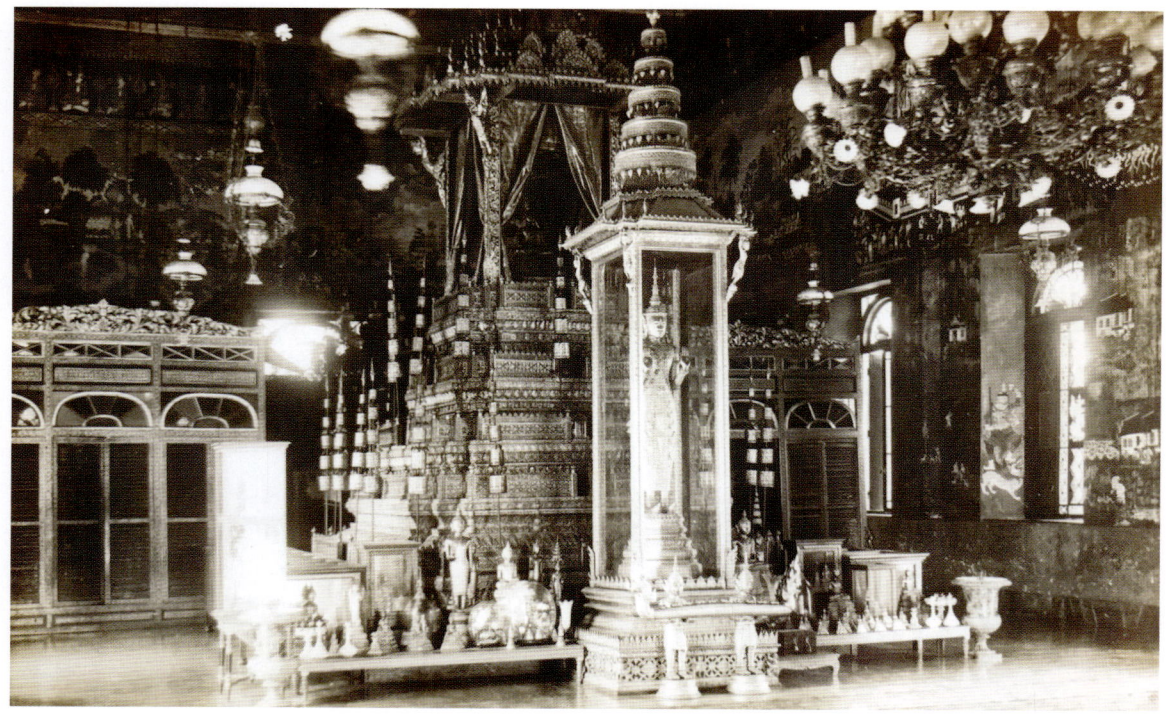

ABOVE: **Throne Hall, Royal Palace.** Phnom Penh. Postcard. ca. 1900. Delcampe International.

LEFT: **View towards the National Palace.** Phnom Penh. ca. 1892. Jules Agostini. Bibliothèque nationale de France.

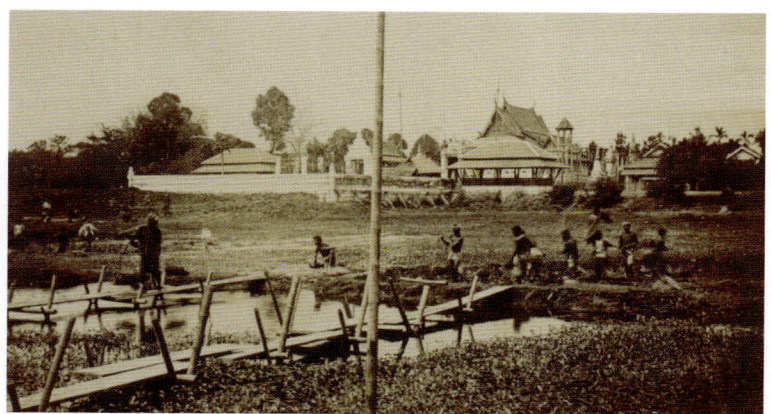

Pageants and Politics

After Norodom was crowned, the French commissioned a new palace complex to be built facing the river at Chaktomuk in Phnom Penh. Started in the late 1860s, the main halls were constructed of solid whitewashed masonry, fine timbers, and iron finials that pointed to the heavens. It was the new political and administrative hub of the kingdom, while the temples of Angkor remained the symbolic spiritual center. The extended royal family and high officials occupied the buildings from where they assisted in religious ceremonies and in administering the kingdom, while receiving official visits and taking part in royal parades. Travelers were naturally drawn to this world of arcane protocol and the interwoven networks of patronage and power.

The Royal Elephants. Phnom Penh. 1925. Attributed to George Groslier. National Museum of Cambodia.

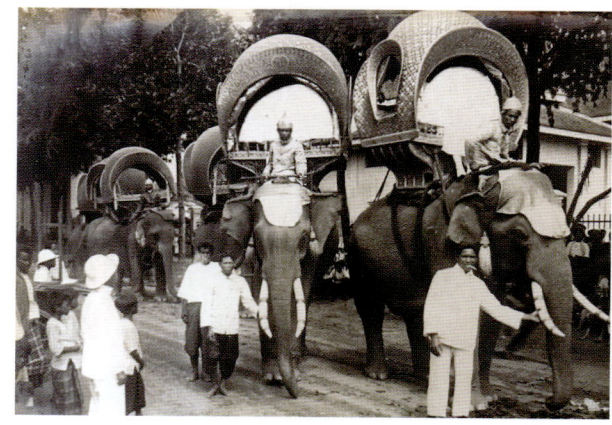

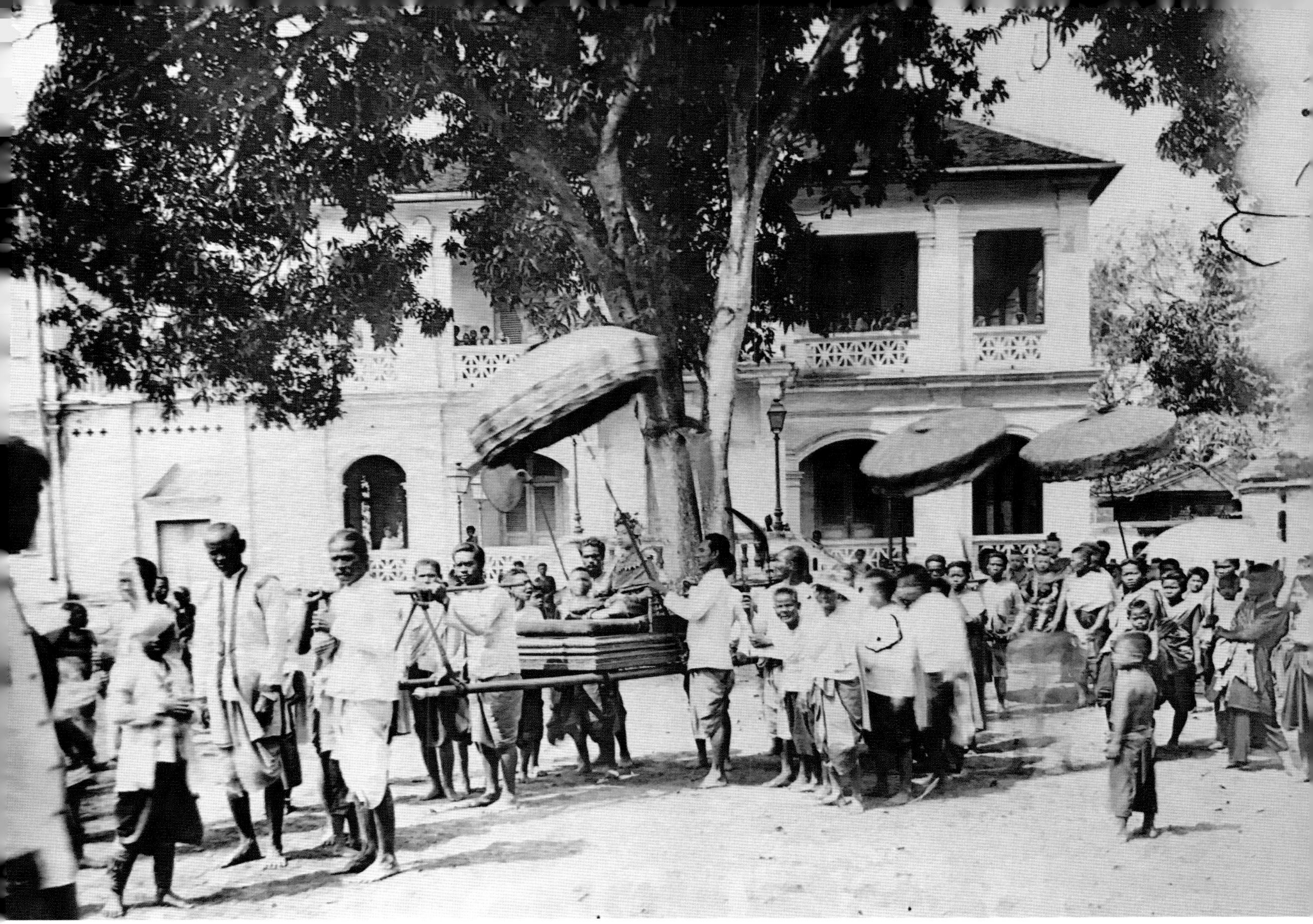

Procession of a royal princess. Phnom Penh. 1899.
Photographer unknown. Philippe Damas Collection, Singapore.

Prince Sisowath and his retinue. Detail. Cochinchina. 1866. Emile Gsell. Metropolitan Museum of Art, New York.

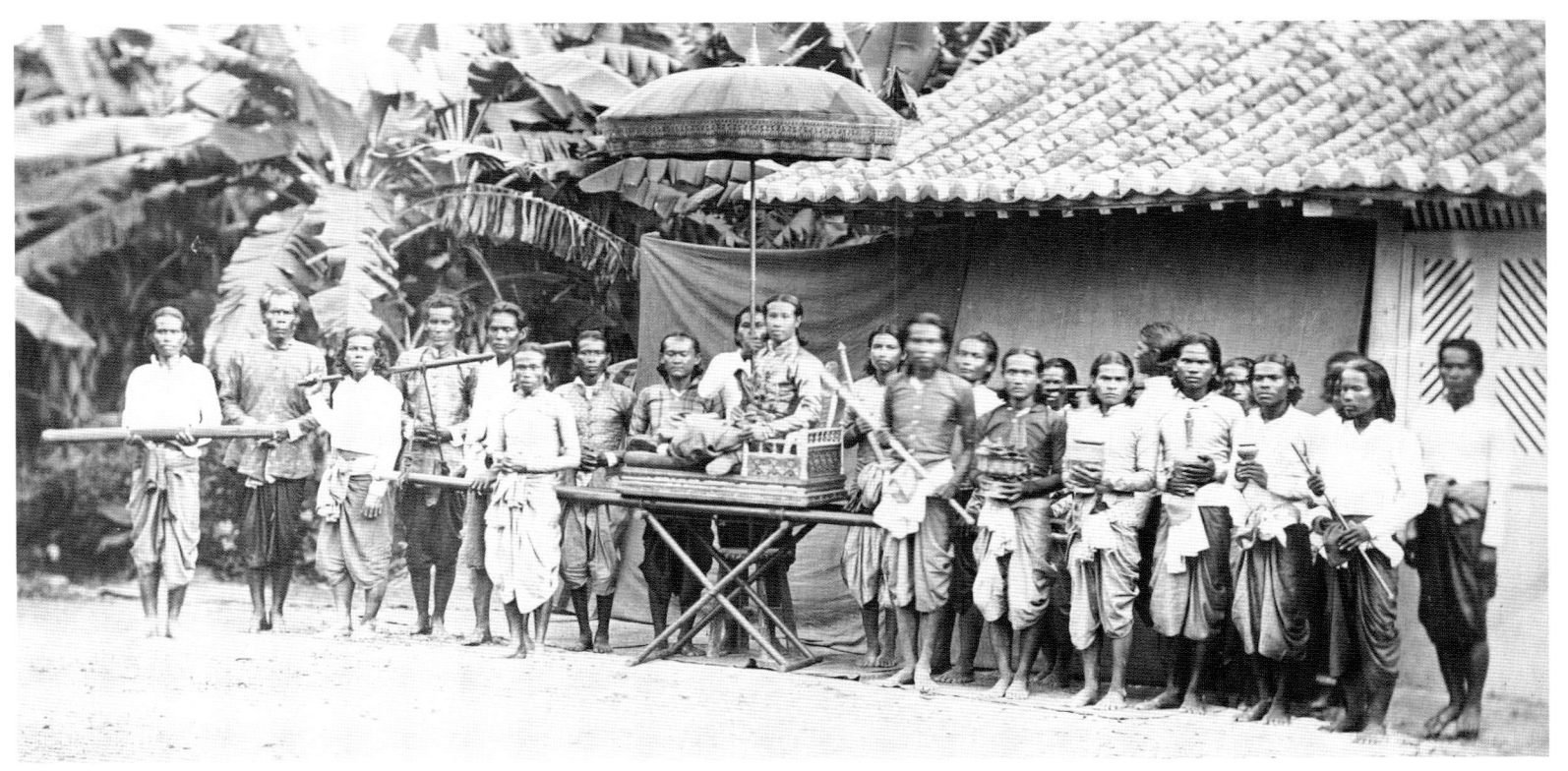

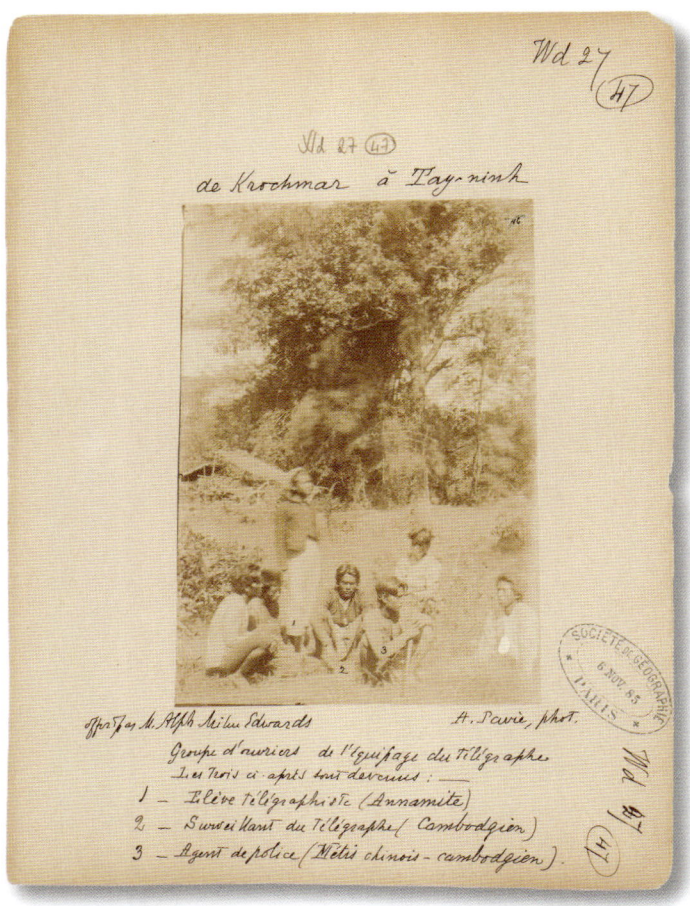

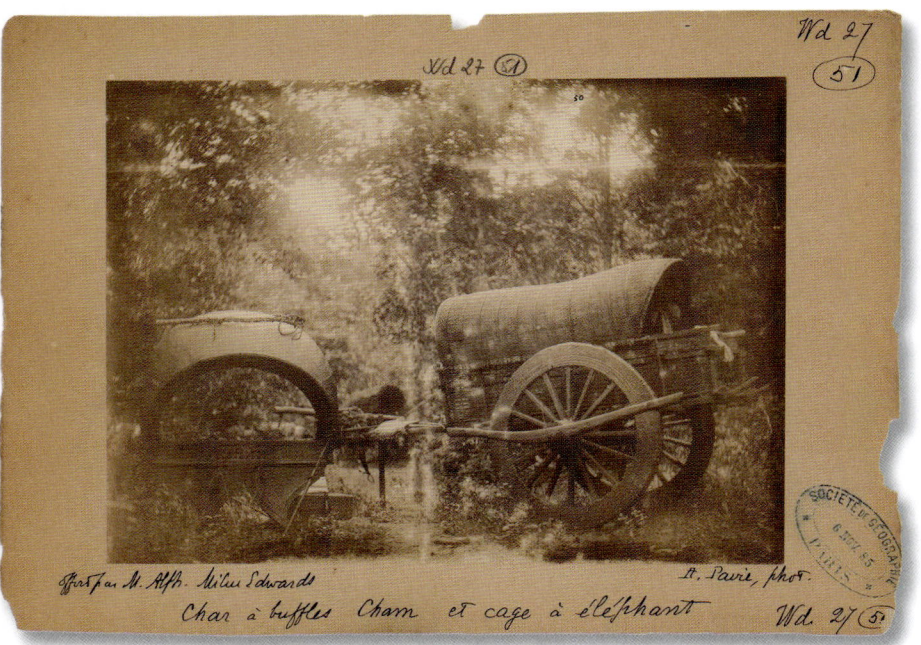

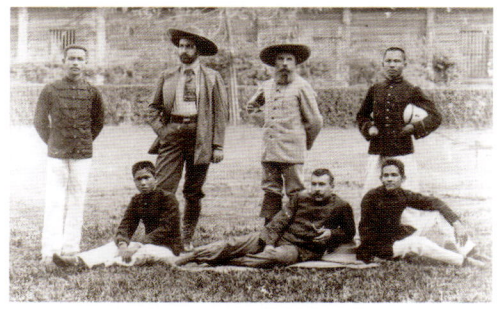

An Explorer and Diplomat

Auguste Jean-Marie PAVIE (1847–1925) belongs firmly in the colonial-gone-native tradition; someone who eschewed the conservative establishment yet was recognized by his peers for his rapport with Cambodian and Lao cultures. After employment in the French army and fighting in the Franco-Prussian War, he was sent to work at the post office in Kampot. This small provincial town enabled him to immerse himself in Khmer culture. He was commissioned to lead numerous overland scientific expeditions, resulting in a meticulously plotted mapping of Indochina. He also oversaw the installation of the first telegraph line from Phnom Penh to Bangkok. Towards the end of his career, he won renown for his remarkable regional diplomacy. With his musketeer-style broad-brimmed hat, Paive appealed directly to the idea of the adventurous "officer-explorer" in the popular imagination of fin-de-siècle France.

TOP: **Cambodian and Annamite staff of the expedition.** "Kandol-Cheroum." 1879–82. Bibliothèque nationale de France.

ABOVE: **Buffaloes and buffalo carts.** "Kandol-Cheroum." 1879–82. Société de Géographie, Paris/Bibliothèque nationale de France.

TOP RIGHT: **Auguste Pavie and Cambodian staff.** Phnom Penh. 1884. Bibliothèque nationale de France.

A Chinese Theater

Colonial engineer and photographer Jules AGOSTINI (1859–1930) traveled extensively throughout Southeast Asia and the South Pacific. Perhaps inspired by Jules Verne's *Around the World in Eighty Days* published some twenty years earlier, Agostini produced his own *Illustrated Book of Travels around the World by Sea and Road* in 1896. This unusual photograph, taken when Agostini visited Cambodia between 1893 and 1894, is intriguing. Is it a temple, a theater facade, or a temporary shrine with bamboo scaffolding propping up its sides? With its three tiers, richly decorated panels of guardian demons, and sumptuous oil lamp chandelier hanging at the entrance, it reflects the wealth and influence of the Chinese merchant community who were the engines of Phnom Penh's commercial success.

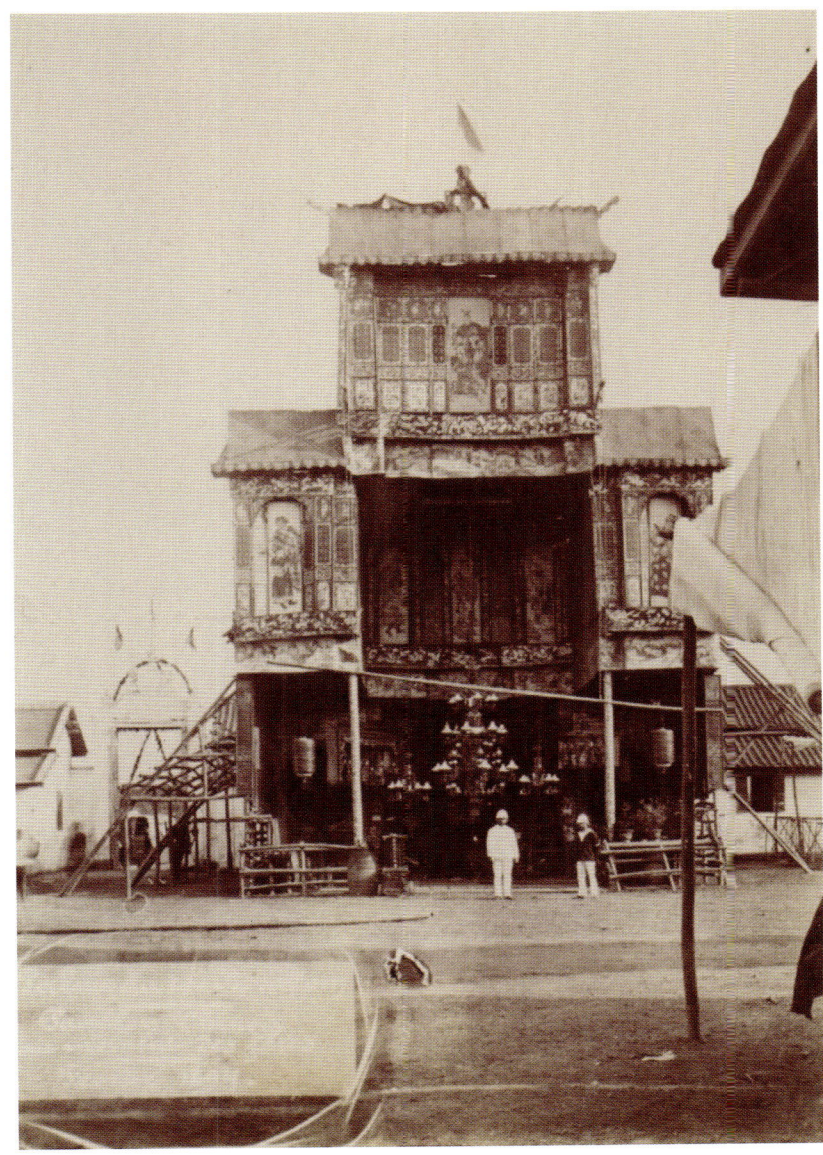

Chinese theater. Phnom Penh. 1893. Jules Agostini. Bibliothèque nationale de France/Société de Géographie, Paris.

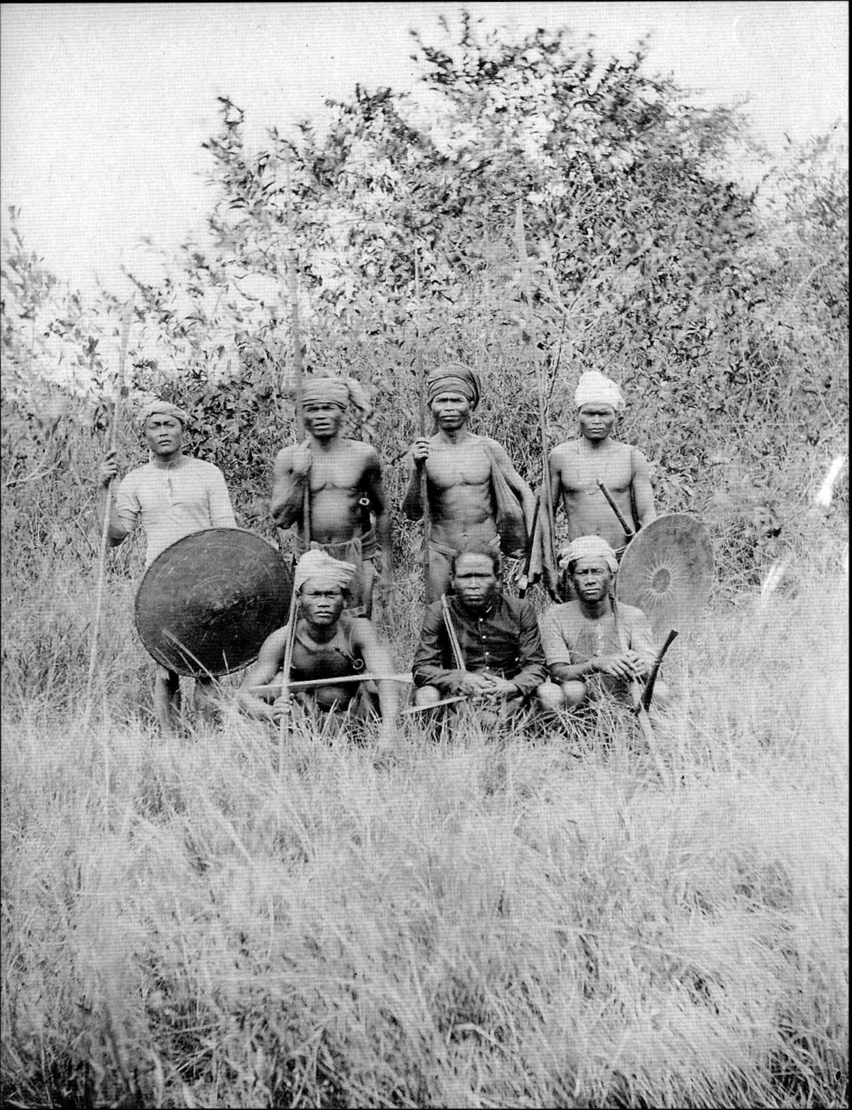

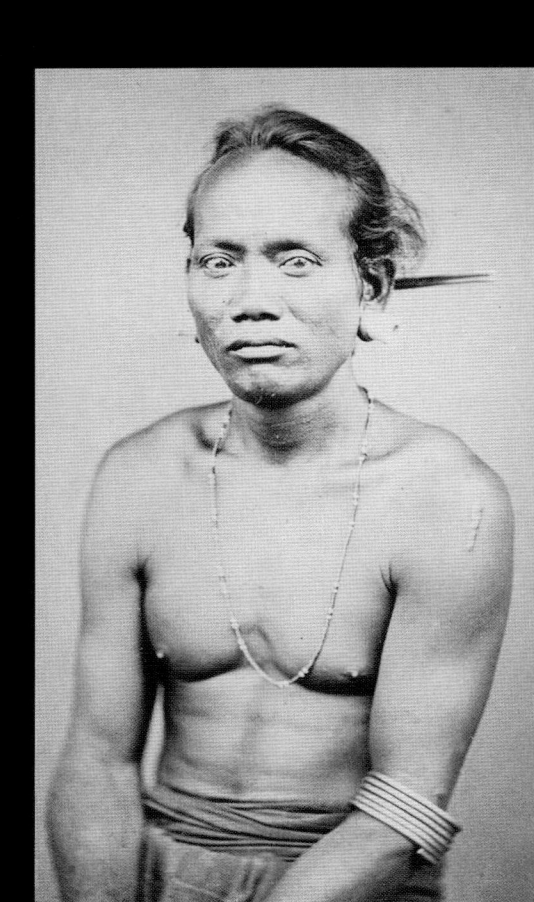

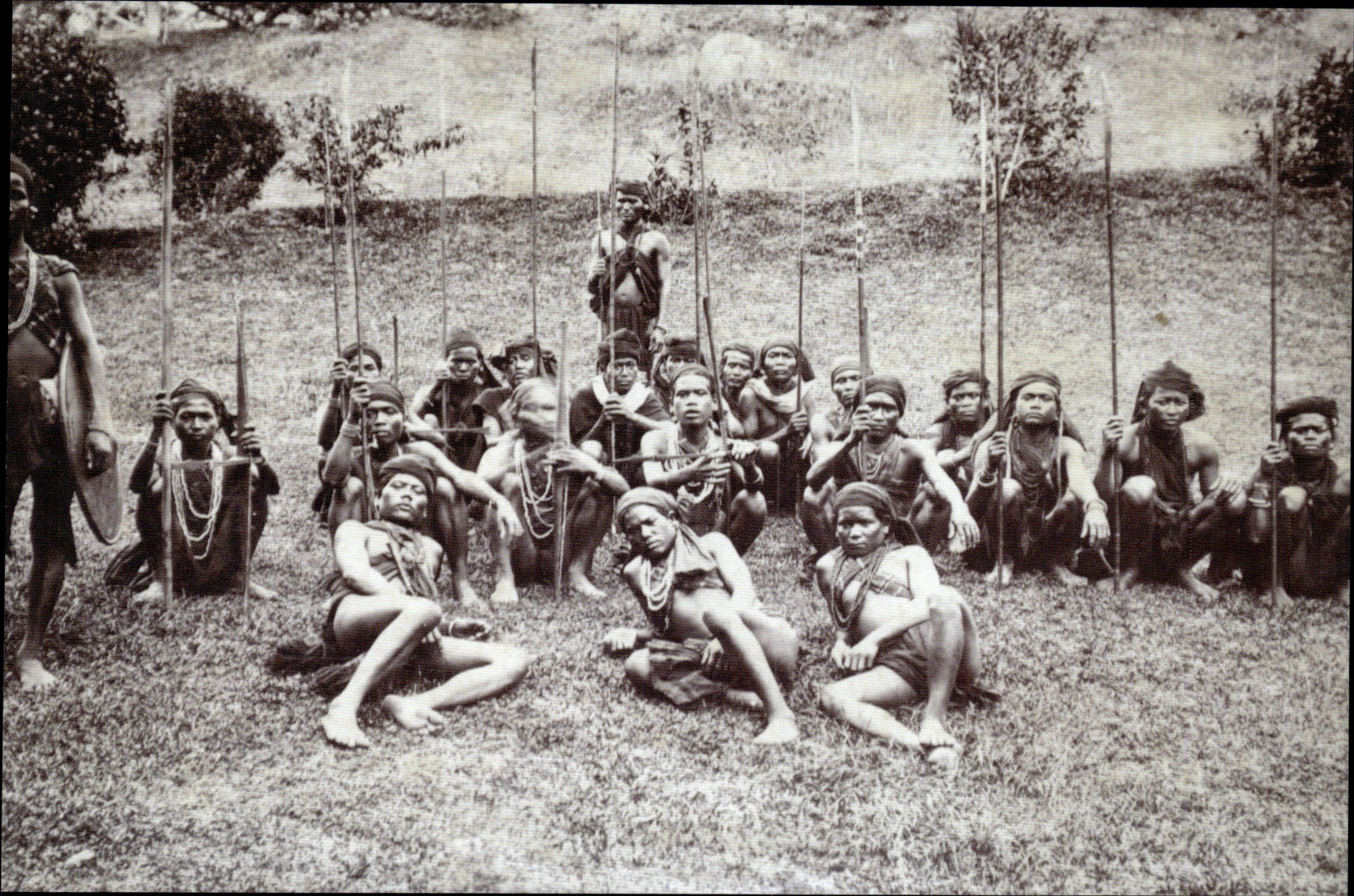

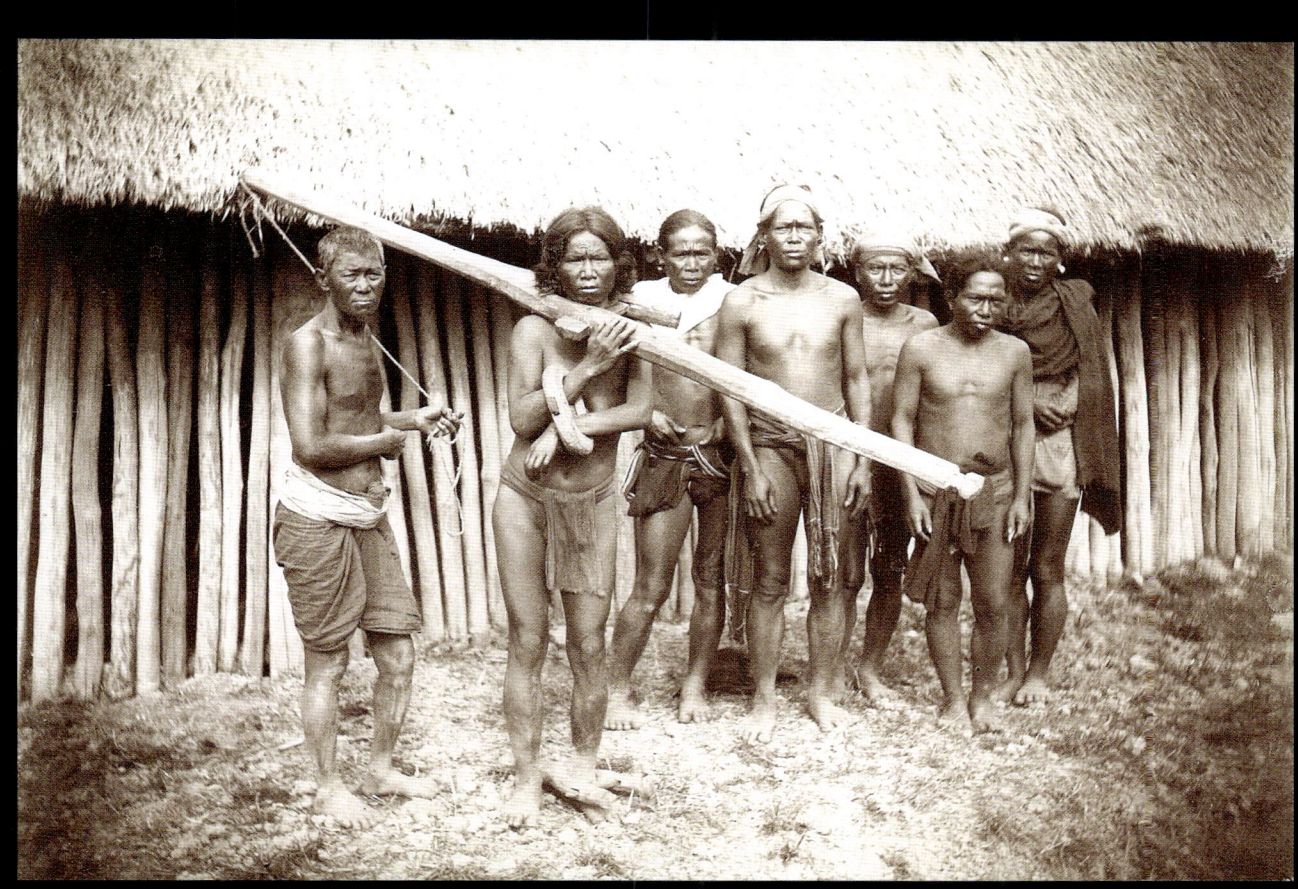

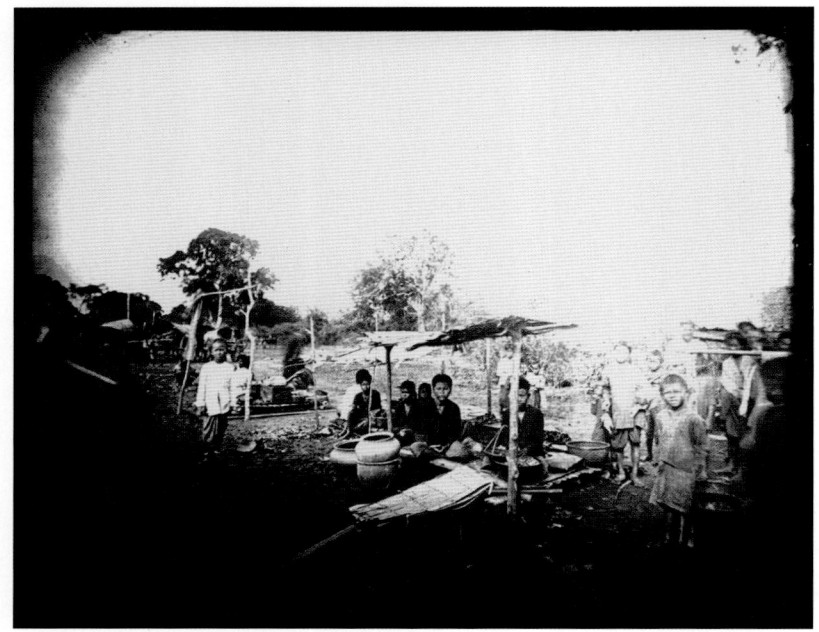

TOP LEFT, CLOCKWISE: **Musicians.** Kampot. 1874–81.

Annamite hut in a flooded forest. Perhaps Tonlé Sap. 1874–81.

Cambodian markets. Kompot. 1874–81.

Photographs: Marie-Joseph Guedson. Bibliothèque nationale de France/Société de Géographie, Paris.

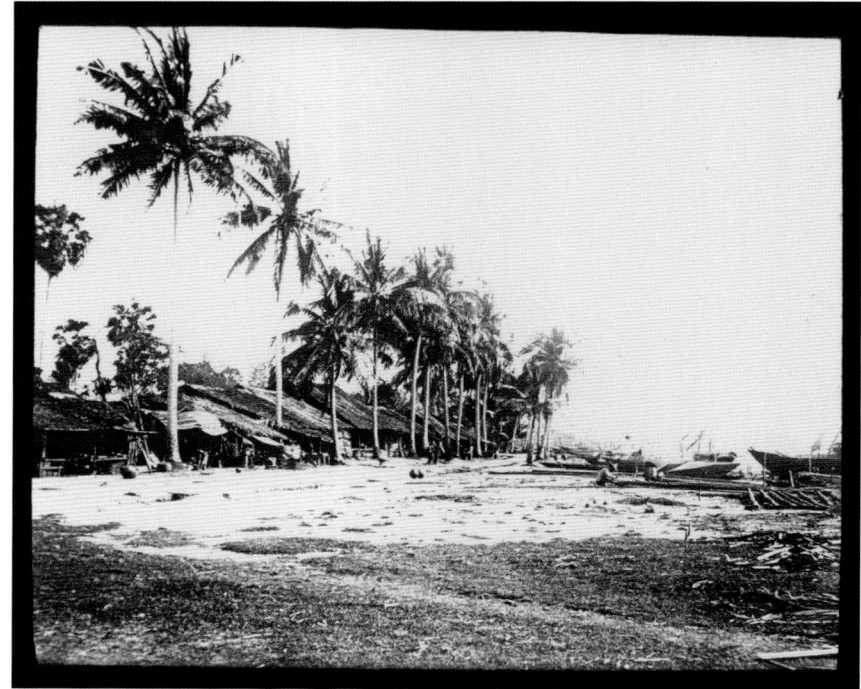

The Linguist and Typographer

Father Marie-Joseph GUEDSON (1852–1939) was a Jesuit priest with a gift for languages. On his arrival in Cambodia in 1882, he embarked on a study of the Khmer language and began to collect Cambodian and Laotian manuscripts. During the course of his research, Guedson took many photographs of the Cambodian worlds around him. On his return to France in 1888, he drew up a map of Cambodia with Khmer-language place-names, and presented it to the Geographical Society in Paris. Later, in Hong Kong, Guedson was instrumental in designing a Cambodian-language type for use in printing. His 1,200-page *Complete French-Cambodian Dictionary*, which included a transcription of Khmer characters, was published in 1930. The dictionary may have been compiled with the help of interpreter Son Diep (b. 1855).

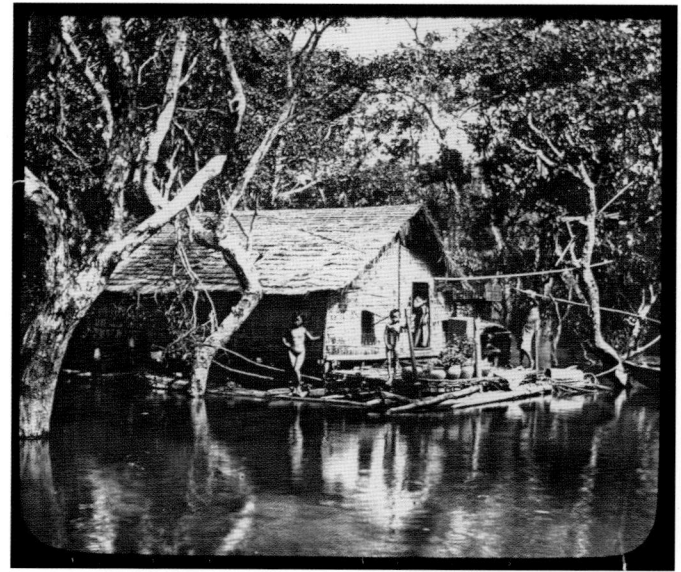

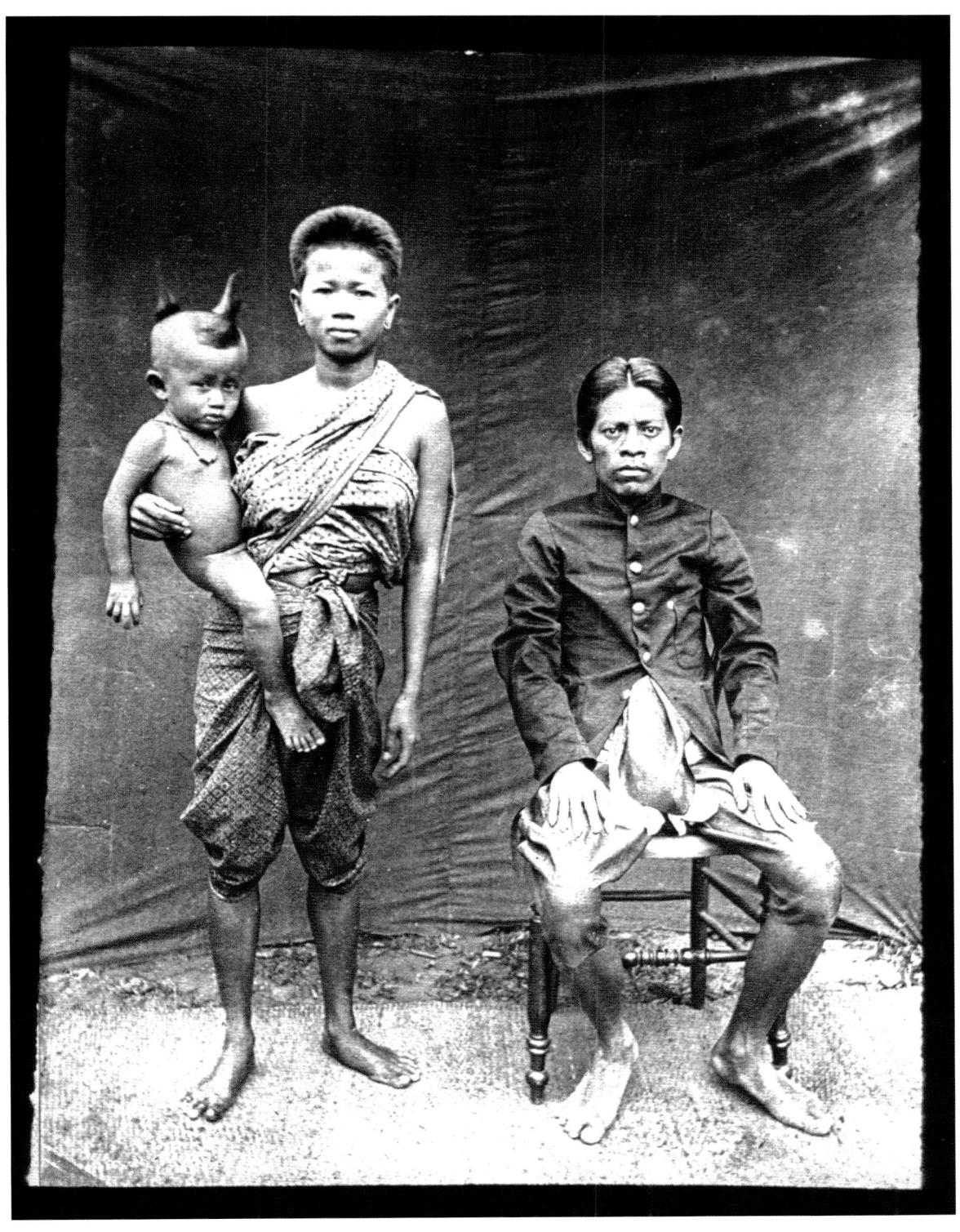

A Cambodian family. Takeo. 1874–81. Marie-Joseph Guedson. Bibliothèque nationale de France/Société de Géographie, Paris.

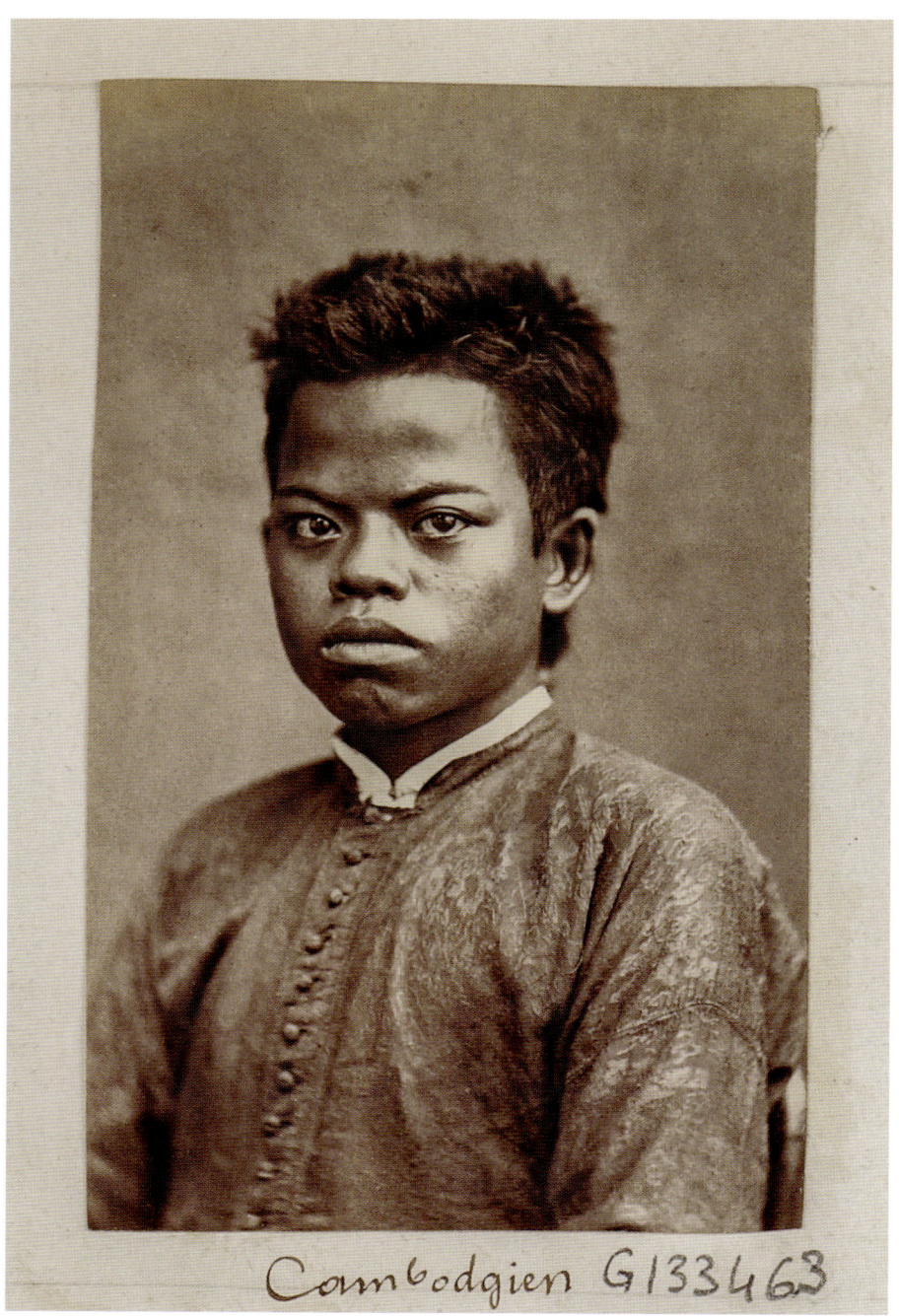

Portrait of Chhun. Phnom Penh. 1866–73. Emile Gsell. Bibliothèque nationale de France/ Société de Géographie, Paris.

Portrait of Chhun

One of the earliest portraits of a non-royal Cambodian, the confrontational stare of the young man suggests a less than amicable relationship with the photographer, Emile Gsell. The man's multibuttoned jacket with its removable collar lining, indicates he came from a well-to-do family, while his cropped haircut was fashionable for the nineteenth-century elite. Chhun was a young and talented interpreter for Ernest Doudart de Lagrée, leader of the French Mekong Expedition of 1866–68. Later in life, Chhun was to serve in many government ministries and was finally appointed as head of the Ministry of Justice. As a consequence of being used for the cover of *Cambodia Captured* (2016) by the late Jim Mizerski, this image is one of the most well-recognized nineteenth-century portraits in contemporary Cambodia.

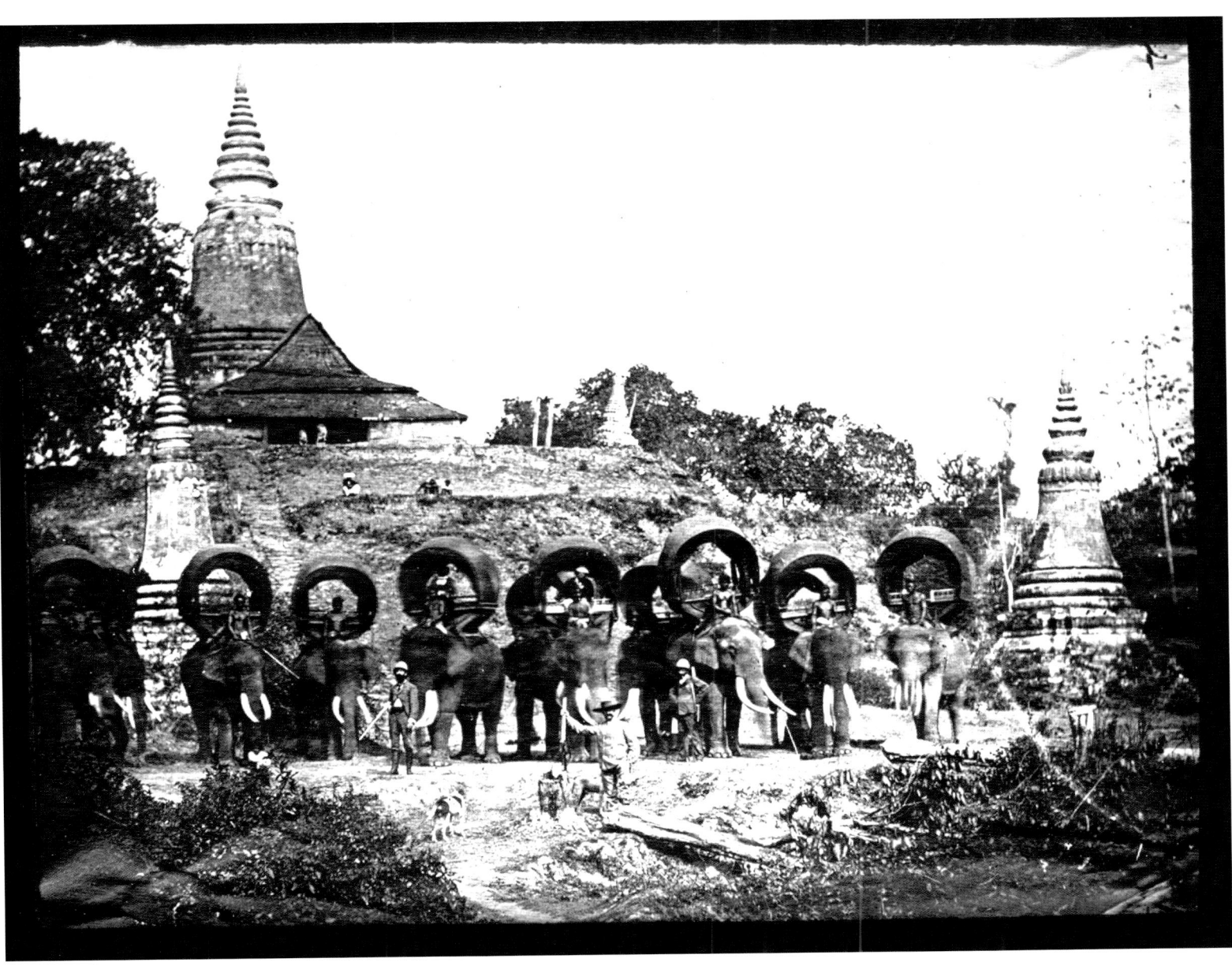

The Hunting Party

Elephant party setting off from Wat Phnom. Phnom Penh. ca. 1893. Fernan Blanchet. Bibliothèque nationale de France/Société de Géographie, Paris.

After training as a hydrographic engineer in Paris, Fernan BLANCHET (1853–1914?) became a director of the Compagnie des Messageries fluviales de Cochinchine in 1890. As well as a fleet of passenger and freight steamers, the company had lucrative postal concessions along the Mekong. During his extensive travels on the river, Blanchet took many photographs, including this magnificent hunting party of eleven elephants, rifle-bearing gentlemen, and their hounds, about to set out from Wat Phnom, the spiritual epicenter of Phnom Penh. The hill is devoid of trees, revealing a rudimentary wat or reception hall built in front of the monumental stupa.

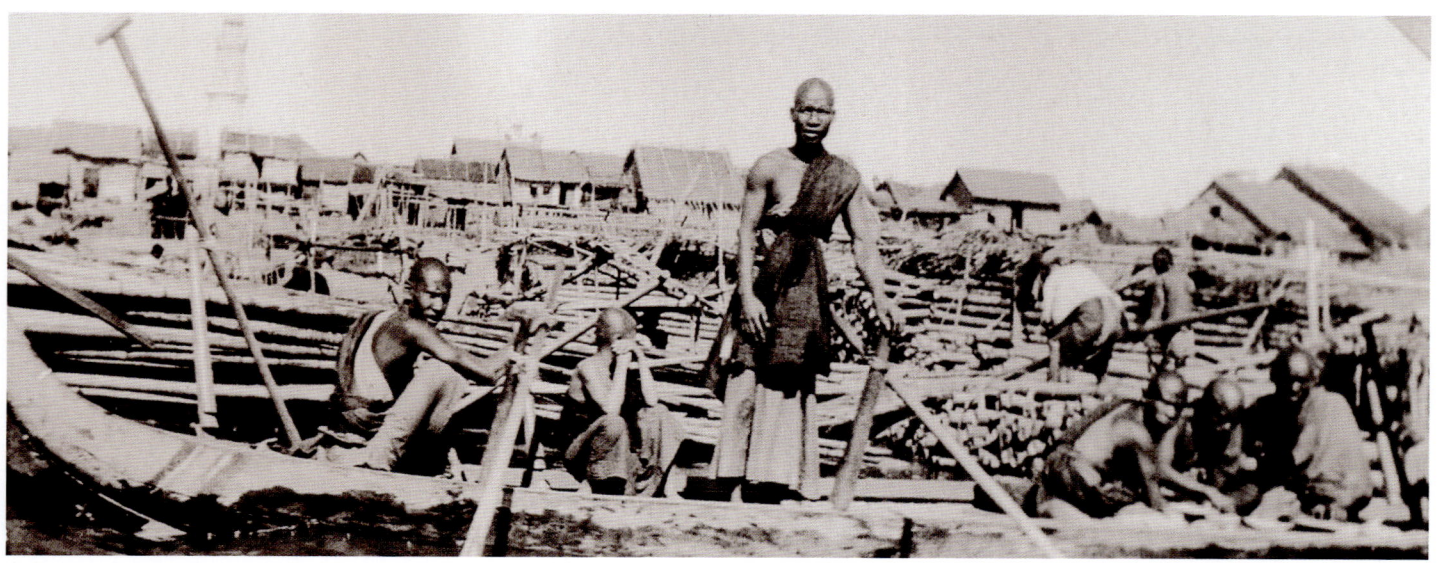

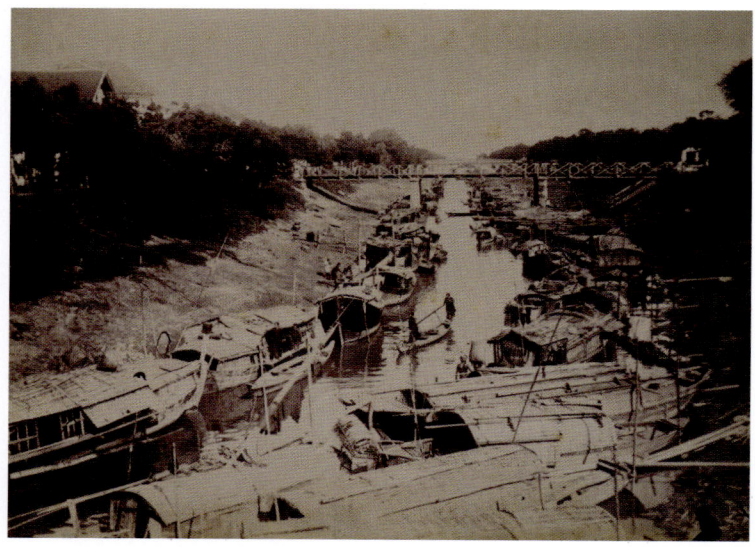

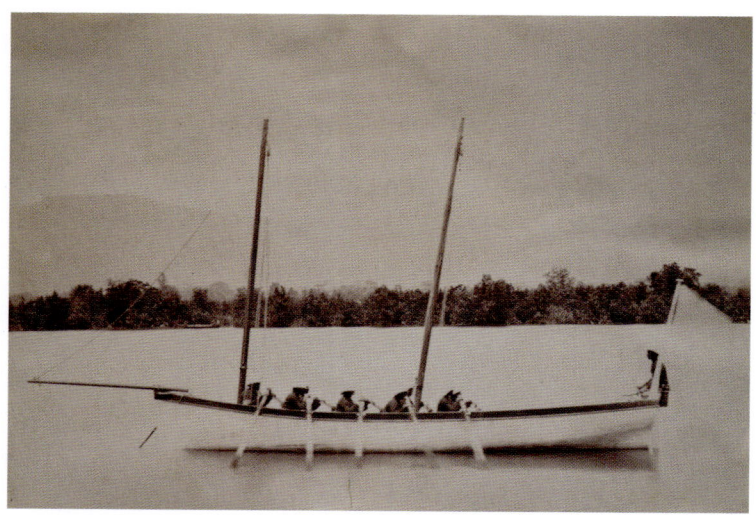

The Colonial Administrator

Adhémard LECLÈRE (1853–1917) was a colonial administrator in Cambodia from 1890 to 1911. For sixteen years, Leclère served as resident of Kampot and Kratié-Sambor, and then as resident mayor of Phnom Penh, before finally being appointed an advisor of the resident-superior. A former journalist with strong left-wing views, he learned Khmer and immersed himself in Cambodian culture and tradition. He took hundreds of photographs of daily life. While interior photographs were rare at this time, the snapshot opposite top was taken while seated, of his mayoral office, with its lightweight Thonet chairs, translucent silk screen, and abundant hanging plants. It offers a fascinating, if somewhat claustrophobic glimpse into the administrative life of the French Protectorate at the fin de siècle. It is a world away from the domesticated, sun-drenched interiors of the French Nabis painter Pierre Bonnard.

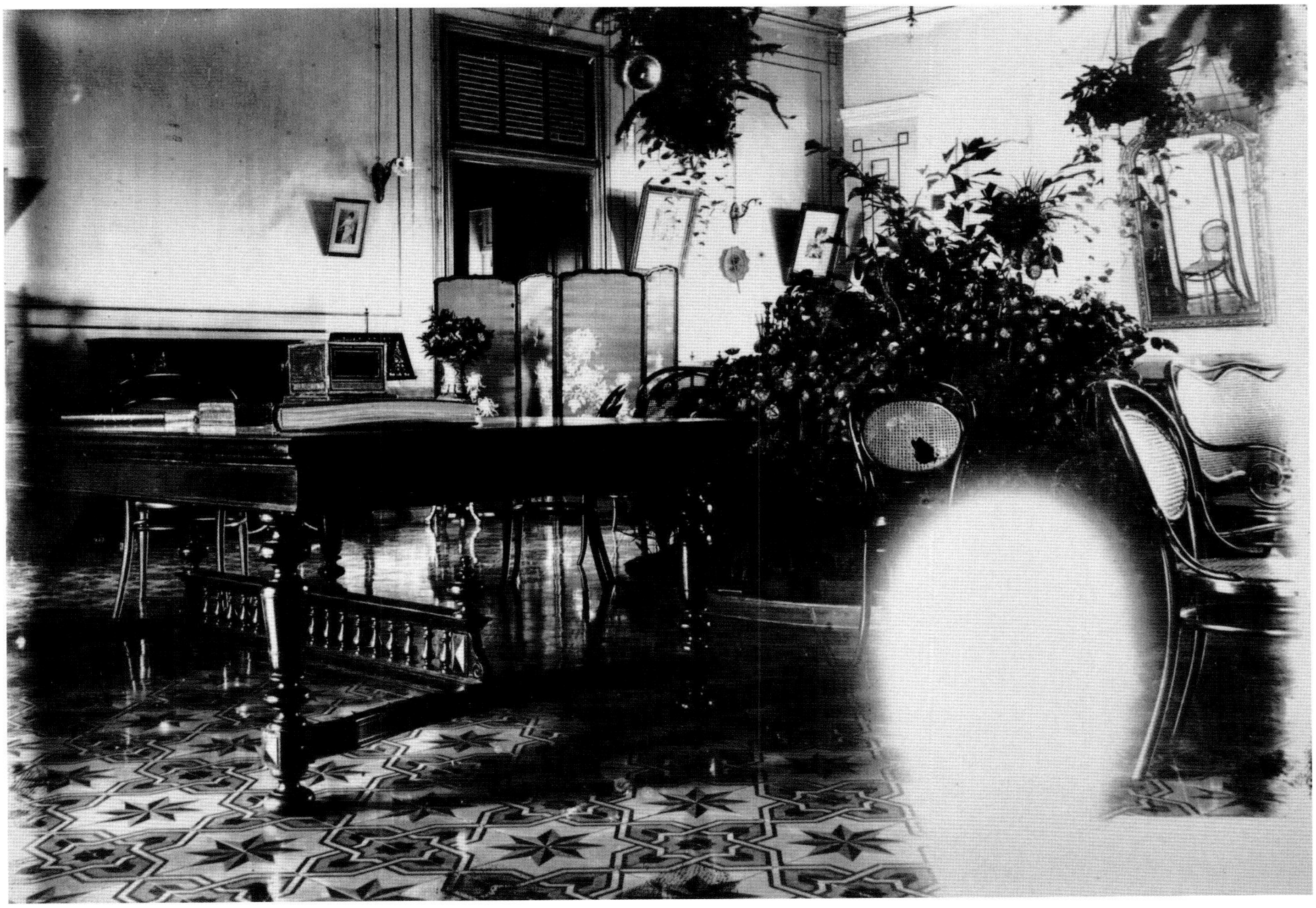

OPPOSITE, FROM TOP: **Monks in a canoe.** Phnom Penh waterfront. ca. 1880s.

De Verneville Canal. Phnom Penh. After 1894.

French gaf-rigged schooner under oars. Kampot. ca. 1880s.

Photographs: Adhémard Leclère. Musée des Beaux Arts et de la Dentelle, Alençon/National Archives of Cambodia.

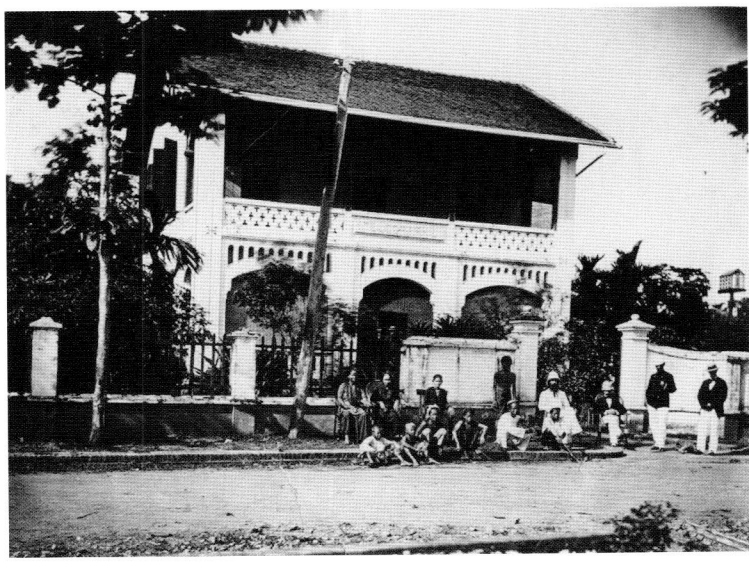

TOP: **Office of the mayor.** Phnom Penh. Adhémard Leclère. 1889–1903.

ABOVE: **Telegraph Office.** Phnom Penh. 1884. Adhémard Leclère. Musée des Beaux Arts et de la Dentelle, Alençon/National Archives of Cambodia.

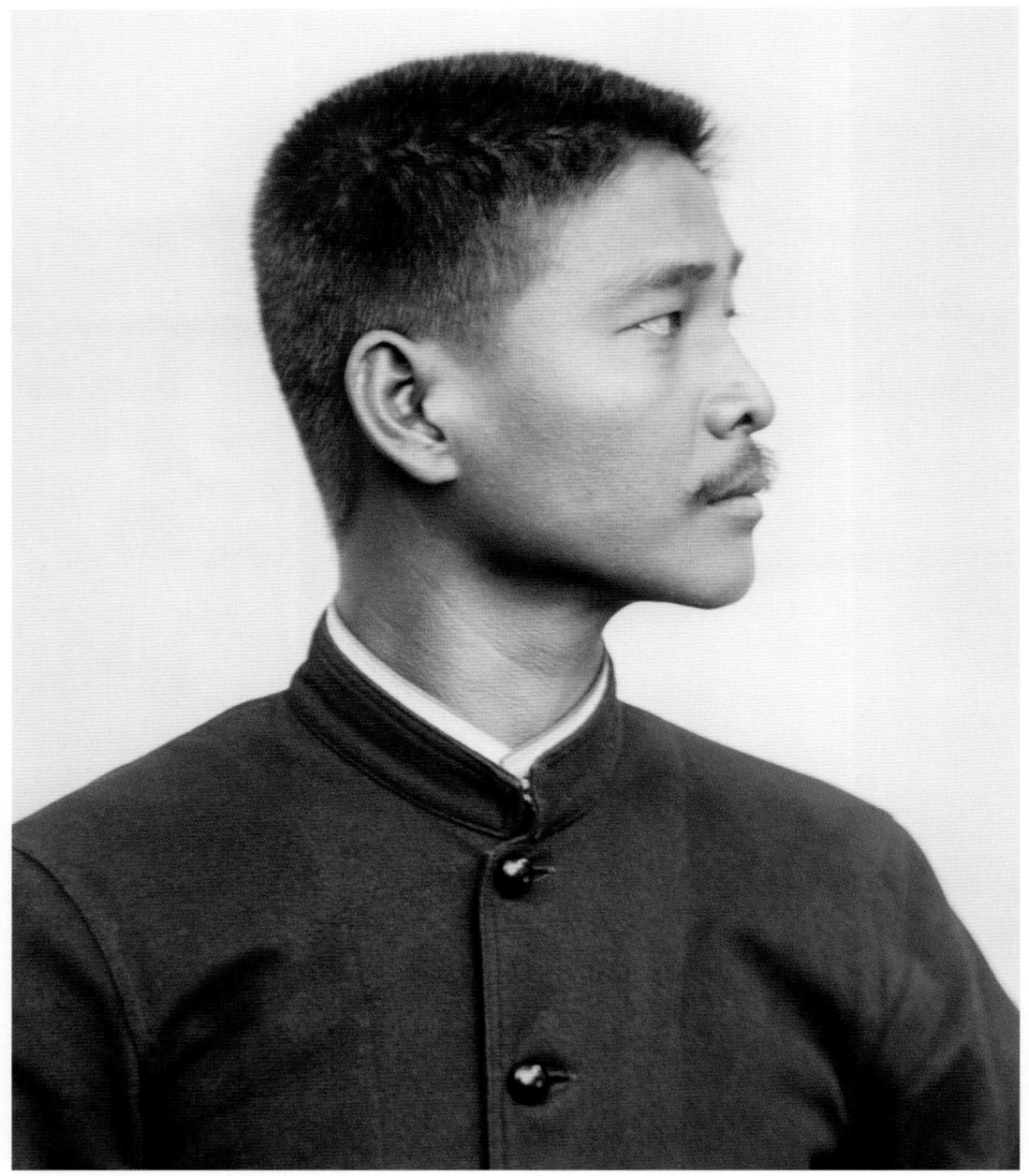

LEFT: **Khmer-Annamite officer.** Phnom Penh. 1898. André Salles. Bibliothèque nationale de France/Société de Géographie, Paris.

The Khmer-Annamite Officer

When André SALLES (1860–1929) visited Cambodia in 1893, he was already a prolific photographer, no doubt making use of the smaller, lighter wooden camera that George Groslier would be using so successfully twenty years later. He traveled across Indochina for three years, photographing people, places, and activities. As a very active member of the Société de Géographie in Paris, he donated hundreds of negative plates to their archives. This photograph of a stylish Khmer-Annamite officer taken in Phnom Penh, whom Salle also photographed in frontal view, shows the subject calm and assured before Salles' anthropological lens. It was a rare and dignified portrait of one of his trusted companions.

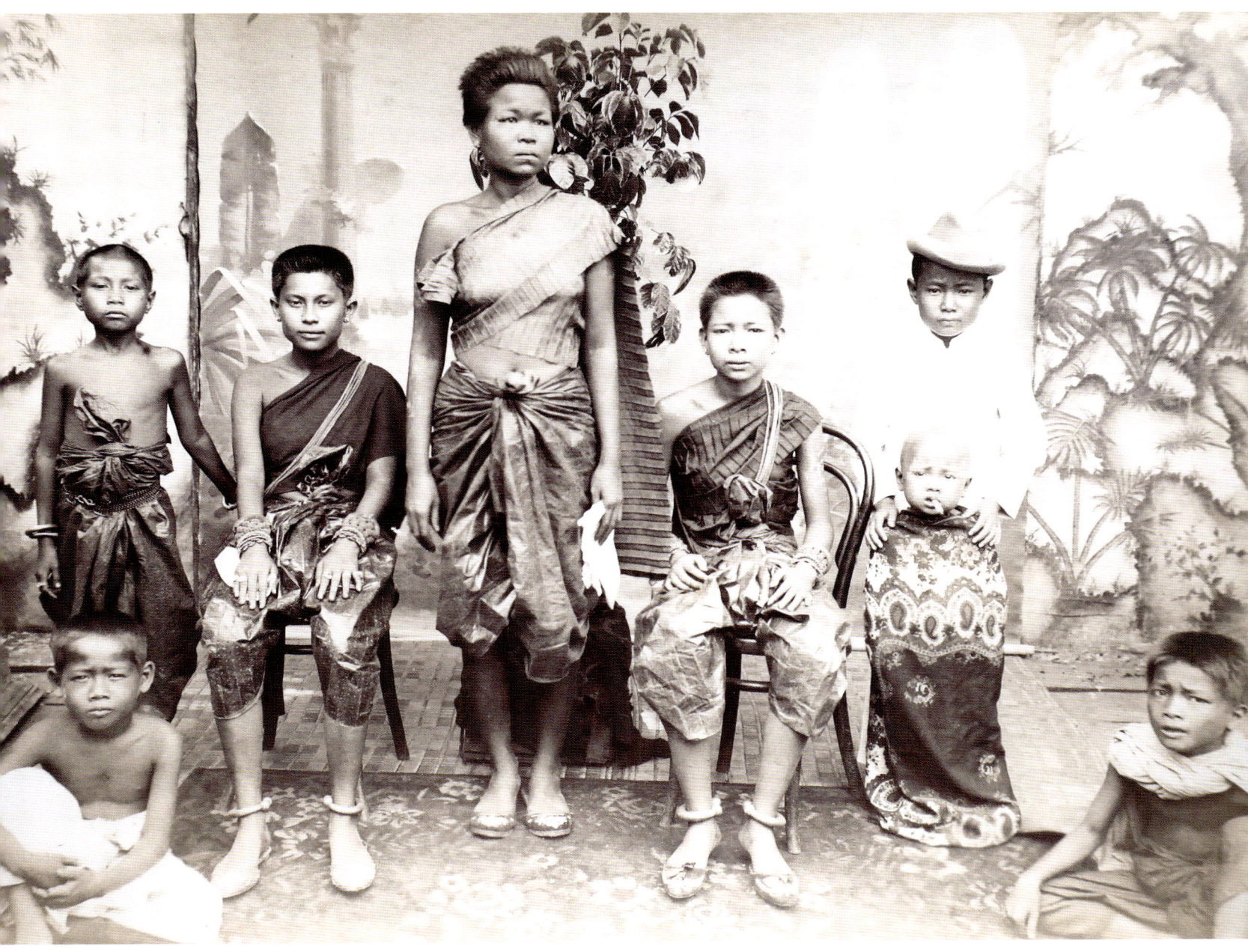

Wealthy Cambodian Women and Children

Three well-dressed women are positioned center stage in this formal studio group portrait. Framed by five children, one of them, wearing a fine felt fedora, has wrapped his younger sibling in an imported French scarf and popped a sweet in his mouth, perhaps to quieten his restlessness before the photographer. There were a few commercial studios operating in Phnom Penh by the early twentieth century. The exotically painted canvas backdrop, with the base of a wooden column to the left and narrow floorboards (a palatial residence would have wider polished hardwood), all suggest the group of eight had left their residence for this special studio ensemble. At least one other photograph was taken at the time, and it was reproduced as a postcard by the Saigon lithographer and printer Monsieur Claude. That image shows the youngest boy naked and the three women holding Western umbrellas, a fashionable accessory for the elite.

ABOVE: **Studio portrait of children of a wealthy household.** Phnom Penh. ca. 1890s. Photographer unknown. Philippe Damas Collection, Singapore.

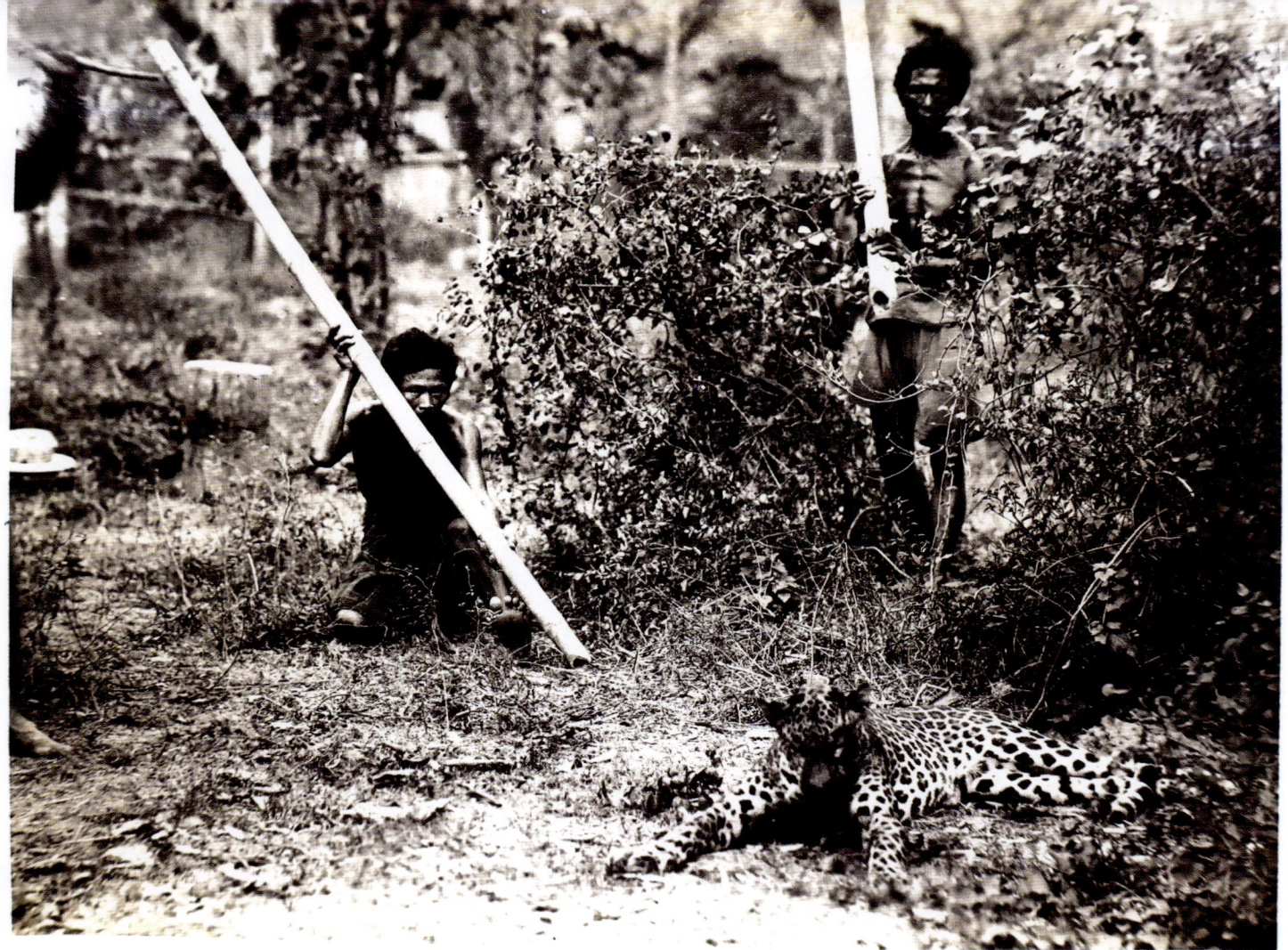

Panther, in d. Vorstadt P.P.'s erlegt. 1899.

Posing With a Leopard Kill

Two Cambodian men, posing for the camera with bamboo poles, mock threaten a leopard. Whether the animal is alive, in a comatose state, or dead is unclear, but the rough fencing in the background suggests a settled rather than a remote or wild location. Was the animal intruding into a village looking for an easy kill from the chicken coup? No "proud white hunter" is evident, with one foot astride the fallen carcass. Nowadays, trophy hunting photography arouses disapproval at the callous pride of the hunter, or, less often, an ode in his defense that celebrates the natural cycle of the hunter and the hunted. Whatever the perspective, in late nineteenth-century Cambodia, this feline was most probably prized for its pelt.

ABOVE: **Posing with a leopard kill.** Location and photographer unknown. Print dated 1899. Philippe Damas Collection, Singapore.

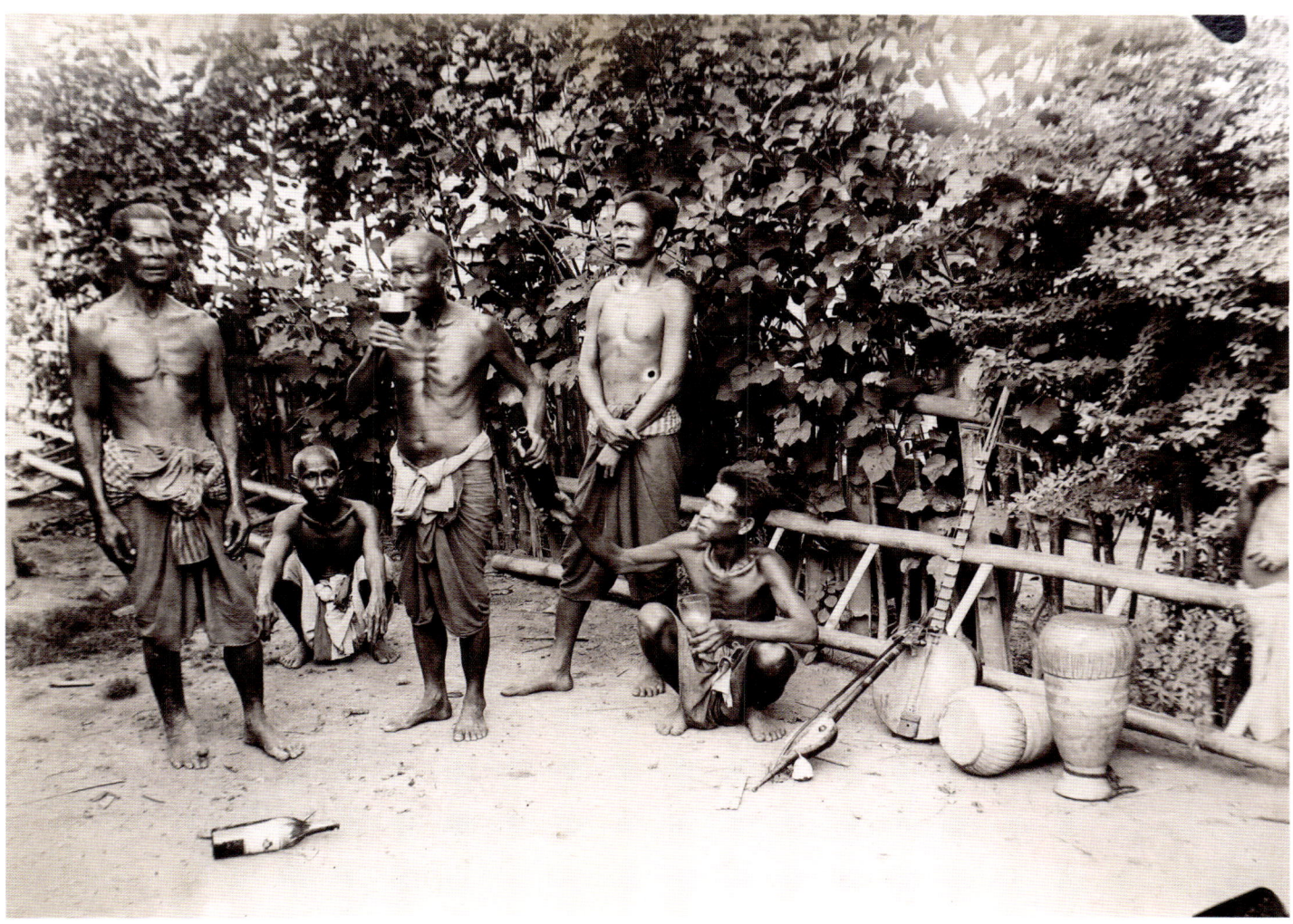

Cambodj: Musikanten

The Drinking Musicians

ABOVE: **Musicians posing as drinkers.** Probably Phnom Penh. ca. 1900. Photographer unknown. Philippe Damas Collection, Singapore.

Five musicians, with their instruments placed next to a bamboo ladder on their left, play-act a drinking scene with a couple of large wine glasses and two wine bottles as props. They seem less than enthusiastic about the caper. Who set up this scenario and who took the photograph? Was it a European, clumsily mocking a supposed attempt at sophistication on the part of a "timid and docile race"? Or was it a Cambodian photographer poking fun at some of the "colons" who were driven to alcohol and opium by loneliness, tropical heat, or the failure of their local businesses? It is an awkward image and difficult to interpret, as evidenced by the bemused child on the extreme right. From an ethnomusicologist perspective, however, it is the set of musical instruments in the photograph that shine.

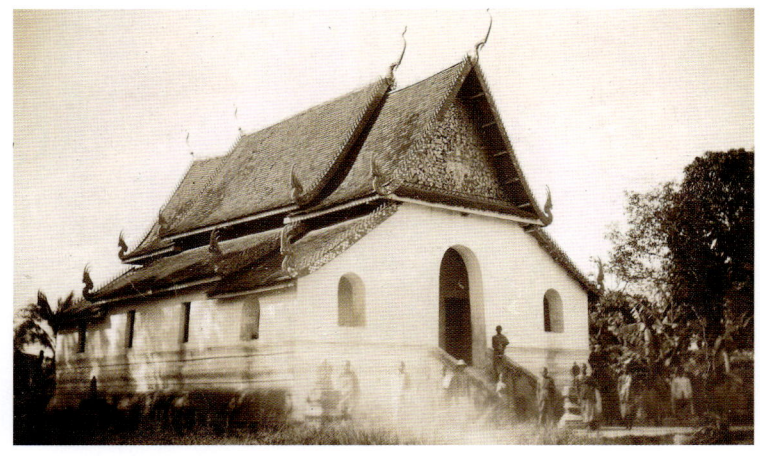
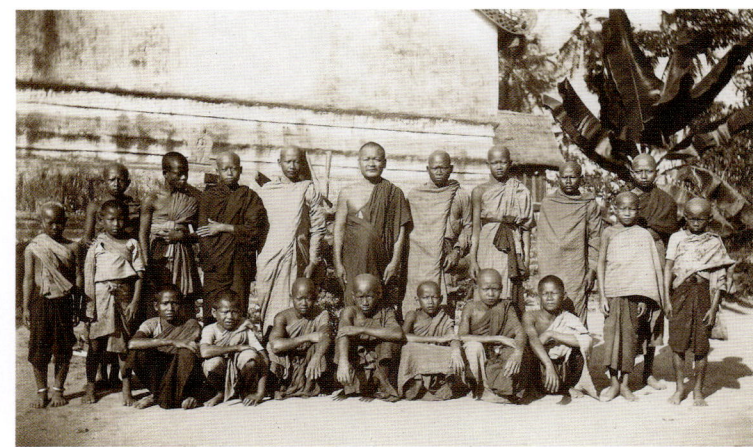
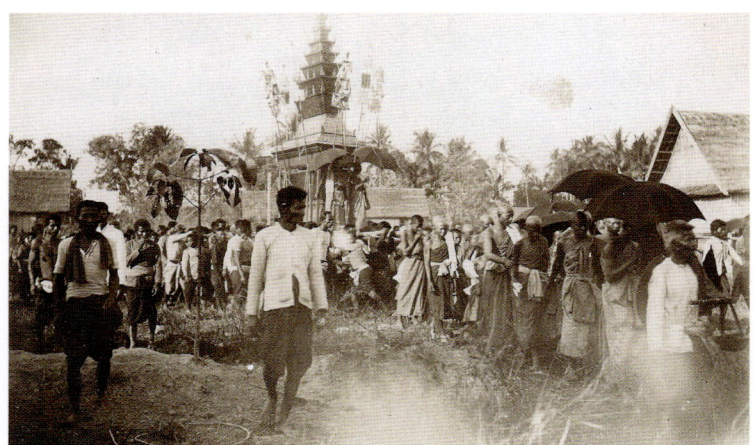
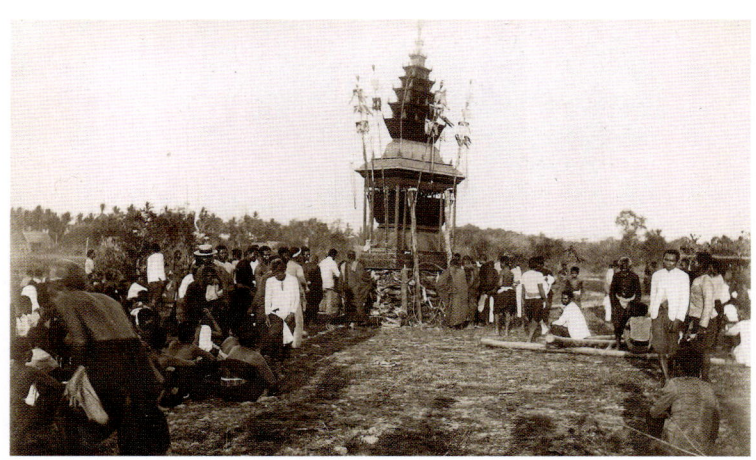
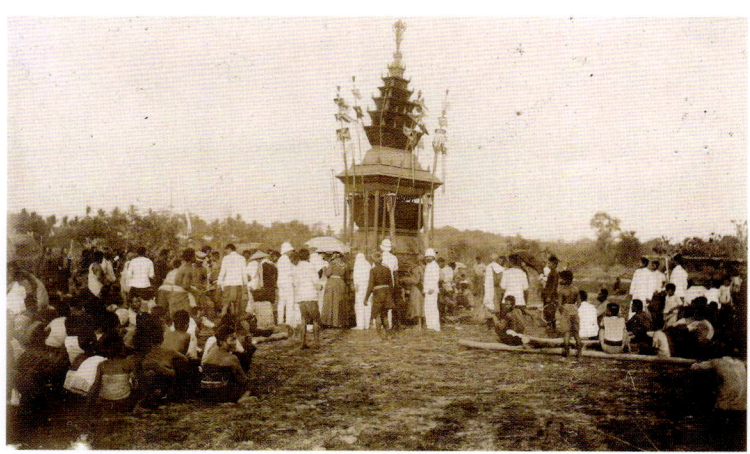
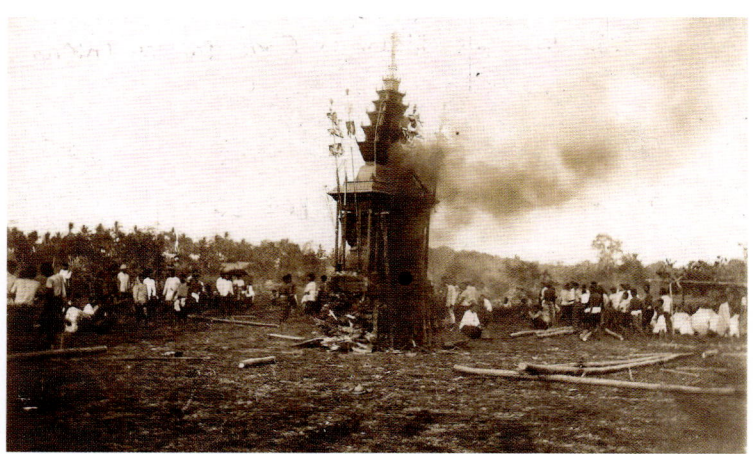

TOP LEFT, ZIG-ZAG DOWN: **The local wat; the head monk, monks, and novices before the wat; mourners carrying the catafalque to the cremation ground; placing the catafalque on the funerary pyre; lighting the pyre, with observing French families; the catafalque consumed by fire.**

Photographs: Stung-Treng. ca. 1903. Albert Tajasque. Marine Pommereau Collection.

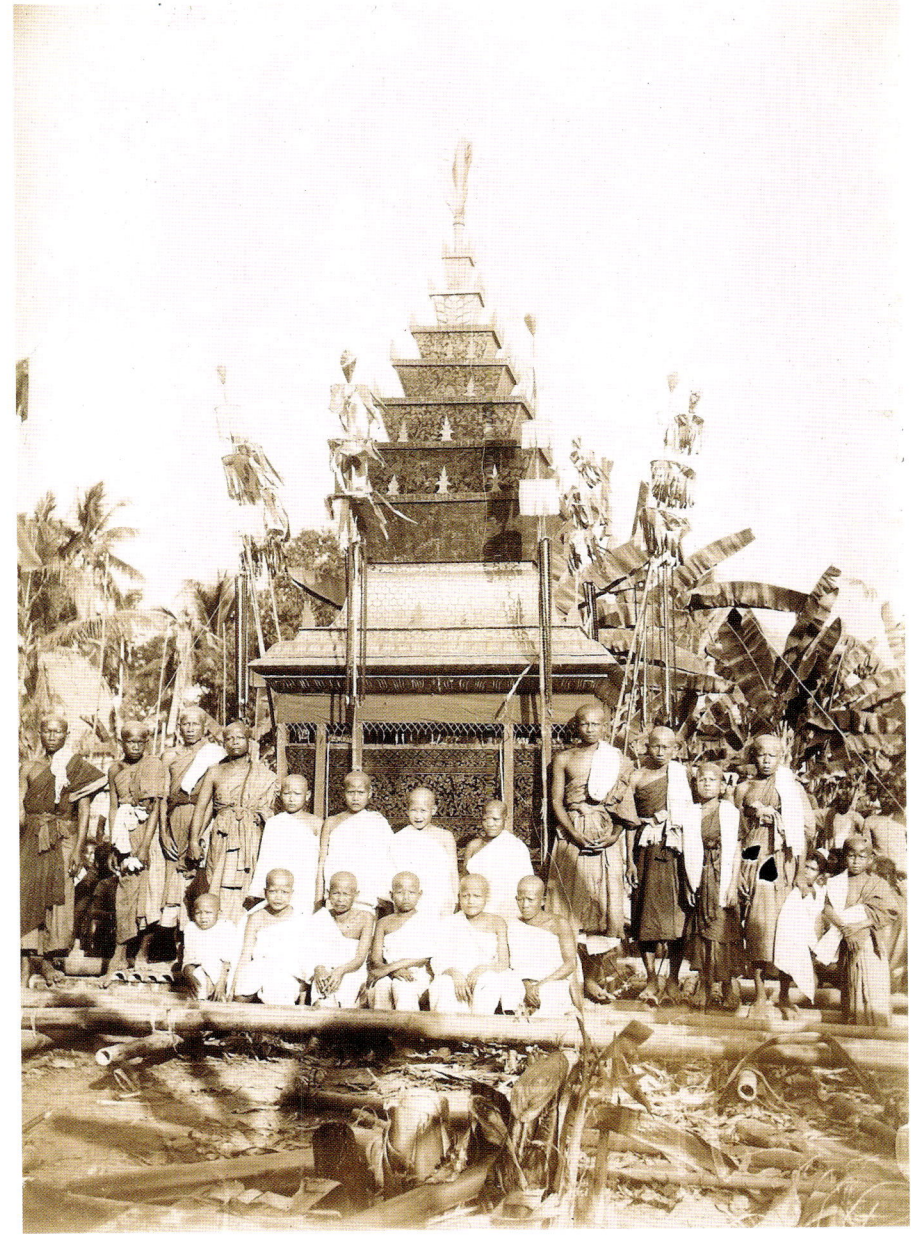

Family mourners and officiating monks before the catafalque. Stung-Treng. ca. 1903. Albert Tajasque. Marine Pommereau Collection.

A Funeral Procession in Stung-Treng

François Albert Louis TAJASQUE (1877–1959) was a dedicated public servant who worked in the colonial administration from 1903 to 1909. He was seconded to Strung-Treng in 1907. While in residence at this isolated post, he documented the cremation of a respected Chan-Hmnong elder. First, he photographed the head monk and his functionaries at the local wat, and then again in front of the paper and bamboo catafalque used to hold the deceased remains (right). Next, he showed the funeral procession on its way to the cremation grounds, with the curious French residents observing the lighting of the pyre. Finally, we see the lazy pall of black smoke that heralded the conflagration. These photographs, taken at the same location and within a few hours of each other, arguably represent one of the first photojournalistic essays in Cambodia's photographic history.

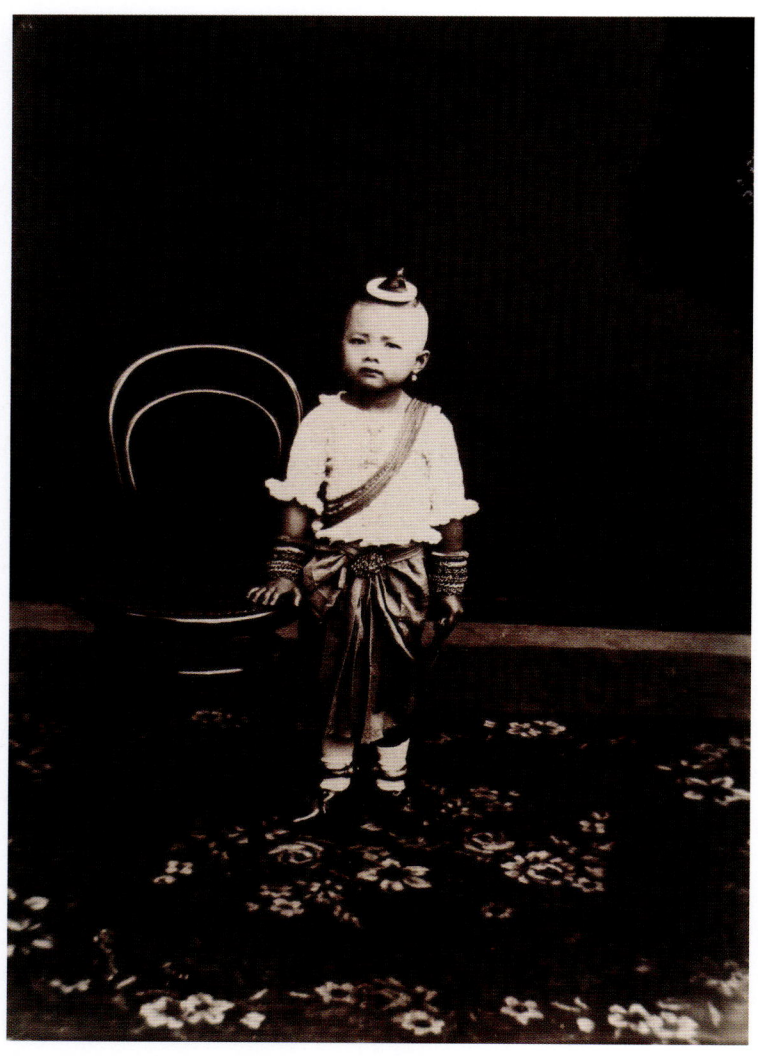

LEFT: A child of a wealthy family. Probably a Phnom Penh studio. ca. 1900. Photographer unknown. Philippe Damas Collection, Singapore.

OPPOSITE: Dancer of the Royal Palace. Probably a Phnom Penh studio. ca. 1900. Photographer unknown. Philippe Damas Collection, Singapore.

A Child of a Wealthy Family

Looking up to the photographer, the subject, perhaps a young royal, holds a frank and attentive stare, befitting an honored child. The darkness of the backdrop and carpet highlights the galaxy of textured curves: the floral coronet atop the child's head, the single pearl earring, the woven metal sash across the frilled blouse, the heavy annealed bracelets and bronze anklets, and next to her, the shiny back of a Thonet bentwood chair. The dark trousers or *sompot chong kben*, are made of tightly woven *ikat* silk, the dense weave and dark color creating a deep luminance. Her feet, clad in patent leather shoes, are spread apart, anchoring her pose.

A Dancer of the Royal Palace

The intense pattern making between the luxuriously dressed dancer and the repetitive machine-printed backdrop creates a shimmering camouflage, disguising the dancer's form, while her whitened face creates a masked calm. Studio portraits like this were often reproduced as postcards to provide enticing glimpses of the exotic East. Twenty years later, George Groslier would photograph dancers in more austere costumes but in more dynamic poses in an attempt to capture a Cambodian art form he felt was disappearing.

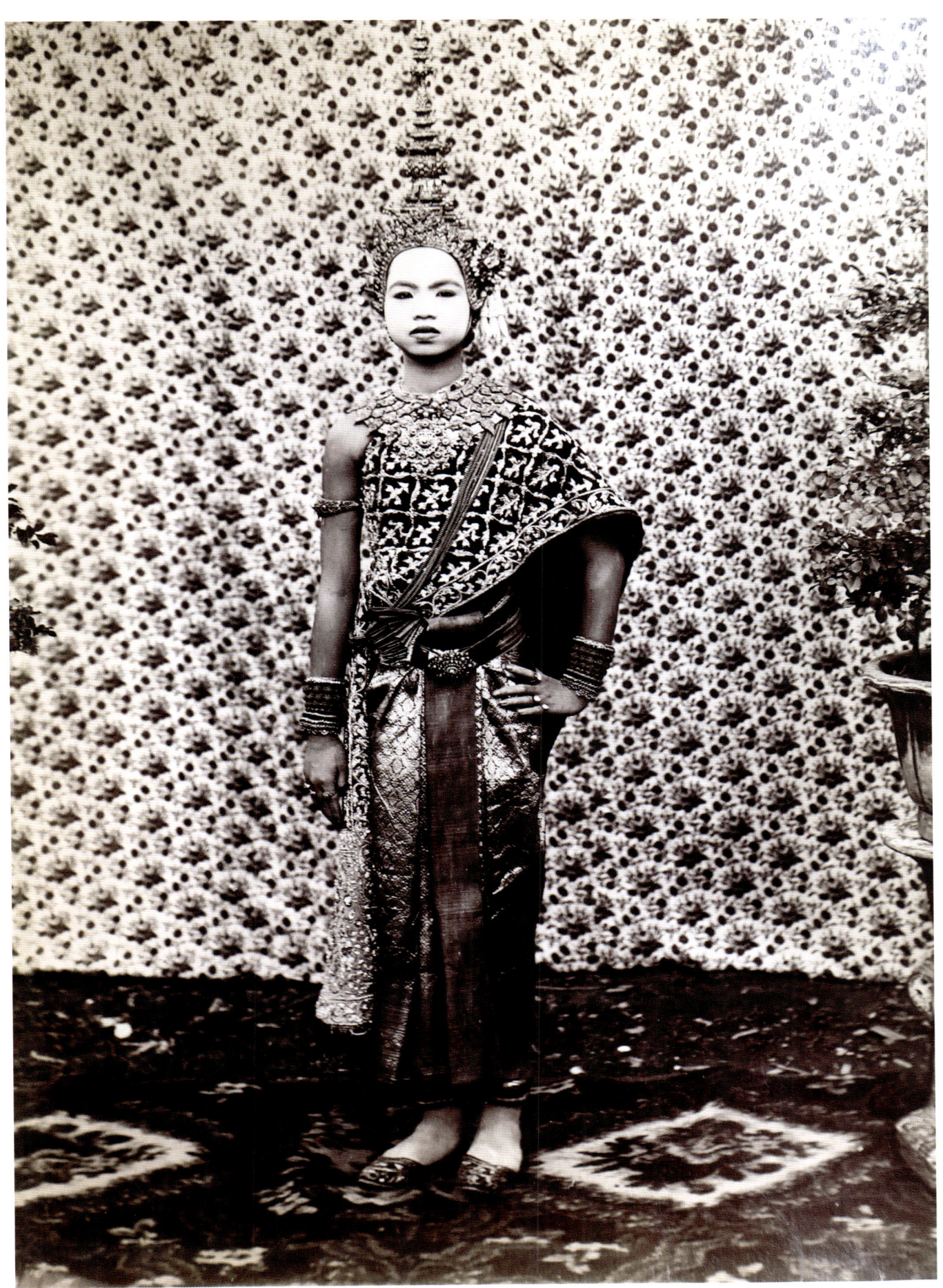

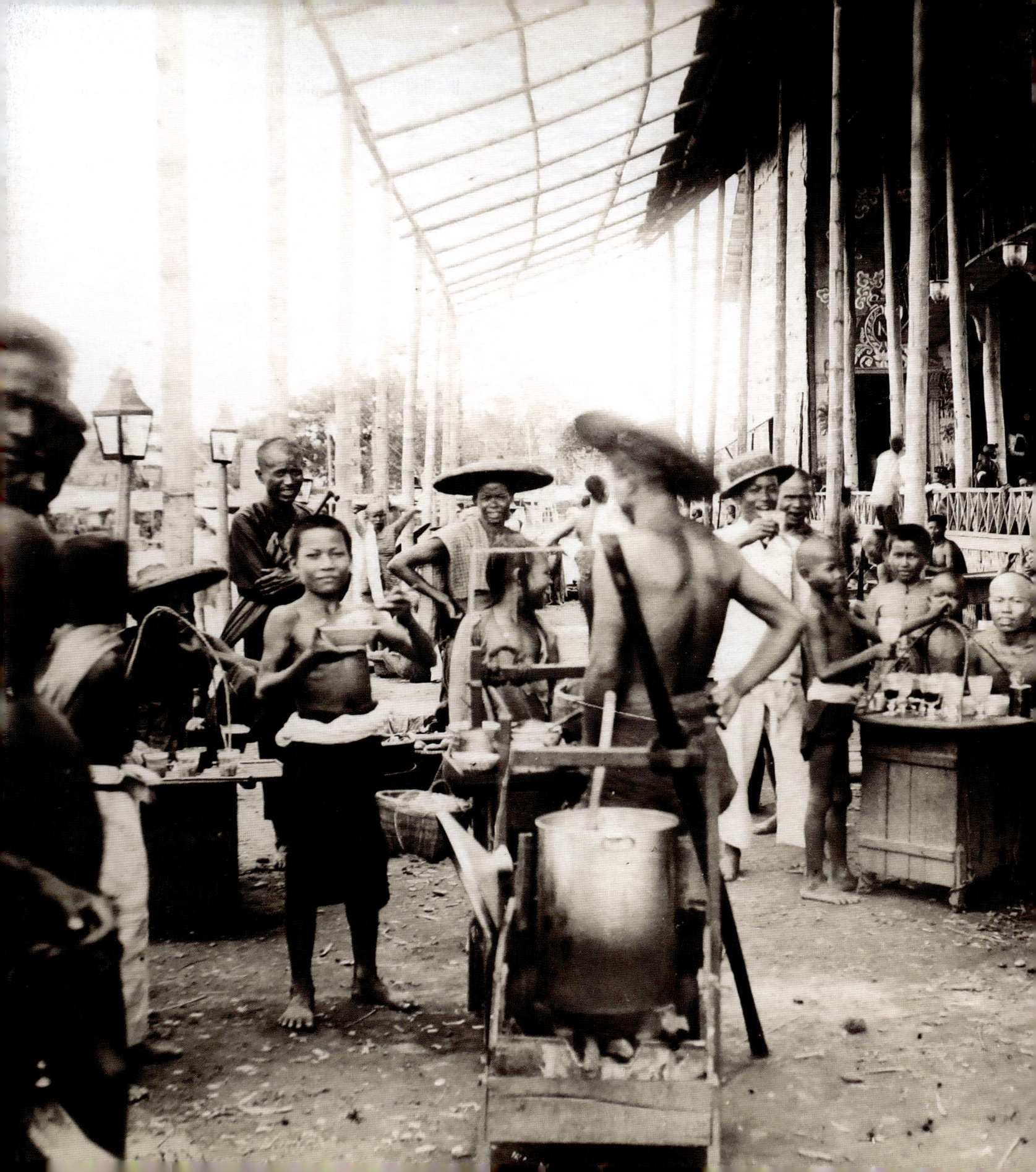

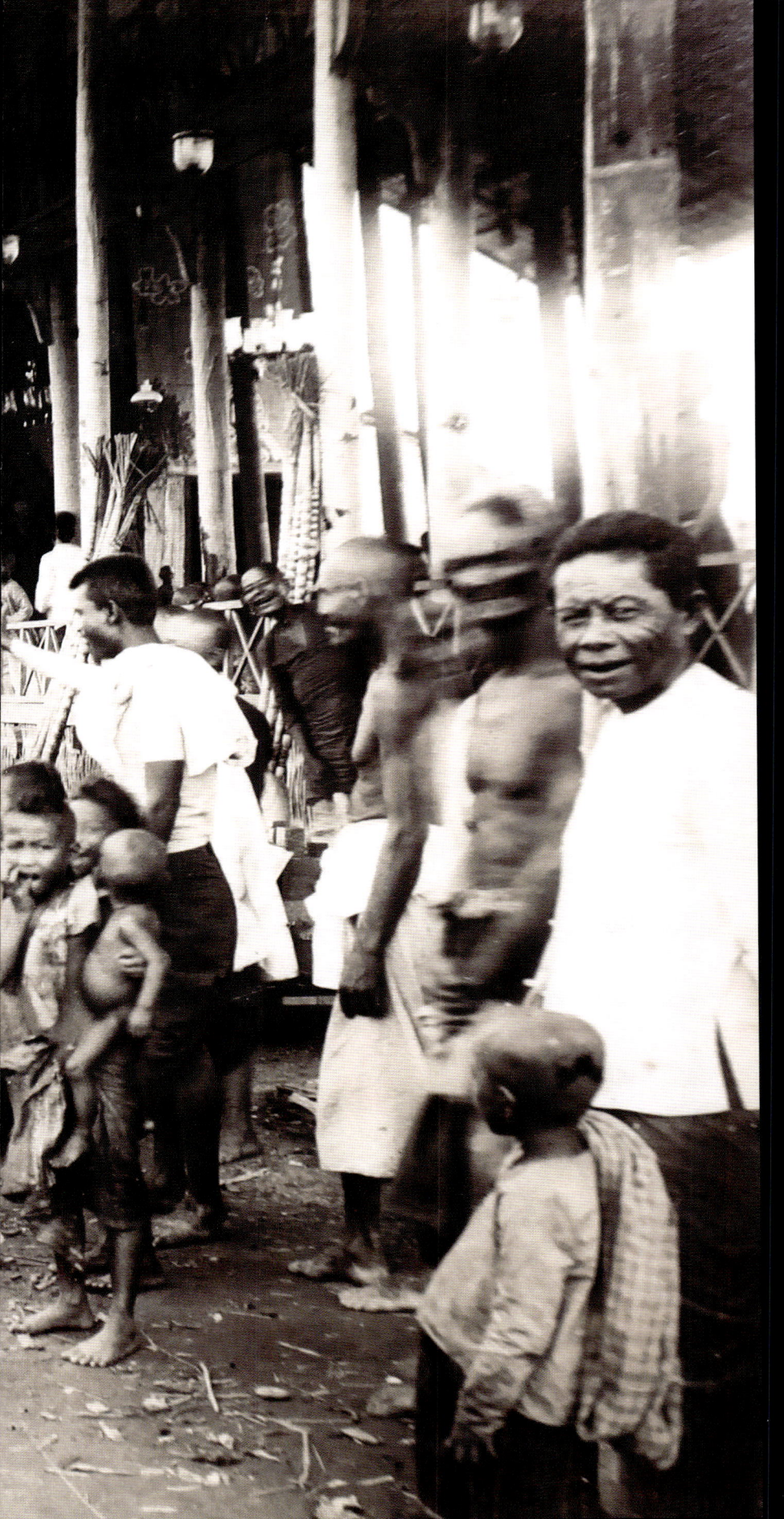

Food Hawkers at the Phochani Pavilion

A group of food hawkers have been drawn to feed the hungry performers and their retinue at the Phochani Pavilion in the royal compound in Phnom Penh. The pavilion was used for rehearsals and performances of the royal dancers, who apparently numbered in the hundreds during Norodom's reign. It is a bustling scene: moving bodies, tea stalls, soup cauldrons, babies, and noodle bowls. Whoever the photographer was, he had an easy rapport with the crowd as he nestled into the scene, set up his camera, and captured the moment. Customers acknowledge the action, raising their beverages, hoisting their food bowls; a jaunty straw boater, hands on a hip, a conversation, laughter, and chatter abound. Perhaps the pavilion is undergoing a renovation, or is a rehearsal soon to commence? The pavilion was built between 1907 and 1912. This image, not of a king, a governor, or the wealthy elite, but of everyday life, reveals a rich cross-section of the populace as colonial Cambodia moves into the twentieth century. If every collection has its masterpiece, this is the one. This dance pavilion should not be confused with the grander, iconic Chanchhaya Pavilion, the most public of structures that sits astride the palace's eastern walls.

1906–1927
The Reign of King Sisowath

The reign of King Sisowath (1840–1927) saw an intensification of French political control and cultural influence in Cambodia. The first twenty years of the new century also saw a major development in the mechanics of photography. No longer the preserve of a knowledgeable few, photography was to become a passion for many with the advent of the Kodak Box Brownie and other easy-to-use cameras with prepackaged film. At the same time, new photomechanical techniques of printing established in the late nineteenth century enabled photographs to be reproduced with greater efficiency and speed. A postcard craze swept the world. Printed in Europe, millions were bulk-imported into Indochina, bought by tourists and colonial officials, penned with messages of love and colonial adventure, and then posted back to Europe.

Sisowath was the first Cambodian monarch to visit France when he attended the Colonial Exhibition held in Marseille in 1906. The following year, Siam, which had annexed the three provinces of Siem Reap, Battambang, and Sisophon in the late eighteenth century, returned them to Cambodia under French diplomatic pressure. The ritual center of the kingdom—the famed temples of Angkor—were once more under Cambodian sovereignty.

In 1908, the newly established École française d'Extrême-Orient (EFEO) built a base at Siem Reap to work on the restoration of the Angkorian monuments. Historians and archaeologists such as Henri Parmentier (1871–1949) and Charles Carpeaux (1825–70), as well as the linguist Louis Finot (1864–1935), not only photographed the monuments but also landscapes, native peoples, and cultural activities. Over the coming century, an enormous archive of images was accumulated. In the same year that the EFEO was established, Joseph Ferdinand Perrot (1873–ca. 1928), with an eye on the prevailing understanding of criminality in Europe, created the Cambodian Criminal Identity Service based on photographic records. His craft appealed to the colonial bureaucracy. Less than ten years later, even midwives needed photographs to confirm their identity.

In Phnom Penh, a few private photographic studios like the Union and the Royal created personalized mementos for the elite. Saigon, however, situated on the mouth of the Mekong and with its larger population, remained the popular commercial capital and gateway to Cambodia. Dozens of photographic studios, such as those owned by the prolific Pierre Dieulefils (1862–1937) and the graphically inventive Ludovic Crespin (b. 1873), competed for audiences with quick turnaround portraiture and readily assembled souvenir albums brimming with imagery. In 1920, a new museum and a school of arts were built in Phnom Penh. The founder, George Groslier (1887–1945), realized the value of photography to document the museum's expanding collections.

With the age of steamships at its zenith, the decade saw a surge in international travelers from beyond the Francophone world. Reporters and writers like Harry L. Foster (1894–1932) and Helen Churchill Candee (1858–1949) used their cameras to illustrate their travel writing, while commercial photographers like J. Dearden Holmes (1873–1937) saw there was money to be made providing enthralling images for cigarette cards.

King Sisowath at the Royal Palace.
Phnom Penh. 1906. Photographer unknown.
National Archives of Cambodia.

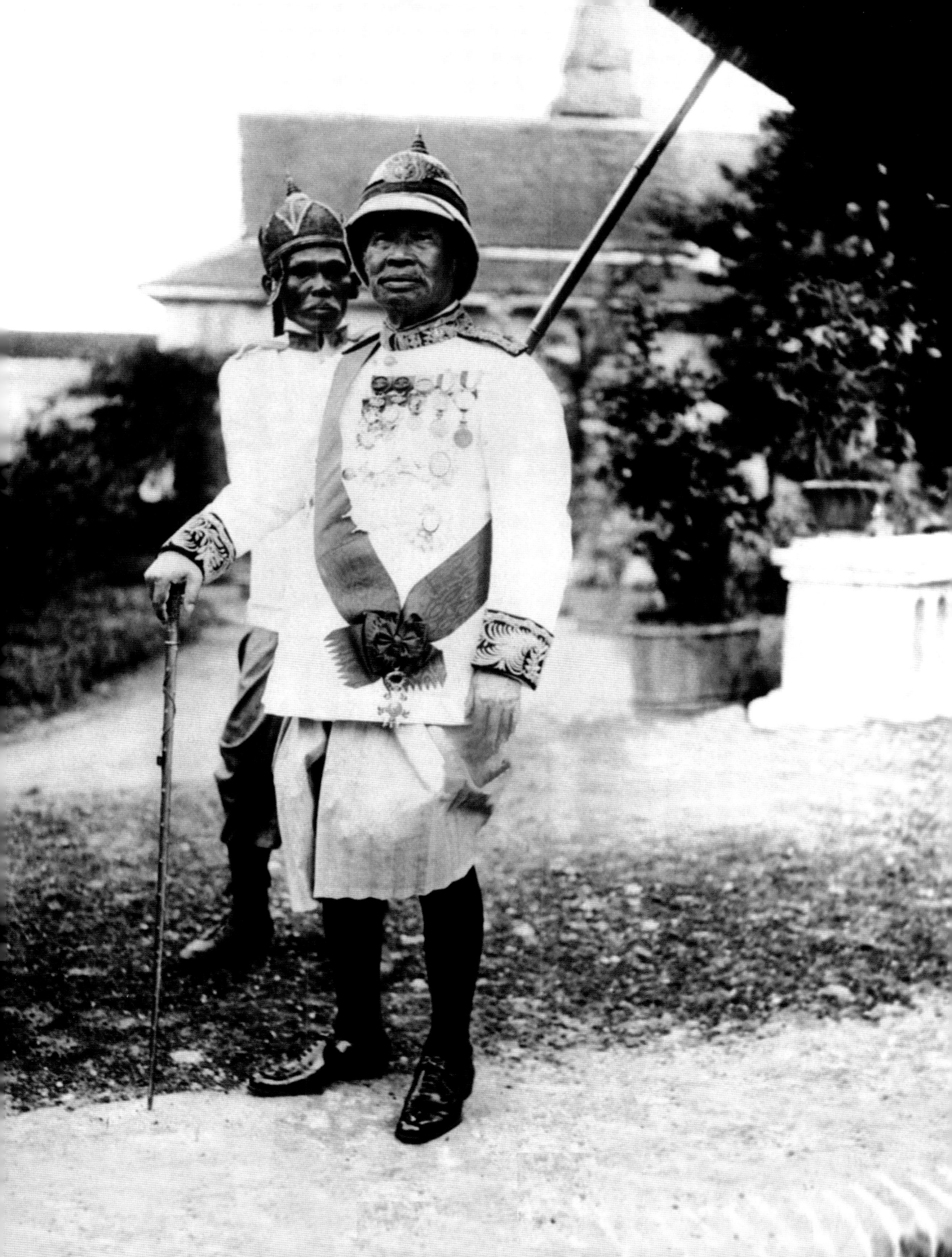

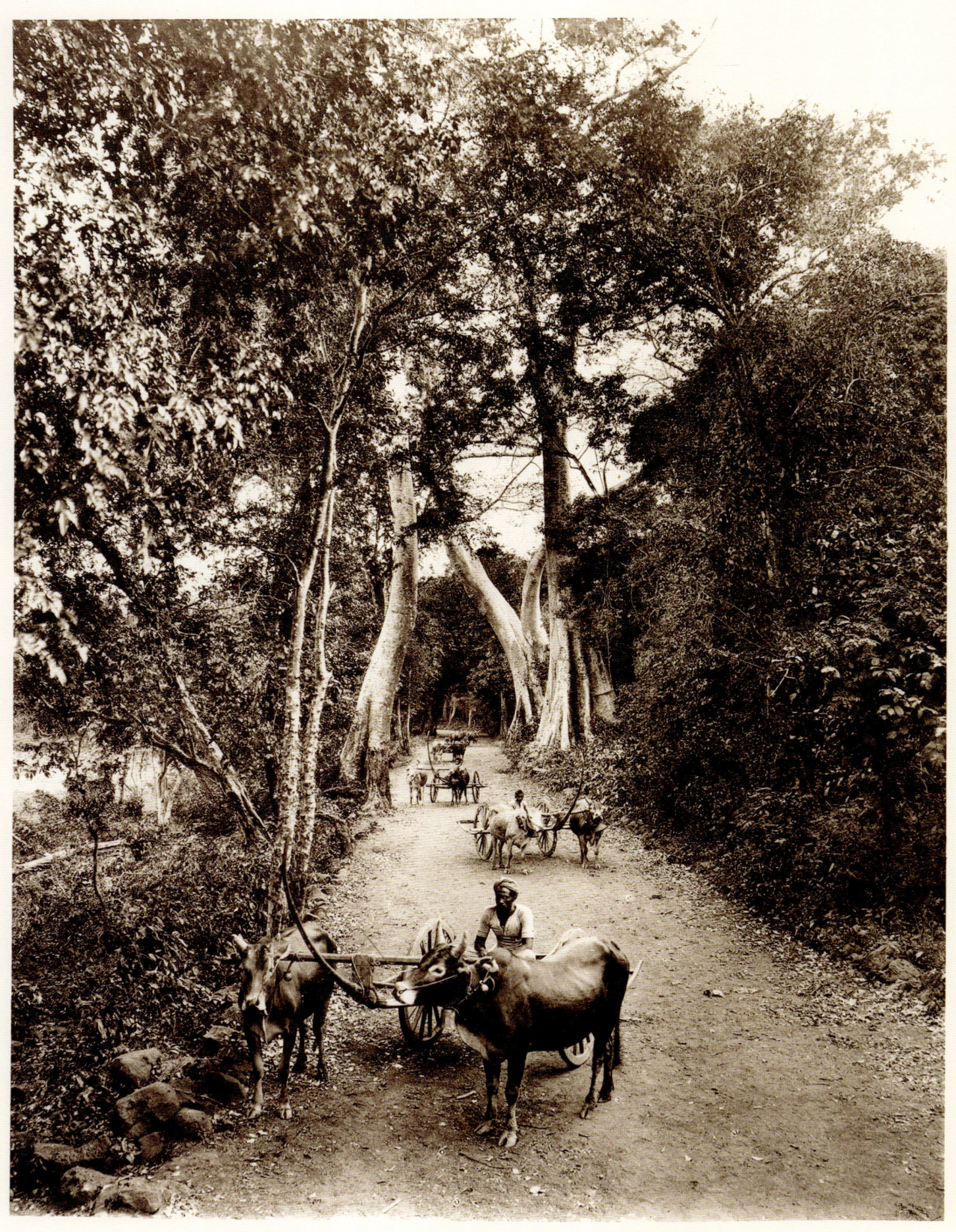

KOMPONG-CHAM — ROUTE DE VAT-NOKOR DANS LA FORÊT

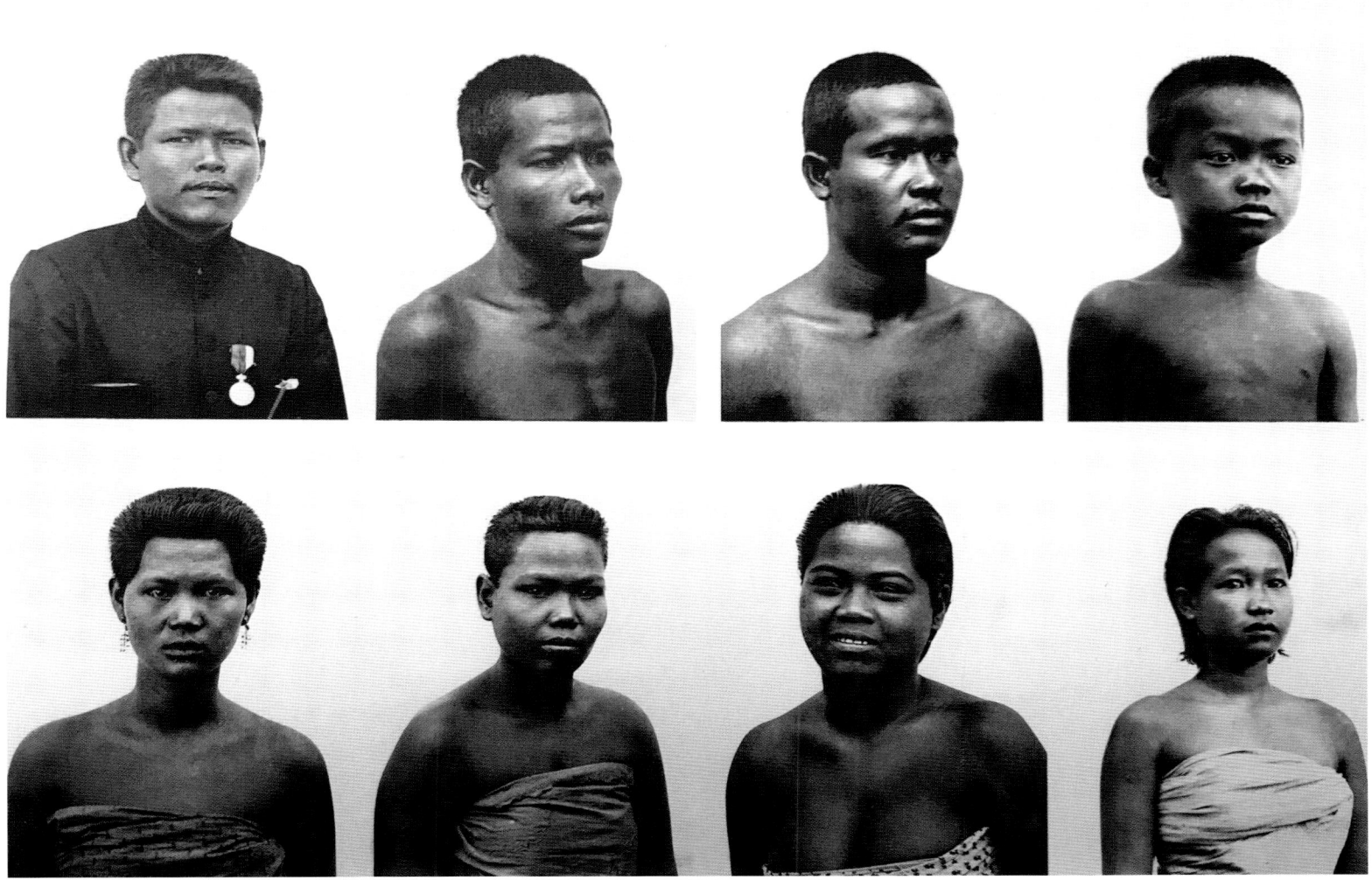

Ruins of Angkor Cambodia in 1909

ABOVE: **Types of Cambodians: men, women, children.** 1909.

LEFT: **Route to Wat Nokor and the forest.** Kompong Cham. 1909.

Source: From the first French edition, *L'Indo-Chine Pittoresque et Monumentale: Cambodge et Ruines d'Angkor*. P. Dieulefils. Paris. 1909. National Gallery of Australia.

Pierre DIEULEFILS (1862–1937) arrived in Indochina in 1885 and quickly established himself as a commercial photographer with a studio in Hanoi. Four years later, his images were displayed at the Exposition Universelle held in Paris in 1889. He is known for his prodigious output, with more than 4,500 photographs, many of which were turned into postcards attributed to his studio. Most he took himself, others he acquired or swapped with other photographers. In 1909, Dieulefils published three major photographic books devoted to Indochina, with the images printed in the sophisticated photo-gravure technique. The Cambodian volume, images from which are reproduced here, was introduced by Etienne Aymonier (1844–1929), the renowned archaeologist and Cambodian linguist, whose endorsement no doubt added prestige to the publication.

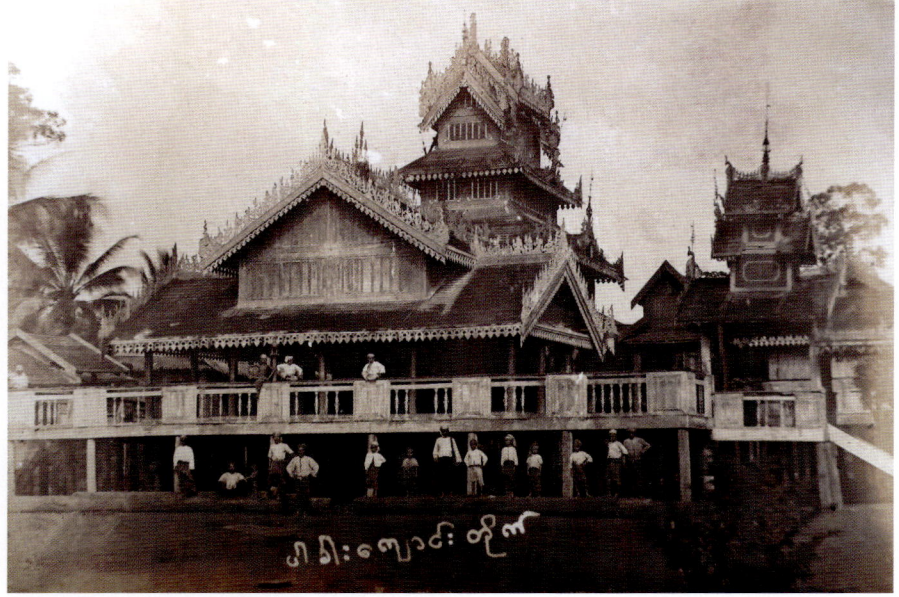

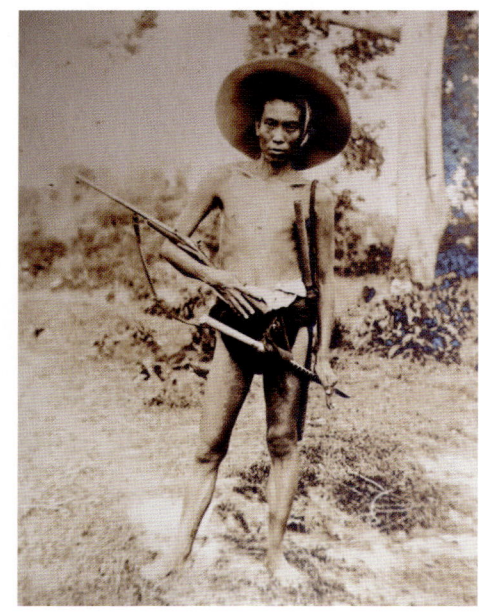

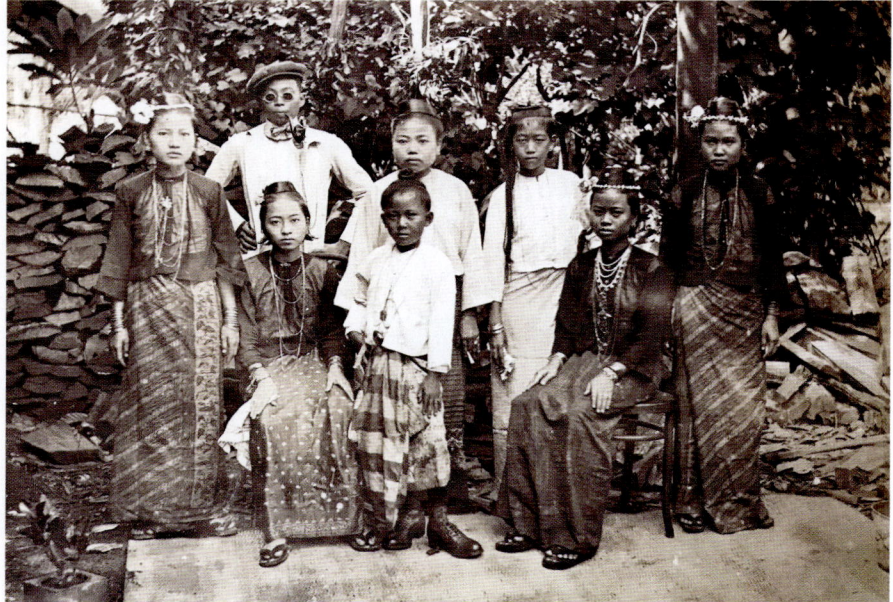

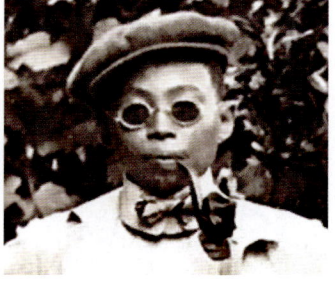

TOP LEFT: **Burmese pagoda of Boyaka.**

TOP RIGHT: **Koula hunter.** (Note the rifle and dagger.)

LEFT: **Burmese family.**

ABOVE: **Detail of left, showing the well-dressed male of the family.**

OPPOSITE: **Studio photograph of two young Burmese women.** Pailin. 1917. Photographer unknown.

Source: "Pailin Album." 1917. Photographer unknown. Philippe Damas Collection, Singapore.

The Burmese of Pailin

This beautiful but badly water-damaged album of blue paper-framed photographs focuses on the Burmese people who controlled the gem trade in Pailin Province on the western border of Cambodia with Thailand. The album appears to have been a gift to the then resident-superior, François Marius Baudoin. The photographer, however, remains unknown. Included are photographs of an elaborate timber temple dripping with fretwork, a dapper patrician wearing a cravat, motoring beret, and dark glasses, and a stuffed toy lion and dog barking at the feet of the two young women in front of a canvas backdrop (opposite). The images suggest a sophisticated community comfortable with its prestige and wealth.

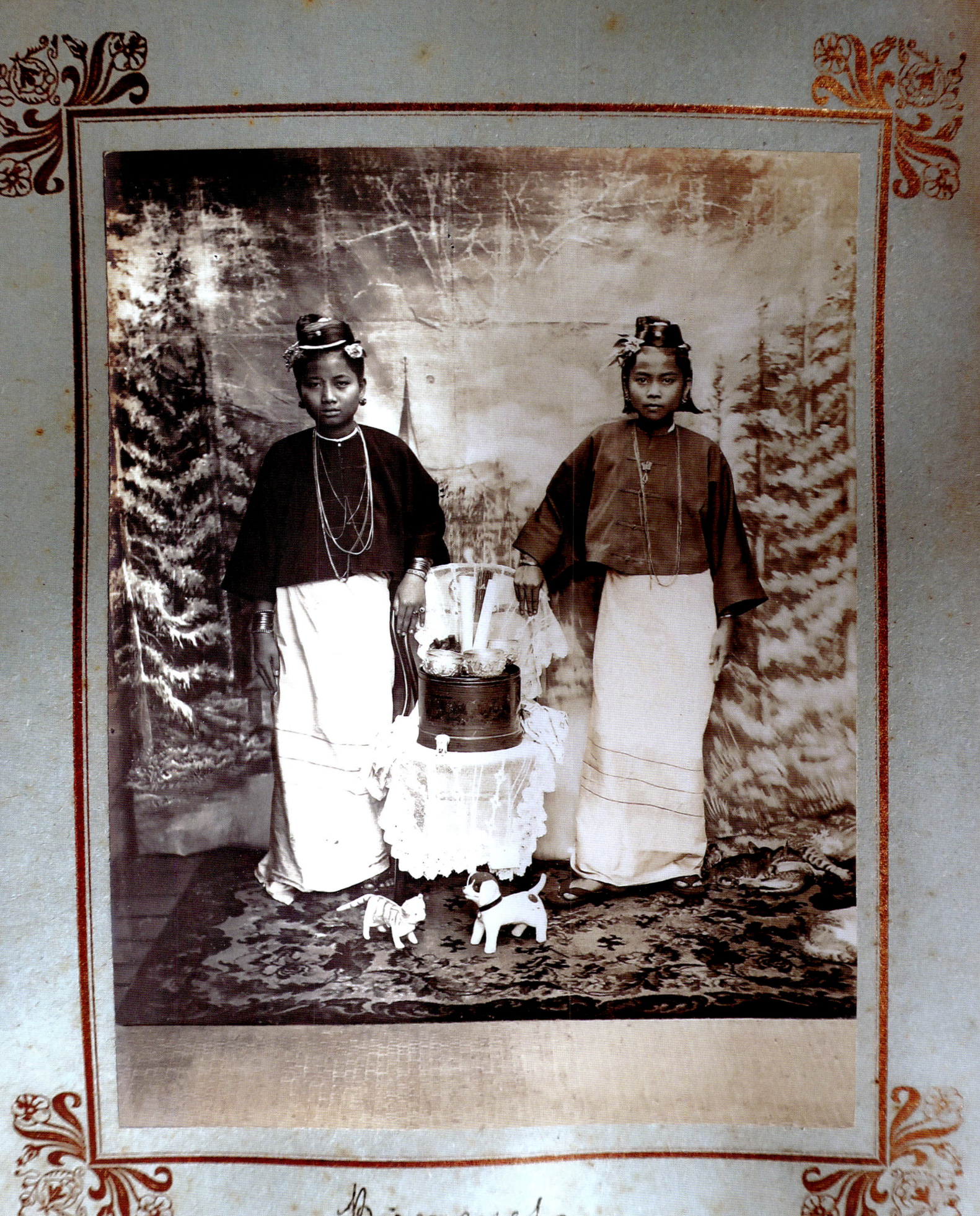

Burmese

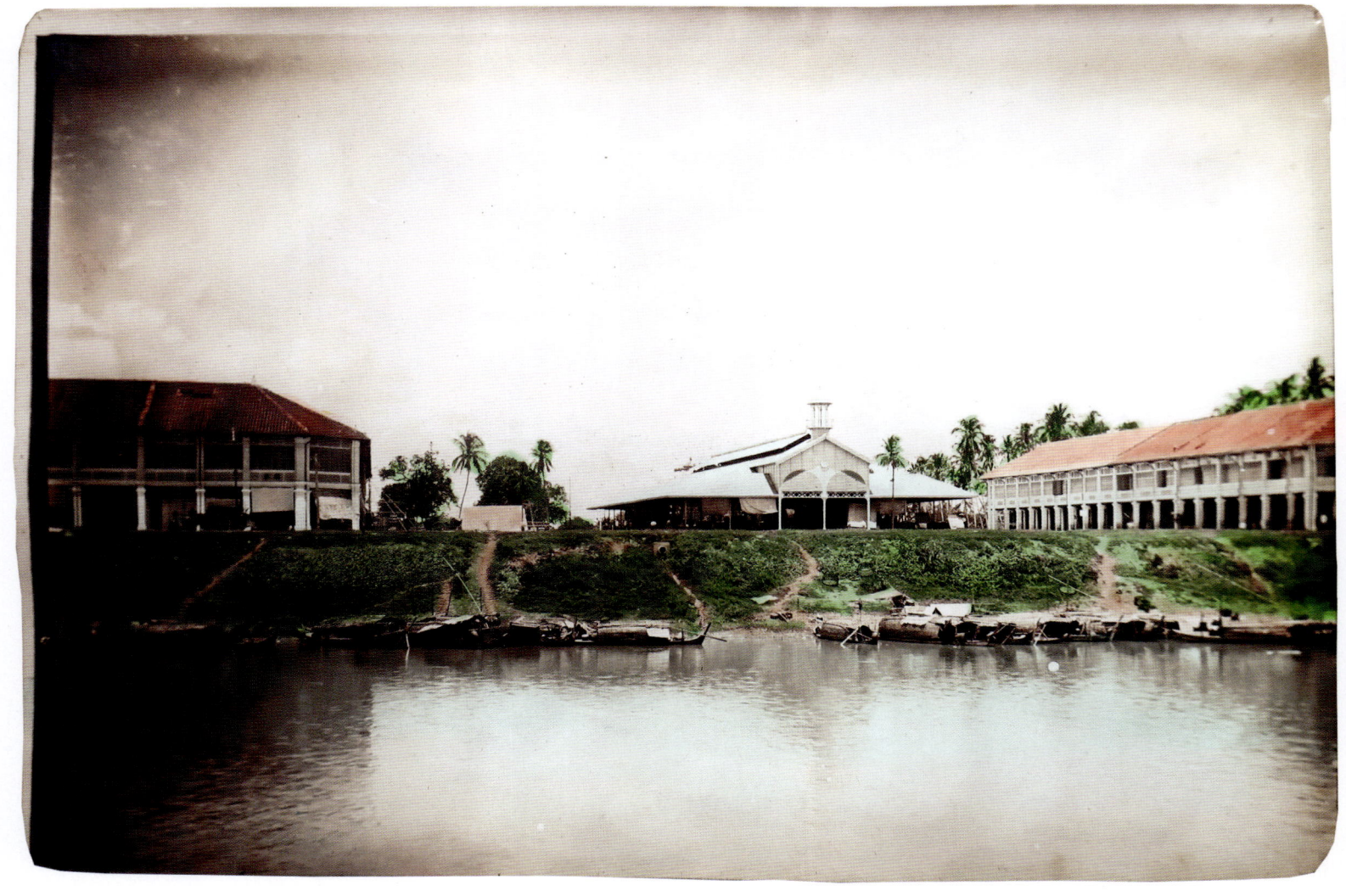

A Hand-Colored View of Battambang

This hand-tinted view of Battambang, looking north across the Sangker River, shows the original Battambang market with two-story shophouses on both sides. It comes from a rather sober collection of photographs, perhaps taken by a proud municipal engineer documenting the new colonial buildings of the township. The photographs show solid structures befitting a provincial capital, where the post office, courthouse, bridges, and distillery needed to be run with economic efficiency. At the time, the outskirts of Battambang were being opened to vast rice estates to develop exports for the country's cash economy.

Overlooking the Sangker River to Phsar Leu (upper market). Battambang. 1917. Photographer unknown. Philippe Damas Collection, Singapore.

The Cambodge Photomontage

Ludovic CRESPIN (b. 1873) founded a photo studio with his wife in Saigon in 1900. For over twenty-three years they were successful entrepreneurs, expanding their business, opening new studios, and buying out competitors. They published postcards and albums of thematic collections of photographs using the monogram of a cloverleaf as their logo. The artful montage below was used as a chapter divider for a printed album of images called *A Souvenir of Cochine China and Cambodia*. It predates by forty years the work of magazine graphic designers during Sihanouk's reign in the 1960s. Crespin lobbied hard for his panoramic photographs of Indochina to be included as official exhibits at the 1922 Marseille Colonial Exhibition. His wish was granted, and this honor for the couple was perhaps the crowning achievement of their careers.

Cambodge. Album divider. From *A Souvenir of Cochine China and Cambodia*. Ludovic Crespin. Saigon. ca. 1920. Philippe Damas Collection, Singapore.

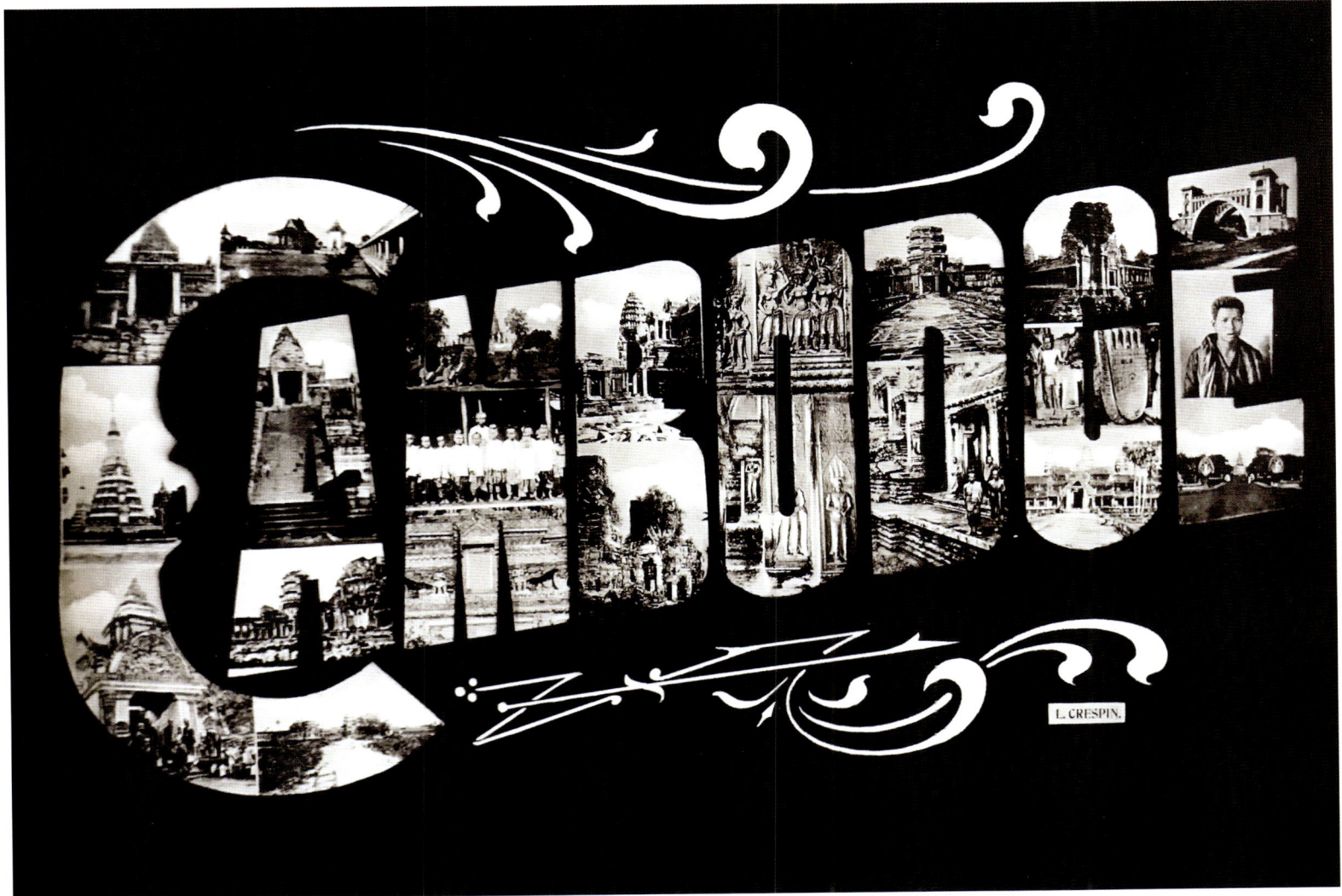

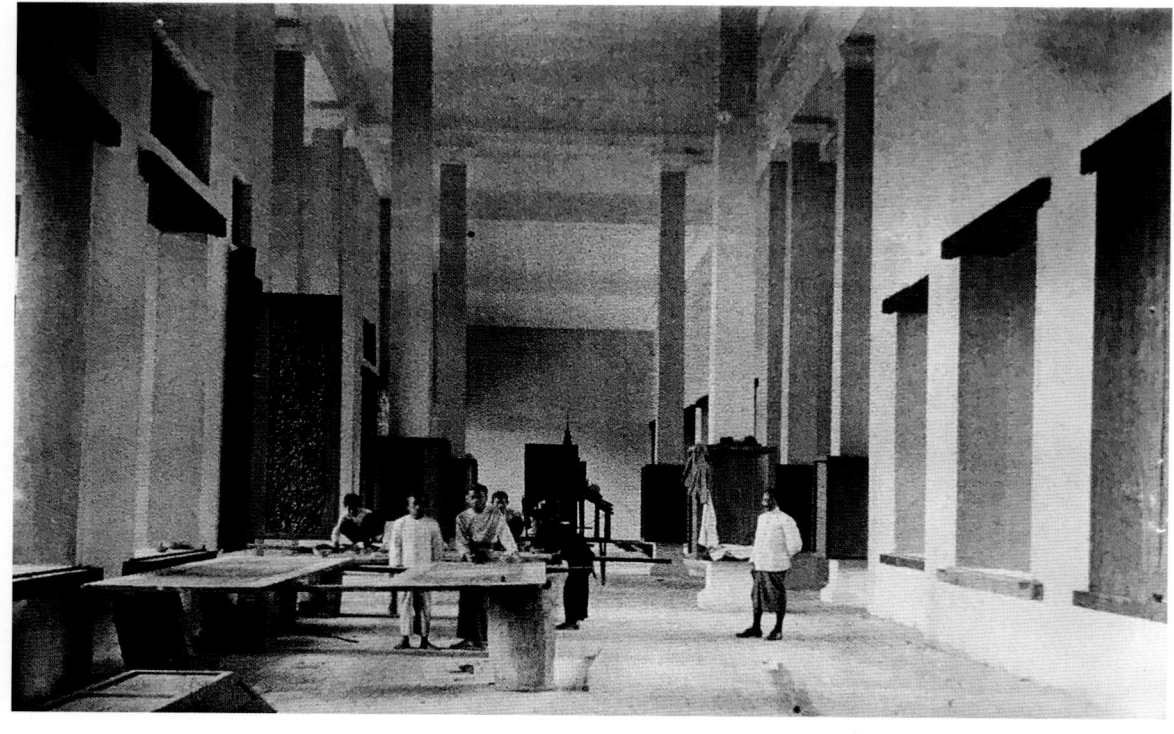

Entrance Gallery. Students from the School of Art decorate the window panels. Musée Albert Sarraut, Phnom Penh. 1919. Attributed to George Groslier. Commemorative booklet for the opening of the museum. 1920. National Museum of Cambodia.

Preparing the Museum

The construction of a new museum in Phnom Penh was an important recognition of the wealth of Cambodian material culture and the need for a permanent home to display historical artifacts and items of cultural significance for public education and enjoyment. It also marked a symbolic shift of power. The cultural heritage of the nation was now part of the public domain, rather than something that was "owned" by the monarchy. The sheer size of the internal spaces matches that of the palace architecture nearby. This redefining of a nation's heritage from the divine patrimony of the king to public ownership was not only a specific aim of the French "mission civilisatrice" in relation to its colonies, but also reflected changing attitudes in the West to the culture of other (non-Western) peoples. Taking advantage of an adjoining school of arts behind the museum, students decorated the massive wooden window shutters with *kbach* floral patterns. These superb window panels can still be seen at the museum, now known as the National Museum of Cambodia.

A Divinity Destroyed

The reflection of the sun in the water has been masked by the fallen torso of the deity Vishnu, to whom the magnificent early twelfth-century temple of Angkor Wat was dedicated. According to Hindu cosmological myth, it is Vishnu who dreams the universe into reality, and who represents one of the three fundamental forces through which the universe is created, maintained, and destroyed in an everlasting succession. The sculpture has been wrenched from its pedestal and dumped in a depression flooded by monsoon rains. The four arms of the mighty god that held symbols of his attributes have broken off, as have the head and feet, an ignominious end to the creator of the universe.

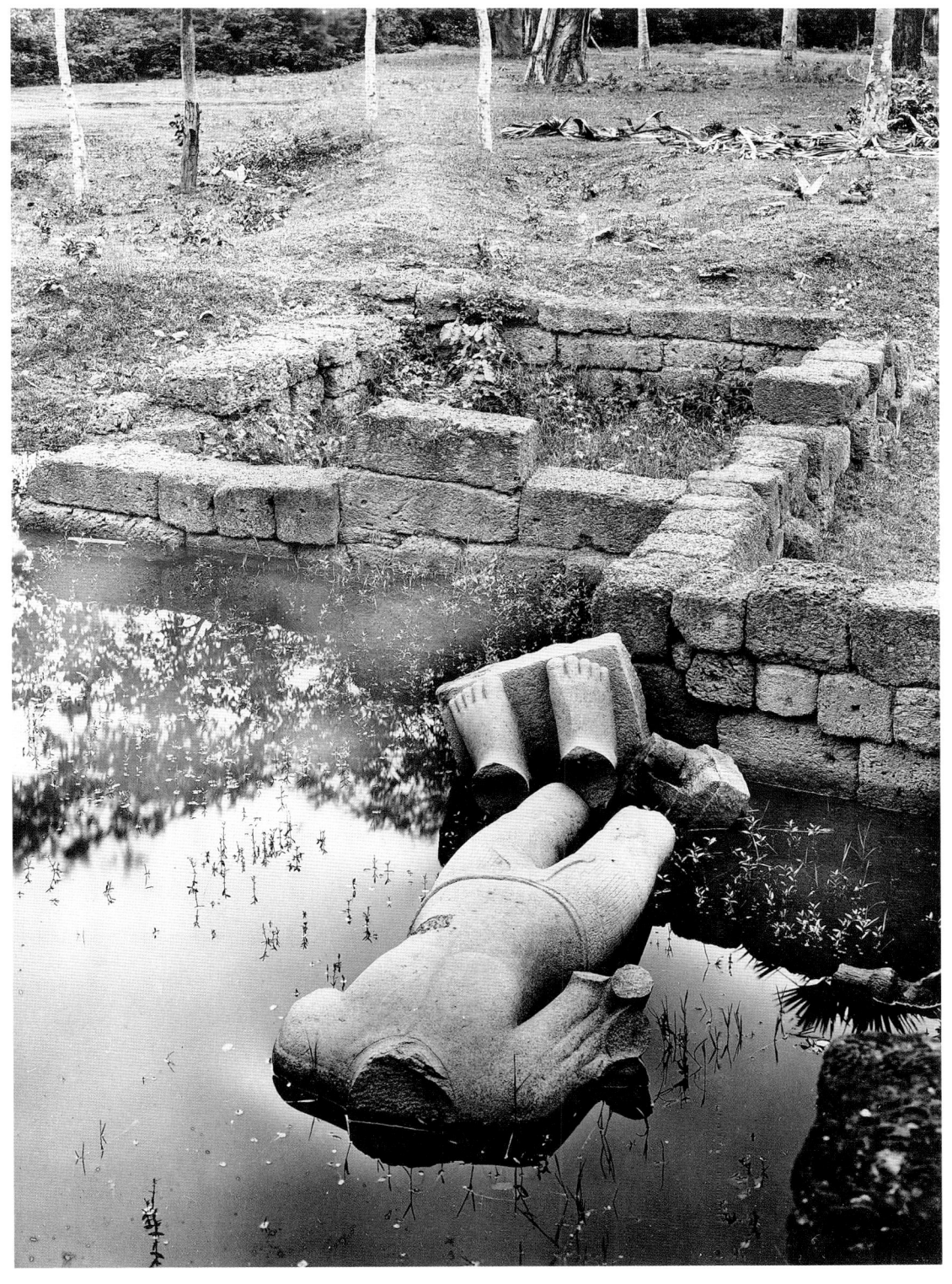

A fallen sculpture of the god Vishnu.
1910s. Photographer unknown.
École française d'Extrême-Orient.

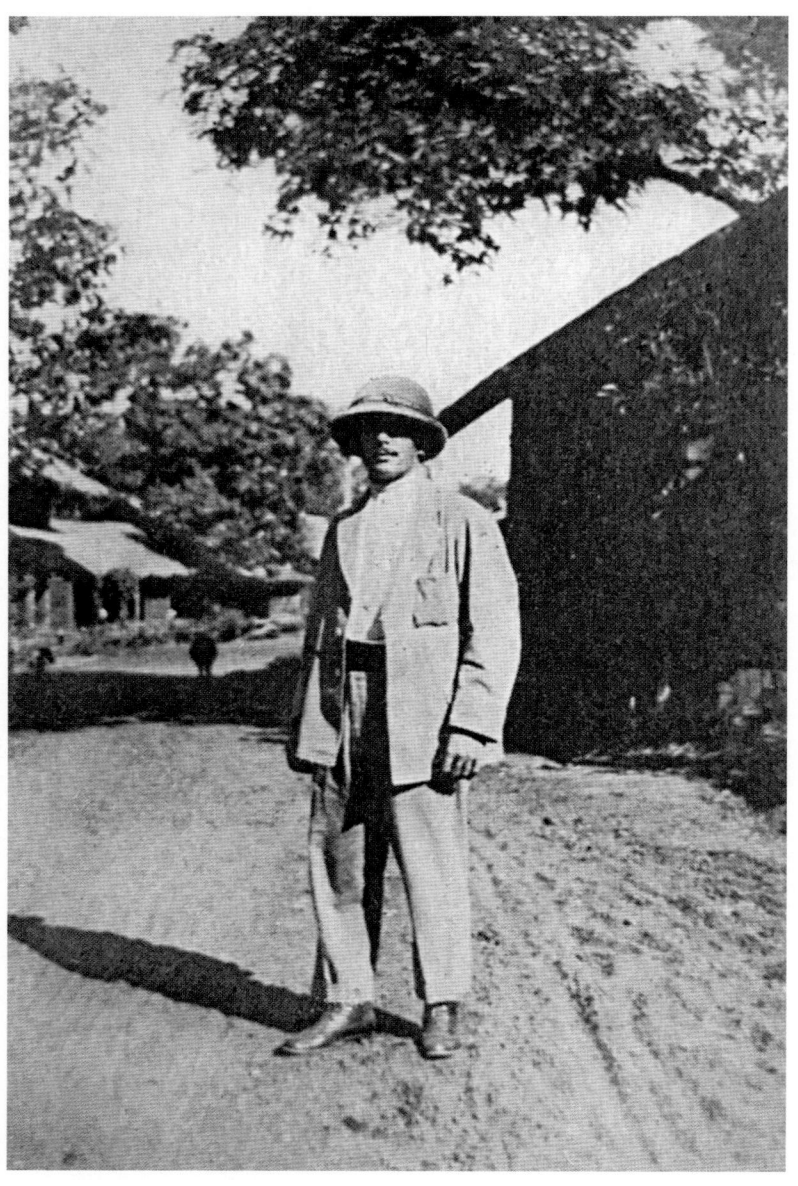

Henri dressed like a dude but he hiked like a He-man. Pailin. 1923. Harry L. Foster. From *A Beachcomber in the Orient*. John Lane, The Bodley Head, Ltd. (1925) Author's Collection.

A Beachcomber in the Orient

A World War I veteran seized with wanderlust, Harry L. FOSTER (1894–1932) adventured in tropical South America and Southeast Asia during the 1920s, taking jobs wherever he could. In his best-selling travel adventure, *A Beachcomber in the Orient* (1925), he describes being "tempted to buy a camera, a somewhat relic of Kodak, from a Chinese pawnbroker" in Hanoi. His adventures continued through Cambodia by river steamer and *sampan* to Battambang, where he befriended Henri Lesseur, the inspector of posts and telegraphs. Bypassing Angkor, Harry and Henri called at Pailin on a "circus parade" of oxcarts and local assistants, fighting off tigers, managing a "frothing epileptic buffalo," and traveling on the hand-pushed narrow-gauge railway near Battambang, which is still popular with tourists to this day. Harry considered Henri, with his manicured nails and polished boots, and his penchant for *vin rouge*, "a true He-man" as he inpected the telegraph line constructed forty years previously by Auguste Paive.

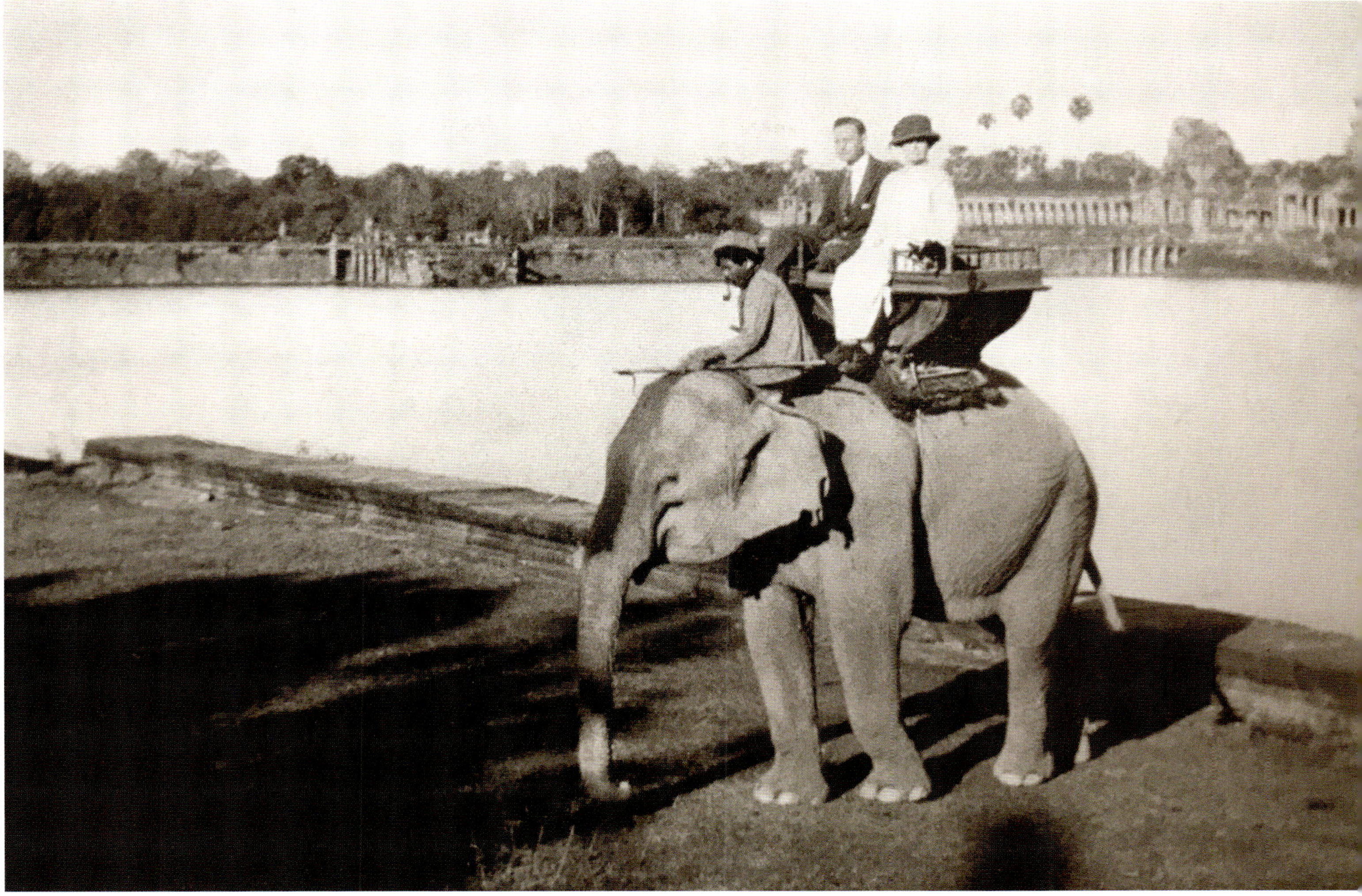

The Authoress, the Beguiler, and Effie

Born into one of America's most august families, Helen Churchill CANDEE (1858–1949), after suffering a disastrous early marriage, went on to become a successful writer, columnist, and essayist on women's rights, education, and interior décor. Her background held her in good stead as a socialite and social commentator. In 1912, she survived the sinking of the "Titanic," and her subsequent essay on that drama cemented her reputation as a writer. After World War I, she began to travel to an exotic Asia. Her *Angkor the Magnificent* (1924) was considered a classic travelogue about Cambodia, which inspired many an Anglophone reader to journey "East." This photograph of Candee and her beloved son Harold riding Effie the elephant before Angkor Wat, is typical of wealthy colonial travelers posing in front of the temple.

ABOVE: **The authoress, the Beguiler, and Effie.** Siem Reap. ca. 1922–23. Photographer unknown. State Library of New South Wales.

RIGHT: **Embossed spine illustration.** From *Angkor the Magnificent*. Helen Churchill Candee. Frederick A. Stokes Co. 1924. State Library of New South Wales.

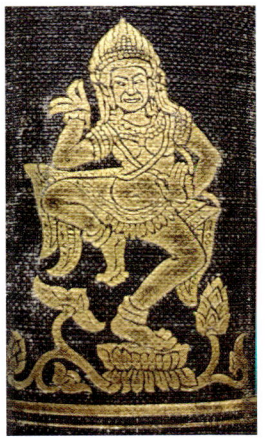

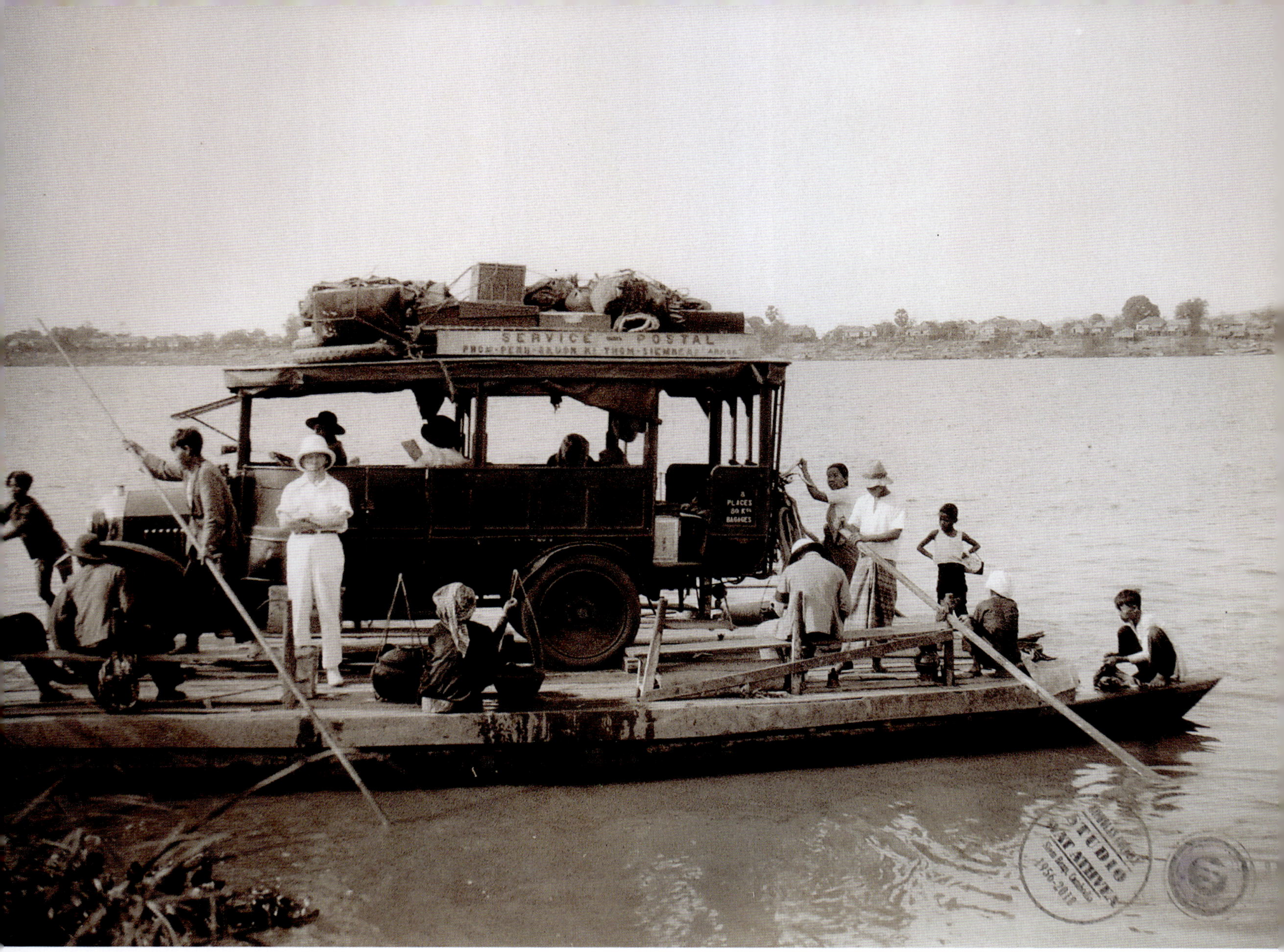

The Smoking Entrepreneur

Traveling across Cambodia by road in the 1920s was either a dusty or mud-bound adventure depending on the season. A fleet of privately owned French autobuses carried chickens, goats, bicycles, postal packages, even humans, as they crisscrossed the pot-holed roads, fording swollen rivers on hand-pulled punts to deliver their battered cargo across the country. Some travelers were luckier than others. The London photographer J. Dearden HOLMES (1873–1937) was sponsored by a cigarette company to take hundreds of stereographic photographs as he traveled the world. The photographs would be printed on card to be inserted into a German-made folding metal viewer, creating a novel and magical stereoscopic image. They were packaged in sets of 24–36 cards and included in cigarette packets to reward loyal smokers.

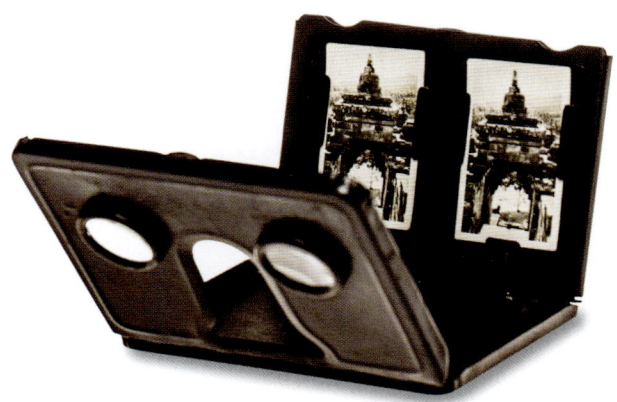

TOP: **Autobus being punted across the Mekong.** Location unknown. ca. 1925. J. Dearden Holmes. Author's Collection.

ABOVE: **Folding stereoscopic viewer for cigarette cards.** Germany. ca. 1930. The Old Post Office Arts Centre, London.

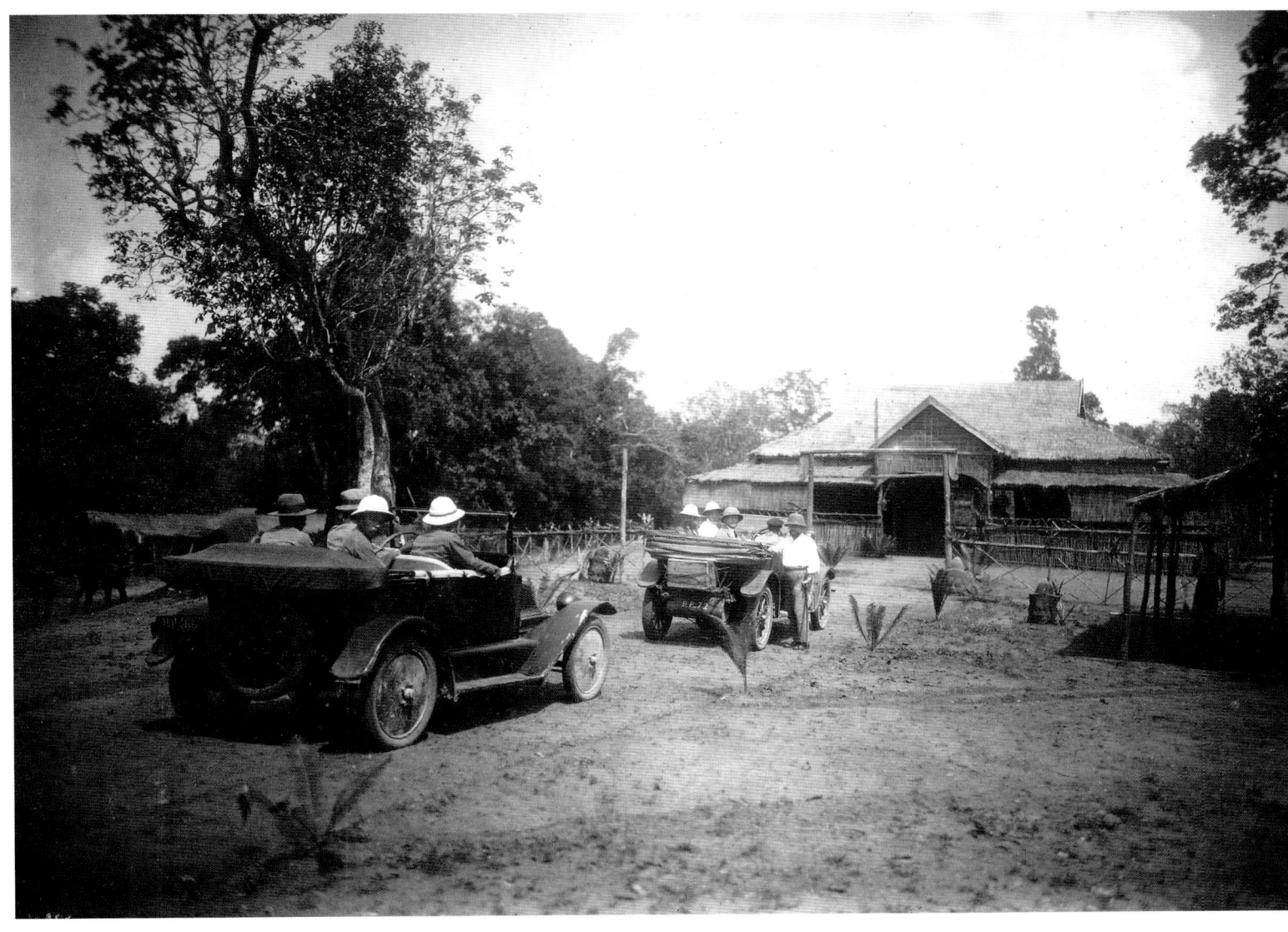

A Road Trip to Banteay Chhmar

In 1924, George GROSLIER (1887–1945) and invited guests set off from Phnom Penh on a long and dusty road trip for a tour of inspection of the remote temple of Banteay Chhmar, 37 miles (60 km) north of Sisophon. When the cavalcade arrived at the temple administrator's bungalow at midday (note the shadows), an unknown photographer asked them to stop and then staged this image of the resident welcoming the entourage. Bordering the garden are stone heads that would have come from the temple's causeway sculptures.

George Groslier and friends arrive at the administrator's bungalow.
Banteay Chhmar. 1924. Possibly George Groslier. National Museum of Cambodia.

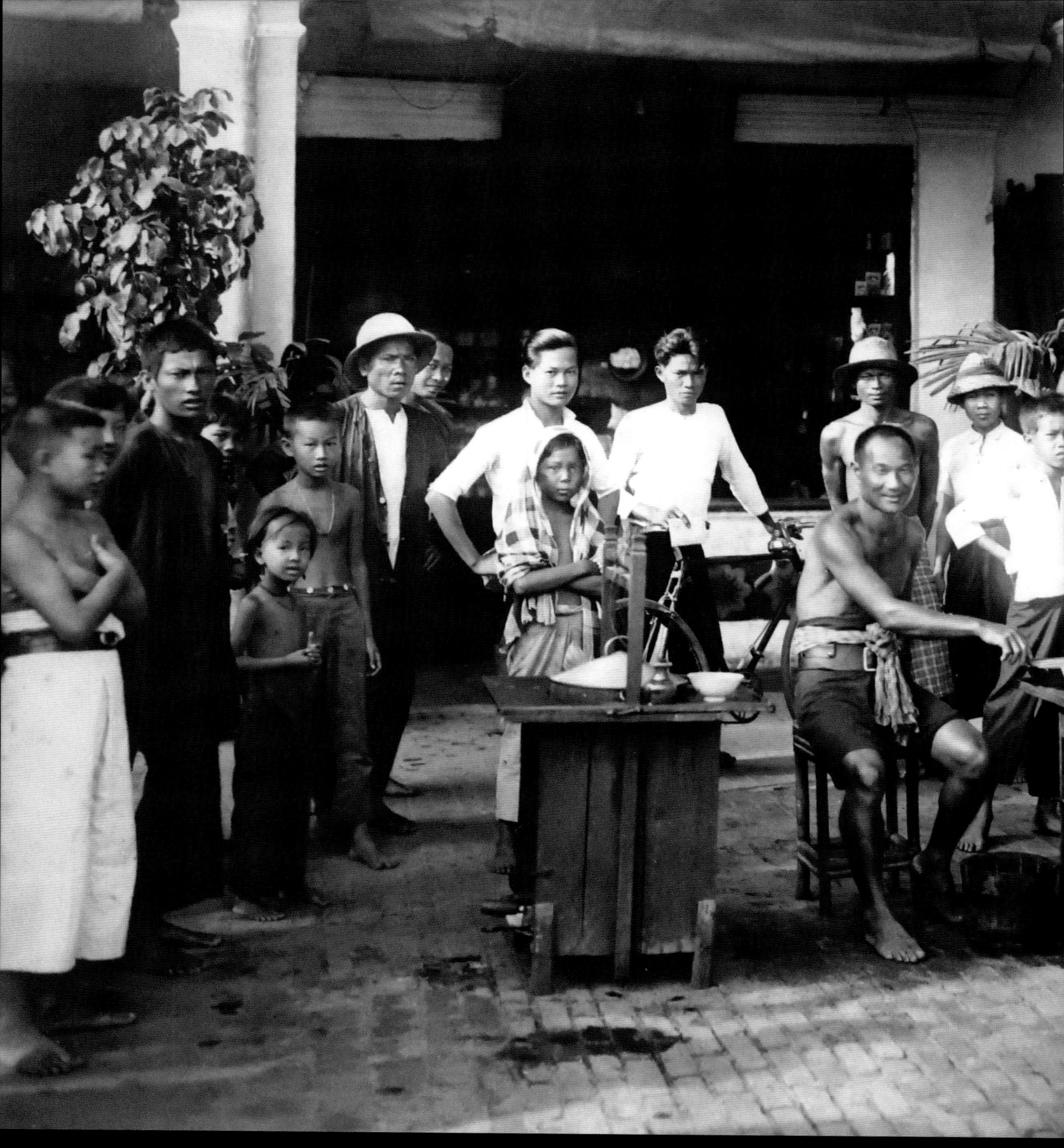

Chinese food hawker. Phnom Penh.
ca. 1924. Attributed to George Groslier.
National Museum of Cambodia.

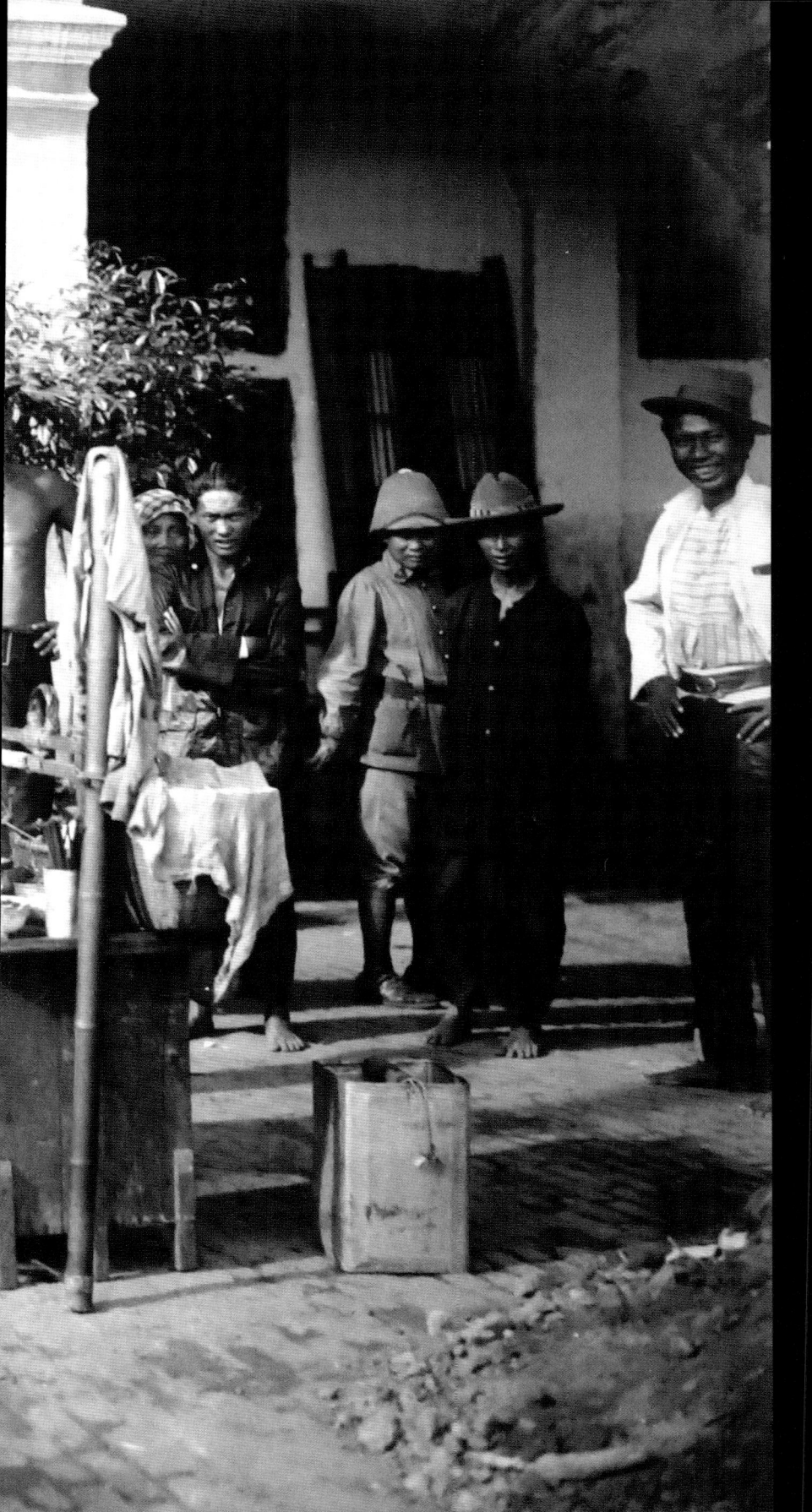

A Chinese Food Hawker

Itinerant food hawkers remain a characteristic feature of street life in Southeast Asia. Offering a limited but reliable menu, often just one specialty dish at an agreeable price, they afford a convenience food for the many migrant workers who rent rooms without the luxury of a kitchen. Sitting on a wooden stool, the hawker reaches to a cupboard of ingredients with soup bowls stacked below. To his right is the broth box, warmed by a charcoal brazier hidden below and topped with a conical metal lid. He wears his cotton *krama*, that ubiquitous, all-purpose item of Cambodian apparel, tied around his waist. The surrounding onlookers are well-groomed, with fashionable felt fedoras and *sola topi* much in evidence. In the background shadows stands a man dressed in military uniform, perhaps a member of the *police indigène*. The child with a *krama* over his head is probably the hawker's assistant.

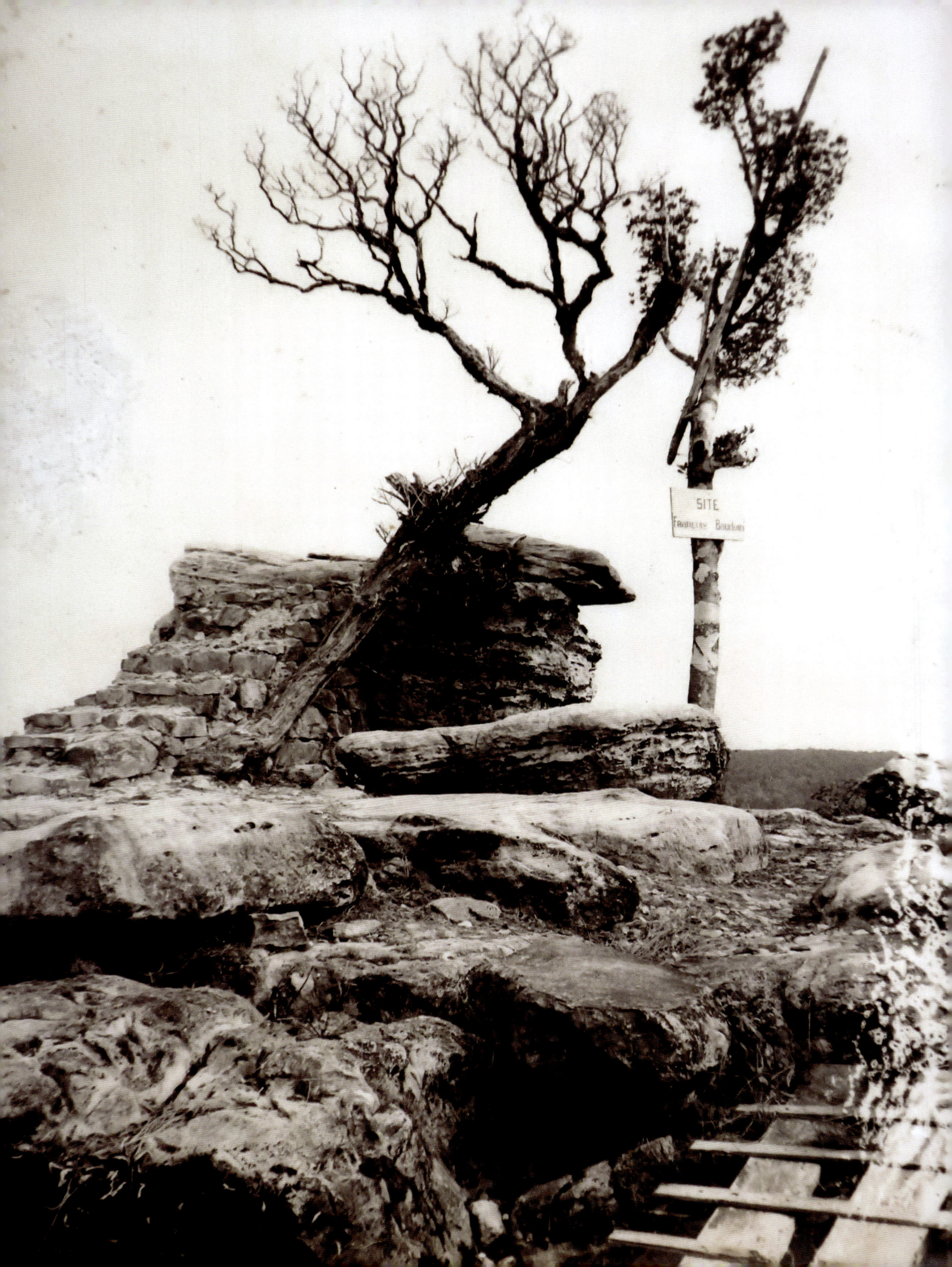

LEFT: **Bokor lookout.** Kampot.

RIGHT: **Three monks.** Location unknown.

BELOW: **Fisherboy holding his catch.** Location unknown.

BELOW RIGHT: **Cambodian countryside.** Kampot.

Photographs: Attributed to George Groslier. ca. 1923–24. National Museum of Cambodia.

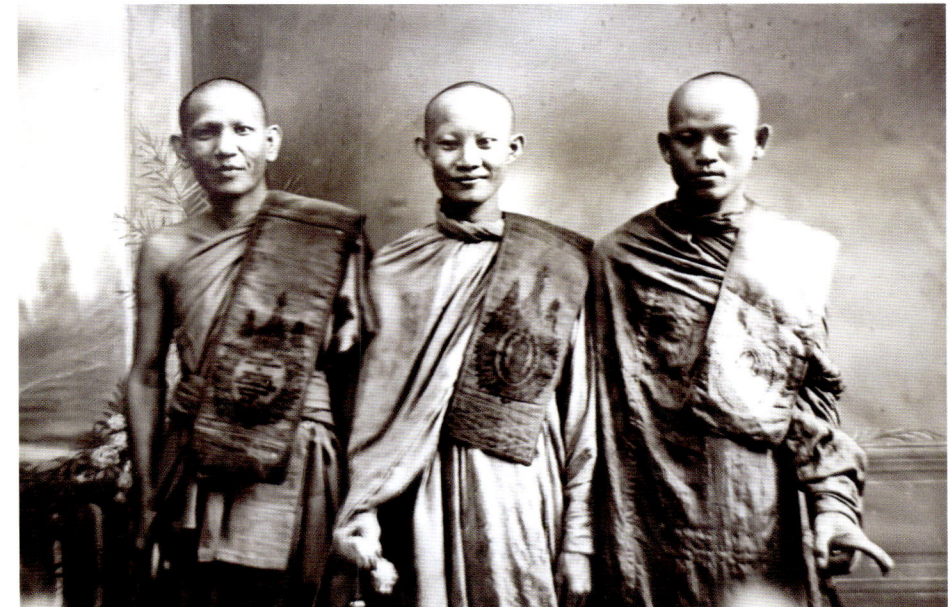

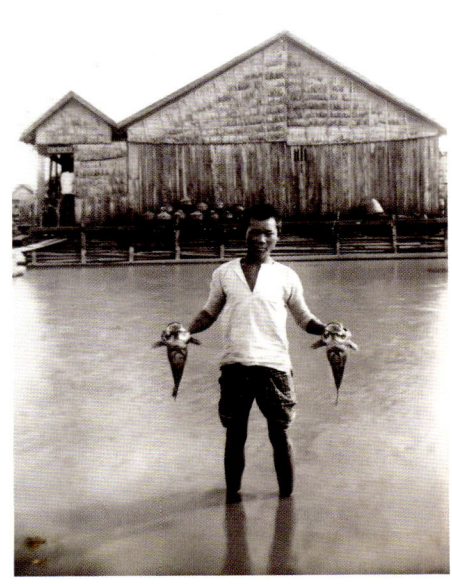

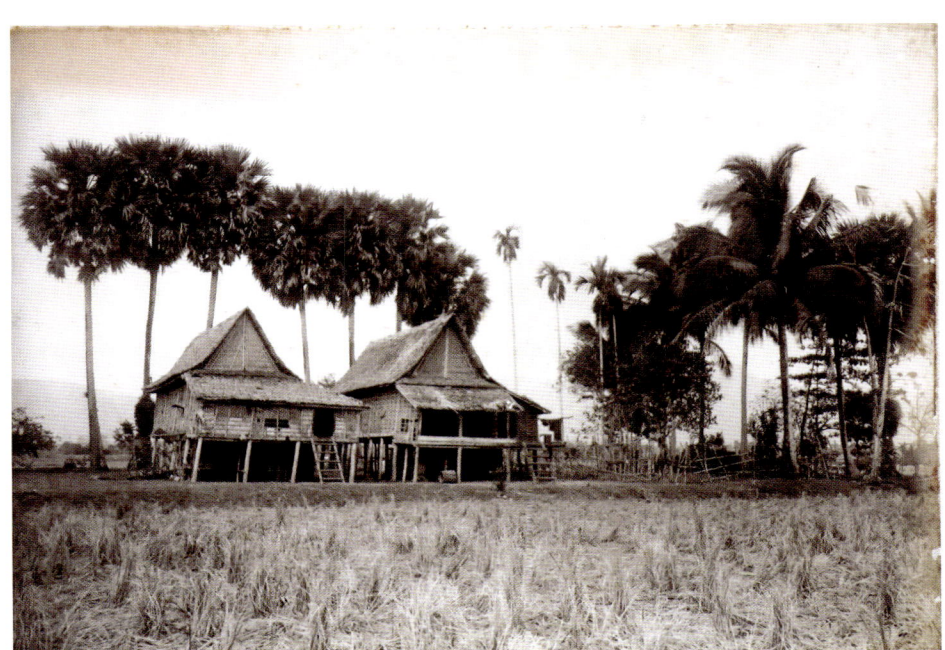

A Beloved Country

Cambodian-born George Groslier lived his entire life in the country. During his lifetime, he amassed a huge collection of photographs. A tour of the country between 1923 and 1924 resulted in an assembled album of 273 images. Each of the photographs is neatly numbered but, unfortunately, the index is lost, making a difficult task for scholars to identify locations. Nevertheless, a close inspection reveals Groslier's love of his country as he photographed a multitude of places and the people he encountered. His images ranged from the most noble of views of tortured trees and decorated church interiors to the humblest of street hawkers, traditional timber houses and colonial buildings, and a proud fisherboy dangling a catch in each hand.

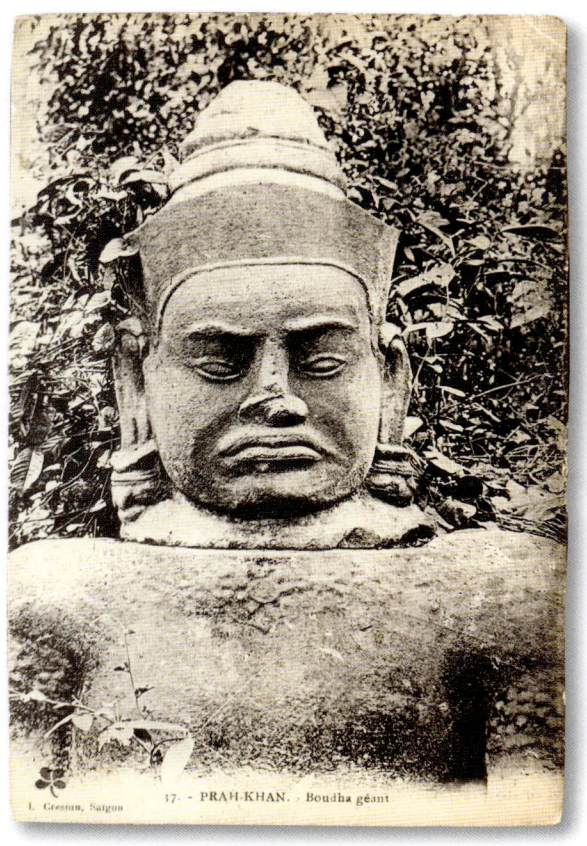

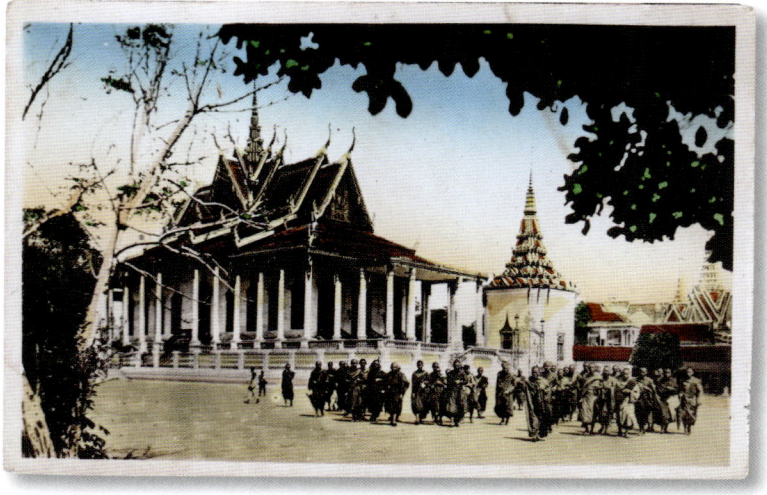

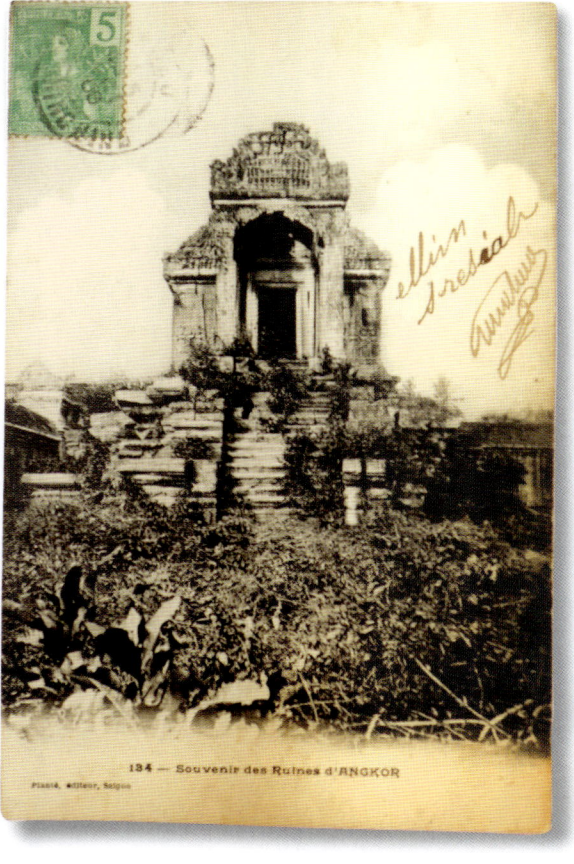

LEFT: Giant statue of Buddha at Preah Khan. Angkor. ca. 1906. Ludovic Crespin.

BELOW LEFT: Souvenir of the ruins of Angkor. Postmarked Saigon. 1909. Planté (editor).

ABOVE: Monks in front of the Royal Palace at Phnom Penh. Postcard. ca. 1910. Agence des colonies.

Source: Darryl Collins Collection, Siem Reap.

"Wish You Were Here"

In the early twentieth century, three things came together to ignite a postcard boom. First was the technological innovation of fast and cheap photomechanical printing in Germany. Then, in 1907, the International Postal Union allowed both an address and a space for writing on the back of a printed picture card. Finally, the emergence of an expanding global middle class with the money for travel but not necessarily the means to afford a camera. The mania for postcards effectively turned the tables on professional photographers with their treasured technical skills. Now, everybody could send views of the delights of Cambodia, its everyday life, and glimpses of a colonial world. As Harry Hervey wrote in 1926 in *King Cobra*, his adventurous colonial quest for an Angkorian temple, "Still further along, I paused to look into a window where pictures of Angkor were displayed. 'Tourisme de l'Indochine' said the lettering on the glass. These photographs, so carefully catalogued and in precise rows, frightened me. Was this a hint of what I should find at Angkor?"

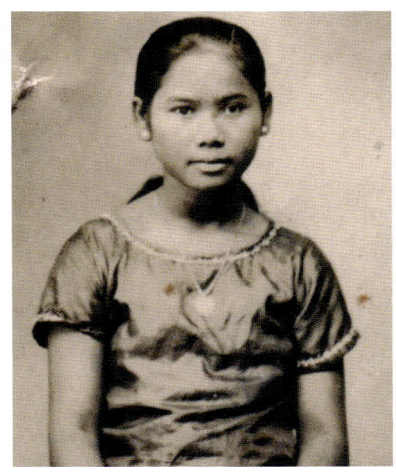 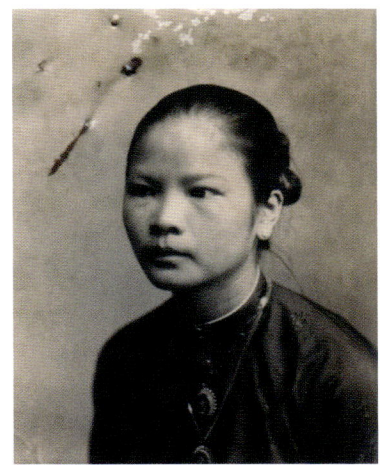 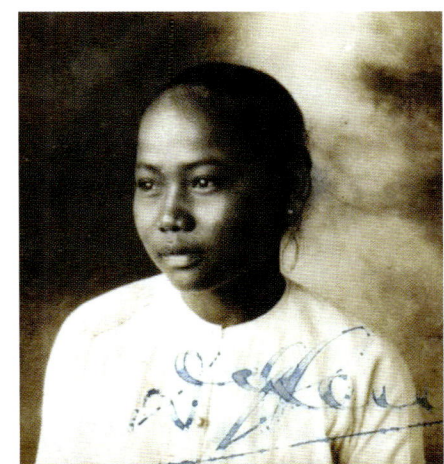

Midwives and Beautiful Babies

Alexandre VARENNE (1870–1947) was governor-general of French Indochina between November 1925 and August 1928. He arrived at a time when Saigon was engulfed in political demonstrations and intellectual upheavals, while in Cambodia there was the electrifying murder of government resident Felix Bardez by local villagers in Kompong Chhang. Perhaps for Varenne, to have attended a good-natured baby beauty contest in Phnom Penh would have been a wholesome distraction from these political affairs. Little is known about this delightful event. However, the formal registration of midwives had been in progress for over a decade, and by 1931 the French had built the Marie Baudoin Crèche in Phnom Penh to tend to the newborn.

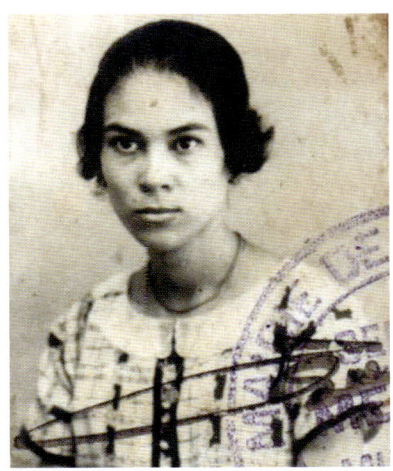

TOP LEFT, CLOCKWISE: **Unknown midwife.** Phnom Penh. 1920s.

Unknown midwife. Phnom Penh. 1920s.

Midwife Sous Kuong. Phnom Penh. 1920s.

Midwife Alice Reynaud. Phnom Penh. 1920s.

RIGHT: **Baby beauty contest during the visit of Governor-General Varenne to Phnom Penh.** 1925. Attributed to Fernand Nadal.

Source: National Archives of Cambodia.

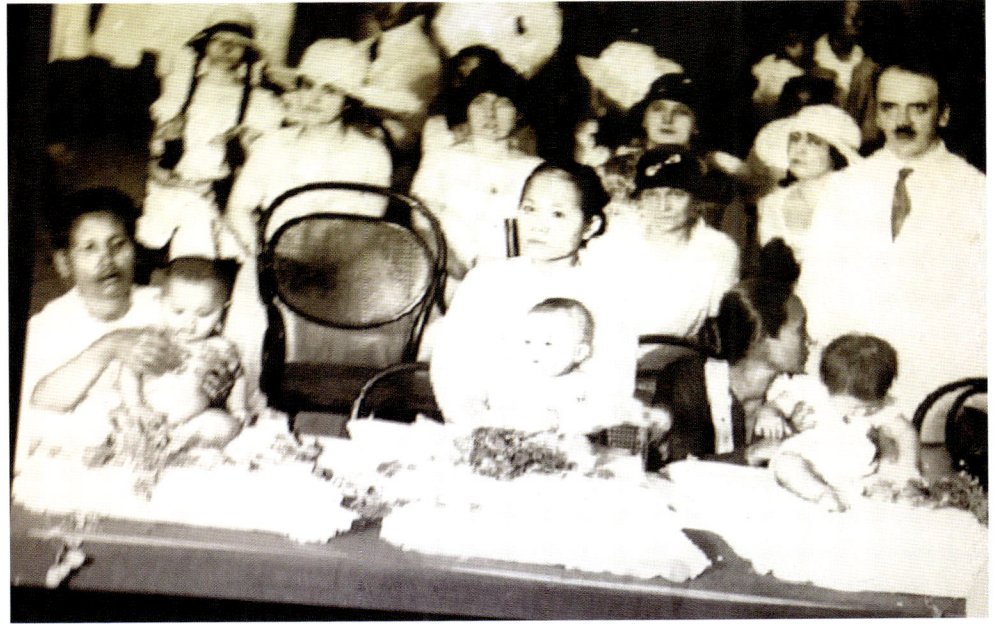

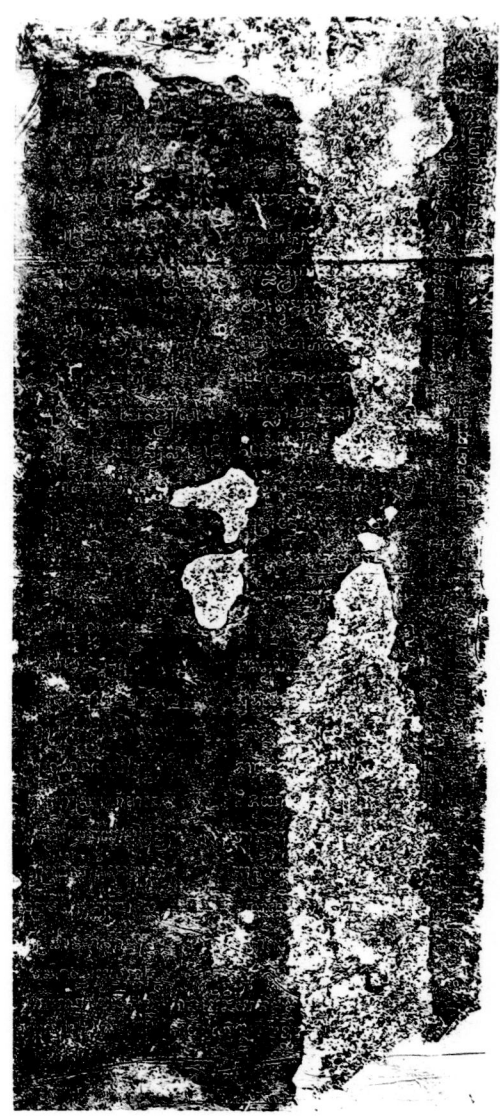

The Inscriptions of Angkor

Louis FINOT (1864–1935) was a scholar who studied the ancient inscriptions carved on the sandstone doorways and stele (ceremonial stone markers) of the Angkorian temples. "Epigraphy" is the name given to this skill. By interpreting the text, he could pass on to archaeologists and historians valuable information about the sponsors and builders of individual temples, and determine the temple's wealth and reach into the surrounding countryside. Often a camera could not capture the fidelity of a shallow inscription, so large sheets of moist paper were pressed against the stone and a ball of inked cloth was daubed across the paper, highlighting the carvers' marks beneath. The paper could then be returned to the studio for close reading. In 1898, Finot sailed to Hanoi to become director of the archaeological mission for Indochina, which transformed into the scholarly École française d'Extrême-Orient (EFEO).

Rubbings of Stele Inscription No. 10. Angkor Thom. Face C and Face D. Louis Finot. From *Mèmoires Archéologiques I: Le Temple d'Içvarapura.* École française d'Extrême-Orient. 1926. Center for Khmer Studies Library, Siem Reap.

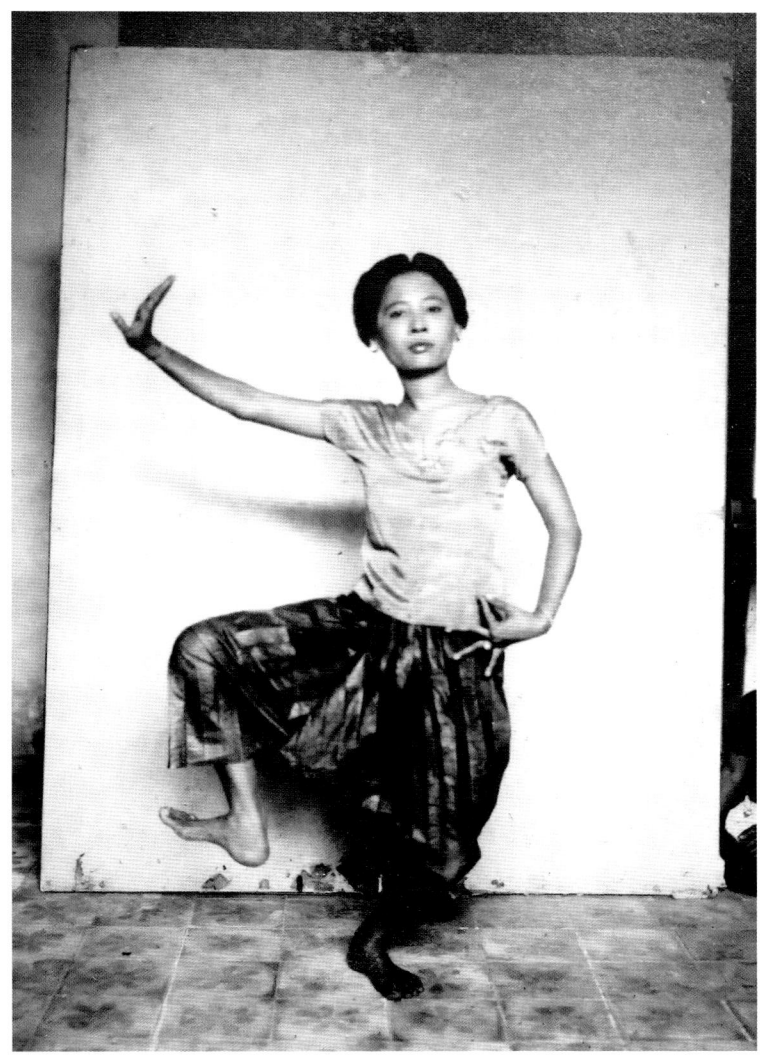 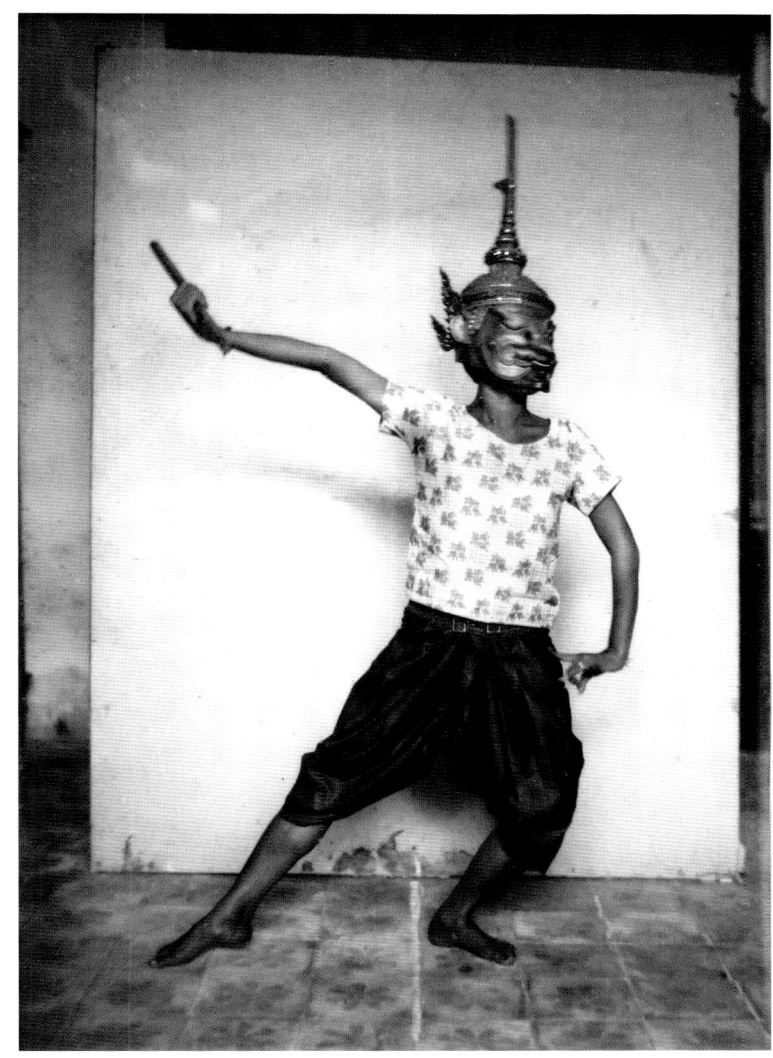

Recording the Royal Dancers

Royal Ballet dancer Nou Nâm posing within the National Museum. Phnom Penh. 1927. George Groslier. National Museum of Cambodia.

George GROSLIER (1887–1945) was the founding director and architect of the Musée Albert Sarraut in Phnom Penh. He was fascinated if not obsessed, with Khmer culture, both antique and contemporary. Groslier was concerned that the pervasive French influence would corrode the purity of the traditional Khmer classical dance form and its performative language would be lost. The carved female dancers on the temples of Angkor suggest an august, even celestial lineage, one that Groslier was keen to extend into the twentieth century. With royal assent, he asked some of the great masters of the art to come to the museum. In what is now the stone conservation workshop, he set up a temporary fabric backdrop and asked the performers to pose in the key choreographic positions of their repertoire, without their elaborate costumes. The 450 glass-plate photographs he took have become both a treasure of the museum's collection and an intangible heritage of the nation.

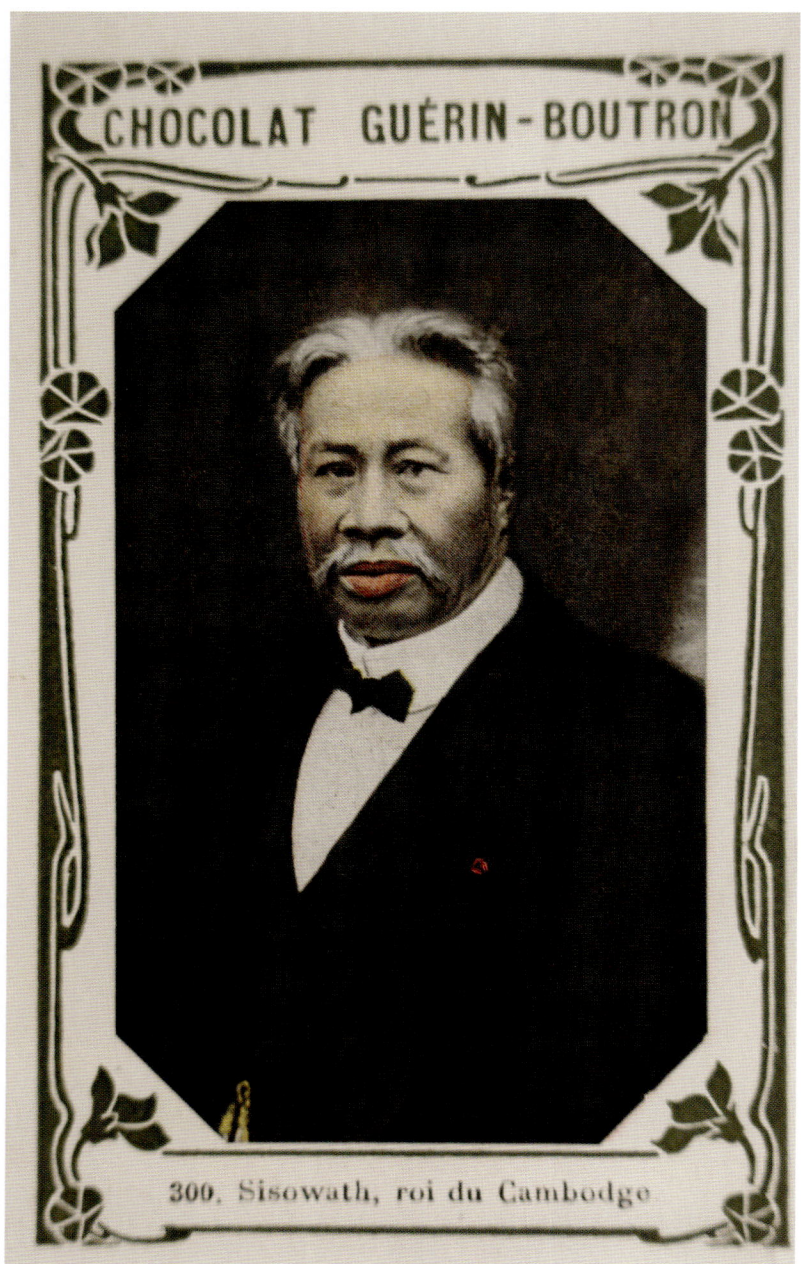

Sisowath and the Chocolate Box

Trade cards enjoyed their heyday from the 1870s onwards, ending just as the twentieth century began. Popularized by the development of color lithography, these novelties were typically inserted into product packaging as a prize or bonus, often as collectible sets. Maison Chocolat Guérin-Boutron commissioned this design of the Cambodian monarch Sisowath who was visiting France for the Marseille Colonial Exposition in 1906. It would have burnished the credentials of their exclusive treats, made with exotic colonial ingredients; in this instance, the cocoa was imported not from Indochina but from another French colony, Côte d'Ivoire.

ABOVE LEFT: **Novelty trade card 300, featuring Sisowath, king of Cambodia.**

LEFT: **Reverse of the trade card showing advertising text.**

Source: Maison Chocolat Guérin-Boutron, Paris. ca. 1906. Author's Collection.

Three Cambodian Gentlemen

Three well-dressed gentlemen and a timid child pose before the camera. They are probably provincial functionaries, as evidenced by their awareness of contemporary fashions and the status symbols embedded in their eclectic synthesis of European and Cambodian sartorial styles—bowler hats, *sola topi*, fob chains, britches, and leather shoes mixed with traditional wrapped pants (*sompot chong kben*). This blending of fashion and function was only natural since the governance of remote areas, mainly for the purpose of collecting taxes and organizing statutory labor days, was left to a thin scattering of European colonial officers supported by an established hierarchy of local officials. Although the gentleman in the center of the photograph has the appearance of a police officer, he is most likely a member of a colonial militia of indigenous guards in whose hands lay the real responsibility for policing the countryside.

Three Cambodian gentlemen. Location unknown. Photographer unknown. 1890s–1900s. École française d'Extrême-Orient.

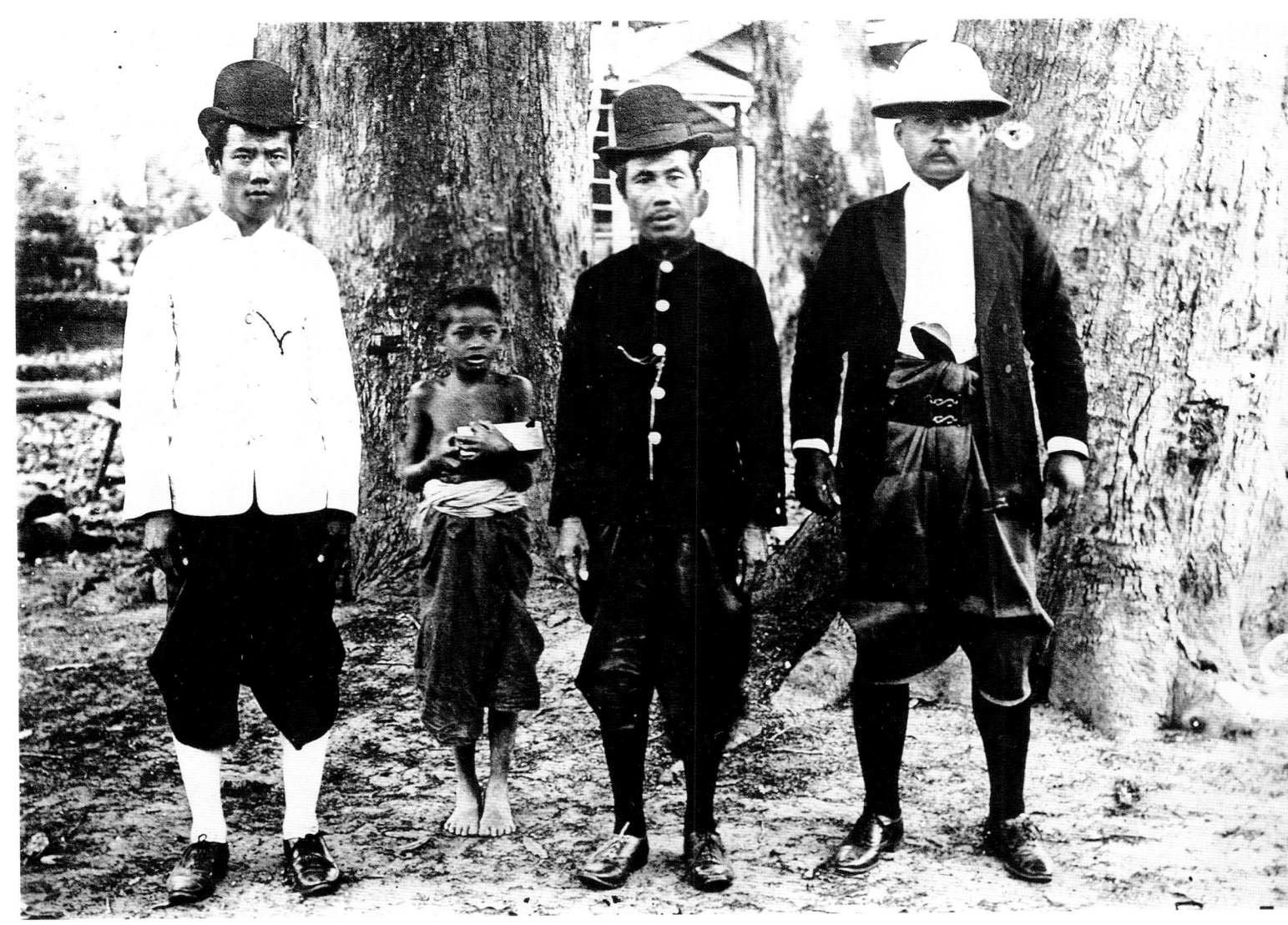

1927–1941
The Reign of King Monivong

By the time King Sisowath Monivong (1875–1941) ascended to the throne in 1927, the French had cemented their control of the Cambodian protectorate. The popularity of the motorcar and the military demands of World War I (1914–18) had ignited a rubber boom in Indochina. Rubber plantations flourished across the Kompong Cham plateau, with entrepreneurs like H. C. A. Elmiger (b. 1894) managing large self-contained factory estates. An avid amateur photographer, he took images of processing buildings and workers' housing, as well as the family's magnificently furnished bungalow.

As the cost of steamship travel dropped, tourism increased. Small launches plied the inland waterways, including the Tonlé Sap to Siem Reap, where motorcars ferried tourists from their hotels to nearby temples. In the 1920s, the young American Hal Llippincott (1908–91), the French performer Georges Portal (1887–1958), and the Zurich-based publisher Martin Hurlimann (1897–1984) toured the country bringing their lighter and more affordable cameras with them to document their journeys. In 1929, Hurlimann used the subtle tones of photogravure printing to produce one of the finest travel photography books about Asia, *Ceylon Und Indochina*.

The 1931 Paris International Exposition, with its captivating replica of Angkor Wat, highlighted Cambodia as a must-see destination for rich European travelers. Daring aviators began to traverse the monsoon skies. The adventurer-aviatrix Elisabeth Sauvy-Tisseyre (1897–1966), epitomized the underlying decadence of the era with her audacious theft of a Buddha's head from Angkor Wat, while aerial photographs of the temple complex in its jungle setting fitted perfectly with an enthusiasm for advenerous travel to faraway places. For the École française d'Extrême-Orient's archaeologists, a bird's-eye view from above the thick jungle canopy offered an unprecedented opportunity to see the interconnectedness between individual Angkorian temples. On a terrestrial level, archaeologists labored away at the Herculean task to restore the monuments. This would be one of the most enduring legacies of the French Protectorate. The EFEO's extensive photographic archives reveal the mainstream archaeological practices that focused on the brick-and-stone structures, their wall carvings, the stone sculptures, and the unearthed metal artifacts. But there are also sociological and ecological observations of villages and landscapes and the surrounding waterways and countryside, as well as photographs that inadvertently reveal the changing dress codes and fashion trends amongst Cambodian workers.

In Phnom Penh, a small Cambodian urban elite graduated from the kingdom's first high school, Lycée Sisowath. Employed in the colonial administration, they bought the first Khmer-language newspaper, *Nagara Vatta*. On opening the pages, they would have read about the war developing in Europe and the disastrous fall of France to the German army in 1940. For all the countries and European colonies across Southeast Asia and Indochina, World War II (1939–45) was to have a profound impact on the prevailing assumptions of power and privilege.

King Sisowath Monivong at the funeral service of his father.
Royal Palace, Phnom Penh. 1927.
Photographer unknown. National Archives of Cambodia.

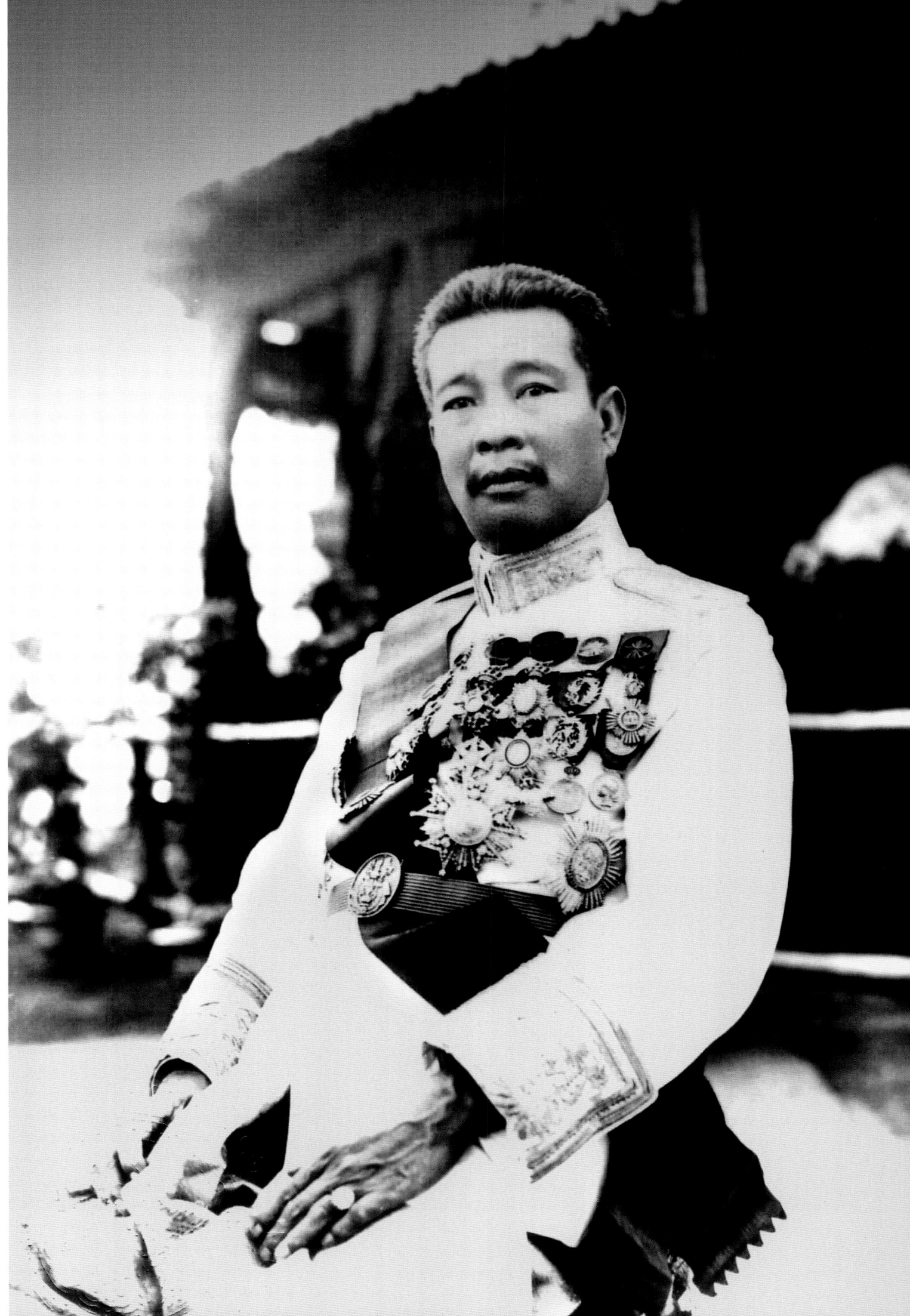

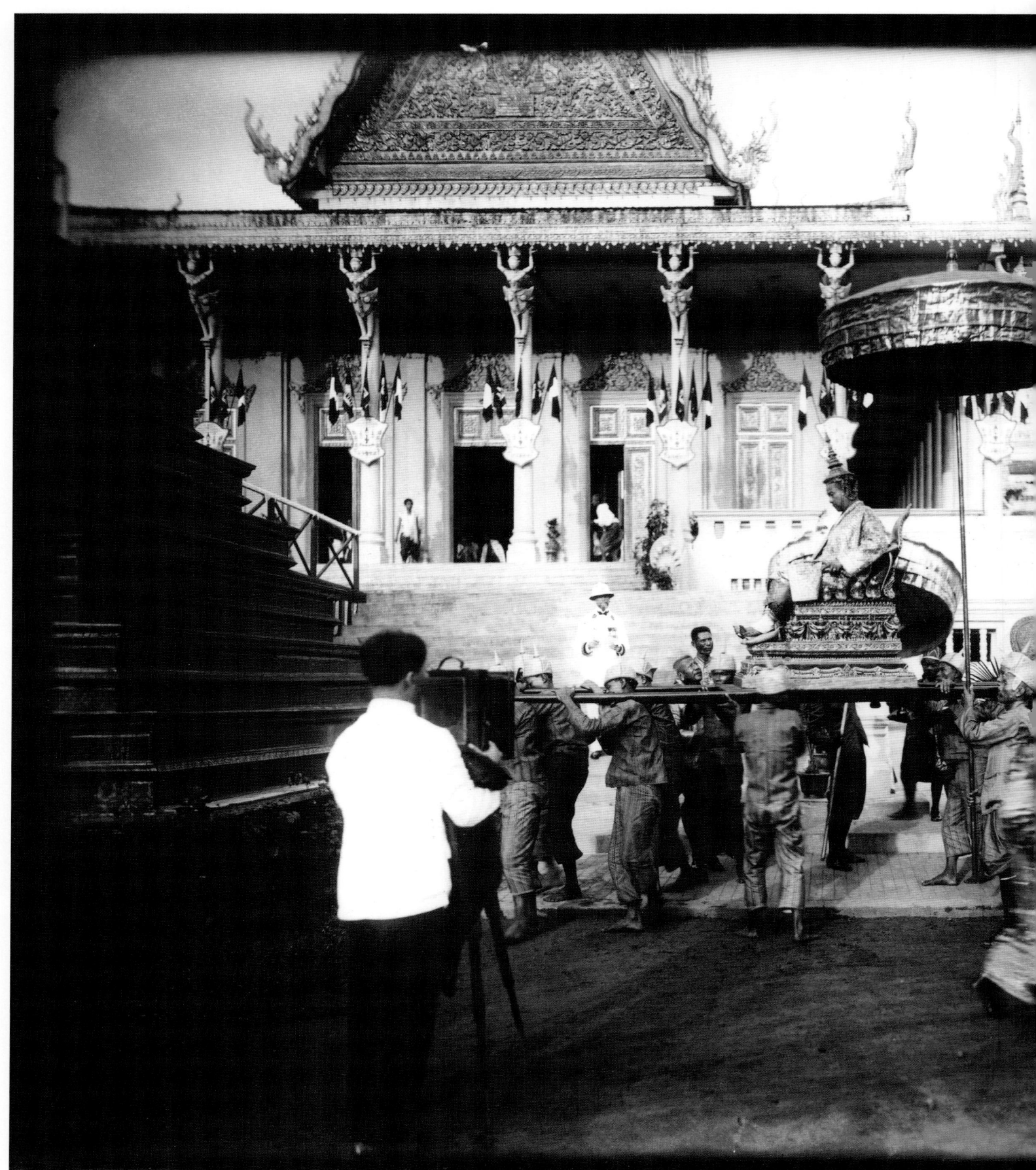

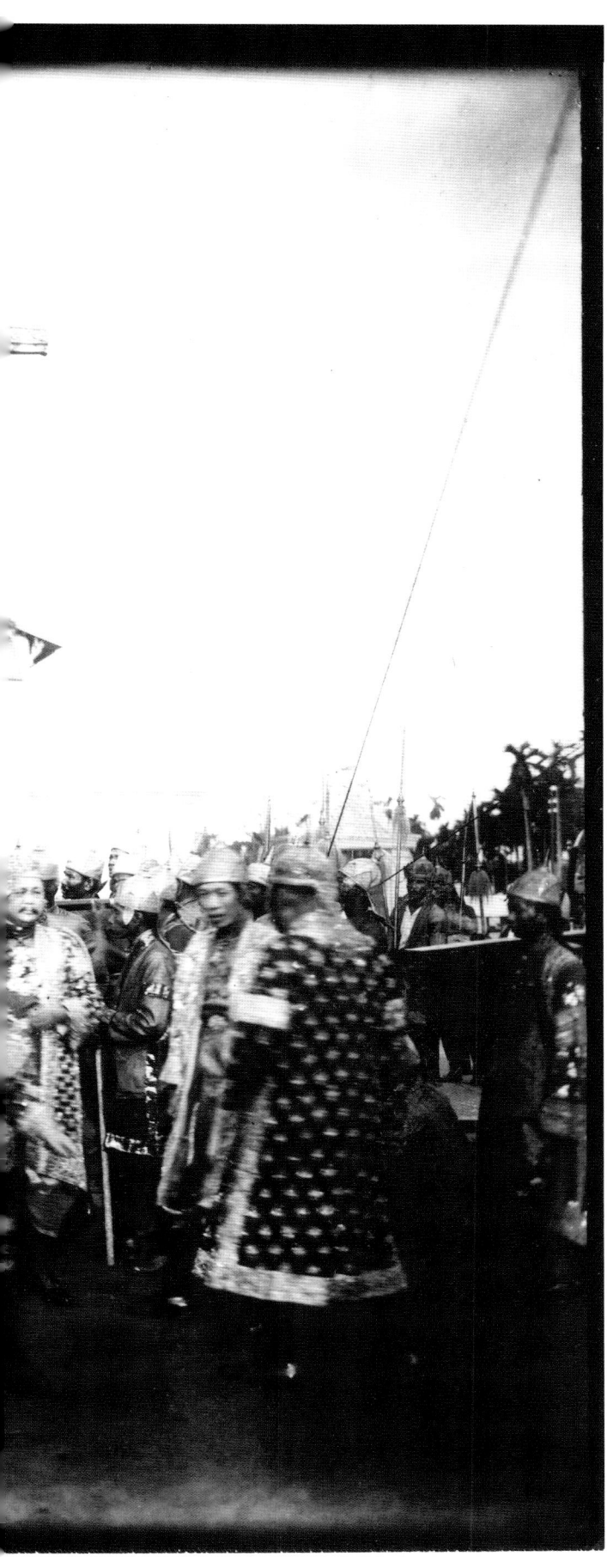

The Coronation of King Monivong

This photograph of the coronation of King Monivong shows all the symbols of Cambodian royal culture: the blur of elaborately costumed officials, the flag-draped backdrop of the palace, and center stage, functionaries laboring under the weight of carrying the newly crowned monarch on a gilded palanquin. Monivong is shaded by an umbrella, signifying his semidivine status. Behind, on the steps to the throne hall, is a French official, with palace servants watching from above. To the left, an unknown foreign photographer (most likely George Groslier) is using a glass-plate camera to capture the ceremony. Monivong's reign was to be the last of a line of kings who observed a conservative, opaque etiquette. It was to end with his death in 1941, and the unfolding repercussions of World War II.

The Coronation of King Monivong.
Royal Palace, Phnom Penh. July 20, 1928. Photographer unknown. Possibly George Groslier. National Archives of Cambodia/Charles Meyer Collection, Paris.

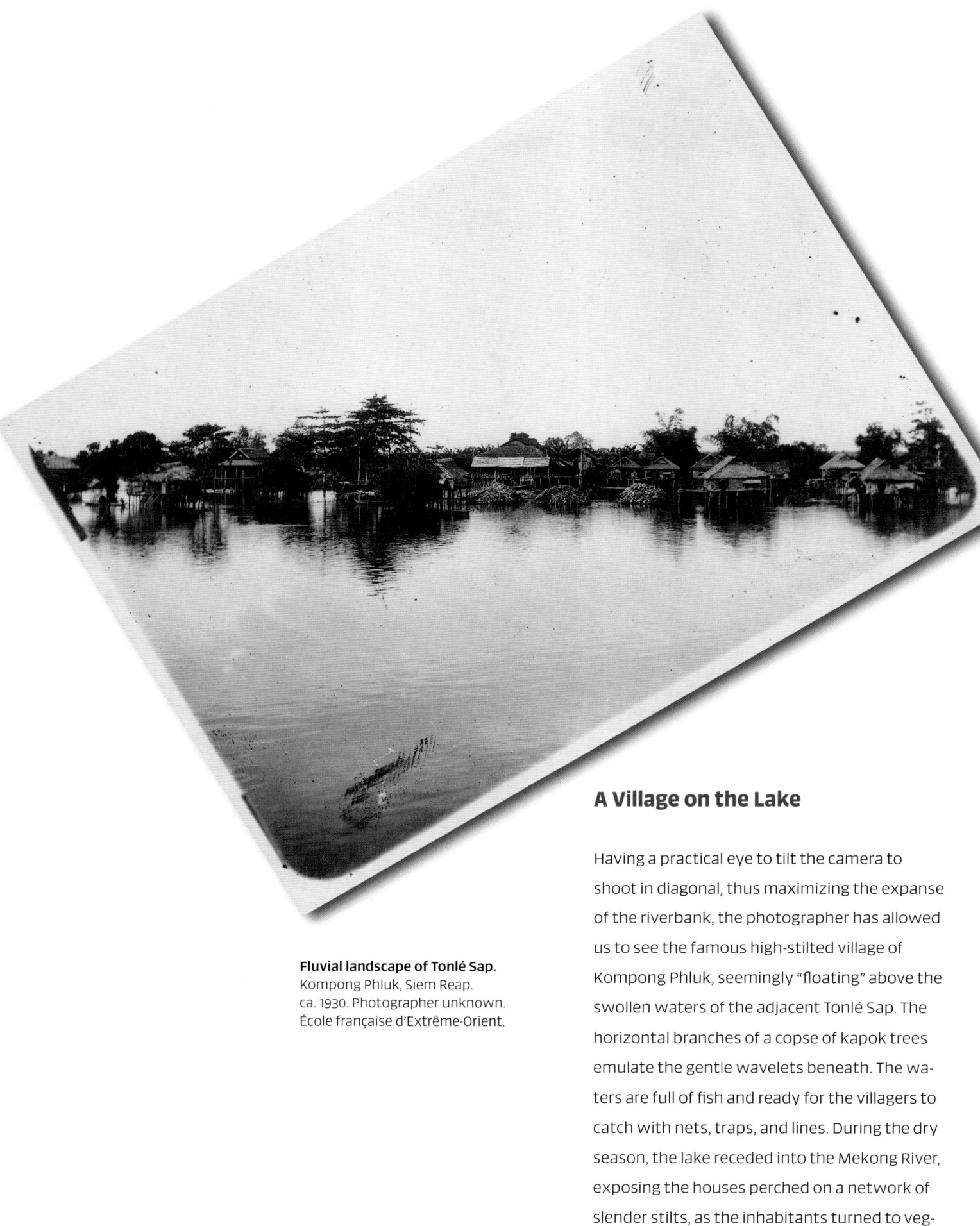

Fluvial landscape of Tonlé Sap.
Kompong Phluk, Siem Reap.
ca. 1930. Photographer unknown.
École française d'Extrême-Orient.

A Village on the Lake

Having a practical eye to tilt the camera to shoot in diagonal, thus maximizing the expanse of the riverbank, the photographer has allowed us to see the famous high-stilted village of Kompong Phluk, seemingly "floating" above the swollen waters of the adjacent Tonlé Sap. The horizontal branches of a copse of kapok trees emulate the gentle wavelets beneath. The waters are full of fish and ready for the villagers to catch with nets, traps, and lines. During the dry season, the lake receded into the Mekong River, exposing the houses perched on a network of slender stilts, as the inhabitants turned to vegetable farming on the silt-covered banks.

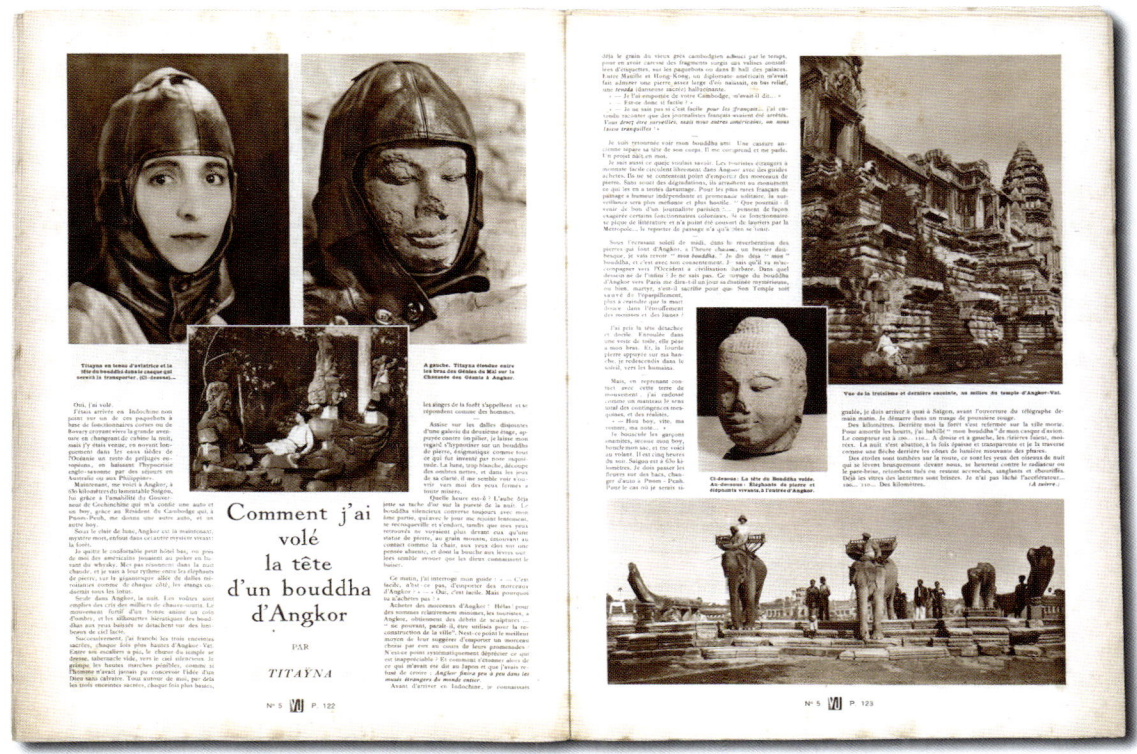

An Audacious Aviatrix

"Buddha from Angkor Stolen," said the headline of the April 1928 edition of VU Journal de la Semaine magazine. The cover showed a dramatic montage of the aviatrix Titaÿna admiring a photographically enlarged stone head of a Buddha. She had stolen the sculpture from the temples of Angkor. Perhaps she was foolishly emulating the theft of Angkorian treasures by the young André Malraux five years earlier. A following spread of images shows her provocatively—and naively—dressing the life-size head with her leather flying helmet. Titaÿna was a French adventuress and reporter whose real name was Elisabeth Sauvy-Tisseyre (1897–1966). The theft was sensational news in Paris, and together with the radical artwork of Man Ray (1890–1976), helped promote VU as one of the leading illustrated magazines of the day.

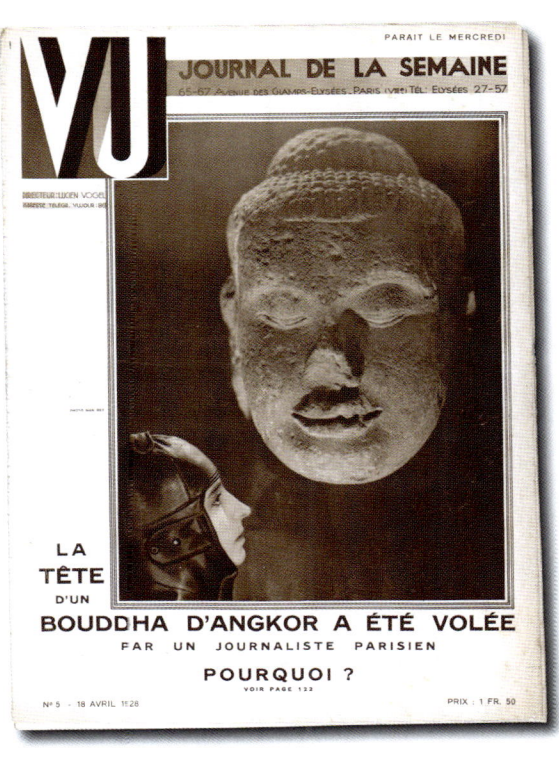

Front cover and pages 4 and 5, *VU Journal de la Semaine.* April 1928. Guy Carrard. Graphic design by Man Ray. Musée Nicephore Niépce.

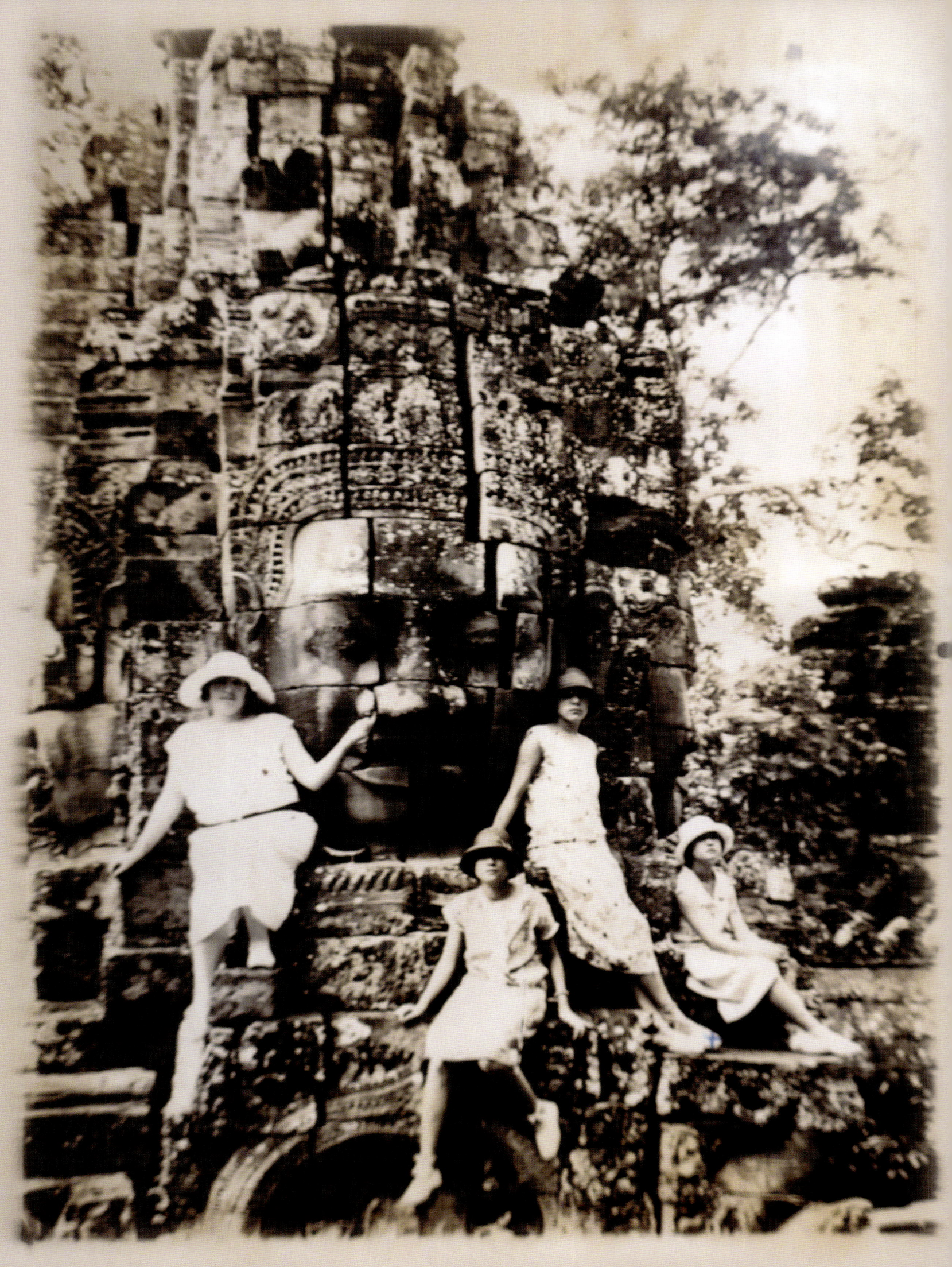

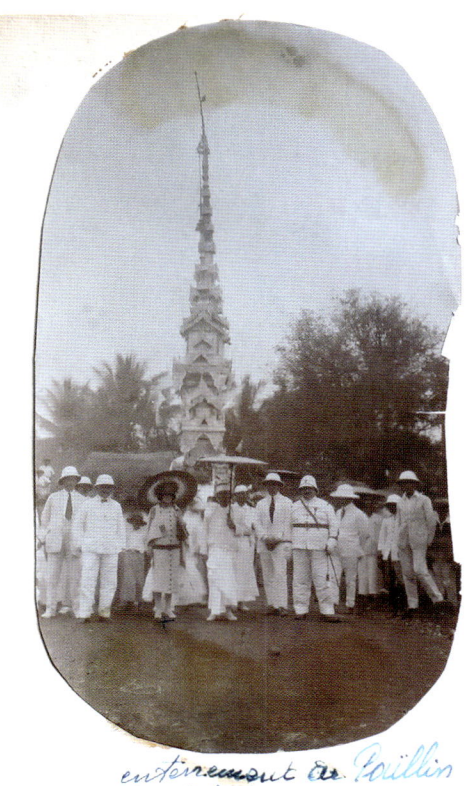
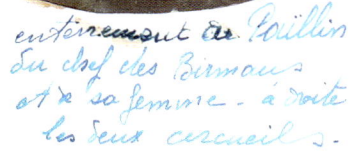
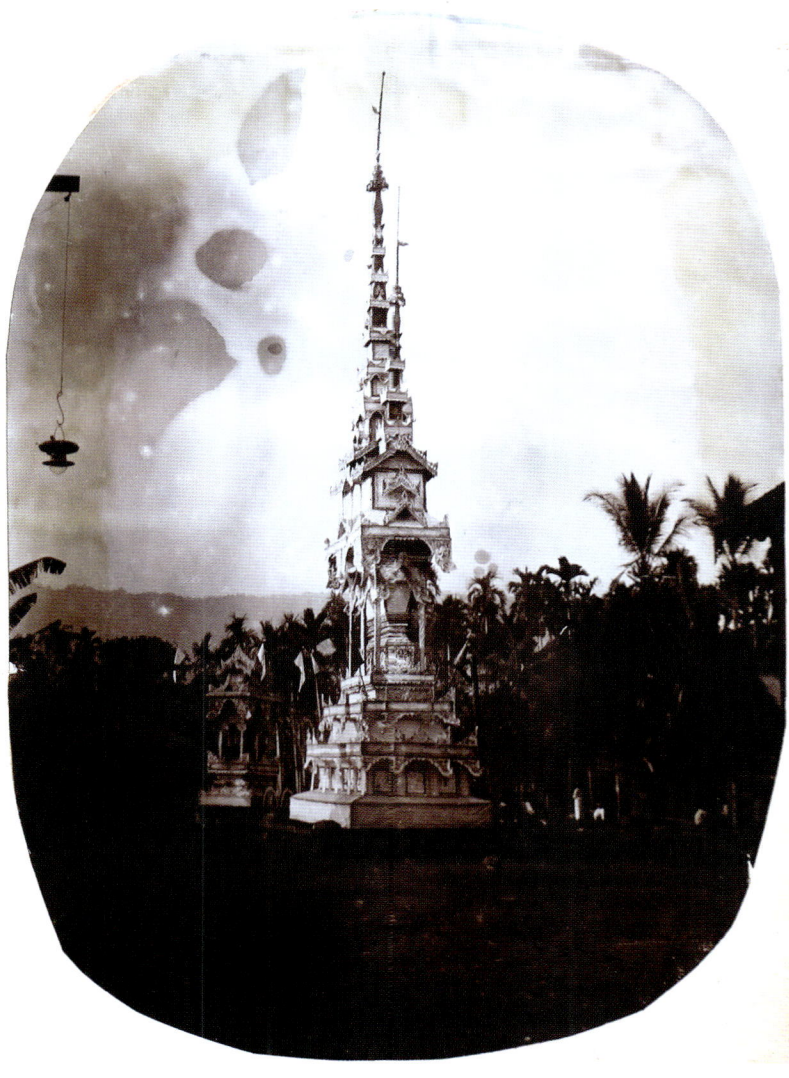

A Sojourn Through Cambodge

OPPOSITE: **Four women at the Bayon temple.** Siem Reap. 1928.

ABOVE LEFT: **Burial in Pailin of the chief (leader) of the Birmans and his wife.** Pailin. 1928. (Le Fol is most likely the gentleman wearing the Sam Browne leather belt.)

ABOVE RIGHT: **Funeral catafalque.** Pailin. 1928.

Photographer unknown.
Source: Philippe Damas Collection, Singapore.

The three photographs on this spread are taken from the same album. Annotations beneath some of the photographs date them to 1928, midway through the two-year term of the resident-superior, Aristide Eugène Le Fol. As a tour of the important provincial cities was expected of an officer of his rank, we can presume the elegant women at the Bayon monument (opposite) were part of his retinue. Their loose clothing, casual demeanor, and exposed arms are indicative of the modern "jazz" age of political and cultural reform, as are the sensible array of wide-brimmed cloche, picture, and musketeer hats to protect them from the tropical sun. The hand-trimmed photographs of a funeral in Pailin (above) show a towering catafalque made of bamboo and decorative paper, its nine-tiered spire and prayer flags guaranteeing the soul of the deceased will reach the heavens. In the photograph of the funeral catafalque (top right) can be seen in the shadows beneath the treeline, the decorated funeral chariot, which would have been the focus of the final parade by mourners from the local wat to the cremation grounds.

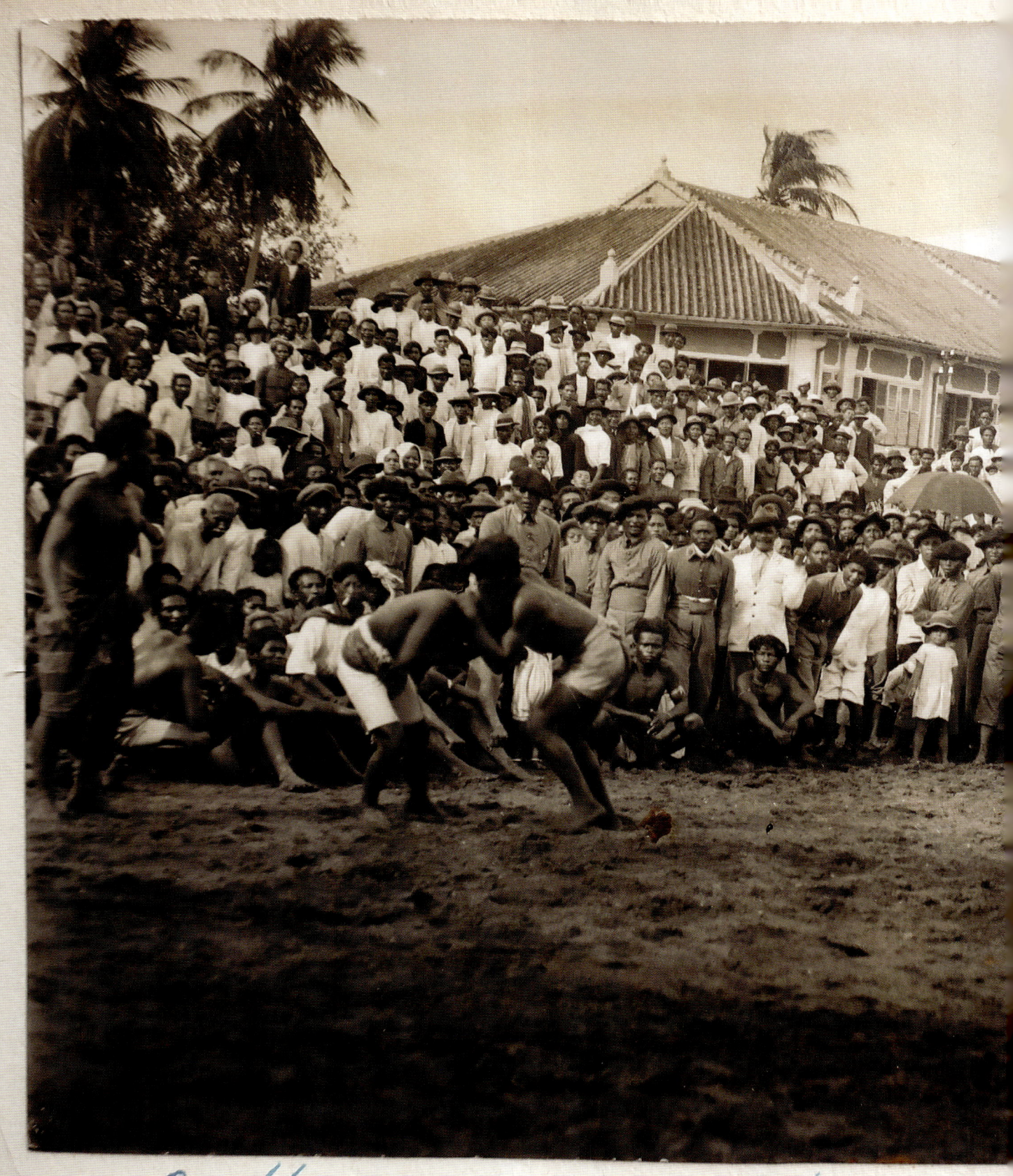

Battambang 14 juillet 1925

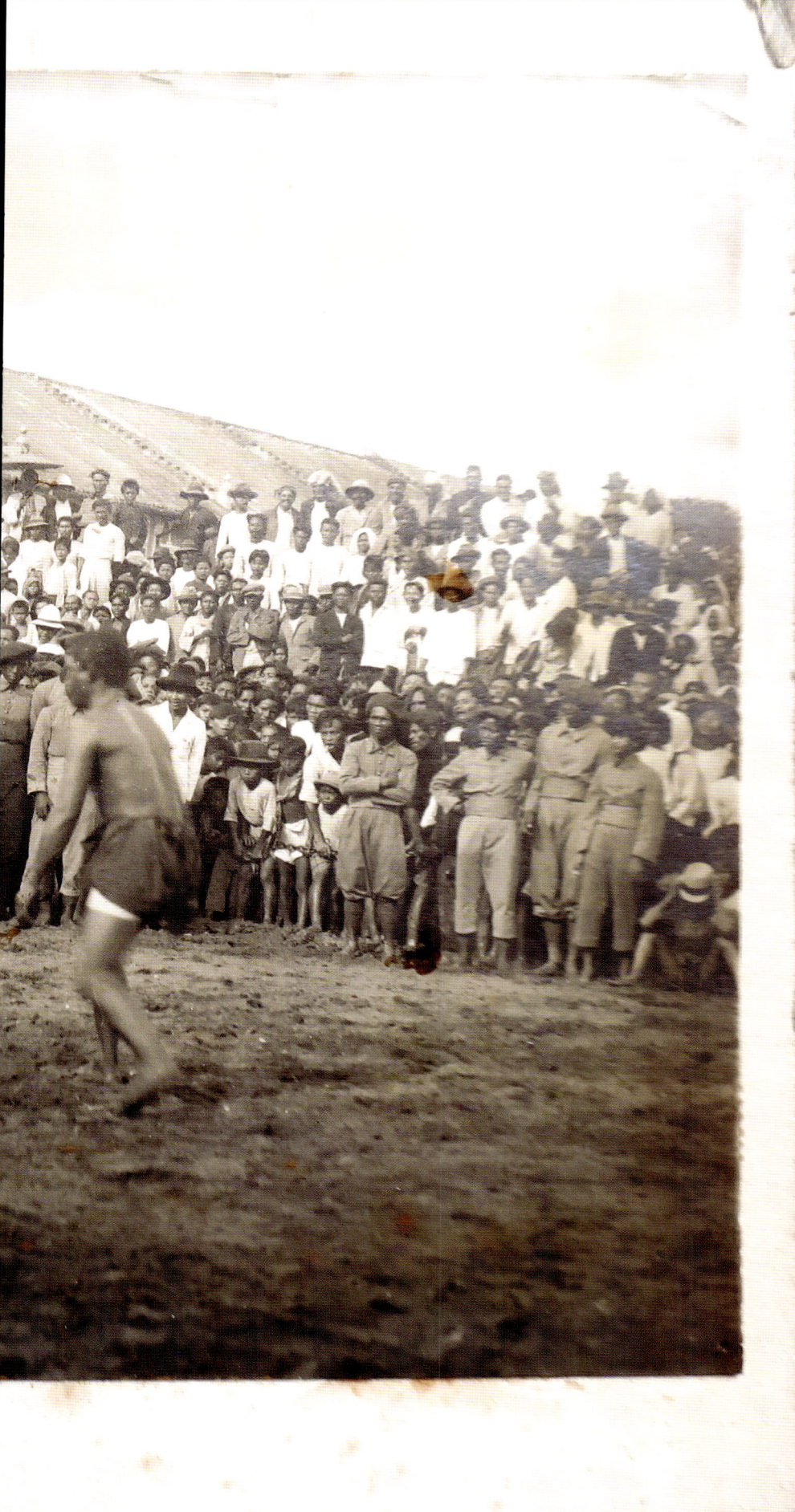

The Battambang Wrestling Match

Hundreds of mainly male onlookers crowd around as two young wrestlers fight for the prize during celebrations for the French National Day (Bastille Day). The spectators are wearing a wide array of headgear. Felt fedoras of various shapes and colors appear to be the most popular, while a Muslim cap, a *sola topi*, and traditional head scarves also make an appearance. Standing on benches, the spectators obscure the lower floors of the shophouses behind them, which were probably situated on the riverbank close to the main market, the social center of Battambang. Sixteen riflemen line the inner circle of spectators. Their uniforms, particularly the oversized berets, have not changed since World War I. Wrestling is an ancient sport in Cambodia, and bas-reliefs of long-ago contestants locked in combat can be seen on the galleries of the thirteenth-century Bayon temple.

Wrestling match to celebrate Bastille Day. Battambang. July 14, 1928. Photographer unknown. Philippe Damas Collection, Singapore.

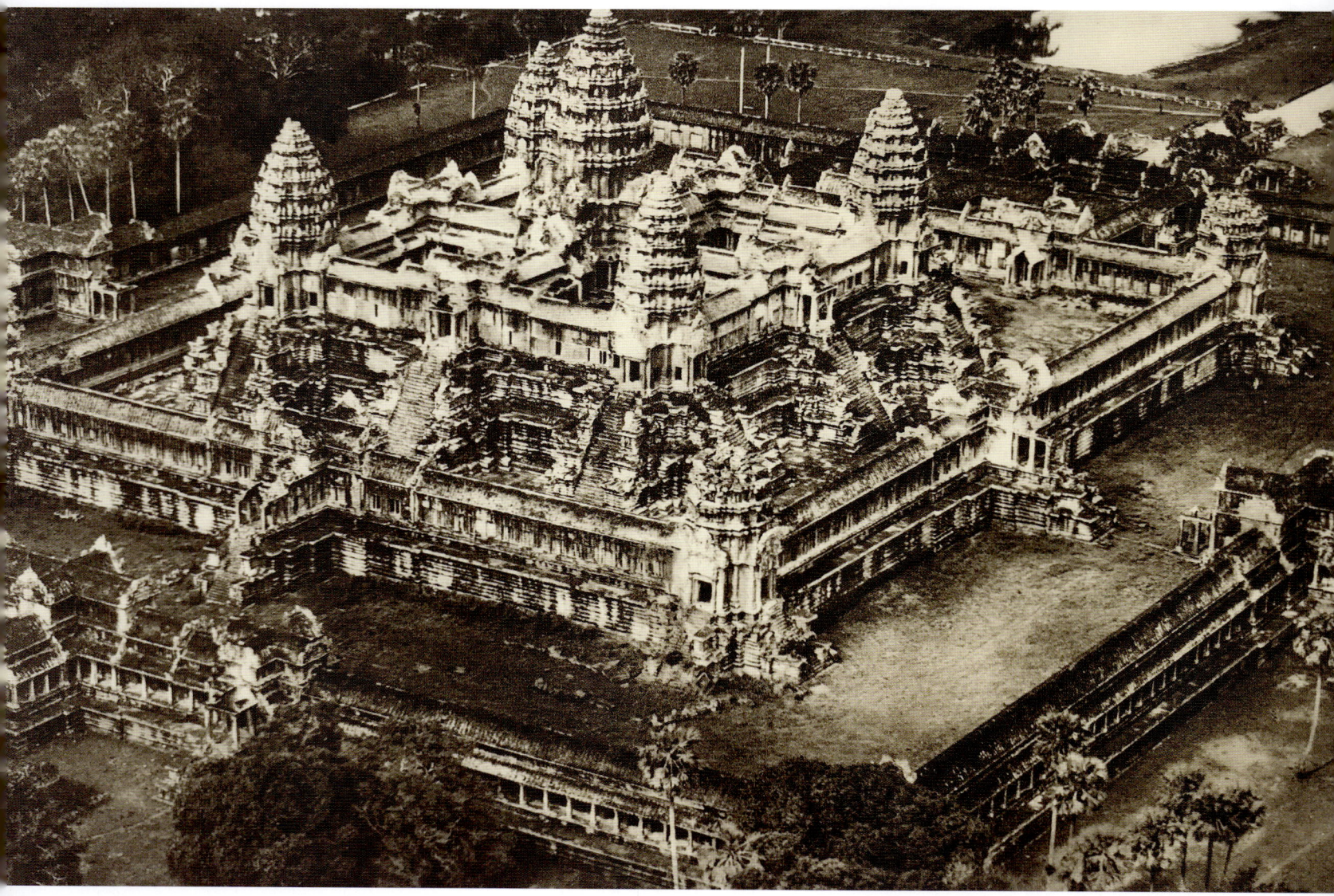

An Aerial View of Ankgor Wat

World War I saw huge advances made in the field of aviation. Postwar, the French had great hopes for the future of powered flight in Indochina as a means of consolidating, developing, and protecting their interests in the region. In reality, the impact of aviation was less than spectacular. Flying was uncomfortable and dangerous, while the Great Depression of the 1930s and Indochina's difficult terrain further crimped its expansion. There were, however, notable exceptions, such as the spectacular flight made by a hydroplane from Phnom Penh to Siem Reap in 1928, where it landed at the West Baray in front of a large crowd of Buddhist monks. By the following year, there was a small fleet of twin-engine hydroplanes landing on the same West Baray ready to pick up adventurous tourists for scenic flights over Angkor Wat. The use of aerial photography by archaeologists had a larger impact. It enabled a bird's-eye perspective of the thick jungle, suggesting that temples which had previously been thought of as independent entities were actually elements of a greater city-complex interconnected by canals and roadways.

Aerial view of Ankgor Wat.
1925–34. Photographer unknown. Author's Collection.

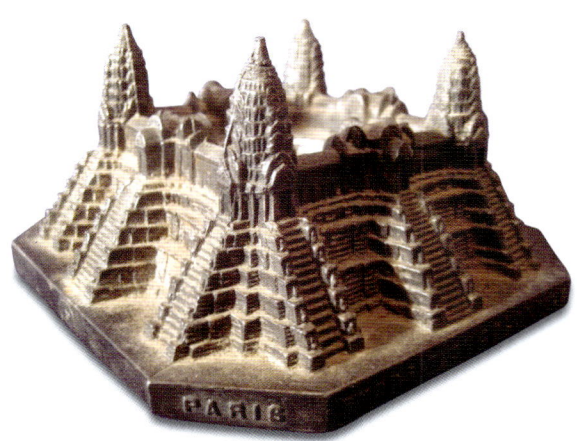

ABOVE: **Souvenir lead inkwell in the form of Angkor Wat.** 1931. Archives Photographiques, Musée Guimet.

BELOW: **Montage of a night view towards the main entrance of the Angkor Wat pavilion.** Paris International Exposition. Photographer unknown. 1931. Archives Photographiques, Musée Guimet.

The 1931 Paris International Exposition

Reconstructions of sections of the iconic Angkor Wat were a hallmark of French expositions from the 1870s through to 1931. Like the Taj Mahal for the British, the Angkorian temples were the glittering jewel of France's imperial possessions. The 1931 International Exposition at Vincennes near Paris attracted enormous crowds—some 30 million visitors during the summer months of 1931. Perhaps this reconstruction, with its tapered pinnacle rather than an historically correct lotus bud, was a sly reference to the Art Deco Chrysler Building finished in New York two years earlier. The Expo was full of merchandise, such as mini-Angkor Wat inkwells and printed postcards that advertised Cambodia as an exotic destination full of oriental mysticism and allure.

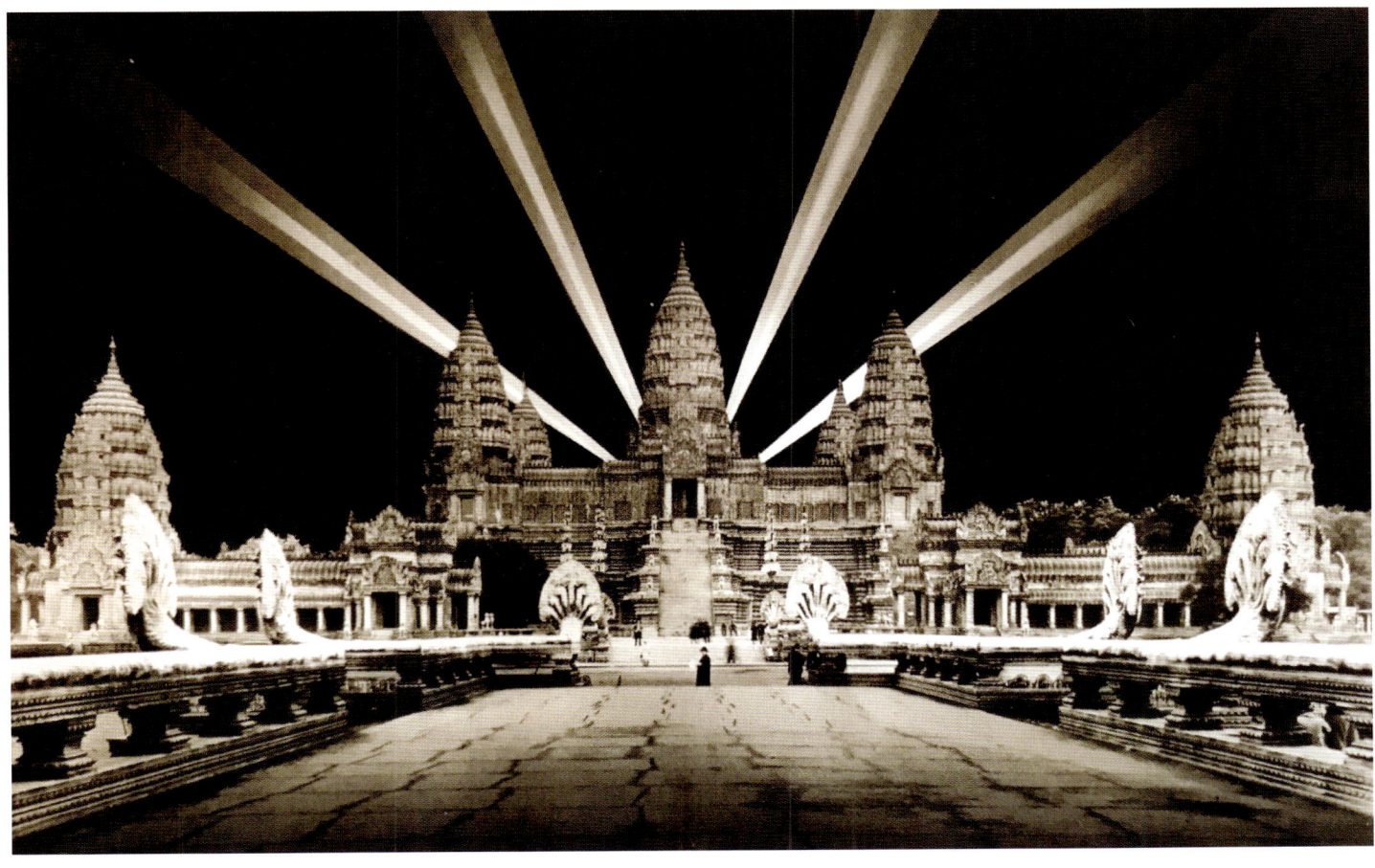

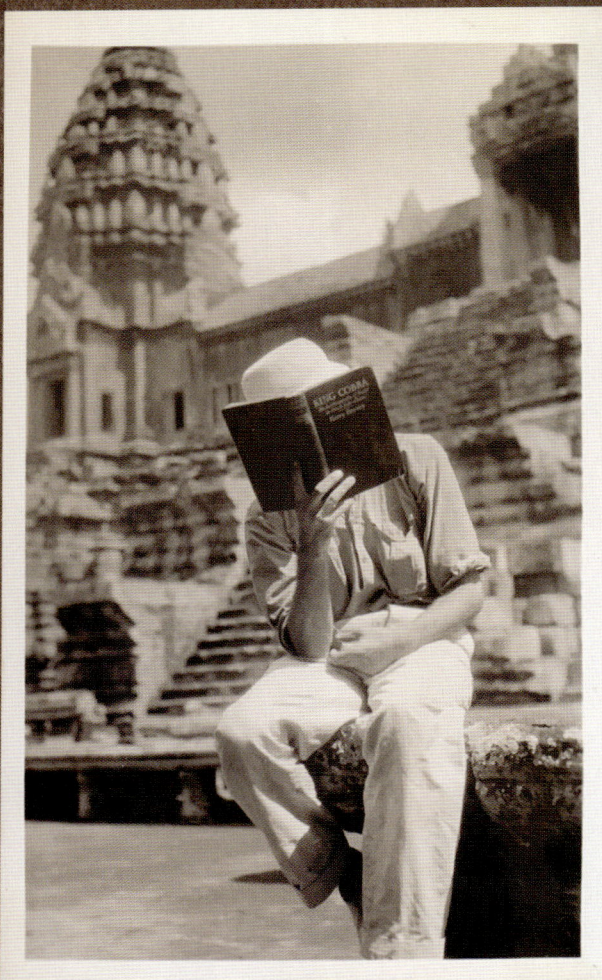

Mort gets some dope on Angkor Vat from friend Harry Hervey.

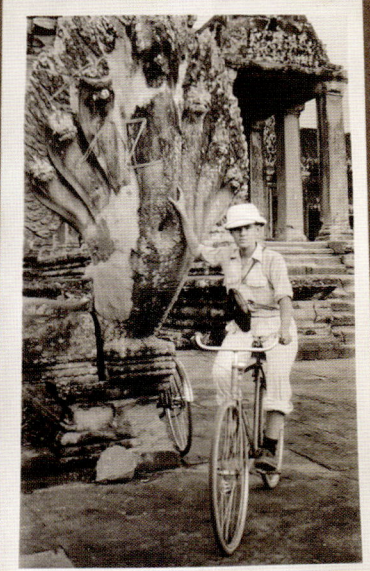

A cobra fan-tail.

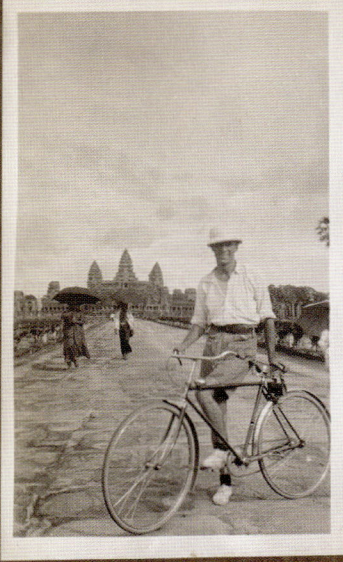

Riding a bike is the best way for a vagabond to see the extensive ruins of Angkor.

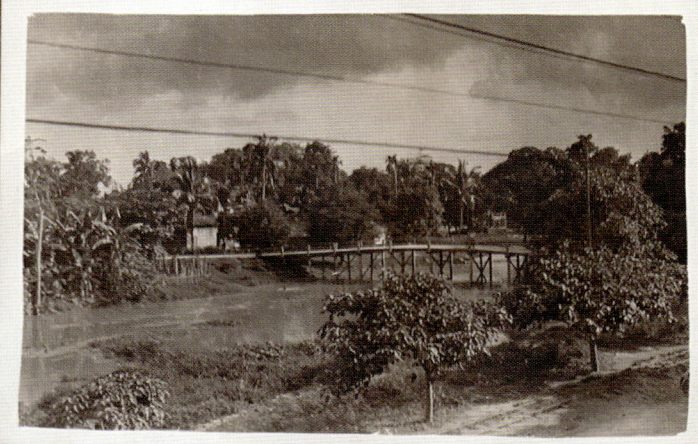

Seim Reap River, from my hotel.

"Getting the Dope on Angkor Wat"

The twenty-one-year-old American Hal LLIPPINCOTT (1907–91) circumnavigated the world between 1928 and 1929, keeping a hilarious yet meticulous diary of his exploits and thriftly living on US$3 a day. He visited Cambodia in the dry season, traveling by bus and ferry as he stayed in cheap Chinese hotels wherever he went, often being bitten by bedbugs and mosquitoes. His natural charm and engaging disposition allowed the nomadic Llippincott to pick up friends and fellow travelers despite his insectivorous companions. Here he sits in front of Angkor Wat reading the first edition of Harry Hervey's renowned Indochinese travel guide, *King Cobra*.

I took a train from Bangkok to the Indo-Chinese border. This took the better part of a day. Just before dark I rented a car with three Chinamen and we tore about 200 miles over a jungle road to Phnon Penh. We arrived at 2 A.M. I spent the night in a cheap Chinese hotel, and the next in a park. The following morning I took a bus 150 miles to Seim Reap. Mosquitos necessitated sleeping indoors so I stayed in a cheap chinese hotel till bed-bugs drove me out the second night. I walked the streets that night, and the third night took a bus back to Phnon Penh. We stopped at a village half way to Phnon Penh to spend the night. I couldn't sleep in the bus because of mosquitos so again walked the streets till dawn. The next night I spent in the park at Phnon Penh— till I was arrested some time past midnight. I warmed a wooden bench in the police station till they shipped me out of town the following morning.

OPPOSITE TOP LEFT, CLOCKWISE: "Must get some dope on Angkor Vat from friend Harry Hervey."

"A cobra fan-tail."

"Riding a bike is the best way for a vagabond to see the ruins of Angkor."

"Siem Reap River, from my hotel."

Photographs: Hall Llippincott. Siem Reap. 1929. Cindy Lippincott and Bob Berman Family Archive, Oregon.

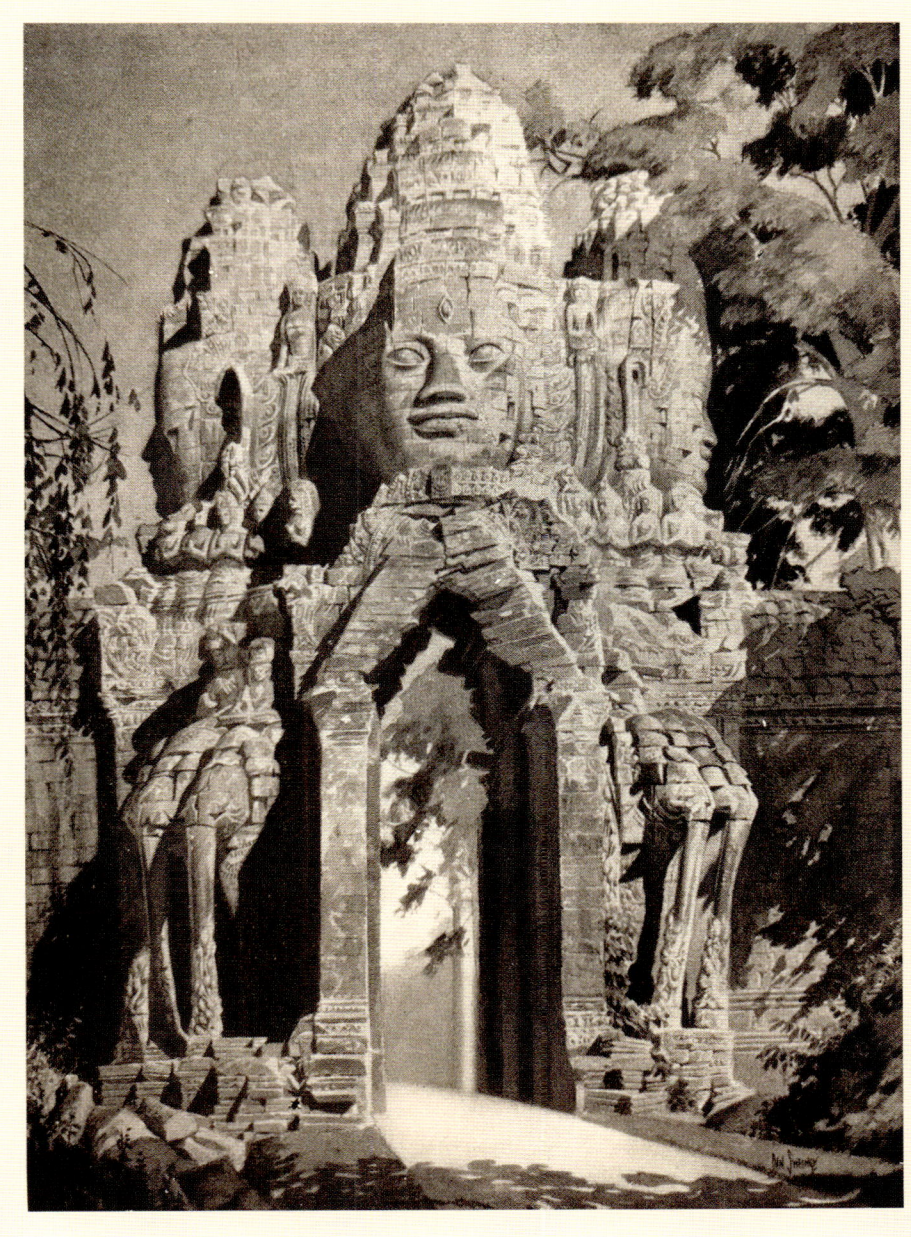

RIGHT: "The God of Destruction looks down from the South Gate of Angkor Thom well pleased with his great jest." Dan Sweeney. 1928. In *Four Faces of Siva: The Detective Story of a Hidden Race*. Robert J. Casey. Blue Ribbon Press/Bobbs-Merrill Company. 1929. Author's Library.

The God of Destruction

Dan SWEENEY (1880–1958) was a highly regarded American illustrator for newspapers, magazines, and theater and travel posters. He sailed to the Orient in the late 1920s, where he was commissioned to create numerous hotel baggage labels for luxurious Shanghai and Hong Kong hotels. While Sweeney designed a label for the Continental Palace Hotel in Saigon, there is no evidence he motored overland to the temples of Angkor to execute this work; the illustraion above was probably taken from a photograph and was used to introduce readers to the 1929 novel *Four Faces of Siva: The Detective Story of a Hidden Race* by the popular columnist and foreign war correspondent Robert J. Casey (1890–1962) who was traveling around the Pacific at the same time. With both being Americans in the publishing game, and at the peak of their careers, perhaps they met at a Saigon bar one evening and the commission was sealed.

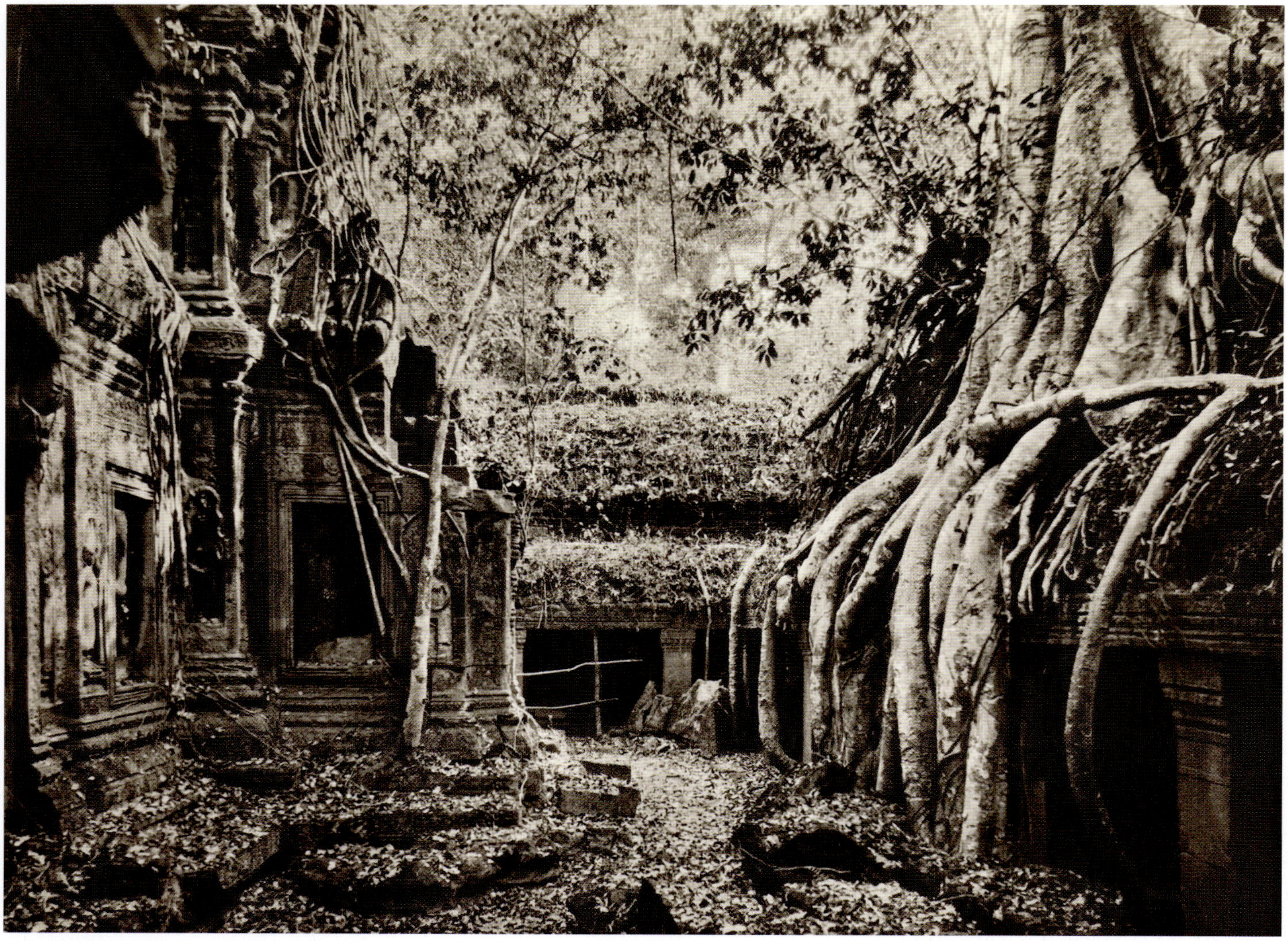

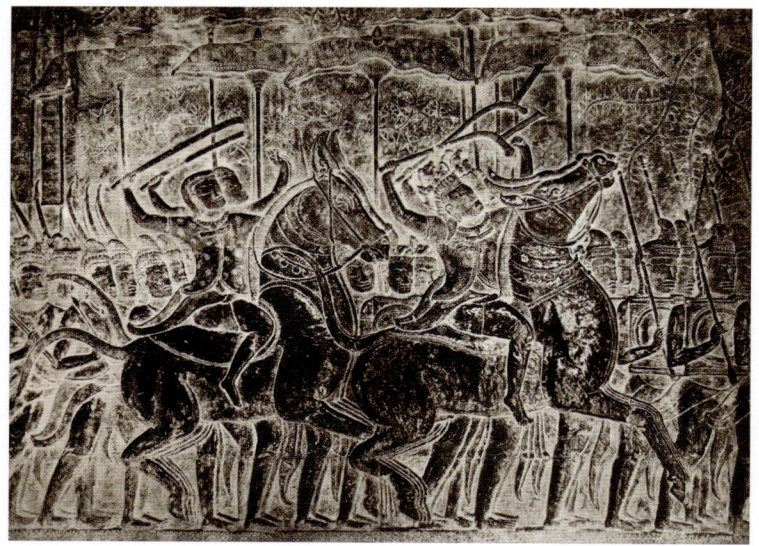
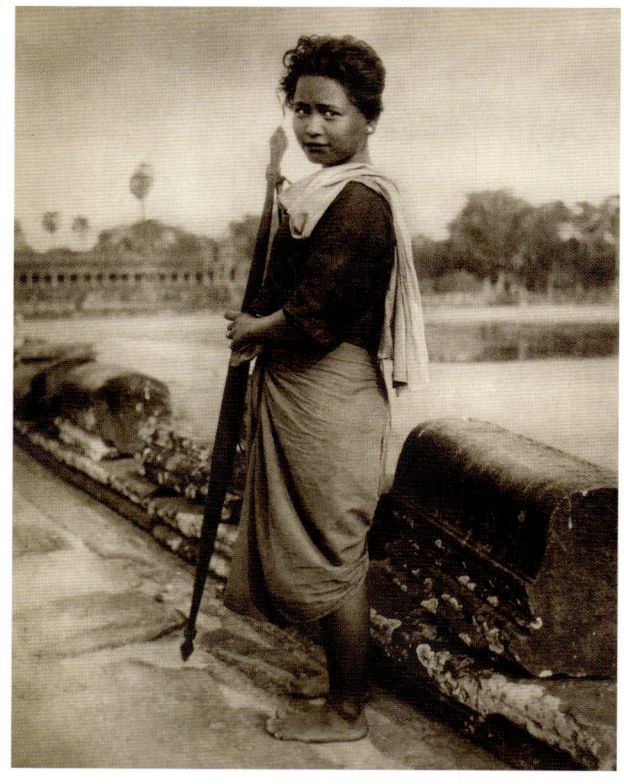

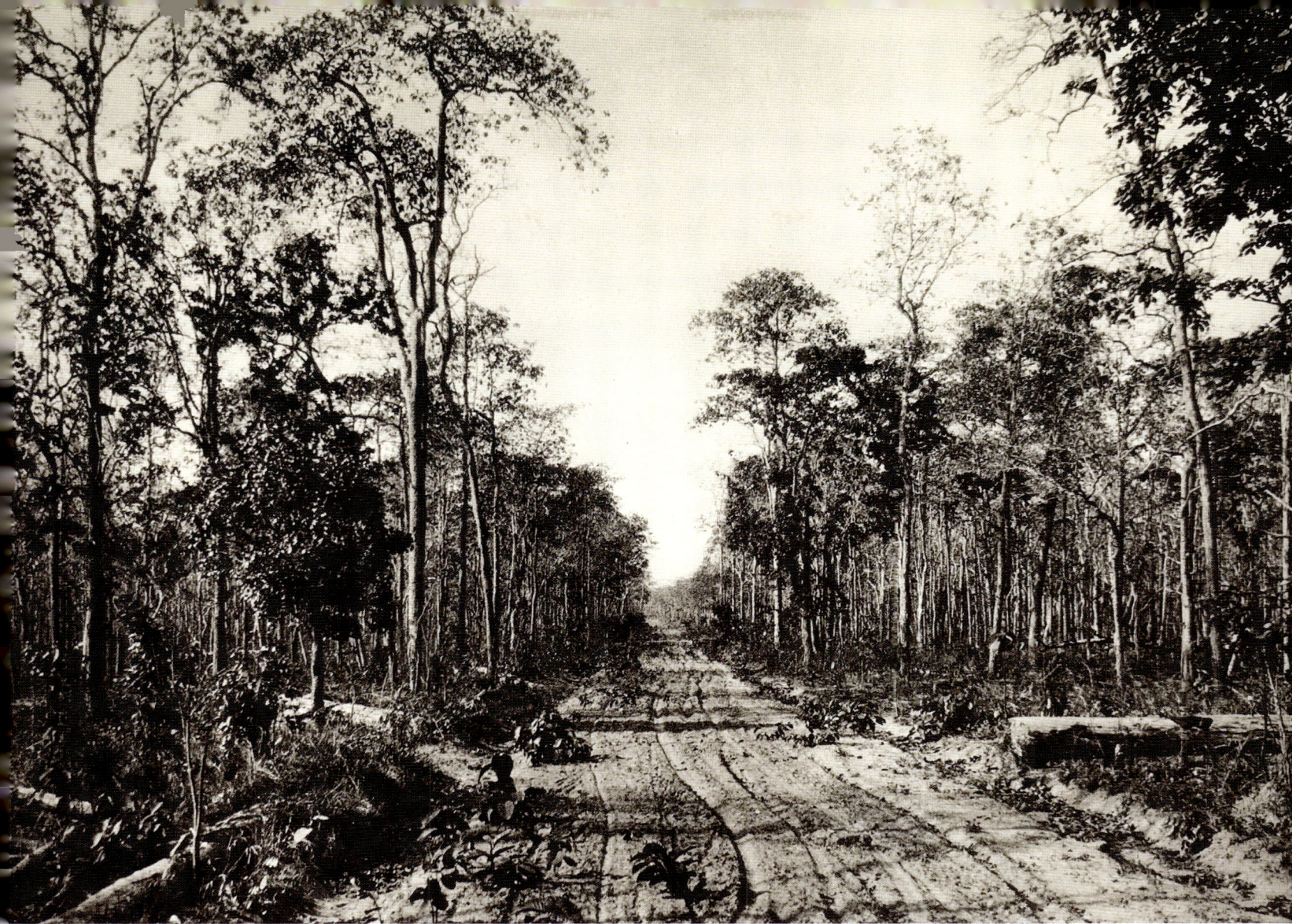

OPPOSITE TOP, CLOCKWISE:
Angkor. Ta Prom. Siem Reap.

Cambodian woman with a bamboo carrying pole near Angkor. Siem Reap.

Angkor Wat. Riders in the army. Siem Reap.

ABOVE: **Forest in west Cambodia.**

Photographs: Martin Hurlimann. 1929. From *Ceylon Und Indochina: Baukunst, Landschaft und Volksleben*. Ernst Wasmuth A.G. Berlin. 1929. Author's Library.

The Photographer and Publisher

Based in both Zurich and Berlin, Martin HURLIMANN (1897–1984) founded the newspaper *Atlantis*, which specialized in international travel stories. He was a prolific travel photographer, arriving in Cambodia in 1929. Hurlimann used his Sinclair Una camera and Zeiss lens to frame formal landscapes with a strong depth of field. Paradoxically, his photograph of a woman with a bamboo carrying pole on the causeway at Angkor Wat almost appears to have been taken in a studio. A year later, in 1930, an English edition of his photographs was published as *Ceylon and Indochina: Architecture, Landscape and Popular Scenes*.

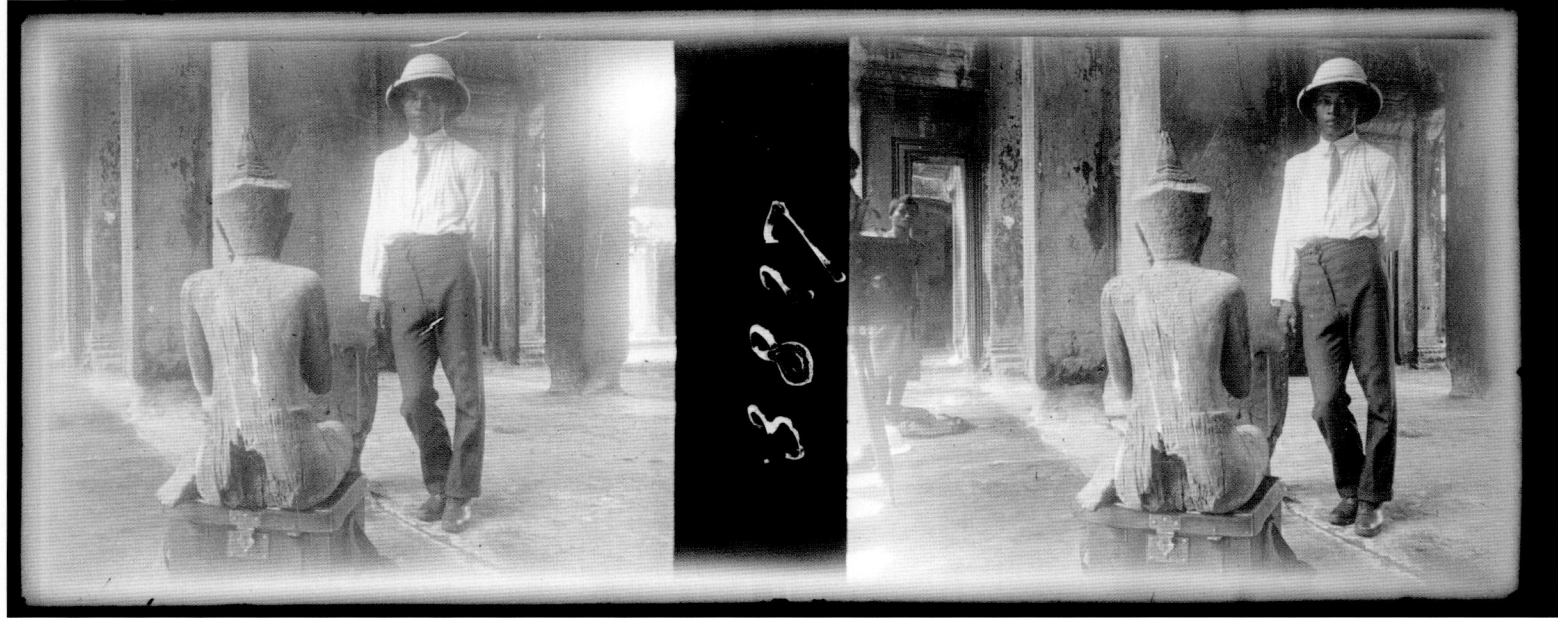

The Archaeologist and the Camera

This photograph, attributed to Henri PARMENTIER (1871–1949), was taken around 1933. It is difficult to tell what the principle focus for the photographer was in this scene. Perhaps, looking straight at the camera, it is the smartly dressed Cambodian wearing polished leather shoes, collar and tie, and pith helmet. He would seem to be standing in the monumental halls of Angkor Wat. The fact that his head is covered and he is wearing shoes on such hallowed ground is unusual for a Cambodian. Or is Parmentier's focus on the badly damaged wooden Buddha sitting precariously on the leather camera box? To the extreme left of the right-hand image is the support leg of a large-format camera, with the silhouette of a second Cambodian operator and an assistant peering into the scene. No names of the onlookers are recorded. Parmentier, who was head of the École française d'Extrême-Orient from 1904 to 1932, had formally retired when this photograph was taken.

Cambodian and wooden Buddha, Angkor Wat. Siem Reap. ca. 1933. Stereoscope. Attributed to Henri Parmentier. École française d'Extrême-Orient.

The Buddha of Vat Tep Pranam

The Buddha of Vat Tep Pranam is captured towering over the photographer in monumental serenity, sitting in the "calling the earth to witness" pose, a pivotal point in the Buddha's defeat of Mara and his enlightenment under the Bodhi tree. Surrounded by the ancient Angkorian monuments of Angkor Thom, this Buddha was carved from massive sandstone blocks, possibly sourced from nearby monuments, and sited on a cruciform terrace that hints of the large timber pavilion (since disappeared) that would have originally protected the image.

In 1917, the eminent archaeologist Henri Marchal noted that looters had severely damaged the statue. Believing that treasures were hidden within, they had chipped and wedged apart the blocks that configured the torso, almost toppling the majestic structure and leaving the statue like an eaten apple core. By the time this photograph was taken, the sculpture had been restored by the École française d'Extrême-Orient. Early European travelers may have believed it to date to Angkorian times, linking it to the faces of the Bayon monument. However, it was constructed in the late fifteenth century.

This photograph, probably taken in 1939 by the Comtesse Gilberte de Coral-Rémusat, a friend of the prolific author Alan Houghton Brodrick, appeared on the cover of his book *Little Vehicle: Cambodia and Laos*, published after World War II, in 1949.

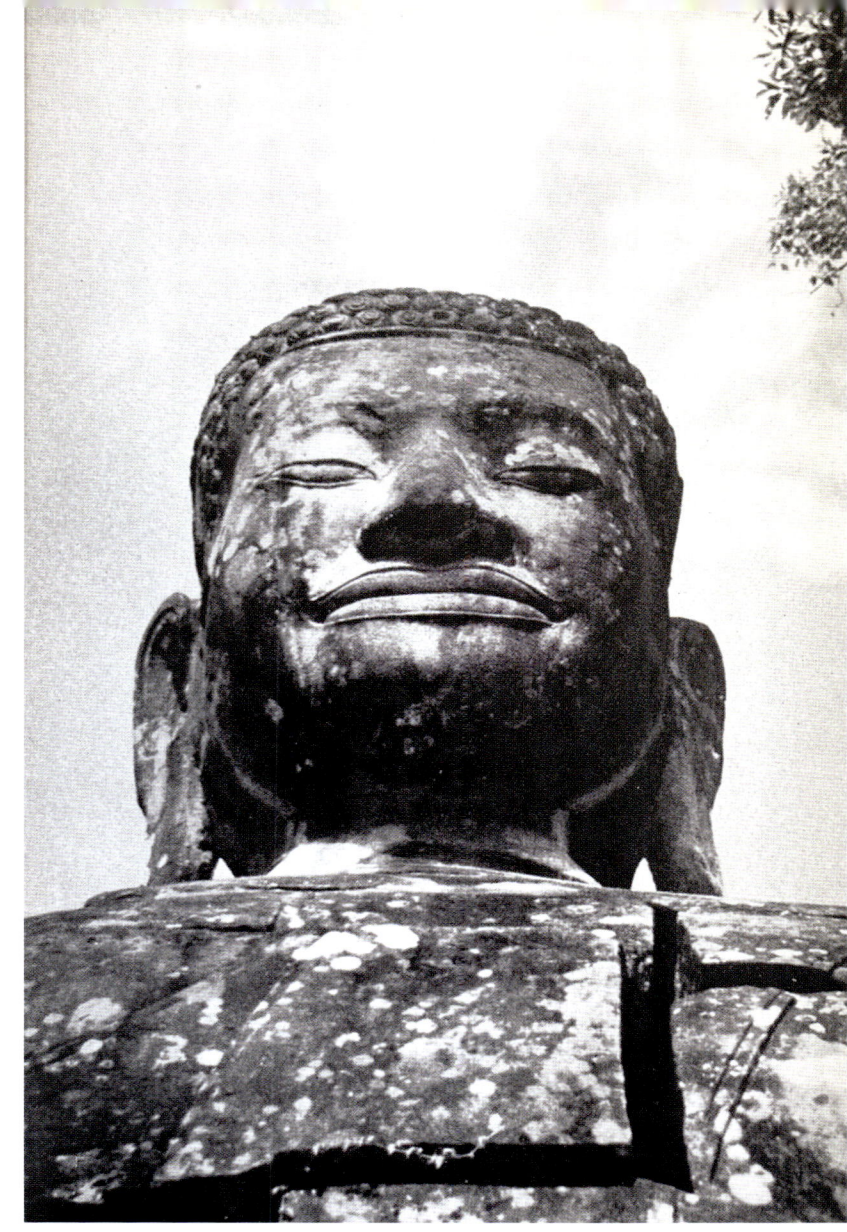

ABOVE: **The Buddha of Vat Tep Pranam**. Angkor Thom, Siem Reap. 1939. Probably Comtesse Gilberte de Coral-Rémusat. From *Little Vehicle: Cambodia and Laos*. Alan Horton. 1949. Author's Library.

LEFT: **The Buddha of Vat Tep Pranam**. Angkor Thom, Siem Reap. ca. 1935. Photographer unknown. Author's Collection.

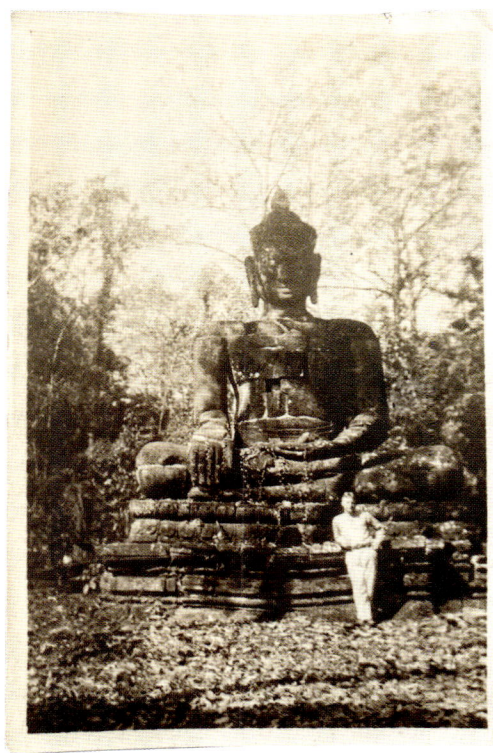

1941–1955
The Reign of King Sihanouk

The death of King Sisowath Monivong in 1941 enabled the now Vichy French to put the eighteen-year-old Prince Sihanouk (1922–2012) on the throne. He reigned for two terms (1941–55 and 1993–2004), then abdicated in favor of his son Sihamoni. Shortly after his coronation, Sihanouk bought his first 16 mm movie camera, and for the next twenty-five years he became a prolific film-maker and master of the photograph to promote both himself and an image of his country.

World War II temporarily shifted the focus of photography towards reconnaissance and propaganda. After the Japanese surrendered, urbanized Cambodians began to see their relationship with the French in very different terms. In 1949, after sustained political agitation, Cambodia was granted limited autonomy within the French Union. A French military presence continued, however, as the First Indochina War of 1946–54 engulfed nearby Tonkin China. Photographers like Varoqui Raymond worked for the military-controlled Service d'information française (SPI), documenting the working lives of soldiers in remote Cambodian outposts and civilian life in towns. As the war escalated, Sihanouk, frustrated with French intransigence regarding full independence, declared martial law in 1953, dissolved the governing assembly, and toured the world on a public relations offensive. It was a dramatic maneuver, but his gamble succeeded. Full independence was granted. Ninety years of French dominion over Cambodia came to an end.

As the new Cold War enveloped the globe, Sihanouk was determined to distance his newly independent kingdom from the competing spheres of communism and capitalism. Like the governments of other postcolonial countries in Southeast Asia, such as Indonesia, Laos, India, and Burma, Sihanouk adopted a non-aligned stance. Both the Soviets and the Americans attempted to win his favor, offering financial and military aid, screening soft propaganda films, presenting displays of photography, and offering courses in film-making. From these early interventions, a nascent Cambodian film industry was born. Young graduates found jobs as photojournalists, layout artists, and cine cameramen.

By the early 1950s, the slow rhythm of daily life and the Angkorian monuments continued to attract international holiday-makers and local expatriate families to tour the country. Women photographers like Mimijac Palgen (1918–95), who worked for Radio Cambodge, and Margaret Parx Hays (1912–2008), who was with the American diplomatic service, created a new perspective on the photography of Cambodia. Palgen's image of a tabletop of fried spiders (page 107) remains a landmark in Cambodian still life photography. After visiting the war zones in Cochin China, Werner Bischoff (1919–54), the renowned German photographer, traveled through Cambodia, forefronting rural life with composed calm, while for the École française d'Extrême-Orient (EFEO), the 1950s and 1960s were considered a mini "golden age" for monument conservation.

By the mid-1960s, Sihanouk was unhappy at the way his "children" were governing the country. The government was becoming increasingly fractious and unstable as entrenched elites were incapable of compromise to pursue long-term policies for development. Sihanouk was about to engineer another of his famous stunts.

Sihanouk meeting a village elder. Location unknown. ca. 1950s. Photographer unknown. Possibly a Forces armées royales khmères (FARK) photographer. Charles Meyer Collection, Paris/National Archives of Cambodia.

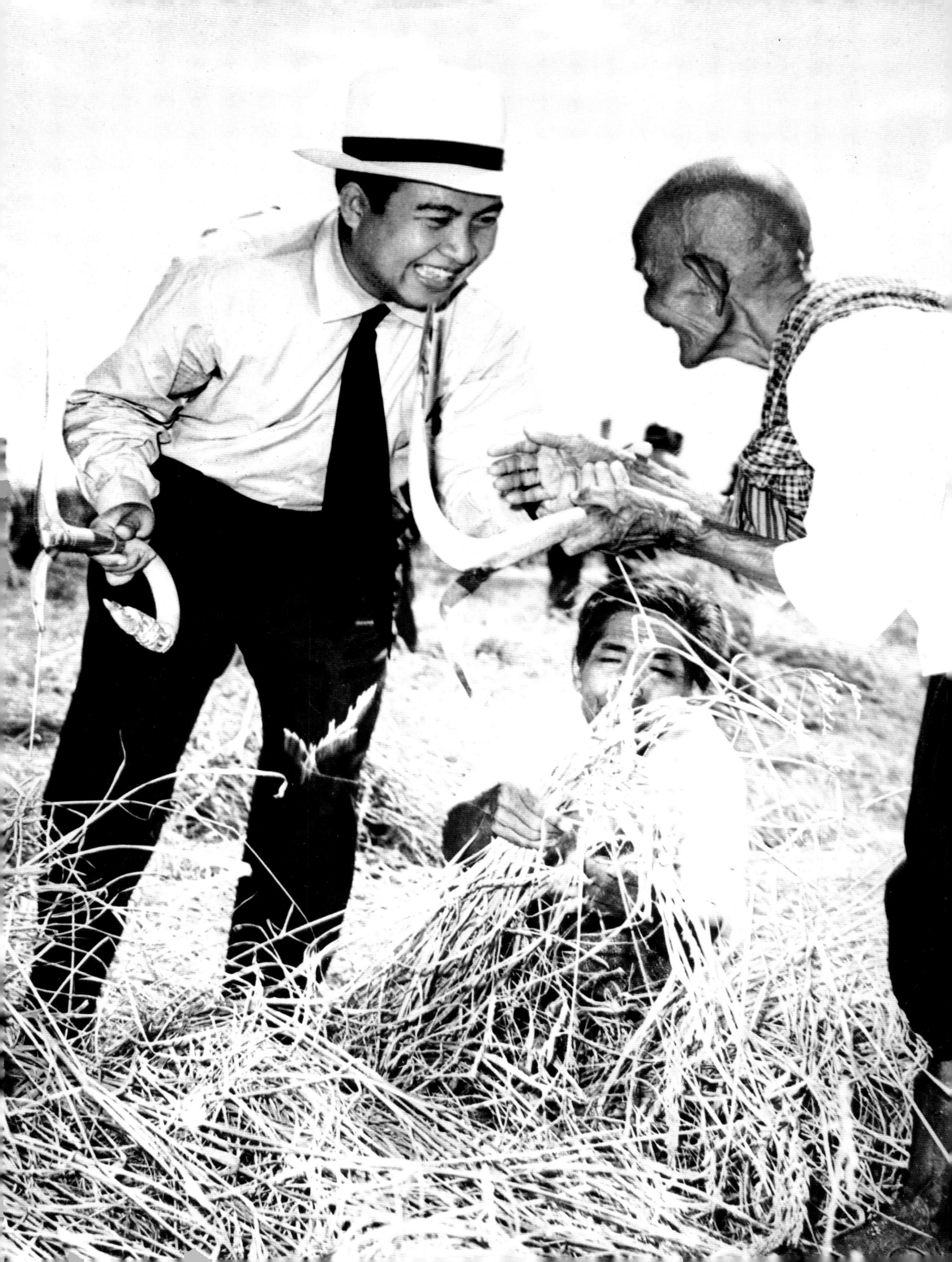

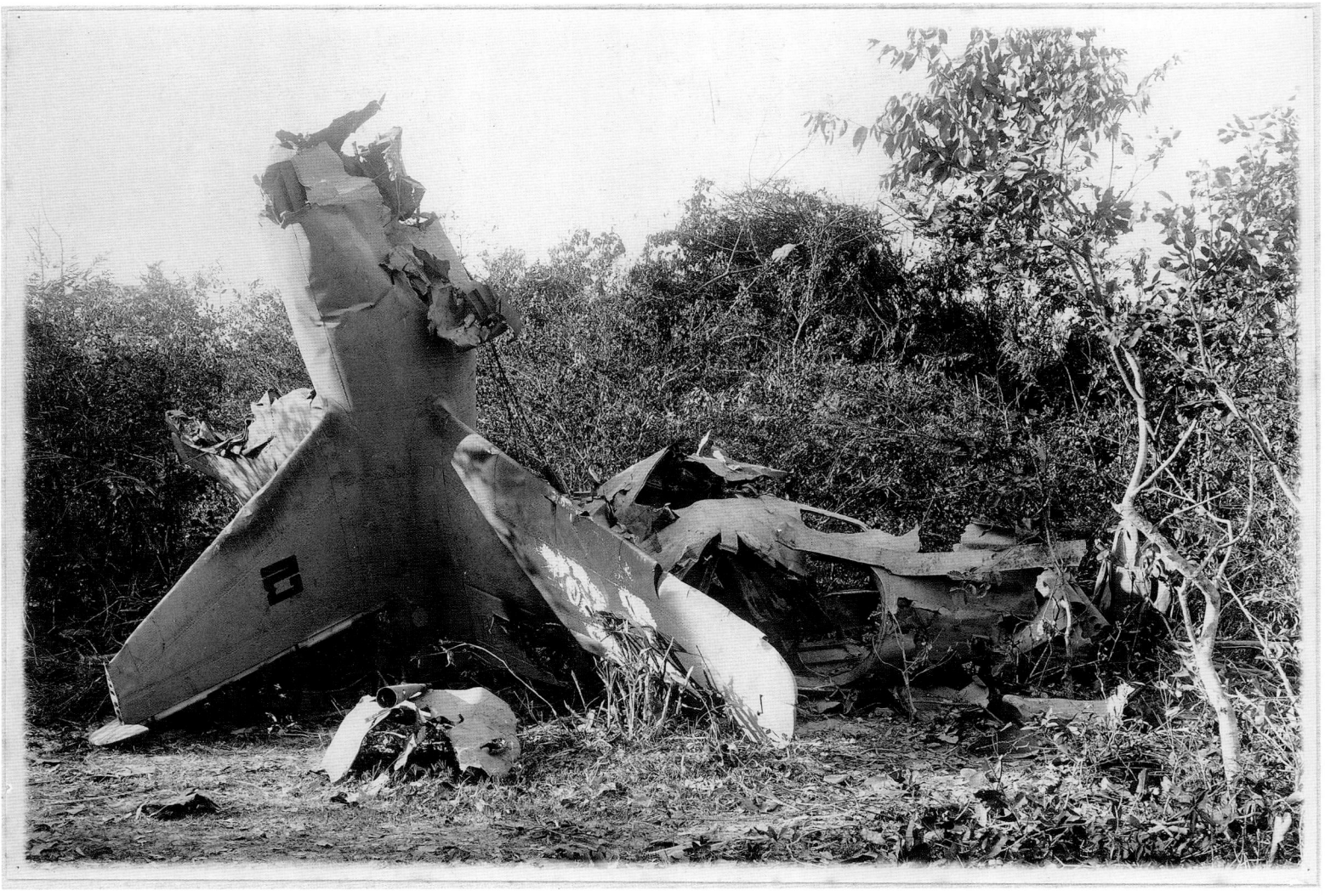

Crashed Thai Bomber

The twisted wreckage of a Thai aircraft intended to bomb the French airfield of Siem Reap lies within a kilometer of Angkor Wat. Based on the shape of the tail fin (branching to the left) and the horizontal stabilizer, the aircraft is most likely a Mitsubishi KI-30 light bomber. The rest of the fuselage lies in complete ruin. It is a graphic memorial to the short war in the first few months of 1941, fought between the Vichy French forces of Indochina and Thailand. Their aircraft, armies, and naval vessels engaged in a conflict that seesawed back and forth on multiple fronts. With Japan's invasion of Indochina in September 1940, the Thais were hoping to take advantage of a weaker France to regain vassal territories ceded to France thirty-four years earlier. The warring parties were coerced into peace by the Japanese. What the Thais could not get militarily, they gained diplomatically, as the French were obliged to return the five northwestern provinces of Cambodia, including Siem Reap, for the duration of World War II.

Downed Thai light bomber. Siem Reap. 1941. Photographer unknown. École française d'Extrême-Orient.

Indochina Bombing Map

By late 1943, with Japan in control over much of Southeast Asia and the Pacific, Allied forces retook the initiative. Knowledge of the enemy's supply chains was essential for victory. Phnom Penh was important as a transshipment port, connecting Saigon via the Mekong River to the east and the railway line to Bangkok to the northwest. Using American and British intelligence, maps were printed for Allied pilots that showed potential bombing targets in Phnom Penh: the railway station and the goods yards, the power plant, and the port facilities along the river. The Americans used these maps to guide the bombing of Phnom Penh in January 1945, during which they mistakenly hit Wat Ounalom, killing many civilians and monks. Perhaps from the air, to an untrained eye, religious spires and industrial smokestacks looked similar. In the larger scheme of things, Cambodia was lucky to avoid the brunt of the war's devastation, as the Japanese occupiers surrendered peacefully in August 1945.

Air Objective Folder, Phnom Penh. Washington, USA. 1944. Photographer unknown. Office of the Assistant Chief of Air Staff. Intelligence. Washington, D.C. National Archives Research Center, Washington.

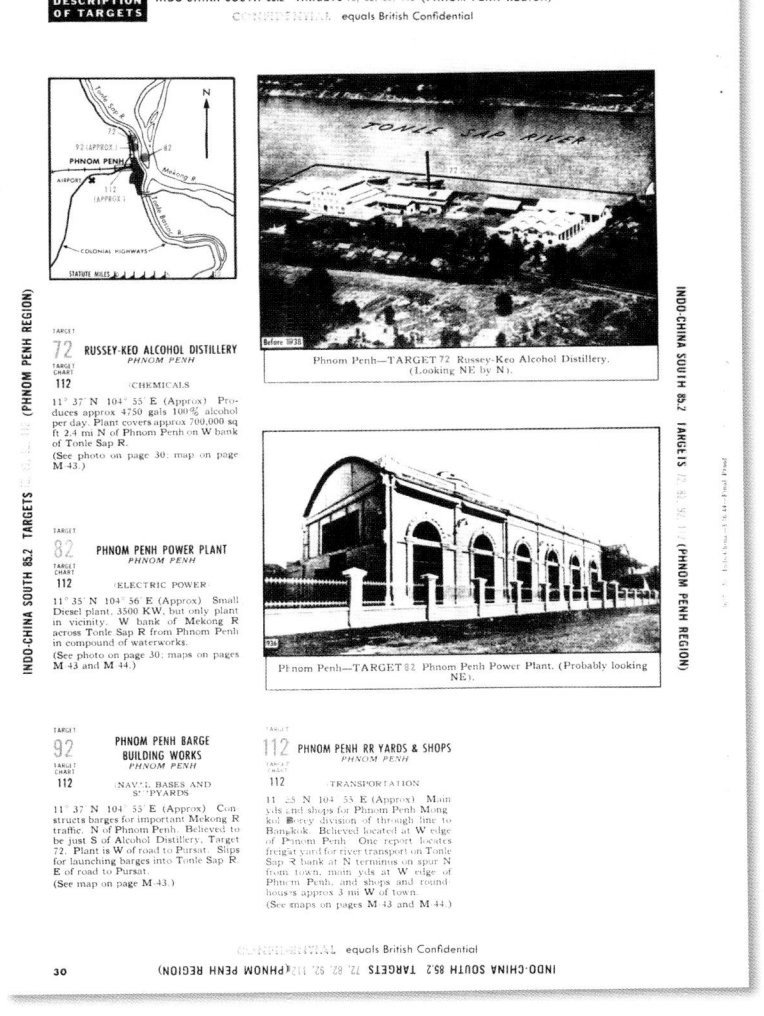

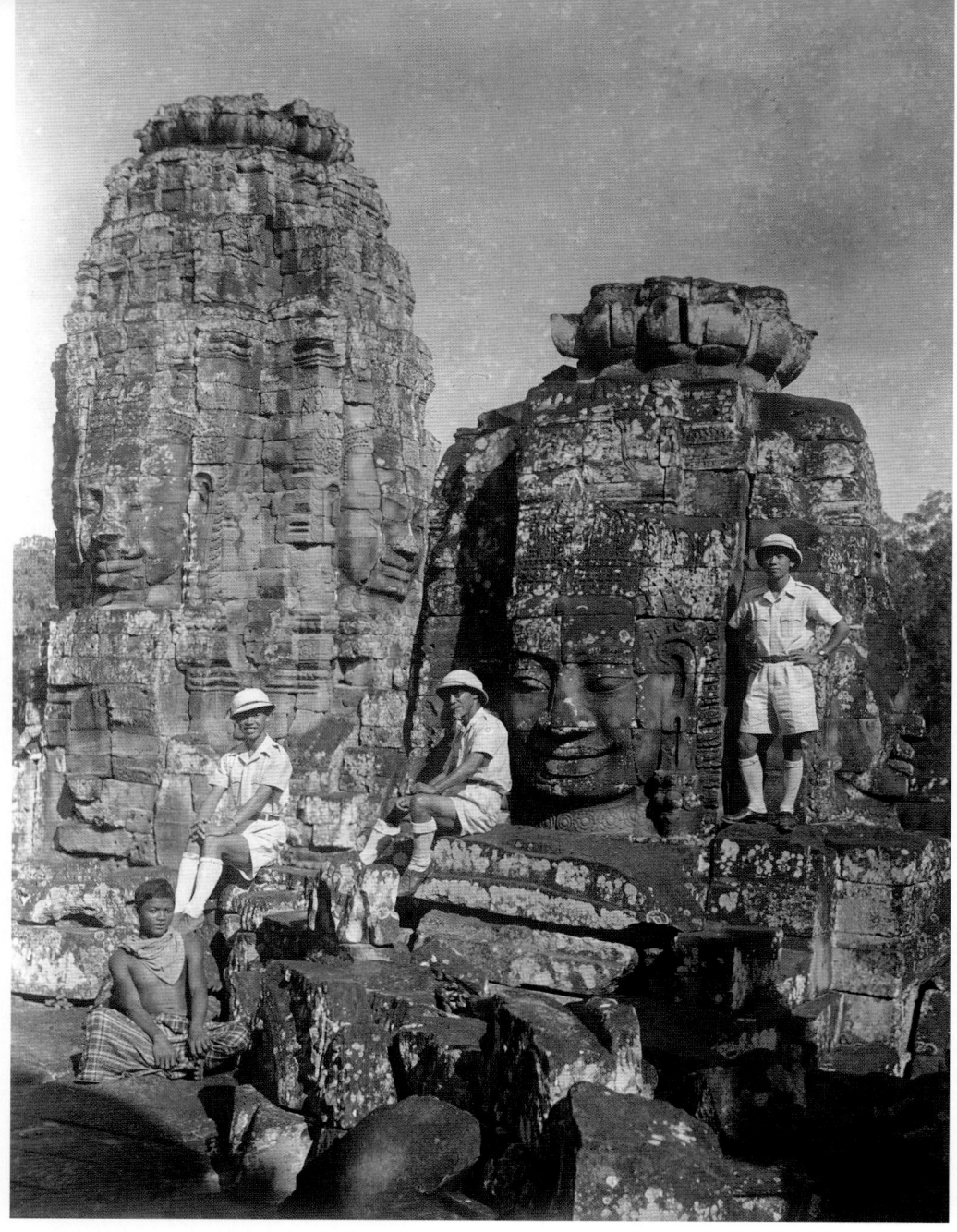

Japanese cultural research team at the Bayon temple.
Siem Reap. 1943. Nomura Naotaro. Masaharu Asada Collection, Tokyo.

A Japanese Cultural Delegation

Taking advantage of the ruins of the great Bayon temple, photographer NOMURA Naotaro artfully balanced his team across the tumble of fallen stones. He was the photographer accompanying twelve Japanese artists and scholars who traveled to the Angkor monuments over the 1942–43 dry season. They were led by Sugitomo Tetsuro, a painter of Buddhist art, who came from the Jodo Shinshu Buddhist sect based in Kyoto. Nomura took hundreds of 120 x 165 mm dry-plate photographs. The old-fashioned technology was still commonly used in Japan until the 1960s, when it was finally superseded by the advent of the popular 35 mm camera. The collection of fifty-three original glass-plate images was bought at auction by Masaharu Asada, who realized they were indispensable in assisting the Japanese archaeological team's restoration work of the temples.

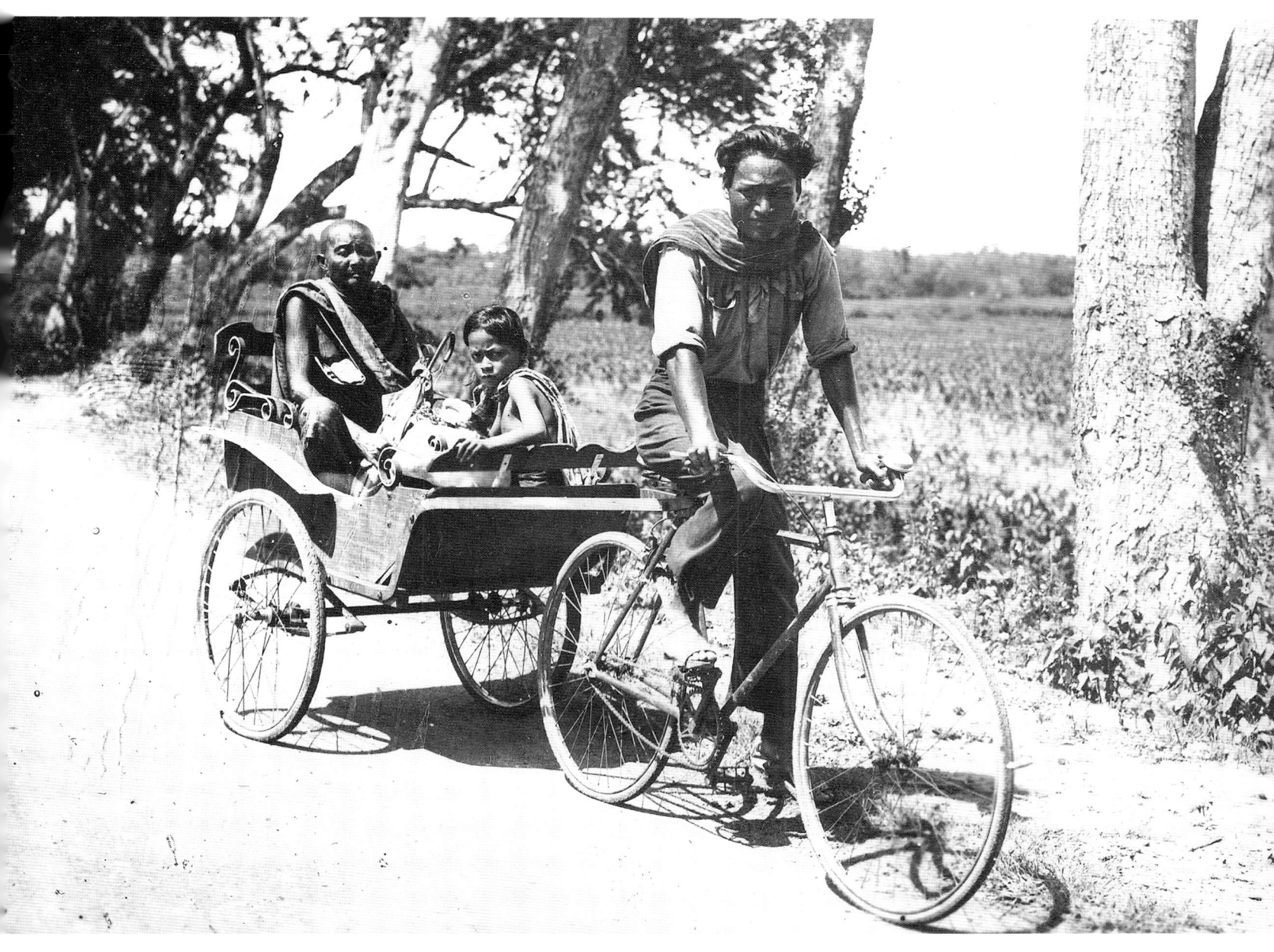

Modern Mobility

The *remorque-kong*, or bicycle trolley, has been a unique part of Cambodian locomotion since the early twentieth century. Its economy of structure and ease of construction and repair, yet ability to transport an entire family or a week's worth of shopping from the local wet market, made it a ubiquitous part of Cambodia's roads and laneways. Structurally, the bicycle trolley probably descended from earlier Chinese rickshaws. In 1936, the pneumatic *cyclo-pousse* was introduced to Phnom Penh by a Frenchman, where a bicycle pushed, rather than pulled, the passenger's carriage. They became popular across Asia. The *remorque-kong*, however, continued to be used alongside the *cyclo-pousse*, retaining the "cow-pulling cart" model but with mudguards and suspension added to the carriage. With the arrival of inexpensive and reliable Japanese motorbikes in the 1960s, the carriage became larger and a canopy was added. This motorized version, the *remorque-moto* [*tuk-tuk*], is still a popular mode of transport in the kingdom.

Family cycling on a *remorque-kong*. Location unknown. March 1948. Photographer unknown. École française d'Extrême-Orient.

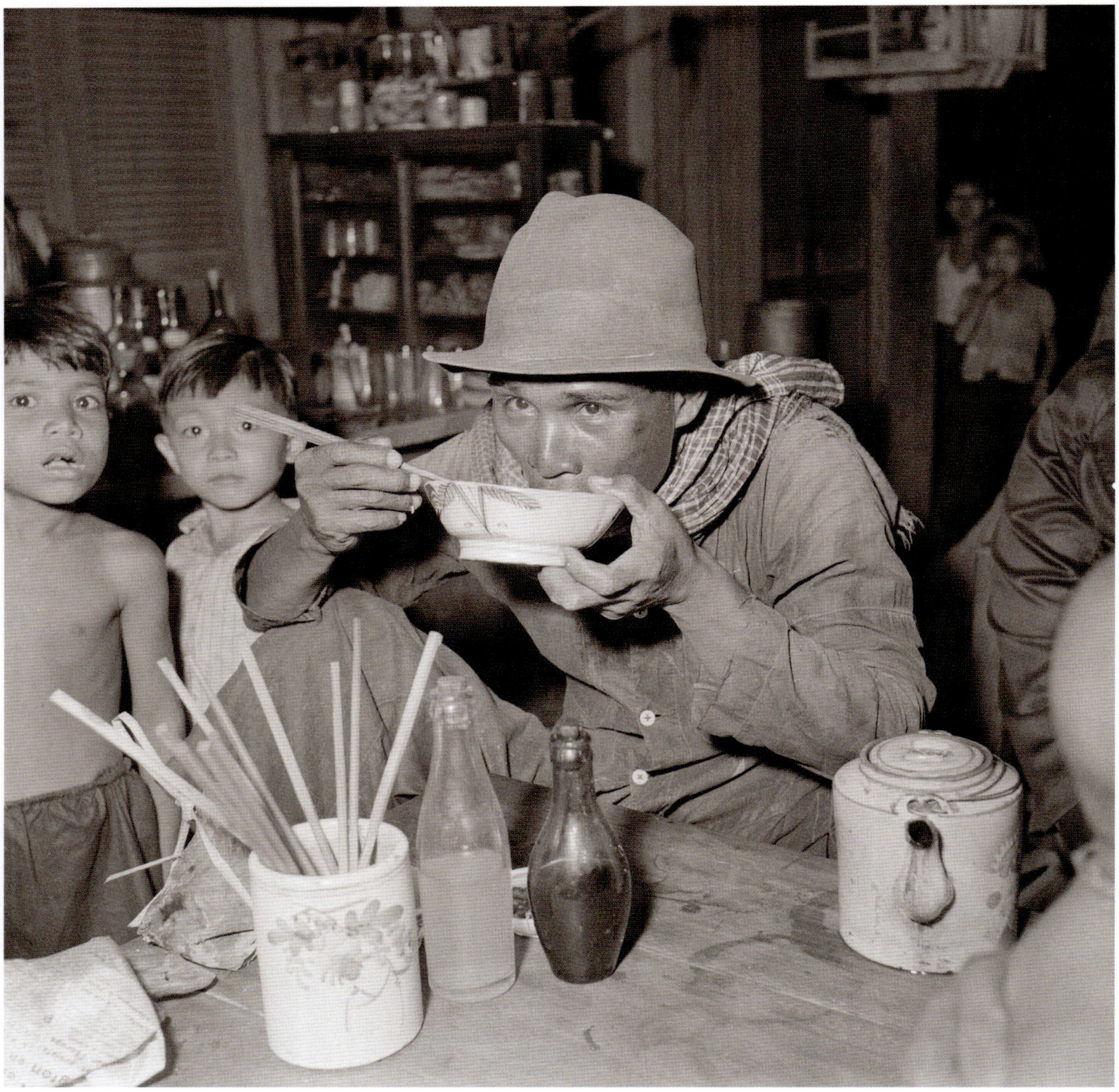

Night Café

Photographers working for the French Information Service (Service d'information française), ostensibly to document French military operations in Indochina, often took a great interest beyond their soldierly focus. Caught in the glare of a camera's flash, this Cambodian worker casually slurps his evening meal of noodle soup. He has his right leg propped up on a stool to steady his "red rooster" bowl. Two young boys, agape at the French photographer, and two shy women in the back doorway, are also caught in the glare. While the fork and spoon are common Cambodian eating utensils, this is a Chinese-owned establishment, hence the chopsticks.

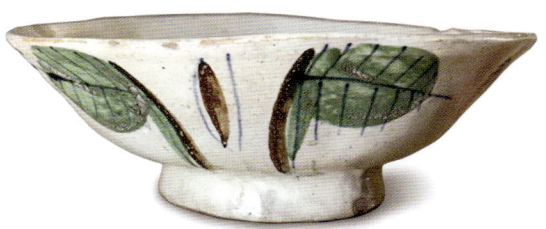

TOP: **Night café.** Phnom Penh. 1952. Gahery. Agence d'images de la Défense, Paris.

ABOVE: **Rooster bowl.** Made by Chinese potters in Vietnam. ca. 1930s. Douglas Gordon. Darryl Collins Collection, Siem Reap.

Angkorian Bronze Mirror Support

At 14 inches (35 cm) in height, this beautifully proportioned bronze mirror support proudly defines the space above for a missing mirror. The Khmer have always viewed bronze as a noble material, signifying prosperity and success. In the Khmer empire it was the preferred material for giving form to divinities and household objects commissioned for the temples, palaces, and private chapels of the nobility. Although the surface is badly pitted by corrosion, the figure's bejeweled body and finely detailed crown suggest that she, too, was an object of great worth and a source of pleasure for her owner living within the walled enclave of Angkor Thom.

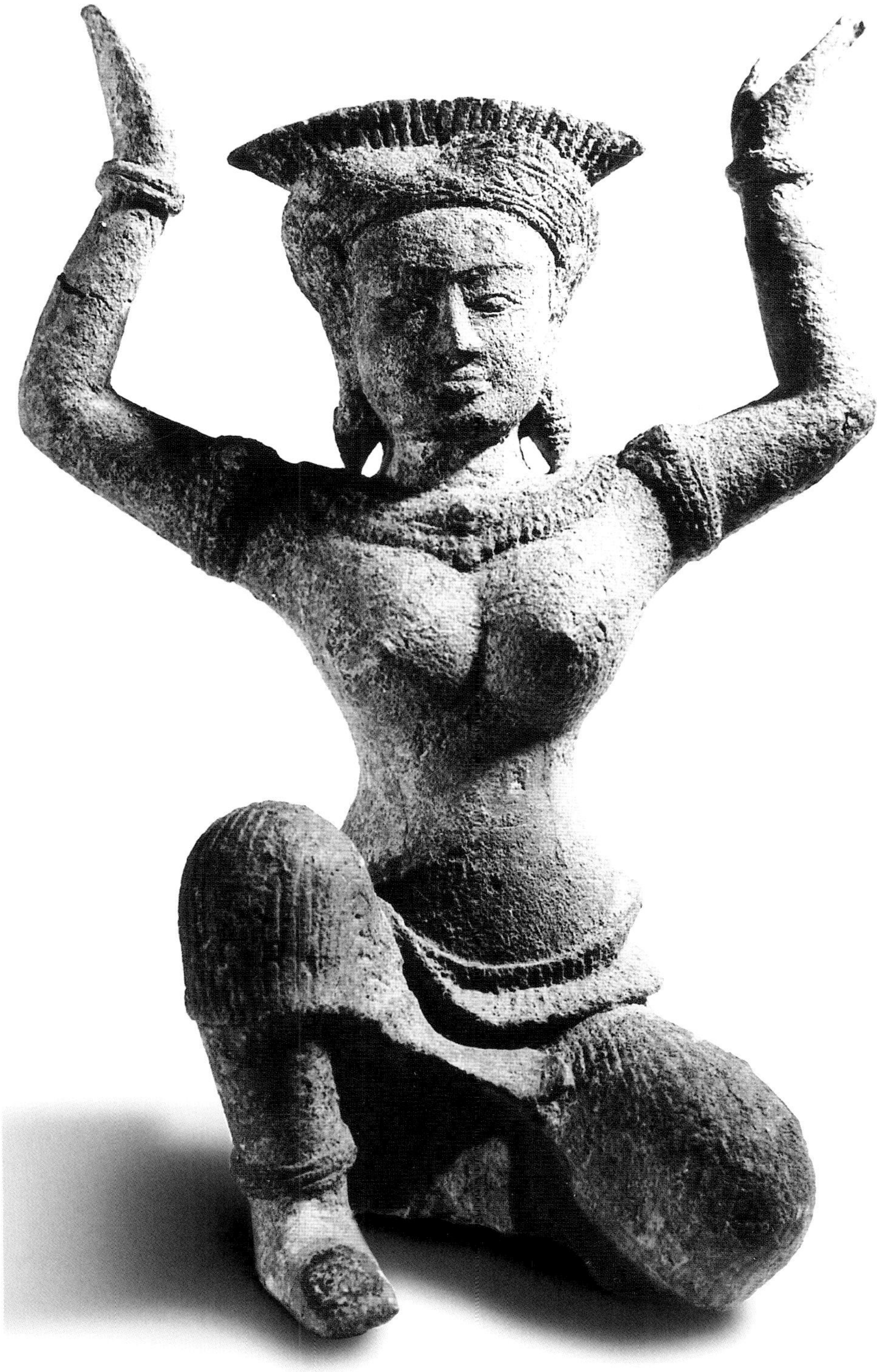

Angkorian bronze mirror support, Bayon period. Siem Reap. 1953. Photographer unknown. École française d'Extrême-Orient.

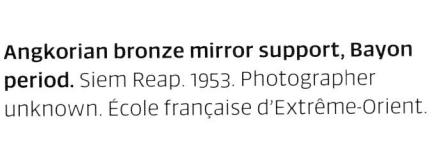

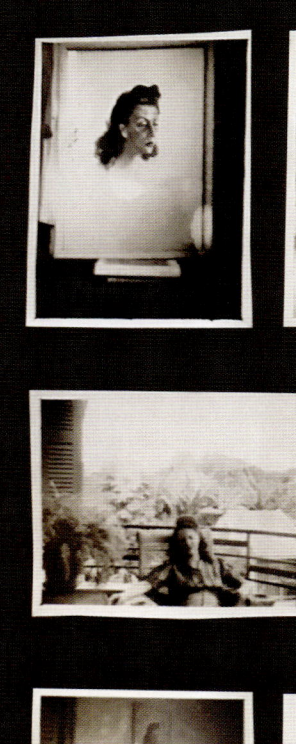
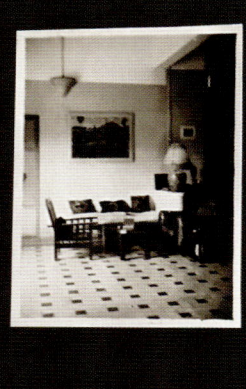
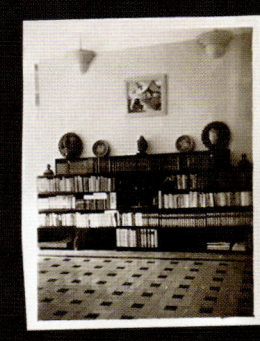
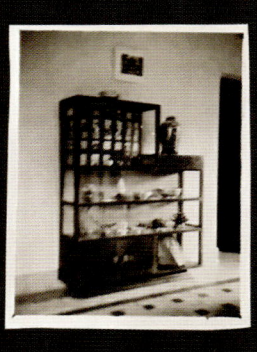
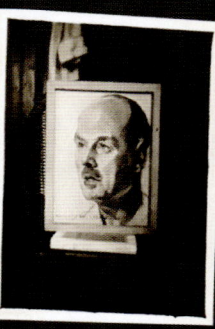
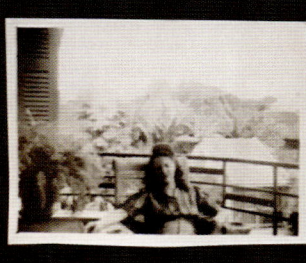
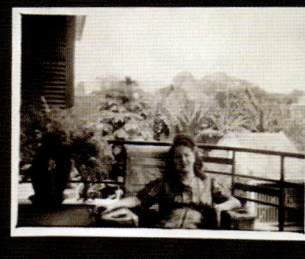
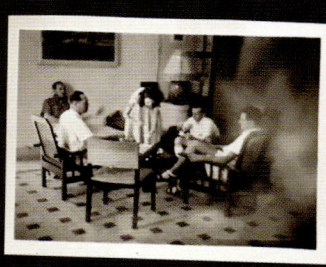
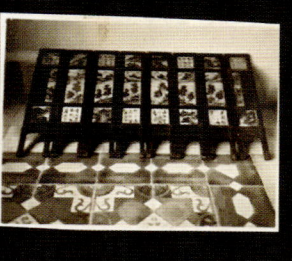
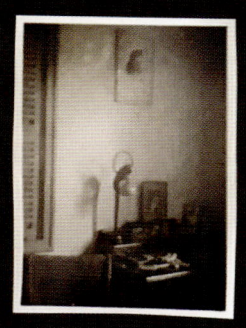
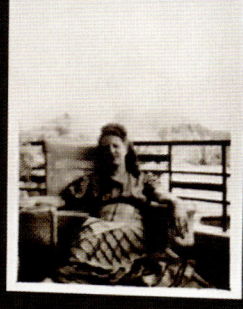
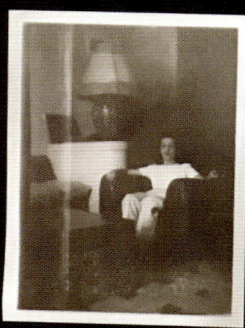
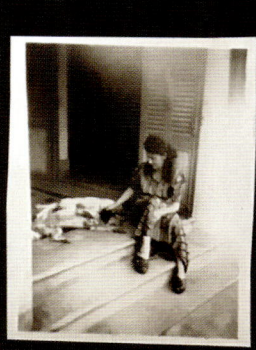
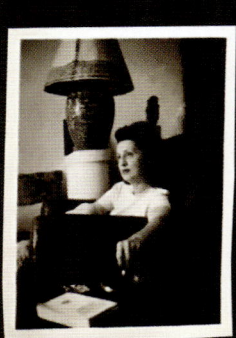
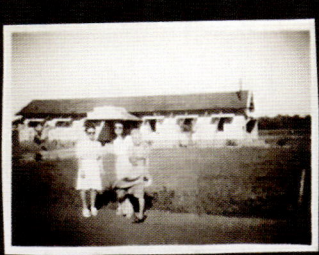
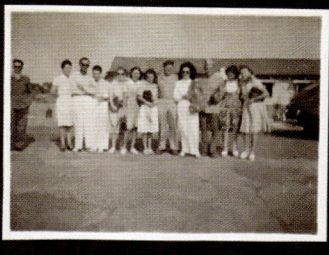
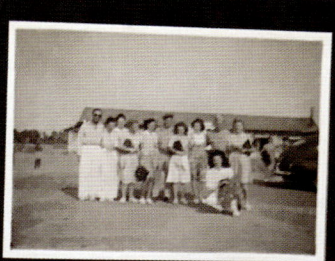
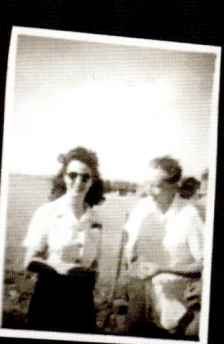
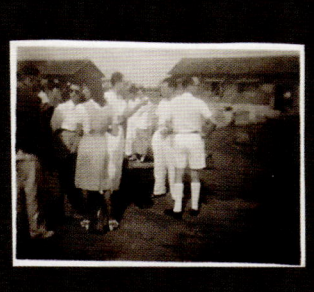
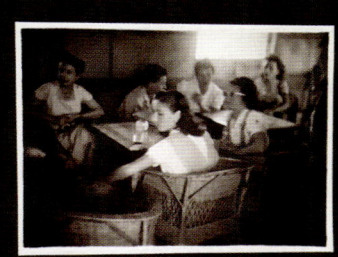
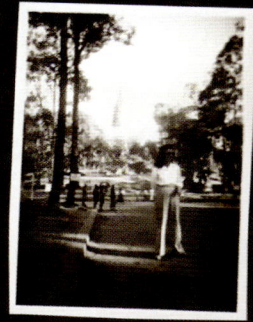
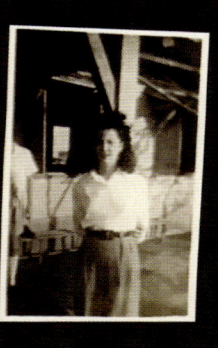
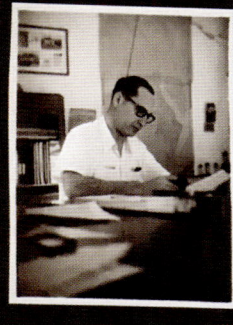
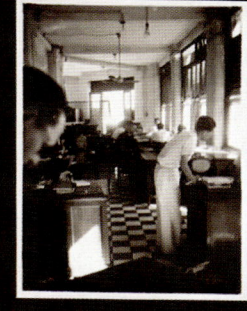
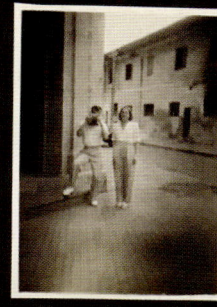
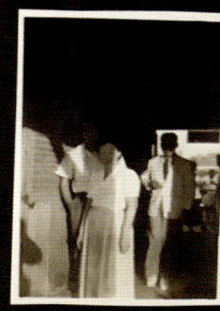
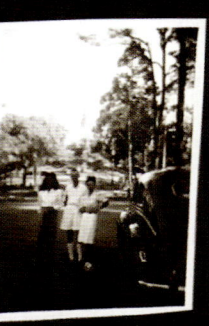

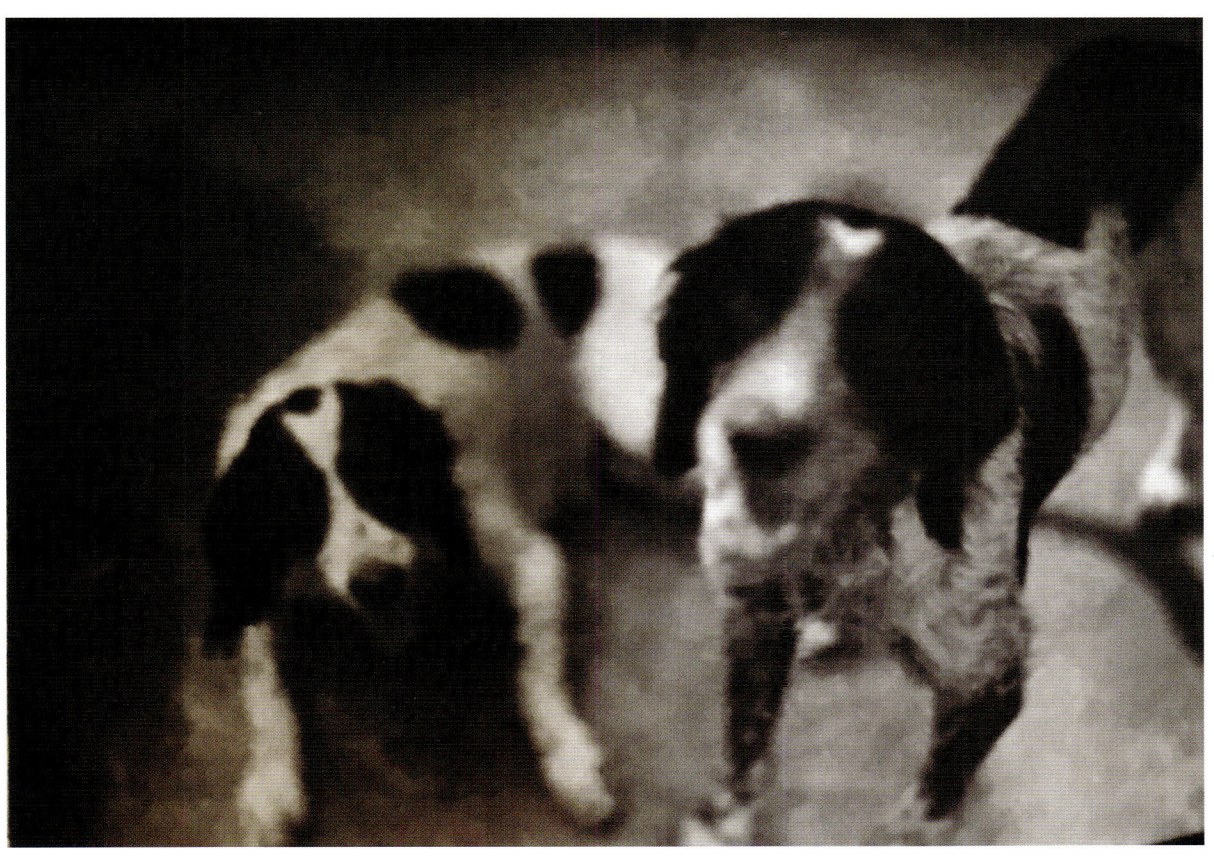

The "Shell" Family Album

An unknown family's album of photographs documents their daily lives as they lived on Boulevard Doudart de Lagree (Norodom Boulevard) in Phnom Penh in the 1940s. Small-format prints are pasted on each leaf of the album, interspersed with handwritten notes penned on glassine pages. The images show family life and home interiors, afternoon drinks, boisterous pets, motorcar visits around the city, and mundane work at the office. The father managed various country operations for the Shell Company, a global petroleum supplier. As well as visits to Annam and Tonkin, their travels took them to China, France, and the Belgian Congo. The album is an intimate, detailed observation of the life of a professional French family at work and play in Cambodia in the immediate postwar years.

ABOVE: **Attentive dogs.** Phnom Penh. 1941–47.

OPPOSITE: **Phnom Penh page from the family's album.** Phnom Penh. 1941–47.

Photographers unknown. Philippe Damas Collection, Singapore.

Service d'information française

At the end of World War II, France established a Far East Expeditionary Corps to restore its sovereignty over Indochina. The newly appointed commander-in-chief, General de Lattre de Tassigny, combined the existing military and civilian news-gathering services into a single entity, the Service d'information française. Their archives are an illuminating collection of photographs of the everyday lives of Cambodians, including scenes from a Chinese opera, a mother with children, a Chinese boy painting a café advertisement, and Picassoesque musicians. The three musicians (opposite), detainees of the French security forces, sit for the camera, two with handmade traditional two-stringed *tro sor* and the one in the center, rather incongruously, with a banjo. Their mixed instruments, jaunty felt hats, and back-to-front singlets reflect the make-do lifestyle of imprisonment, while the sarongs suggest that two of the musicians may be from the Cham community. The French would probably have suspected that the prisoners were communist insurgents or sympathizers.

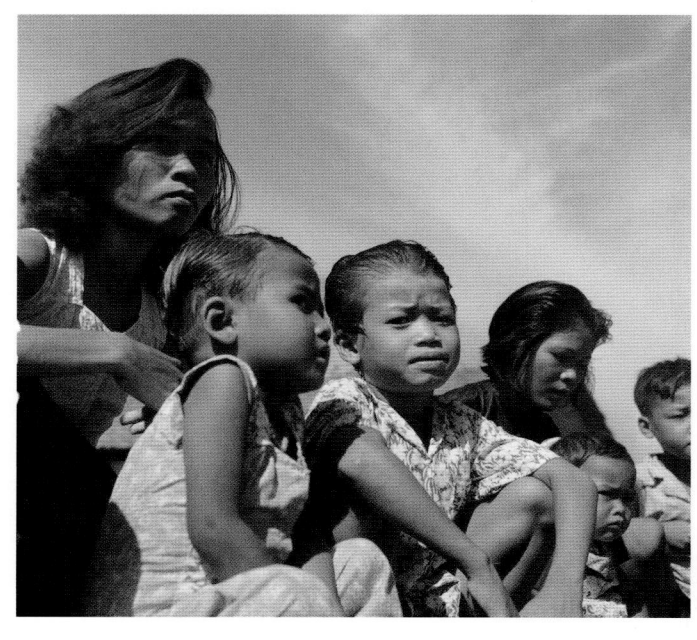

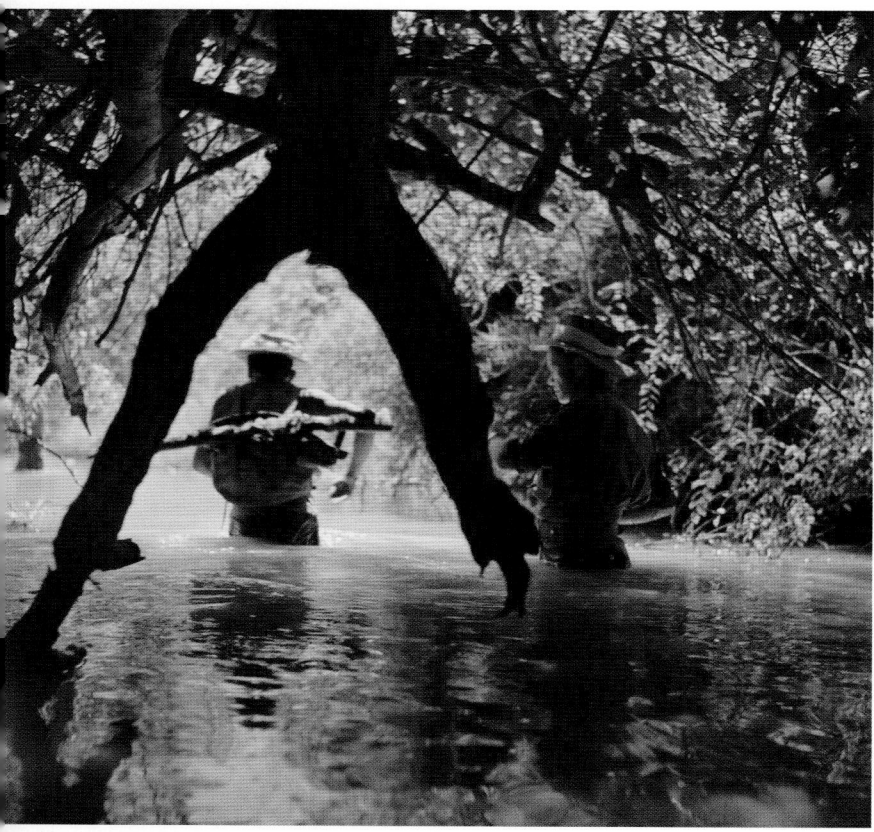

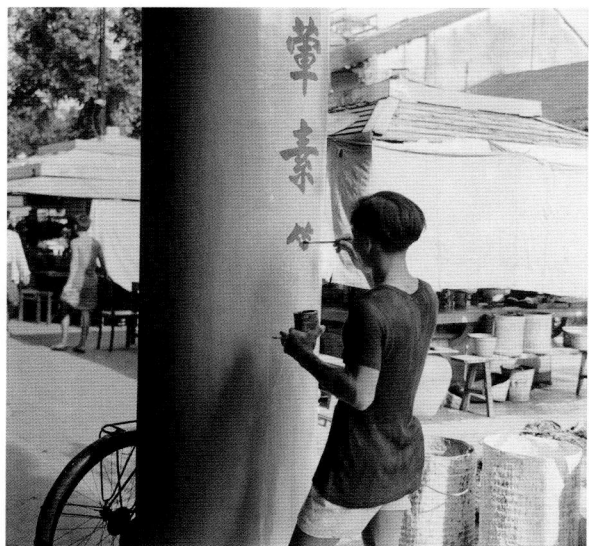

TOP: **Faces of Cambodian children.** Phnom Penh. Surel. 1953.

ABOVE: **Chinese Boy painting a café sign.** Phnom Penh. Photographer unknown. 1953.

LEFT: **Reconnaissance patrol advances along a stream.** Mimot. Raymond Varoqui. 1953.

Source: Agence d'images de la Défense, Paris.

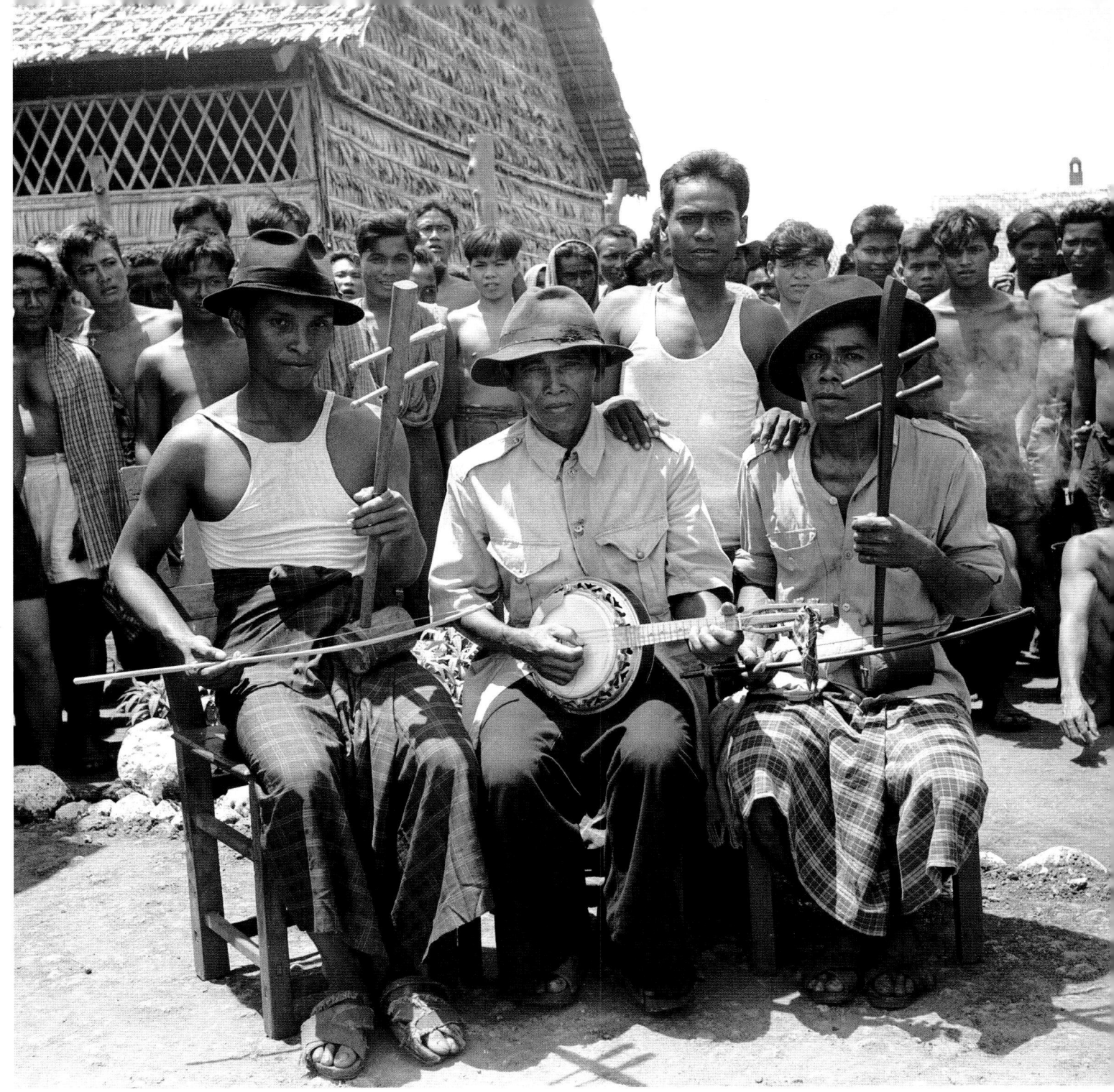

Musicians at prisoner-of-war camp.
Kompong Cham. 1952. Photographer unknown. Agence d'images de la Défense, Paris.

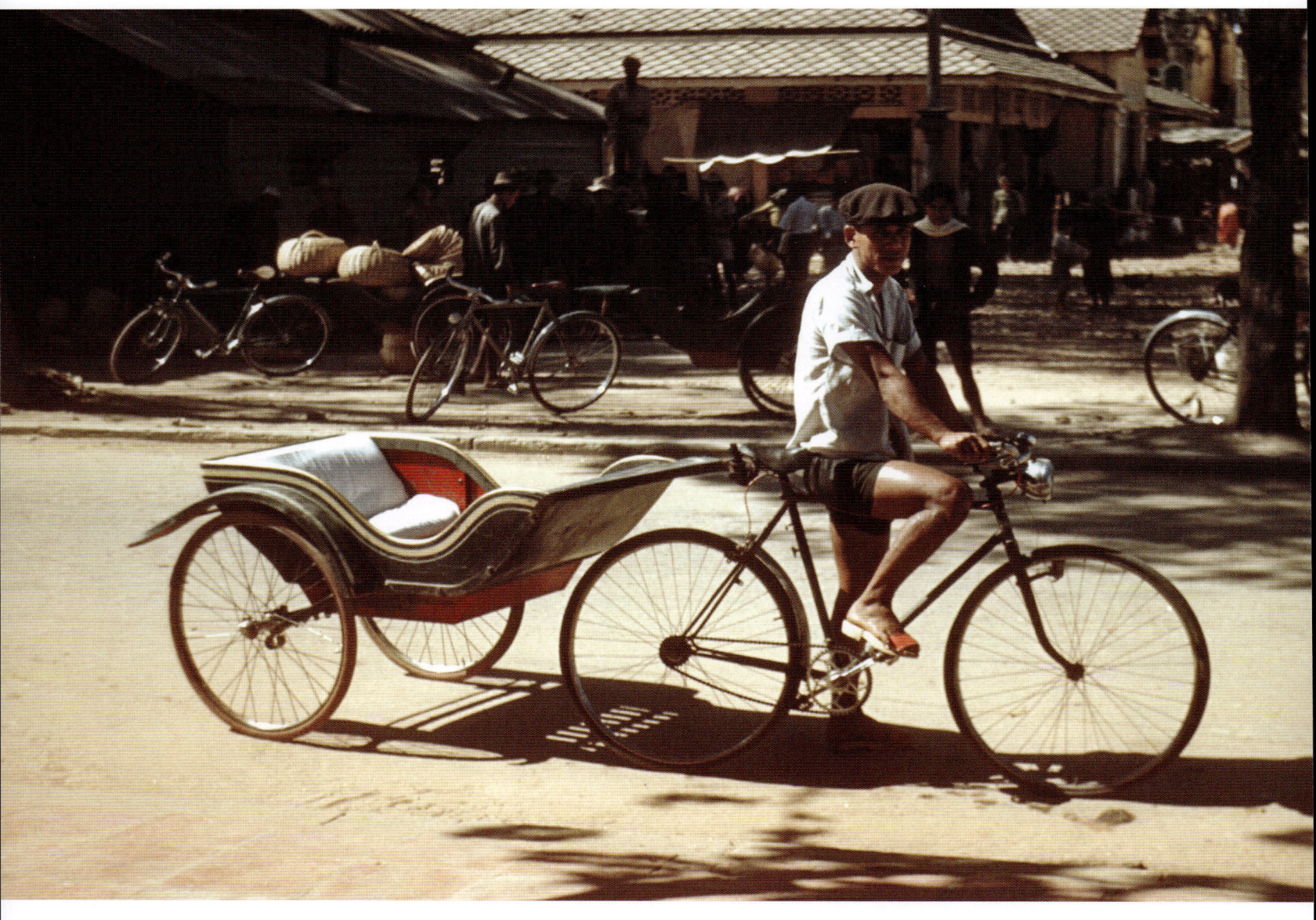

A Christmas Holiday in Siem Reap

In the 1950s, Margaret Parx HAYS (1912–2008) was working in the consular service of the American Embassy in Manila. The job gave her access to international travel and allowed her to indulge her passion for photography. For her summer holidays of 1954, she traveled with two colleagues to Siem Reap. Using 35 mm color slide film, they walked around the central market and along the banks of the Siem Reap River and out to Phnom Krom on the edge of the Tonlé Sap. She took photographs of everyday life, such as strolling monks, food carts, and this hawker on his elegant *remorque-kong* (bicycle trolley), used to ferry passengers and their shopping from market to home.

Hawker on his *remorque-kong* (bicycle trolley). Siem Reap. 1954. Margaret Parx Hays Papers. Madison Library, University of Wisconsin Digital Collections.

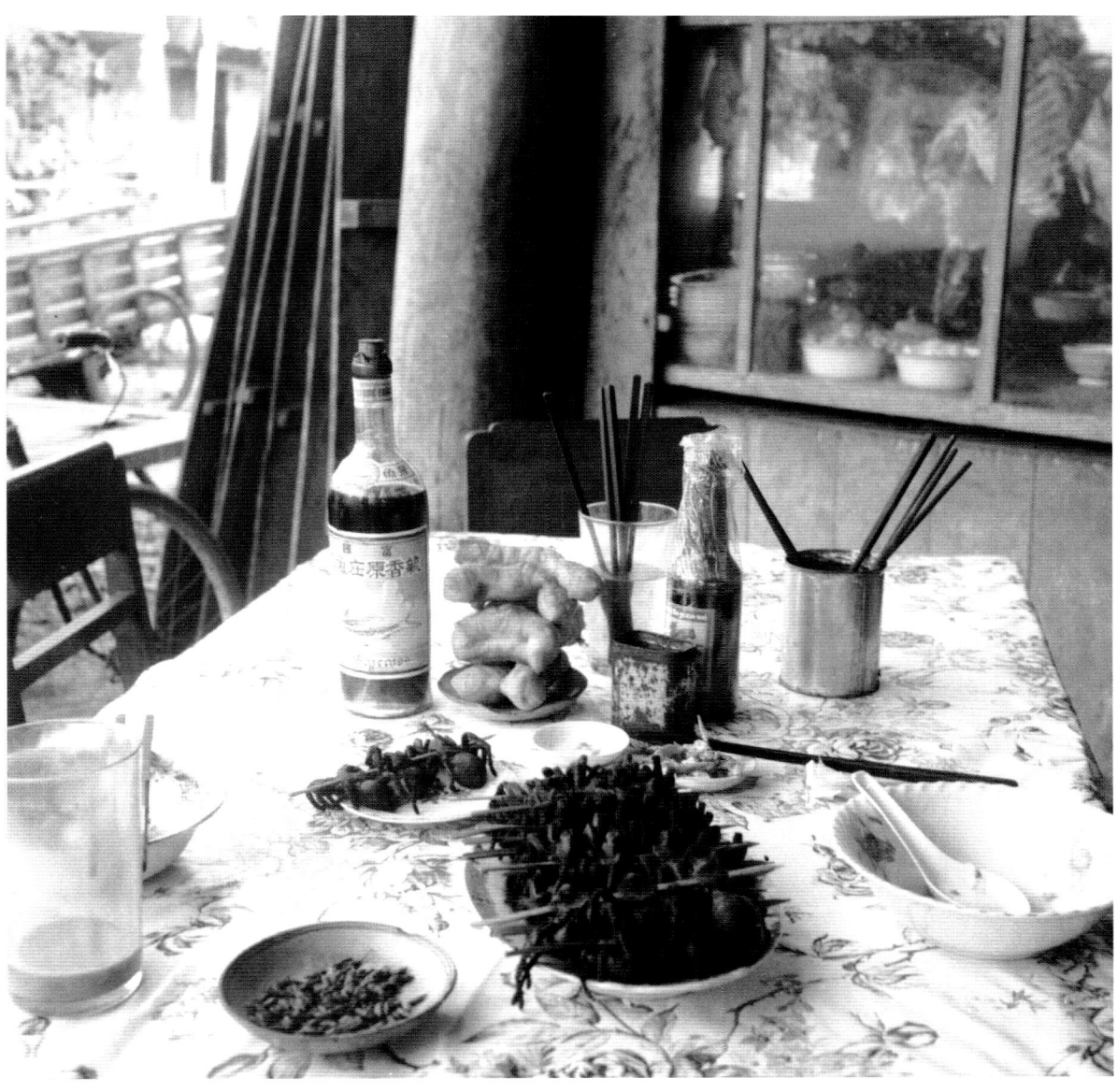

Fried Spiders, Skuon

Mimijac PALGEN-MAISSONEUVE (1918–95) was employed at Radio Cambodge in Phnom Penh from 1946 to 1962. While living in Cambodia, she carried her Rolleiflex wherever she went, taking over 1,000 black-and-white photographs and developing the film herself. She regularly visited the Angkorian monuments. On the long dusty journey by road between Phnom Penh and Siem Reap, it was customary to stop at the town of Skuon, popular for its tasty snacks of deep-fried spiders. On the café table are plates stacked high with skewered fried tarantulas and Chinese fried breadsticks, along with chopsticks in a recycled tin container and bottles of soy and fish sauce. Palgen's photograph mixes the genres of still life and travel documentary, provoking both a sense of appetite and the traveler's momentary passage of time.

Chinese street café serving fried spiders. Skuon. 1949–62. MimiJac-Maissoneuve Palgen. MimiJac Palgen Memorial Collection, Arizona State University Library.

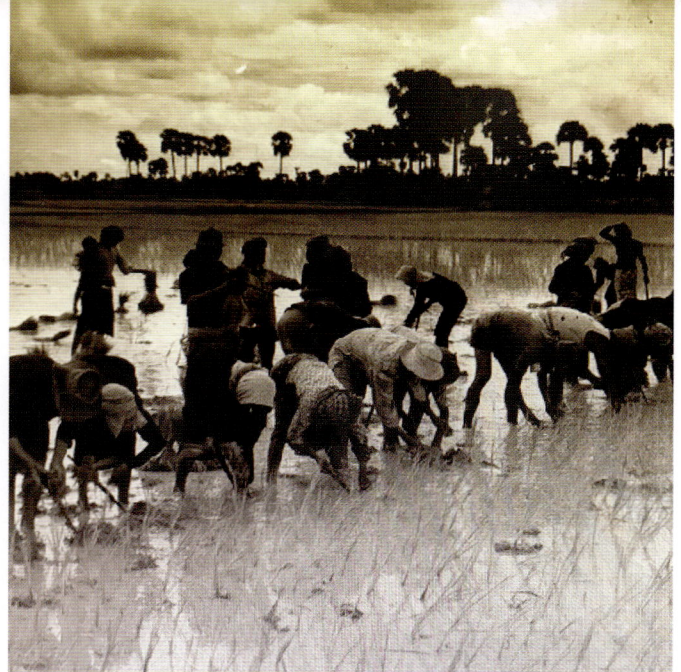

LEFT: **Transplanting rice seedlings.** 1960s. Photographer unknown. Charles Meyer Collection, Paris/National Archives of Cambodia.

BELOW LEFT: **Fisherman with juvenile Greater Adjutant stork.** Siem Reap market. 1960s. Photographer unknown. Charles Meyer Collection, Paris/National Archives of Cambodia.

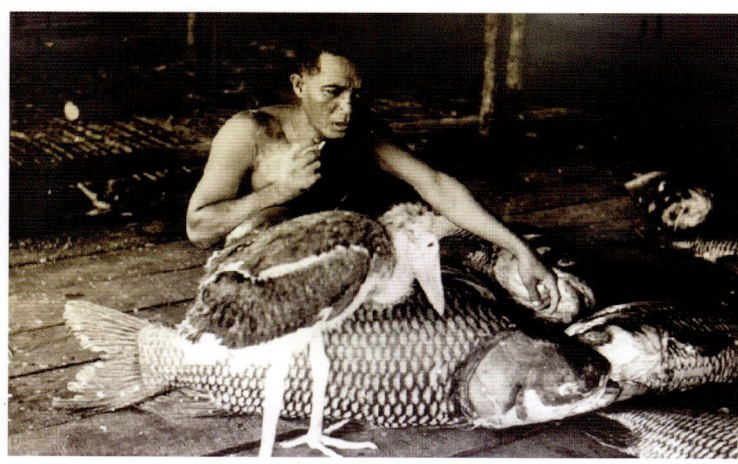

Cambodian Rhythms

For thousands of years, the rhythm of life for the people of Southeast Asia has been regulated by the seasonal ebb and flow of the southwest monsoon. As annual rains nourish the fields, rice seedlings are transplanted and the Tonlé Sap in the center of Cambodia begins to fill with water flowing down the Mekong, a combination of the river's tributaries and ice melt from the Himalayas. During the dry season, rice is harvested and, as the lake retreats, the fishing season begins, affording a valuable source of protein. The photograph at top shows a steady line of villagers communally planting rice seedlings in a flooded field, while the photograph above shows a fisherman guarding his catch from a juvenile Greater Adjutant stork as it pokes around for scraps.

Portrait of a Young Khmer

By the early 1950s, Swiss-born Werner BISCHOFF (1919–54) was at the height of his international career. He had gained a reputation as a humanist photographer after documenting the destruction of Germany at the end of World War II. In 1952, at the beginning of the Cold War, he made his first trip to Asia. As he traveled through Vietnam he witnessed the bloody conflict of the First Indochina War (1946–54) between the colonial French and the independence-seeking communist Viet Minh. Being independent from the French-controlled Service d'information française, he photographed without censorship. He also took time to record a more peaceful life, capturing with his extraordinary eye for composition and lighting a distracted Cambodian youth looking beyond the camera.

RIGHT: **Young Khmer, Angkor.** Siem Reap. 1952. Werner Bischoff/Magnum Photos.

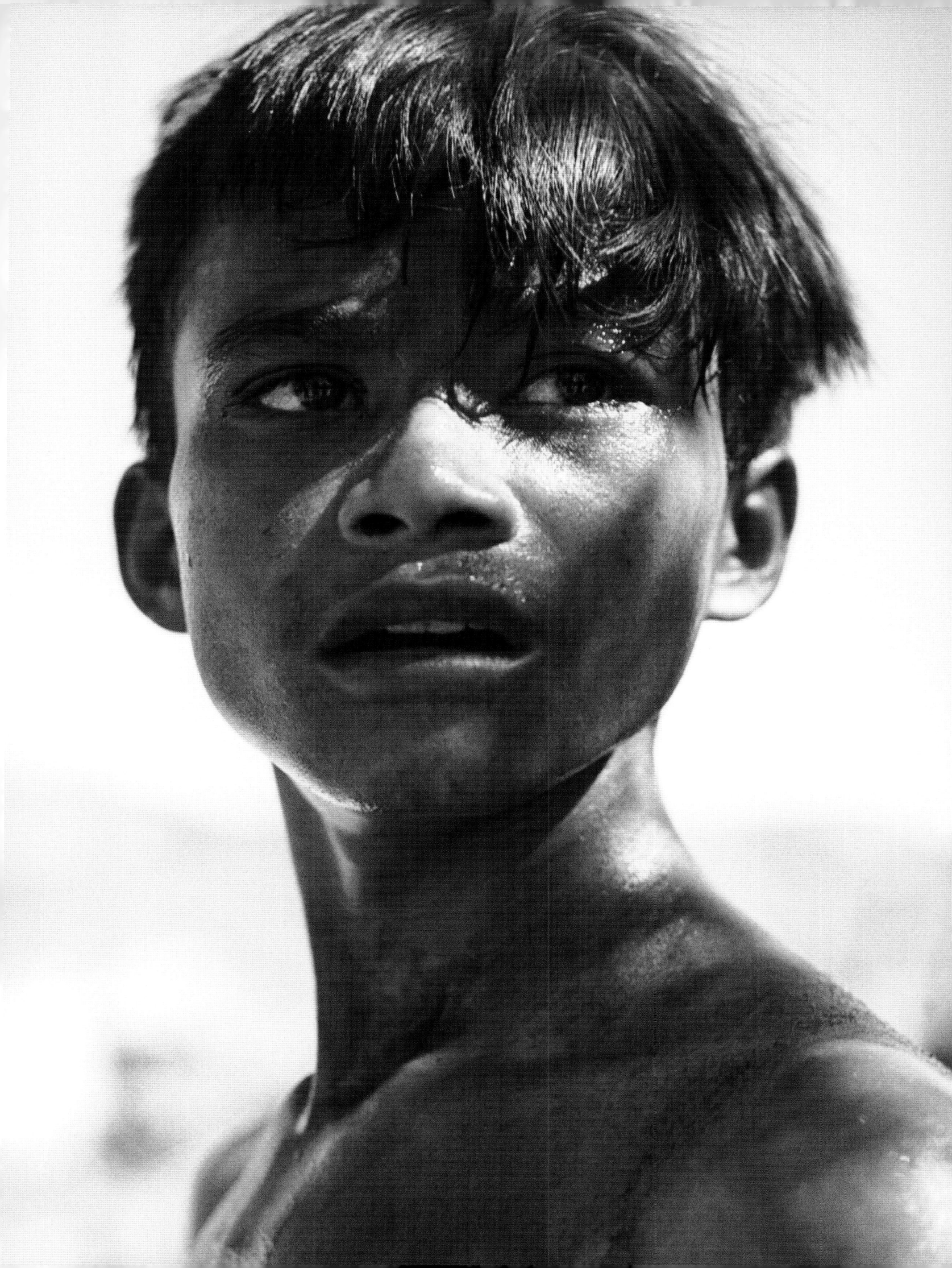

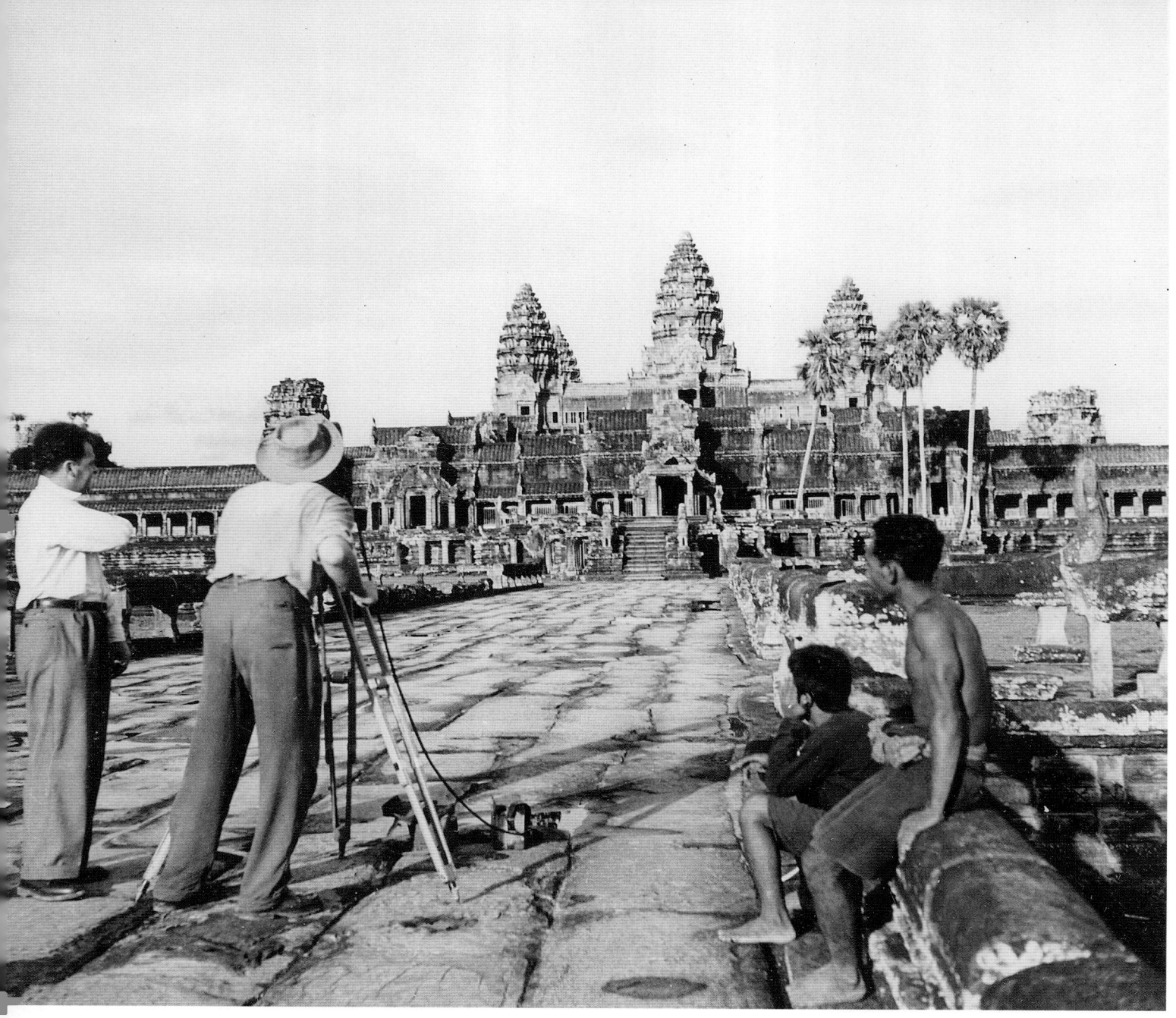

École française d'Extrême-Orient

After World War II, there was a renewed effort on behalf of the French to study and restore ancient Khmer monuments. New scientific techniques enabled better conservation methods to be used in their reconstruction, although the brutal functionalism of the massive mobile timber crane (opposite top) might suggest otherwise. In 1950, in concert with the move towards independence, the Albert Sarraut Museum and the artifacts belonging to the Conservation d'Angkor were transferred to Cambodian ownership. Henri Marchal was seventy-four when the photograph was taken of him working with a young Cambodian assistant (opposite below left). Marchal had spent a lifetime working on the archaeology of Angkorian monuments using, as far as possible from the 1930s onwards, the original materials for their restoration.

Mr. Blanc and Mr. Moride photographing Angkor Wat. 1952. Photographer unknown.

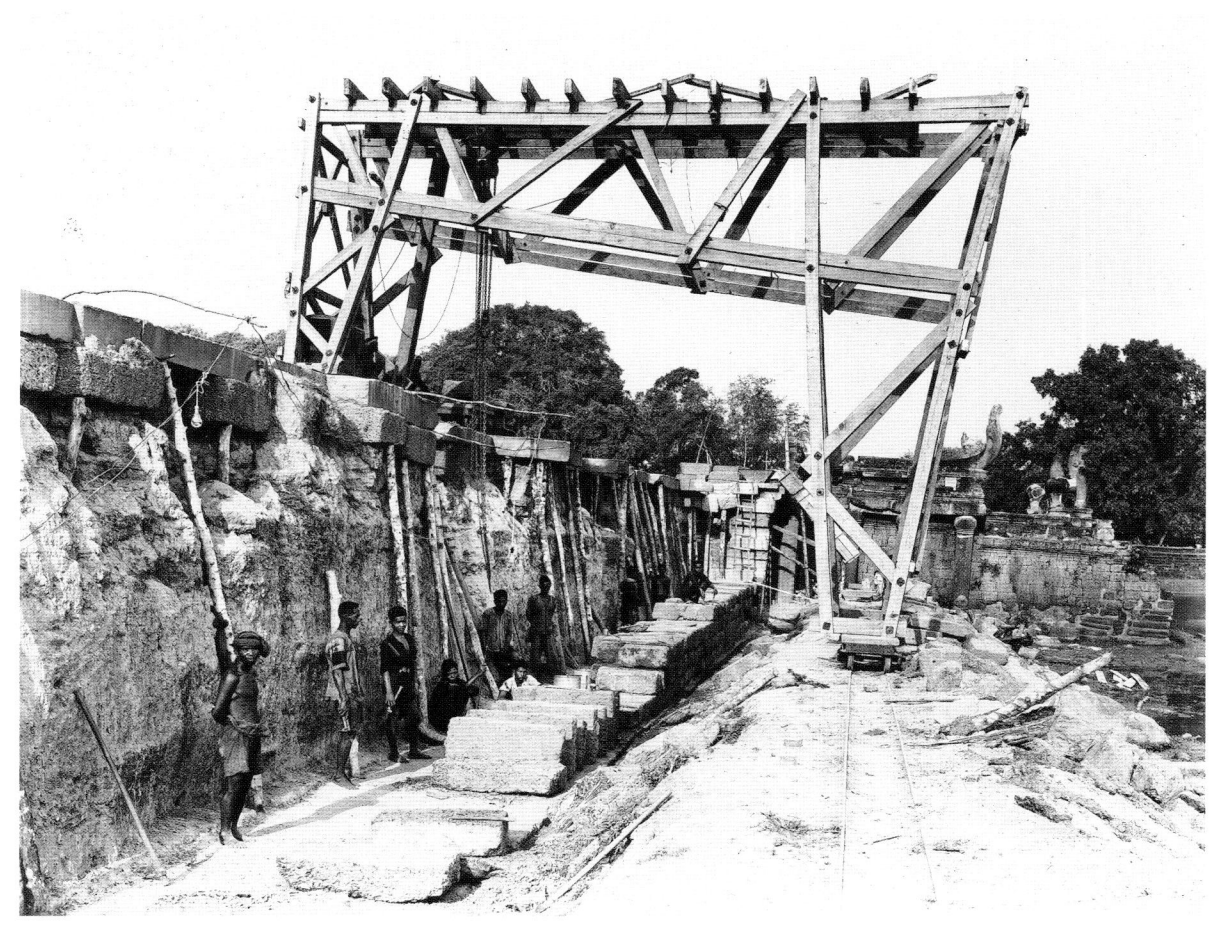

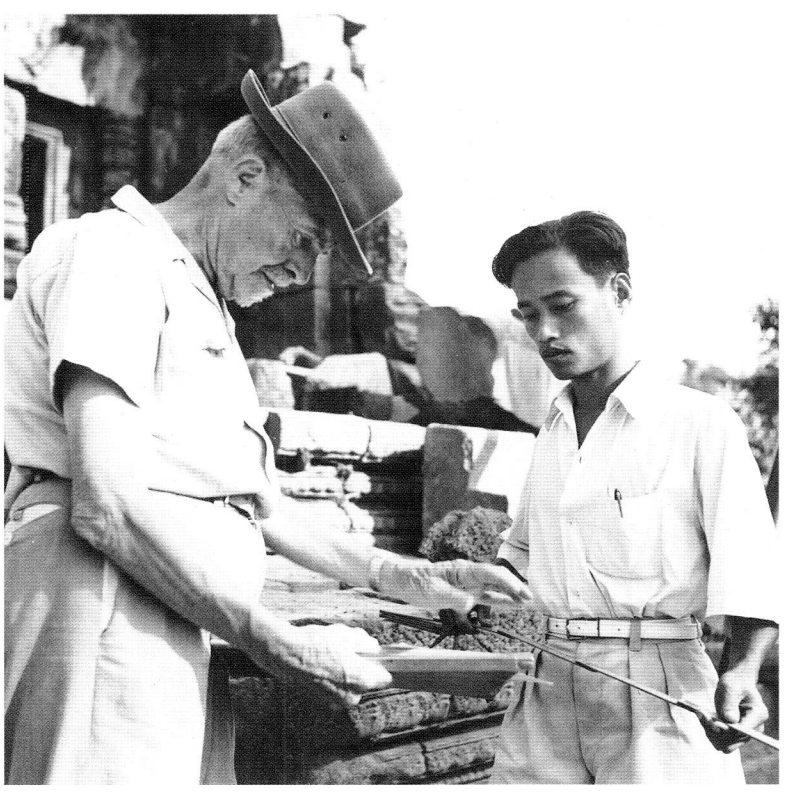

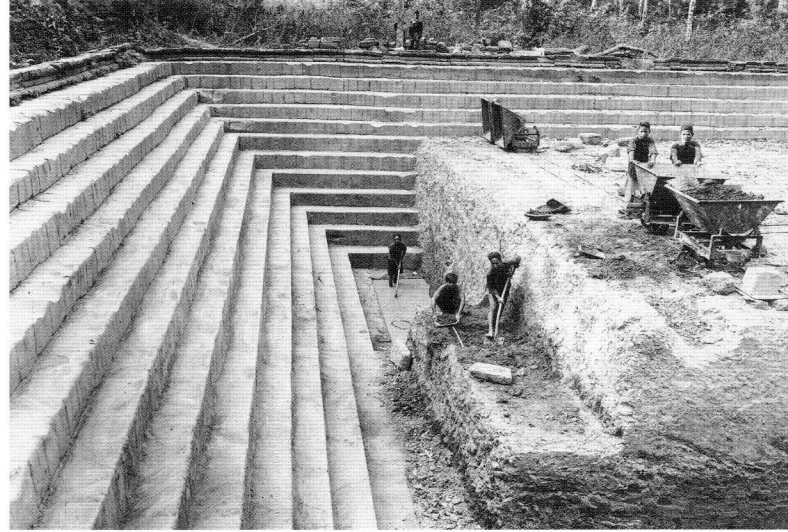

TOP, CLOCKWISE: **Removal of laterite foundation blocks.** Angkor Wat. 1954. Photographer unknown.

Removal of debris from the Eastern Basin, Royal Palace. Siem Reap. 1954. Photographer unknown.

Henri Marchal and assistant. Banteay Srei. 1952. M. Moride.

Source: École française d'Extrême-Orient.

1955–1970
The People's Socialist Community

In what historians claim was a masterstroke of political strategy, Sihanouk abdicated his kingship in 1955 and created his own political party, the Sangkum Reastr Niyum (the People's Socialist Community). He dissolved parliament and called for fresh elections. By using a combination of fraud, intimidation, charisma, and manipulation of the press, he won every seat in the parliament. At the outset, there was genuine enthusiasm for the Sangkum. Sihanouk had given Cambodia a decade of relative peace, a golden postindependence glow, and a touch of cultural glamor. He now began to modernize the country. New buildings with a contemporary style and tropical character expressed the country's new values. The "Pearl of the Orient" became a pleasant posting for diplomats like Yves Coffin (1924–2016) and a port of call for the Malaysian cinema magnate Loke Wan Toh (1915–64). Schools and universities were built across the country. Students wore Western-style uniforms, and the end-of-year class photograph became a common rite of passage. Chinese family-run studios offered affordable photography for an emerging middle class. Cambodia's music and cinema industries flourished, while photographs of pop stars were montaged onto bright album covers. The palm-fringed town of Kep became a popular weekend resort for the urban elite. Jacqueline (Jackie) Kennedy visited the country in 1967, with a phalanx of international photographers in tow, providing a dash of American soft power. Cambodia's transformation looked appealing in Sihanouk's self-edited monthly fanzines like *Le Sangkum* and *Le Cambodge*, where designers often used novel photomontage techniques that reflected international trends in graphic design. Sihanouk employed French photographers like Micheline Dullin (1927–2020) and Raymond Chauchetier (1920–2021), who used medium-format cameras to document the prince's travels across the country, while Cambodian photographers were embedded within the army's security ranks to get close-up, candid photographs of Sihanouk's personal meet-and-greet with adoring followers. For the first time, Cambodian photographers could see their work in popular print, often in color. Rarely, however, were they credited for their efforts. Foreign tourists flew on commercial jetliners to arrive at glamorous glass-fronted terminals with cafés and waiting lounges.

The first few decades after World War II were renowned for their informal style of behavior, which promoted a more casual and relaxed engagement between photographer and subject, evident through the lenses of Michael Vickery (1931–2017) and the young French schoolteacher Marie-Françoise Châtel (b. 1940). At the same time, the anthropologist May Makyo Ebihara (1934–2005) immersed herself in village life, exploring and uncovering the hidden complexities of an apparently simple rural community. By the end of the 1960s, however, the Vietnam War was intensifying as the National Liberation Front of South Vietnam, better known as the Vietcong, and the North Vietnamese Army battled the United States. This conflict spilled over the border into Cambodia where the communist insurgency destabilized the countryside. The economy floundered, university graduates, with their limited practical skills, found little work, and the illusory appeal of those color magazines promoting the Cambodian good life began to fade.

"When the eyesight is failing, the hands are used as a substitute." Location unknown. 1968. Possibly Royal Cambodian Armed Forces (FARK) photographer. *Kambuja Monthly Illustrated Review*. Center for Khmer Studies Library, Siem Reap.

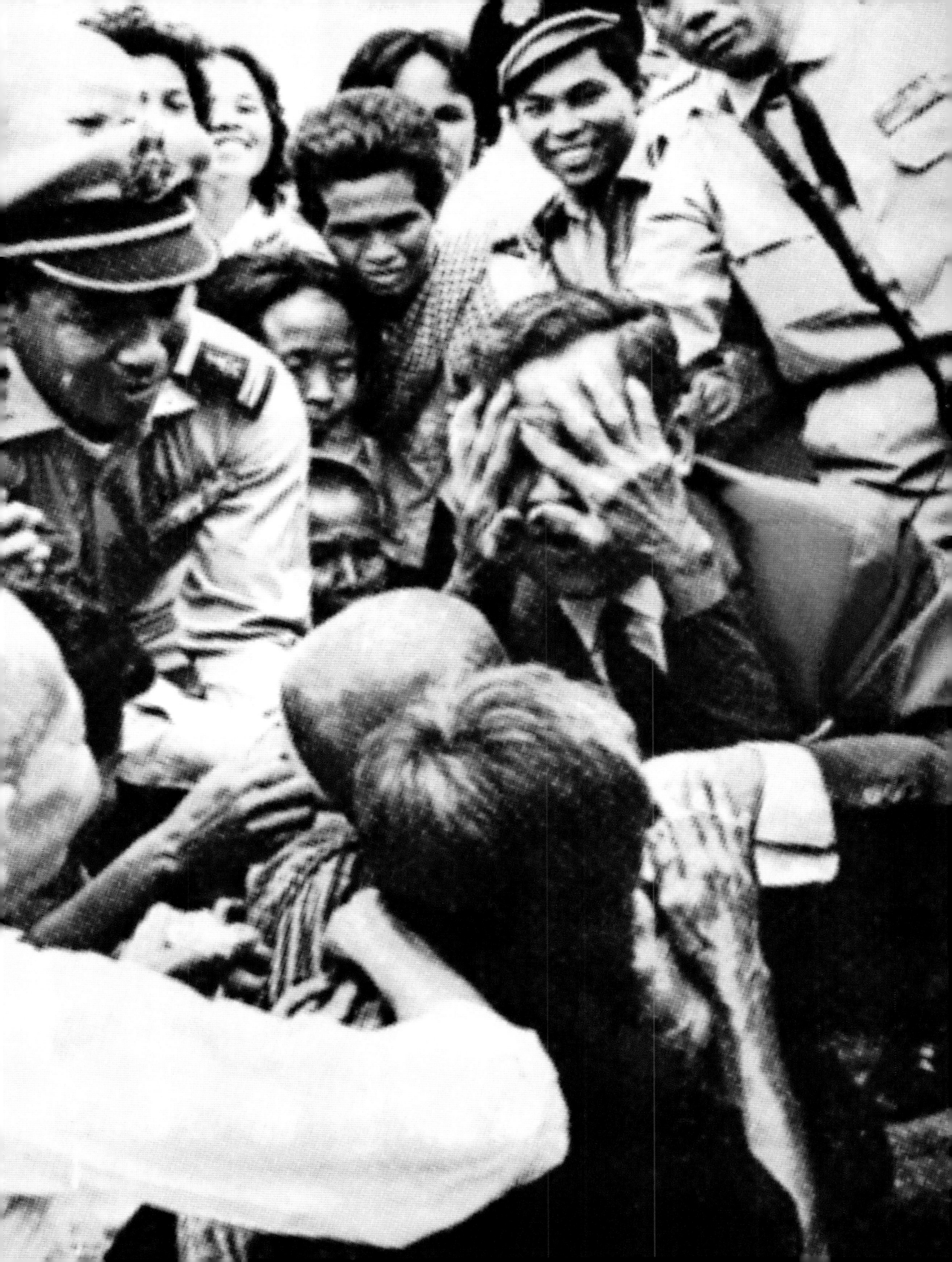

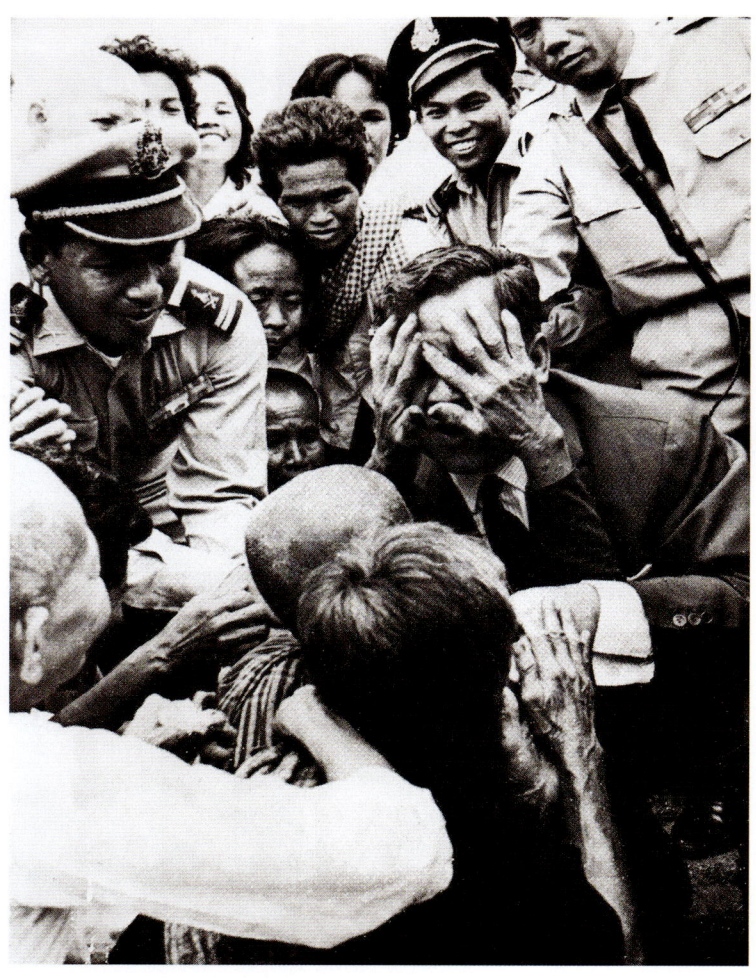

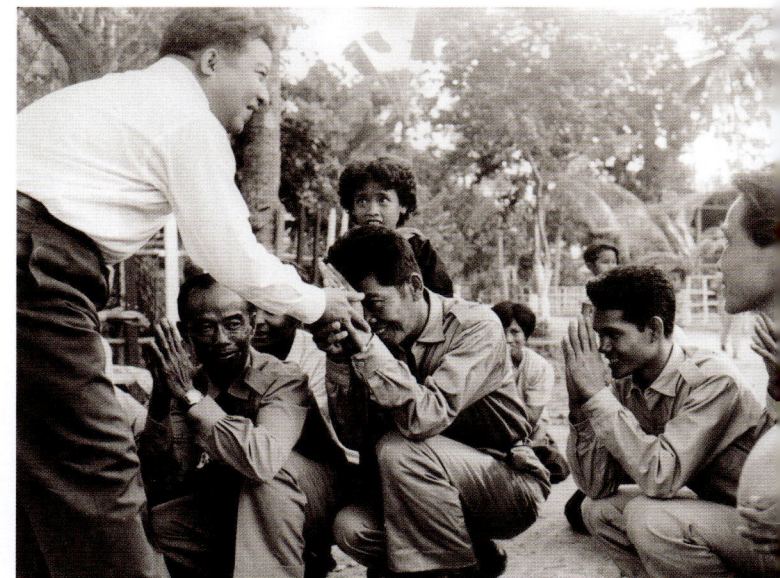

LEFT: "When the eyesight is failing, the hands are used as a substitute." Location unknown. 1968. Possibly FARK photographer. *Kambuja Monthly Illustrated Review*. Center for Khmer Studies Library, Siem Reap.

ABOVE: Sihanouk greeting soldiers. Location unknown. 1960s. Photographer unknown. National Archives of Cambodia/Charles Meyer Collection, Paris.

BELOW: An audience with Sihanouk in the Royal Palace. Phnom Penh. ca. 1959. National Archives of Cambodia/Charles Meyer Collection, Paris.

Politics of the Sangkum

Sihanouk's public profile was a complete break from previous generations of royal indifference and palace seclusion, where public appearances were enacted through formal, ceremonial pageants. In the 1960s, Sihanouk famously said, "I am Sihanouk and Cambodians are my children." While this comment suggested an aloof patrician, Sihanouk was anything but. The photograph above shows Sihanouk kneeling to allow a poor blind woman to "read" his face, an outrageous breach of established royal protocol. He encouraged an image of himself as a man of the people, greeting soldiers, farmers, children, and the disabled with an apparent warmth and genuine affection. His photographic portraits and displays of his achievements were distributed widely across the kingdom.

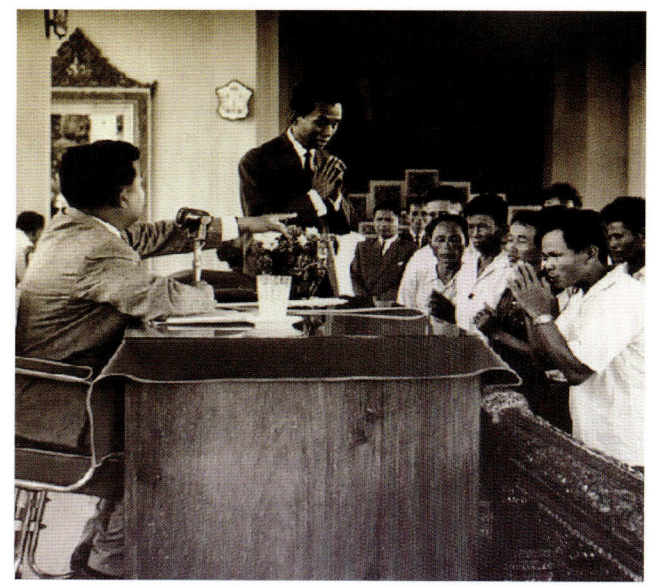

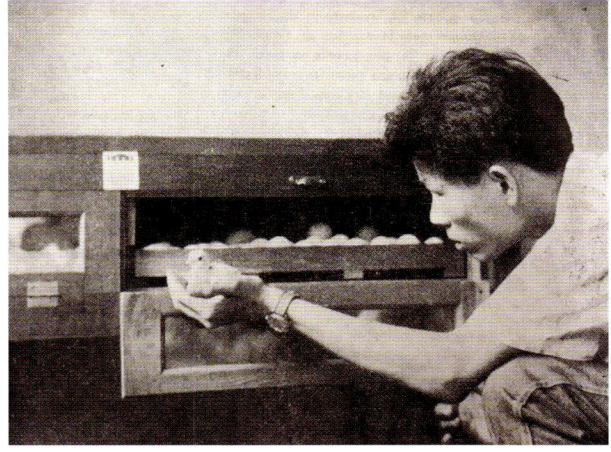

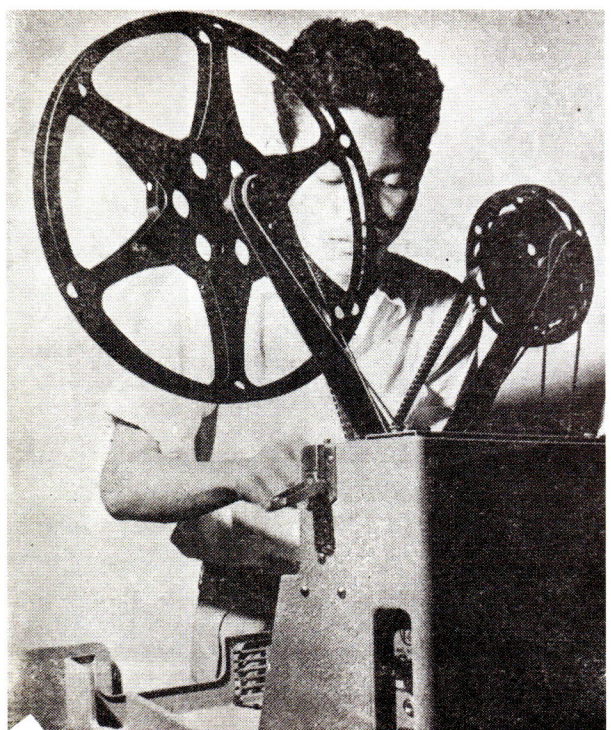

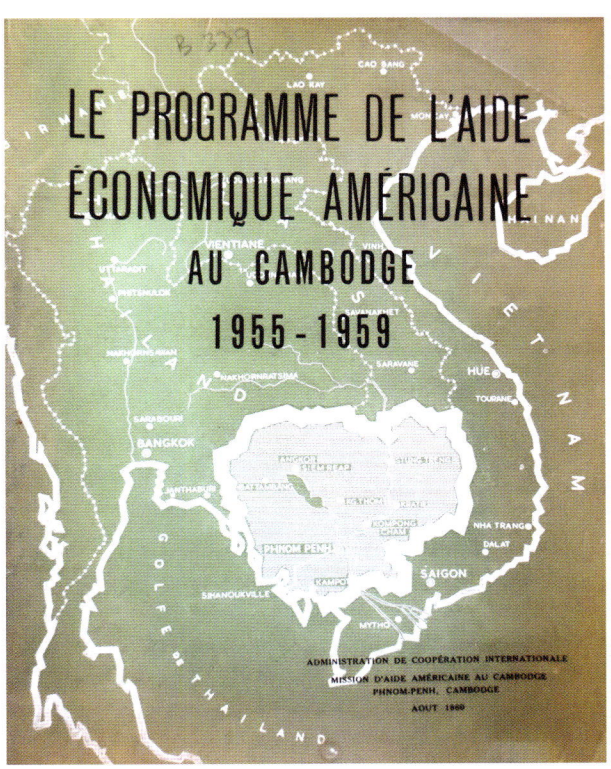

American Aid Review

In 1958, the commander-in-chief of the Pacific Command, when analyzing the rising influence of communism in the region, wrote that Cambodia was "the hub in the wheel of Southeast Asia." Propping up Sihanouk was essential, despite his mercurial behavior and support for a non-aligned policy. This booklet, compiled in 1959, reviews the United States' economic, cultural, and military aid, previously extended to the recently independent country. Published in French, the magazine's audience would have been government officials and the urban elite. The diversity of American involvement was highlighted by the variety of images, ranging from the man nurturing chickens in an incubator to a young Khmer attending a film projection class, and finally, the coarse-screened image of a military tank.

LEFT, FROM TOP: **"Better chicks are produced by the Veterinary Service and distributed to Cambodian growers."**

An audiovisual workshop.

Front cover artwork.

BELOW: **US military tank.**

Source: *Le Programme de l'aide Economique Americane au Cambodge 1955–1959*. The American Aid Mission to Cambodia. Phnom Penh. 1960. Photographers unknown. National Archives of Cambodia.

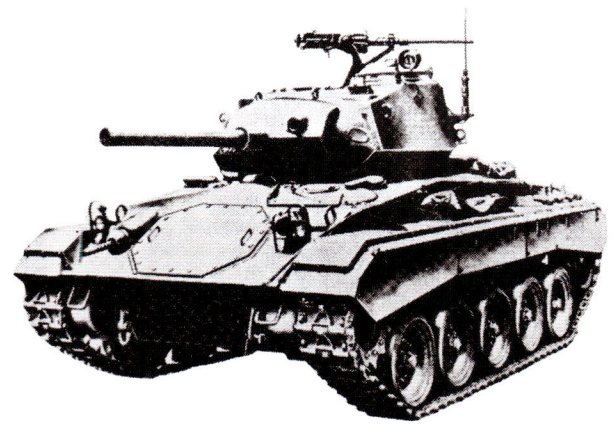

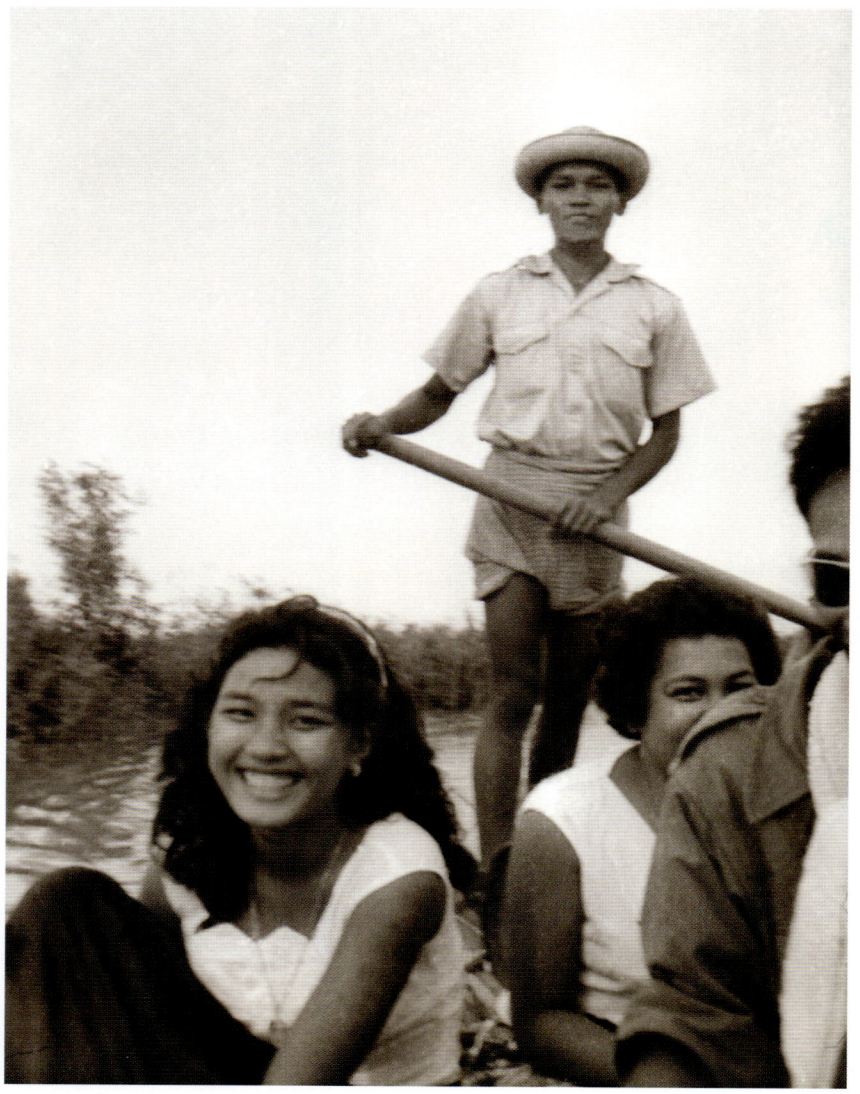
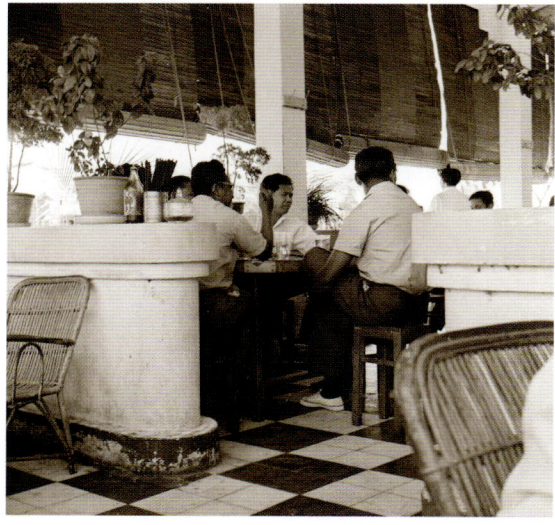
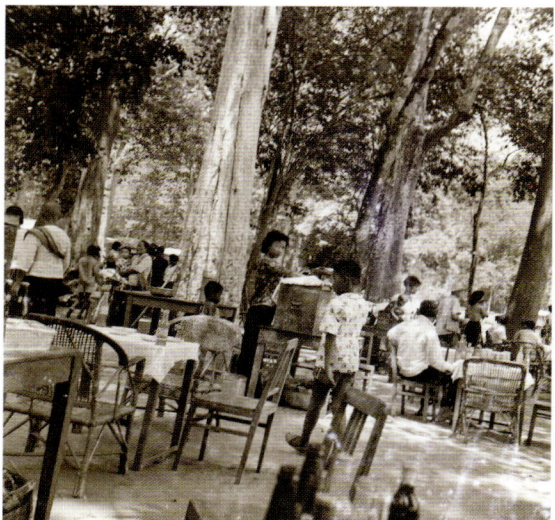

A Teacher in Kampong Thom

Michael VICKERY (1931–2017) was an English teacher at the Lycée de Kompong Thom from 1960 to 1964. His young age and informal, personable manner enabled him to develop an engaging relationship with his Cambodian students and friends. His gift for languages also helped. The "distance" of earlier colonial photographers had vanished as he captured a natural, relaxed relationship between himself and his students. Over the next three decades, Vickery was to become a giant of Cambodian scholarship, celebrated for his writings on both Cambodia's classical and modern history.

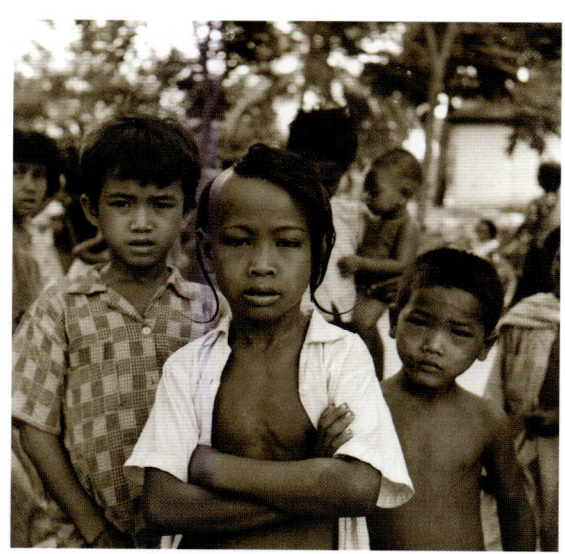

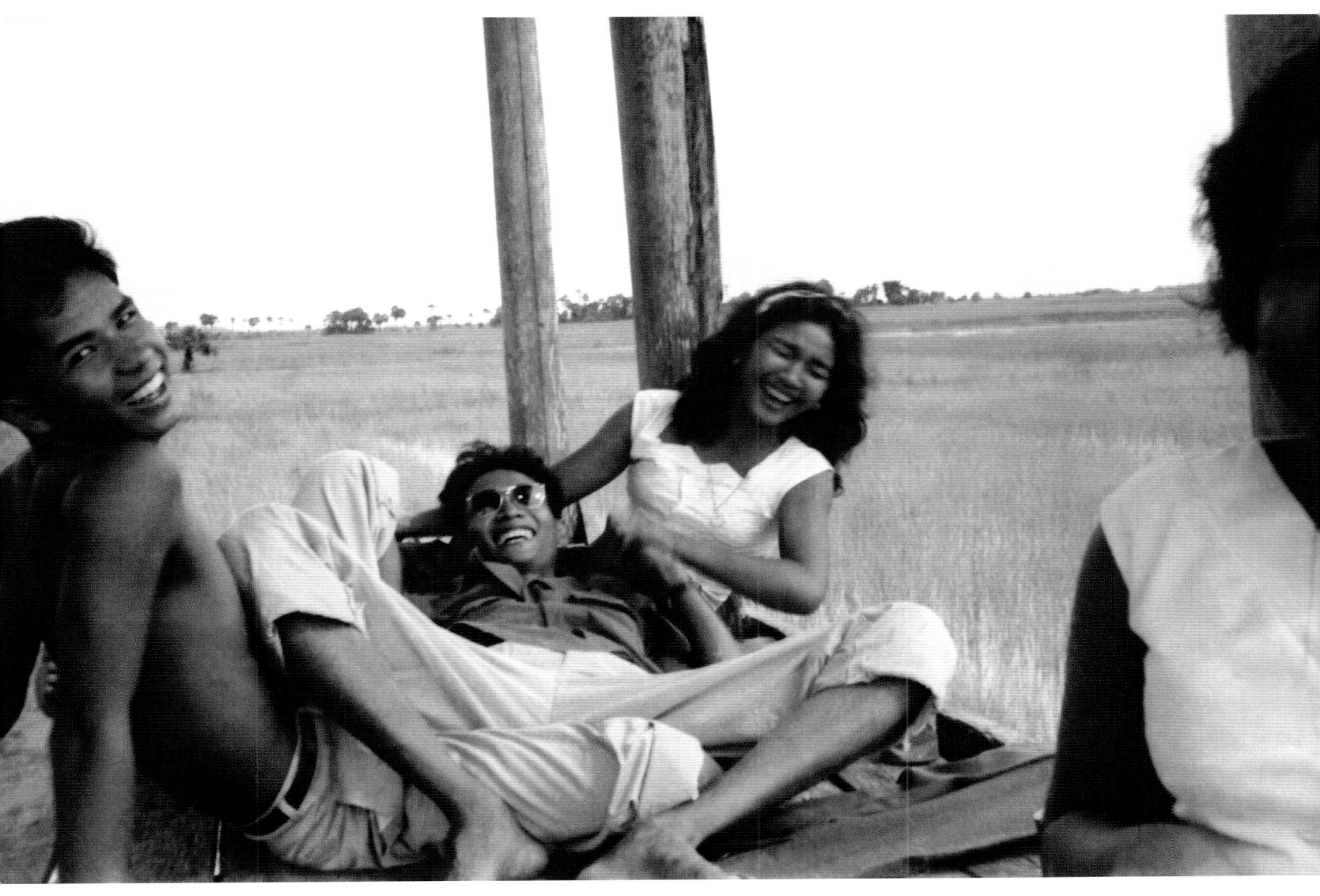

OPPOSITE TOP LEFT, CLOCKWISE:
Friends on a boat. Battambang. 1961.

Café. Kompong Thom. 1961.

Outside café. Possibly near Angkor Wat. Siem Reap. 1961.

Minority boy. Battambang. 1961.

Photographs: Michael Vickery.
Michael Vickery Collection, Chiang Mai.

ABOVE **Four friends relaxing near rice fields.** Battambang. 1961.

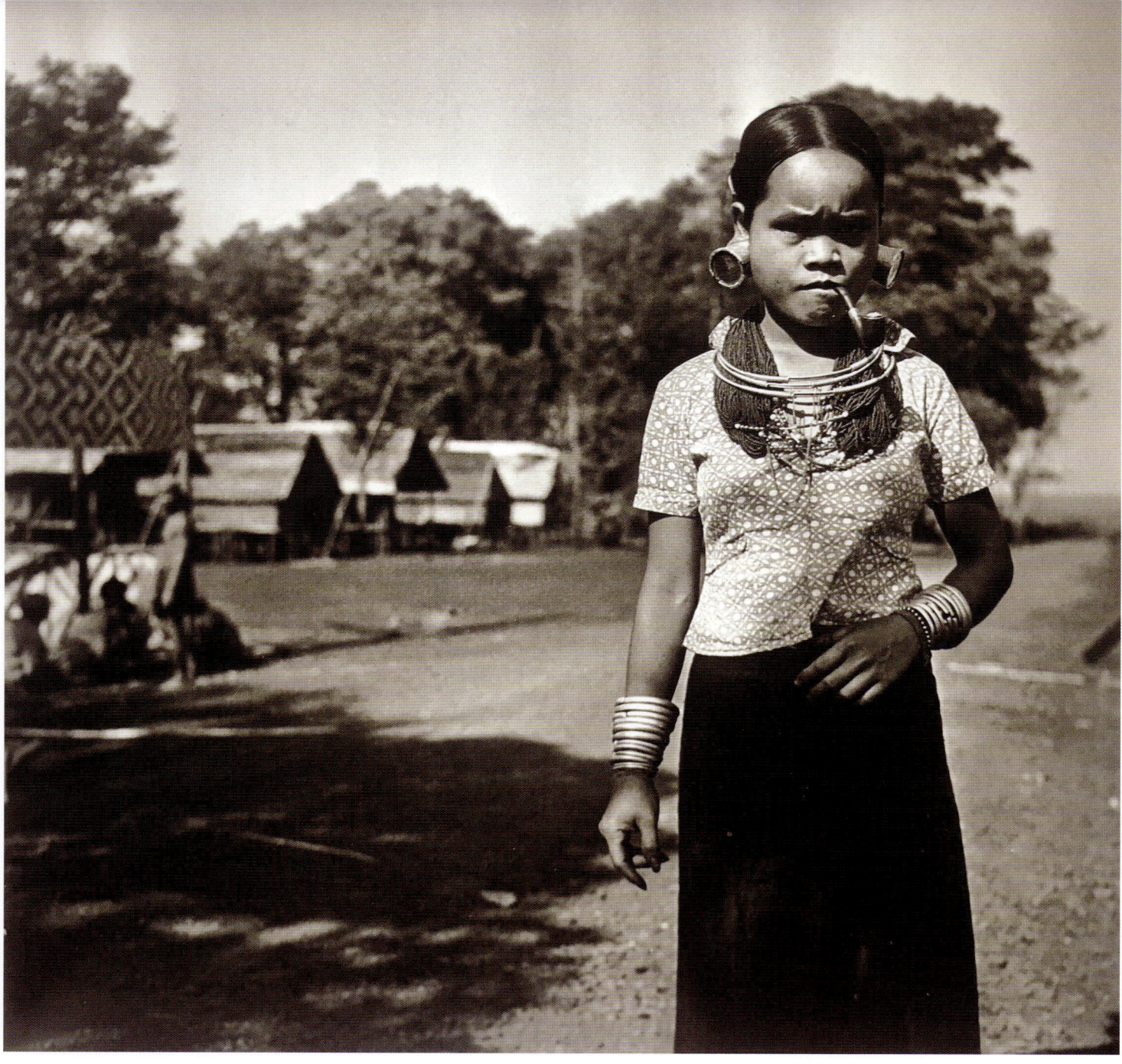

The Prince's Photographer

Minority woman. Ratanakiri and Mondulkiri region. ca. 1961. Micheline Dullin. Micheline Dullin Archive, Paris.

This masterful portrait of a young pipe-smoking indigenous woman strengthens both her sense of self as well as place, with the thatch-roofed houses and meeting of villagers beyond. By using the filtered light through the unseen trees above, Micheline DULLIN (1927–2020) overcame the technical difficulty of overexposing the bright patterned shirt the woman wears; a similar device was used by Emile Gsell a hundred years earlier. Traveling to Cambodia with her photographer husband Robert Favart between 1958 and 1964, they became the official photographers for King Sihanouk, being invited to all the ceremonies and events that he attended as he toured the country. She used the popular Rolleiflex square-frame camera to capture these moments.

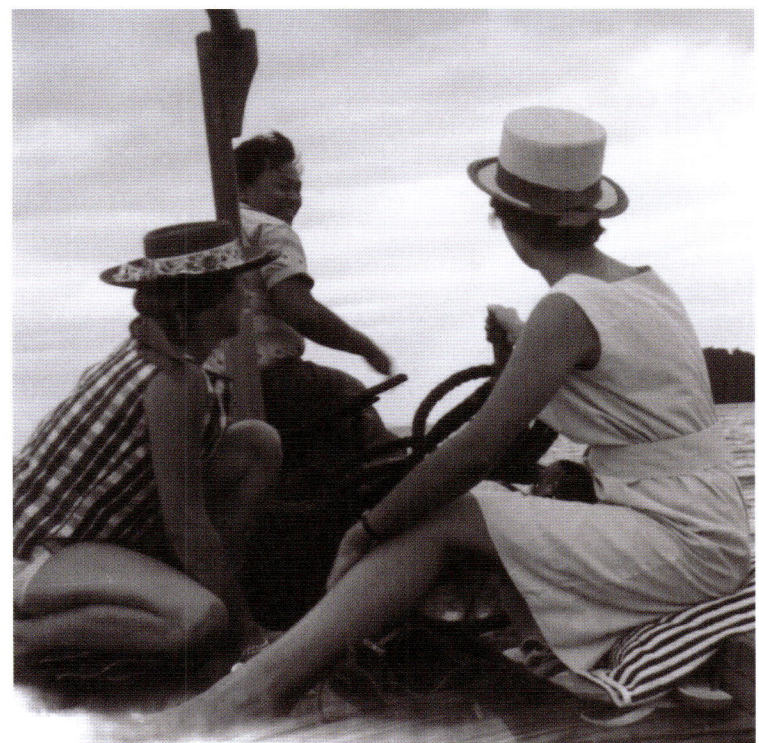
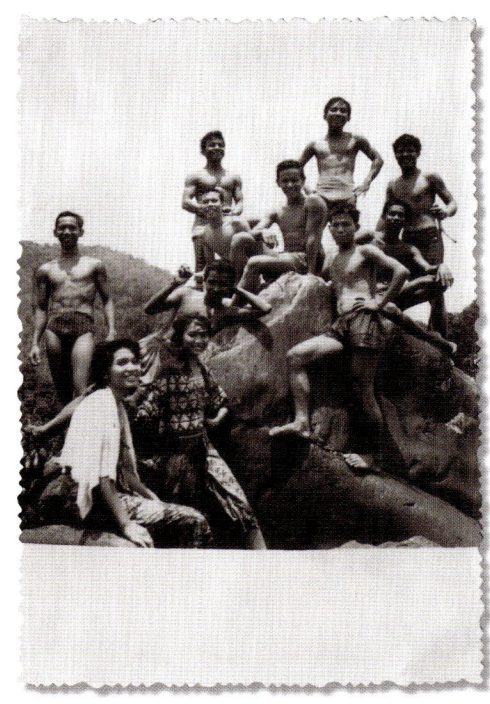
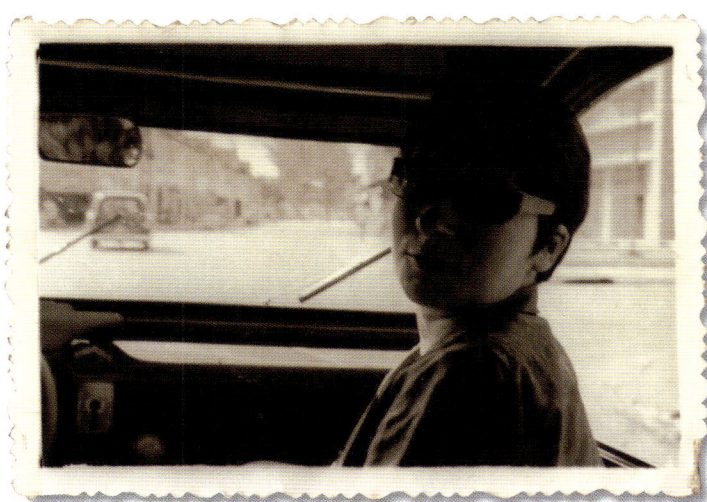
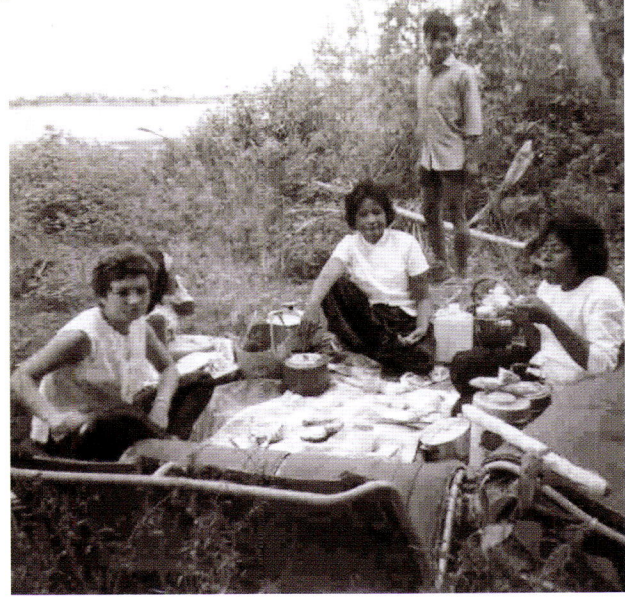

A Teacher in Kampot

Marie-Françoise CHÂTEL (b. 1940) was a young French schoolteacher who worked at the Lycée Preah Reach Samphear in Kampot during the first few years of Cambodia's independence. From 1960 to 1964, she took photographs of fellow teachers and their lifestyles in their rented houses, moving back and forth between government bungalows to private shophouses as school terms finished and contracts were renewed. The teacher–student bond grew over the years as they shared their educational experiences, as well as the school band with its Western electric guitars, outings to the nearby river, picnics, and shopping, and, after the jubilation of graduation, the poignant final departure from each other's company. She returned in 2005 to renew acquaintances.

TOP LEFT, CLOCKWISE: **Marie Françoise Châtel (right) and fellow teacher boating.** Kampot. ca. 1963.

Student outing, Kampot River. Kampot. ca. 1963.

Picnic with Maria, Phon, Anne-Marie, and Madmoiselle Dactylo. Kampot. 1964.

Driving through Kampot. ca. 1963.

Photographs: Marie-Françoise Châtel.

From Malaya to Cambodia

Born in Kuala Lumpur, Malaysia, LOKE Wan Tho (1915–64), was a prominent cinema magnate in Singapore. One of his close friends, Malcolm MacDonald, was the British commissioner-general for Southeast Asia. While visiting Cambodia as a guest of Sihanouk in 1955, MacDonald noticed there were no English-language guidebooks for the country, only French guides. Loke and MacDonald returned in 1957, and over the next two years worked on a guidebook, with Loke taking 112 elegant black-and-white photographs as they toured the country. Ten thousand paperbacks were printed in 1958 and shipped, free of charge, to various hotels around Cambodia.

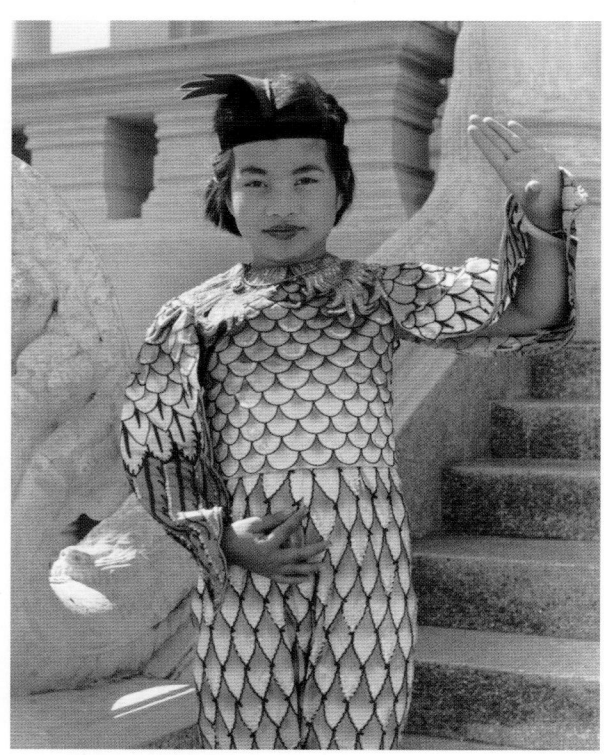

Young dancer in bird costume. Phnom Penh, perhaps the Royal Palace. ca. 1955. Loke Wan Tho. National Museum of Singapore/National Heritage Board.

The Cultural Diplomat

Yves COFFIN (1924–2016) was part of the French consular service posted to Phnom Penh in the 1960s after Cambodia's independence. During his time in the diplomatic service, he became interested in the architecture and sculpture of Southeast Asia's classical Hindu-influenced cultures. Between 1955 and 1970, to enrich his research, he systematically photographed examples of Khmer, Cham, and Javanese artwork that he saw both in the field and in national galleries and museums. His Cambodian collection alone totals 1,700 images of sculptures and monuments from across the country.

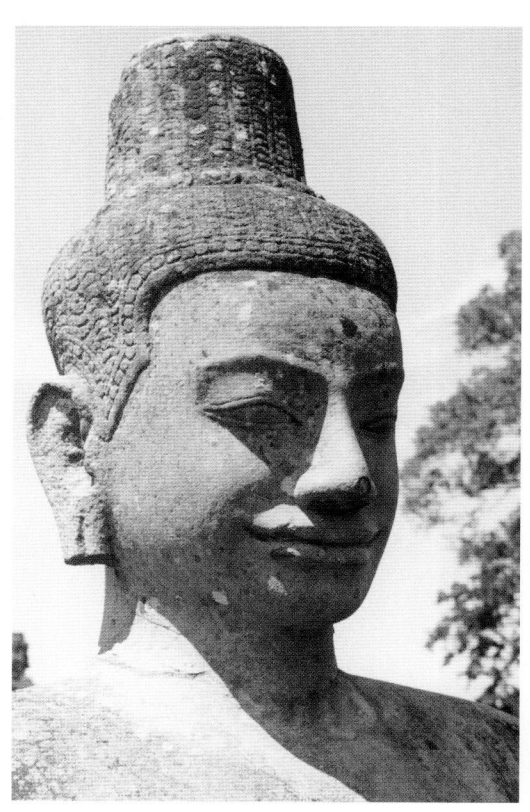

Head of Vishnu, Bakong. Siem Reap. ca. 1965.

Photographs: Yves Coffin. National Library of Australia.

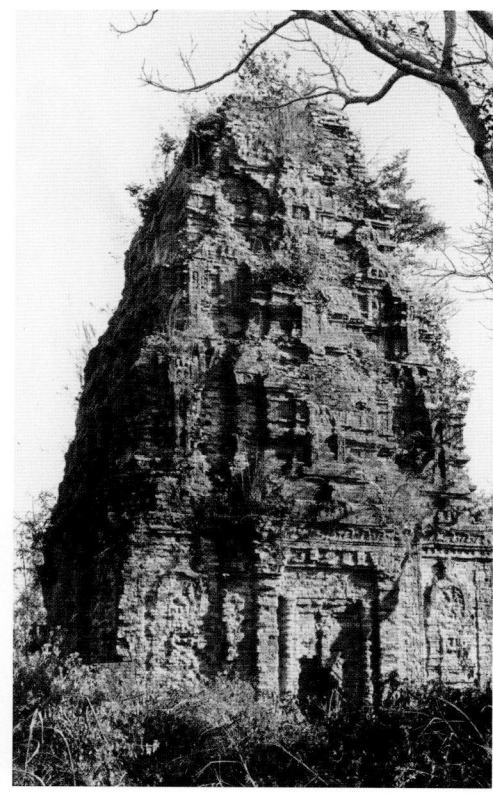

Prasat Phnom Ba Yong. Takeo. ca. 1965.

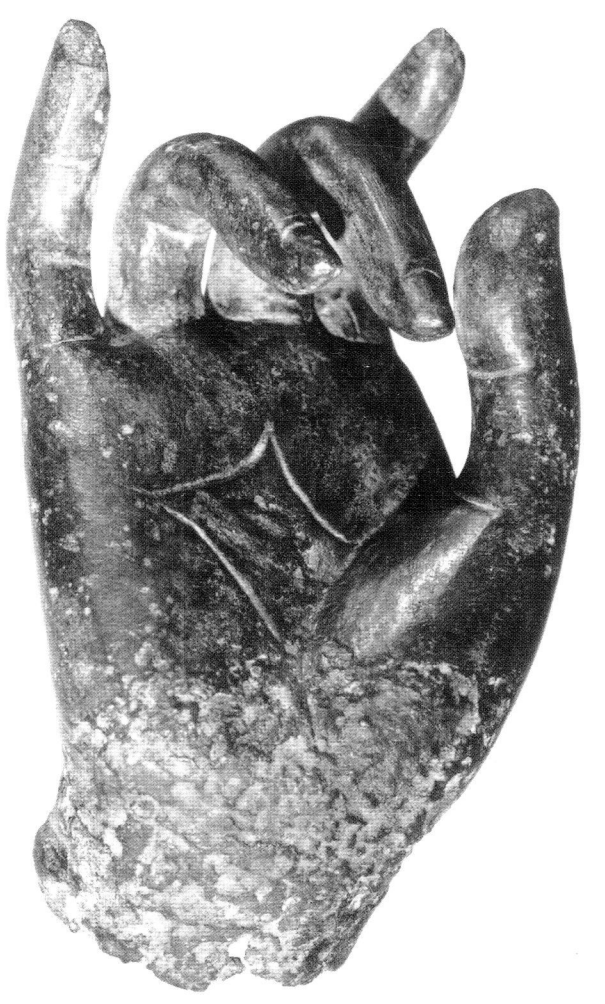
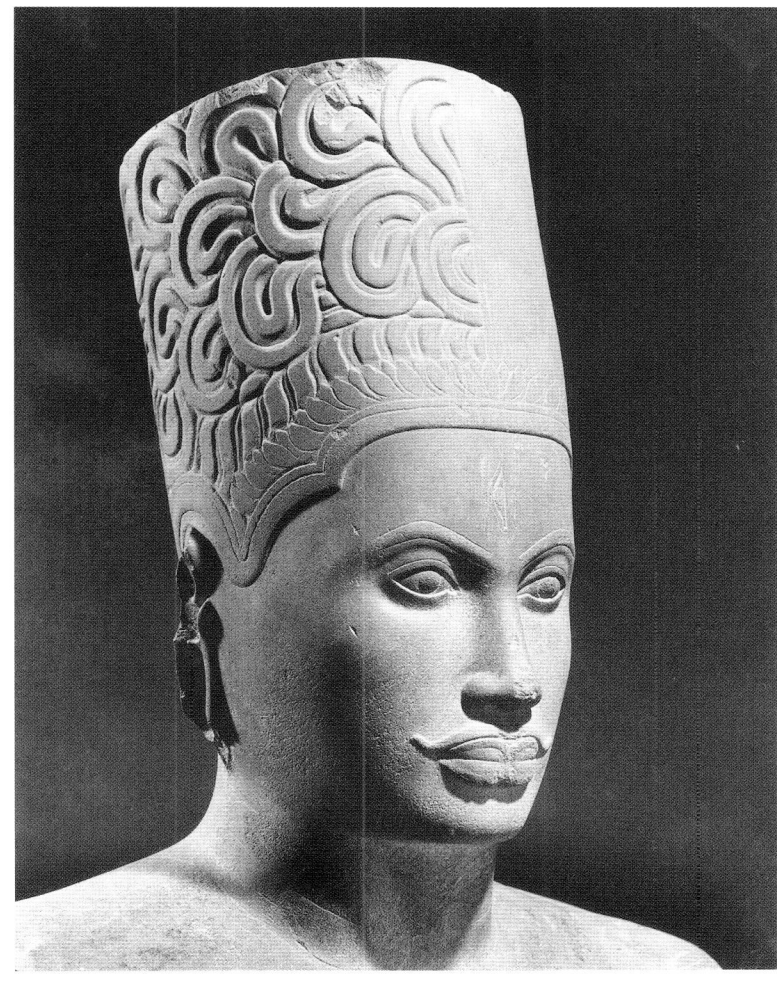

ABOVE LEFT: **Bronze hand of an unknown Angkorian diety.** Length 5 inches (12.5 cm). Provenance unknown. 1968. Photographer unknown.

ABOVE RIGHT: **Early Angkorian Harihara sculpture.** Prasat Andaet, Kompong Thom. 1965. Photographer unknown.

Source: École française d'Extrême-Orient.

École française d'Extrême-Orient: The Postwar Years

While the pleasures of the Sangkum were being enjoyed by urbanized Cambodians, the countryside was being destabilized by civil war. Sculptures of gods and guardians were being looted from unattended temples. To alleviate this, the EFEO built an armory in Siem Reap to safeguard many of these priceless moveable relics. The magnificent head of the Hindu god Harihara (above), with his fine moustache, extended earlobes, and penetrating eyes, masterfully captures the attributes of a deity representing both Vishnu and Shiva in a single form. By 1970, most EFEO staff had left the Angkor site. The Khmer Rouge guerrillas had control of the sacred heart of the kingdom, and the symbolic power of *vitarka mudra* (the hand sign of Buddha symbolizing the wheel of the law (above left), had dissipated.

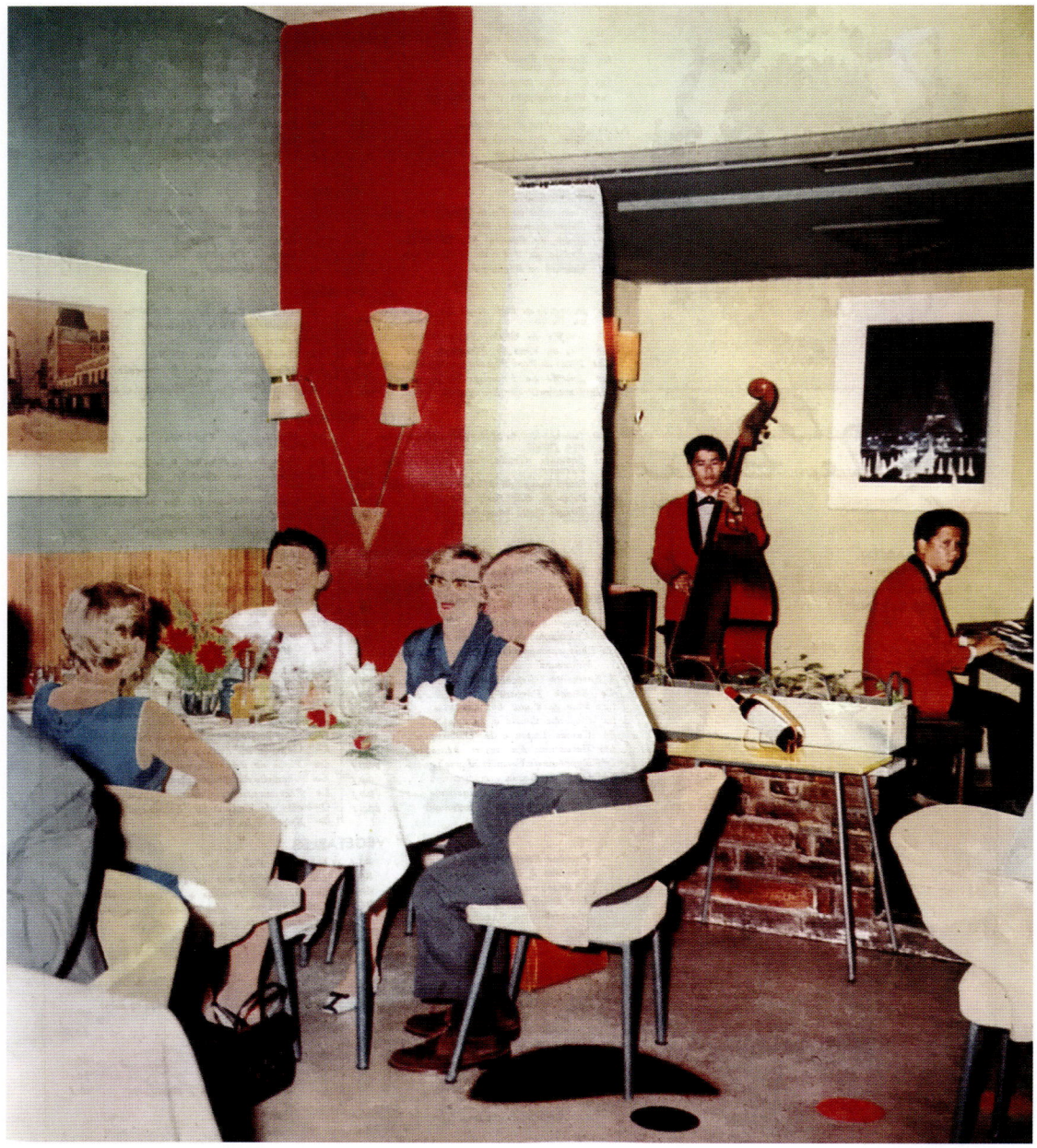

Café du Paris

Patrons dining at the Café du Paris, Phnom Penh. 1966. Photographer unknown. *Kambuja Monthly Illustrated Review*, October 15, 1966. Center for Khmer Studies Library, Siem Reap.

When the Café du Paris opened its doors on Kramoun Road, Phnom Penh, in the middle of 1966, it was celebrated, rather breathlessly, by the reporter working for the *Kambuja Monthly Illustrated Review* as "the temple of French gastronomy in Cambodia." The portly owner, originally from Corsica, ensured the restaurant's décor was the height of postwar 1960s chic, with contemporary furniture and wall-mounted light fittings, a Miroesque pattern on the floor, and framed prints on the modishly colored walls by the works of the French painters Utrillo and Renoir. An orchestra played popular French favorites, and an open bar with ruby red stools completed the enviable scene. This was very much an establishment for the Francophone elite.

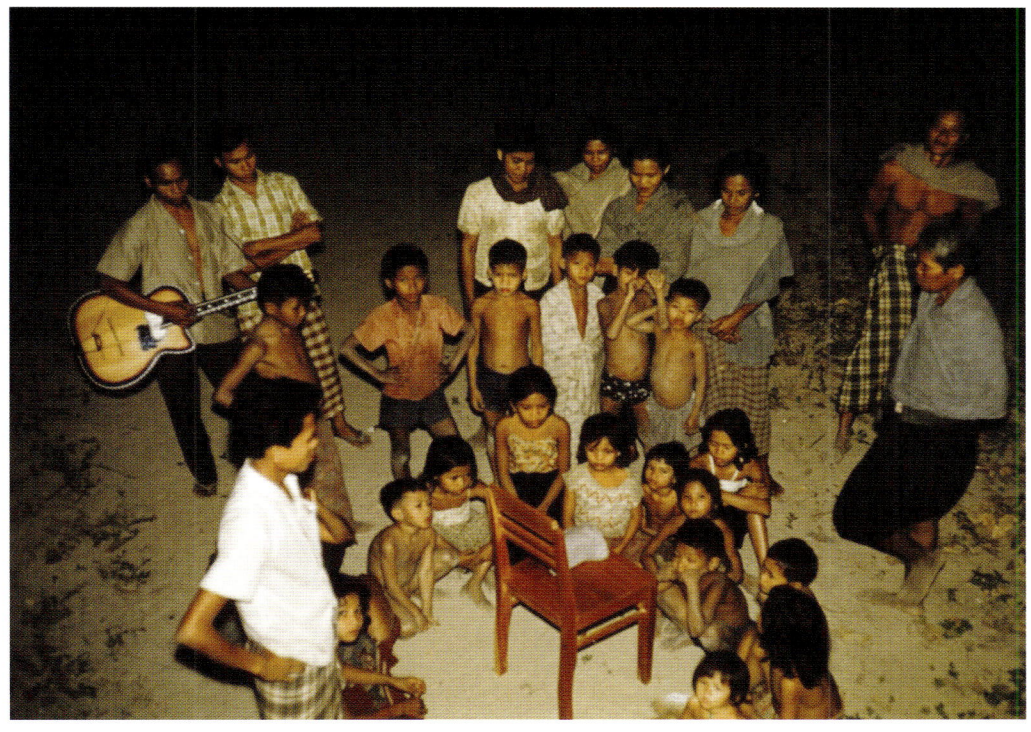

LEFT: **"Villagers listening to a radio in my front yard."** Svay Village, Kandal. 1959–60.

BELOW: **Au in rice fields.** Svay Village, Kandal. 1959–60.

Photographs: May Mayko Ebihara. May Ebihara Digital Collections, Northern Illinois University Libraries.

An Anthropologist in Svay

Between 1959 and 1960, the American anthropologist Dr May Mayko EBIHARA (1934–2005) conducted two years of field research among the inhabitants of the rice-growing village of Svay, 18 miles (30 km) south of Phnom Penh. Her studies revealed a detailed picture of village life, its social structure, and the devotion to animist and Buddhist beliefs, as well as local agricultural practices. Taken from her balcony at night, the photograph above shows villagers listening to a radio propped on a chair. The children appear transfixed by the broadcast. Was it a galvanizing political speech by Sihanouk or popular music aired by Radio Cambodge? After the Khmer Rouge devastation, Ebihara returned in the late 1980s to follow up her earlier research. While meeting the son of her adopted grandparents in the village, he shook his head sadly, reflecting on the past. "Things are not what they were," he said.

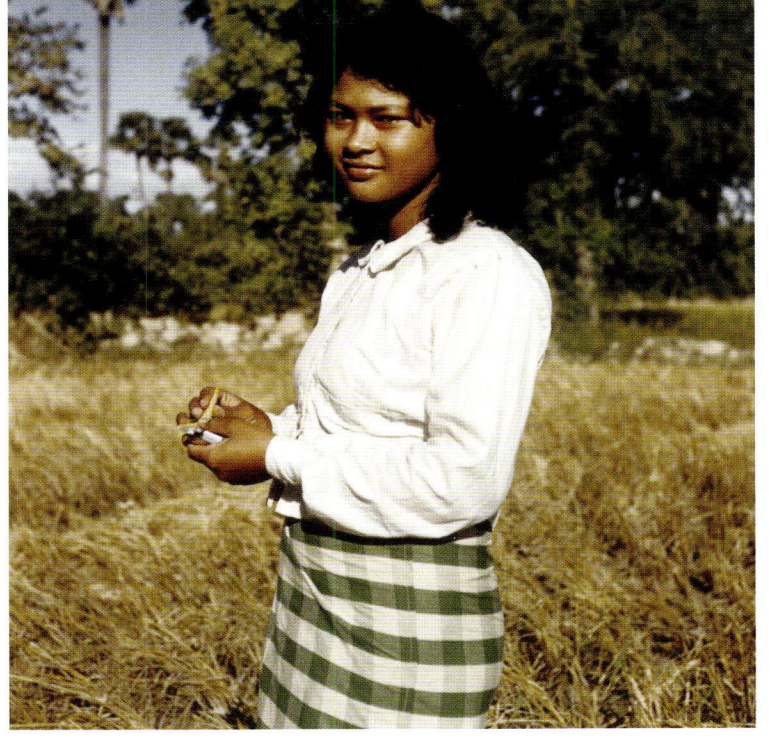

Kep Sur Le Mer

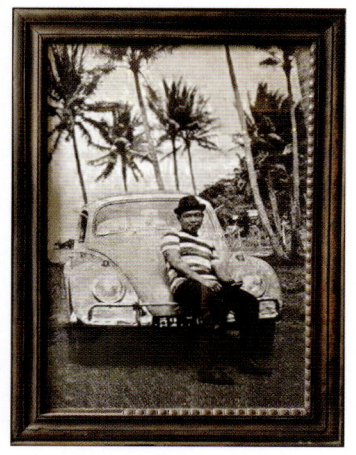

Originally a remote provincial outpost during the French Protectorate, Kep came to prominence when an American-funded highway between nearby Sihanoukville and Phnom Penh was completed in 1959. The fishing town's natural beauty—coconut groves, quiet beaches, and a sea breeze that buffeted the surrounding jungle-covered hills—attracted a new holiday elite. They built large bungalows in the latest modern styles, and even Sihanouk commissioned a villa to entertain diplomatic and family guests. Successful businessmen, well-paid public servants, and the artists and musicians of Phnom Penh motored south, driving their imported American and European vehicles, for weekend getaways. At the beach, they laid out mats for seafood picnics, lit up an Apsara cigarette, and changed into bathing costumes to enjoy a paddle in the surf.

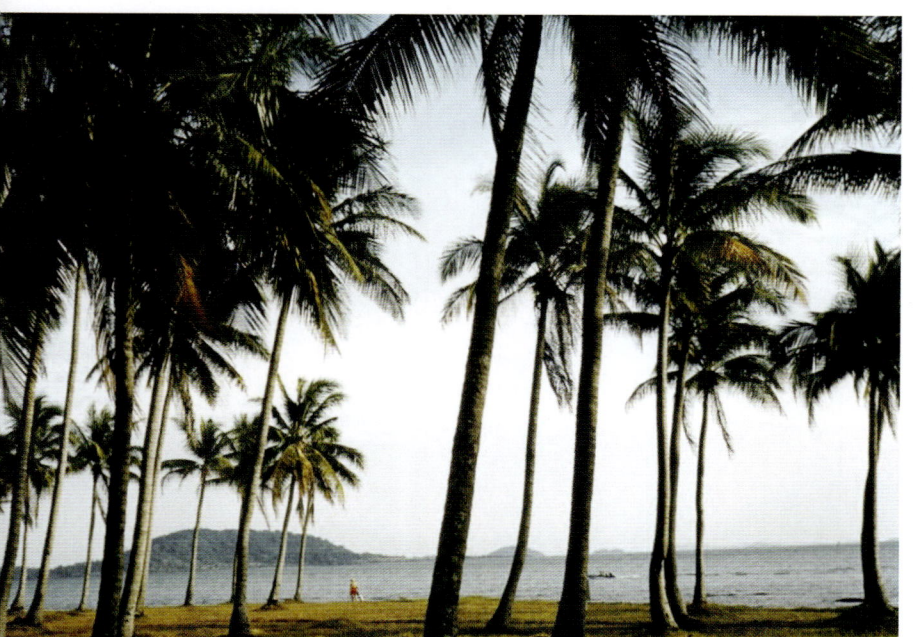

TOP LEFT: **Sinn Sisamouth and his Volkswagen.** ca. 1960. Photographer unknown. Lee Peng Heng Collection, Phnom Penh.

LEFT: **Kep shoreline.** 1959–60. May Mayko Ebihara. May Ebihara Digital Collections, Northern Illinois University Libraries.

BOTTOM LEFT: **Postcard of Kep beach.** 1964. Photographer unknown. Pinterest.

BOTTOM RIGHT: **Hubert Elmiger with Jost.** Kep. 1942. H. A. C. Elmiger Archive/National Archives of Cambodia.

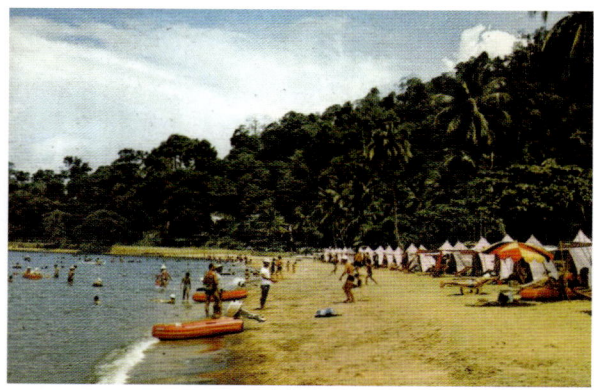
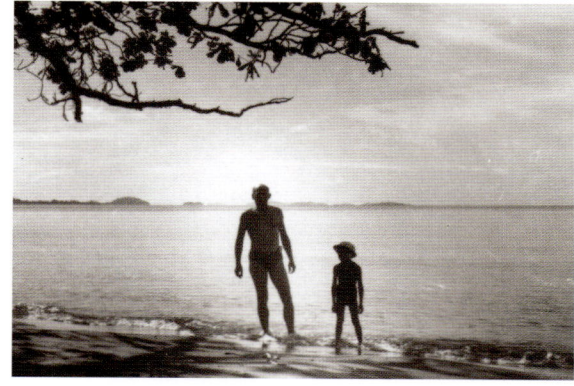

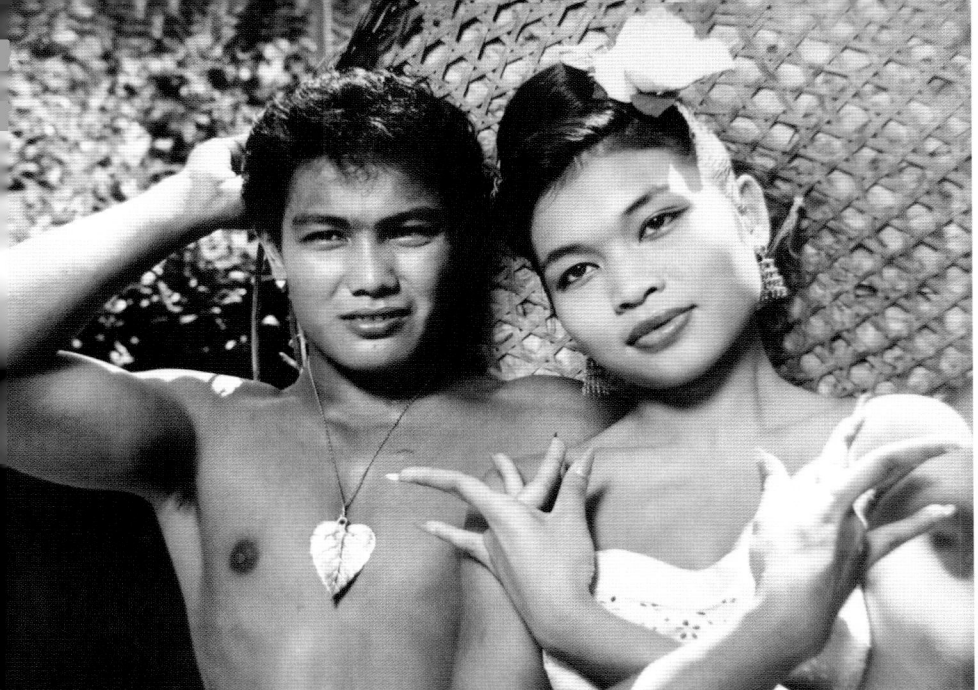
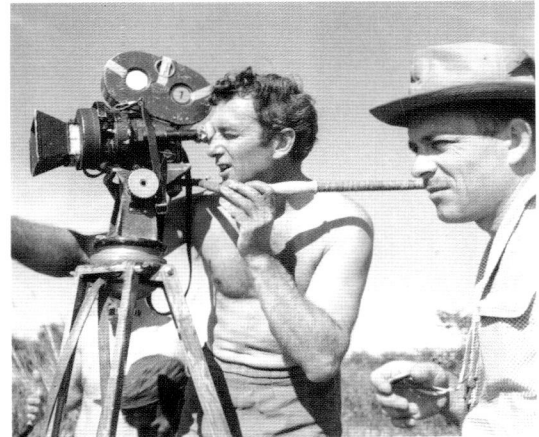
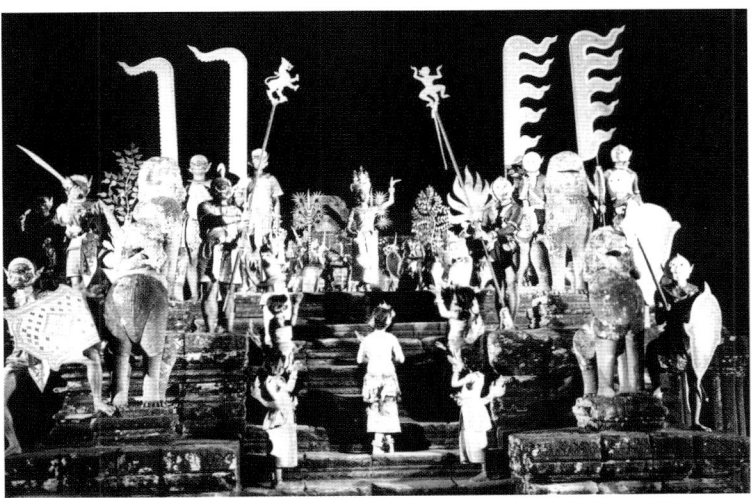
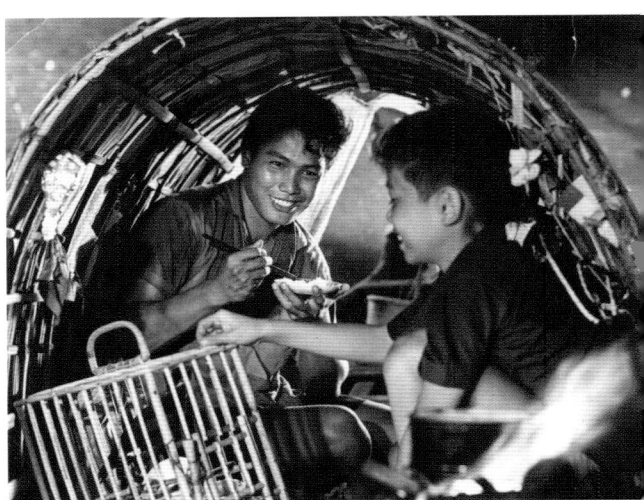

Bird of Paradise

After his *Black Orpheus* movie was released to critical and popular acclaim in 1958, Marcel CAMUS (1912–82), decided to repeat the formula in a Cambodian setting. Starring two young amateur performers, Hem Narie and Nem Nop, *Bird of Paradise* (*L'Oiseau de Paradis*, 1962) contrasted dazzling Angkorian spectacle and sophisticated city locations against intimate village scenes to explore a fated and frustrated love between a handsome young itinerant worker and a temple dancing girl. Filmed in Phnom Penh studios and on location at Angkor Wat, the production was able to give Cambodians working experience in the professional environment of European cinema-making. A stills photographer recorded important scenes for continuity and to groom the movie's public image. These photographs were used as raw material for creating film posters, large cinema street banners, smaller images to be displayed in cinema foyers, and for distribution to fan magazines.

TOP LEFT, CLOCKWISE: **"Lovers" production still.** Phnom Penh. 1962. Author's Collection.

Marcel Camus (behind camera). Siem Reap. 1962. National Archives of Cambodia/Charles Meyer Collection, Paris.

"The boat" production still. Phnom Penh. 1962. National Archives of Cambodia/Charles Meyer Collection, Paris.

Dance sequence at Angkor Wat. Siem Reap. 1962. National Archives of Cambodia/Charles Meyer Collection, Paris.

The stills photographer has not been recorded in production credits.

The Cham and Muslim World

Photographs taken in 1962 by little-known Salle ISSA (aka Sales ISA) record the journey of five men on a Haj pilgrimage to Mecca, center of the Muslim faith. There is a chance that Salle is the young man to the left, leaning into the group after clicking the timer on his camera. The KLM flight bag hanging on the rough timber wall behind the men hints at an earlier, more salubrious travel mode. We know little of Salle's life. The Cambodian National Archives notes he was from the Chruoy Changvar peninsula, sandwiched between the confluence of the Mekong and Tonlé Sap rivers. The lower images, from the Charles Meyer Collection, do not record the photographers. They show a vibrant, engaging Muslim community that was to be devastated by Khmer Rouge chauvinism and persecution between 1975 and 1979.

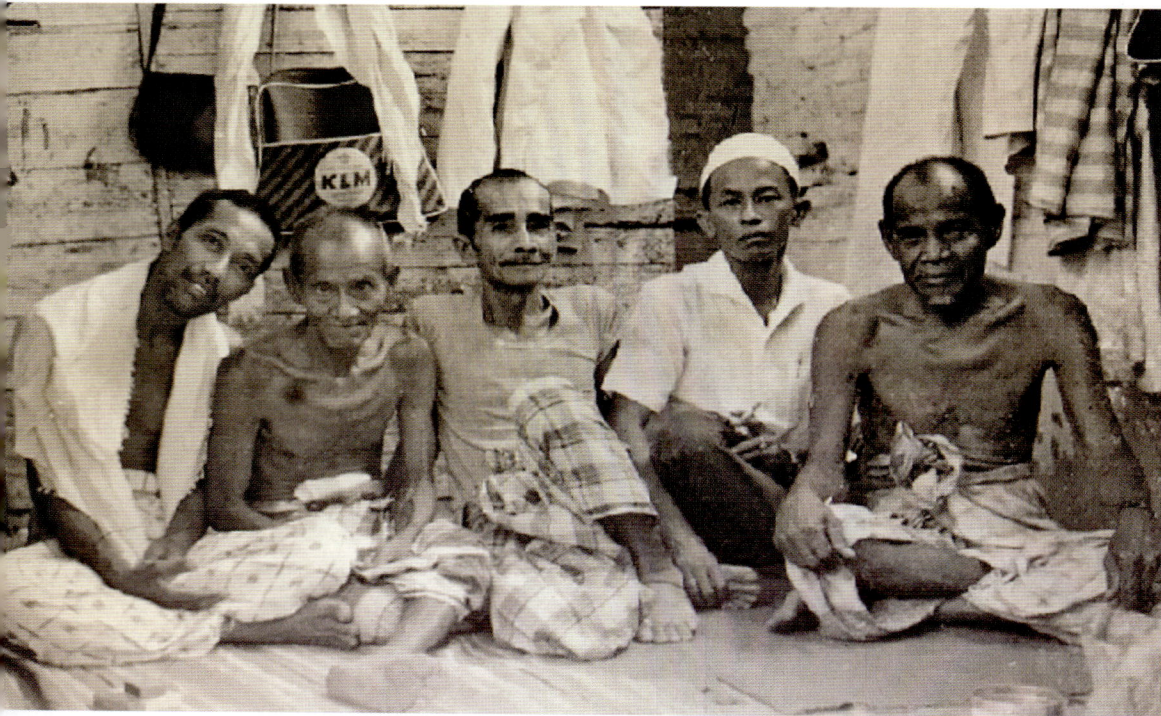

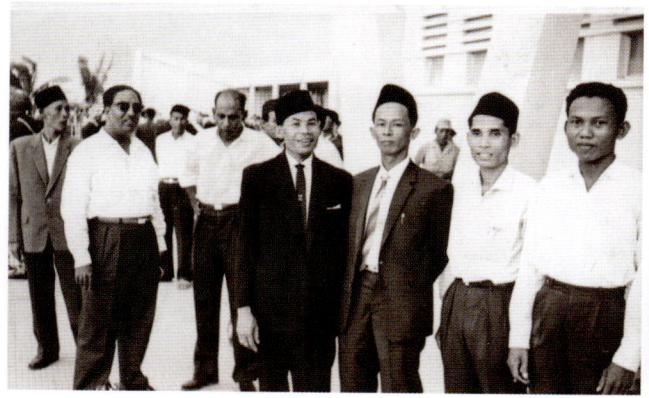

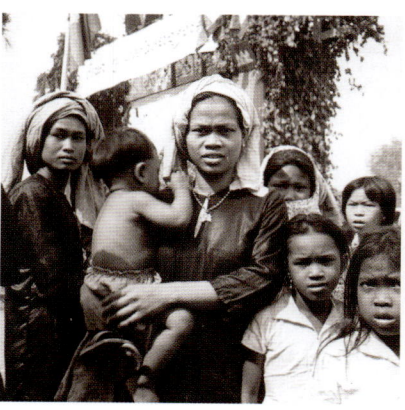

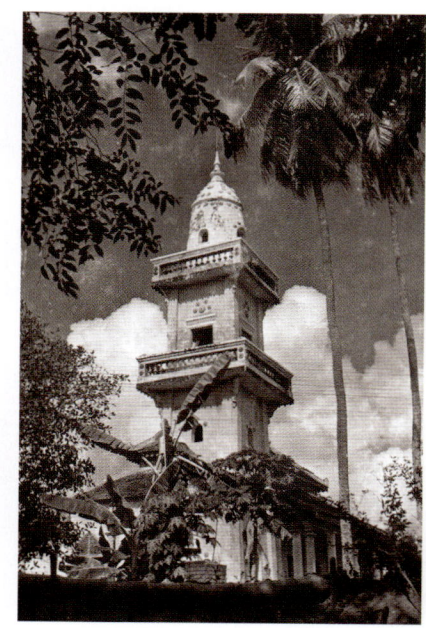

LEFT, CLOCKWISE: **Pilgrims on their journey to Haj.** Location unknown. 1962. Salle Issa.

Mosque minaret. Possibly Chruoy Changvar peninsula. 1960s. Photographer unknown.

Cham women and children. Phnom Penh. 1960s. Photographer unknown.

Guests at a Cham wedding. Phnom Penh. 1960s. Photographer unknown.

Source: National Archives of Cambodia/Charles Meyer Collection, Paris.

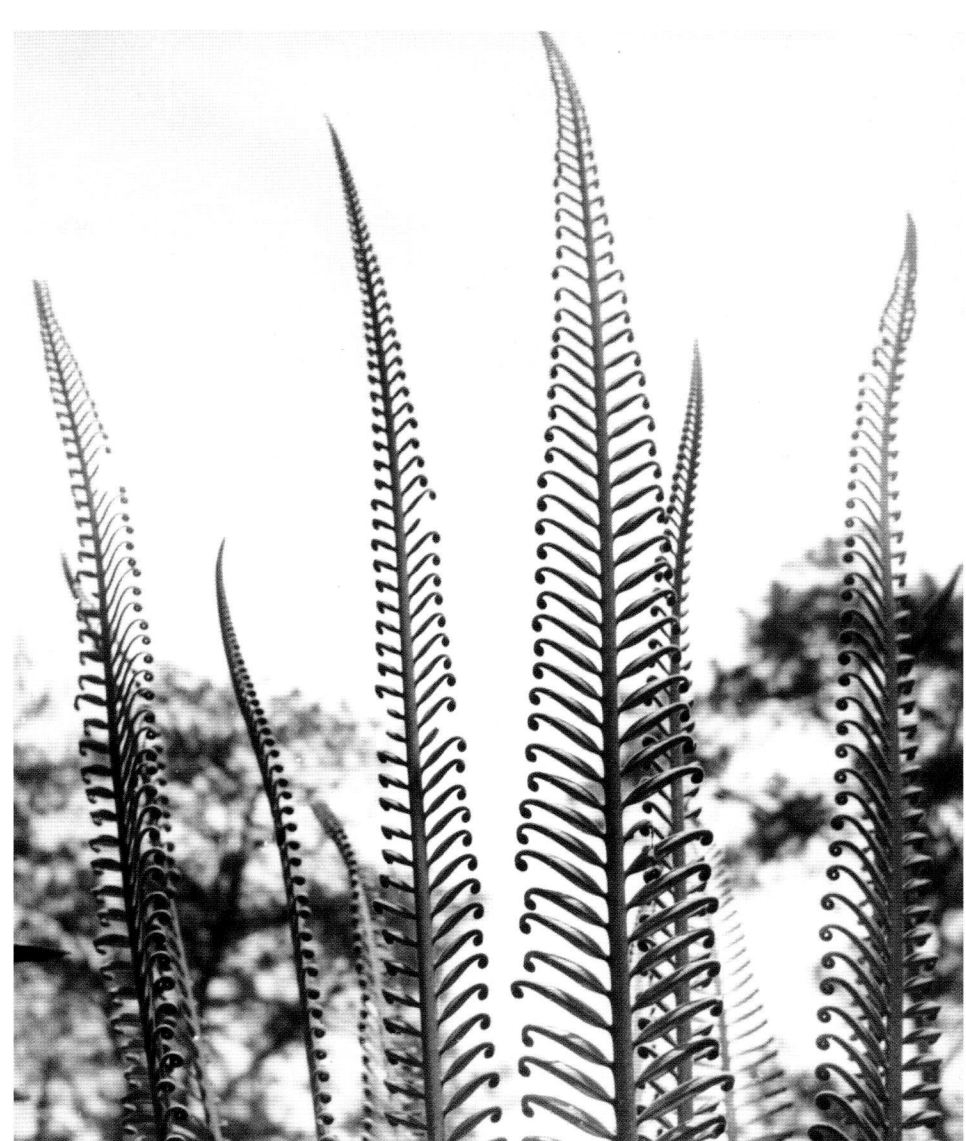

RIGHT: **Fern fronds.** Mimot Estate, Tboung Khmum. ca. 1965.

BELOW: **Gibbon on the driveway.** Mimot Estate, Tboung Khmum. ca. 1965.

Photographs: Jean Boulbet. National Archives of Cambodia/ Charles Meyer Collection, Paris.

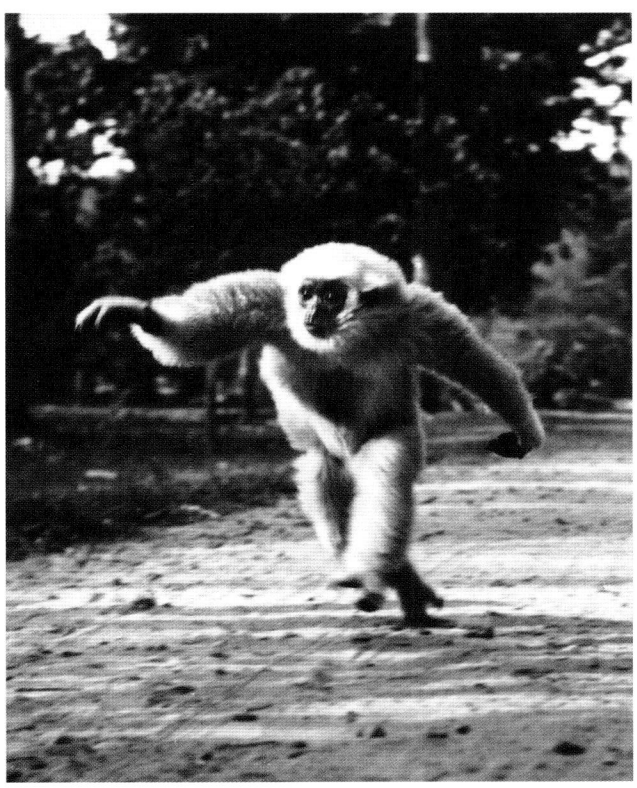

Jean Boulbet's Natural World

Jean BOULBET (1926–2007) was a keen observer of the natural world. In the mid-1960s, he traveled to the eastern province of Tboung Khmum to visit the large Mimot rubber estate, then managed by H. A. C. Elmiger. Boulbet took the morning image of young fern fronds (above), and later in the day, a yellow-cheeked crested gibbon (left), gamboling along the driveway of the estate's bungalow. Boulbet is primarily known as an ethnologist and human geographer. He worked for the École française d'Extrême-Orient in Siem Reap during the late 1960s, where he rediscovered the early Khmer riverbed carvings at Kbal Spean in the Kulen Mountains. By the early 1970s, the Khmer Rouge were closing in towards the north of Siem Reap, making research work at the ancient monuments difficult to continue. He relocated, first to Battambang, and then later to Thailand to escape the emerging civil war.

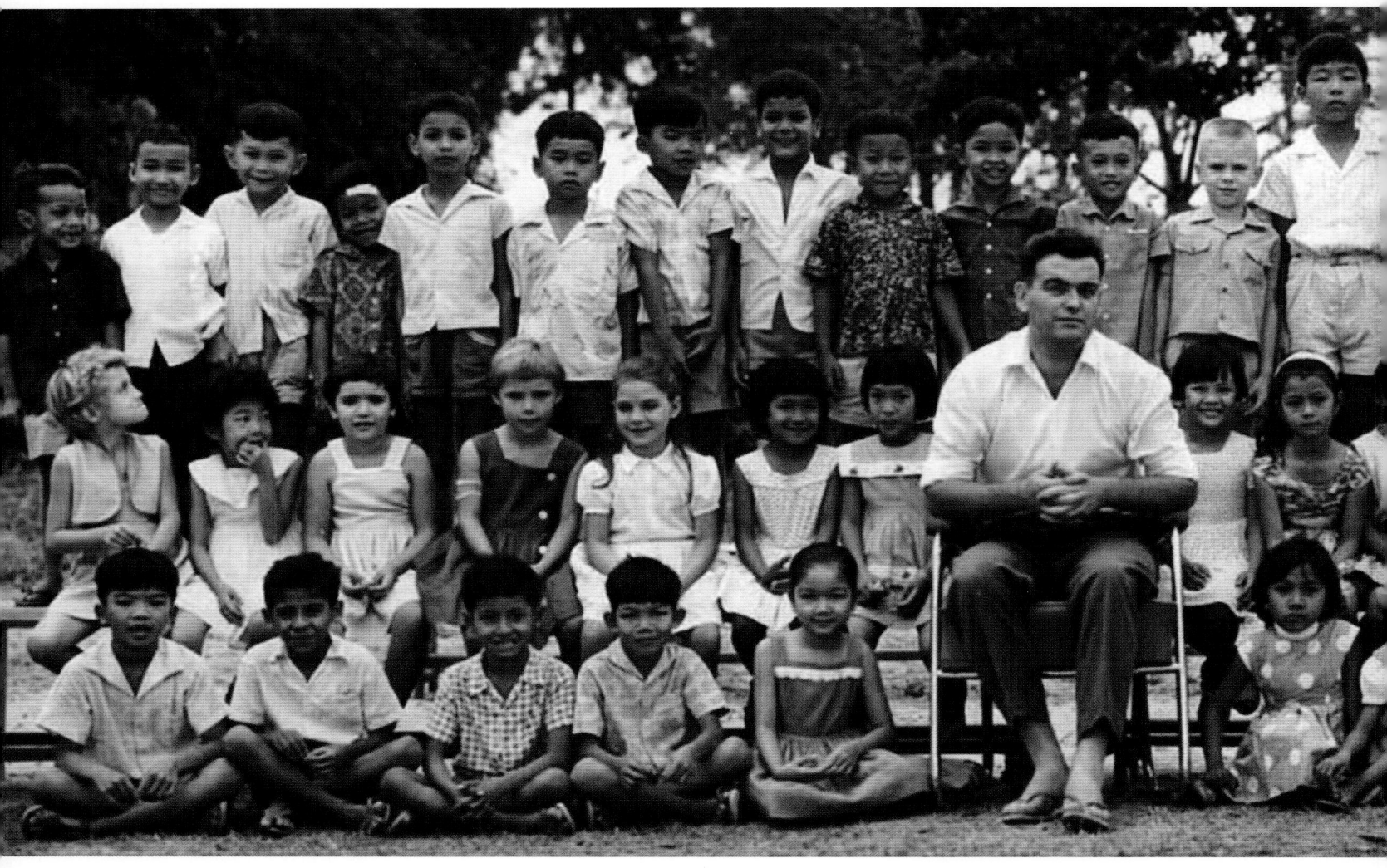

Lycée français René Descartes

Established in 1951 during the last years of the French Protectorate, Lycée français René Descartes quickly gained a reputation as the premier French-language school in Cambodia. Members of the royal family, high officials, and the business elite all wanted their children admitted. After independence in 1953, the teachers adapted what was originally an exclusively French curriculum to include subjects taught in Khmer. The formal end-of-year class photograph—a familiar rite of passage experienced by generations—captures a kaleidoscope of young personalities gaining new social skills within their school environment. With hindsight, we may wonder about the fate of the dancing teenagers (opposite center) as the emerging civil war engulfed Cambodia.

Mr. Chauvin's Year 10 class. Phnom Penh. 1962.

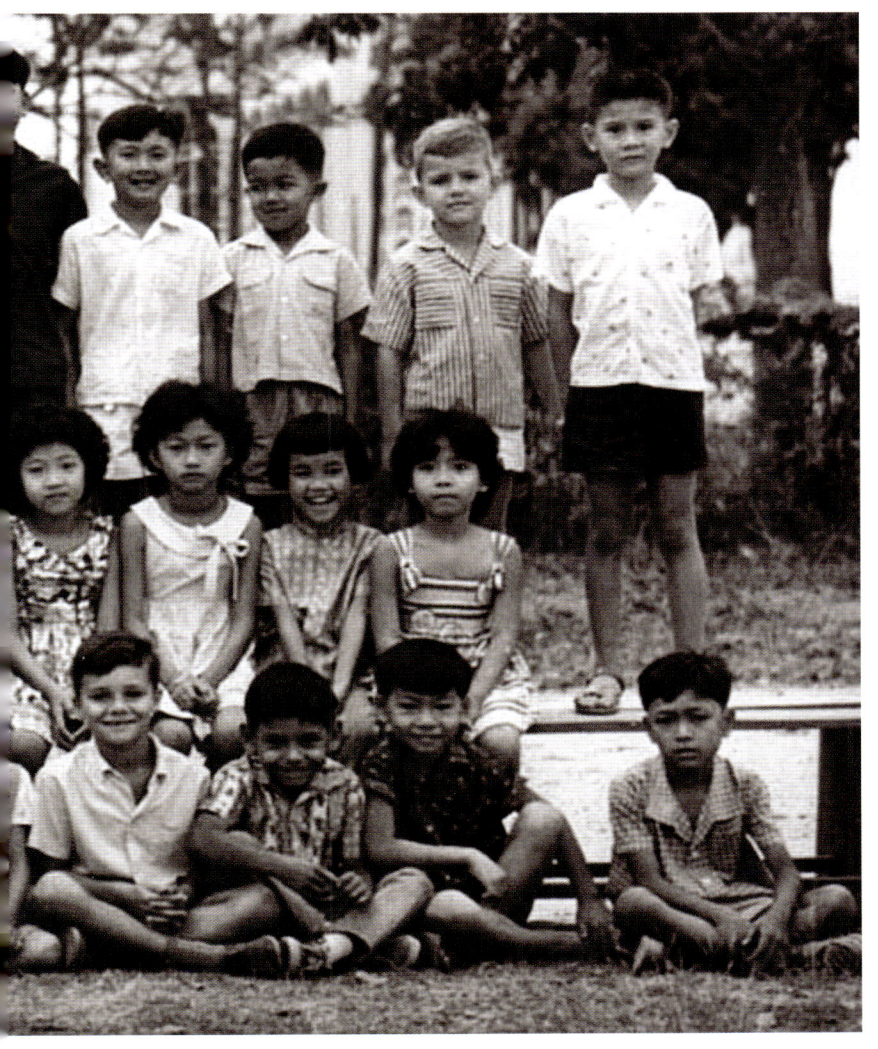

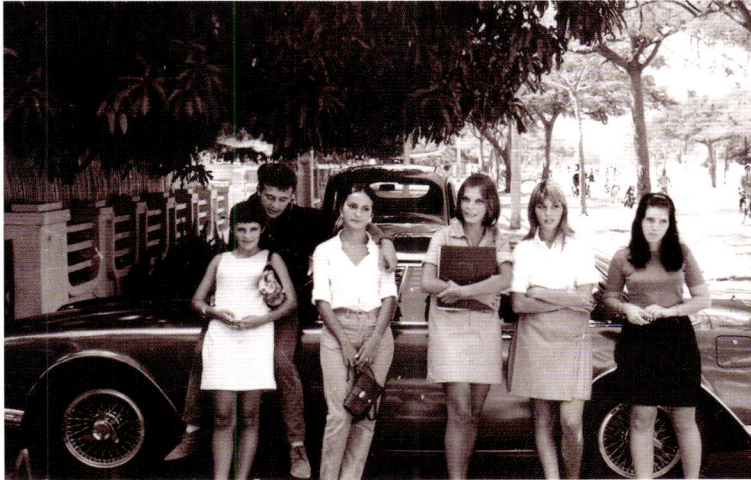

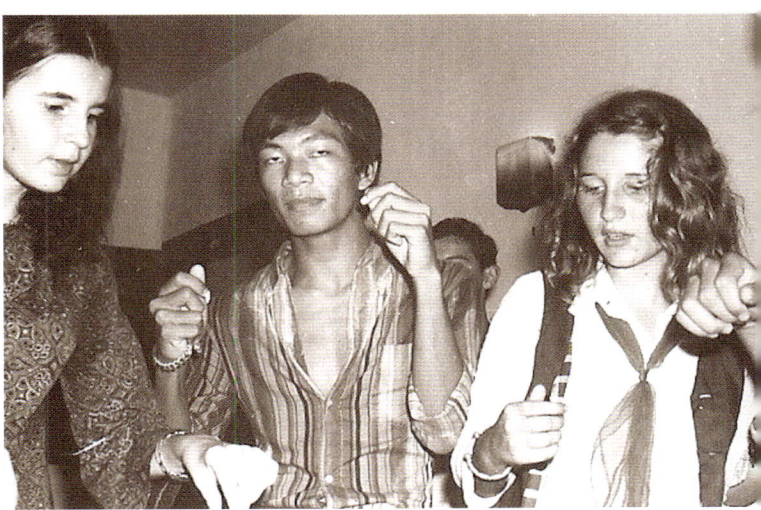

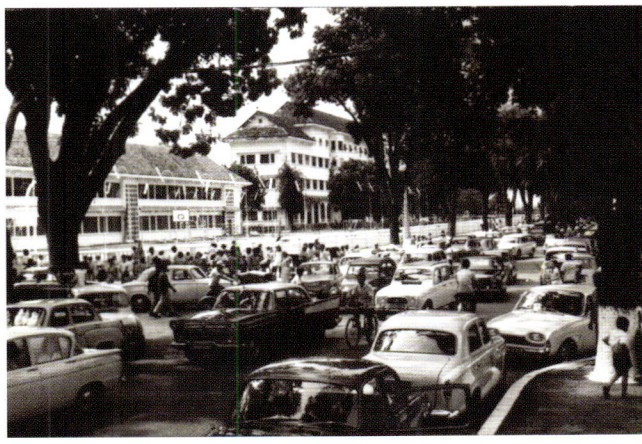

Science class. Phnom Penh. 1955.

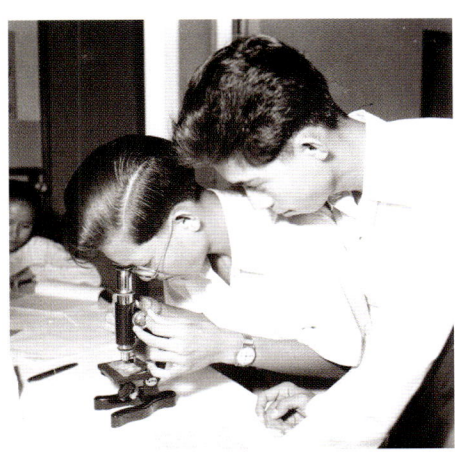

FROM TOP: **Girls in front of Lycée Descartes.** Phnom Penh. 1966.

Student dance. Phnom Penh. 1967.

Families collecting students after school. Phnom Penh. ca. 1960.

Photographers unknown. Overblog Kampot la prospère—années 60/Marie-Françoise Châtel Collection.

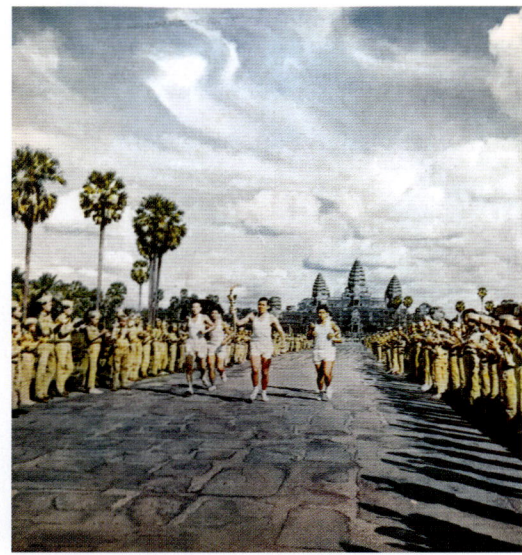
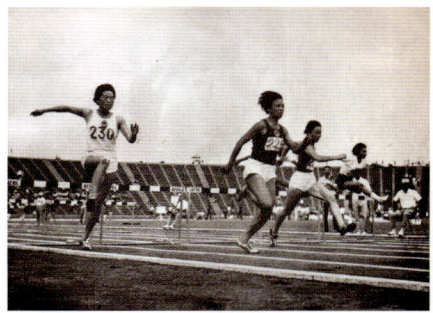
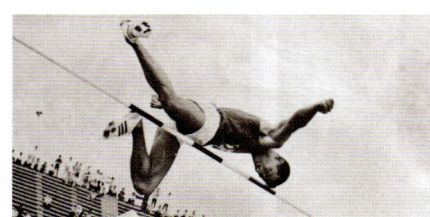
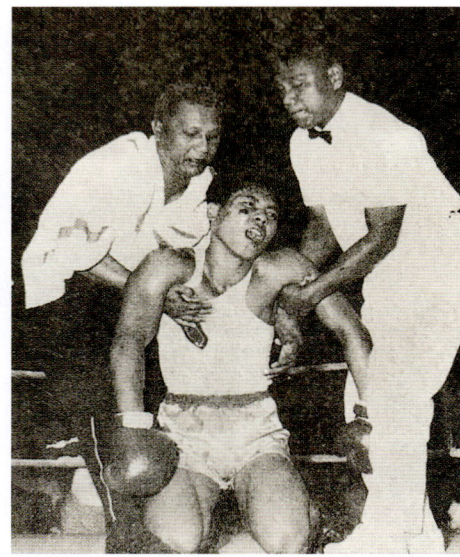
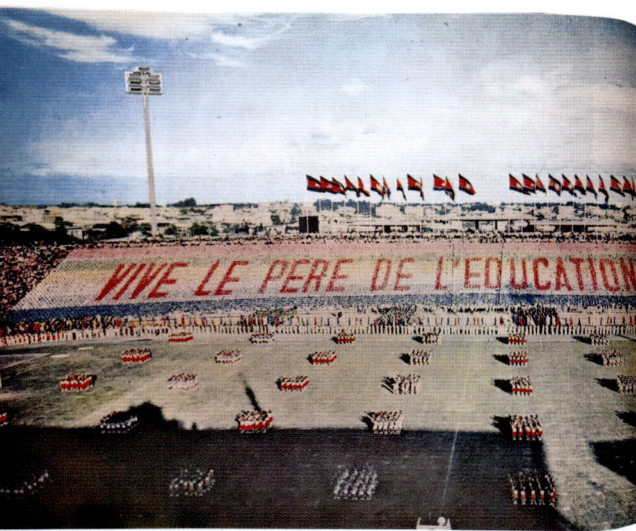
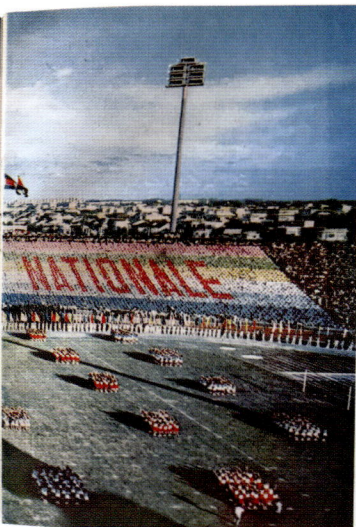
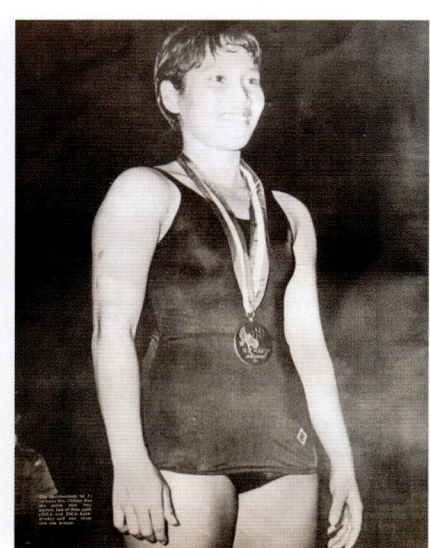

The 1966 Asian GANEFO Games

The Games of the New Emerging Forces (GANEFO) were established in the early 1960s by a group of nations that had achieved independence after World War II. As most of these "emerging nations" had a socialist leaning, they formed GANEFO as a counterpart to the Olympic Games, which they felt was riddled with factional alliances of competing communist and Western countries. The first GANEFO Games were held in Jakarta in 1963 and the second, and last, "Asian GANEFO" Games were held in Phnom Penh in 1966. Naturally, the hosts did well, winning sixty-two medals, the third highest after China and North Korea. The games were an opportunity to showcase the largest construction project in the country, the National Sports Complex, designed by Cambodian architect Vann Molyvann. Throughout the Sangkum years, Cambodian athletes traveled extensively to compete in regional events.

TOP LEFT, CLOCKWISE: **The GANEFO flame leaves the sacred site of Angkor Wat.** Siem Reap. December 1966. Royal Cambodian Armed Forces (FARK) photographer.

The Women's 800-meter hurdles. Phnom Penh. December 1966. Photographer unknown. *Kambuja Monthly Illustrated Review.*

Men's high jump. Phnom Penh. December 1966. Photographer unknown. *Kambuja Monthly Illustrated Review.*

Saw Tunhla exhausted after his fight with Touch Nol. Bassein, Burma. 1966. Photographer unknown. *Le Sangkum.*

Our number 1 sportswoman, swimmer Miss Chhoun Kun. She won four medals, two of them gold. Phnom Penh. December 1966. Photographer unknown. *Kambuja Monthly Illustrated Review.*

11,000 children perform a magnificent tableax. Phnom Penh. December 1966. Photographer unknown. *Kambuja Monthly Illustrated Review.*

Source: Center for Khmer Studies Library, Siem Reap.

National Sports Complex

The construction of the enormous sports complex proved to be a major logistical and engineering feat for the young nation. Inspired by ancient Angkorian models, the architect, Vann Molyvann, took advantage of the swampy land by constructing a network of ponds and canals which helped to both drain and cool the site. He built large *brise-solei* to enclose the smaller indoor stadium. These perforated concrete screens filtered the direct sunlight to illuminate the interior, while tropical breezes passing over the ponds cooled the spaces within. Hungarian photographer Antal GABELICS (b. 1987) visited the site fifty years after its completion. Unlike previous photographers who focused on the dramatic angles of the exterior structure as a metaphor for the aspirations of an emerging nation, Gabelics' work is a more meditative exploration of abstraction and repetition, enabling a reflection on Van Molyvann's appreciation of the harmonic geometry of Angkorian temple architecture.

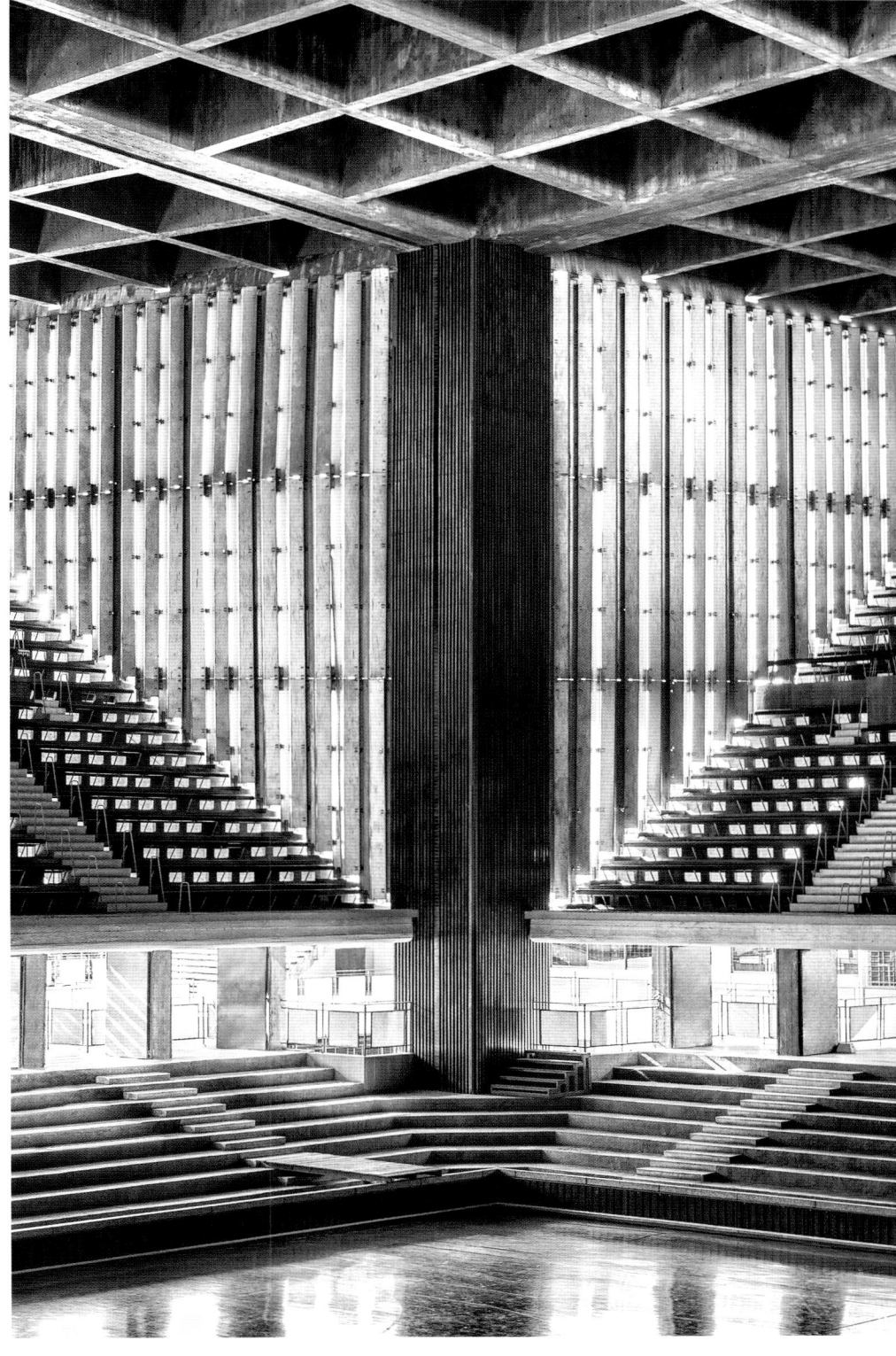

Interior of the National Sports Complex. Phnom Penh. 2017. Antal Gabelics.

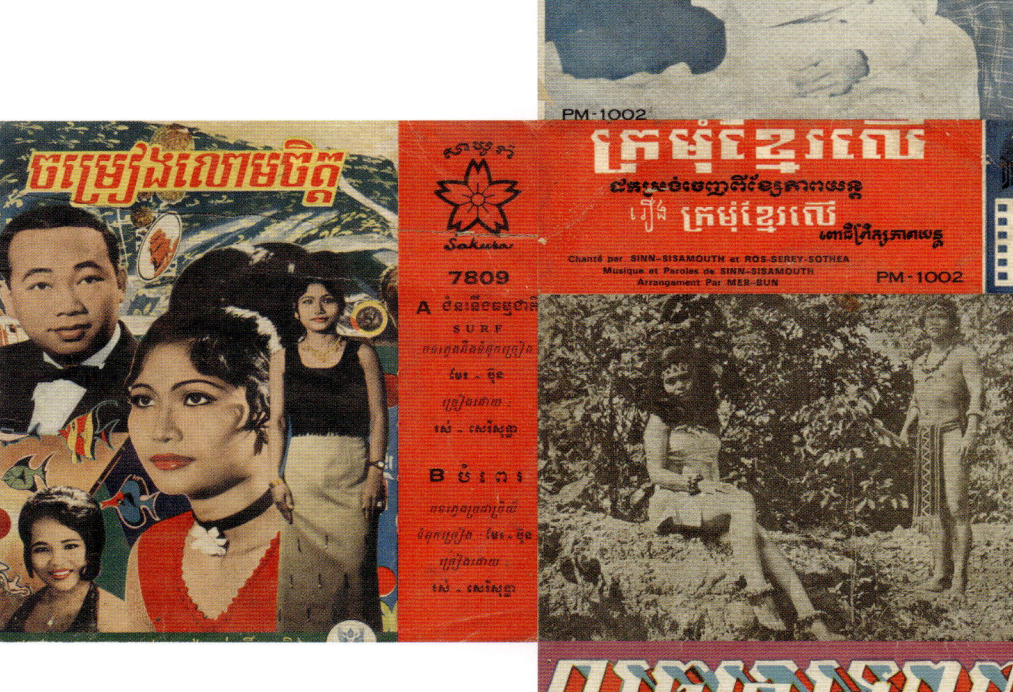

45 rpm vinyl record covers.
1950s and 1960s. Various artists. Chan Yoen Music Collection, Siem Reap.

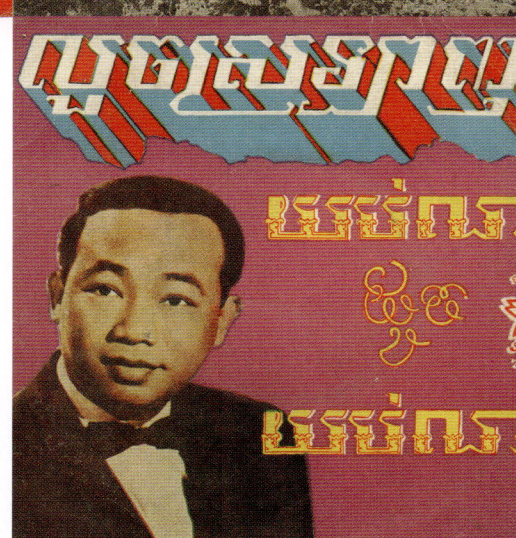

The Art of Selling Music

In the late 1950s, French-inflected swing and jazz gave way to Latin, go-go, and cha-cha as international influences fused with more traditional Cambodian music styles. The same musical revolution was happening in Malaysia, Singapore, and other postindependent Southeast Asian countries. By the mid-1960s, the scene was further influenced by Western rock and soul music disseminated via the US armed forces radio broadcasts from Vietnam. To attract buyers, local record companies commissioned designers to make trendy covers using bright pop colors and montaged portraits of singers against zany backgrounds. When Phnom Penh was finally overrun by the Khmer Rouge in 1975, the young Chan Yoen hid his precious collection of Cambodian music in the walls of his home and in a metal container buried under the nearby cowshed. Chan and his family survived the Khmer Rouge because he was able to trade favors by fixing motorbikes, bicycles, cars, and watches. Exhumed nineteen years later, in 1994, the record collection encapsulates vivid memories of a rapidly changing popular music scene in Cambodia over a twenty-year period.

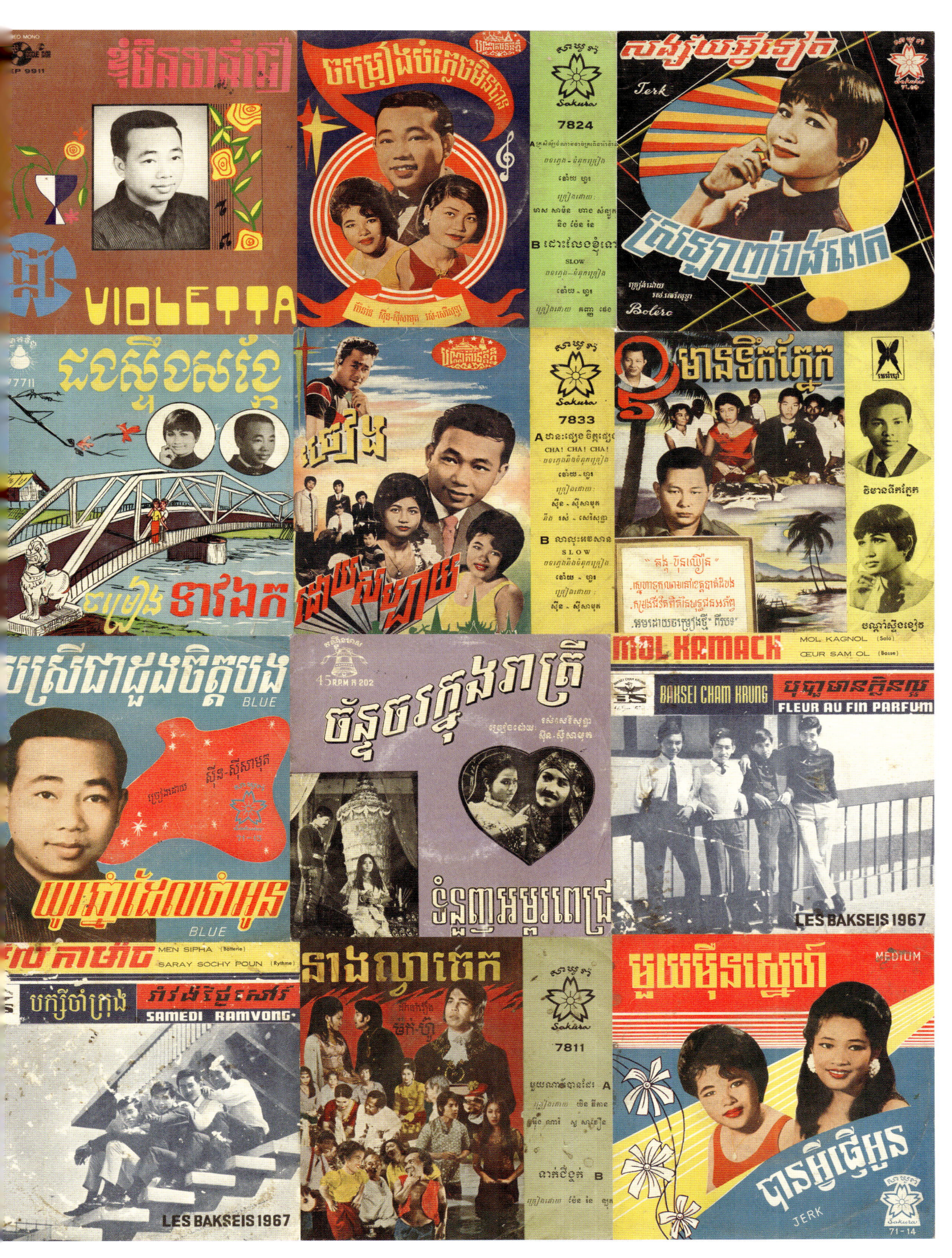

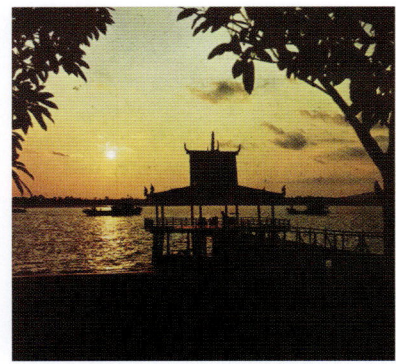
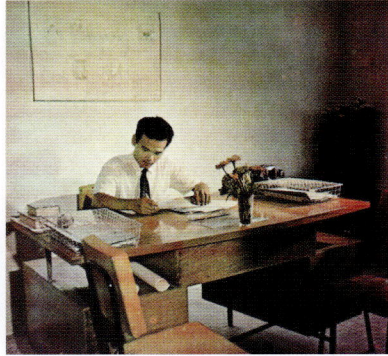
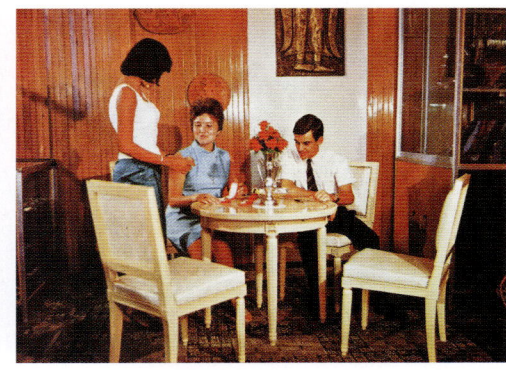
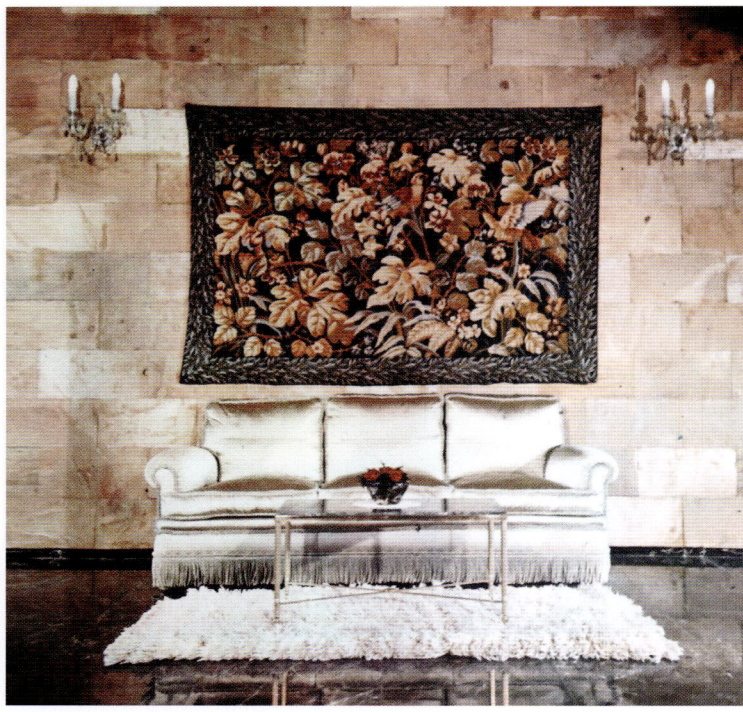
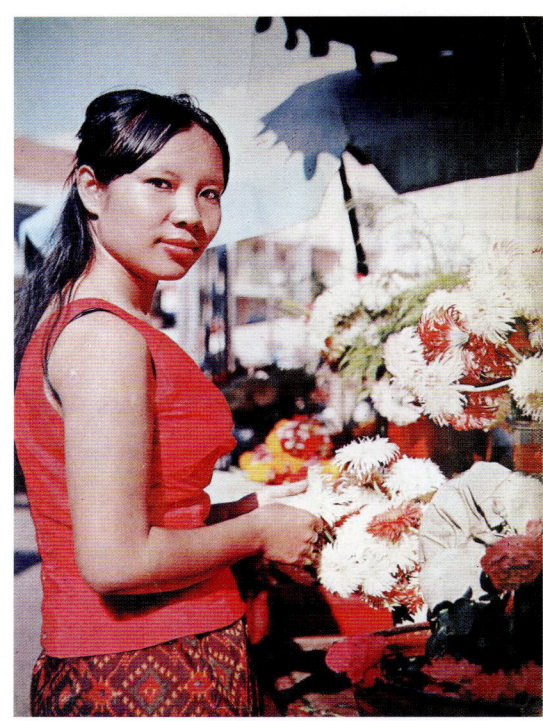

Publishing *Le Sangkum*

During the middle decades of the twentieth century, large-format color magazines flourished. The French *Réalitiés* and American *LIFE* magazines were particularly popular. Sihanouk saw these new media formats as a valuable way to promote industrial progress and cultural sophistication in his rapidly modernizing country. He edited and published the illustrated political review *Le Sangkum* (1965–70) and the *Kambuja Monthly Illustrated Review* (1965–70) to meticulously document his tours of the country. These magazines featured Sihanouk greeting supporters and opening new hospitals, bridges, and schools. Cambodian photographers were needed, and their images could be seen by thousands of readers. Photographs of flower markets, agricultural produce, new tractor factories, and anodyne sunsets were in abundance, as were feature spreads of national ceremonies. Rarely, with the exception of Royal Cambodian Armed Forces (FARK), were individual photographers credited.

TOP LEFT, CLOCKWISE: **Sunset from the State Residency.** Khemarak Phoumin, Kep. 1967.

One of the directors of the National Tractor Corporation. Sihanoukville. 1967.

Opening of a new shop at the departure hall, Pochentong Airport. Phnom Penh. 1967.

A flower seller with roses and asters. Phnom Penh Flower Market. 1967.

Inner gallery with comfortable seating beneath a wool tapestry "Touraine" by Dupont. State Palace, Chamkar Mon. Phnom Penh. 1967.

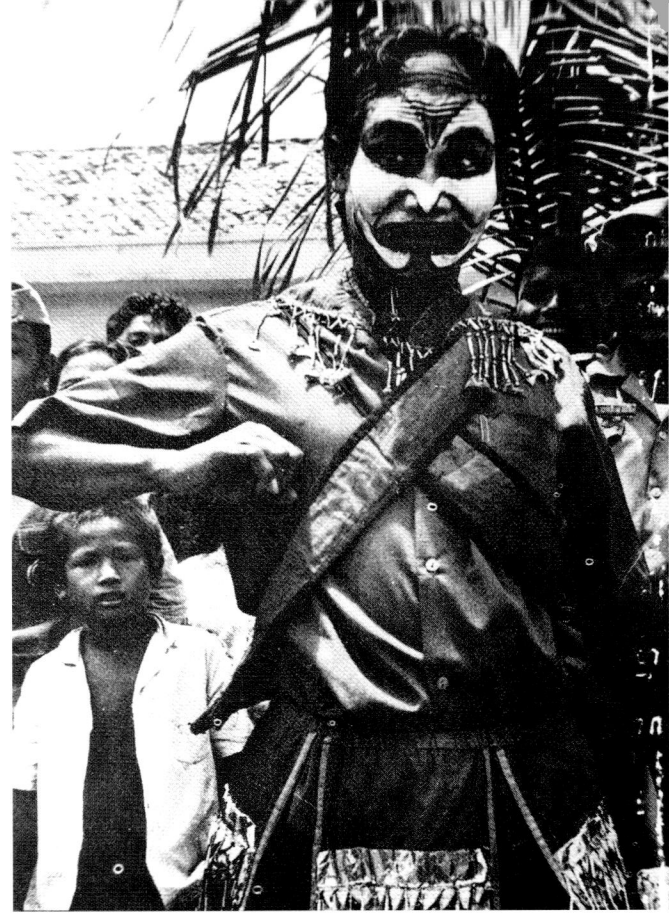
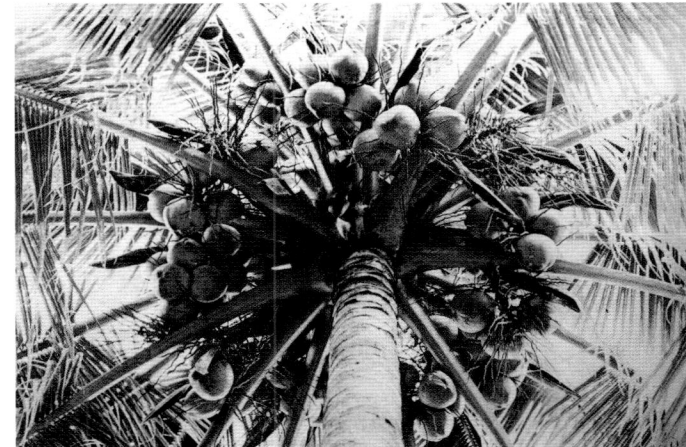
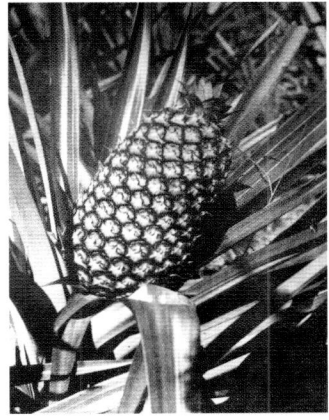
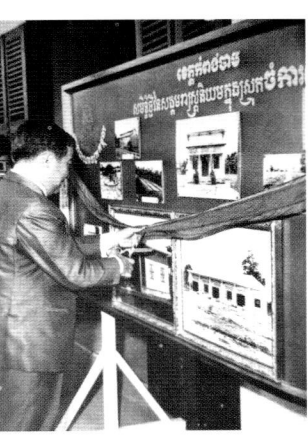

TOP LEFT, CLOCKWISE: **Street performer during the visit of Prince Sihanouk.** Iam Chikang, Kompong Cham. 1967.

Agriculture in Cambodia. Coconut tree. Location unknown. 1967.

Prince Sihanouk opening a photography exhibition of new public works. Prek Po, Kompong Cham. 1967.

"… a crowd comprising the army and youth impeccably in line all around the Monument." Montage. Independence Monument, Phnom Penh. 1967.

Agriculture in Cambodia. Pineapples. Location unknown. 1967.

Source: *Kambuja Monthly Illustrated Review.* No photographers credited. Center for Khmer Studies Library, Siem Reap.

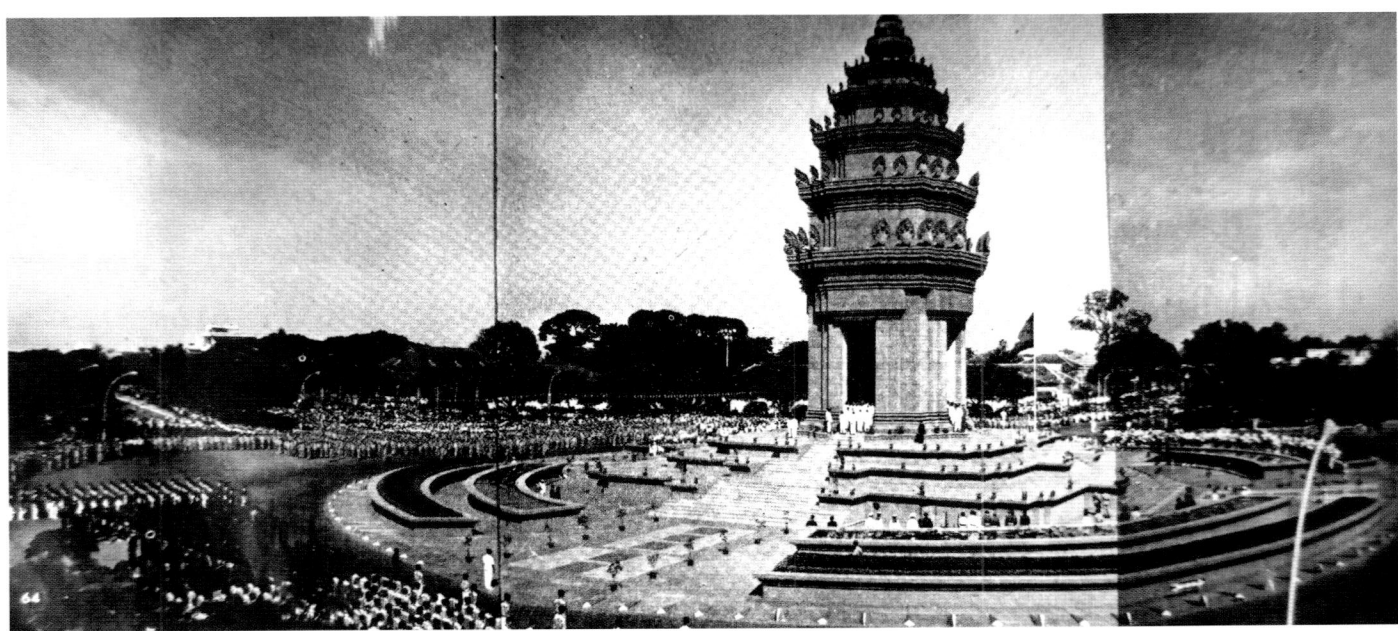

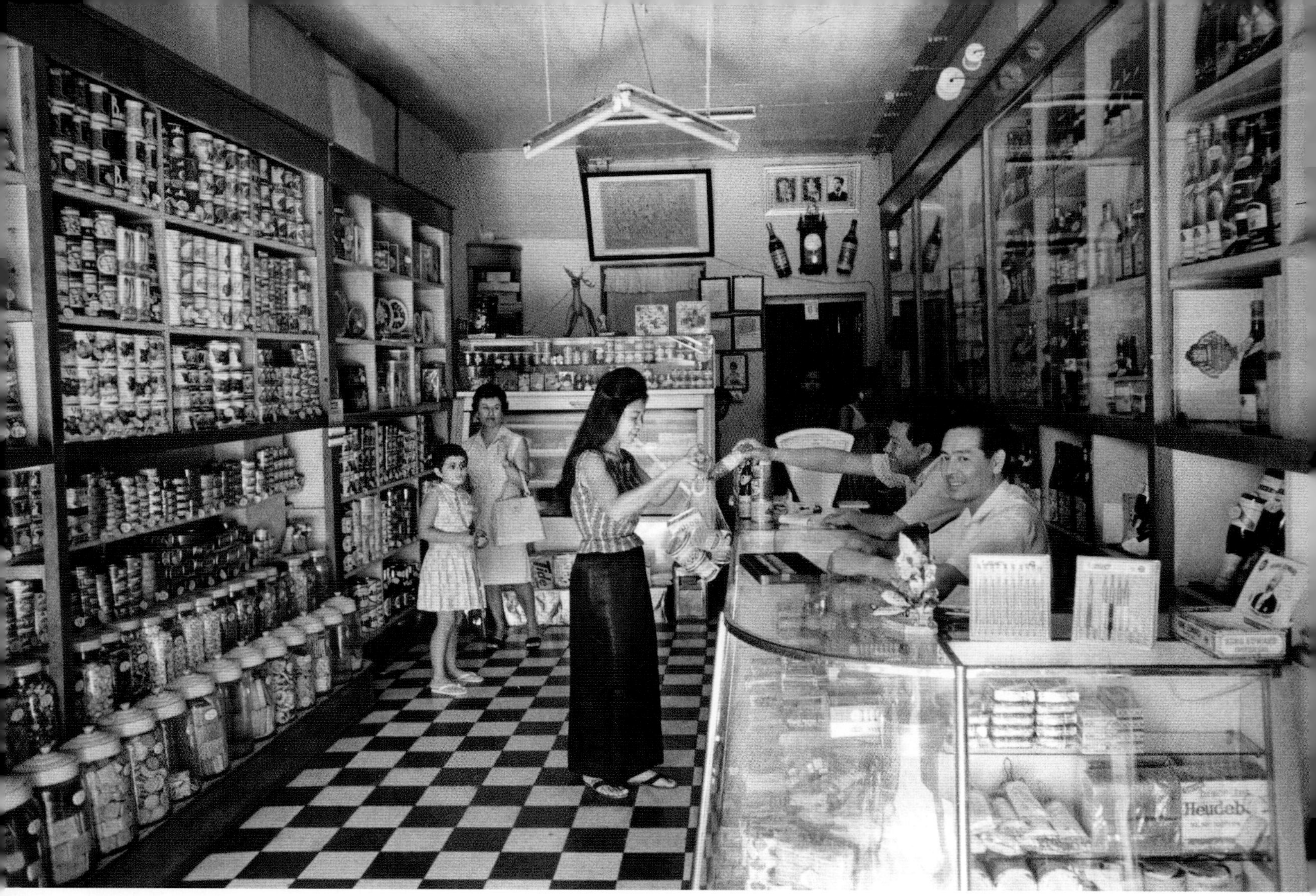

The Retail World

Phnom Penh prospered in the early years of the Sangkum government. American aid flooded in and the effects of the Vietnam War were yet to impact city life. Specialty shops and general stores stacked with goods catered to an emerging urban middle class. Photographic magazines, with their high-quality printing, enabled an output for niche commercial photographers to use their skills to sell products and services to their readers. Mekong Jewelry offered a luxurious cascade of pearl and gold chain necklaces and jewel-encrusted bracelets, topped with a boutique gift, to entice a buyer keen to cement a relationship—or to tie the knot. This advertisement was printed full page in the February 1966 edition of *Le Sangkum*.

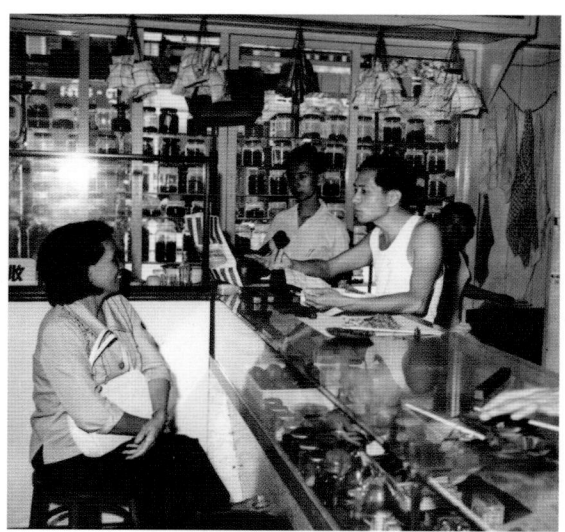

ABOVE AND TOP: **Interior views of Chinese shophouses.** Phnom Penh. Early 1960s. Photographer unknown. National Archives of Cambodia/Charles Meyer Collection, Paris.

RIGHT: **Cadeau de Joie Bijoux Mekong.** Phnom Penh. 1966. *Le Sangkum*, no. 2. Photographer unknown. Center for Khmer Studies Library, Siem Reap.

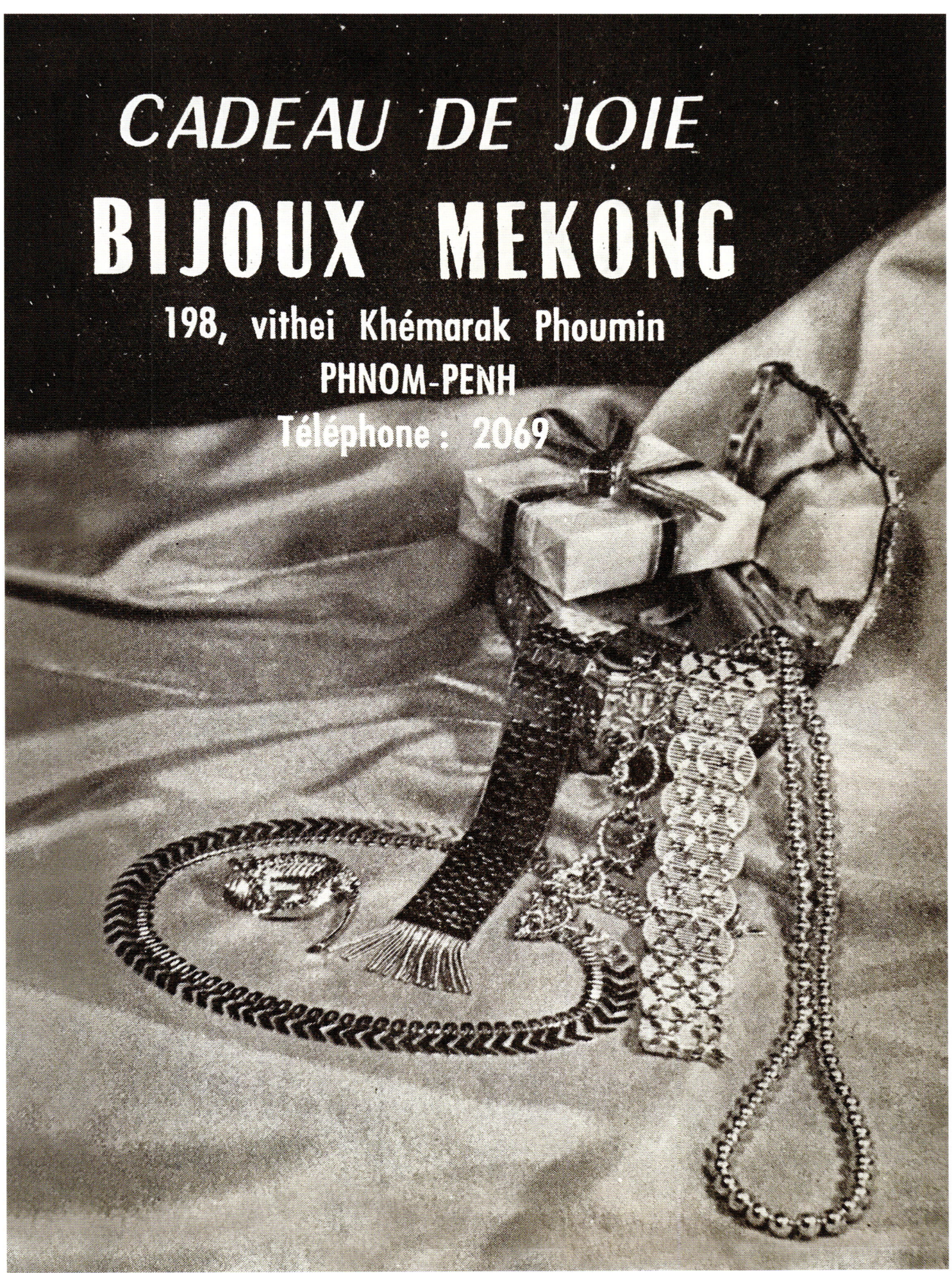

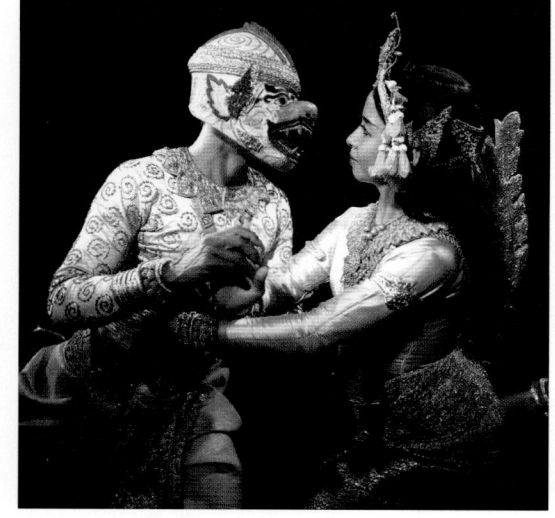

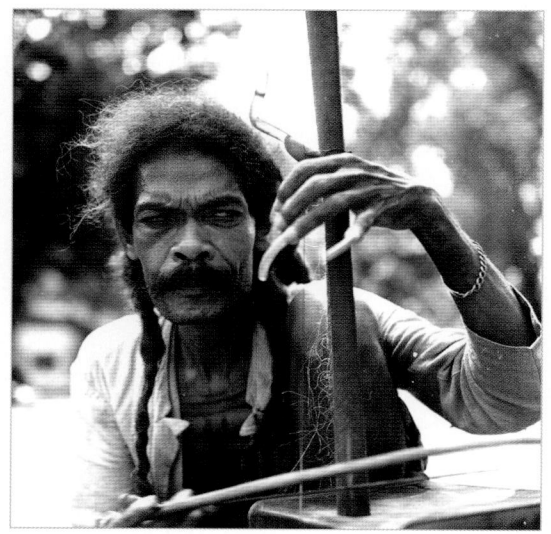

At the Request of the Prince

Raymond CHAUCHETIER (1920–2021) acquired his taste for Asia while working for the French press corps during the First Indochina War (1946–54). He chose a Rolleiflex camera for its robust construction to cope with a difficult environment. Returning to France at the end of the decade, he developed a reputation for intimate and natural photography of actors and directors behind the scenes of the French *nouvelle vague* cinematic movement. In 1967, Chauchetier was invited to Cambodia by Prince Sihanouk to take photographs for the tourism department. For two months he traveled the length and breadth of the country, shooting a dramatic spread of imagery, from aerial views of the capital to theatric shots of ballet performers and everyday characters on the streets. Strong contrast, with subtle mid-tones, identify his work. Sihanouk was delighted with the results, asking him to set up a school of photography. Unfortunately, Chauchetier could not commit. Soon after he finished the project, Sihanouk was deposed and most of Chauchetier's photographs were destroyed.

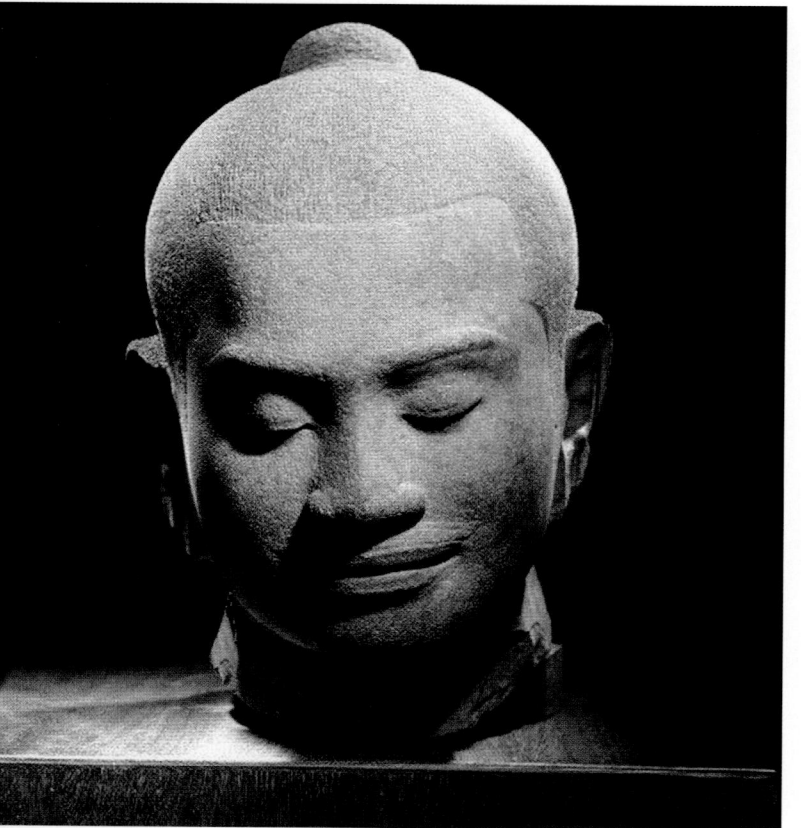

LEFT, FROM TOP: **Performers of the Reamker, Royal Ballet.** Phnom Penh. 1967.

Street musician. Location unknown. 1967.

Head of Jayavarman VII, National Museum. Phnom Penh. 1967.

Photographs: Raymond Chauchetier/James Hyman Gallery, London.

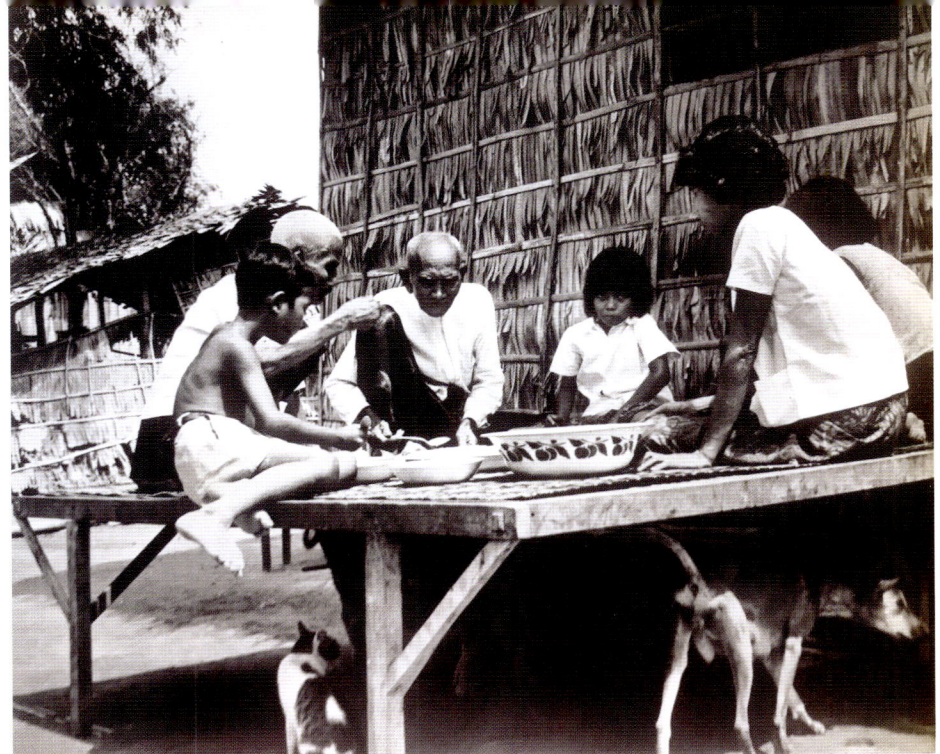
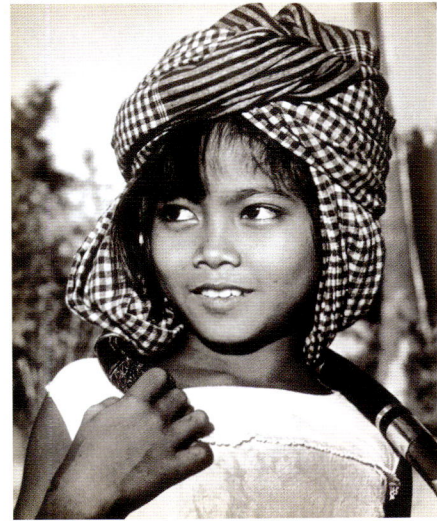

An Idealized Childhood

The "Children of the World" series of picture books took Francophone readers into the adventurous lives of children in foreign cultures. The Cambodian edition, *Sinoun La Petite Cambodgienne*, was created by Odile WERTHEIMER. Using photographs taken from a child's perspective, the book explored an idealized child's world that was becoming far removed from the realities of a country tumbling into war. It used black-and-white photographs, many of them cut out, with the pages often adorned with cerise and green shapes of leaves and traditional artifacts. This created a distinct graphic unity to the "look" of the book. The text was written in poetry and prose. Published in 1970 by Fernand Nathan, the book won the French Bologna Book Fair prize for graphic design in 1971.

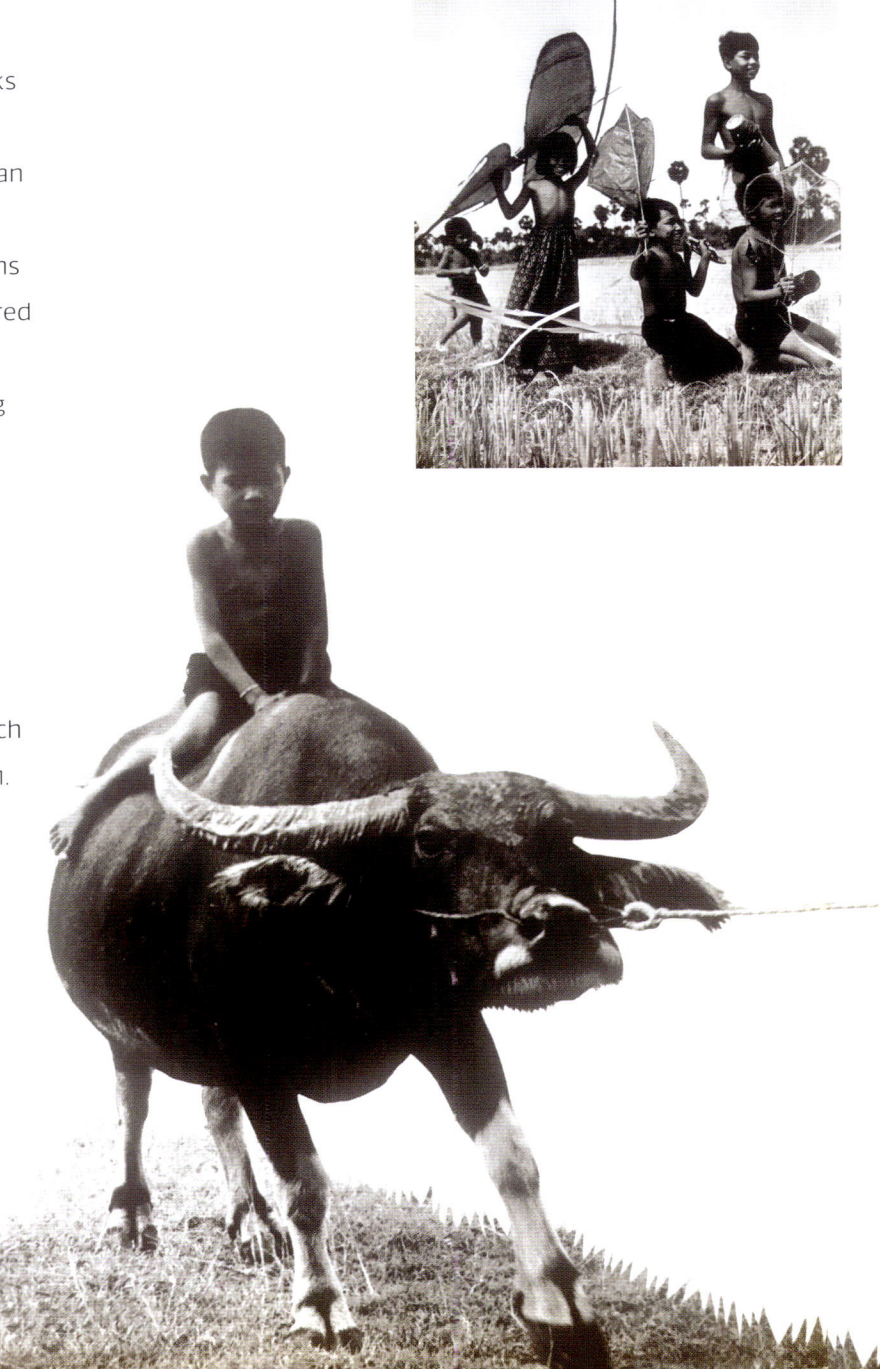

TOP LEFT, CLOCKWISE: **Sinoun's family sharing a meal.**

Portrait of Sinoun.

Flying kites in the dry rice fields.

Vandy riding his water buffalo.
(Cut-out photograph)

Photographs: Odile Wetheimer.
Various locations. 1968. Author's Collection.

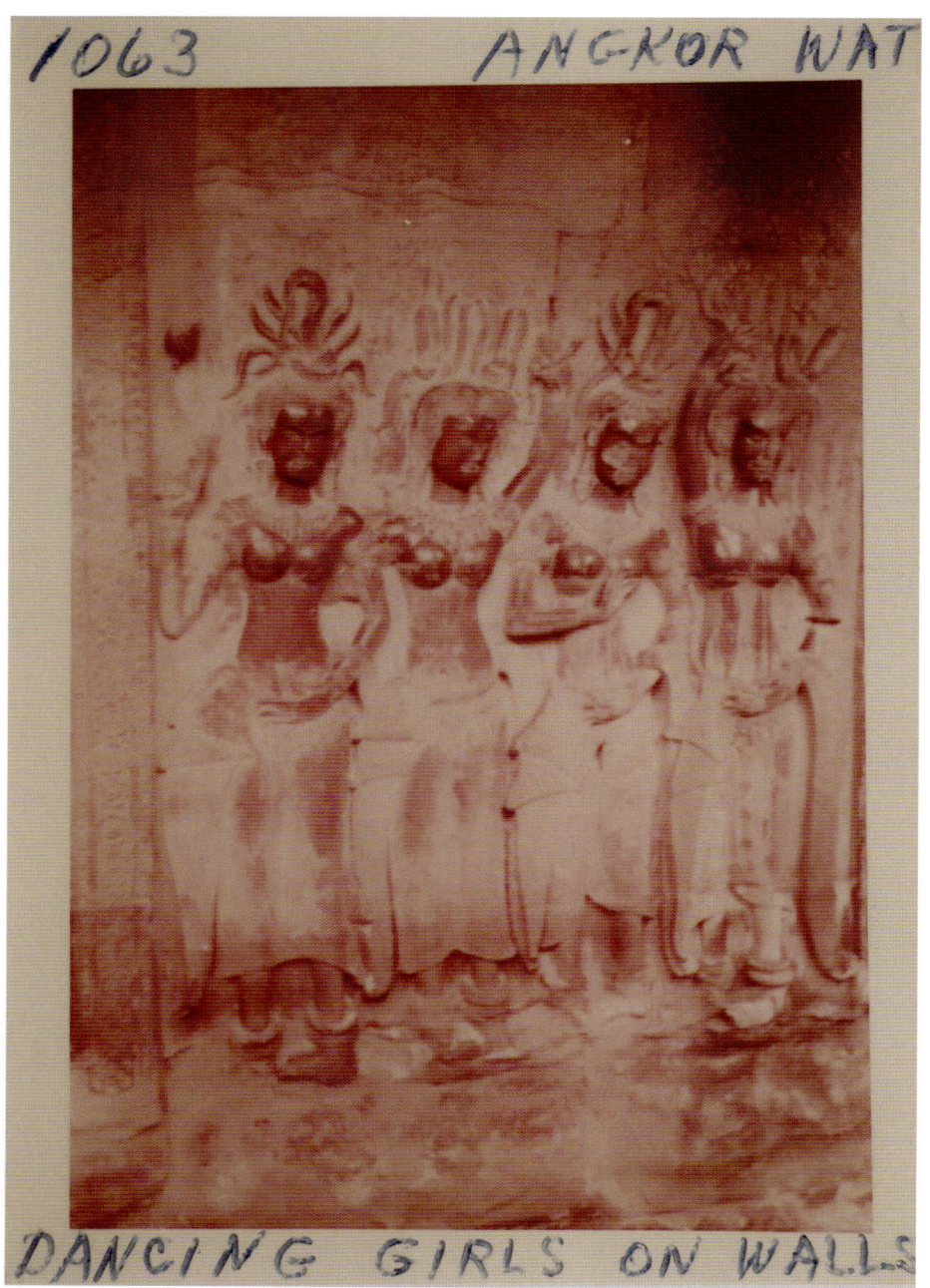

"1063 Angor Wat. Dancing Girls on Walls." Siem Reap. ca. 1960s. Photographer unknown. Author's Collection.

1063 Angkor Wat

The handwritten title on the margins of this faded color print suggest the owner had a potentially large collection; note the number "1063" at the top. Although there is nothing spectacular about this photograph, it is a worthy example of the medium in a more tactile age, before the dominance of digital photography in the twenty-first century. The act of visiting a site, taking a photograph and developing the image as a print, and then creating an index number for the image, inscribed in biro, gives this item its currency. The familiar subject matter—the celestial dancers carved on the stone walls of Angkorian monuments—remains a perennial favorite for generations of visitors.

The Festival of the Nine Emperor Gods

On the ninth lunar month of the Chinese calendar, the Nine Emperor Gods descend from heaven. They are the personification of the stars of the North Ursa Major constellation (the Big Dipper) who control the movement of the planets and, in turn, influence the passage of life for earthbound mortals. In a carnival-like atmosphere, the Phnom Penh devotees dressed in white and carried incense and candles as they paraded towards the river, supposedly the watery avenue for the gods to descend to earth. The gods then enter the bodies of the willing adherents, who fall into a trance and perform ritualized self-mutilation, piecing their cheeks and bodies with metal skewers and knives to absolve their sins. When this photograph was taken in the late 1960s, there were over 110,000 Chinese residents in Phnom Penh. The photograph may have been taken by Micheline Dullin as it has the characteristics of her hallmark style, dating it between 1958 and 1964.

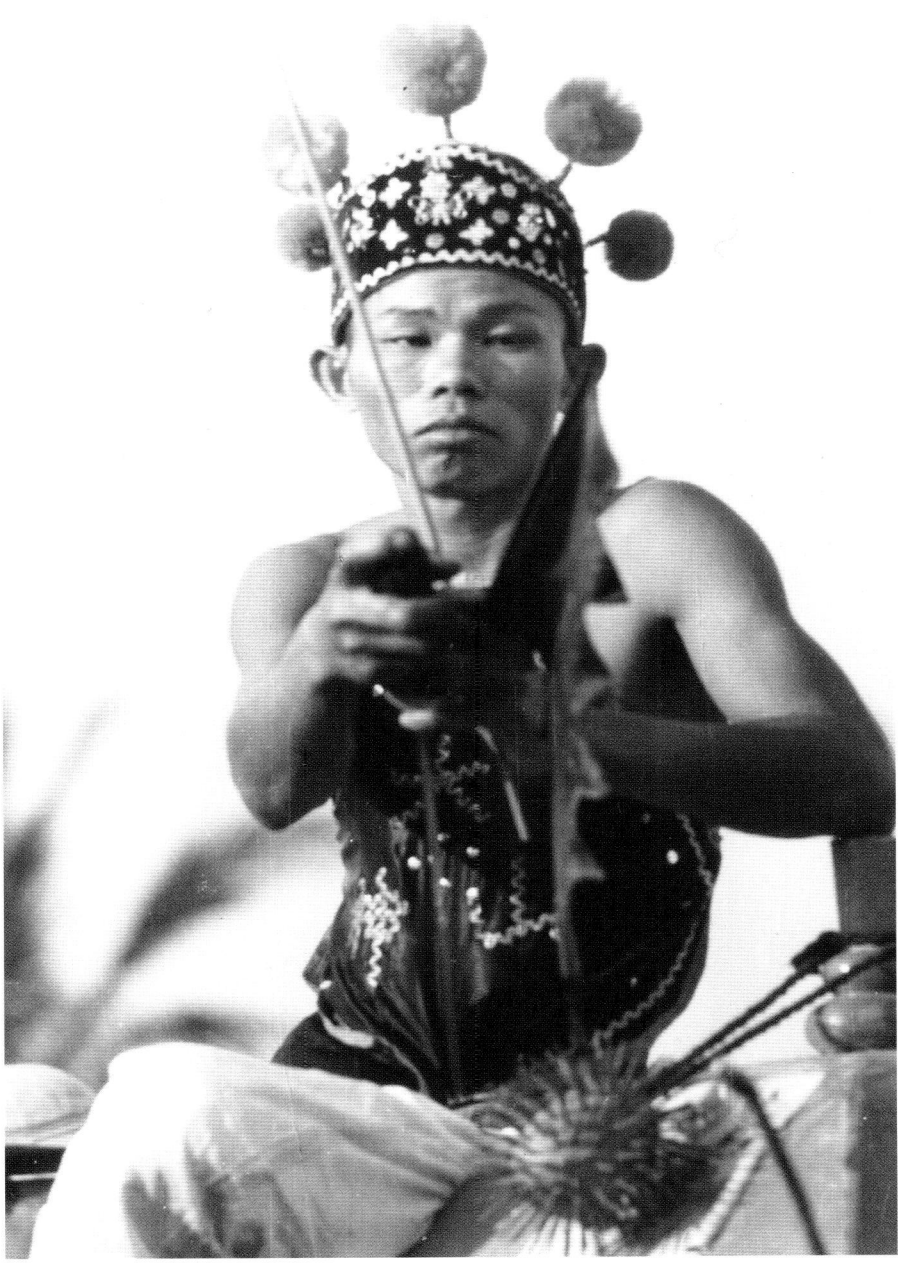

Young devotee at the Nine Emperor Gods Festival. Phnom Penh. ca. 1960. Probably Micheline Dullin. National Archives of Cambodia/Charles Meyer Collection, Paris.

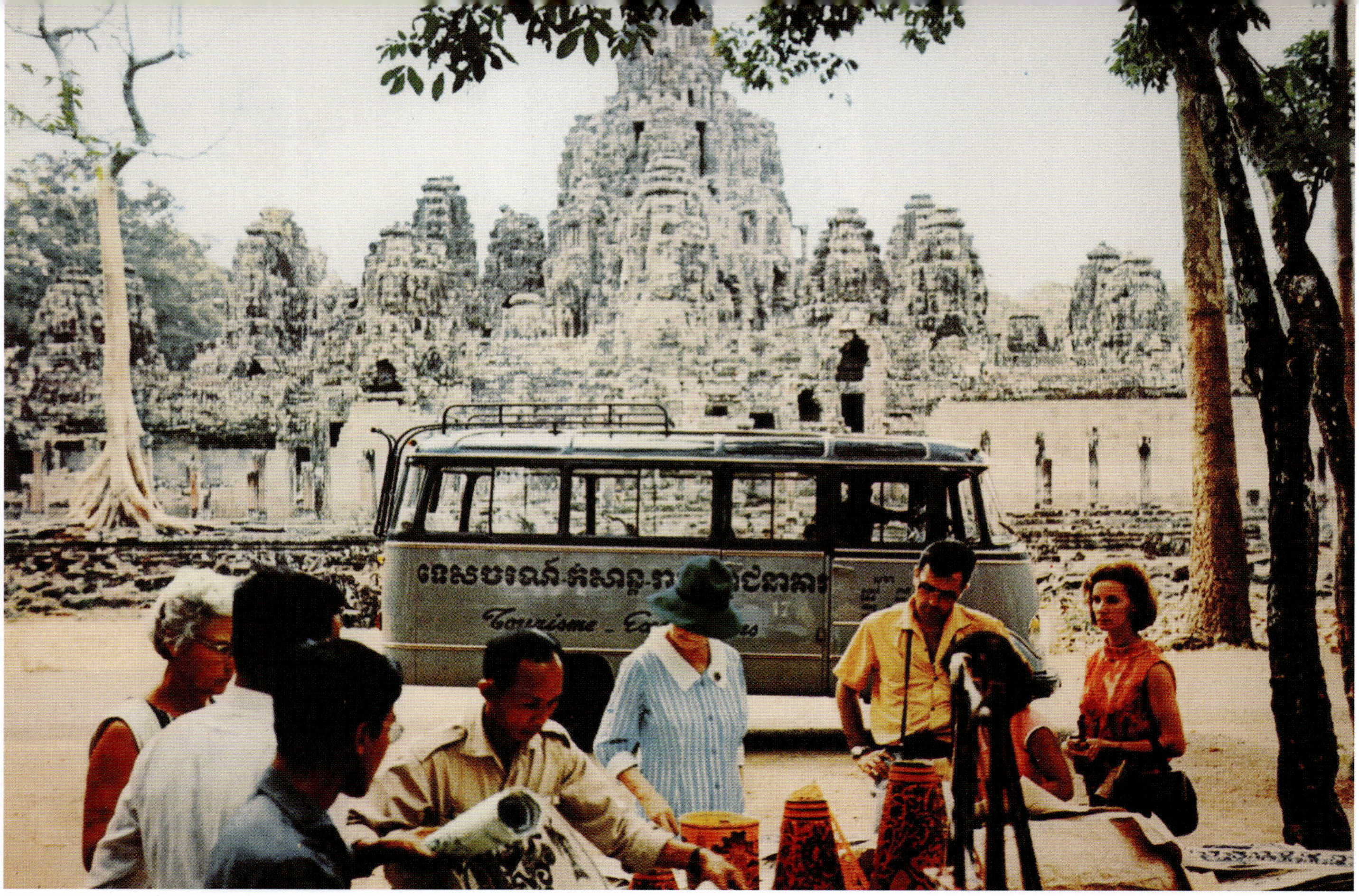

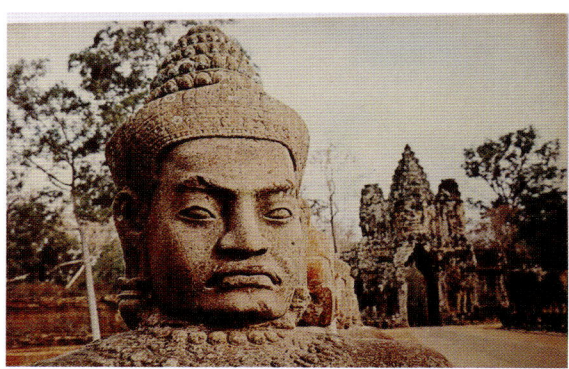

Postcards of the 1960s

The van carrying this tourist group around Siem Reap is a Mercedes Benz. These vehicles were new on the scene, imported during 1959 for the newly opened "Direction du Tourisme Khmer" in Phnom Penh. A *National Geographic* magazine article in which this same image appeared, identifies the production of the postcard at some time after 1960. Parked near the Bayon monument, the tourist group admire souvenirs of waxed paper lampshades and direct rubbings from the bas-reliefs on the monument. The partly obscured sign on the van's side, "Tourisme Excursions," suggests a small but sophisticated tourism infrastructure was developing in Cambodia at that time. Postcards continued their appeal as quick visual clues that tourists had reached their destination. The cargo-passenger liner SS *Cambodge* made its maiden voyage in 1953, and for the next sixteen years connected Marseille through the Suez Canal to Southeast Asian ports and beyond.

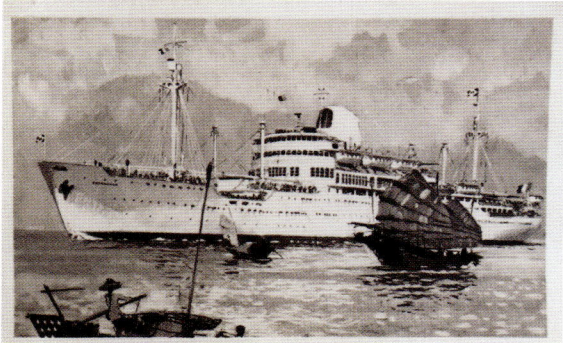

FROM TOP: **Tourists at the Bayon.** Postcard. After 1960. Darryl Collins Collection, Siem Reap.

Demon's head, south gate causeway, Angkor Thom. Postcard. ca. 1965. Darryl Collins Collection, Siem Reap.

The SS *Cambodge*. Compagnie des Messageries Maritimes. Postcard. After 1953. Author's Collection.

The Pottery of Kompong Chhnang

Chhnan, meaning "cooking vessel" in Khmer, is integrated into the culture and identity of Kompong Chhnang. The pottery is produced in two villages, Chrey Bak and Srae Thmei, where the locals take advantage of the smooth, red clay deposits. For generations, families living in these two communities have reproduced a range of essential rounded pots, cooking stoves, and jars. While the men prepare the clay, pot-making is a skill allotted to women, where they use a wooden paddle to form the clay into the desired shape. After open firing, itinerant hawkers load the pots onto bullock carts, buffer the pots with rice straw, then circumnavigate the great Tonlé Sap, selling pots to villagers along the way.

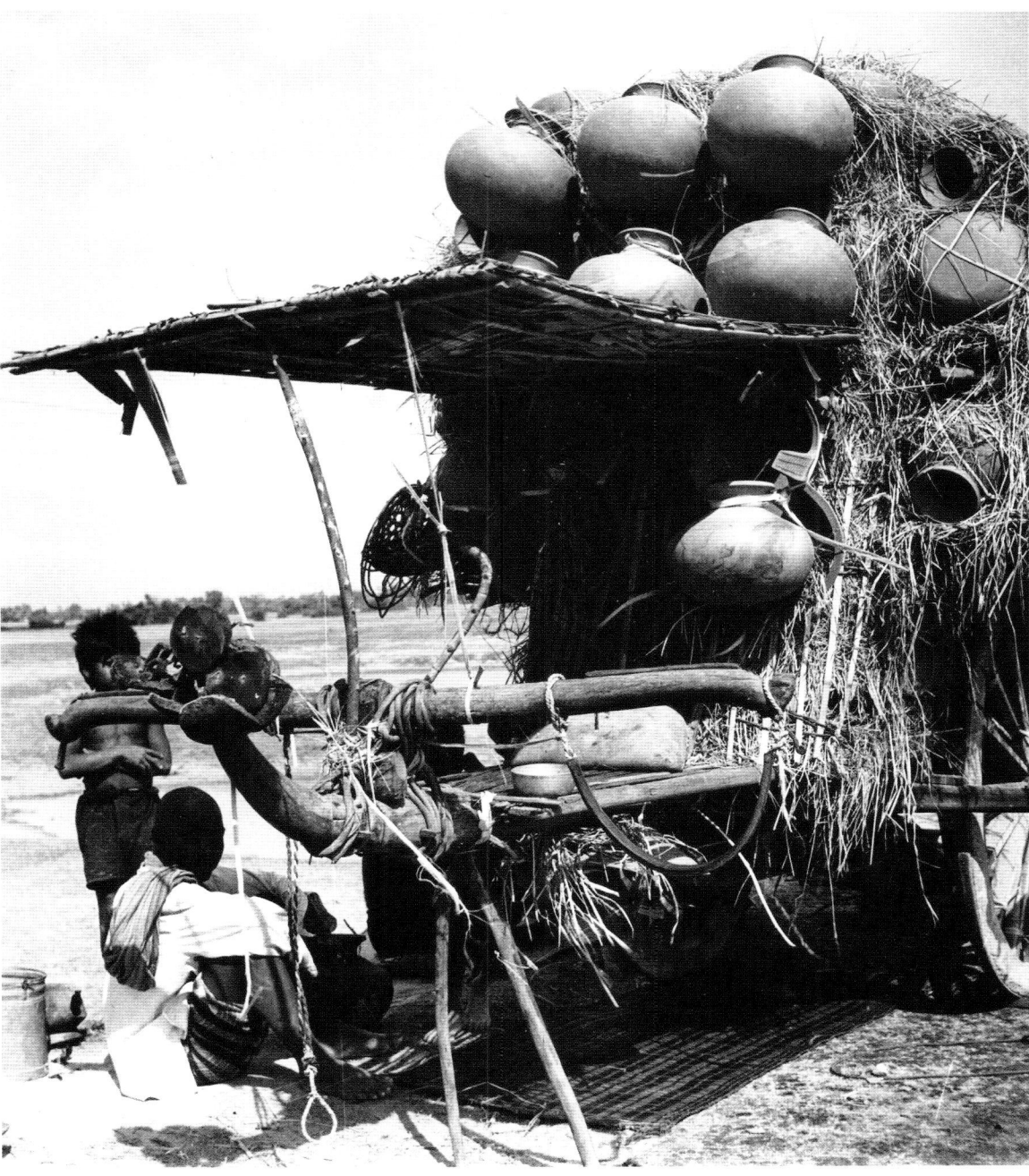

Bullock cart loaded with pottery.
Kompong Chhnang. ca. 1965. Micheline Dullin. Micheline Dullin Archive, Paris.

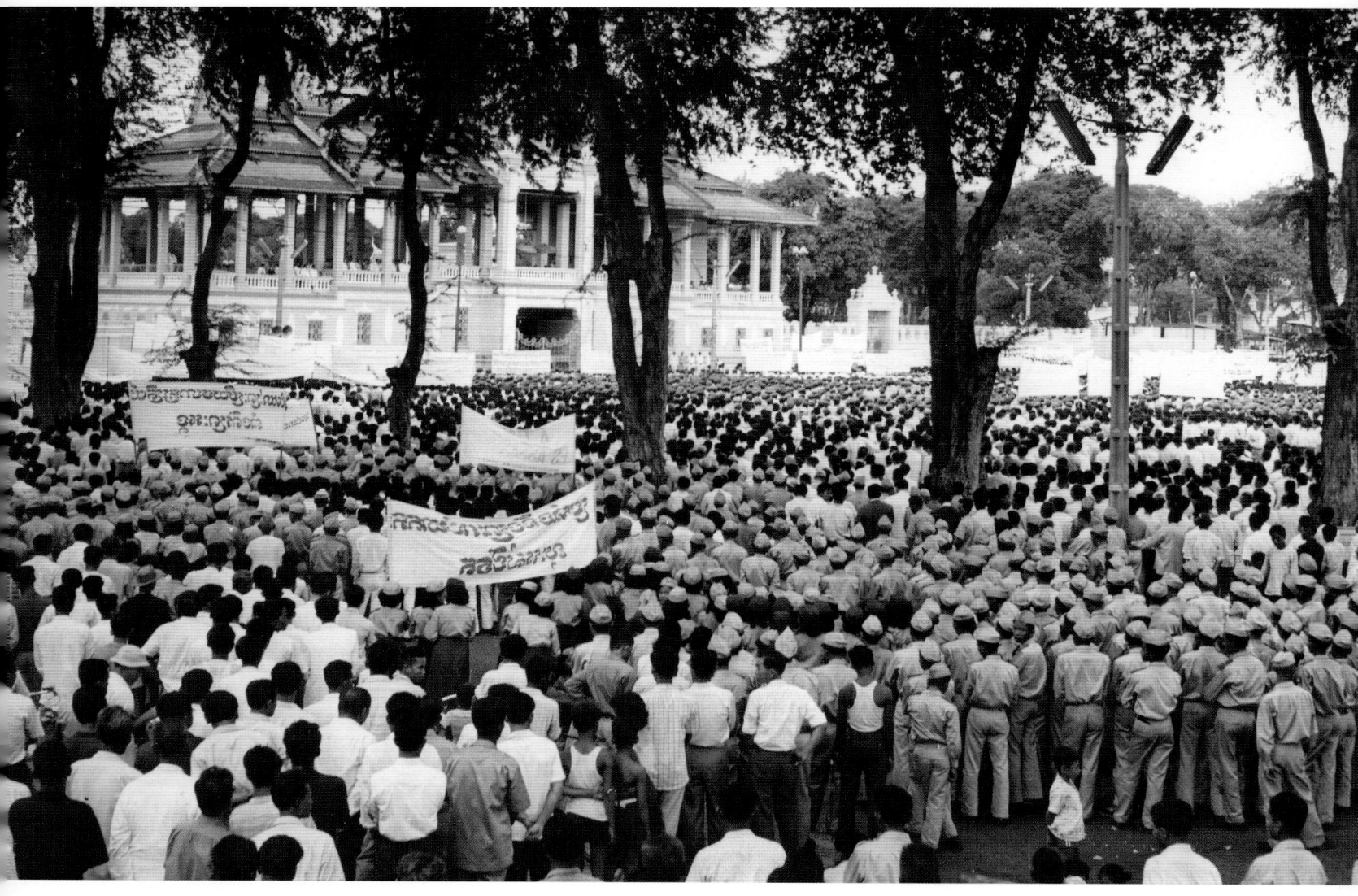

The Sangkum's Legacy

By the late 1960s, Cambodia's economy had stagnated. While the hullabaloo of pop music, watching movies, and enjoying weekend holidays at the seaside for a few thousand well-off urban families was infectious, it could not mask the overall discontent and privation of Cambodia's rural and urban poor, nor the pervasive corruption endemic in successive governments. Sihanouk attempted to contain the situation by supporting, dividing, or dismissing his ministers, but with little effect. During the Sangkum's fifteen years in power, the position of prime minister rotated twenty-two times. This was a period of unprecedented political agitation and participation, public and student rallies, and demonstrations. Despite these difficulties, multiple elections and referenda continued to be held, no matter how dubious their outcomes.

ABOVE: **A pro-monarchist rally in front of the Royal Palace.** The banner reads "The people will protect the king." Phnom Penh. ca. 1967. Photographer unknown.

OPPOSITE TOP LEFT, CLOCKWISE: **Faces in a political rally.** Possibly Pochetong Airport, Phnom Penh. 1960s.

Ford truck as a float at a political rally. Location unknown. 1960s.

Pro-Sihanouk rally. The banner reads "Support the new policy of Samdech Ouv to reform the national economy and finance." Kompong Svay district, Kompong Thom. ca. 1963–64.

Political rally on Monivong Boulevard. Phnom Penh. Late 1960s.

Casting their votes. Location unknown. 1960s.

Political rally. Location unknown. 1960s.

Source: National Archives of Cambodia/Charles Meyer Collection, Paris.

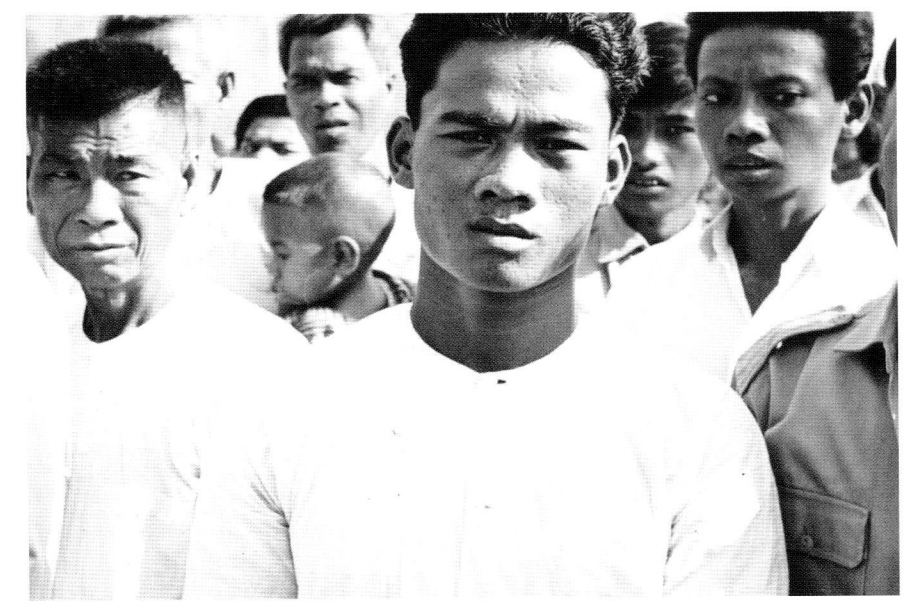
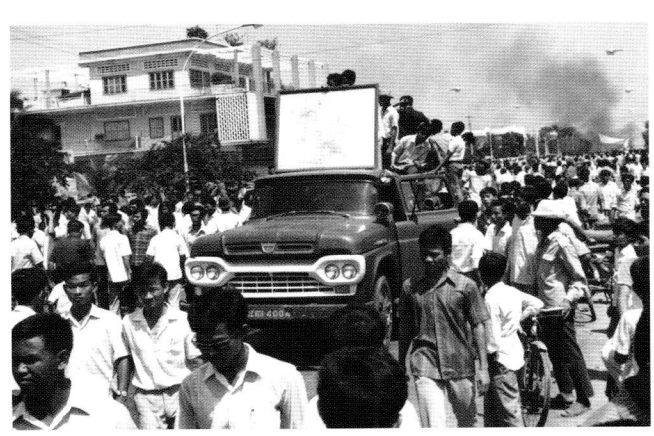
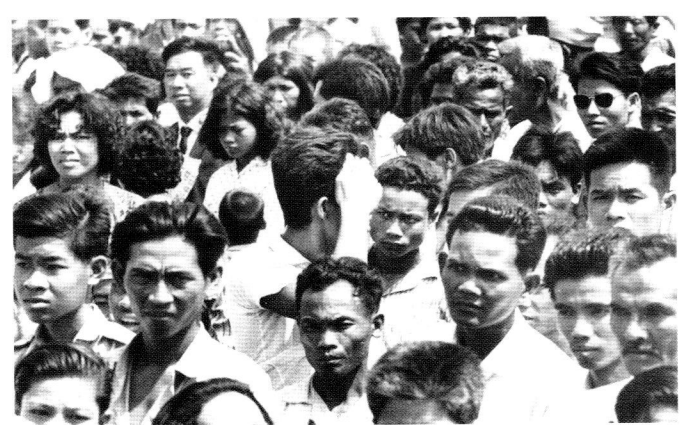
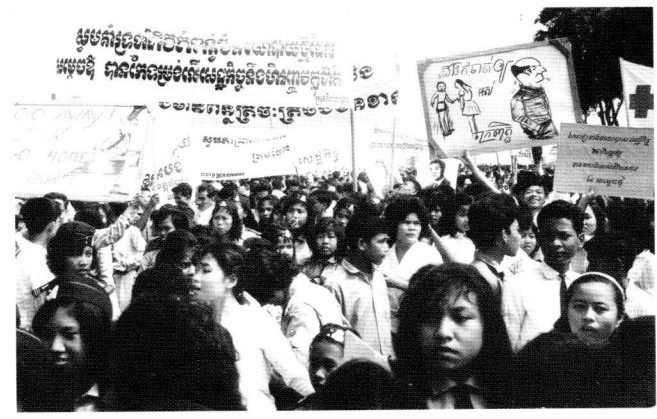
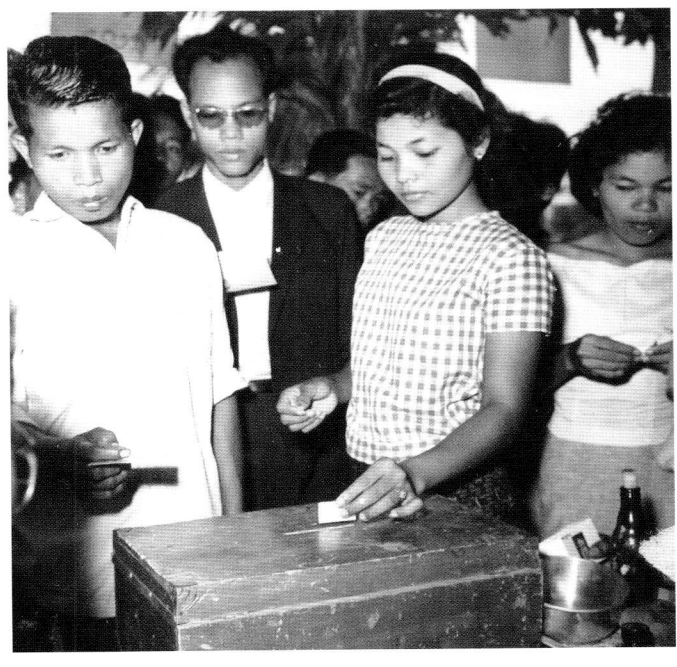
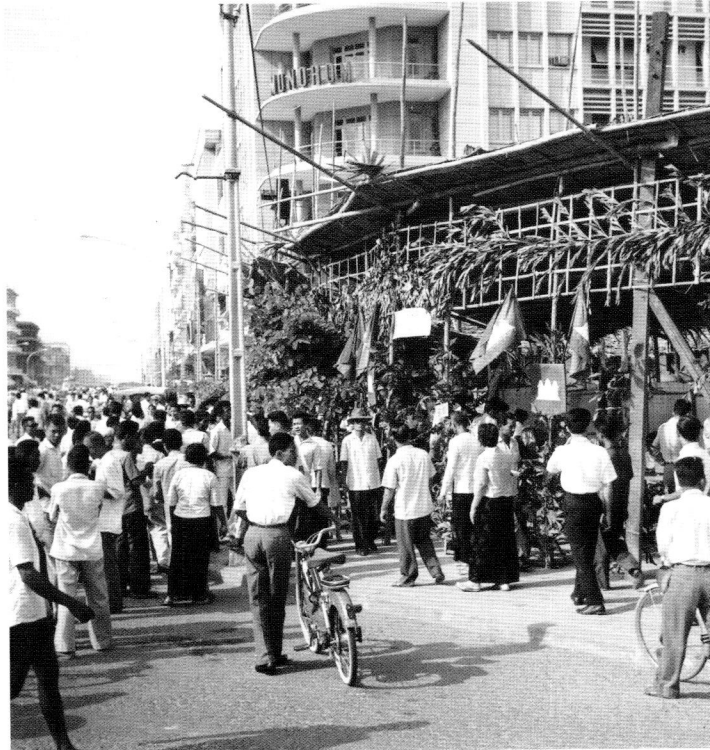

1970–1975
Lon Nol's Khmer Republic

On March 18, 1970, while Sihanouk was overseas, the conservative Prince Sirik Matak (1914–75) orchestrated a parliamentary coup. The National Assembly voted in General Lon Nol (1913–85) as prime minister. The monarchy was abolished. It was a momentous occasion. In one thousand years of Khmer history, this was the first republic.

The faltering economy was refortified with a massive influx of American financial and military aid. Cambodian society was put on a war footing. Recruitment drives saw thousands of enthusiastic young volunteers swell the army's ranks. Major military offences against the communist intruders were launched. They were a disaster. Inefficiency, corruption, and poor training were no match for seasoned guerrilla forces. Within a year, the communists had control of 80 percent of the countryside. Meanwhile, Sihanouk had fled to China, a key political and military supporter of the guerrilla movement. Photojournalists who were covering the Vietnam War flew into the country, many using the robust Japanese Nikon F series of cameras to record the conflict. When they came over to the Cambodian "sideshow," they found a disorganized army command that had little time to help in the management of itineraries for international war correspondents. The reporters turned to literate young Cambodians to act as field assistants, drivers, and local photojournalists. Ironically, Cambodian photographers finally won recognition for their work. Previously they had been nameless assistants seen at the edge of colonial photography or as uncredited photographers in Sihanouk's magazines. Professionals like Chhor Vuthi (d. 1975?), Dith Pran (1942–2008), and Sou Vichith (d. 1975?) worked alongside foreign journalists covering a chaotic, cruel war. Republican-sponsored magazines often printed surprisingly honest stories of the war's devastation. In April 1972, the *Khmer Republic Monthly Illustrated Magazine* published a ten-page photo essay by Tea Kim Heang (d. 1975?) documenting the destruction of Phnom Penh's Tul Kork district by incoming Khmer Rouge rockets. He was the first Cambodian photographer ever to be credited in print. As the war continued, Phnom Penh's 400,000 population swelled to over two million refugees. The beleaguered capital became the lens of a savage and inhumane conflict. Younger and younger recruits were called into service. It became a child-fight-child war. Photographers like Kouy Sarun (d. 1977?) and Thong Veasna (d. 1975?) covered the descent. Many foreigner correspondents and photojournalists disappeared or were killed during the brief five years of the republic's life. In April 1975, the city's defences collapsed. "Operation Eagle Pull" was launched by American forces to frantically evacuate diplomatic and civilian personnel and their Cambodian colleagues. Then all went eerily quiet. A few days later, after five years of war and over half a million deaths, an army of teenage soldiers emerged from the countryside. They were the Khmer Rouge. After they took control of the city, almost all Cambodians who had worked in journalism disappeared, presumed murdered. Dith Pran was a rare survivor.

Hanuman and the buffalo demon.
Independence Park, Phnom Penh. ca. 1974.
Colin Grafton.

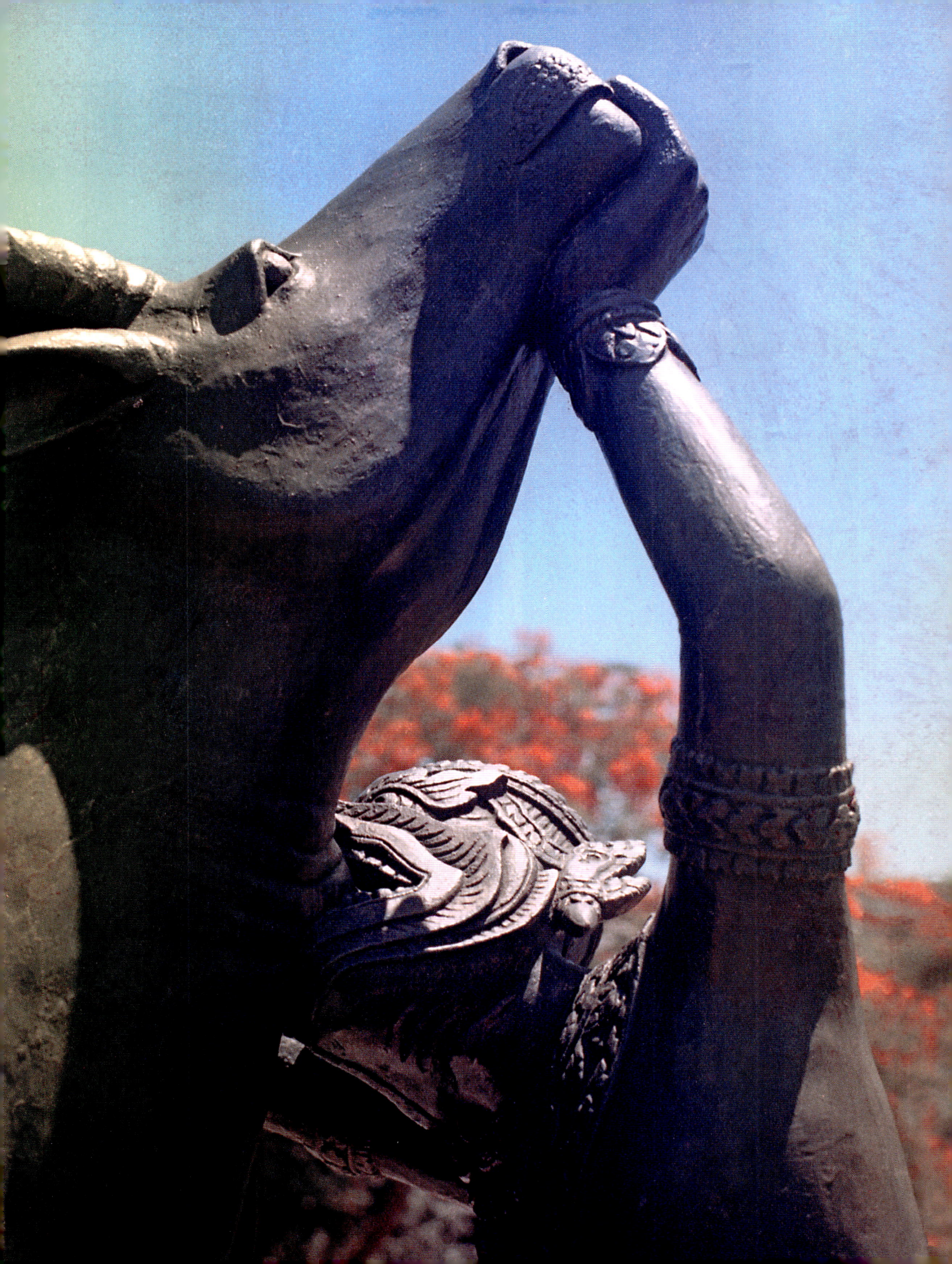

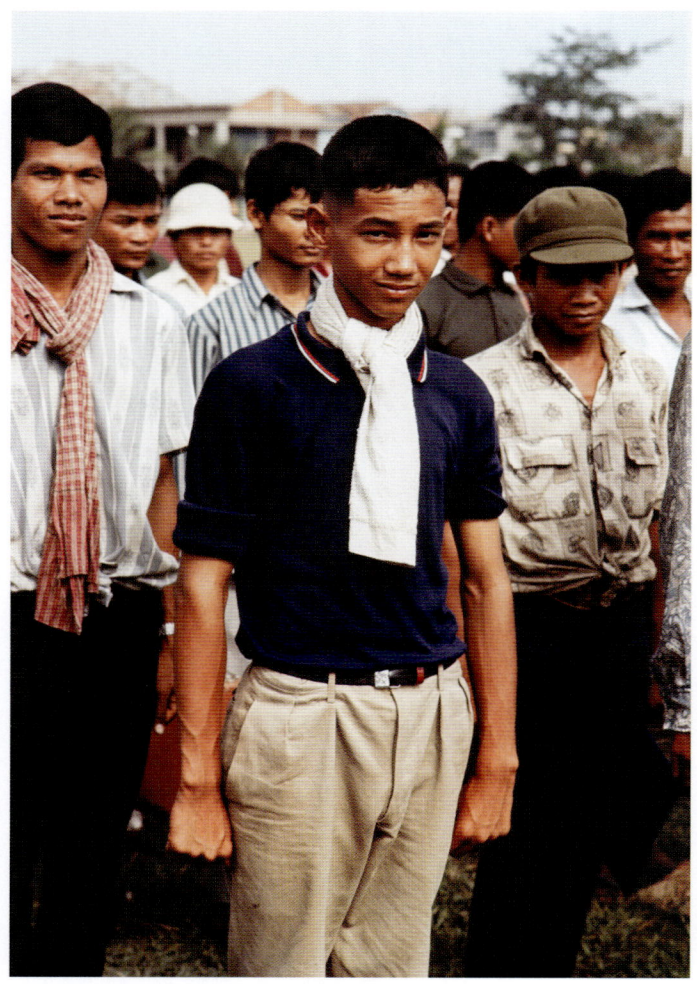
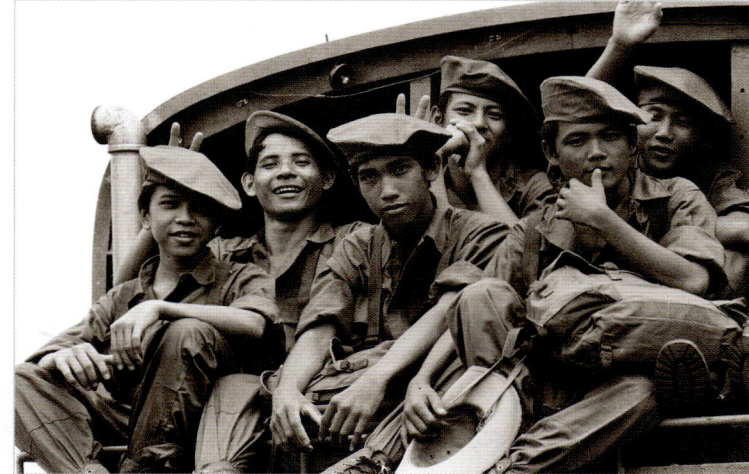
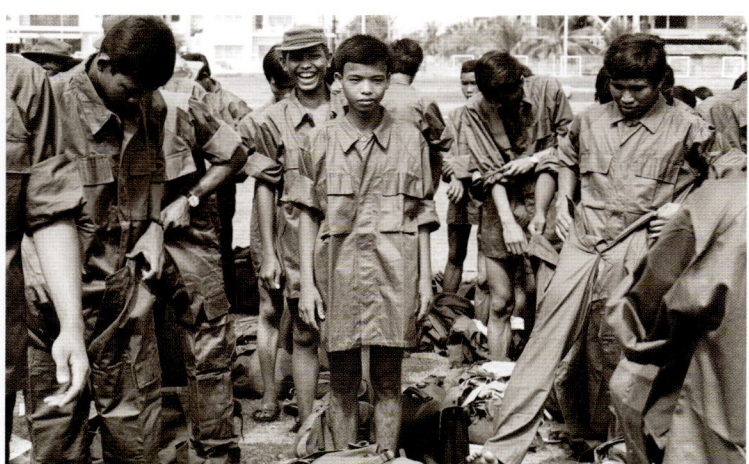

The Recruitment Drive

LEFT, CLOCKWISE: **Volunteers in civilian clothes.** Phnom Penh. 1970.

Volunteers being trucked to barracks. Phnom Penh. 1970.

Volunteers trying on US-provided uniforms. Phnom Penh. 1970.

Photographs: Gilles Caron.

Days after Lon Nol's coup in 1970, French photographer Gilles CARON (1939–70) photographed these eager volunteers. In April, Operation "Chenla 1" was launched by the renamed Republican Army to retake from the communists the vast rice plains in the northwest of Cambodia. It was strategically ineffective but trumpeted as a great success by the republican-controlled media. Operation "Chenla 2," launched the following year, was a disaster. The government forces suffered severe casualties and equipment loss. Vast swathes of eastern and northwestern Cambodia were overrun by the communists. Caron was in the republic for only two weeks when he disappeared along with reporter Guy Hannoteaux and lawyer Michel Visot as they ventured into the battle zone to the east of Phnom Penh. Over fifteen other journalists and photographers disappeared or were killed in combat during these early tumultuous weeks.

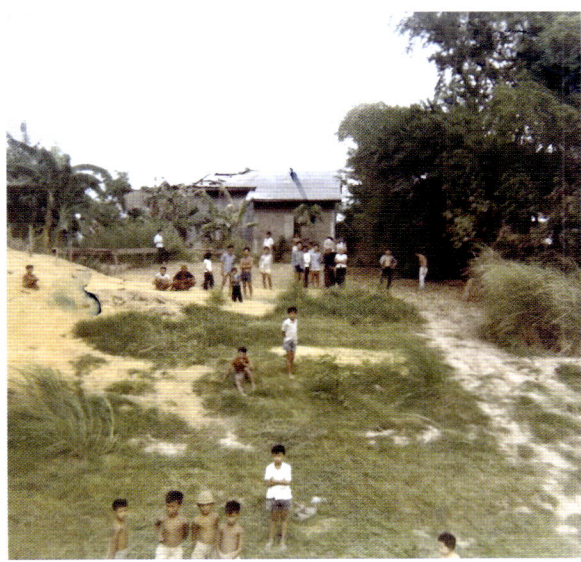
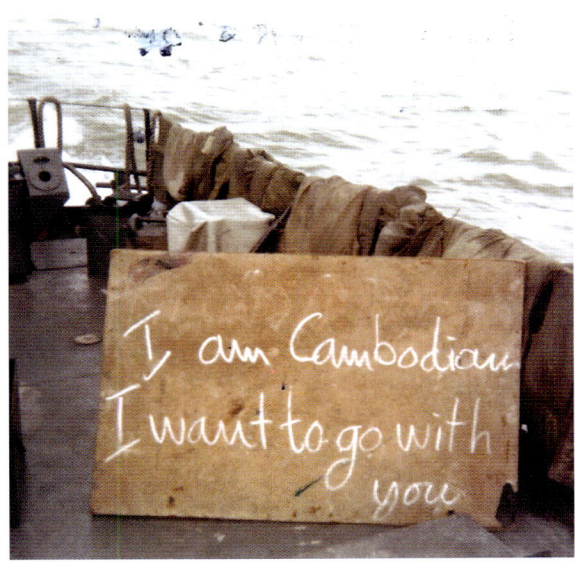

"I want to go with you."

In May 1970, US Naval officer "Jack" Edwin SPRATT was a gunner on a patrol boat squadron that was defending the Mekong River, a strategic supply route from Saigon to the besieged capital of Phnom Penh. On May 10, as the boats were passing through Prey Veng, he saw a young man on the riverbank holding a handwritten SOS sign. It was Chim Senyint, who was in imminent danger of being arrested and executed by Khmer Rouge infiltrators in his home village. Local informants had told the communists of Chim's recent travels to Phnom Penh, where he had participated in an anti-Vietnamese student demonstration. The patrol boat slowed, then circled back. Chim jumped into the swirling muddy river. As he clambered on board seeking refuge, he offered, with his trilingual skills, to become an interpreter. He was a lucky young man as he had been studying at the Beng Trabek High School, the only school in the capital that taught both English and French. In 2014, in the United States, Commander Spratt gave these photographs to Chim Senyint to commemorate his serendipitous swim to safety.

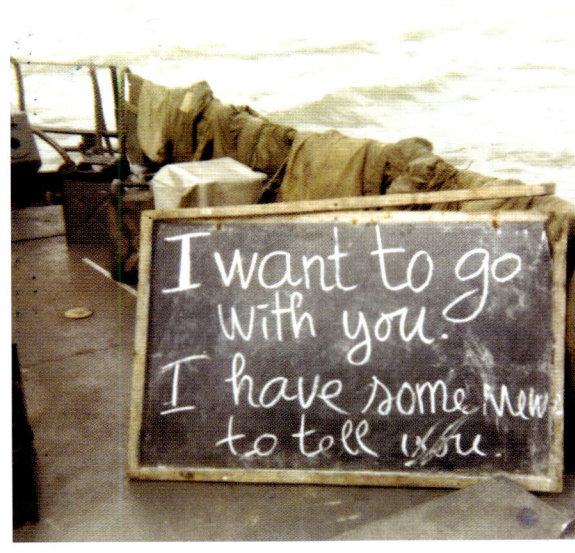
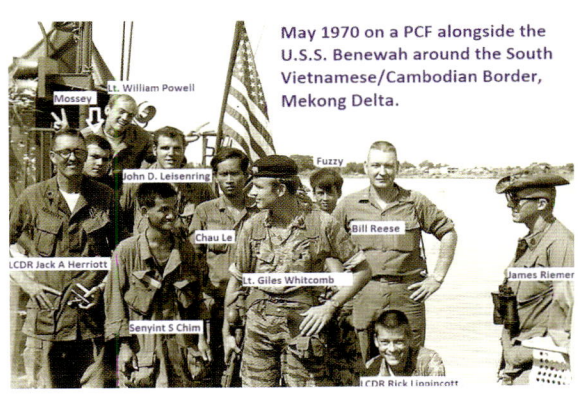

TOP LEFT, CLOCKWISE: **Riverbank from where Chim Senyint swam to the patrol boat.** Peam Chor village, Prey Veng. 1970.

"I am Cambodian. I want to go with you." Prey Veng. 1970.

"I want to go with you. I have some news to tell you." Prey Veng. 1970.

Chim Senyint and the crew of PBF 56. Viet-Khmer border. 1970.

Photographs: "Jack" Edwin Spratt.

The Looted Photograph

On September 4, 1970, a republican heavy machine gunner and his bearer struggle with their equipment while trying to set up their roadside position near Srang, 30 miles (48 km) southwest of Phnom Penh. The framed photograph was looted from a nearby home. Images of classic Chinese landscapes were popular wedding gifts within the Chinese community, and the last four characters on the left-hand side—新婚之喜 ("Congratulatory gift to the Newlywed")—confirms this. The upturned eaves and lakeside view suggest Suzhou or Fuzhou, implying the home province of the receiver. In the late 1960s, Ghislain BELLORGET covered the Vietnam War as a freelancer out of Saigon before moving to Phnom Penh to cover Cambodia's conflict.

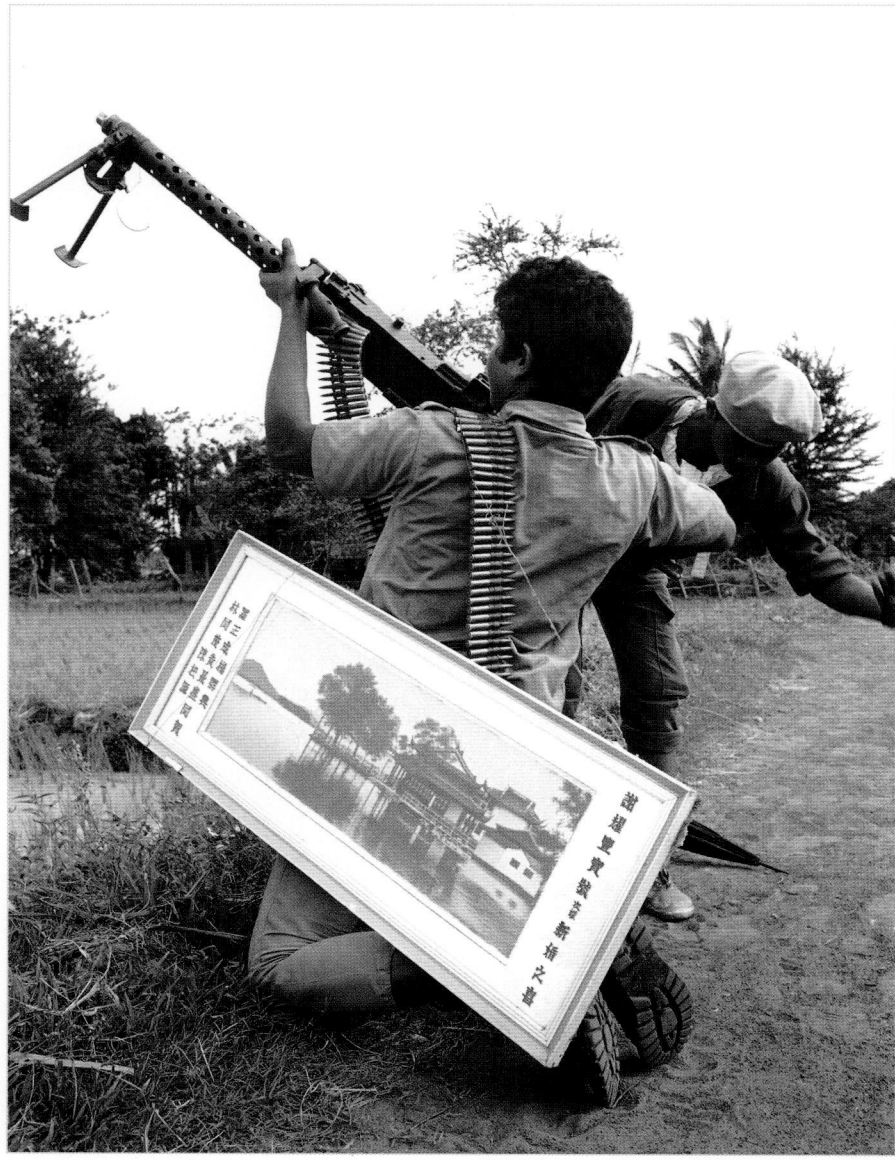

The looted photograph. Southwest of Phnom Penh. 1970. Ghislan Bellorget/Associated Press.

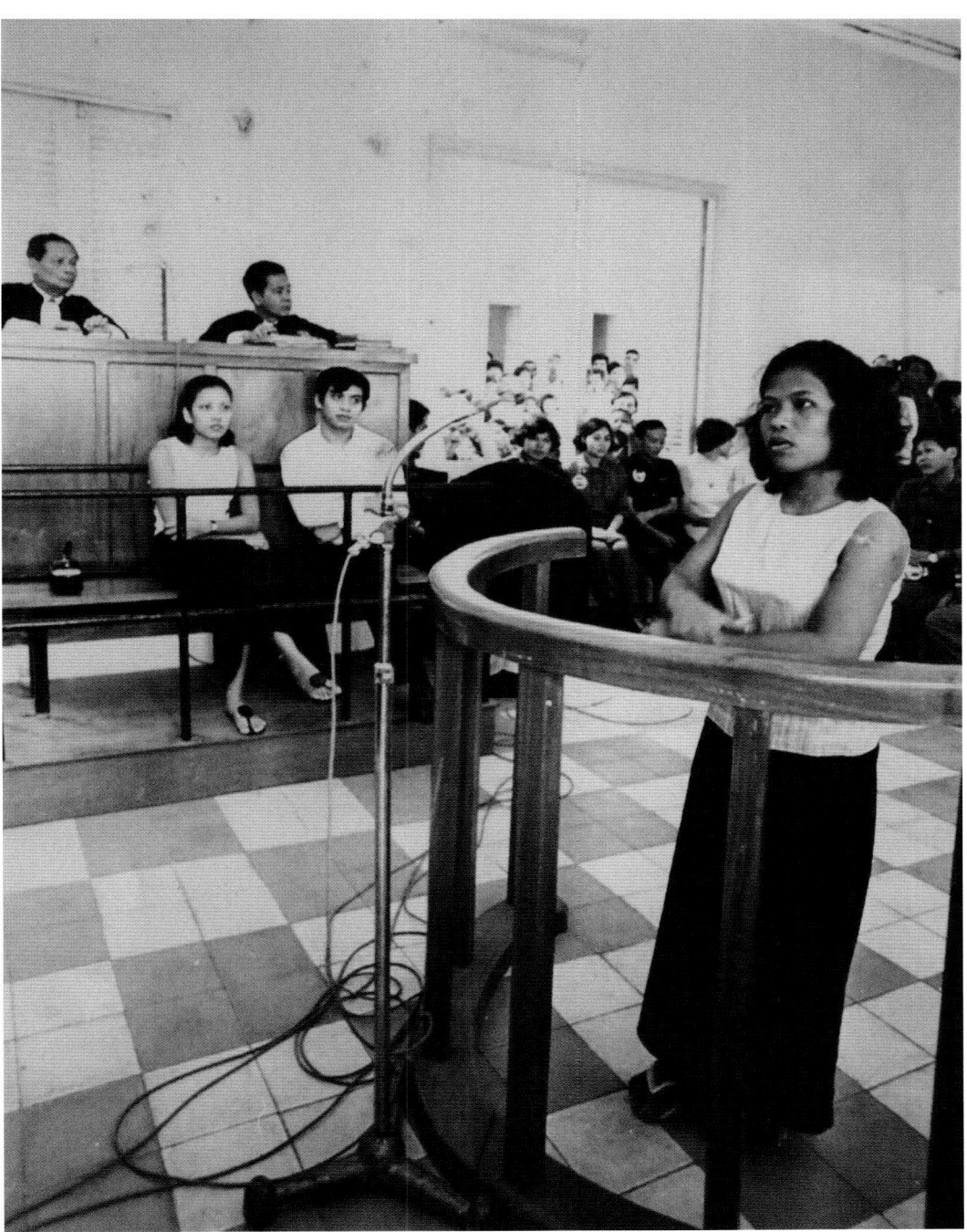

The trial of Prince Naradipo. Phnom Penh. 1971. Ghislan Bellorget/ Associated Press. Author's Collection.

The Trial for Treason

A maid from the Royal Palace testifies at the treason trial of Sihanouk's son, Prince Naradipo (seated background second from left). Naradipo's previous education at Peking University, under the personal supervision of former Chinese Premier Zhou En-lai, and his fluency in Chinese, would have been ample reason for the new Lon Nol regime to have him arrested after the coup against his father. He was sentenced to five years hard labor, but in 1973 was exiled to China. When Lon Nol's republic was defeated by the Khmer Rouge in April 1975, Prince Naradipo returned to Cambodia with his father. It was a fateful move. He was arrested by the Khmer Rouge and disappeared, presumed killed, in the 1976–77 dry season.

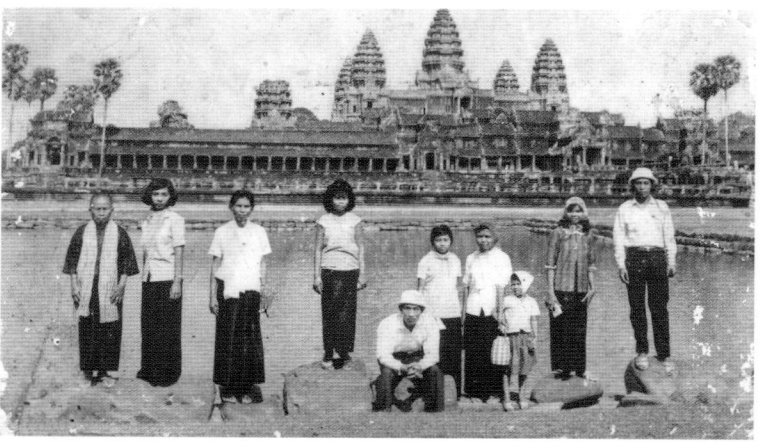
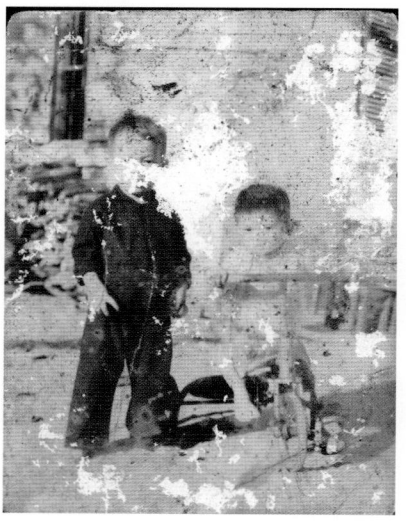
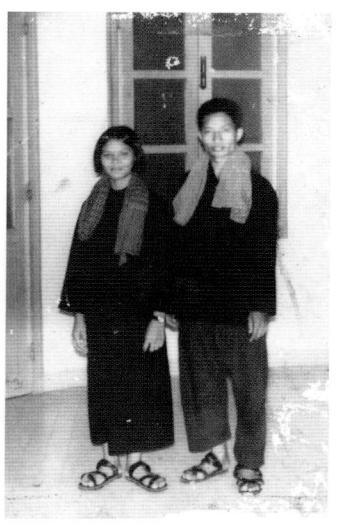
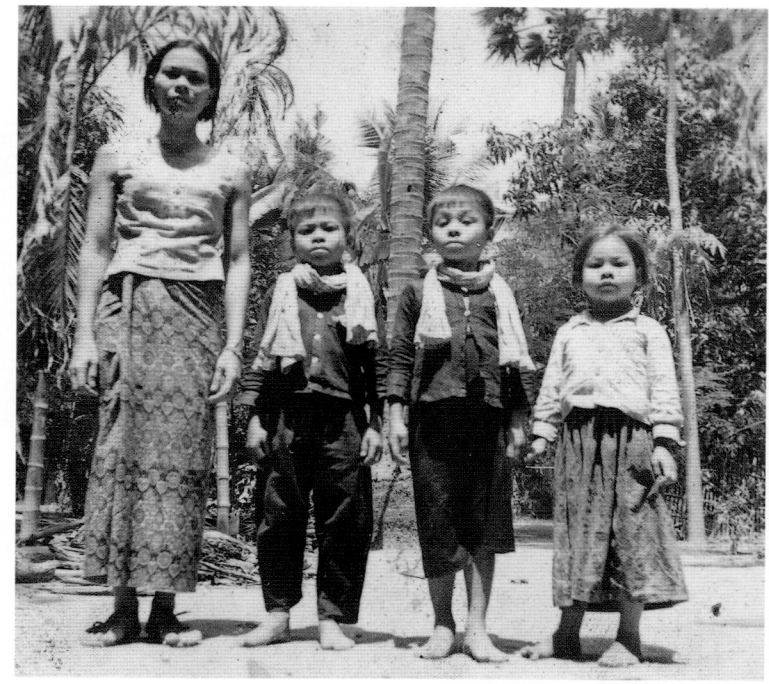

TOP LEFT, CLOCKWISE: **Ban Savoeun's extended family at Angkor Wat.** Siem Reap Province. 1960.

Ban Savoeun, factory worker, and three of her children: Ek Chandy, Ek Chanda, and Ek Phornny. Kang Meas, Kampong Cham Province. ca. 1975.

Ban Savoeun's sister Ban Saran (aka Lin) and her husband Ol. Location unknown. ca. 1975.

Ban Savoeun's son Ek Sithy and niece Srei Nakk. Kratie Province. ca. 1978.

Source: Stilled Lives Project/ Documentation Center of Cambodia (DC-Cam). Photographers unknown.

Ban Savoeun's Family Photographs

Angkar, the Khmer Rouge's political arm, was an opaque organization that nevertheless implemented complete control over all aspects of people's daily lives. There are remarkable instances, however, where small caches of family photographs have managed to evade the regime's machinery of surveillance, confiscation, and destruction. They provide insights into changing family fortunes across decades of upheaval. Over an eighteen-year period, Ban Savoeun's collection of photographs records moments from a family holiday at Angkor Wat in 1960 (top left), through to when their Kampong Cham Province was overrun by the Khmer Rouge in 1975 (note the change in her sister's and husband-in-law's clothing in the later photographs). Considered by the Khmer Rouge a "base family"—coming from original farming stock—would have helped the family survive. Four years into the life of Democratic Kampuchea, Sovoeun was fortunate to have a photographer capture an image of her son and niece.

Dancing Ting Mong Puppets

Every year in Cambodia, Buddhist temples host the Bon Phka ceremony aimed at soliciting donations from the local community in order to build a local *wat* or repair village infrastructure. At the front of the land reserved for the *wat*, 10-ft (3-m)-high female and male *ting mong* puppets would bounce in ungainly sways and bobs to entertain the crowds, accompanied by the noisy drumming of a *chhay yam* band. Related to farmers' scarecrows, many Khmer youngsters were frightened by these large and fearful puppets. Traditionally, each puppet has a giant papier mâché head mounted on a woven bamboo body wrapped with paper or fabric. In November 1972, the *Khmer Republic Monthly Illustrated Magazine* published a double-page spread of color photographs simply titled "Le Cambodge en Images," which included this uncredited photograph.

Soldier-musicians participating in their local Bon Phka ceremony. Location and photographer unknown. *Khmer Republic Monthly Illustrated Magazine*, November 1972. Center for Khmer Studies Library, Siem Reap.

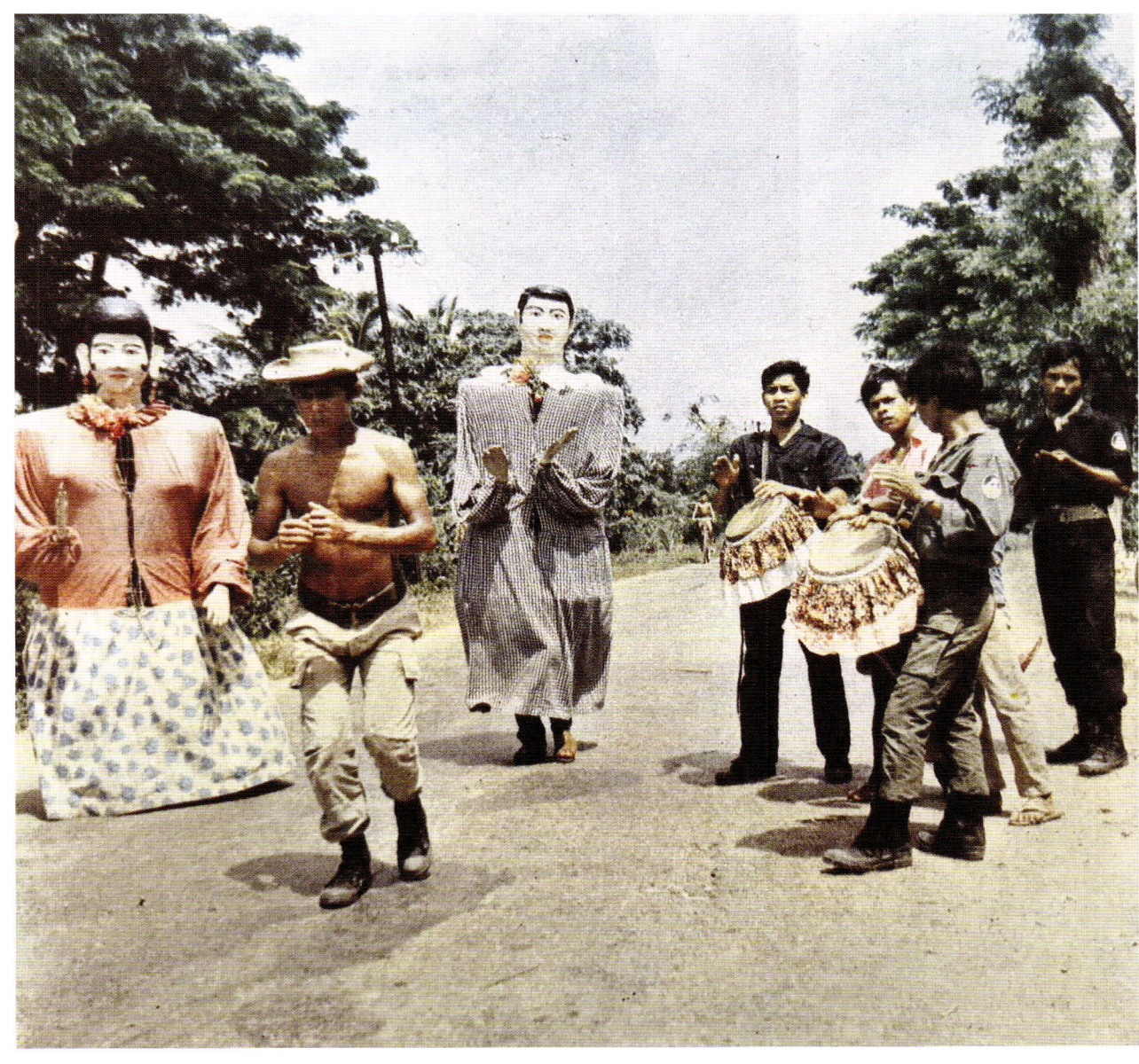

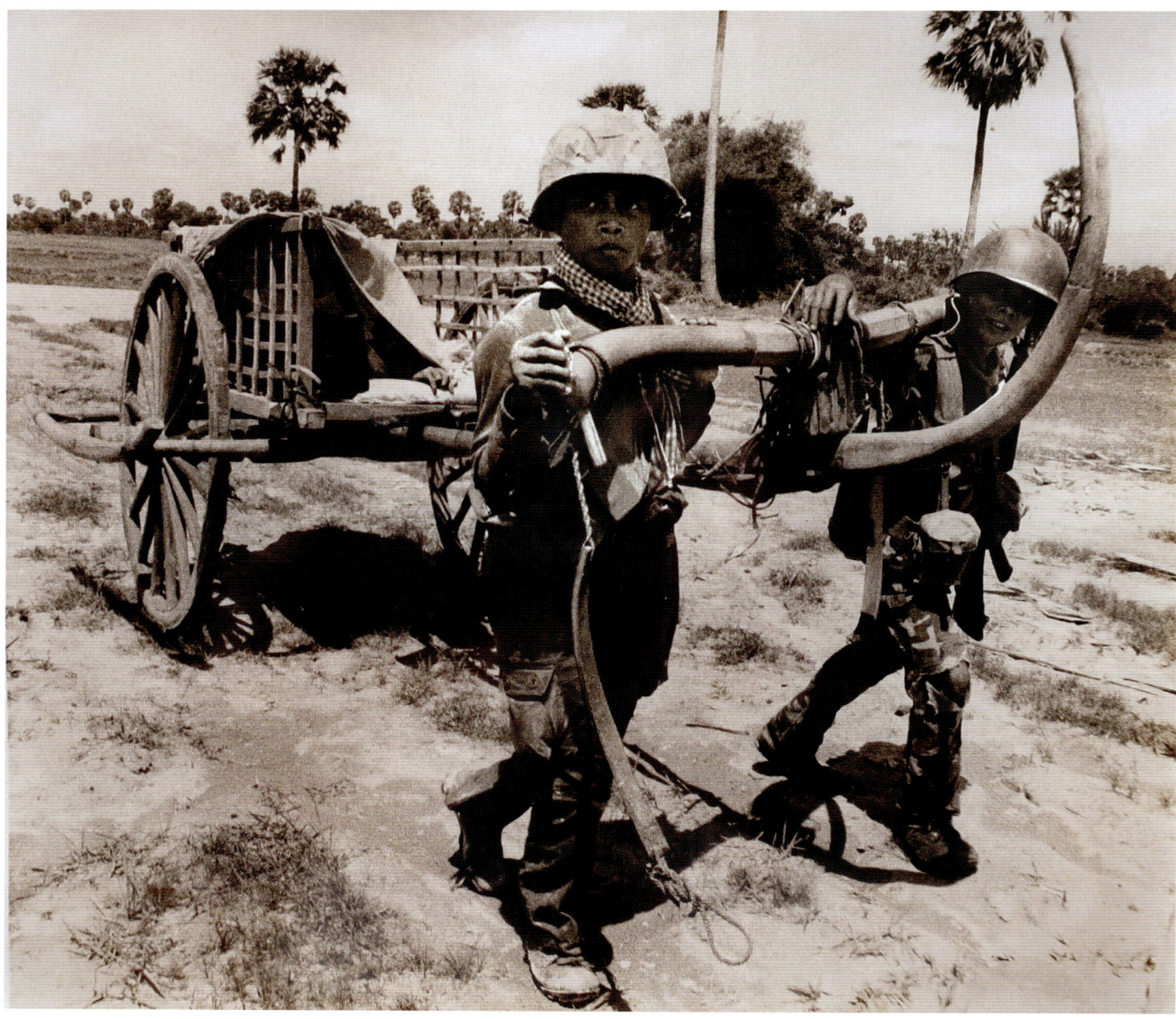

The Collapse of the Countryside

Throughout the short, five-year life of the Khmer Republic, the United States poured over two billion dollars of military hardware and financial aid into the country. Often munitions and supplies were resold to the highest bidder by corrupt high-ranking officers, sometimes even across enemy lines to the communist insurgents. Gasoline was one such liquid commodity. Françoise DEMULDER (1947–2008) took this photograph of two republican child foot soldiers who had commandeered a farmer's bullock cart for their war effort. This was not an uncommon sight. A similar image was published in the 1971 edition of the *Khmer Republic Monthly Illustrated Magazine*. In that instance, the boys who pulled the cart were denied the luxury of army boots and went barefoot.

Republican soldiers pulling a bullock wagon. 1971. Françoise Demulder. Author's Collection.

The Nights the Rockets Rained

Over the nights of March 20–21, 1972, hundreds of Soviet-made 122 mm rockets rained down on a densely populated shanty town on the eastern edges of Tuol Kok, Phnom Penh. Some 122 people died and 248 were wounded in the carnage. Taken from a low perspective, this photograph of a shocked survivor was published as part of a major photo-essay about the incident in the *Khmer Republic Illustrated Monthly Magazine*. The man later died in hospital. Photographer TEA Kim Heang (d. 1975?) worked closely with the foreign press corps and the Associated Press, earning great respect amongst his colleagues. A year later, he was last seen walking with his family as they joined the lines of forced evacuees departing the capital.

Injured man. Tuol Kok, Phnom Penh. March 1972. Tea Kim Heang. *Khmer Republic Monthly Illustrated Magazine*, vol. 1, no. 2. Center for Khmer Studies Library, Siem Reap.

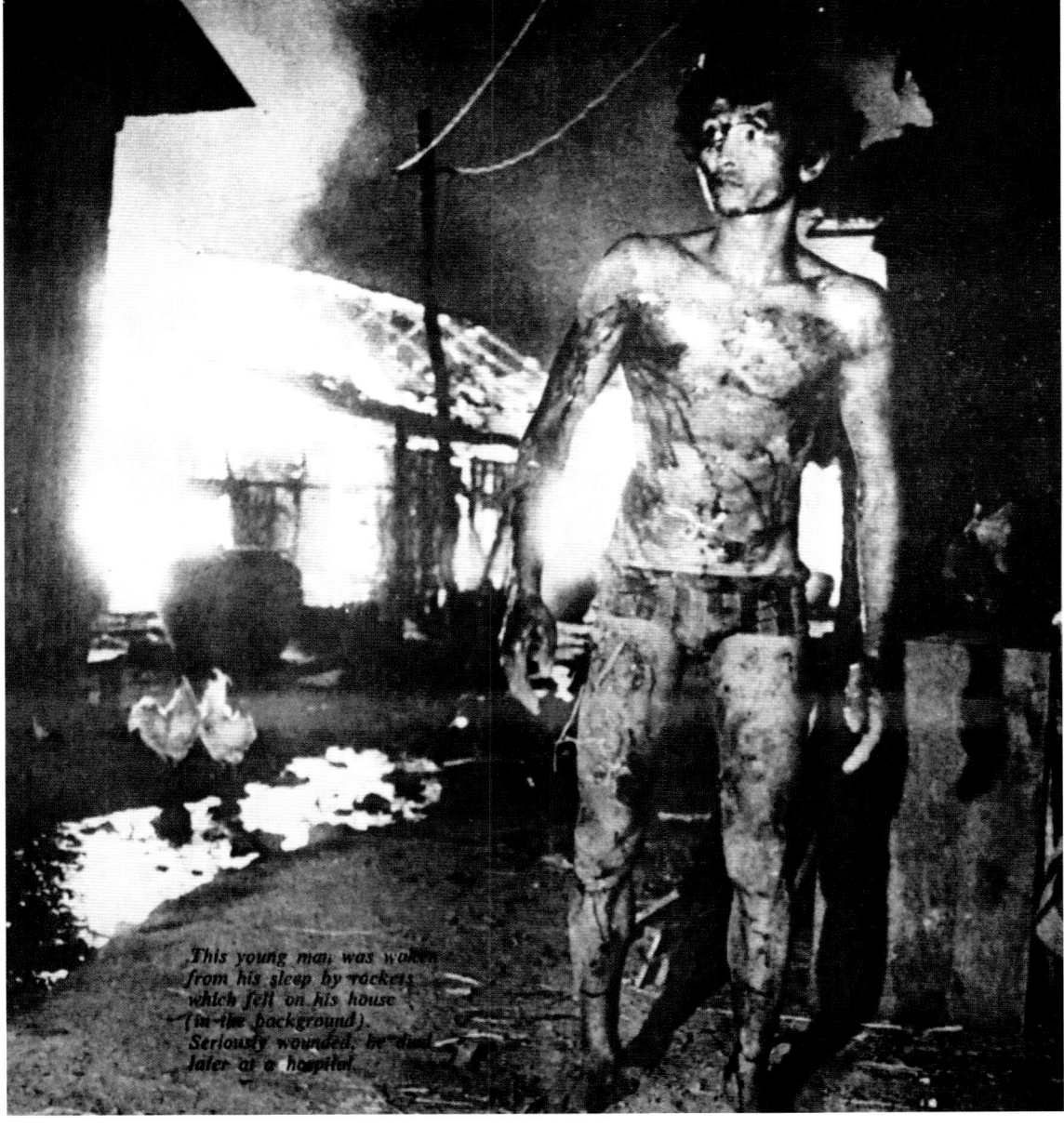

KHMER NATIONAL ARMED FORCES 1955-1969 VICTIMS OF DEFEATISM

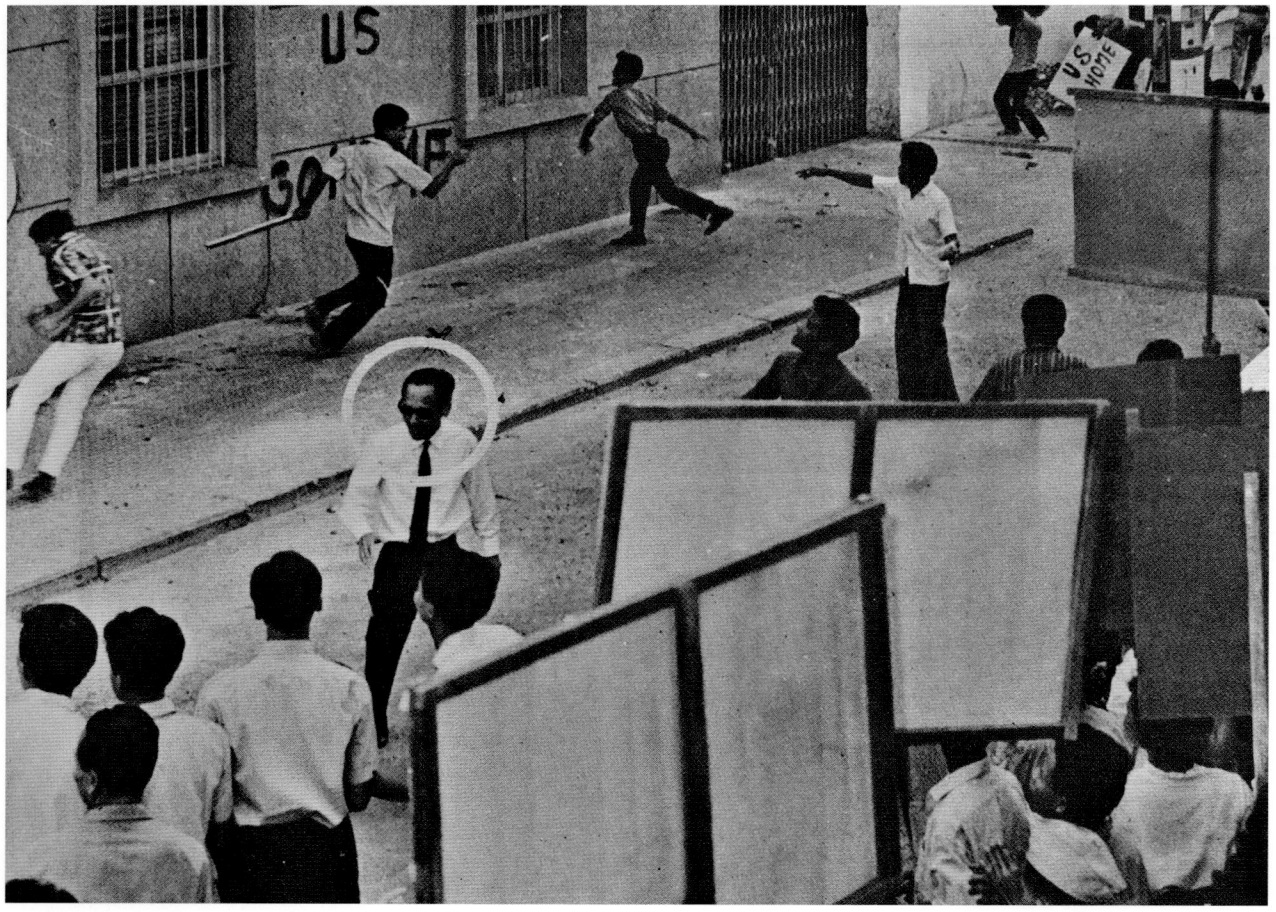

Victims of Defeatism

"Here Chau Seng is seen exhorting riot against the US Embassy." Phnom Penh. 1954, edited 1972. Photographer unknown. *Khmer Republic Monthly Illustrated Magazine*, vol. 1, no. 2. 1971. Center for Khmer Studies Library, Siem Reap.

The *Khmer Republic Monthly Illustrated Magazine* was the pictorial mouthpiece for Lon Nol's regime. Like Sihanouk's *Le Sangkum* and *Le Cambodge*, it covered a wide range of topics—the war effort, social and cultural events, and reflections on Cambodia's past. This archival photograph, used by the magazine's editor Chhan Song, apparently shows a demonstration outside the American Embassy in 1954. The person circled is Chau Seng, who was a close political ally of Prince Sihanouk during the Sangkum years. Now in the hands of a conservative pro-American press, the photograph is manipulated to construct the history of the Royal Cambodian Armed Forces (FARK) and how they were stalwart supporters of Cambodia's peace and prosperity against Chau and fellow leftist "defeatists." The headline above the photograph shows the influence of international typographic styles on the Cambodian press in the 1970s.

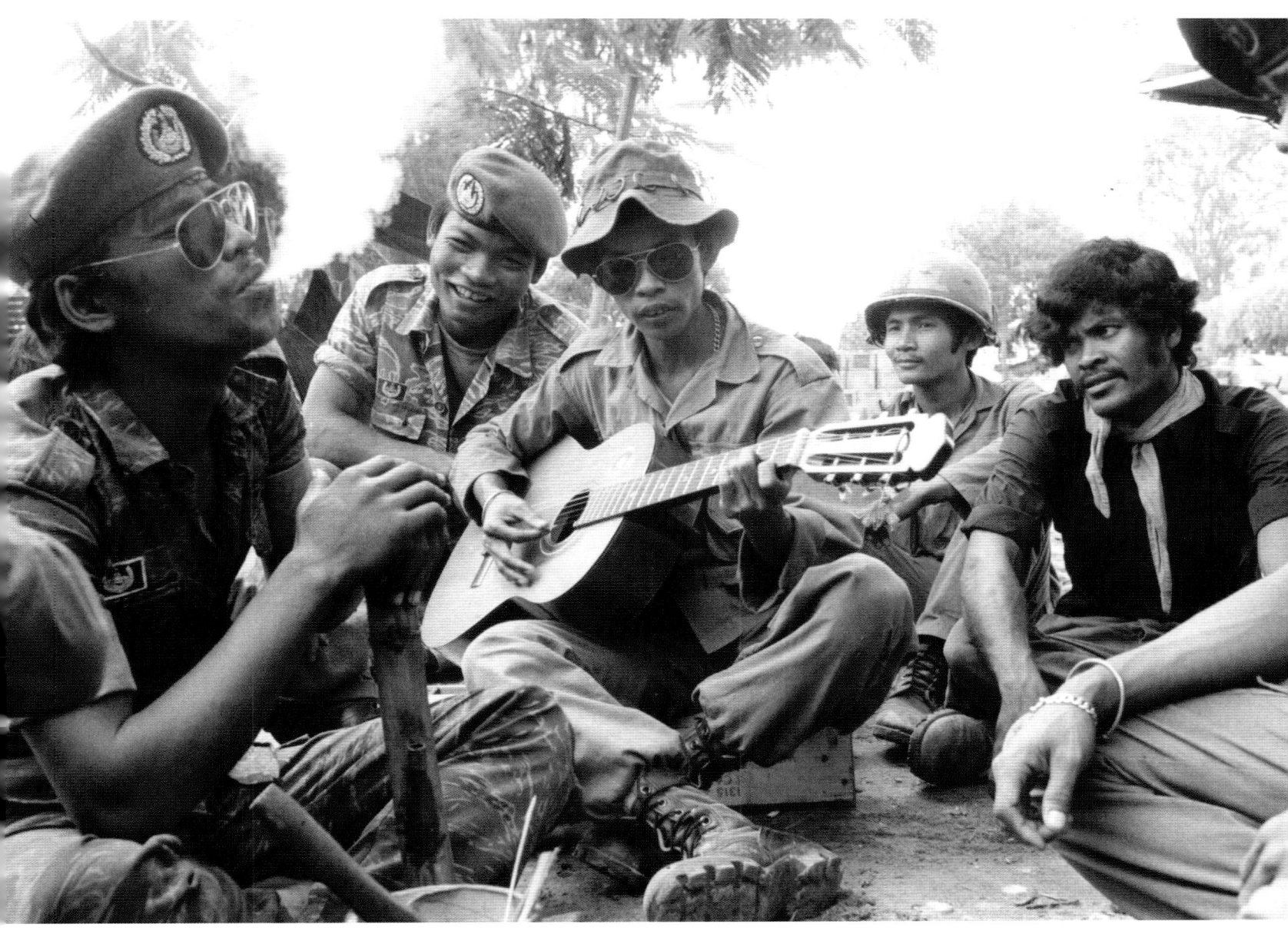

Stoned Behind the Battleline

From the perspective of military history, we can read this photograph by CHHOR Vuthi (d. 1975?) in contrasting ways. Either it is an intimate portrait of the camaraderie of soldiers behind the frontlines of war or it is an indictment of everything that was wrong with the Republican Army—the lack of discipline, the ad hoc preparation, and soldiers stoned under the influence of drugs as they went into battle. When Chhor Vuthi took this image, he was working for the Associated Press as one of Cambodia's youngest war photographers. A year after this photo was taken, he was wounded in the arm, but quickly returned to the field. He was presumed killed by the Khmer Rouge after the fall of Phnom Penh in April 1975.

Republican soldiers. Phnom Penh. 1973. Chhor Vuthi. Tim Page/Indochina Media Memorial Foundation (IMMF) Project.

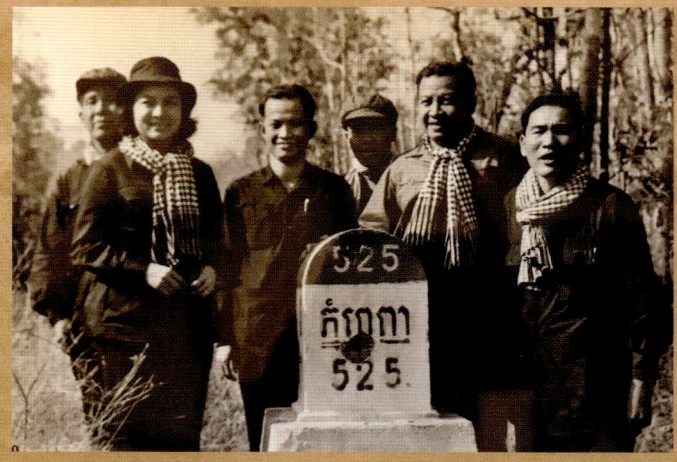

Sihanouk and his wife Norodom Monineath (Monique) with senior Angkar cadres at the 326-mile (525-km) road marker from Phnom Penh.

中国佛教协会《会务通讯》编辑组
地址：北京市西四阜内大街二十五号
电话：六六零四零三
邮政编码：100034

The background on this page shows the original manila envelope which held this collection of photographs. The envelope is approximately demiquarto in size, with the photographs being slightly smaller.

Sihanouk's Clandestine Journey to Angkor

Following Lon Nol's coup in 1970, Sihanouk was offered asylum in Beijing, where the Chinese sponsored a government-in-exile for Sihanouk's allies, including the Khmer Rouge. In 1973, the Chinese convinced Sihanouk and his wife Norodom Monineath (Monique) Sihanouk to make a clandestine journey into the communist-held territory in Cambodia. This was believed to have enormous symbolic value. In order to get there, they had to travel down the Ho Chi Minh Trail—little more than a path through the mountains of Laos into communist-occupied Cambodia—undoubtedly a very dangerous adventure. They were photographed with Khmer Rouge cadres against the backdrop of Angkorian temples. It was a propaganda coup that reinforced the credentials of the Khmer Rouge as a legitimate alternative to the Lon Nol republic—the king was back with the people, the grassroots of Cambodia. "Join the revolution to liberate the territory for the king," was a popular Khmer Rouge slogan at the time.

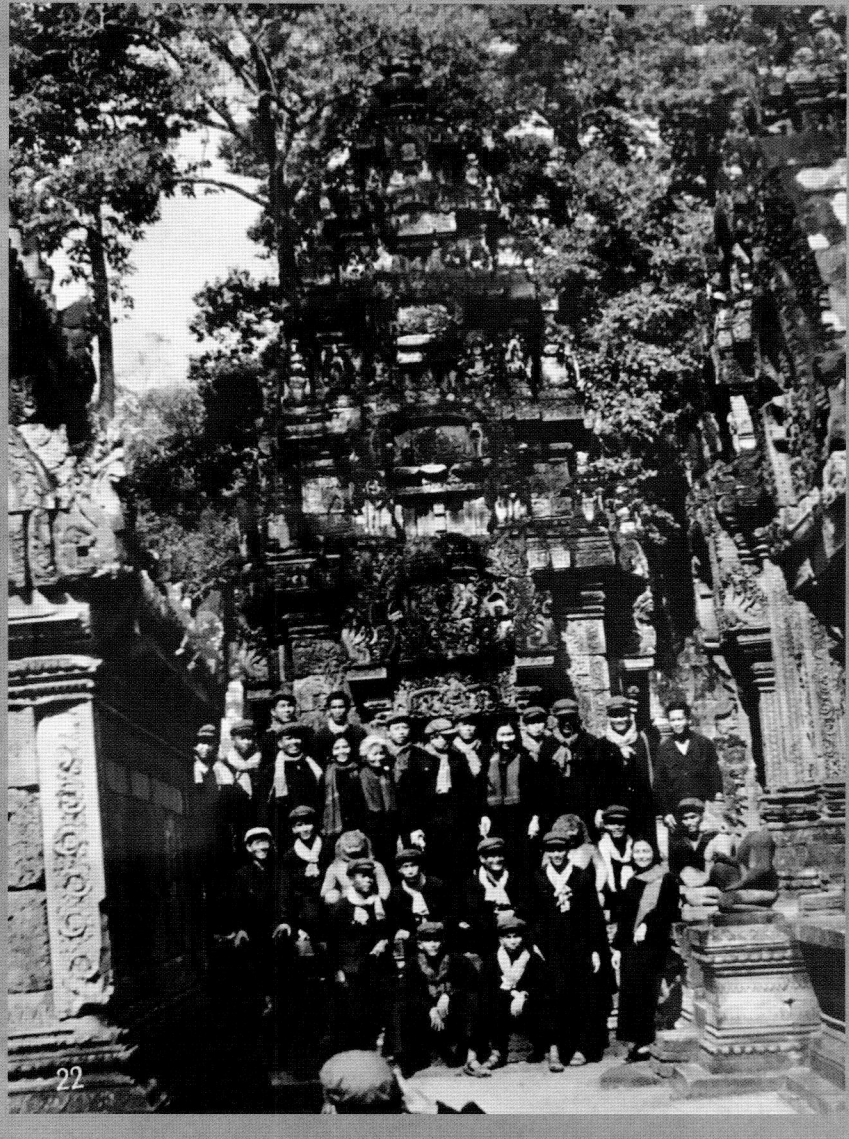

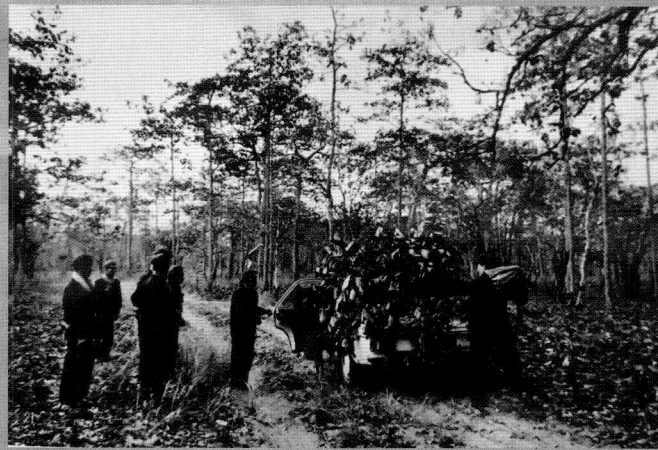

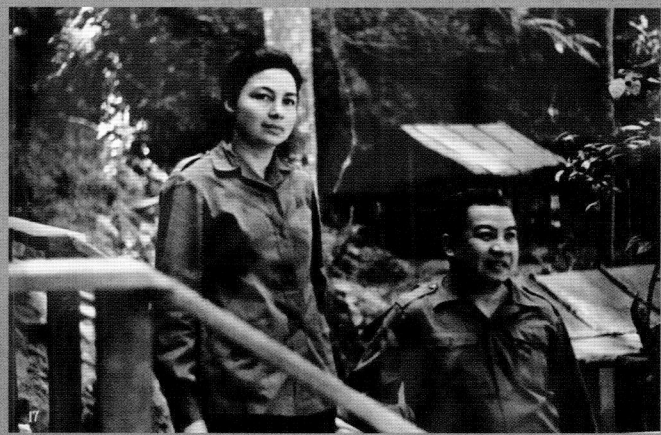

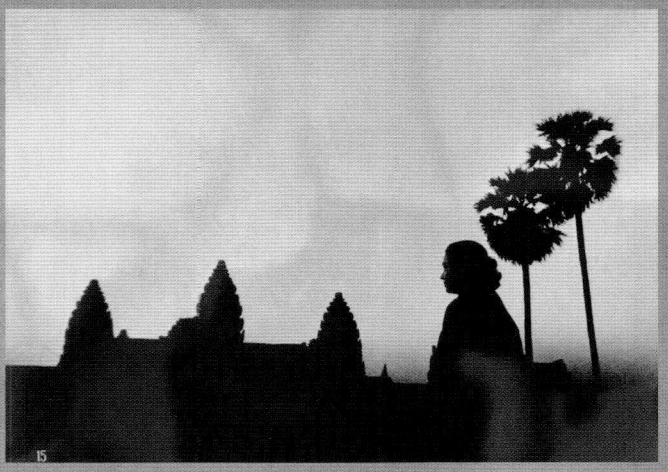

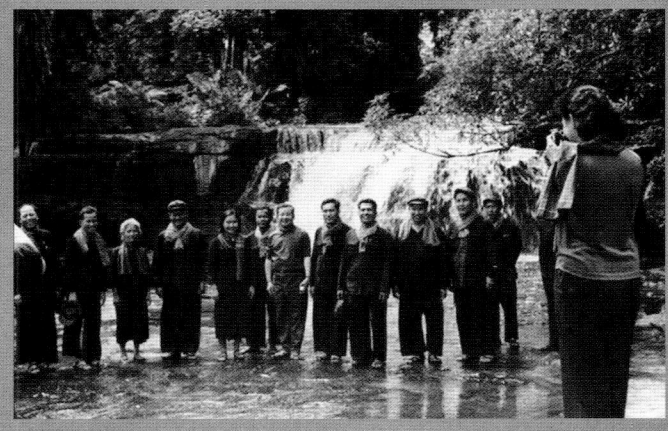

ABOVE, CLOCKWISE: **Sihanouk, Monique, and cadres being photographed at Phnom Kulen waterfall.** Documentation Center of Cambodia (D-Cam).

Motorcar camouflaged against aerial surveillance. Location unknown.

Monique and Sihanouk at a jungle camp. Location unknown.

Monique overlooking Angkor Wat temple.

Photographers unknown. Envelope and prints: Philippe Damas Collection, Singapore.

RIGHT: Not included in the envelope is this image by Norodom Monineath (Monique) Sihanouk, the wife of Sihanouk, taking a snap of the prince and other cadres against the backdrop of a waterfall at Mount Kulen. Did she also take the other propaganda photographs? And who was the photographer taking the photograph of Monineath? Three years later, would they have been part of the group of young cadres selected to go for training in Shanghai with Nhem En?

Photographer unknown.

Searching for Cambodia's Future

We appear to step through the frame of this map of Cambodia, following two soldiers walking into the ruins of a Buddhist *wat* ravaged by battle. They are approaching the temple from the east, the morning sun behind them. At the center, silhouetted against the sky, is a large statue of the Buddha, which would have been enclosed by the walls of the main hall, now destroyed. In the foreground, explosions have knocked off the plaster on the columns, exposing the textured brick core. Photographed in March 1972, the Cambodian audience would have responded to the artwork's symbolism and potent imagery—a country in trauma, searching for a peaceful and compassionate future.

Two soldiers walking into the ruins of a Buddhist *wat*. Location unknown. March 1972. Photograph attributed to Tea Kim Hak. *Khmer Republic Monthly Illustrated Magazine*, vol. 1, no. 2. 1972. Art Director: Dim Nhek, Khun Khut, and Yong Neang. Center for Khmer Studies Library, Siem Reap.

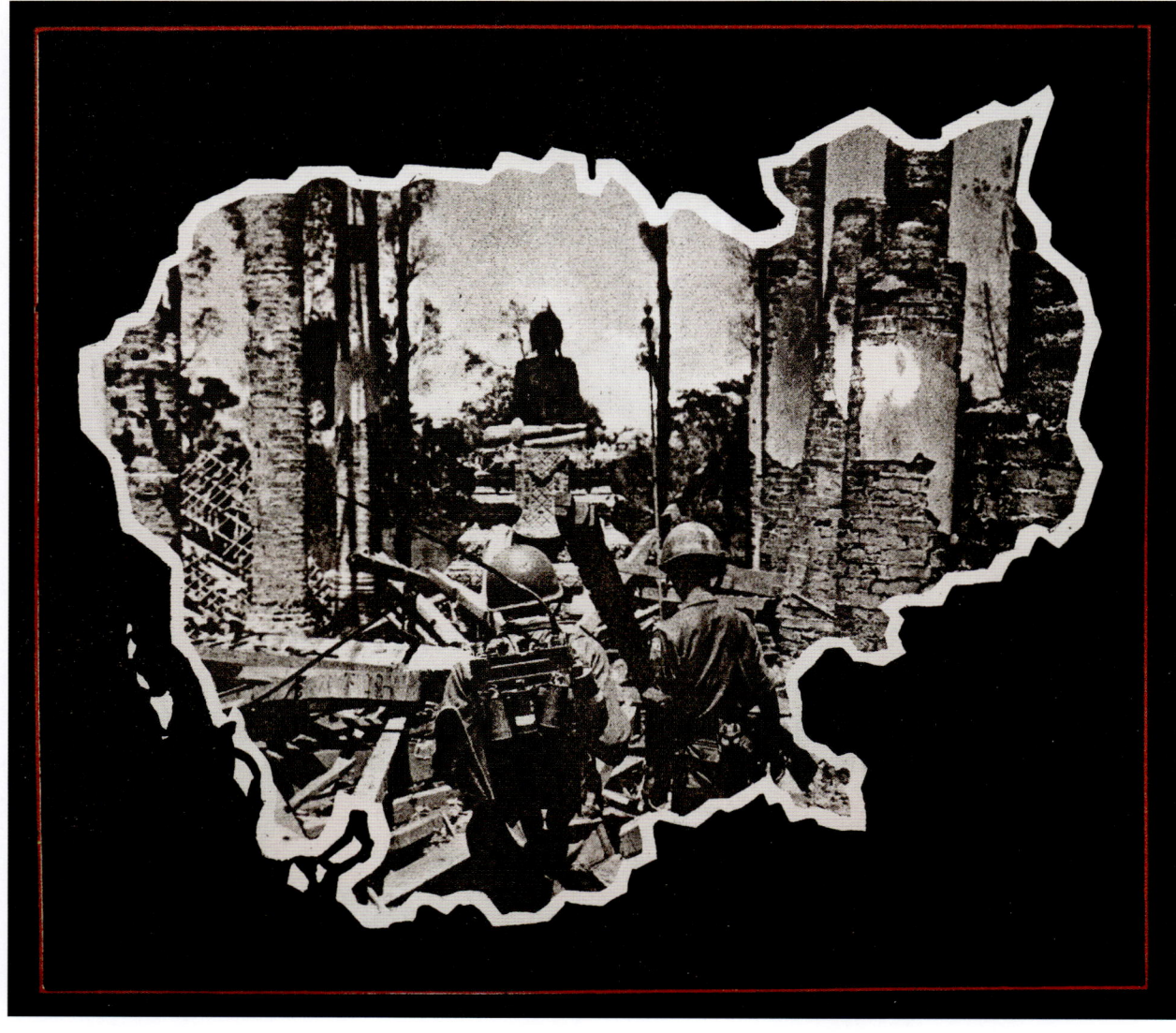

The Massacre of the Children

On December 14 and 15, 1972, the North Vietnamese army and Vietcong troops attacked the old city of Oudong, 22 miles (35 km) to the northwest of the capital. Prior to Phnom Penh, Oudong was Cambodia's royal center for 200 years. The attack was a particularly brutal affair, with many civilians killed, including ten children from the Lycée Tep Pranam. The loss to the communists was both a military as well as a symbolic defeat for the republic. In March 1973, the *Khmer Republic Monthly Illustrated Magazine* printed a four-page feature covering the memorial rites for the children. This bold "D" with the children's photographs pasted within, was part of the graphic headline "DES JUENES MASSACRÉS" (The Massacred Youths). Their loss had a profound effect on the student population of Phnom Penh.

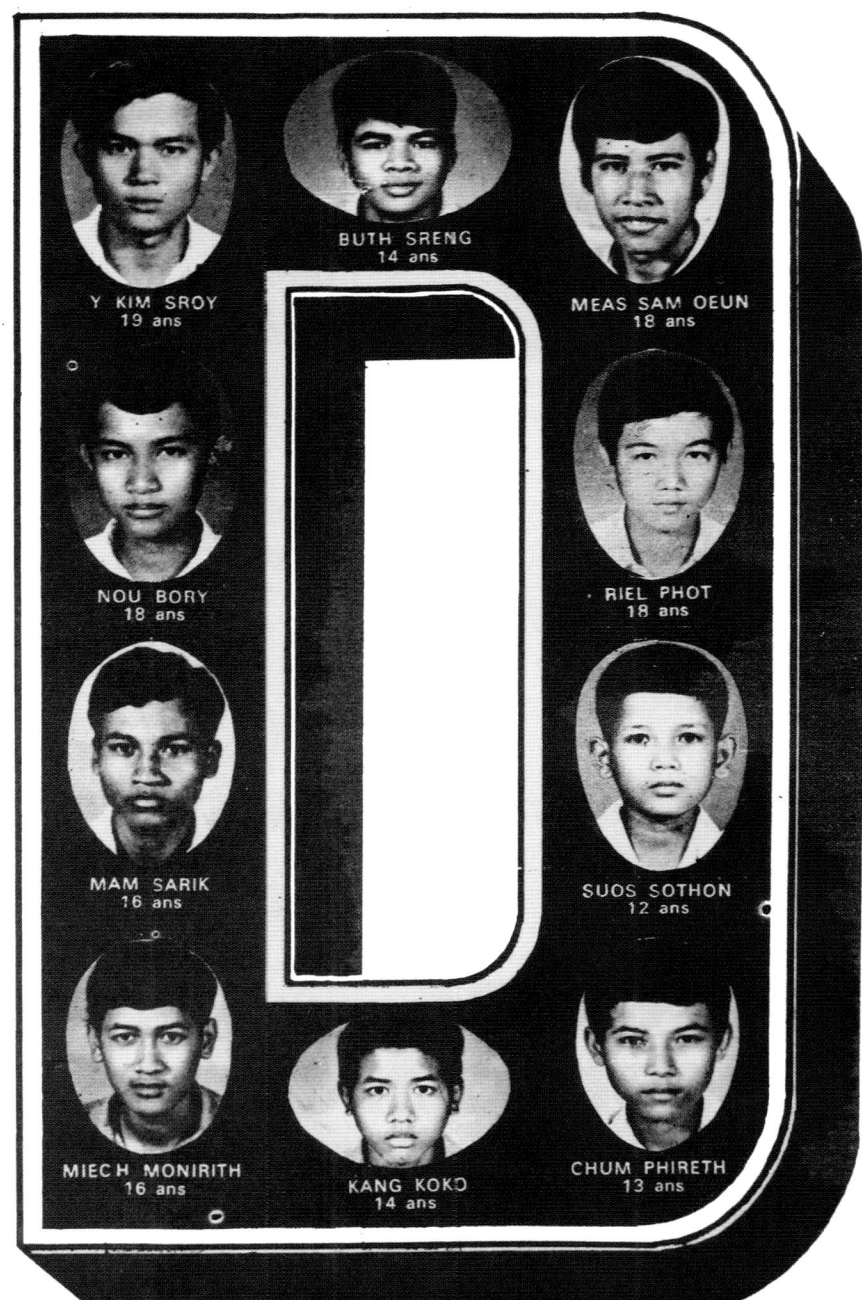

Montaged graphic for a magazine headline, "DES JUENES MASSACRÉS "
Khmer Republic Monthly Illustrated Magazine, March 1973. Artist unknown. Center for Khmer Studies Library, Siem Reap.

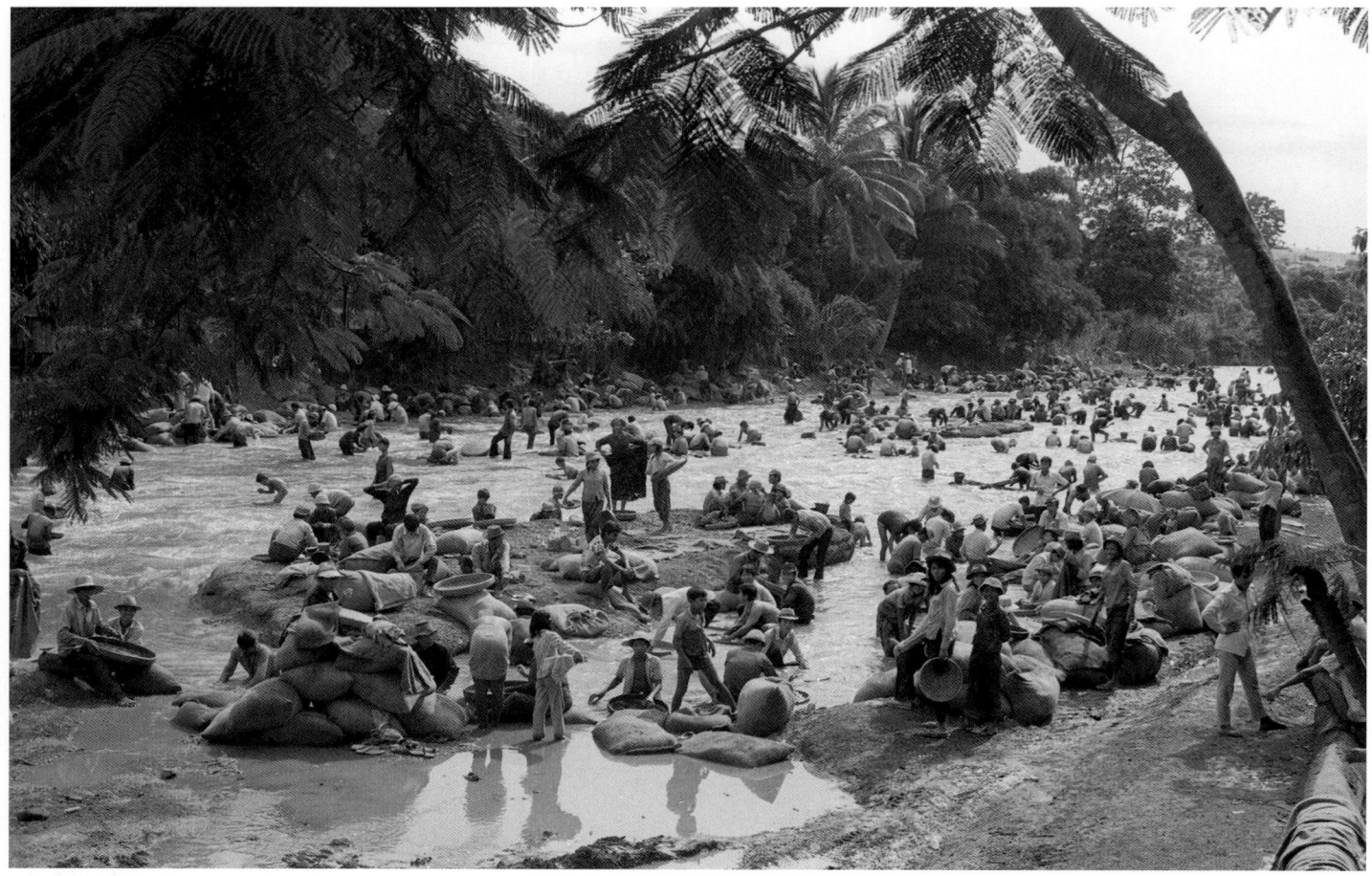

Pailin Gem Hunters

In 1974, Colin GRAFTON (b. 1947) managed to catch a lift on a helicopter to the western border town of Pailin, where he photographed sapphire hunters panning the river sediment. Unlike Phnom Penh, the town was a hive of commercial activity, apparently oblivious to the capital's plight. Grafton had arrived in Cambodia in 1972 to work for a local language school in Phnom Penh. Like teachers Michael Vickery and Marie-Françoise Châtel a decade earlier, this enabled him to be immersed in the local culture and daily life of Phnom Penh's residents, school colleagues, and close friends as they endured the war.

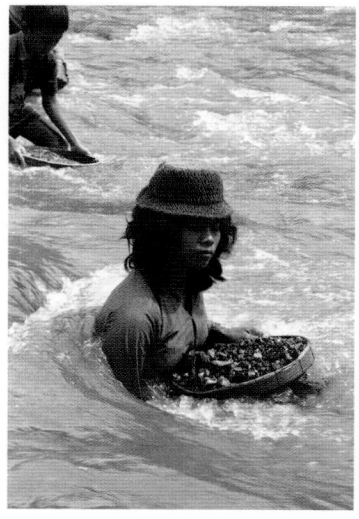
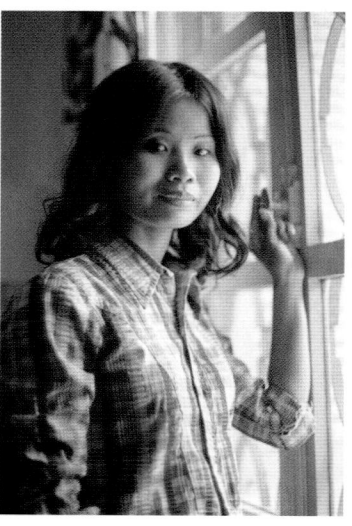
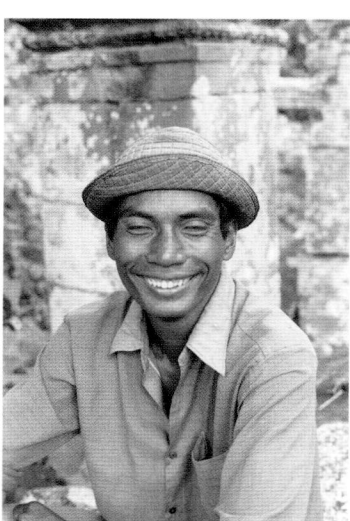

ABOVE: **Gem hunters panning in the Pailin River.** Pailin. 1974.

LEFT TO RIGHT: **Gem hunter panning in the Pailin River.** Pailin. 1974.

Phally. Phnom Penh. 1974.

Moto driver. Banteay Chhmar. 1972.

Photographs: Colin Grafton.

The Republic Disintegrates

Only weeks before the downfall of Phnom Penh, another random rocket attack devastated the capital. The photograph at right, taken by SOU Vichith (d. 1975?), shows a distraught mother holding her dying child. Sou was a prolific photographer. As well as working at the front line, he also documented civilian casualties in the capital. In 1975, as Phnom Penh fell to the communists, Sou and his family took temporary refuge in the French Embassy. Forced out by Khmer Rouge soldiers, Sou was last seen alive by fellow photographer Dith Pran as the family walked out of the city in the direction of the "Killing Fields."

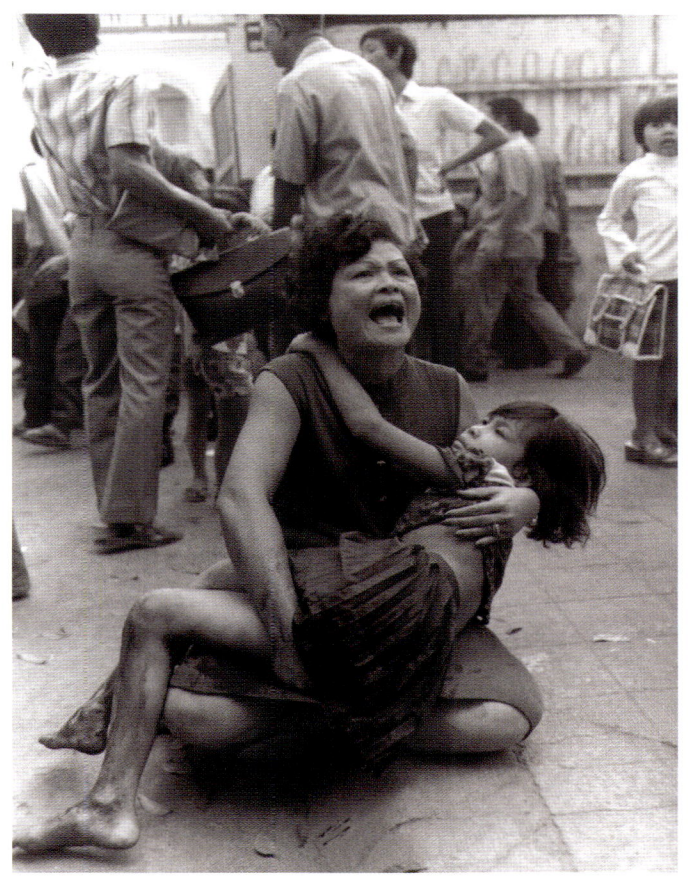

ABOVE: **Mother holding her dying child.** Phnom Penh. 1975.

BELOW: **Refugees fleeing the aftermath of a rocket attack.** Phnom Penh. 1974.

Photographs: Sou Vichith. Tim Page/Indochina Media Memorial Foundation (IMMF) Project.

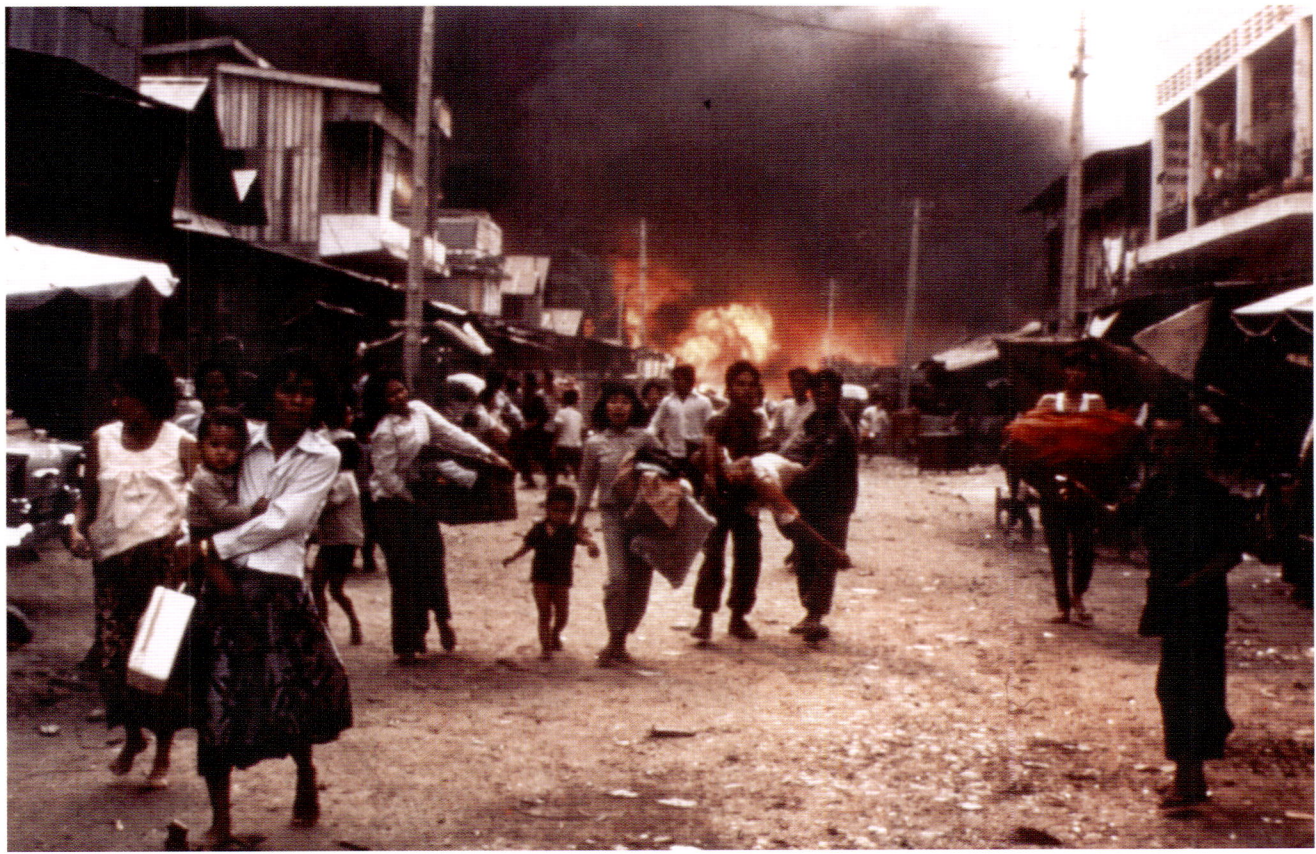

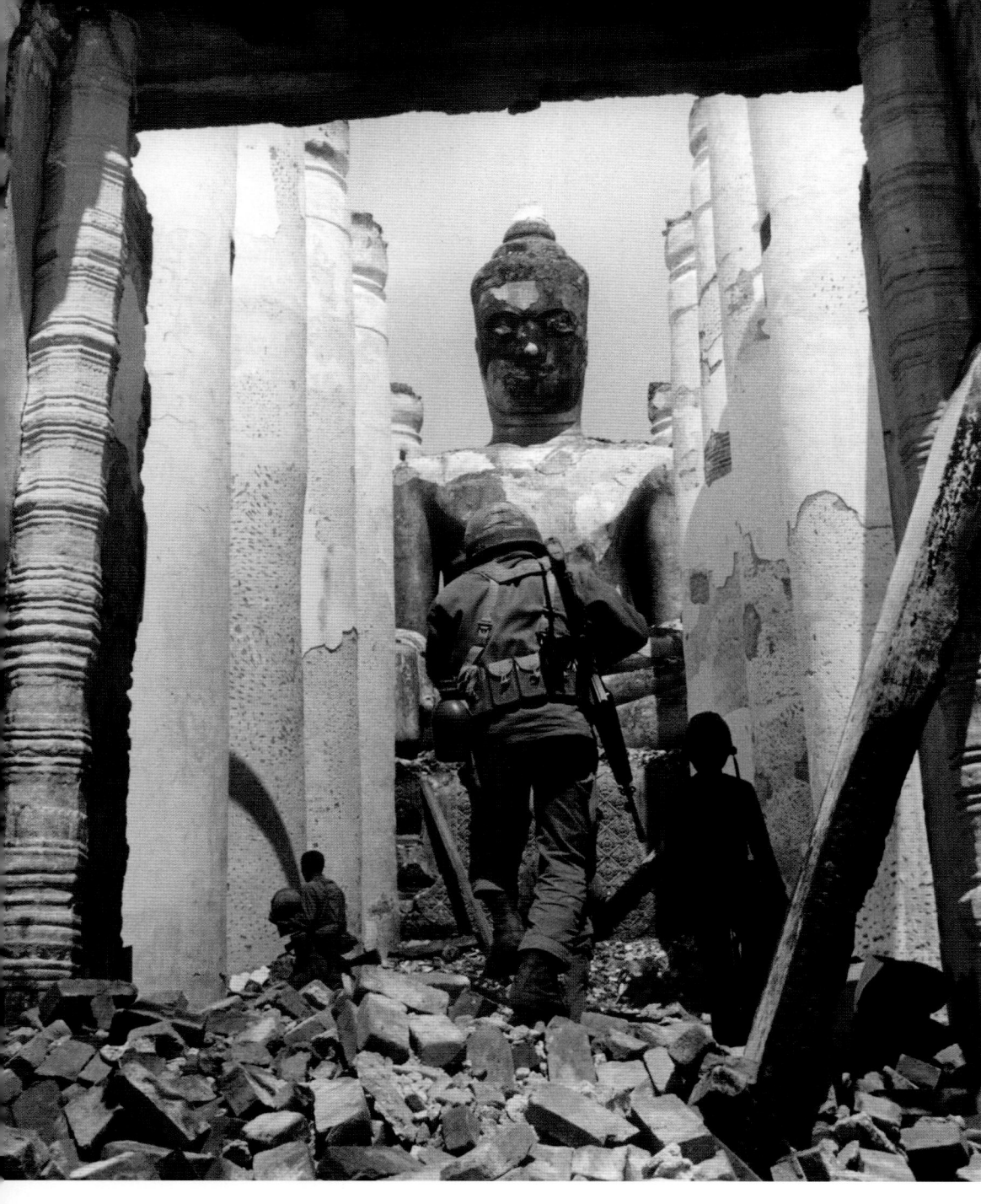

Republican soldiers entering the ruins of Wat Preah Ath Roes. Phnom Oudong. 1974. Pen. Tim Page/Indochina Media Memorial Foundation (IMMF) Project.

The Destruction of Wat Preah Ath Roes

This photograph by PEN (d. 1975?) fixes in time republican soldiers entering the monumental ruins of Wat Preah Ath Roes, atop Phnom Oudong. The mountain, a strategic and symbolic northern gateway to Phnom Penh, had just been recaptured from the communists. The photograph, with its framing and loaded symbolic values, bears a striking similarity to one published a year earlier in *The Khmer Republic Illustrated Monthly Magazine*. Pen, like many Cambodian war photographers at the time, was a stringer, a journalist who contributes content to a news organization on a piece-by-piece basis. He was only paid if the work was published. Pen worked for the Associated Press. As Tim Page and Horst Fass poignantly observe in the biographical notes of their photography book, *Requiem*, "Pen was another stringer for AP who left no trace."

The Comforts of War

Cambodian family members often tagged along behind their soldier-breadwinners into war. The families not only provided food but also social comforts unavailable within the military structure. Perhaps this boy is a temporary guardian of his father's possessions and minder of the family's pet dog. Perhaps he has no mother or home, and the father's military environment is the only survival choice he has. Together, did father and son make what is called "tactic agency"? Did they make a considered survival choice under the extreme pressures of war, that living together on the battlefront they had a better chance of survival than being a fractured family? THONG Veasna (d. 1975?) worked for the Associated Press. We know nothing of his fate after April 1975.

A boy and his pet traveling with his father, a republican soldier. Preak Phnou. 1975. Thong Veasna. Tim Page/Indochina Media Memorial Foundation (IMMF) Project.

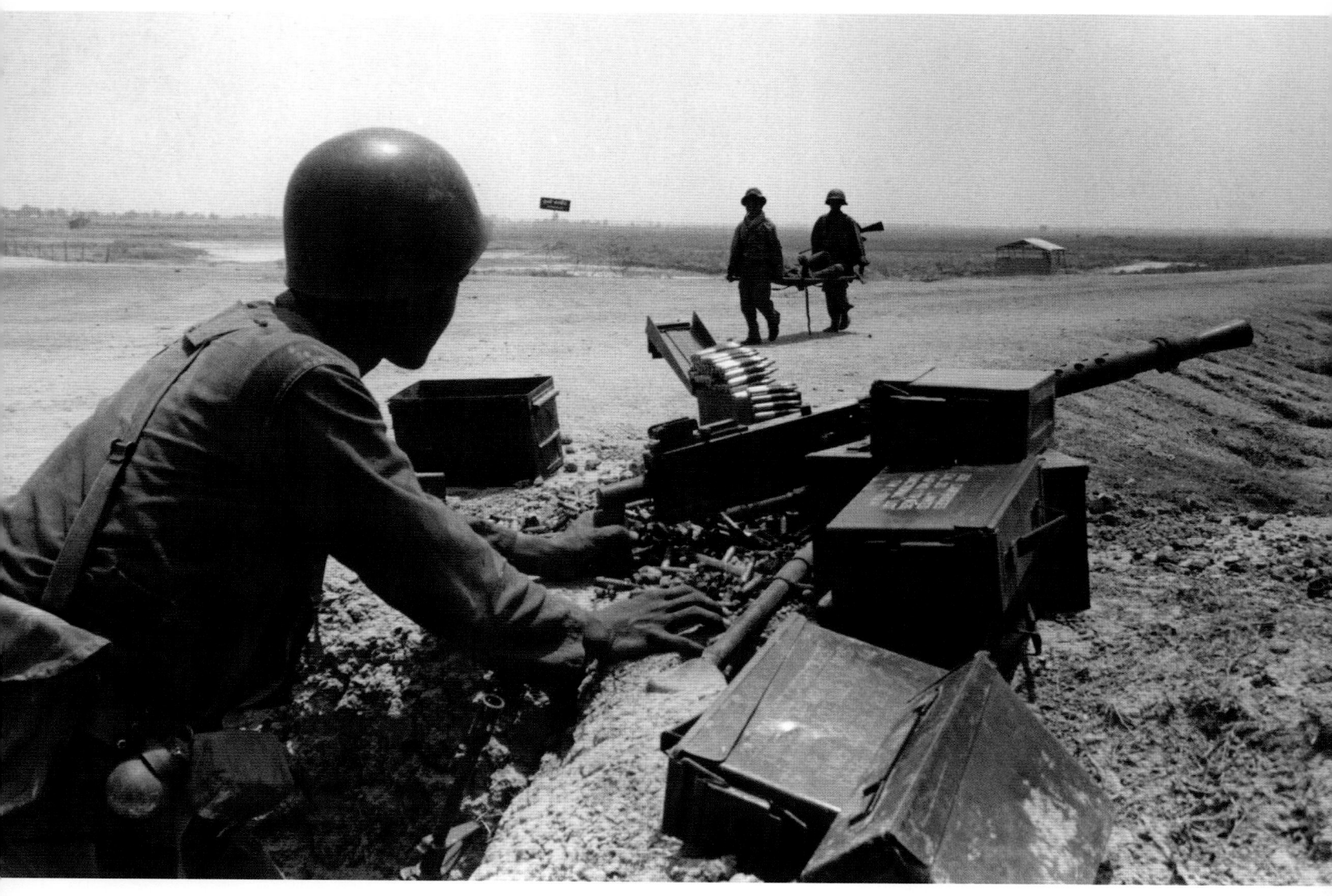

The Wounded Comrade

Like many Cambodians working alongside the international press, KUOY Sarun (d. 1977?) was multiskilled, working as a driver, interpreter, and photographer. He suppied images to a number of news agencies, including the *New York Times*. In this photograph, the searing heat of the Cambodian dry season weighs heavily on the two soldiers carrying their wounded comrade on a stretcher past a makeshift machine gun post. The landscape is bleak and shadeless. The seasons play an important strategic influence in Indochinese warfare. The dry season was an opportunity for well-equipped armies to advance their heavy armor, while the monsoon favored agile, lighter-armed communist troops. Kuoy was believed to have died in 1977.

Cambodian solders carry a wounded comrade past a machine gunner's position on Route 5. North of Phnom Penh. ca. 1974. Kuoy Sarun. Tim Page/Indochina Media Memorial Foundation (IMMF) Project.

Nhem Noeun's Family Photographs

These photographs from the Nhem Noeun family cache traverse the changes in photographic conventions caused by the disruptions of war. On the left, a 1970 Kompong Cham studio photo of the recently married couple sets them against a painted backdrop of an idealized villa, far removed from their humble rural background. The stiffly suited Nhem suggests an aspiration for an urban life, while his wife, Ros Sithat, is more traditionally attired. A few years later, Nhem had risen quickly through the Khmer Rouge ranks to become the district governor of Siem Reap. In 1978, when he took a photograph of his grandmother and his son Nal Sokhin (center), they are wearing drab Khmer Rouge attire and swathed in *krama*, the traditional Cambodian cotton scarf that, for the Khmer Rouge, cemented their identity as authentic "old" people of agrarian stock. By the time his son had reached adolescence, the Vietnamese republic was established and his identity photo (right) now shows him in Western attire.

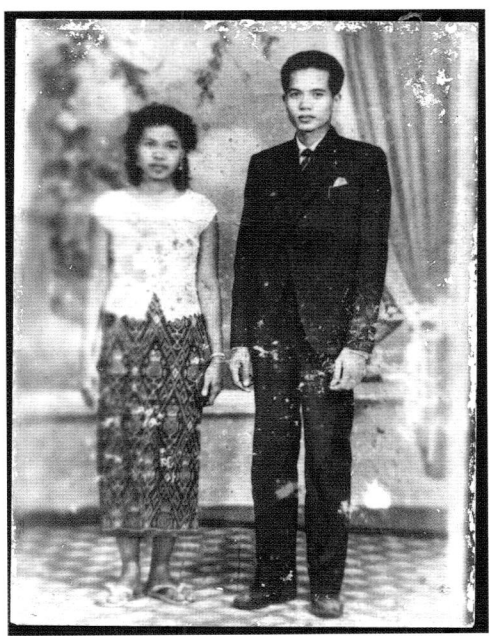
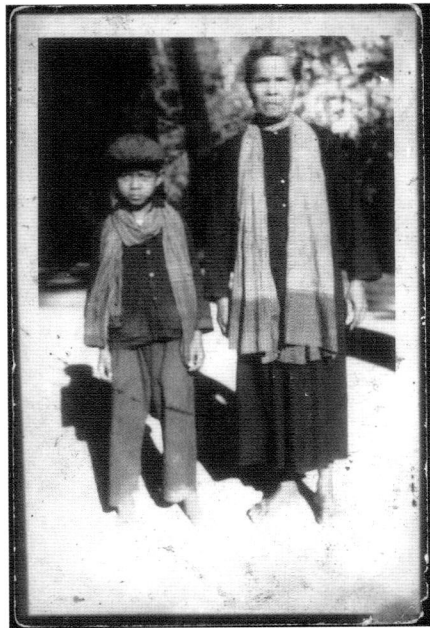
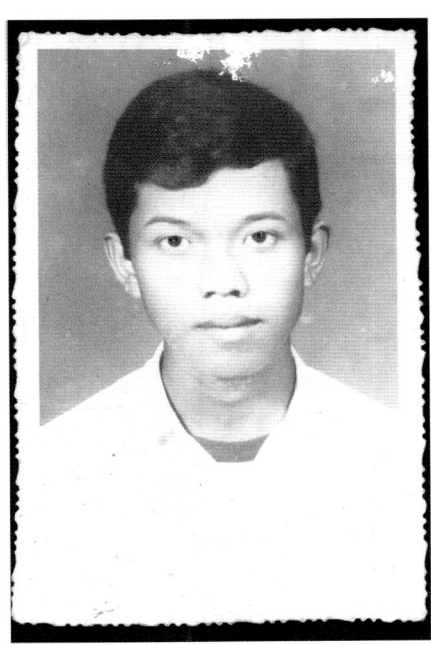

ABOVE, LEFT TO RIGHT: **Ros Sithat and her husband Nhem Noeun's marriage photograph.** Kampong Cham Province. ca. 1970.

Nal Sokhin and his grandmother. ca. 1973.

Nal Sokhin, the son of Sithat and Noeun. ca. 1980s.

Source: Documentation Center of Cambodia (D-Cam)/Still Lives Project. Photographers unknown.

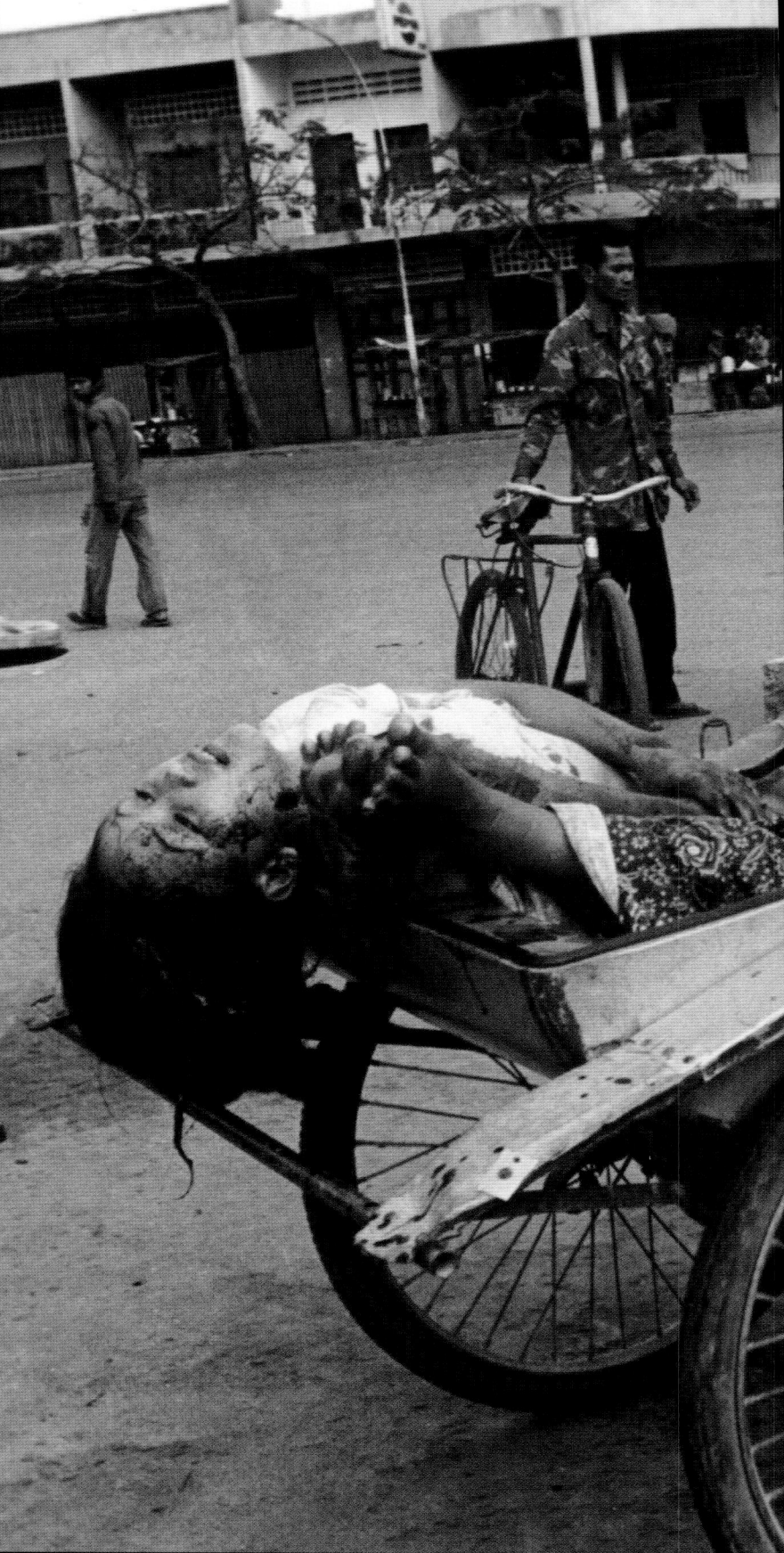

The Wounded Civilians

Moments after a rocket attack on the Pochentong central market, a woman lies slumped in the back of a bicycle-pulled trolley (*remorque-kong*) as a republican soldier adjusts her hair and places a pillow of fabric beneath her head. While the bloodied child appears to be dead, perhaps the mother is unconscious. She is wearing a fashionable summer dress, no doubt in an effort to maintain a dignity of personal style despite the impact of war on everyday life. The driver is moving forward, preparing to mount the bicycle and take his load to hospital. A piece of debris on the roadway hints at the material damage, while civilians gather themselves to continue their lives as best they can, close to the encroaching battle lines.

Wounded civilians in a *remorque-kong*.
Pochentong, Phnom Penh. 1975. Tea Kim Heang. Tim Page/Indochina Media Memorial Foundation (IMMF) Project.

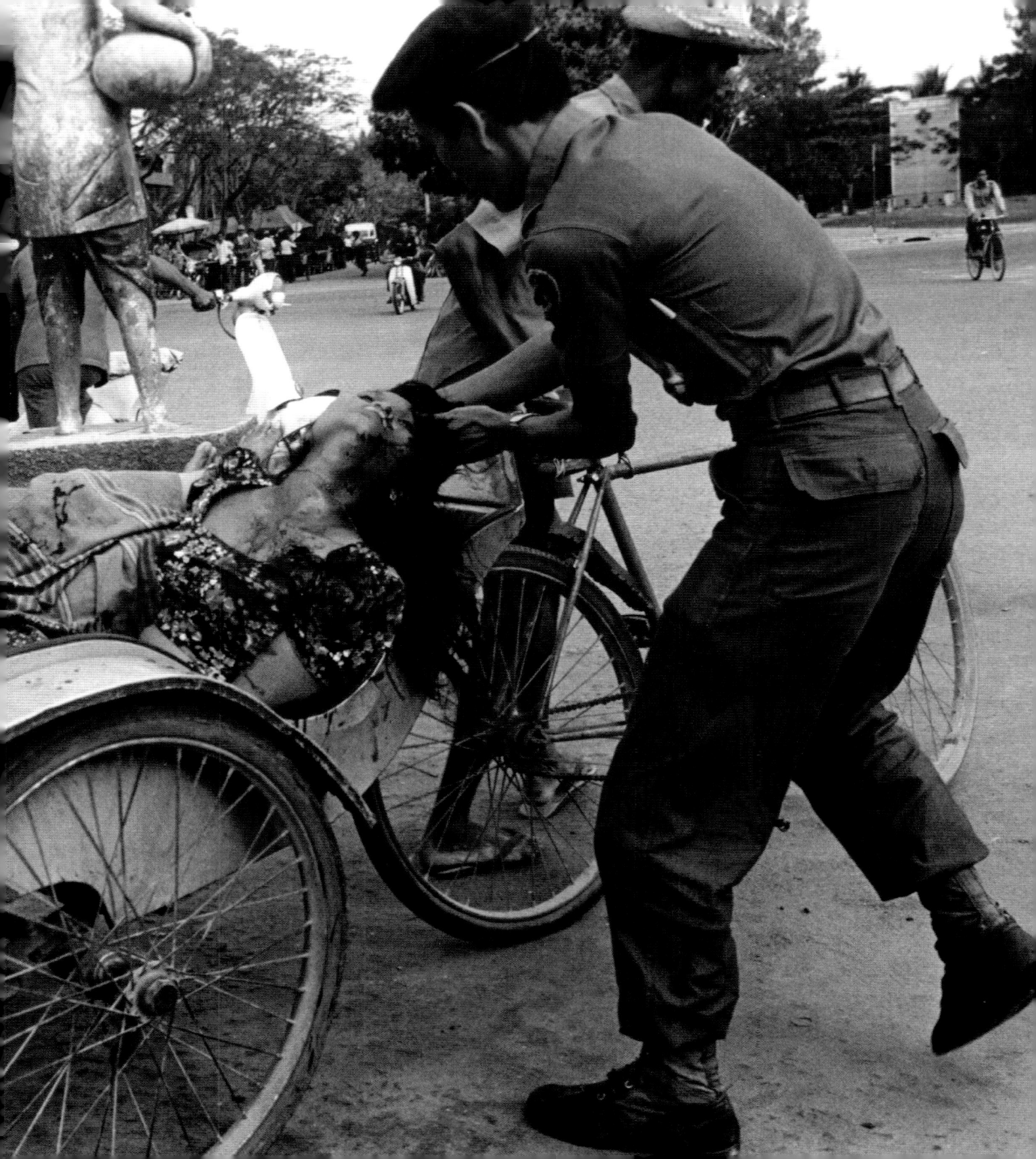

The Hospital Ward

Don McCULLIN (b. 1935) served as an aerial reconnaissance photographer for the Royal Air Force in the mid-1950s. Like the French photographer Gilles Caron, he covered the world's conflict zones of the 1960s, such as Cyprus, Nigeria, Vietnam, and Northern Ireland. As the Cambodian republic collapsed in April 1975, McCullin, like many photographers, stayed to document the unfolding events. In this photograph in one of the crowded hospitals of the city, a young woman is embracing the body of her mortally wounded husband. As they entered Phnom Penh, the Khmer Rouge would have had little sympathy for the soldier's plight.

Cambodian woman holds her dying husband, wounded in the battle of Phnom Penh. 1974. Don McCullin/Contact Press Images, New York.

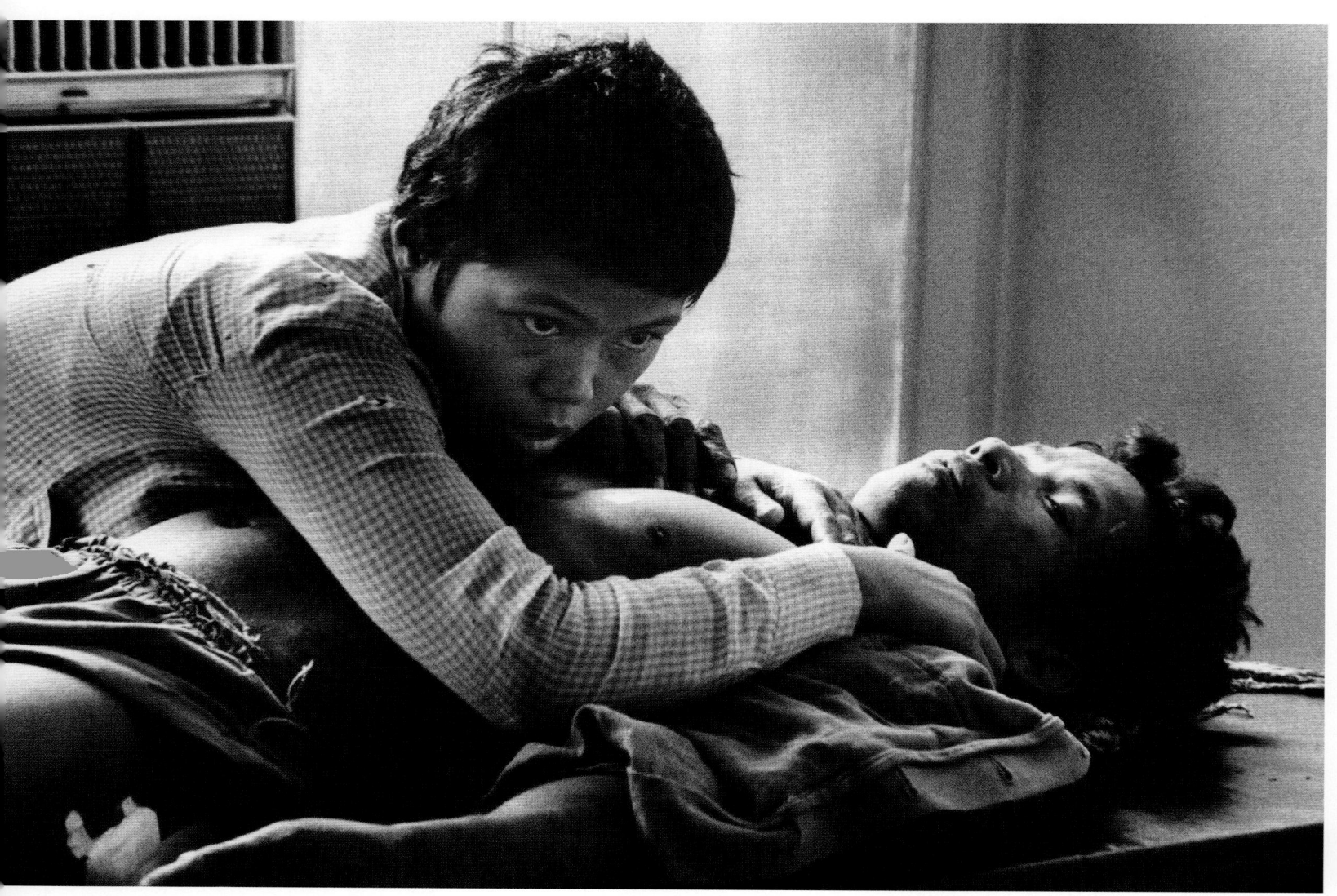

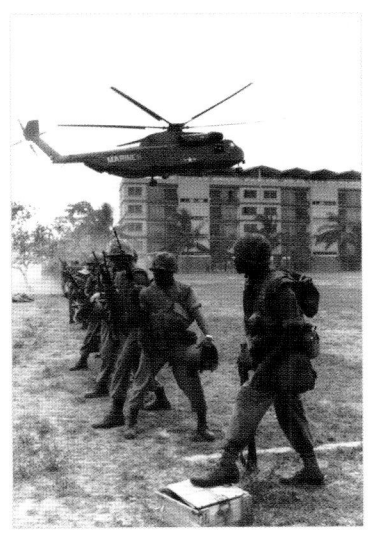
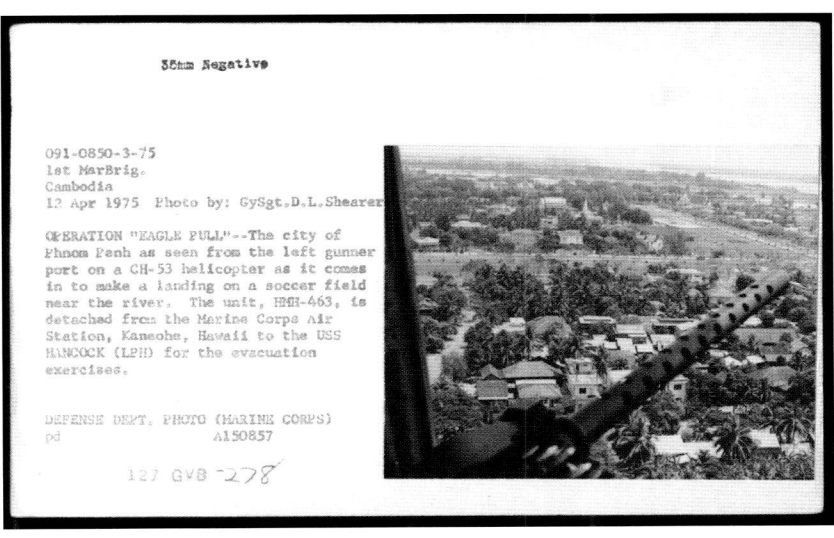
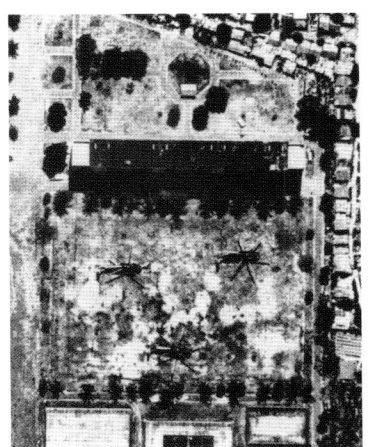
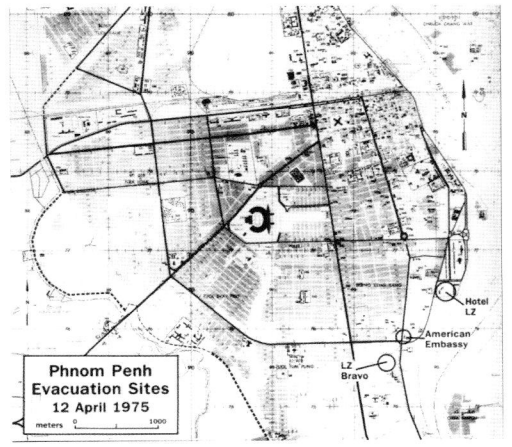
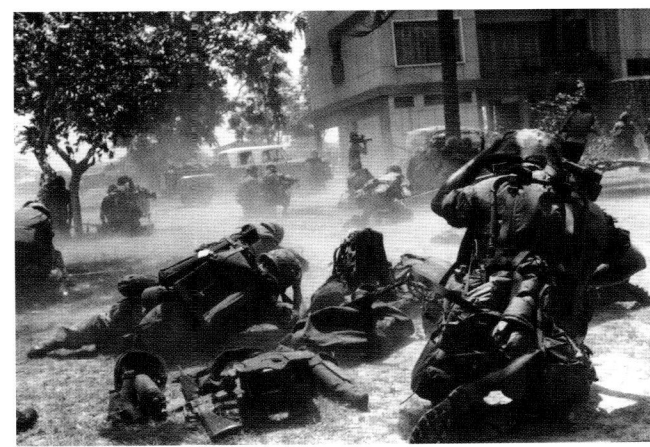

"Operation Eagle Pull"

The last-minute evacuation of Phnom Penh on April 12 and 13, 1975 was recorded from both aerial and on-the-ground perspectives. Gunnery Sargent D. L. SHEARER's photographs, taken from a marine helicopter hovering over the city, offer a panoramic view. Despite the fact that the prints from his 35 mm negatives have been pasted onto documentation cards, with factually typed descriptions of an "evacuation exercise," they have not lost their urgency. Like many others, the civilian journalist Tea Kim Heang covered the ground action at the sports field as American marines formed a defensive ring around the evacuation site. Was this an efficiently executed military operation or a humiliating withdrawal by the United States from a disastrous war? Only two weeks later, Saigon would fall, and for everyone it was all over—except for Cambodians.

TOP LEFT, CLOCKWISE: **Marines form a defensive perimeter around the landing zone for the final evacuation.** Phnom Penh. April 13, 1975. Tea Kim Heang. Tim Page/Indochina Media Memorial Foundation (IMMF) Project.

The city of Phnom Penh as seen from the left gunnery port on a CH-53 helicopter. 1975. D. L. Shearer. US National Archives.

Marines come under rocket attack near the US Embassy. Phnom Penh. April 13, 1975. Tea Kim Heang. Tim Page/Indochina Media Memorial Foundation (IMMF) Project.

Phnom Penh Evacuation Sites map. April 1975. US Defense Department Archives College Park.

Aerial view of three USMC CH-53 helicopters on LZ (landing zone). 1975. Photographer unknown. US National Archives.

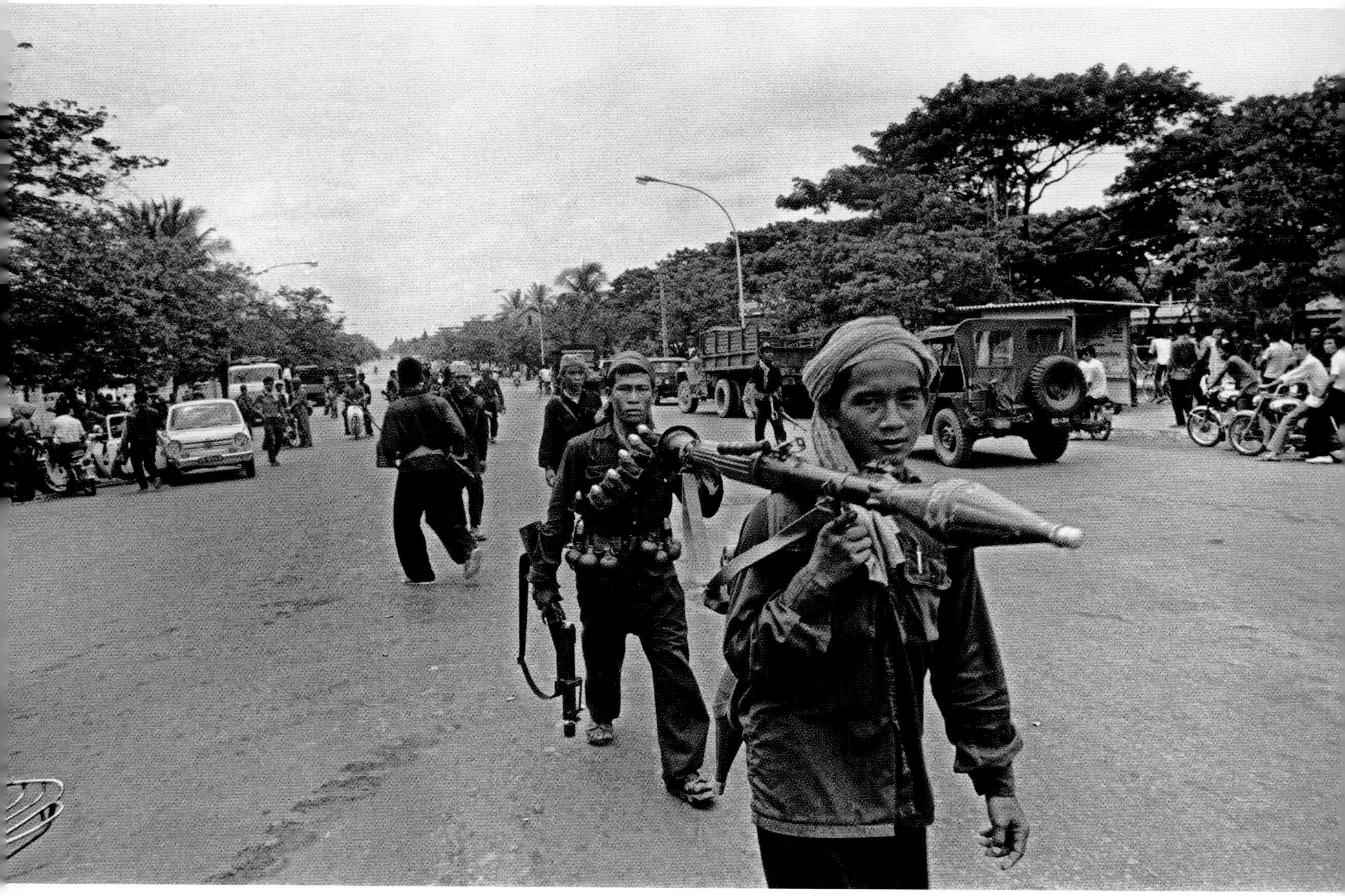

April 17, 1975

After "Operation Eagle Pull," a few days of eerie silence hung over the city. People gathered on the main streets, with nowhere to go and no idea of what would happen next. The French photographer Roland NEVEU (b. 1950) was among the few foreign journalists and photographers who had turned down the US Embassy's last invitation to leave a few days earlier. As the first column of Khmer Rouge troops walked along Monivong Boulevard on April 17, 1975, Neveu photographed a cheeky Cambodian youngster crouching down, keen to be caught by his camera's lens (top right). Another photograph of Khmer Rouge soldiers advancing on the city (above) shows a soldier with a rocket-propelled grenade launcher slung over his shoulder, while civilians on motorbikes watch from the roadside. While that was the "moment captured," the stamps, dates, and notations encrusted on the cardboard mount of the 35 mm transparency show how the image was subsequently propelled along the media lines, passing from photographer to agency, from editor to publisher, and finally to archive.

Khmer Rouge soldiers walk into Phnom Penh. April 17, 1975. Roland Neveu.

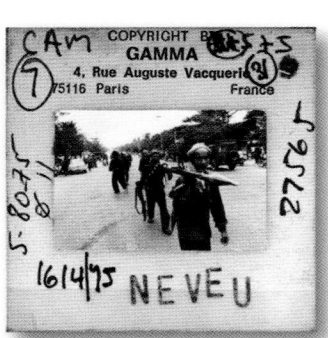

Mounted 35 mm slide.

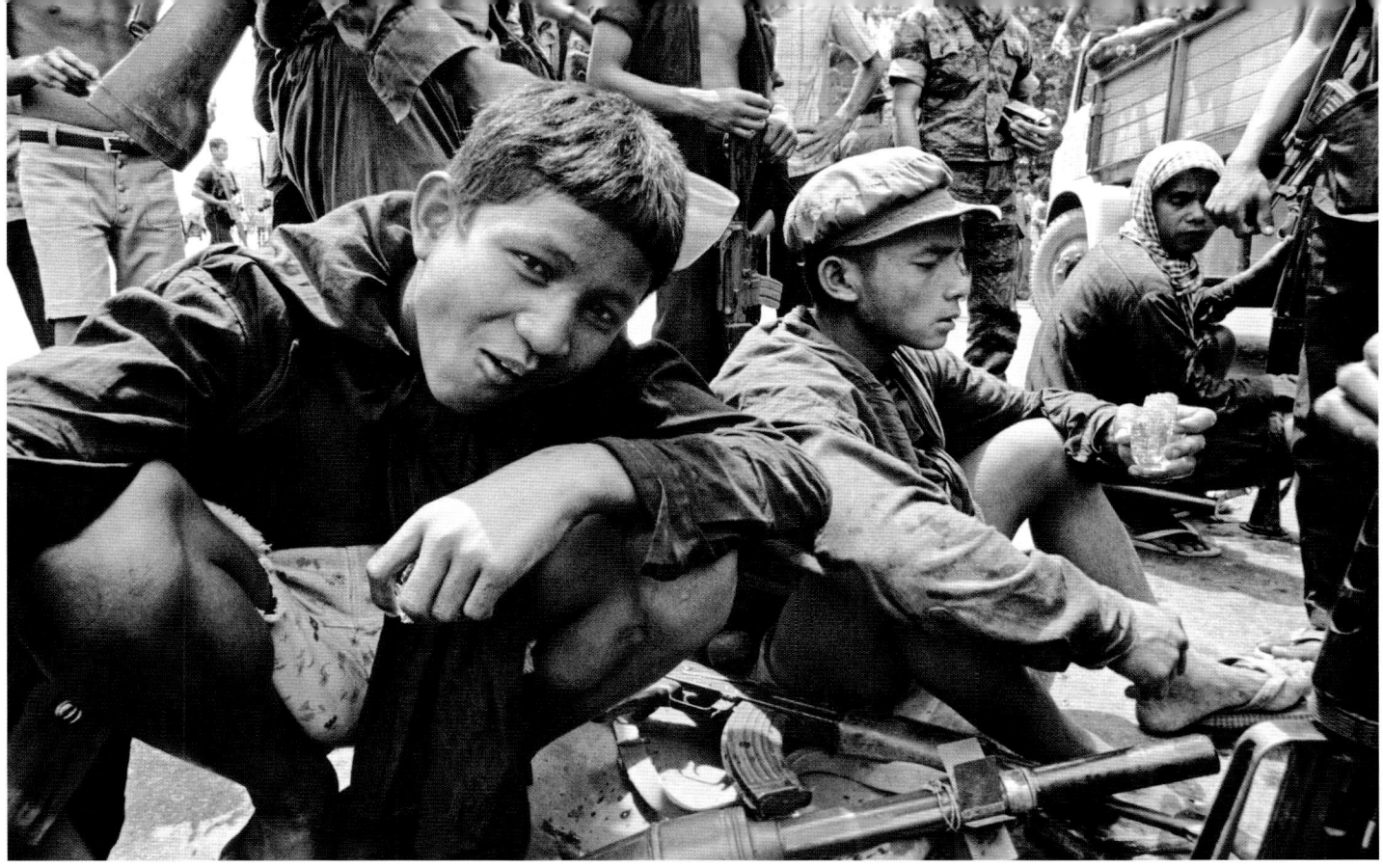

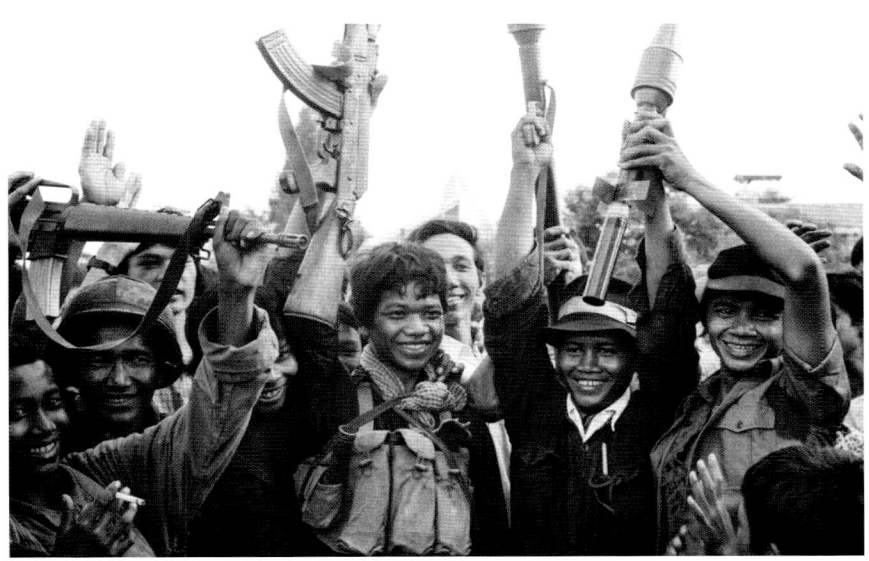

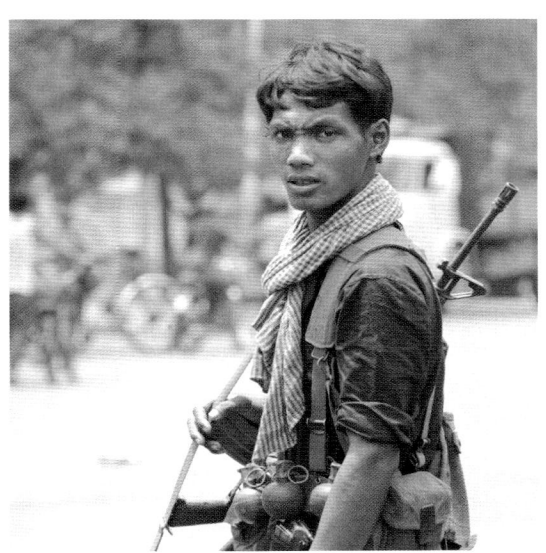

TOP, CLOCKWISE: Young Cambodian soldier looks at the camera.

Portrait of Khmer Rouge soldier.

Portrait of young Khmer Rouge soldier.

Joyous Khmer Rouge and republican soldiers, plus civilians.

Photographs: Roland Neveu. Phnom Penh. April 1975.

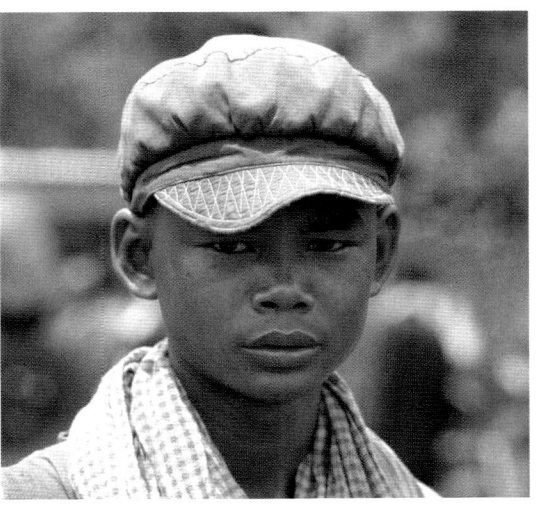

1975–1979
Democratic Kampuchea and the Khmer Rouge Army

Directing the Khmer Rouge foot soldiers as they entered Phnom Penh was the enigmatic Angkar Padevat or "Revolutionary Organization" led by Pol Pot (1925–98). They immediately depopulated Phnom Penh and large towns, including Kampot, Battambang, Siem Reap, and Banteay Chhmar. Families quickly collected the few moveable possessions they could carry, as well as small treasures like photographs of weddings and school friends, wrapping them close to their body or else burying them for safe keeping. Angkar used trains to move tens of thousands of people to the northwest agricultural provinces of Battambang, Pursat, and Banteay Meanchey. Traditional villages, centered around the annual ceremonies of Buddhist life, were abolished and replaced by self-sufficient cooperatives. Canal digging, reservoir construction, and large-scale farming began. Angkar was wiping the slate clean. But poor administration by Angkar and limited agricultural skills on the part of the urban population, combined with intermittent drought, made living conditions harsh. Annual rice production almost halved.

In January 1976, Angkar sent 141 children to Shanghai for military training in radar, battle tactics, and reconnaissance. A few gifted youngsters learned portrait photography, cinematography, projection, and how to use Canon, Yashica, and Rolex cameras. Upon their return, they were sent to document Angkar's achievements, both public and covert. A pictorial magazine, *Democratic Kampuchea Is Moving Forward*, echoed the format of their Maoists benefactors, *China Reconstructs*. Aside from glossy propaganda photographs, an informal use of photography continued, the subjects posed in their obligatory "peasant" uniforms. Paradoxically, unaware of their own hubris, only the politically elite cadres were seen in relaxed compositions. When looking into the archives of the Documentation Center of Cambodia (DC-Cam), it is apparent that across the Khmer Rouge-held countryside loyal cadres, soldiers, and families did have access to cameras, film, and processing facilities. There are personal collections that show individual and family portraits that span those years. Under what sanctions Angkar allowed this photography is unknown. During the five-year Khmer Rouge period, people's clothing loses its individuality, with simple cotton trousers and shirts adorned with the ubiquitous *krama*. Over the 1977–78 dry seasons, Vietnam and Cambodia engaged in irregular conflicts along their shared border. Nurturing an ingrained xenophobia about earlier Vietnamese influence in the Cambodian communist movement, Angkar turned upon itself as bloody purges wracked the eastern provinces. The accused, their families, and associates were bought to Phnom Penh for interrogation. Nhem En (b. 1961) and six other young photographers were assigned to the Toul Sleng (S-21) secret prison. They took black-and-white identity portraits of some 14,000 prisoners as they were tortured for confessions and then trucked to the "Killing Fields" on the outskirts of the city. During the dry season of April 1978, Khmer Rouge soldiers again raided the Vietnamese border, crossing into Ang Giang Province, massacring the civilians of Ba Chuc village. Over 3,150 people were killed and hundreds more died from landmines planted in the wake of the attackers. It led to a devastating blowback. At the end of the dry season in 1979, Vietnamese troops counterattacked and then advanced to liberate Phnom Penh. Like Lon Nol before him, Pol Pot and senior cadres helicoptered to safety.

Khmer Rouge cadre holding her child. ca. 1976. Photographer unknown. Documentation Center of Cambodia (DC-Cam).

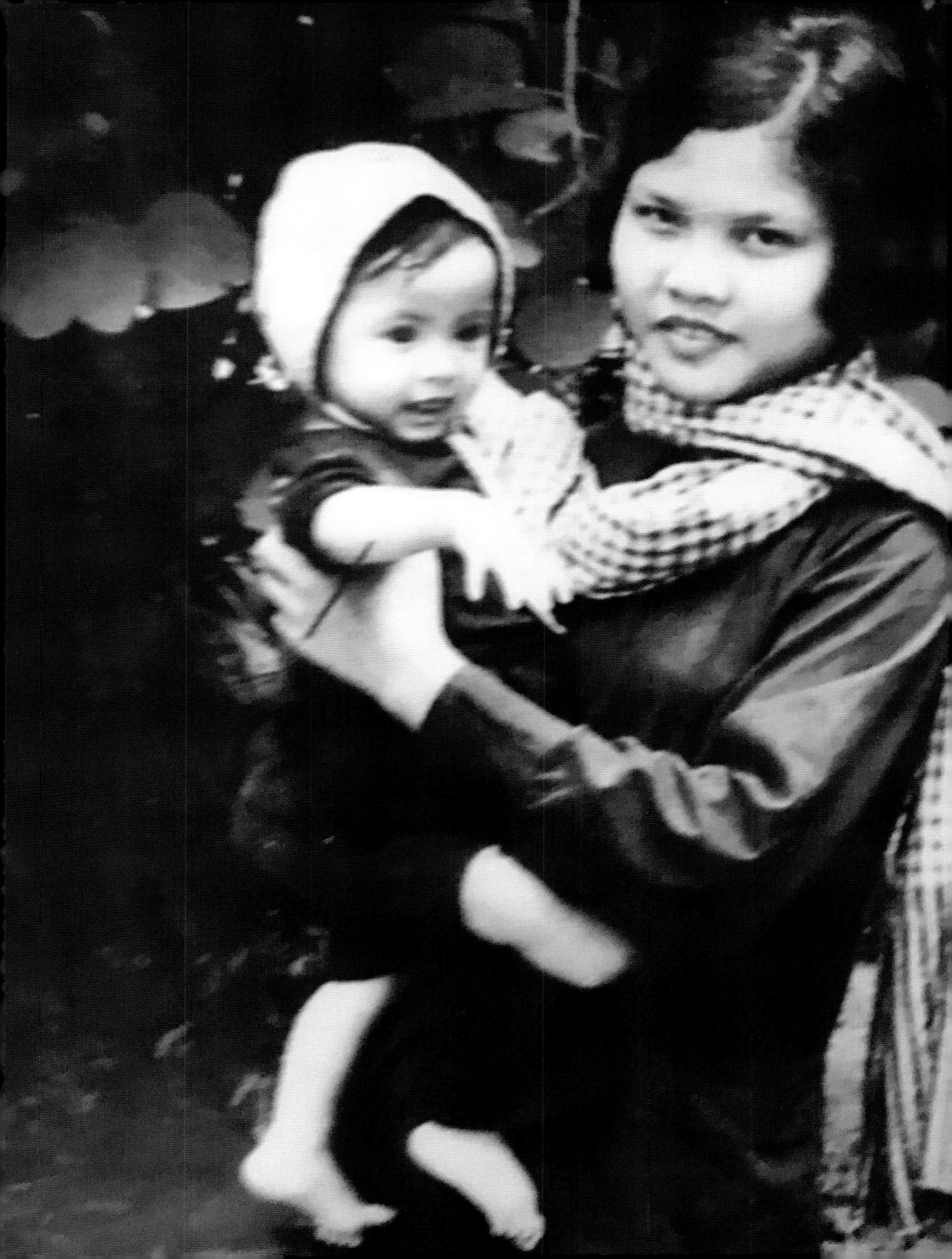

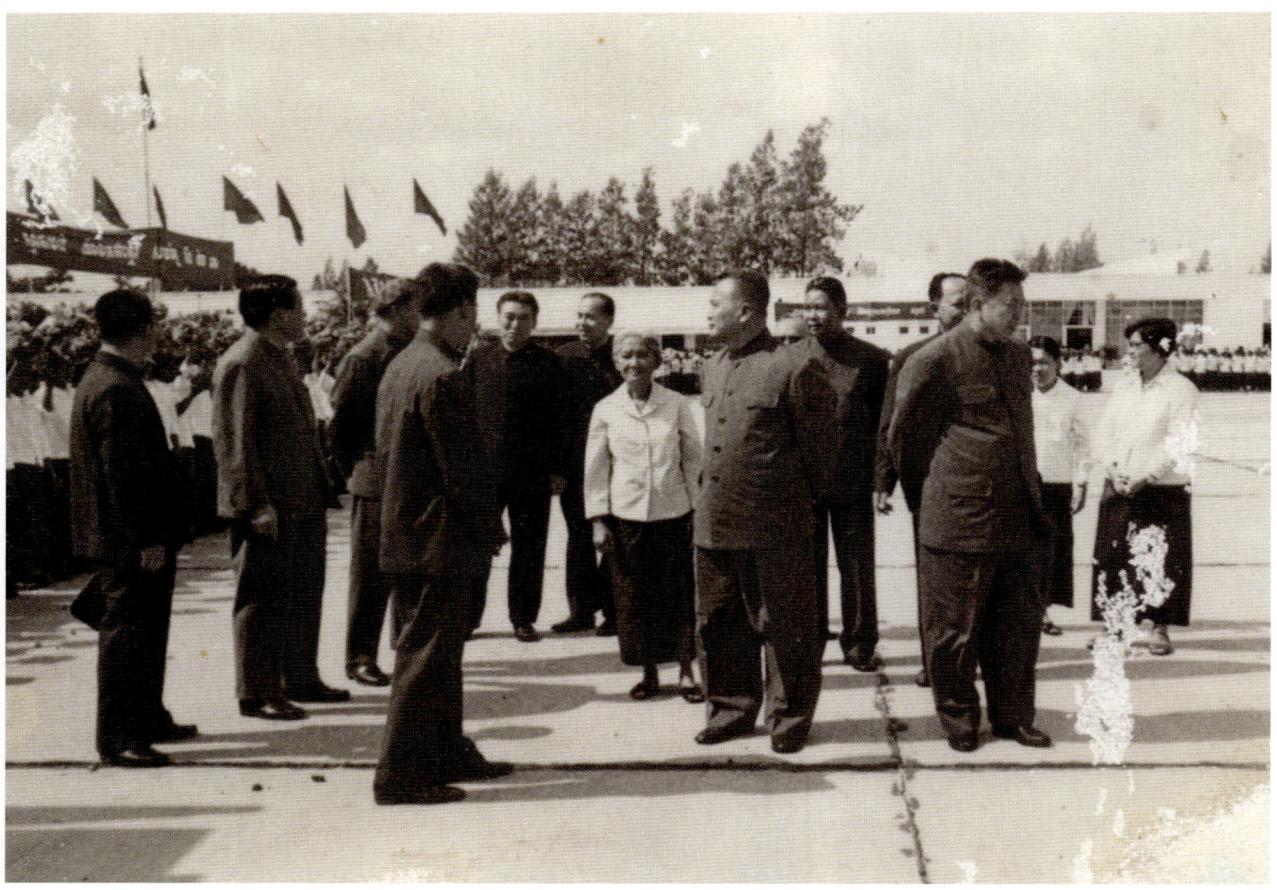

Angkar's Agricultural Utopia

With regards to photography, the Khmer Rouge dictatorship was unique. Unlike Russia or China, or Sihanouk for that matter, there was no mass distribution of portrait photography of political leaders to be displayed in schools and government offices, or large posters erected in public squares. Administration was expressed through whispered word of mouth and notes within envelopes, often delivered by bicycle. During Angkar's brief four-year control of the country, such restraint enforced the sense that the silent, omnipresent Angkar, "the organization," was in complete and total control. There were photographs of senior cadres, but often in surprisingly casual situations; they would have known these images were not for popular scrutiny. Meanwhile, the stock socialist iconography of beaming peasants with their abundant harvests was distributed for foreign consumption.

ABOVE: **Senior Angkar cadres at Potechong Airport.** Phnom Penh. ca. 1975. Photographer unknown. Documentation Center of Cambodia (DC-Cam).

RIGHT: **"Happy and proud to participate in the edification of the new and prosperous Kampuchea with full confidence in their brilliant future."** Photographer unknown. *Democratic Kampuchea Is Moving Forward* magazine, August 1977. Center for Khmer Studies Library, Siem Reap.

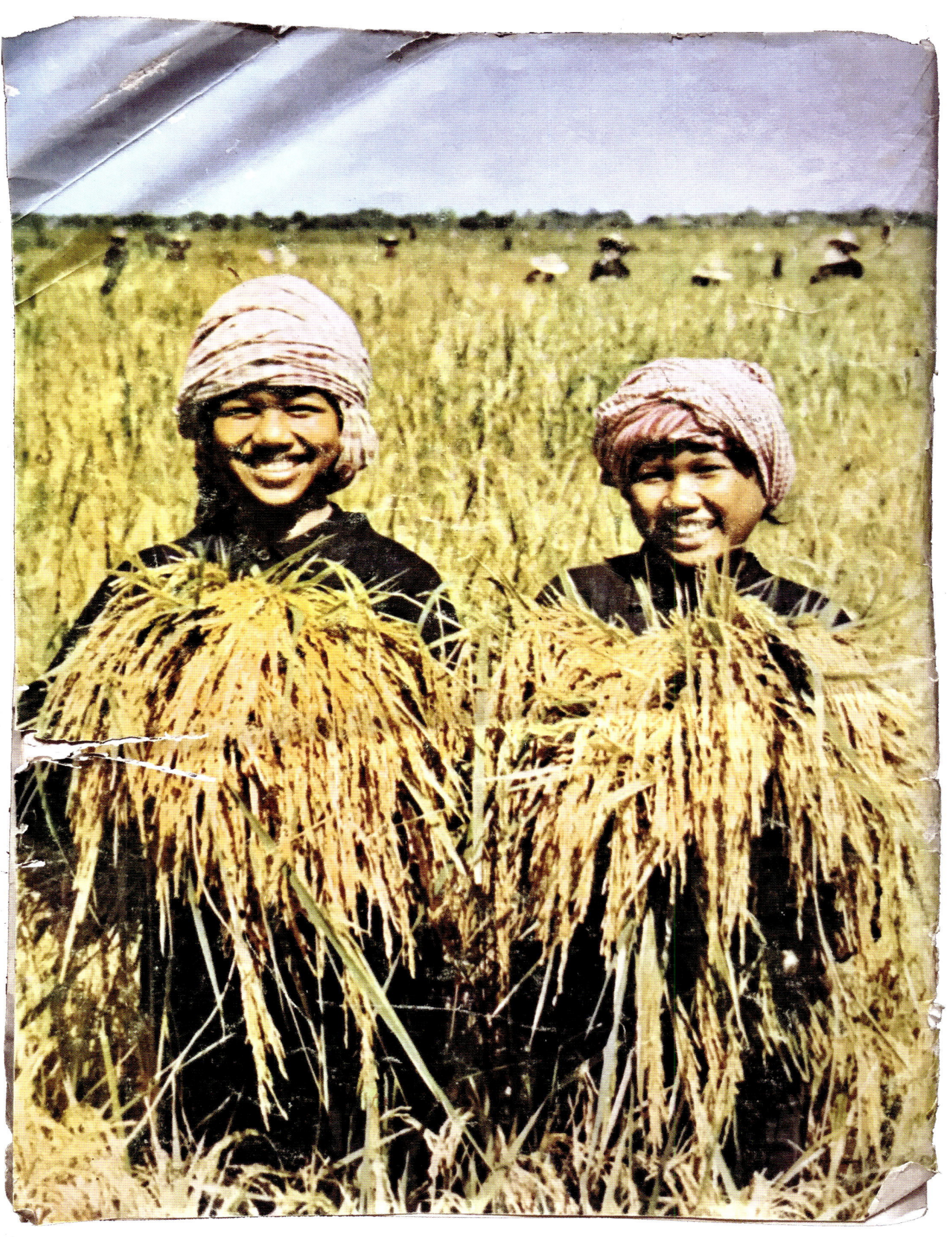

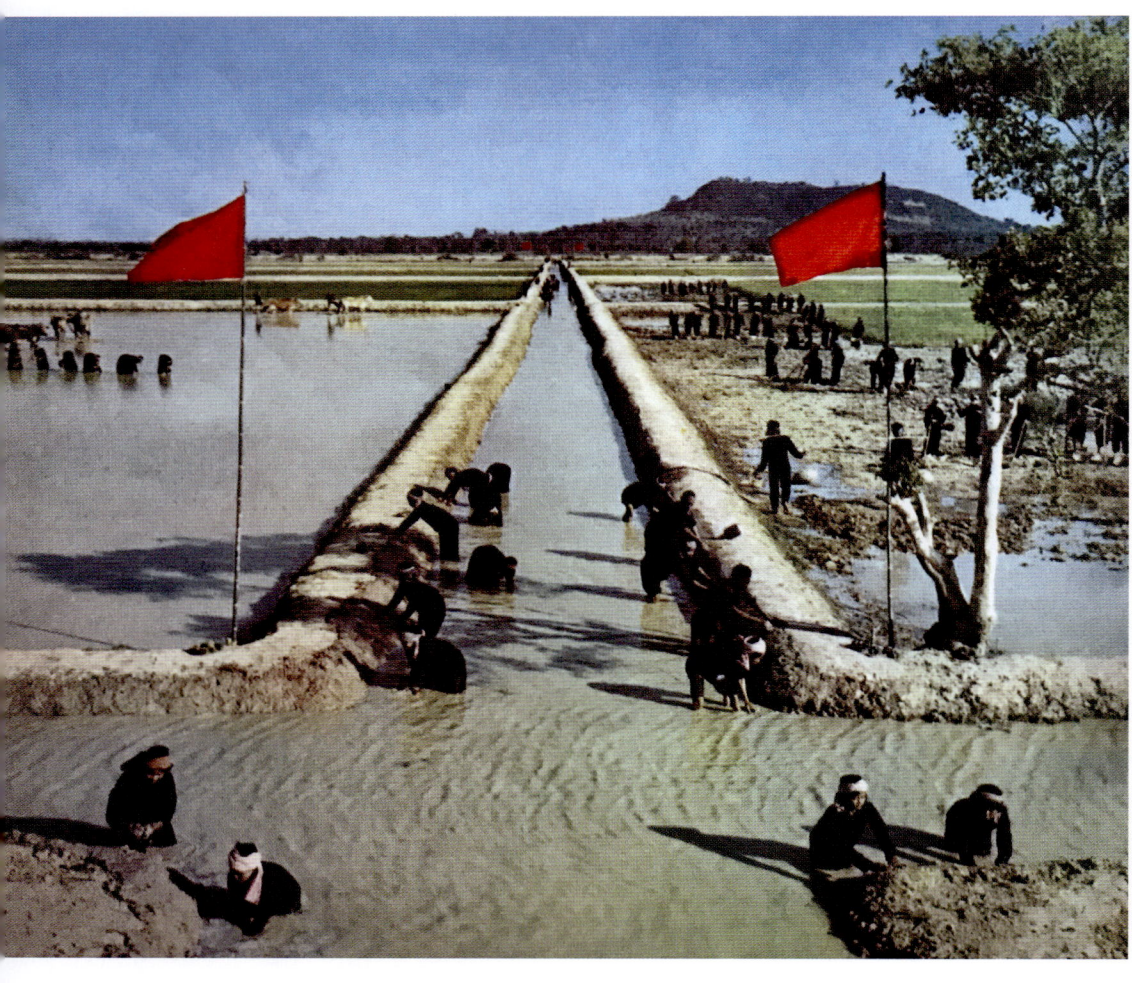

"Harnessing the rice fields in the form of a checkerboard and the systems of irrigation." Phnom Krom, Siem Reap Province.

Democratic Kampuchea Is Moving Forward

During the 1960s, Sihanouk published monthly color magazines. Both Lon Nol's Khmer Republic and the Angkar's Democratic Kampuchea continued this glossy tradition. Angkar focused on agricultural activities and collective labor in factories, where the subjects were photographed from a distance. Close-ups were extremely rare. The individual was subservient to the massed productivity of the state. We do not know if this was a political directive from Angkar, or whether it was a spontaneous expression of lessons newly learned by the young photographers who returned in 1976 from an educational visit to Shanghai. In "Harnessing the rice fields" above, two red flags mark the gateway of the manmade canal receding into the distance, while on the horizon rises Phnom Krom, the rocky hill at the northern end of Cambodia's great lake, the Tonlé Sap. On the summit is a ninth-century Hindu temple. If that mighty Angkorian civilization could rely on human labor to build a complex network of irrigation canals, could not the new Democratic Republic do the same?

OPPOSITE TOP LEFT, CLOCKWISE: "Mobilizing all energies to irrigate rice fields with windmill and pedal bucket chain." Possibly Battambang.

Democratic Kampuchea Is Moving Forward. Front cover, August 1977.

Textile factory. Phnom Penh.

Products in a silk weaving workshop.

Making oxcarts in a cooperative.

Reading the *Democratic Kampuchea* magazine.

Loading rice for export. Kompong Som Port.

Source: *Democratic Kampuchea Is Moving Forward.* August 1977. Photographers uncredited. Center for Khmer Studies Library, Siem Reap.

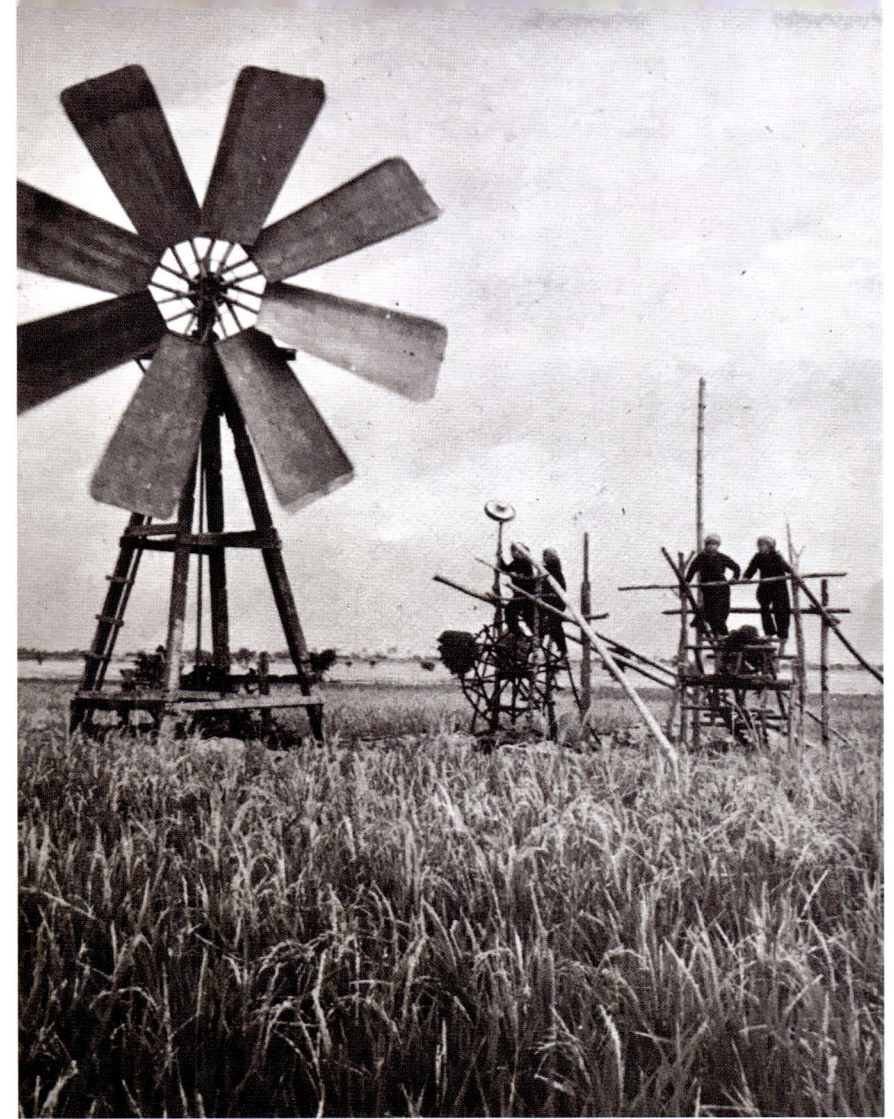
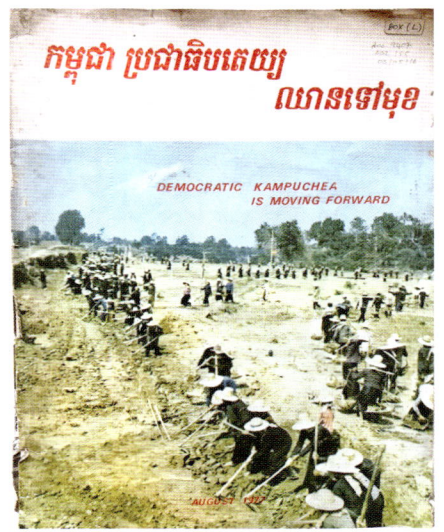
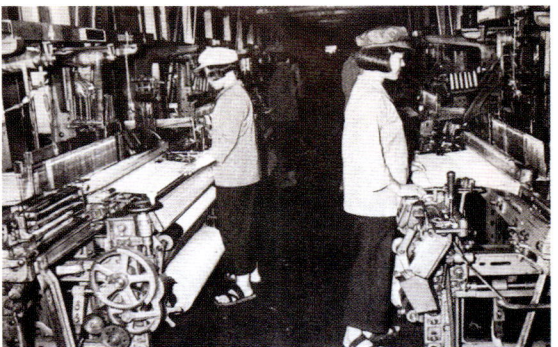
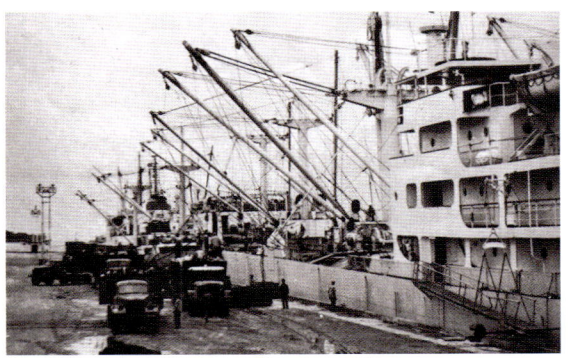
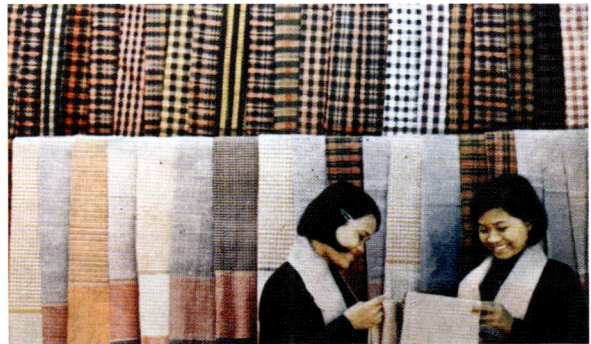
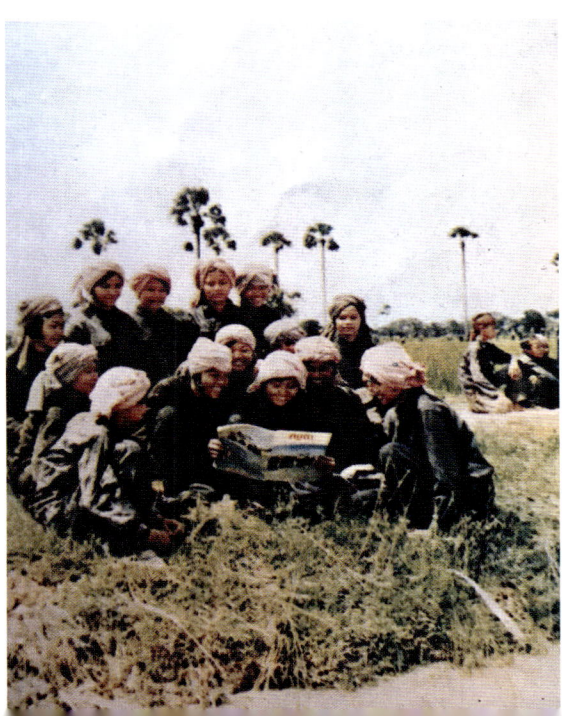
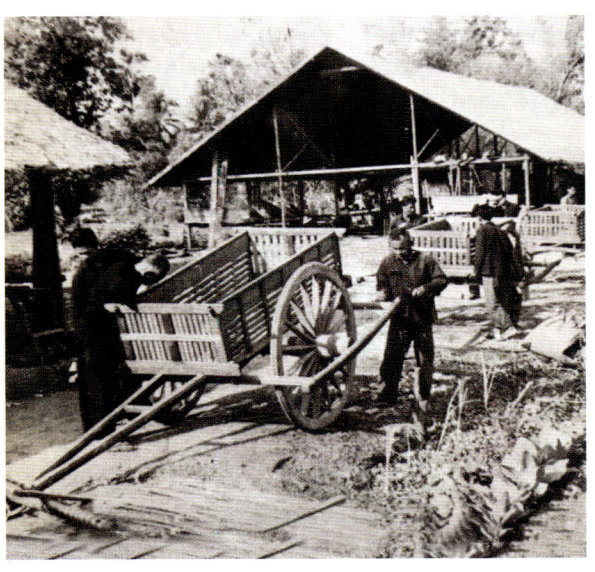

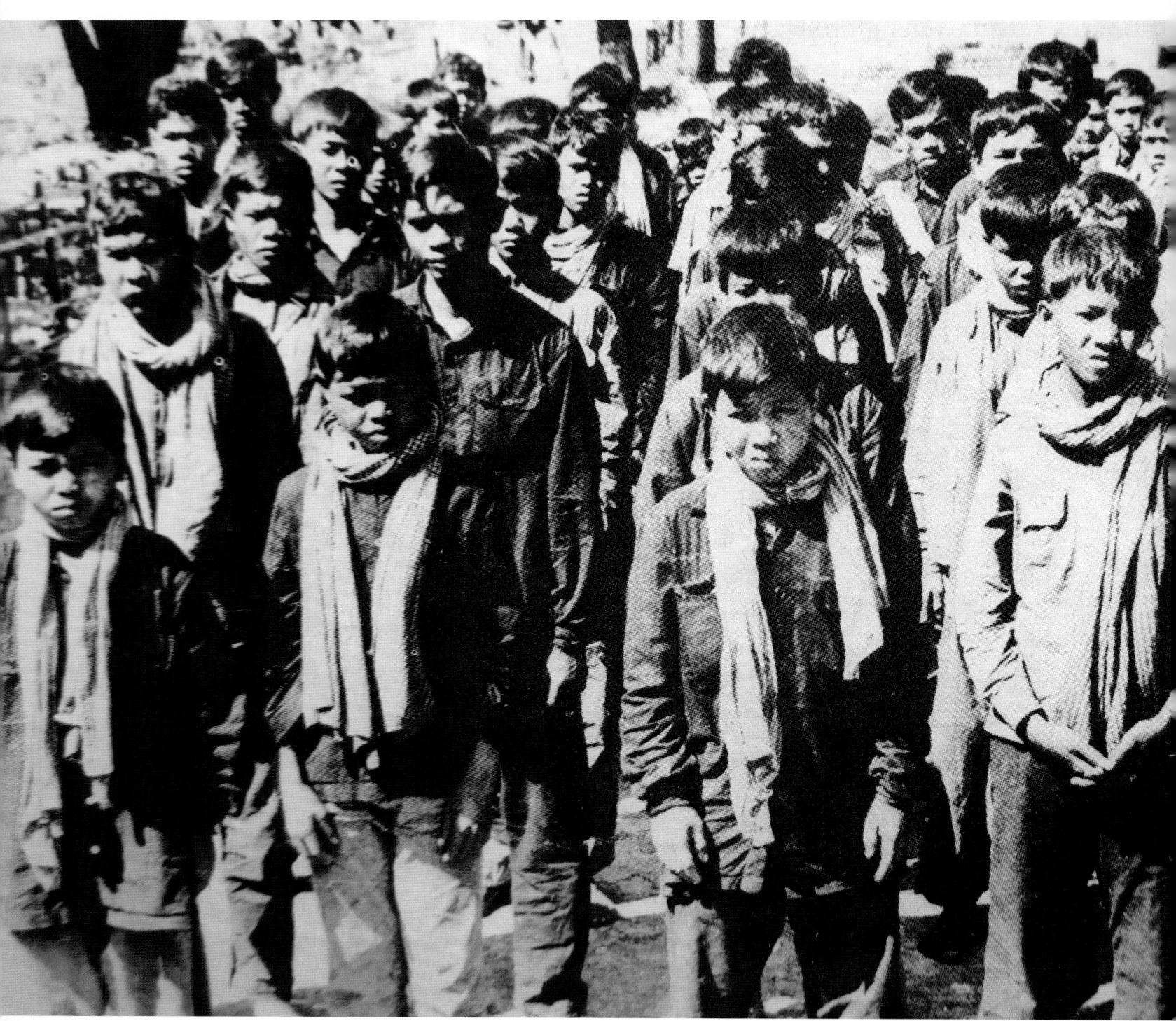

Khmer Rouge army unit.
Unknown location. *Democratic Kampuchea Is Moving Foward.* August 1977. Photographer uncredited. Center for Khmer Studies library, Siem Reap.

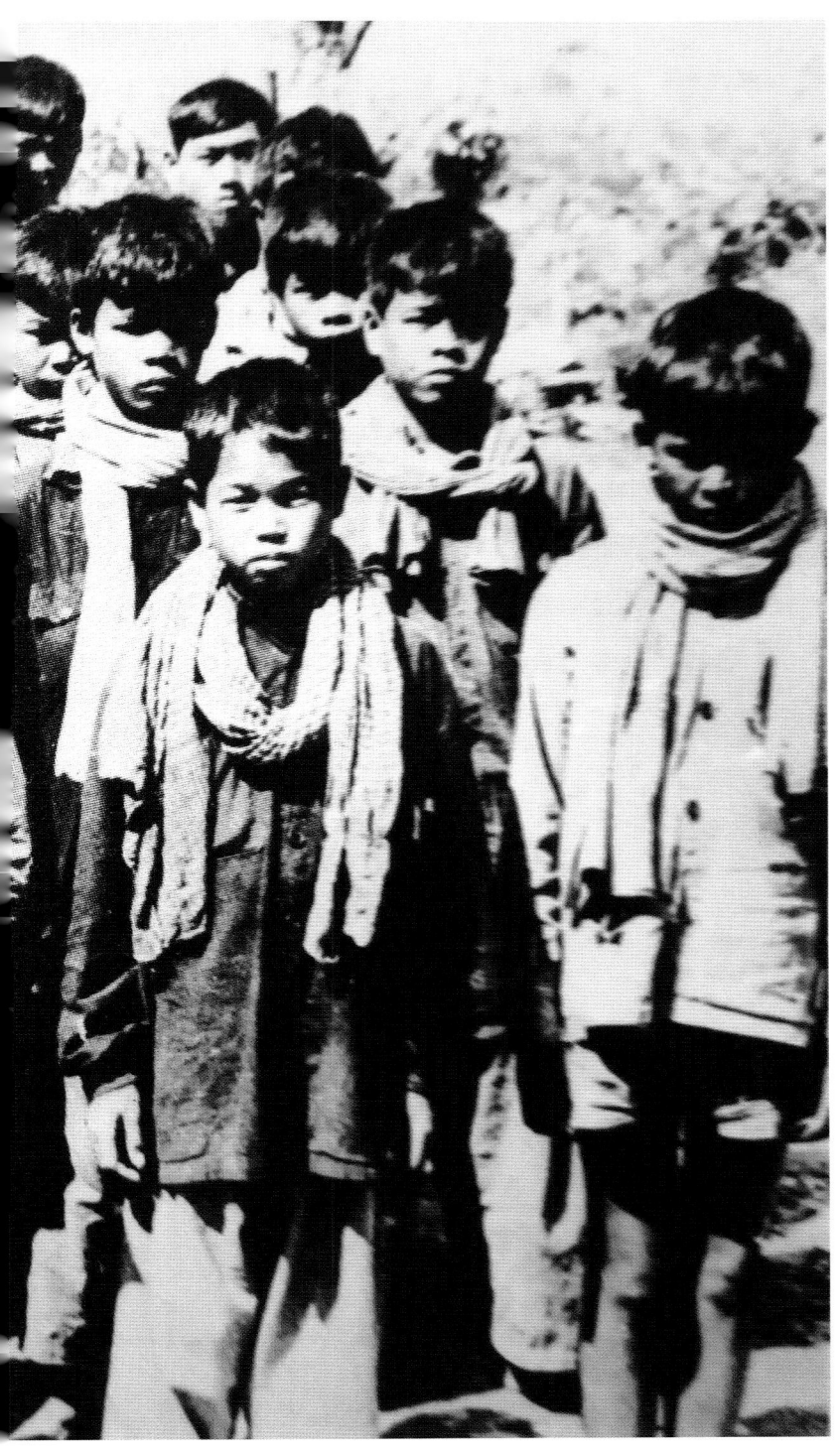

Child Soldiers of the Revolution

In a typical Khmer Rouge army unit, the average age of the soldiers was thirteen to fourteen years. They were mainly children from rural backgrounds with only the most rudimentary education. They were commandeered from communist-held territories and were often traumatized by the indiscriminate United States aerial bombing of the countryside and their exposure to the ferocious technology of modern warfare. Removed from an extended family environment, they were easily inculcated into the Angkar moral spirit, where "the others"—anybody who was not them—were the constant enemy. Uniforms consisted of locally made loose cotton pants and shirt, a traditional farmer's cotton *krama* scarf, and sandals made from recycled rubber tyres. They ate, worked, and slept as a collective. The Khmer Rouge efficiently implemented a plan to completely erase the past society, its politics, and its family structure, together with religion and a justice system. Upon a clean slate, a new agrarian society was to be created. As Teeda Butt Mam said: "They told us we were less than a grain of rice in a large pile. The Khmer Rouge said that the Communist revolution could be successful with only two people. Our lives had no significance to their great Communist nation." And they added, "To keep you is no benefit, to destroy you is no loss." (Teeda Butt Mam. "Worms from Our Skin." In *Children of Cambodia's Killing Fields: Memoirs by Survivors*. Dith Pran (compiler). Yale University Press. 1997.)

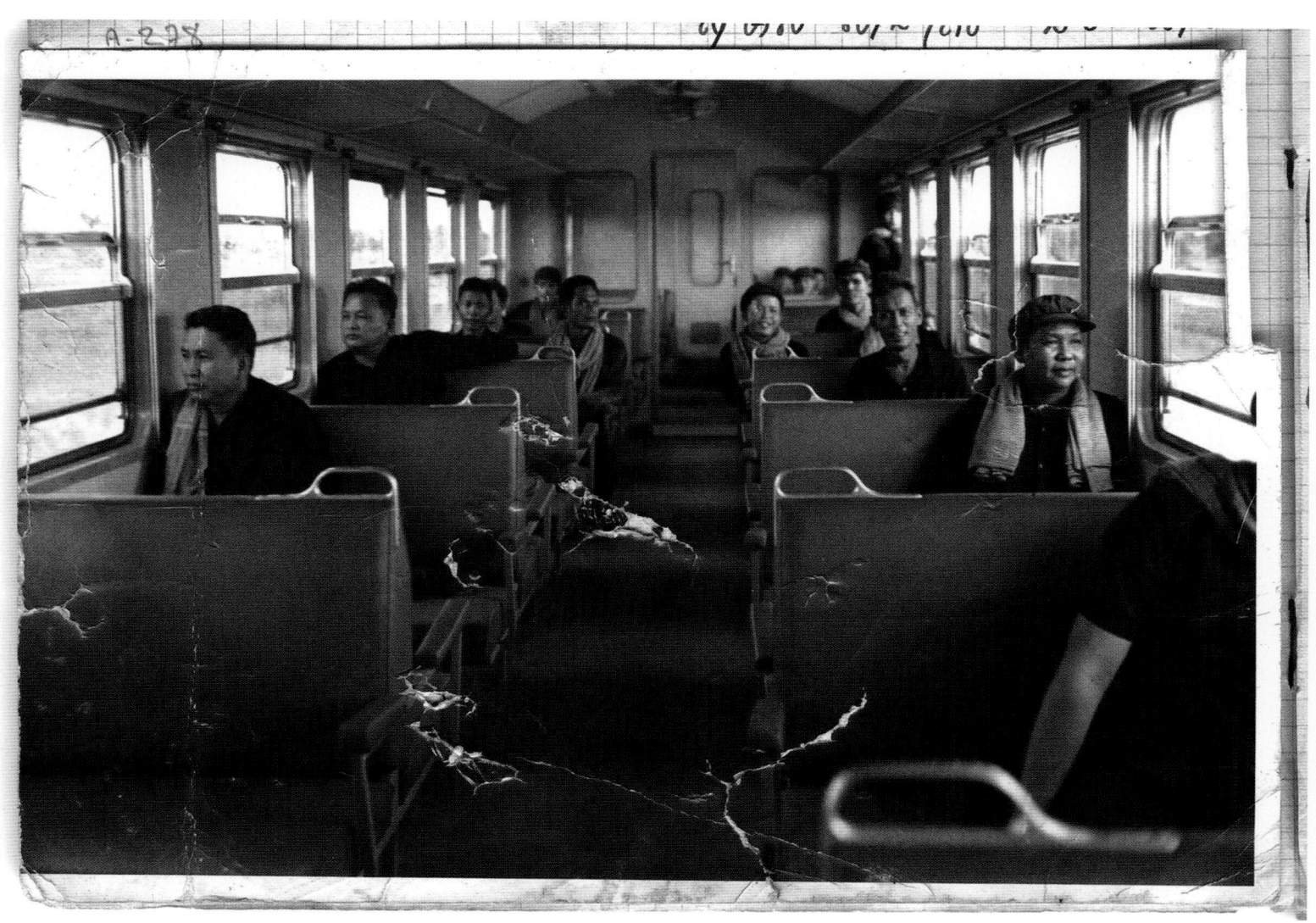

The Train Journey

This photograph is typical of the majority of images of Angkar's senior cadres. They look relaxed and informal, knowing that the photographer and the images he took were under their total control. There is only one senior cadre per seat looking out the windows at the passing countryside in what would ordinarily be a very crowded train. Lower cadres share seats towards the back, and three children poke their faces through the rear window.

Senior Angkar cadres on a train. Possibly the Battambang–Phnom Penh line. ca. 1977. Photographer unknown. Documentation Center of Cambodia (DC-Cam).

RIGHT: **Democratic Kampuchea Navy PC-461-class submarine chaser.** Phnom Penh. August 1978.

BELOW: **Child on a hospital bed.** Phnom Penh.

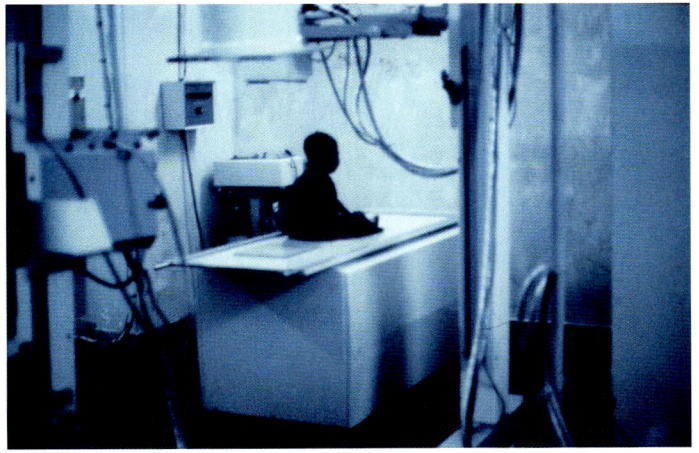

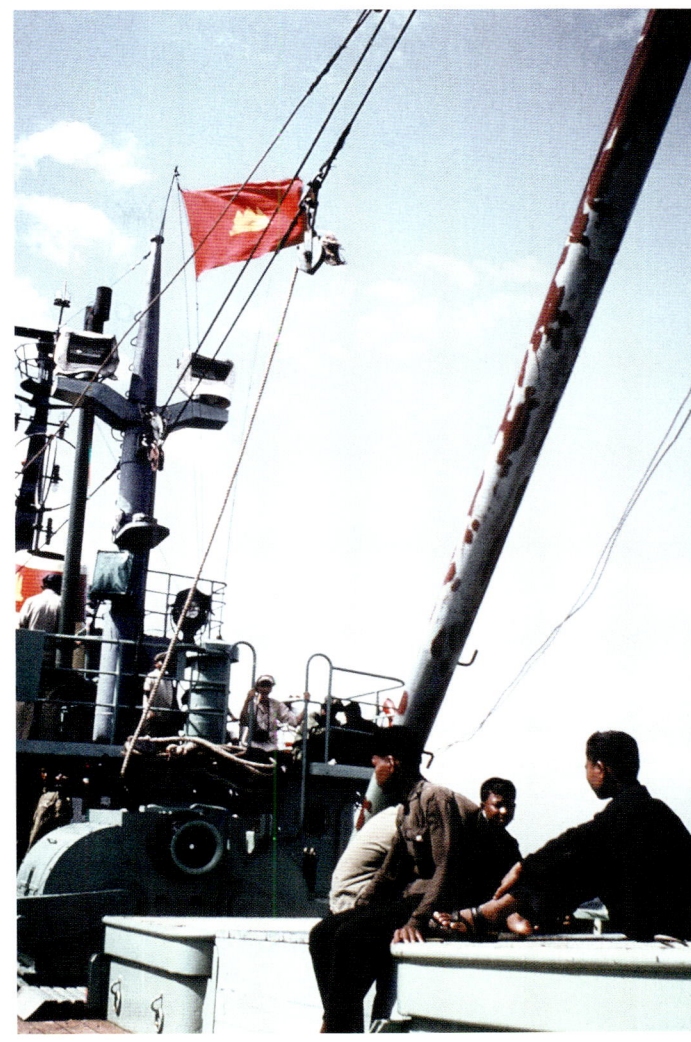

Swedish-Cambodian Friendship Mission

Gunnar BERGSTRÖM (b. 1951) was a founding member of the Swedish-Cambodian Friendship Association, a pro-Marxist organization keen to report on the Khmer Rouge utopia. He was a member of a four-person delegation that was allowed into Cambodia for a two-week tour of the country in August 1978. Their Angkar minders created stage-managed encounters with ordinary Cambodians, arranging visits to hospitals, thriving agricultural cooperatives, and factories. They were even invited to a charmless dinner with Pol Pot. A year later, while his co-travelers remained Maoist apologists, Bergström realized he had been duped by Angkar's propaganda, and that Cambodia was not a splendid rural utopia after all. In 2016, Bergström revisited his journey, offering remorse for his actions to local Cambodians and displaying the photographs he had taken during that initial tour.

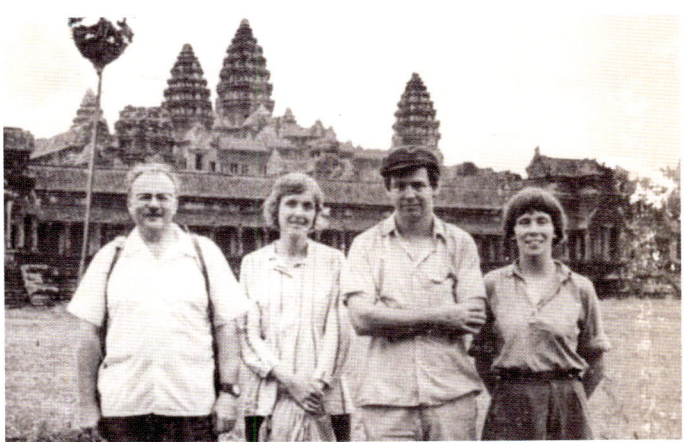

ABOVE: **Members of the Swedish-Cambodian Friendship Association at Angkor Wat.** Siem Reap. August 1978. Photographer unknown. Documentation Center of Cambodia (DC-Cam).

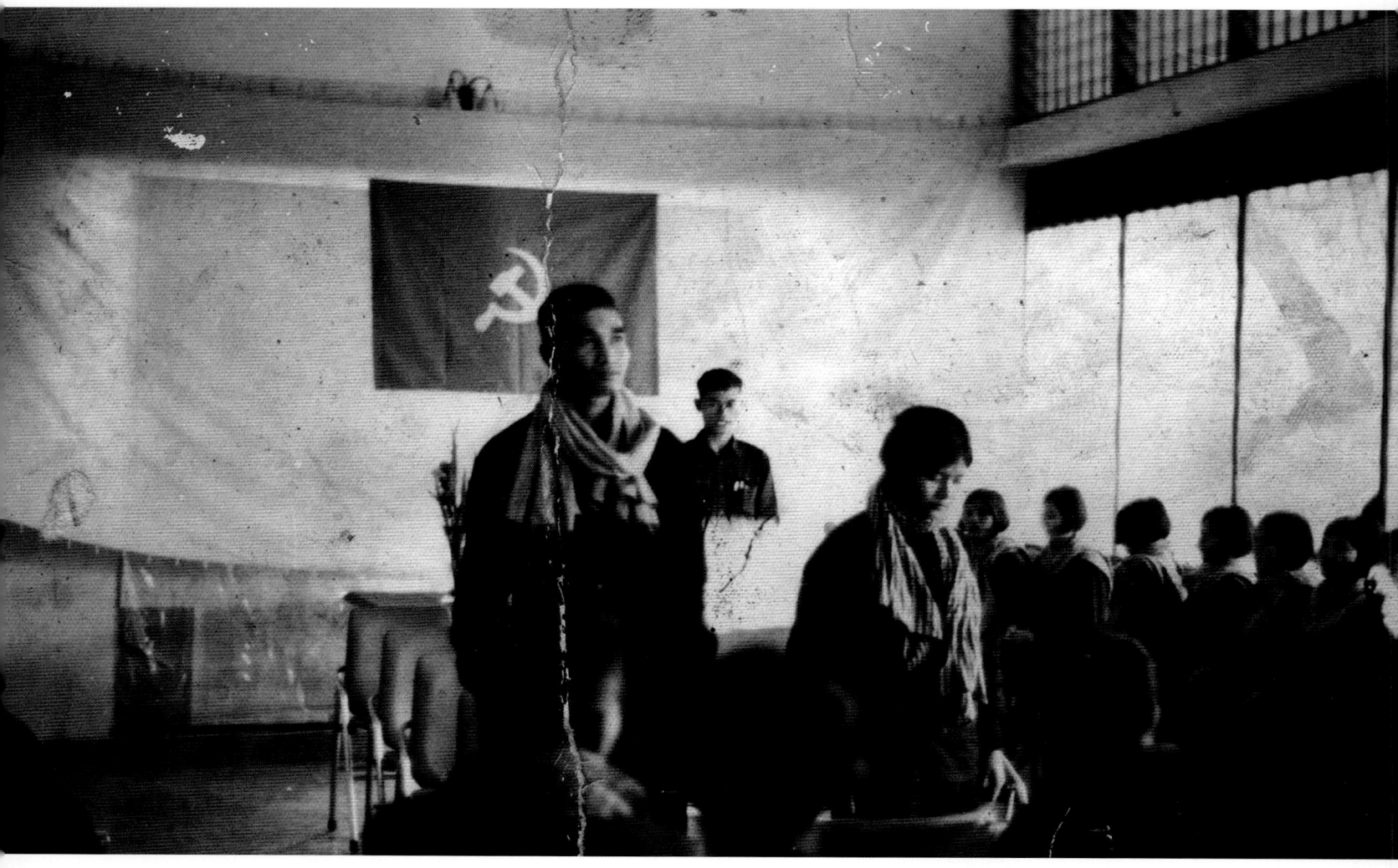

The Forced Marriage

In traditional Cambodian society, courting couples needed to have their families sanction their relationship, often with the mediation of village elders. Spiritual mediums would determine an auspicious time for the marriage, while monks from the local *wat* blessed the union. Special music, dance, and song, as well as ritual paraphernalia, were all part of the occasion. Traditional Khmer life, including these marriage ceremonies, was a key target for Angkar's ground-zero policy, an attempt to break with tradition and build a new society. Photographer NOEM Oem (1953–1977?) was the head of photography at the Tuol Sleng (S-21) secret prison. He took this photograph of the marriage of Nun Huy and Prok Khoeun in the prison headquarters in Prey Sar. Nun Huy served as the head of the Khmer Rouge re-education center at the prison complex. In 1977, he was killed after the escape of his radio operator. Disturbingly, that same year, his wife Prok Khoeun became deputy of an interrogation team at the prison where the photographer of this marriage, Noem Oem, was interrogated and killed.

The marriage of Nun Huy and Prok Khoeun. Prey Sar Re-education Centre (Office S-24), Phnom Penh. ca. 1976. Noem Oem. Documentation Center of Cambodia (DC-Cam).

Incursions at Tây Ninh

In September 1977, the Vietnamese province of Tây Ninh, bordering southeast Cambodia, was the scene of bitter incursions by the Khmer Rouge. They penetrated about 6 miles (10 km) inland, where their army destroyed many villages and killed more than 1,000 Vietnamese civilians. Shortly after, the Vietnamese published booklets documenting the atrocities as well as survivors speaking to the officials. The Vietnamese retaliated in December, quickly overrunning the Khmer Rouge army and advancing into Cambodia. Since neither side could agree to a political solution to solve the conflict, the People's Army of Vietnam withdrew. As they did so, they evacuated thousands of prisoners of war and civilian refugees, including the future political leader of Cambodia, Hun Sen.

Tây Ninh incursion pamphlet. People's Republic of Vietnam. 1977. Photographers unknown. Documentation Center of Cambodia (DC-Cam).

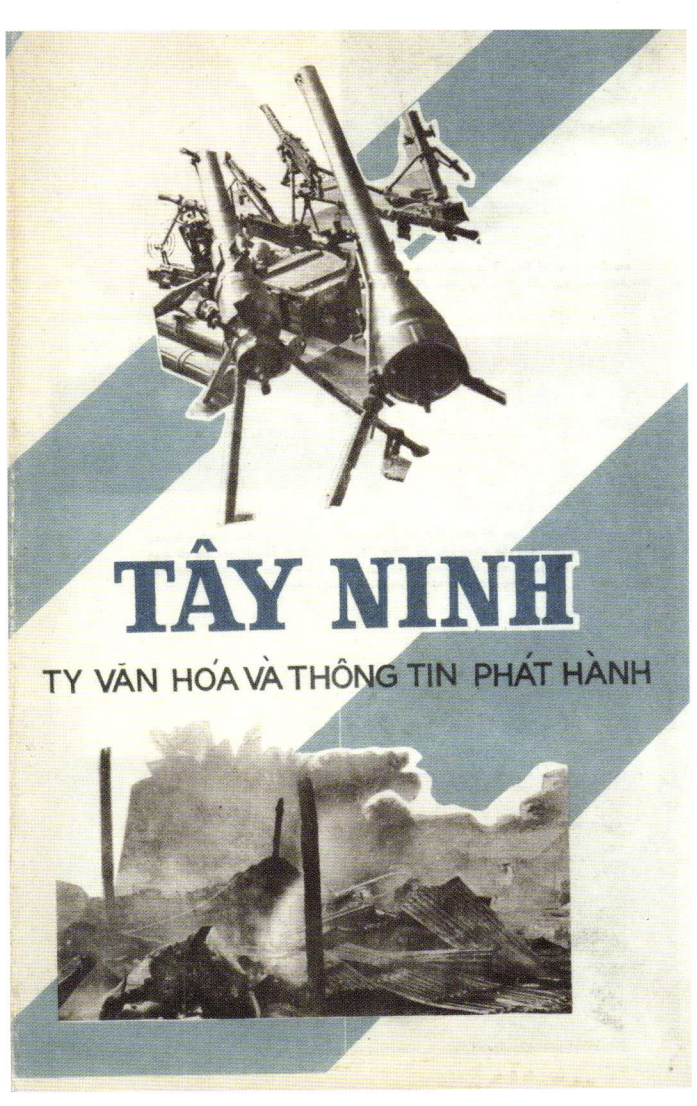
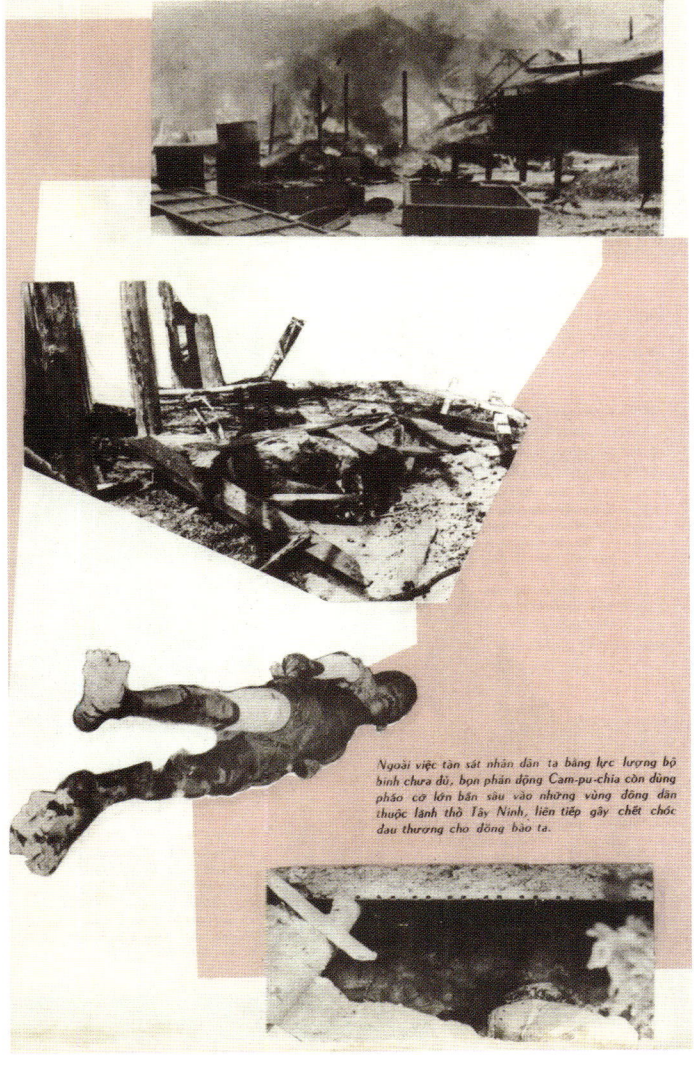

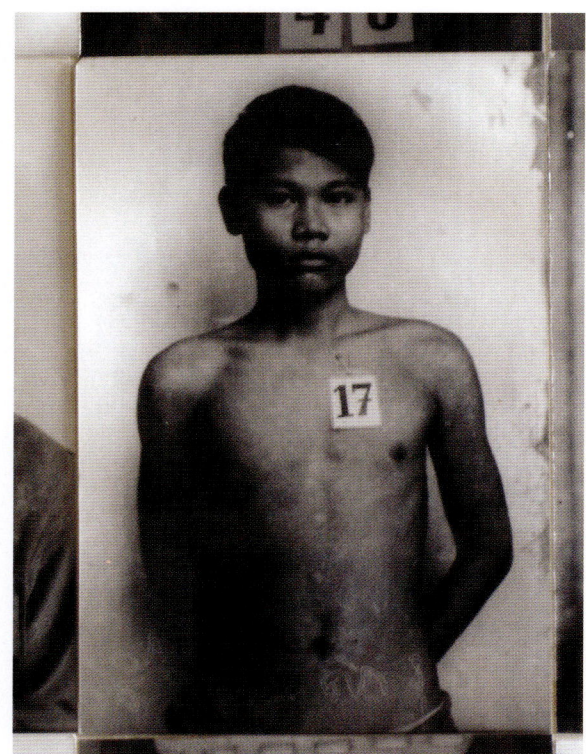

LEFT: **Prisoner 17.** Toul Sleng (S-21) prison, Phnom Penh. 1978. Nhem En. Darryl Collins Collection, Siem Reap.

BELOW: **Prisoner 162.** Toul Sleng (S-21) prison, Phnom Penh. ca. 1977 Photographer unknown. Documentation Center of Cambodia.(DC-Cam).

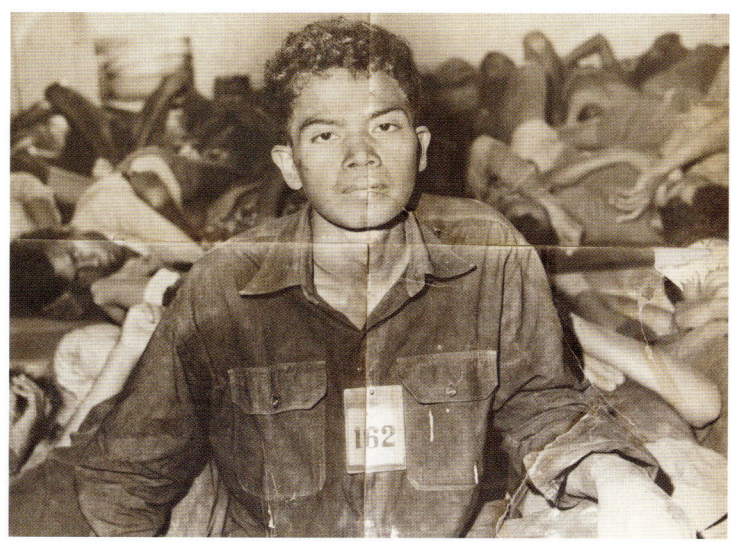

Toul Sleng Prison Photographer

In 1975, fourteen-year-old NHEM En (b. 1961) was sent to China for advanced training in photography. Upon his return, he was assigned with a team of six other photographers to document incoming prisoners at the S-21 prison camp in Phnom Penh. Nhem was a meticulous and diligent photographer, seldom making a technical mistake and refraining from any verbal contact with prisoners to avoid retribution from his boss, the notorious prison leader Kaing Guek Eav (alias Brother Duch). By late 1977, Angkar was imploding with internal purges. Especially vulnerable were the inhabitants of villages which had been temporarily occupied by Vietnamese troops in the tit-for-tat border conflicts. Suspects were sent to prisons for interrogation. Under torture, detailed "confessions" were extracted. Not having a shirt, the newly arrived prisoner 17 had his identity tag pinned directly onto his chest. He was photographed, then tortured for confessions, and trucked to the nearby "Killing Fields" for execution.

Prisoner 162

Amidst the shackled bodies of fellow prisoners lying on a concrete floor, prisoner 162 looks at us with a resigned calm. For many young prisoners, most of them rural "base" people untainted by urban excesses, it is quite conceivable that this was their first encounter with photography, other than perhaps the occasional wedding photograph or studio portrait documenting a rite of passage. While the vast majority of prisoners were taken to a special purpose room to have identity photographs taken, this contextual photograph is unusual. The neutral backdrop of the usual bureaucratic chain of images produced by the Khmer Rouge (as seen in the photograph above left) is absent, revealing the shocking reality behind— prisoners shackled together, lying on a concrete floor.

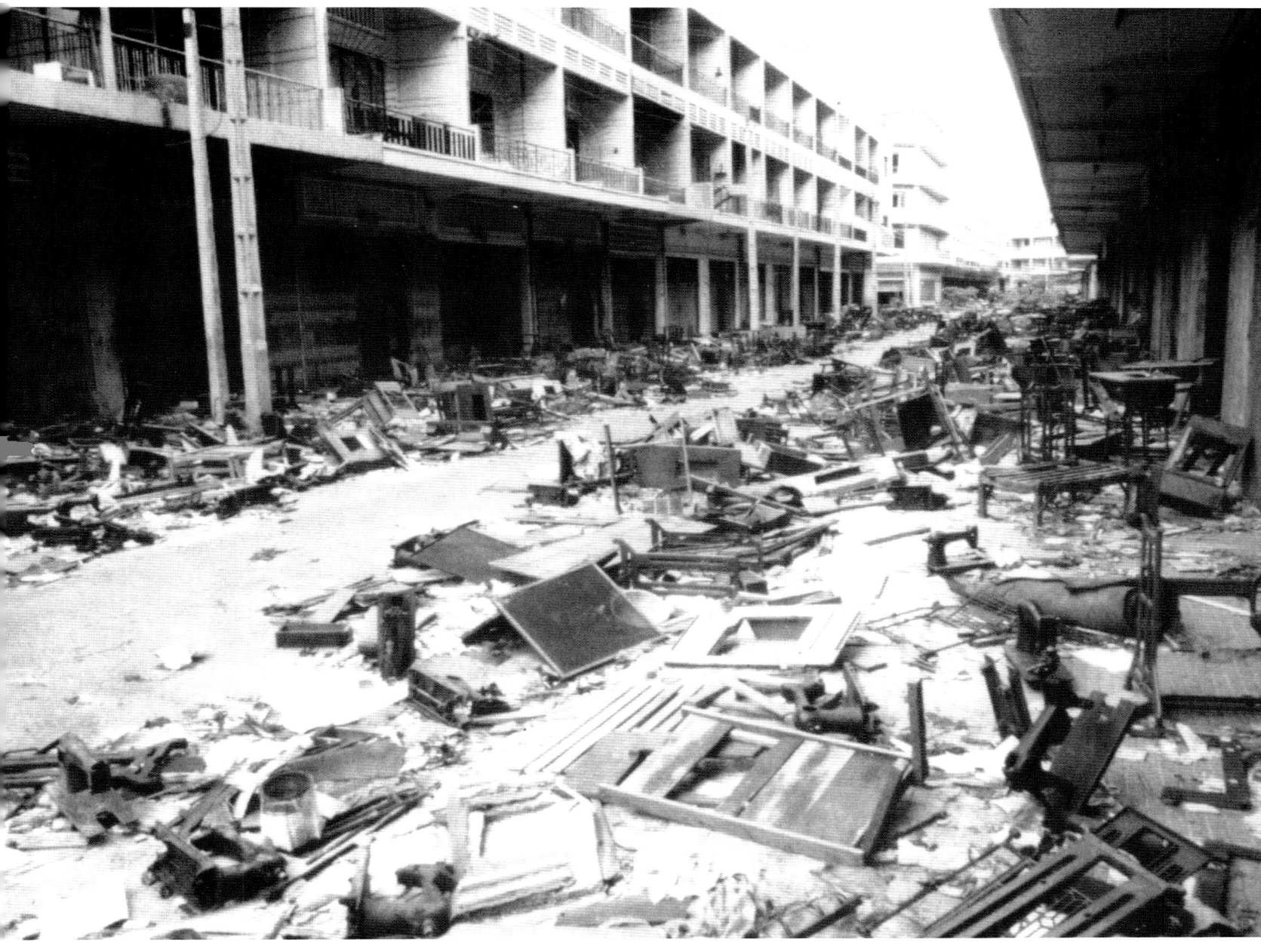

Abandoned Phnom Penh January 10, 1979

Abandoned streets in Phnom Penh. January 1979. Photograph: Possibly Ho Van Tay/AGEfotostock, Spain.

In December 1978, the Vietnamese launched a major offensive against the Khmer Rouge. With its superior weapons and manpower, its army advanced swiftly across the dry Cambodian countryside. On January 10, 1979, the Khmer Rouge army, ill-equipped and demoralized by internal purges, lost control of Phnom Penh. They left behind an exhausted city, with all traces and trappings of the Sangkum and republican years erased. Automobiles were piled in roadside heaps, the streets and boulevards littered with the debris of wanton destruction, and shops and cinemas shuttered. Civilians and refugees soon returned to the city, many squatting in abandoned buildings. Since government records and land titles had been destroyed, there was little leverage for eviction.

1979–2000
The Republic, the United Nations, and the Kingdom

The incoming Vietnamese regime established a new republic, the third for Cambodia in five years. Angkar left behind a failed, traumatized state, with army photographer Ho Van Tay (b. 1931) recording the grim remains of the Toul Sleng (S-21) secret prison. It was transformed into a memorial museum, with Angkar's meticulous photographs of prisoners becoming a riveting cache of human cruelty. With Cambodia's food chain in disarray, hundreds of thousands of people walked to refugee camps along the Thai border, and a new round of UN-sponsored identity photography began. As Angkar retreated to the northwest mountains, its army no longer remained a secretive operation. Photographers like Craig Buck (b. 1952) and Pierre Toutain-Dorbec (b. 1951) slipped across the Thai border to document their daily lives, suggesting that Angkar was receptive to presenting a more nuanced image of themselves.

The new socialist republic maintained a strict control of local media, with only invited foreign correspondents allowed into the country. By the late 1980s, the Cold War was coming to an end and financial support for the regime dried up. Their army left Cambodia in 1989. The country was renamed the State of Cambodia and survived by moving to a free market economy. In 1991, at the Paris Peace Conference, it was agreed that the United Nations would take control and disarm all factions, supervise general elections, and facilitate the return of refugees. Military photographers arrived. Previously restricted, the media landscape flourished. Media means photography, so Cambodians like Heng Sinith (b. 1964) and Mak Remissa (b. 1970) got the jobs. With a congratulatory flurry, Sihanouk returned as titular head. There was a different reception when Khieu Samphan, head of the Khmer Rouge, arrived a few days later for conciliatory talks.

In May 1993, four million Cambodians cast their votes in one of the fairest elections since independence. Jeff Widener (b. 1956), Bruce Sharp (b. 1962), and veteran Tim Page (b. 1944) returned with the international press to record this historic achievement. As the United States authorized the Cambodian Genocide Justice Act in April 1994, the Documentation Center of Cambodia (DC-Cam) was established to record and preserve the visual and written history of the Khmer Rouge regime. In the mid-1990s, the National Archives were rehabilitated after the Khmer Rouge had used the ground floor as a cattle pen. The year 1998 was significant for the revitalization of Cambodia's intangible heritage when Chorn-Pond Arn (b. 1966) started Cambodian Living Arts, and Ly Daravuth and Ingrid Muan (1966–2005) established the Reyum Institute of Arts and Culture.

On April 15, 1998, Pol Pot died in a small jungle hideout. Photographer David Longstreath (b. 1952) used a rudimentary digital camera to record his cremation. As Khmer Rouge cadres dumped his body on a pile of broken furniture, rubber tyres, and a stained mattress, a young soldier squatted down, lit a match, and the ensuing fire engulfed an extraordinary chapter of Cambodia's twentieth-century history. The digital age was born.

Les pionniers du Kampuchea. From *Kampuchea*. Antonín Kubeš (compiler). 1982. Photographer uncredited. Center for Khmer Studies Library, Siem Reap.

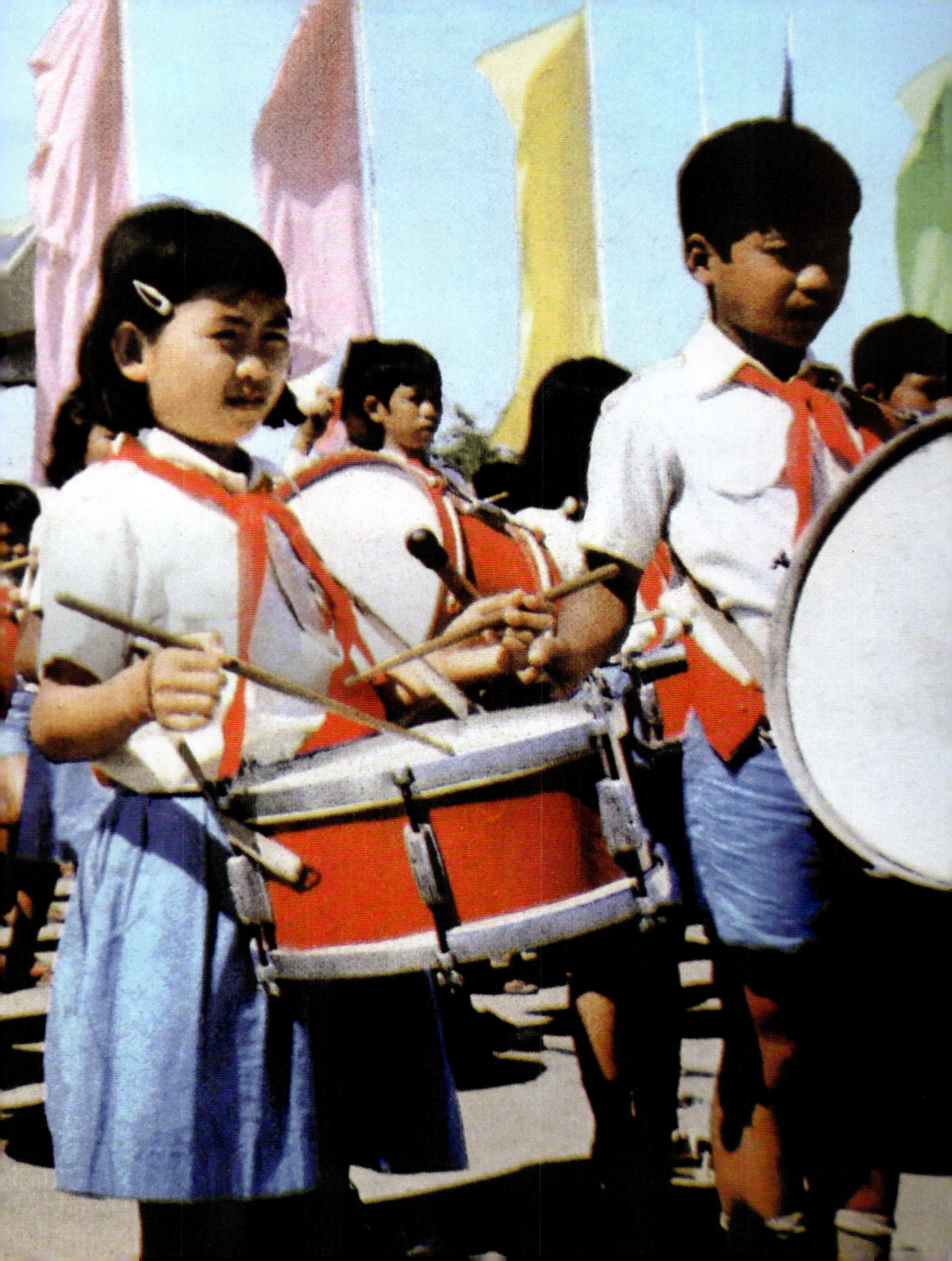

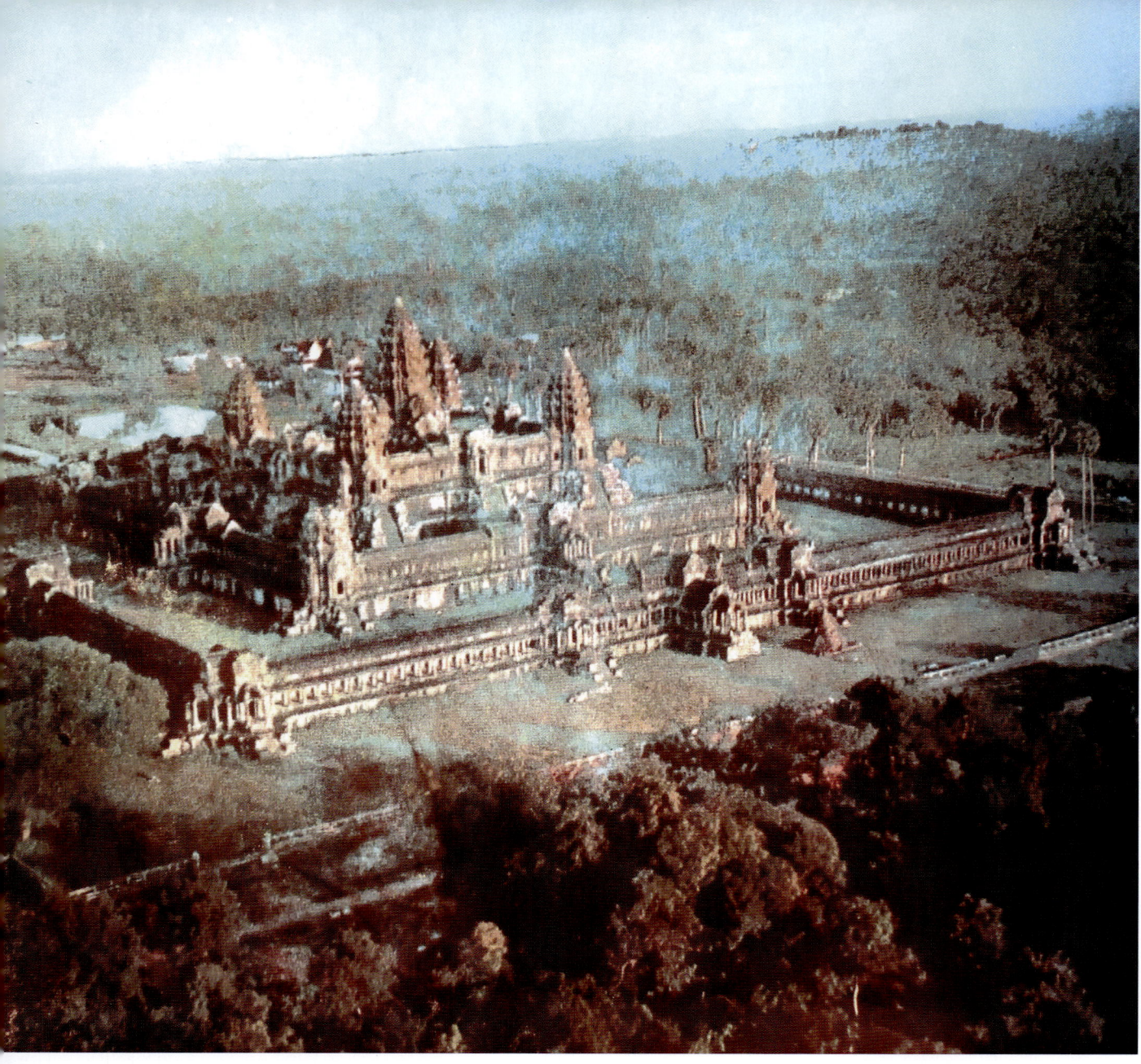

Kampuchea

In 1982, Czech-born Antoniń KUBEŠ compiled the pictorial book *Kampuchea*, containing images gathered from the Czech News Agency (CTK), the Telegraph Agency of the Soviet Union (TASS), and the archives of the Orbis Press Agency in Prague. Kubeš documented the rise of the Khmer Rouge and their four years of control. Positive images of life after the Khmer Rouge were ousted by the Vietnamese (the Czechs and Russians were pro-Vietnam) completed the review. The low-quality color separation and printing gave many of the images a strange enameled copper effect, especially the image of Angkor Wat (above).

ABOVE: **Angkor Wat from the air.** Siem Reap. 1982.

OPPOSITE TOP LEFT, CLOCKWISE: **Senior members of government greet a delegation at Pochetong Airport.** Phnom Penh.

Traumatized child. Location unknown.

In the 1960s, Phnom Penh was known in Europe as "the Swiss of Asia." Phnom Penh.

Women harvesting rice. Location unknown.

Hospital surgery. Phnom Penh.

Irrigating rice fields. Location unknown.

Vietnamese troops on parade. Phnom Penh.

Source: From *Kampuchea*. Antoniń Kubeš (compiler). 1982. Photographers uncredited. Center for Khmer Studies Library, Siem Reap.

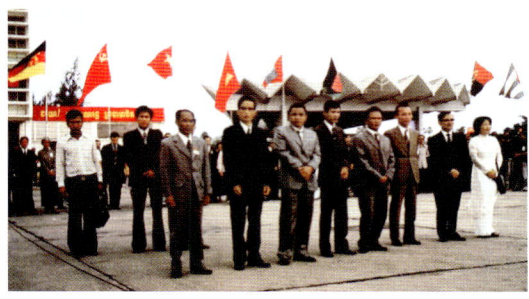
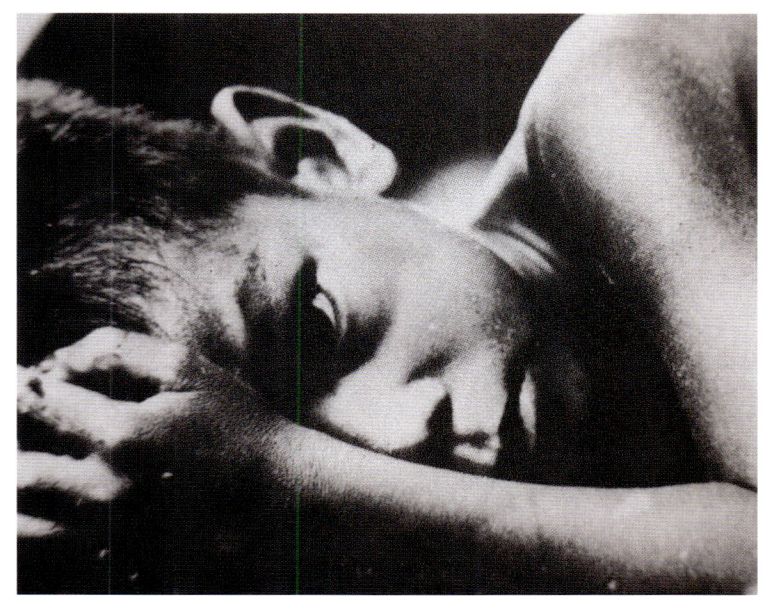
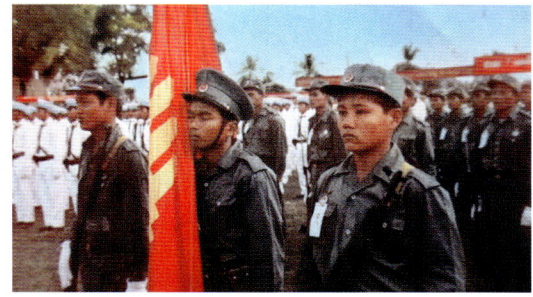
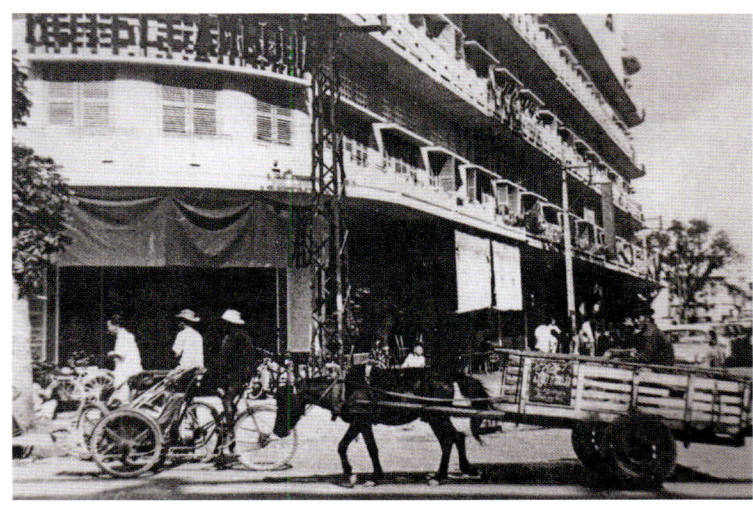
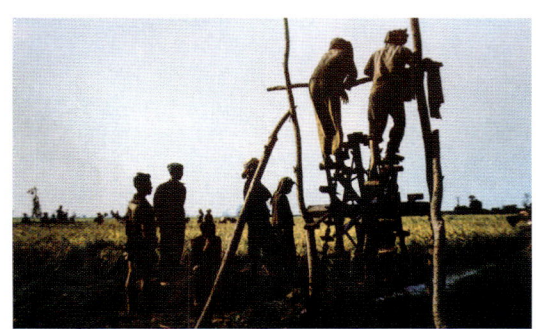
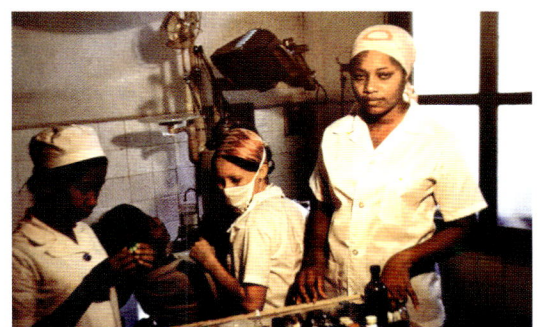
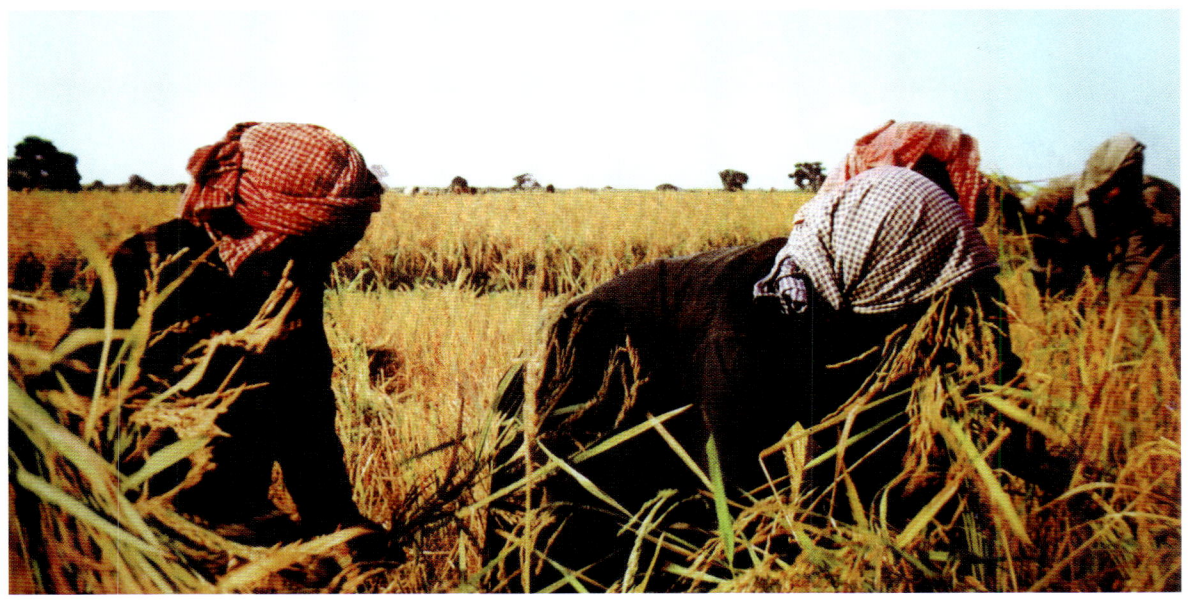

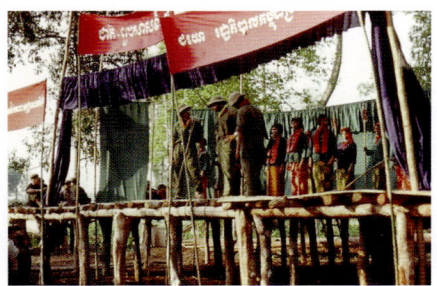
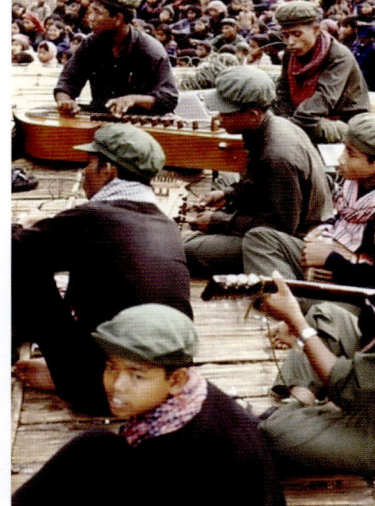
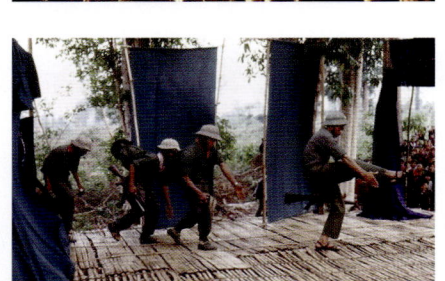
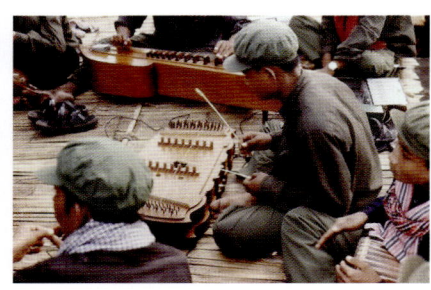
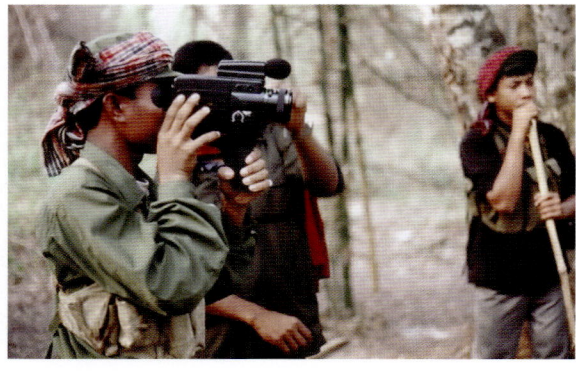
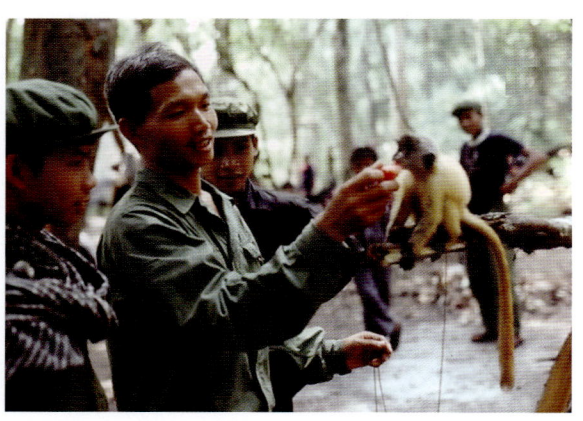

TOP LEFT, CLOCKWISE: **Temporary stage.**

Military orchestra.

Soldier with pet parrots.

Musician playing a *roneat* **(xylophone).**

Soldiers with pet marmot.

Khmer Rouge cadre shooting Super-8.

Performers lampooning Vietnamese troops.

Photographs: Craig Buck. Northwestern territories. 1981.

Crossing the Border

In 1981, Craig BUCK (b. 1952) crossed the Thai border three times into Khmer Rouge-held territory to document the daily life of the soldiers. They lived in temporary camps, constantly changing location to avoid detection by the Vietnamese army. His photographs show young men laughing and joking, playing with pets, and being entertained by a troupe of performers and musicians on a temporary stage. The show lampoons the Vietnamese, belittling their character. It exemplifies the role of propaganda in stereotyping the enemy. Intriguingly, he also took an image of a cadre using his own Super-8 film camera. The all-pervading sense of Angkar's stoic revolution seemed to have dissolved.

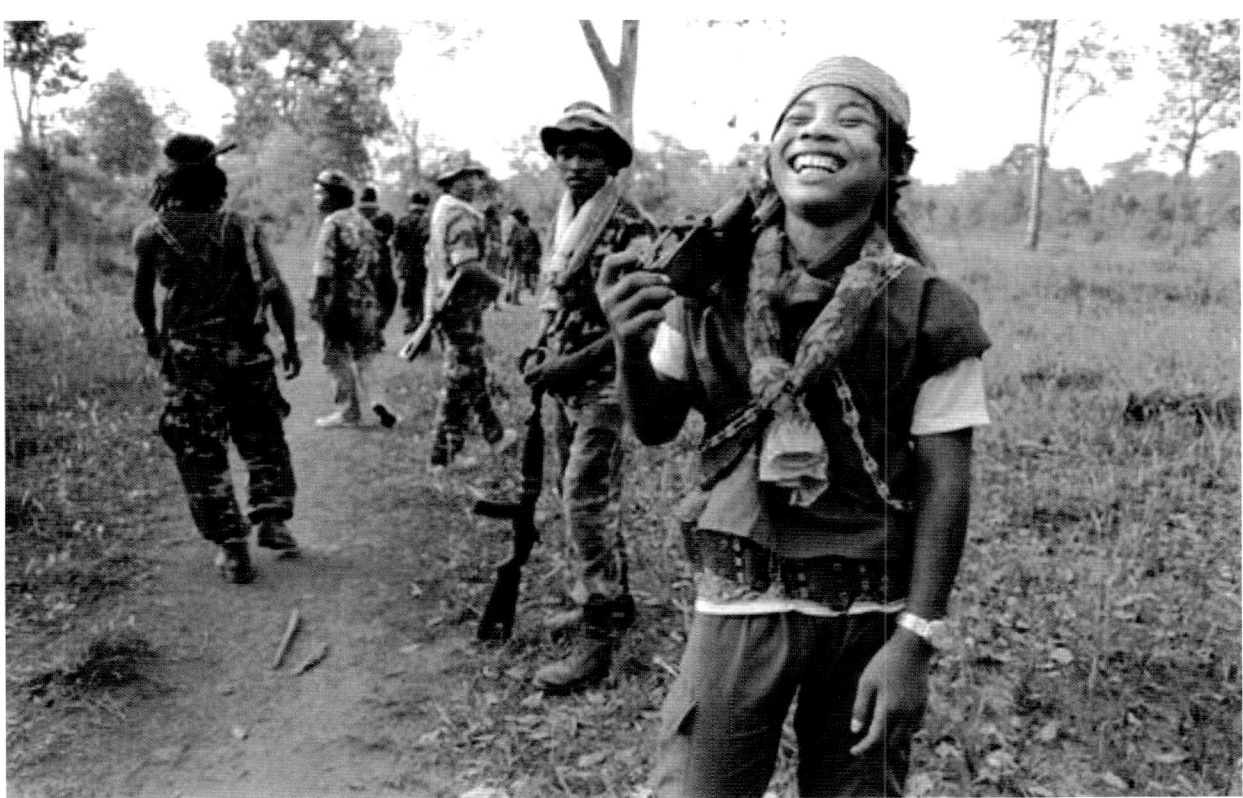

The Khmer Serei

Initially a powerful guerrilla force in the 1960s, the Khmer Serei were both anti-Sihanouk and anti-communist. By the early 1980s, through defections and a lack of centralized leadership, the Khmer Serei had broken into competing bands of militarized warlords. They preyed on outlying villages and refugee camps that had grown up along the Thai-Cambodian border. Like Craig Buck with the Khmer Rouge, Pierre TOUTAIN-DORBEC (b. 1951) photographed the Khmer Serei with an extraordinary intimacy. In his own words: "I was coming back from a tour with the Khmers Rouges, and I was visiting one of the refugee camps on the Thai border (Khao-I-Dang about [12 miles] 20 km from Aranyaprathet), when some refugees came to me. They said: 'Come with us, some armed guys are stealing our rice.' I went and I meet all those Khmer Serei that were indeed stealing the rice that was supposed to be distributed for free to the refugees."

Laughing Khmer Serei soldier. Thai-Cambodian border. 1981. Pierre Toutain-Dorbec.

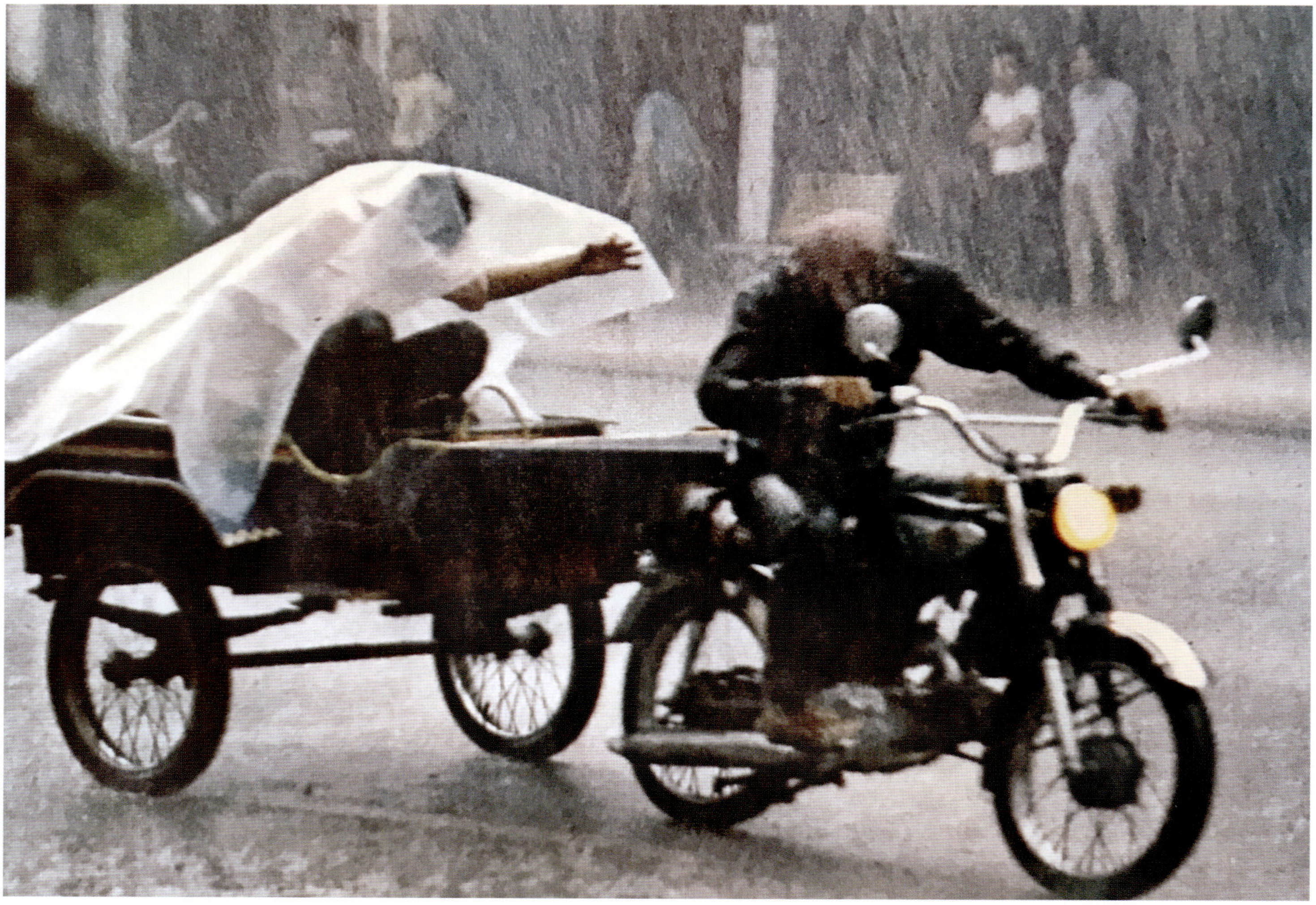

National Geographic

A year after the Vietnamese victory, National Geographic asked journalist Peter T. White and photographer David Alan HARVEY (b. 1944) to create the story "Kampuchea Wakens From a Nightmare." It was in conjunction with an article on the temples of Angkor. While journalists have often spoken about how their itineraries were carefully managed in the first years of the new republic, Harvey's ability to project the National Geographic style of high color, graphic strength, and "the moment" would have delighted the new republic's image makers. Having a wide international readership, the magazine's articles were a major coup for the Vietnamese to legitimize their actions in ousting the Khmer Rouge. Life, in all its colorful moments, had returned. The stories were published in the May 1982 edition of National Geographic.

ABOVE: *Remorque-moto racing through a storm.* Phnom Penh. 1981. David Alan Harvey/Magnum Photos.

BELOW: **Cover of *National Geographic*.** May 1982.

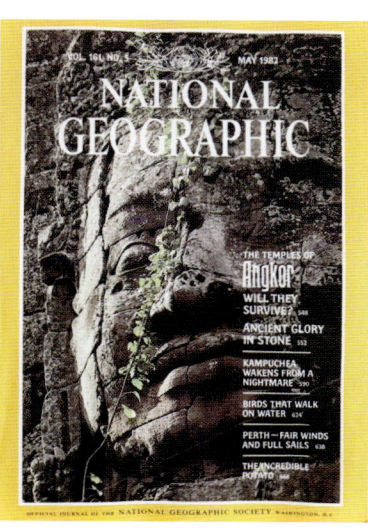

The Hotel Cambodiana

Swiss by birth, Jean-Noel WETTEWALD (b. 1955), worked thirty-four years for the United Nations High Commission for Refugees (UNHCR), with substantial stints in Vietnam and Cambodia. His photograph of the swimming pool and pavilion of the Hotel Cambodiana overlooking the Mekong River, bereft of people, displays forlorn neglect. Designed by Cambodian architect Lu Ban Hap in 1967, the hotel was completed in 1970. From 1975 to 1979, the Democratic Kampuchea regime used it as a fertilizer storehouse. Rehabilitated after liberation, it was popular in the early 1990s with the staff of the United Nations Transitional Authority in Cambodia (UNTAC).

View of the Hotel Cambodiana and swimming pool. Phnom Penh. 1984. Jean-Noel Wetterwald.

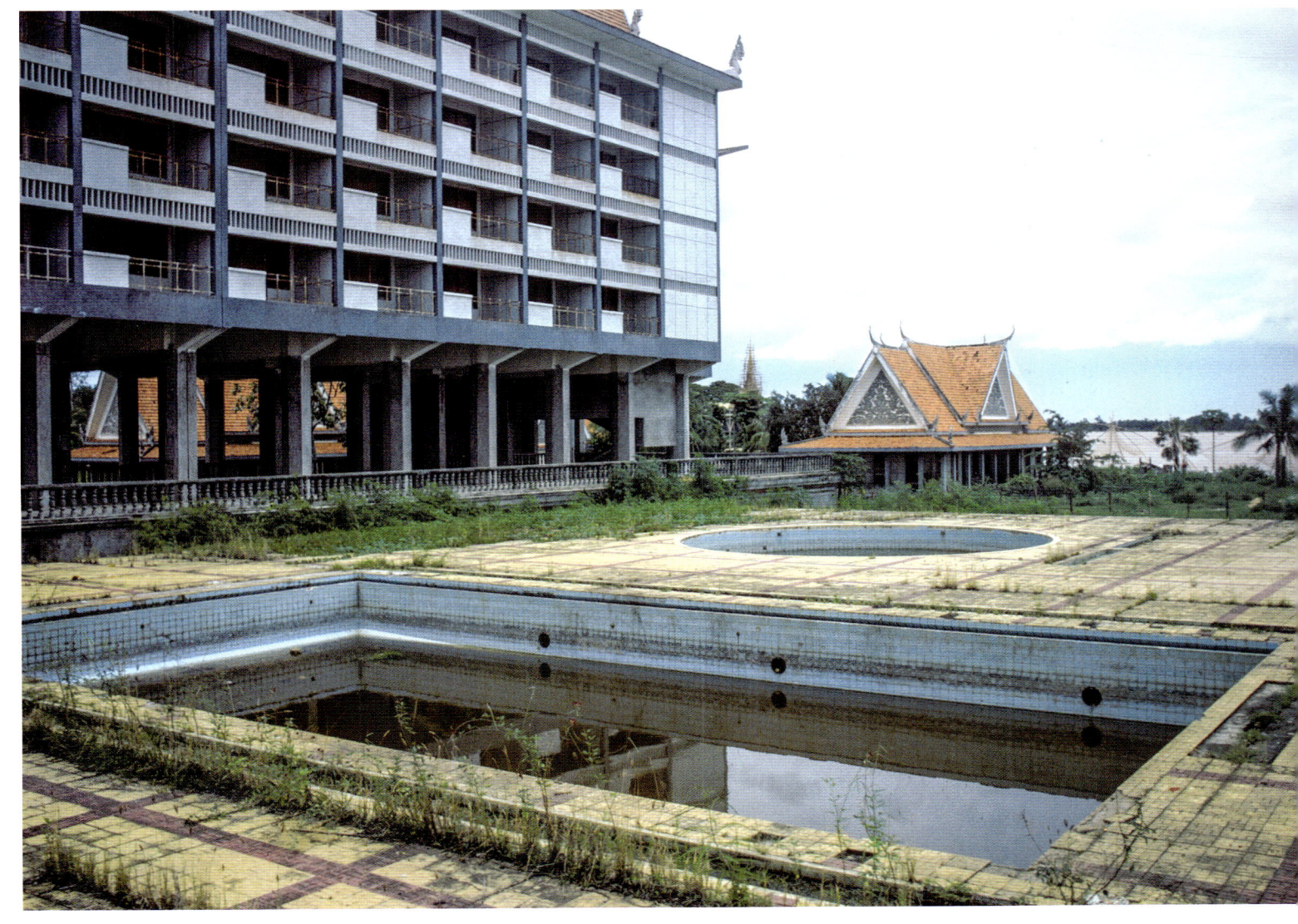

Camp Site II

The researcher, writer, and photographer Sharon MAY (b. 1964) spent two years at the Thai-Cambodian border camps, particularly Camp Site II. May observed the resilience of the older generations of Cambodians who survived the Khmer Rouge persecutions and were passing on their skills of music and dance to a younger generation. May's photographs reveal the resourcefulness essential for survival in such difficult circumstances, as well as the humor embedded in everyday life. "Girl running in camp lane," however, stands out as a photograph loaded with questions—and potential youthful joy.

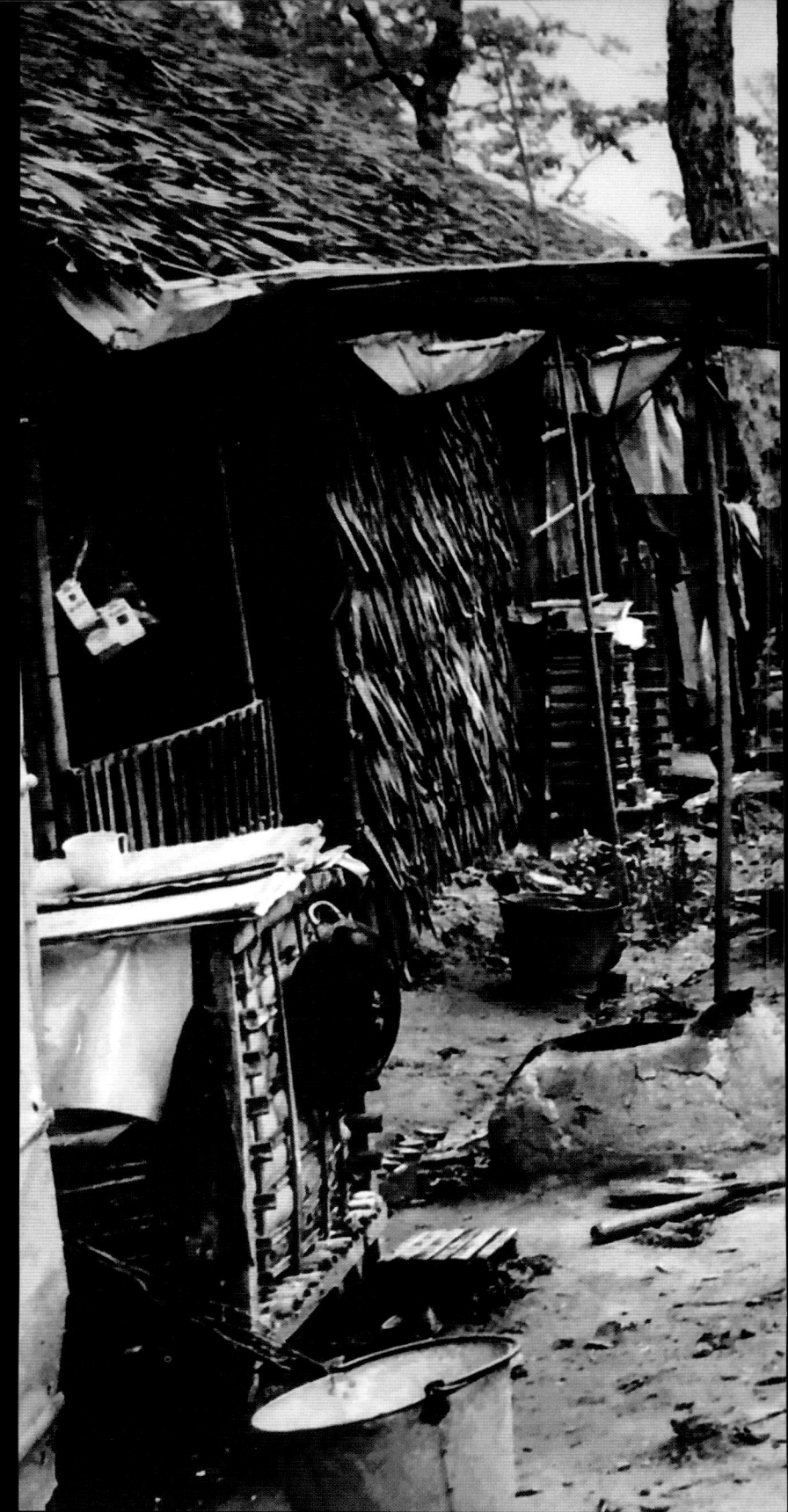

Girl running in camp lane. Camp II. Thai-Cambodian border. 1985. Sharon May.

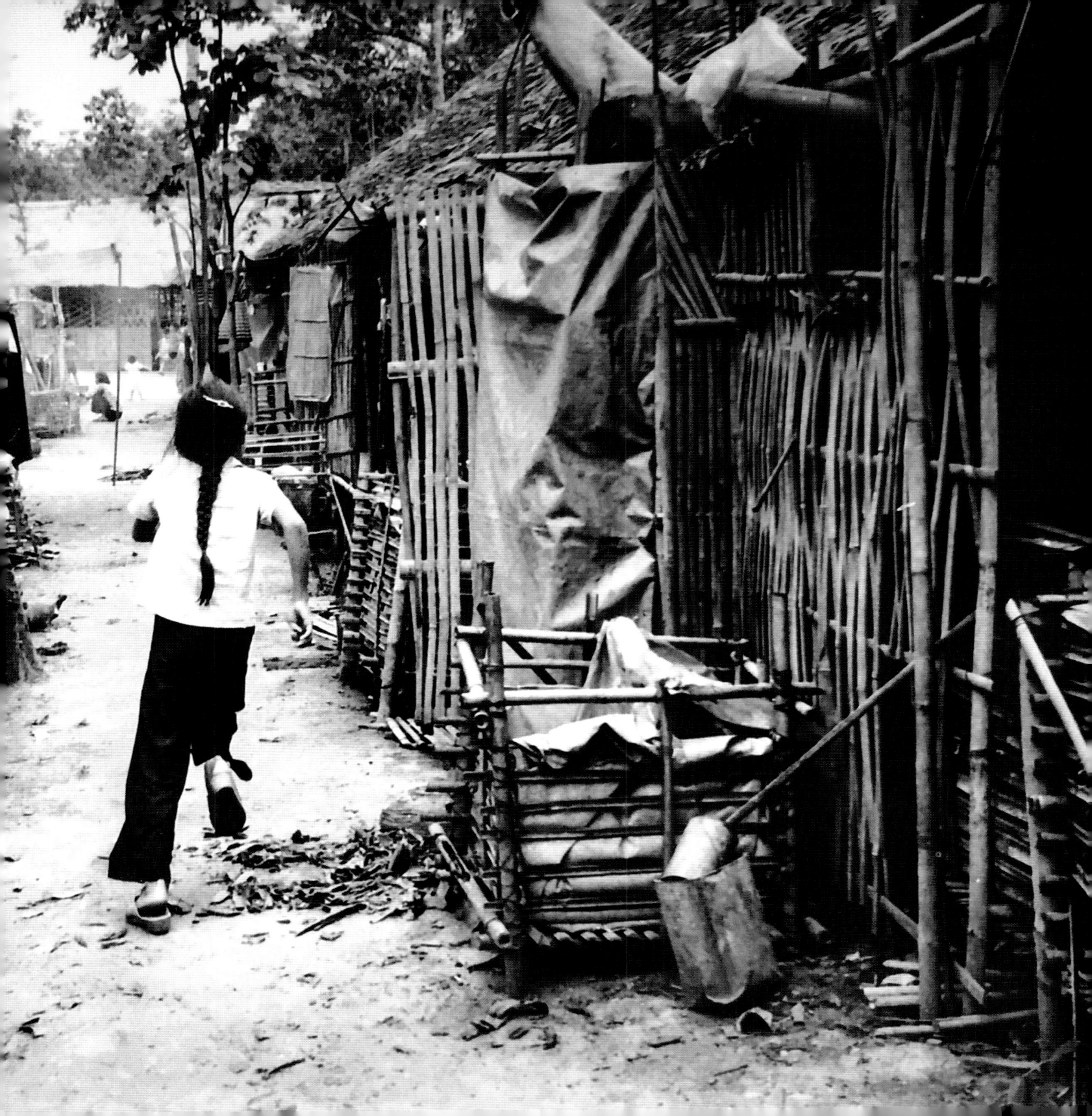

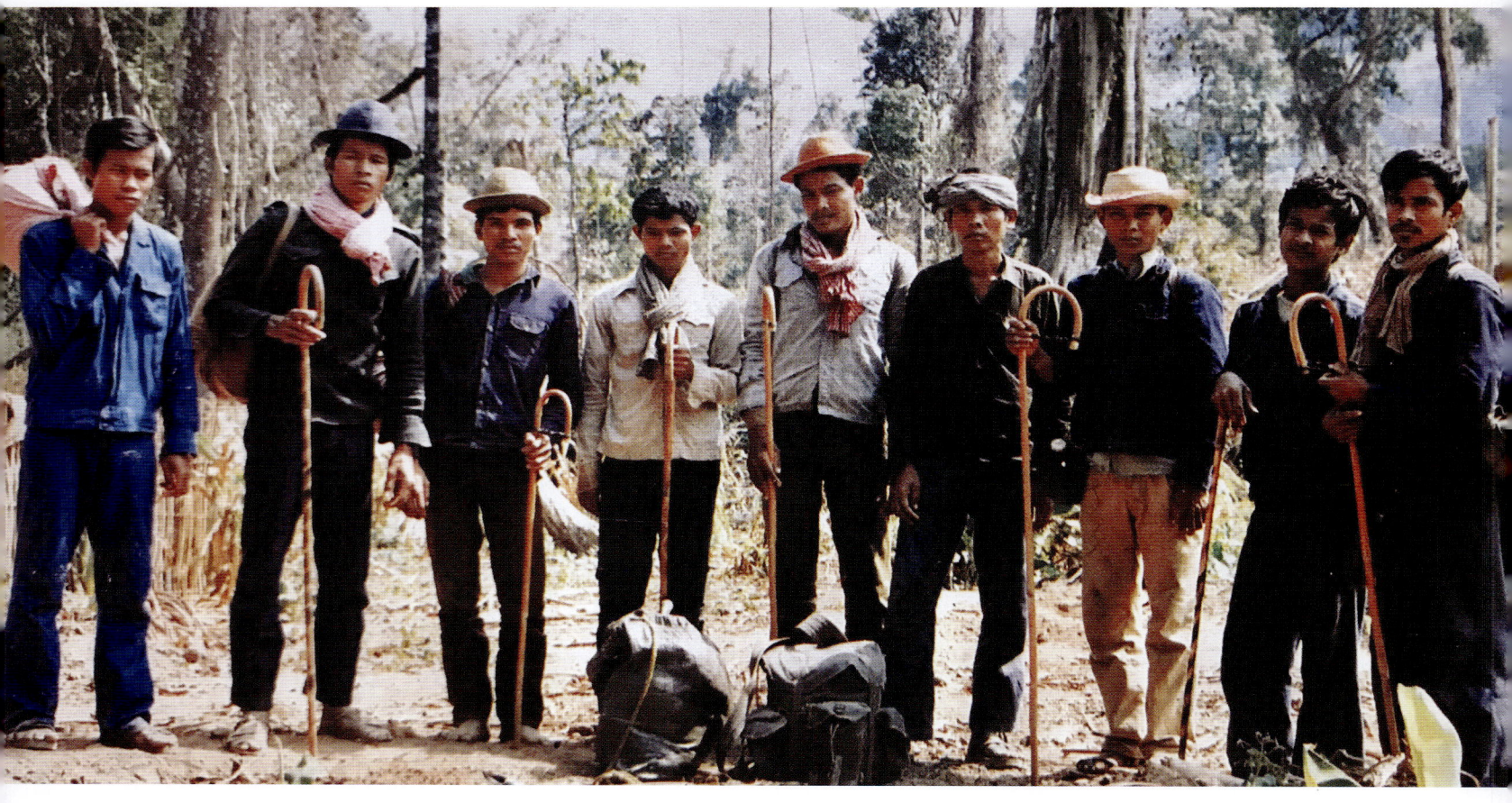

Magazine Wars

Civilians who deserted the Vietnamese K5 forced labor camps. West Kampuchea. April 1987. Photographer unknown. NADK magazine, April 1987. Center for Khmer Studies Library, Siem Reap.

The printing of propaganda magazines with competing stories of political, military, and social success continued into the 1980s. The Vietnamese-backed People's Republic printed their propaganda within Cambodia, while Angkar's renamed National Army of Democratic Forces (NADK), living in the more difficult terrain in the northwest, relied on presses in China. The legitimizing iconography of Angkor Wat continued to be appropriated by both sides. The NADK photograph of civilians who had fled from the Vietnamese K5 forced labor project—a 217-mile (350-km)-long giant earth rampart to keep the Khmer Rouge on Thai territory—unwittingly recalls the work of the German photographer August Sanders, "Young Farmers" (1915), with their hats and walking canes.

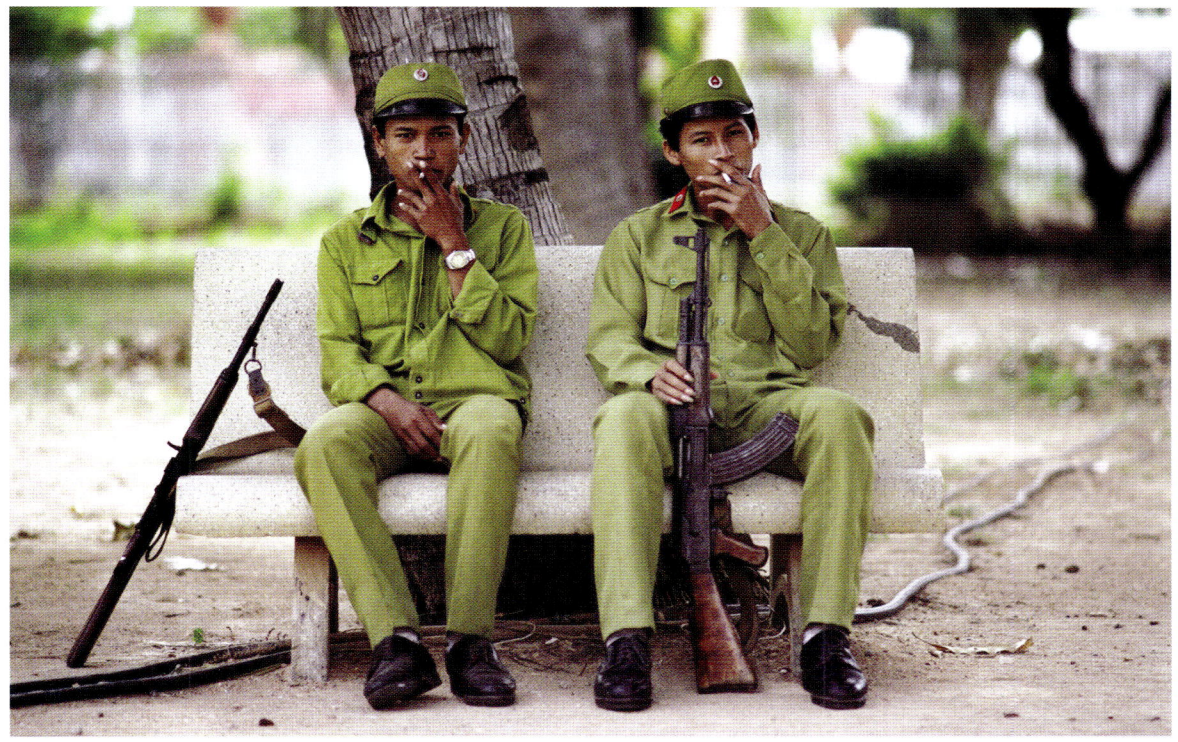

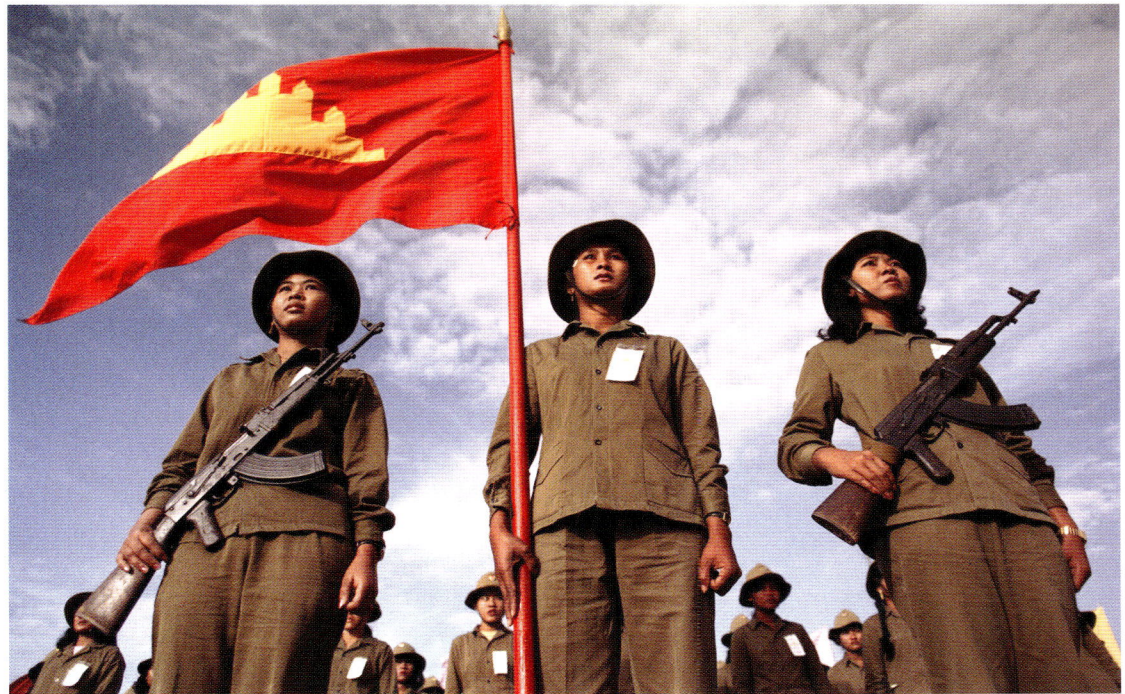

ABOVE: **Gunsmoke.** Phnom Penh. 1988.

RIGHT: **Girls with guns.** Battambang. 1988.

Photographs: Jeff Widener.

The Vietnamese Military

Jeff WIDENER (b. 1956) was the Bangkok-based Southeast Asia pictorial editor for the Associated Press when he covered the unconditional withdrawal of the Vietnamese army from Cambodia in 1989. Over the past decade of fighting, 55,000 Vietnamese had lost their lives trying to quell the Khmer Rouge. The socialist country had started to open to foreigners as Widener stood roadside and covered this historic occasion of their withdrawal. His heroic perspective of the women troops holding the revolutionary flag contrasts with the smoking youth on the park bench. Two years later, the Third Indochina (Vietnamese-Cambodian) War came to a formal end.

The Mugging of Khieu Samphan

By the end of 1991, the United States, China, and the Soviet Union had engineered the creation of a non-aligned Cambodia led by Sihanouk. It was cemented by the historic Paris Peace Accord on October 23. The prince returned from a second exile in Beijing (he had fled Phnom Penh as the Vietnamese advanced in 1979). He arrived at Pochentong Airport and motored into town to adoring flag-waving crowds. Two weeks later, the head of the Khmer Rouge, Khieu Samphan arrived. The crowds were not happy, jeering and abusing him. Bundled into an armored car for safety, he returned to the airport, shaken and bloodied, lucky to have escaped with his life. The American photojournalist Stefan ELLIS (1965–96) headed to Thailand in 1987 to document the Cambodian refugee camps. In 1991, he opened the news bureau of the Agence France-Presse in Phnom Penh. He would remain in the country until after the 1993 national elections. In 2008, the former Khmer Rouge head of state made his first appearance at Cambodia's war crimes tribunal.

Khieu Samphan wearing an army helmet and a pair of bloodied underpants on his head. Pochetong Airport, Phnom Penh. 1991. Stefan Ellis/Agence France-Presse.

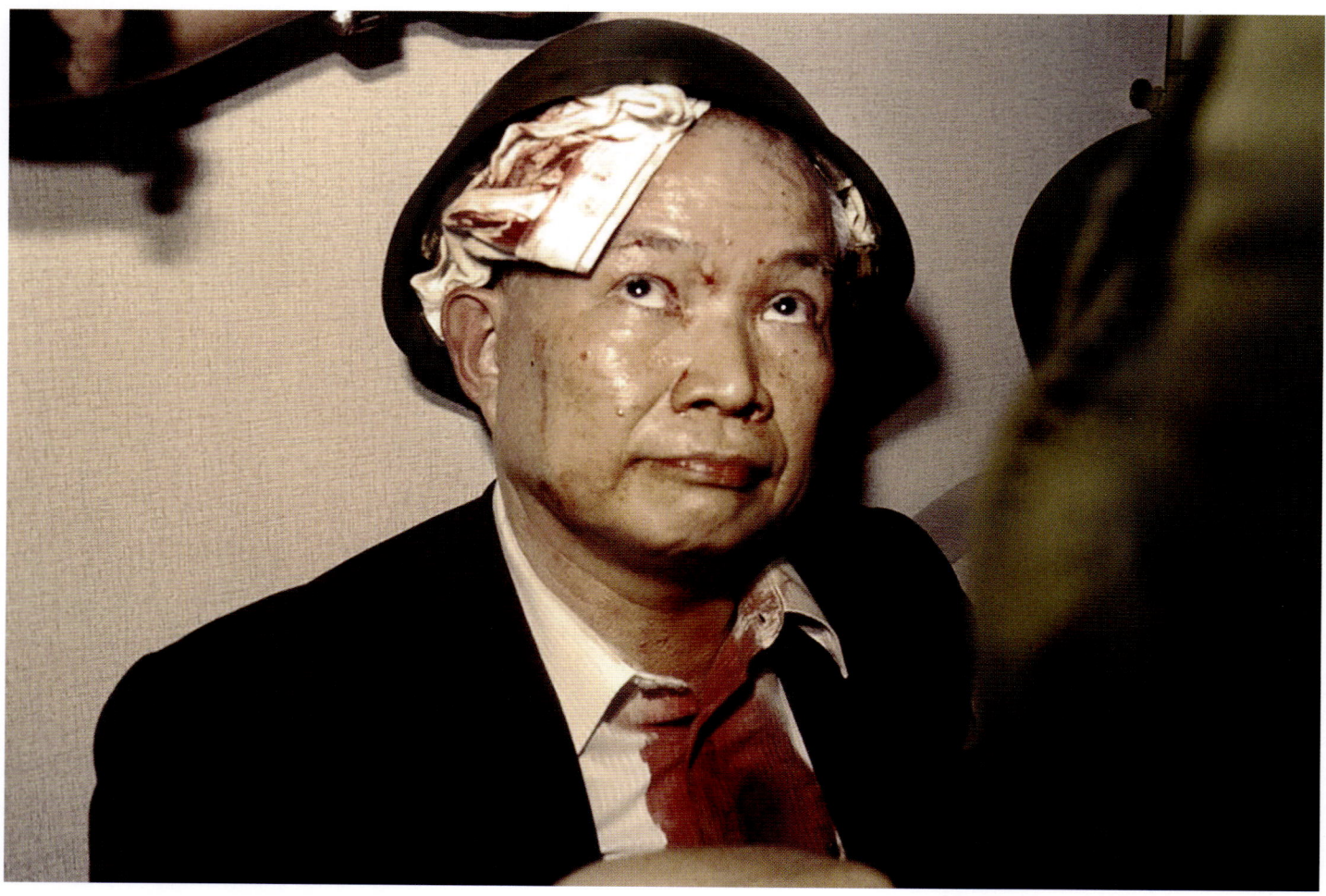

Harvest in Mecklenberg for apprentice Sam Mayany.
Für Dich magazine. German Democratic Republic. 1983. Photographer unknown. Meta House, Phnom Penh.

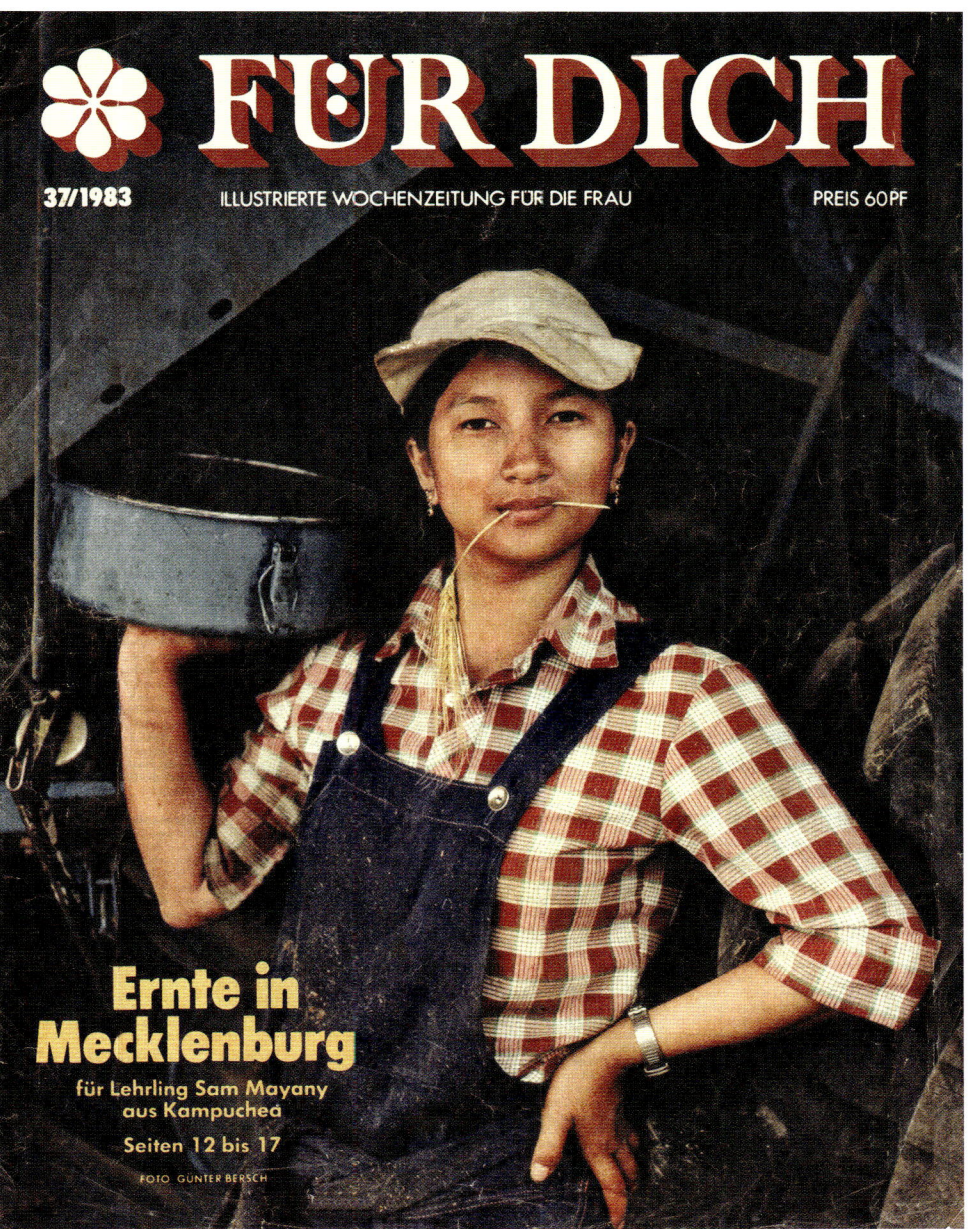

Harvest in Mecklenburg

"Harvest in Mecklenberg for apprentice Sam Mayany from Kampuchea" states the front cover of *Für Dich* (For You), the illustrated weekend magazine targeting women in the German Democratic Republic. An ally of Vietnam, and by association Cambodia, *Für Dich* showed that a woman could conquer male domains and participate in politics, culture, and industry to build the socialist state. The art director had positioned Sam Mayany as a strong working woman with a flair for style and fun, a far cry from the Maoist Angkar's image of woman a decade earlier.

Dayanny So Family Photographs

When the interconnectedness of family generations has been dislocated by war or other trauma, the ephemeral treasures of family photographs take on a profoundly new meaning. These photographs from the Dayanny So Family Archive are part of a larger store of works collected by Charles Fox, a British photographer and academic. His "Found Cambodia" is an online archive which collects social history photography pre- and post-Khmer Rouge. Each image is captioned with the family's story.

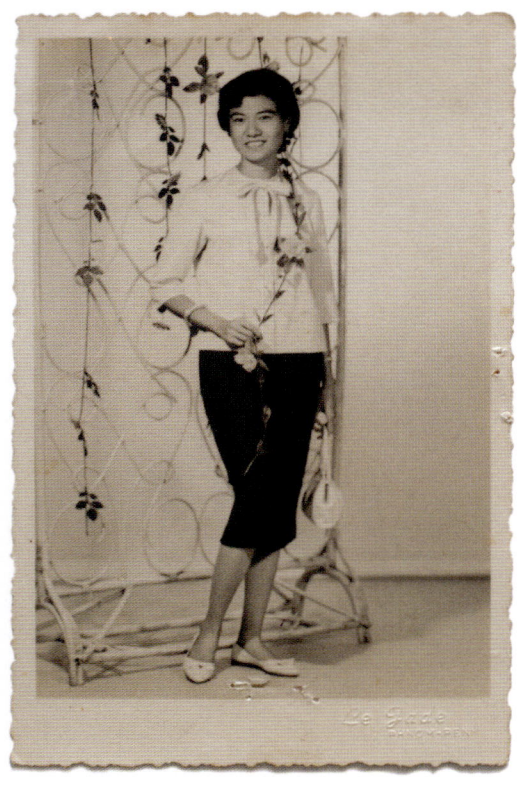

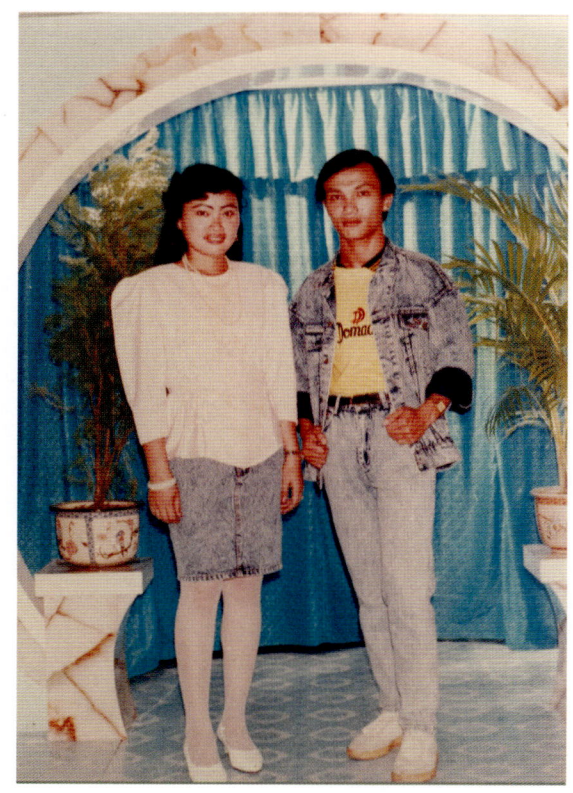

Studio portrait of Auntie. Phnom Penh. 1960s. Photographer unknown.

"Portrait of Auntie in the 1960s, the image was made in a photo studio in Phnom Penh where she had just graduated with the qualifications to become a high school teacher and this photograph was intended to mark the occasion."

Source: Dayanny So Family Archive/Found Cambodia.

Dayanny and sister in denim. Phnom Penh. Studio Laor Penh Chet. 1989.

"This was the first time my sister returned to see us from Russia where she was studying, we went shopping to buy the latest fashions coming from Thailand. At the time we did not have a camera—we had to go to a studio or along the riverside to get your photograph made. We wanted some record of this time together. It was also seen as a treat to go to the studio or have your photo."

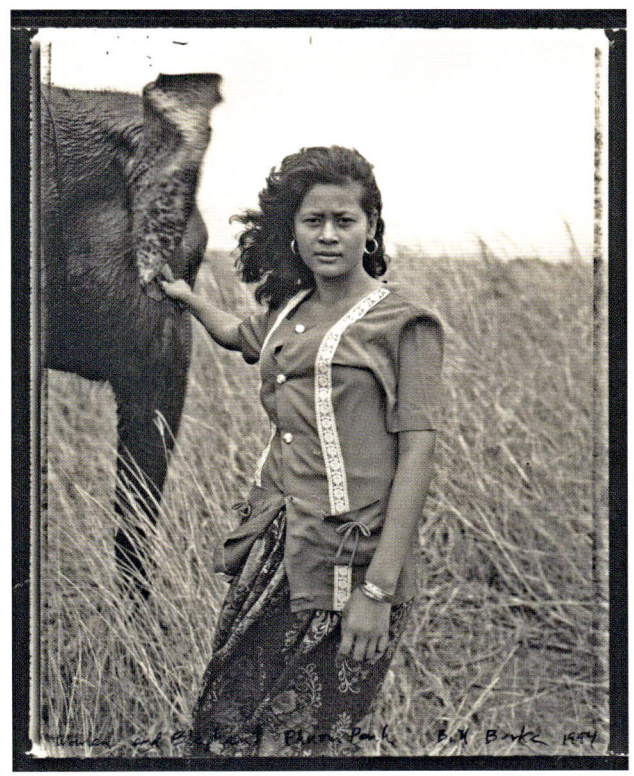

Woman at the waterfront with elephant.
Tonlé Sap, riverbank below the Hotel
Cambodiana, Phnom Penh. 1994. Bill Burke.

On the Riverbank

A woman gently holds an elephant's ear as she looks straight at the camera. The location is a grassy bank of the Tonlé Sap, the river which defines the eastern boundary of Phnom Penh. With fellow handlers, she had taken the pachyderm to feed on grass on the riverbank below the Hotel Cambodiana. The elephant's working days were spent at a local wat, soliciting money for visitors to gain merit. Elephants are the guardians of Buddhist temples and a symbol of strength and steadfastness. Bill BURKE (b. 1943) first traveled to the region as the Soviet-supported Vietnamese regime was beginning to loosen its control of the state-run economy. He used a peel-apart Type 55 Polaroid pack film for his projects. The large 90 x 120 mm format enabled high-resolution enlargements.

Portrait of Sorn Samnang

Spectacles, tailored clothes, and reading books. Just fourteen years earlier, during the Khmer Rouge, such attributes of culture would have been the end of Sorn Samnang. Heide SMITH (b. 1937) was on assignment with journalist Marje Prior following Australian troops working for the United Nations peacekeepers when she took this photograph inside the National Library in Phnom Penh. Sorn was professor of history and dean of the Faculty of History at the Phnom Penh University during Long Nol's Khmer Republic (1970–75). With an insouciant air, he leans against the bookcases originally built in 1925 for both the library and the adjacent archive.

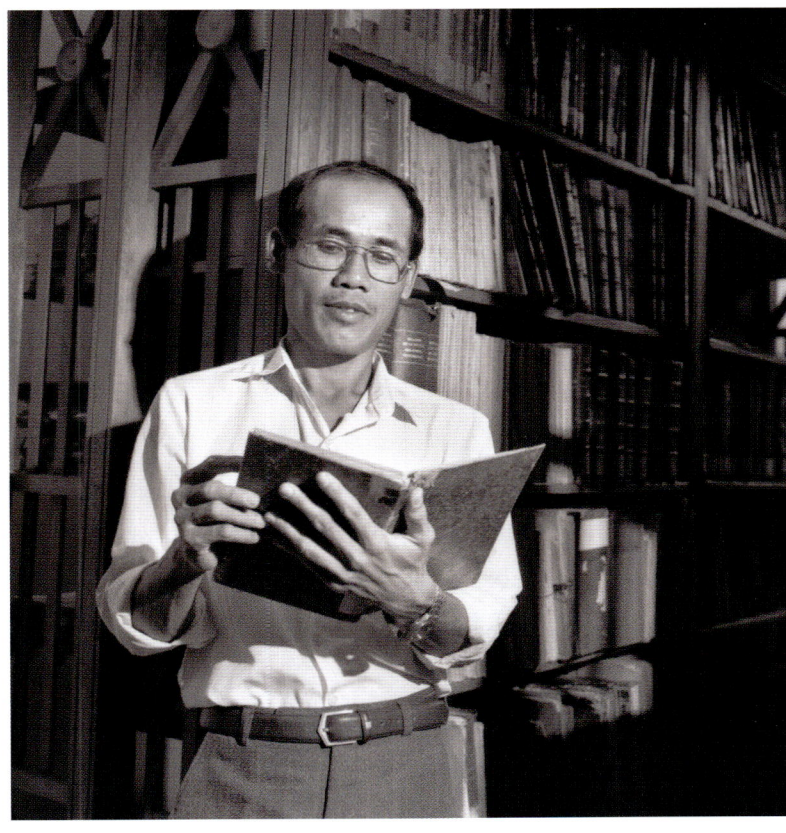

Portrait of Sorn Samnang. National Library, Phnom Penh. 1993. Heide Smith/Australian War Memorial.

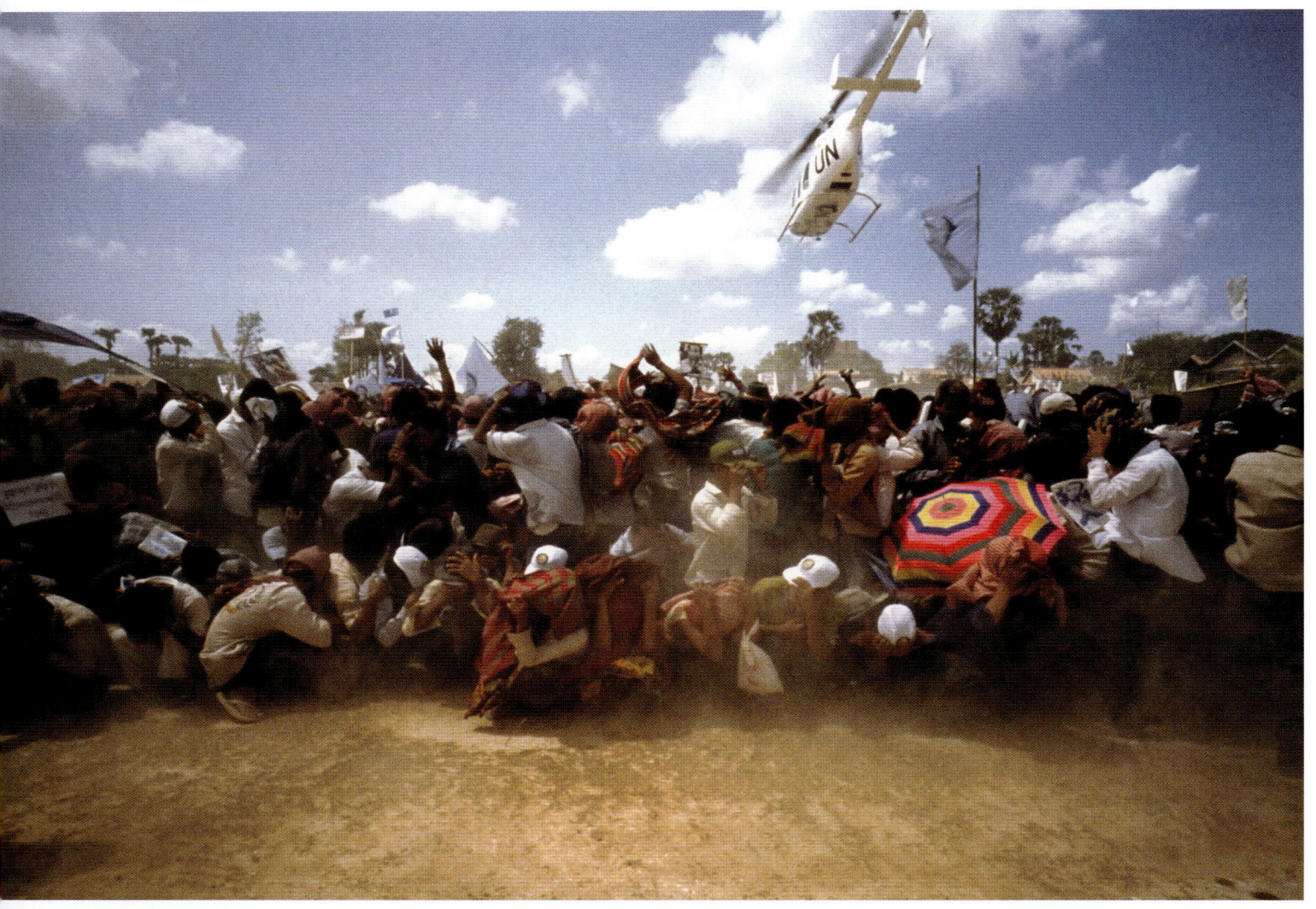

The United Nations Election

Tim PAGE (b. 1944) worked extensively in Vietnam during the Second Indochina War (1955–75). In 1993, he moved to Cambodia to cover the elections managed by the United Nations Transitional Authority in Cambodia (UNTAC). This photograph shows a UN helicopter departing with Prince Norodom Ranariddh after he had addressed a crowd of potential voters. They are cowering from the swirling dust generated by the helicopter's rotors. The contested elections resulted in a negotiated co-prime ministership shared by the prince as leader of the royalist FUNCINPEC party and the incumbent Hun Sen. FUNCINPEC stands for Front uni national pour un Cambodge indépendant, neutre, pacifique, et coopérative.

Helicopter dust. Prey Veng football field. 1993. Tim Page.

Angkor Under Infrared

John McDERMOTT (b. 1955) traveled to Cambodia in 1995 to witness Angkor Wat illuminated by the unnerving "monochromatic, platinum light" of the total solar eclipse. The astronomical phenomena occurred over Cambodia on October 24. The gloom lasted for just over two hours, reaching its zenith at 4:15 p.m. Inspired by the experience, he experimented with infrared film to recreate the moment. After years of photojournalists recording war, conflict, and misery, McDermott's work pioneered the return of photography to Cambodia that looked beyond a direct record of the human condition, towards a meditation on landscape and place.

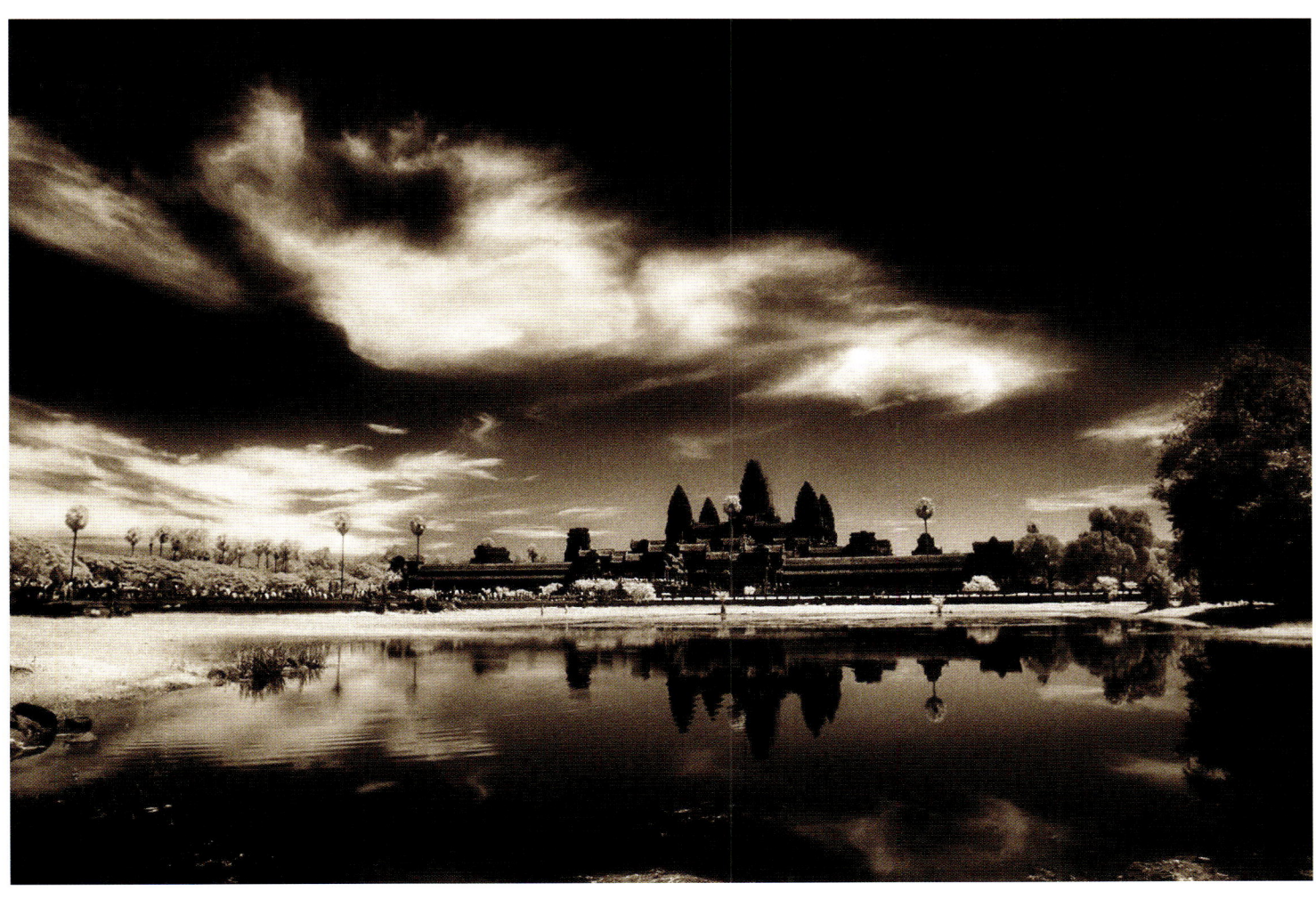

Panorama of Angkor Wat. Siem Reap. 1995.
John McDermott.

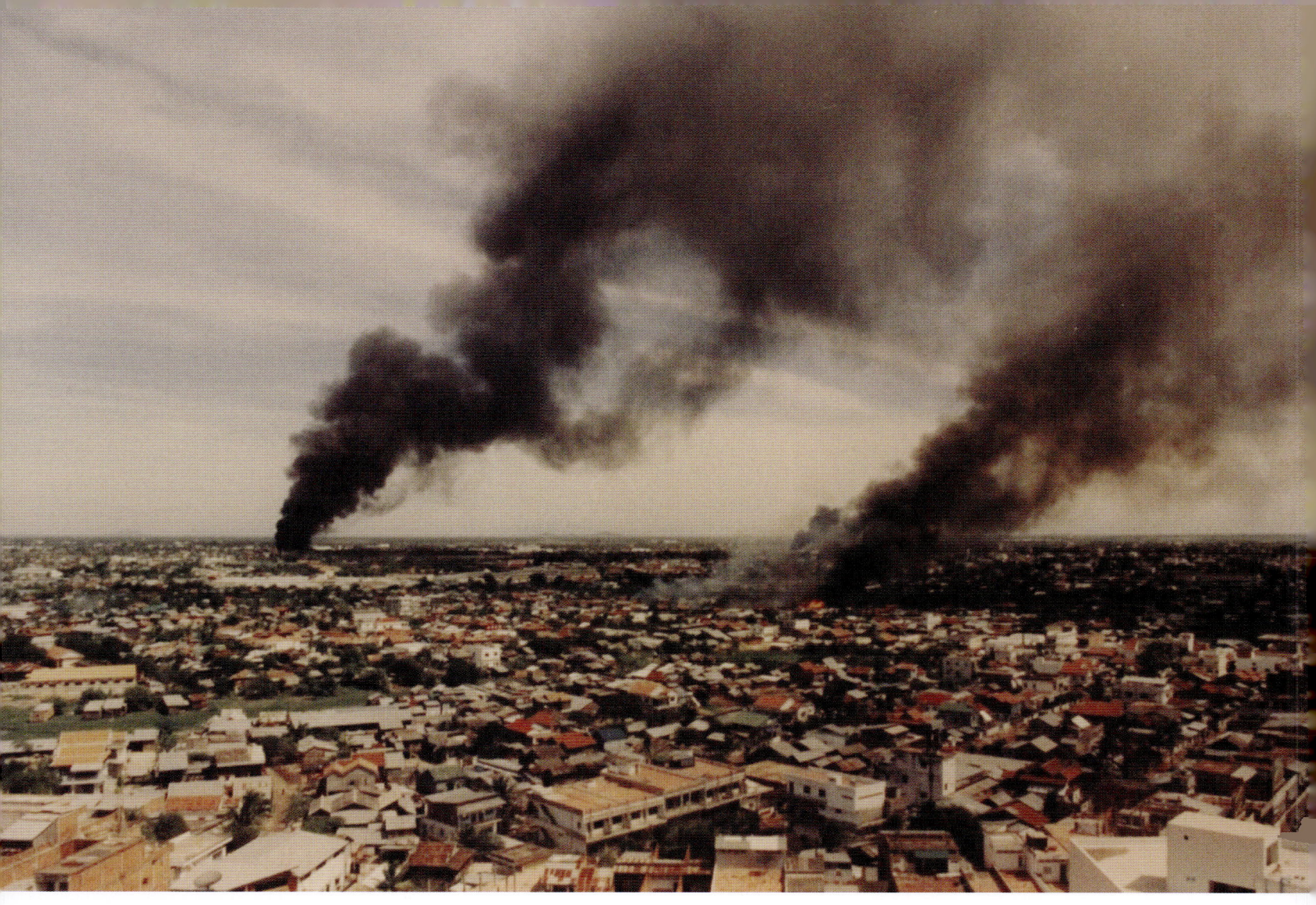

Smoke Rises Over Phnom Penh

Arriving in early 1995, Huw WATKINS (b. 1960) spent four years as a journalist in Cambodia. Following the 1993 United Nations-sponsored election, a coalition of two political parties with two prime ministers was cobbled together comprising the Cambodian People's Party (CPP) led by Hun Sen, on the one hand, and its erstwhile FUNCINPEC "partner" headed by Prince Norodom Ranariddh, on the other. In July 1997, their mutual loathing quickly unraveled among escalating violence—grenade attacks, assassinations, and shoot-outs between rival police and military units—from which the CPP emerged decisive victors. This photograph looks west from the roof of the Hotel Intercontinental and records the opening shots on July 7.

Smoke rises over Phnom Penh. 1997.
Huw Watkins.

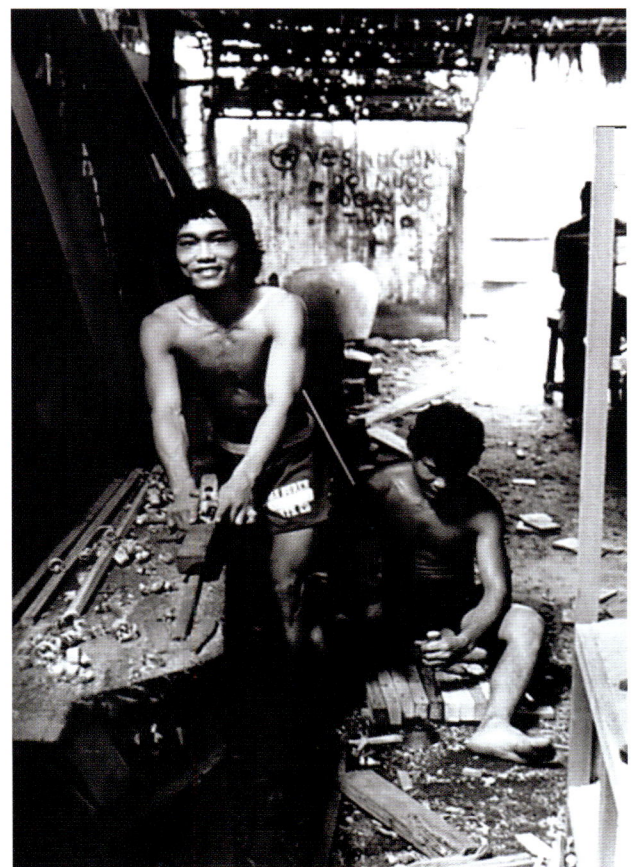
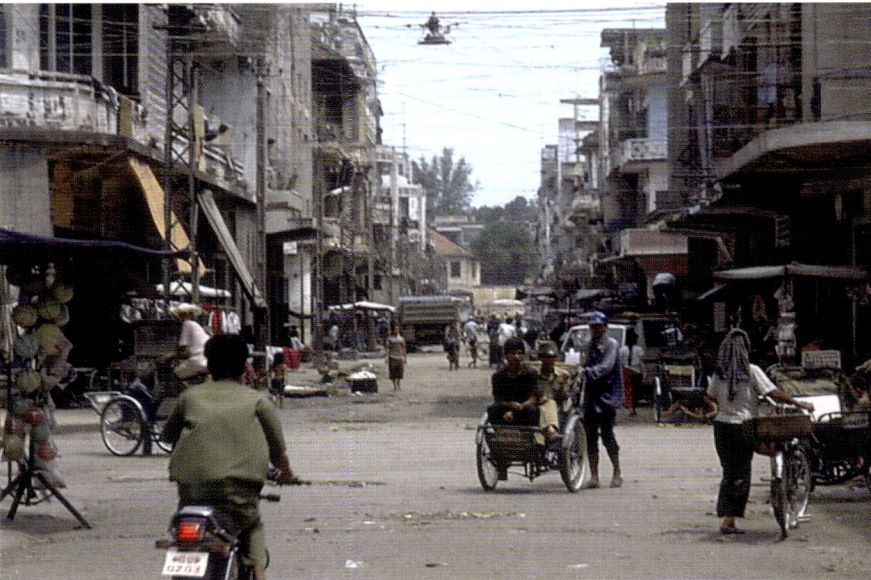
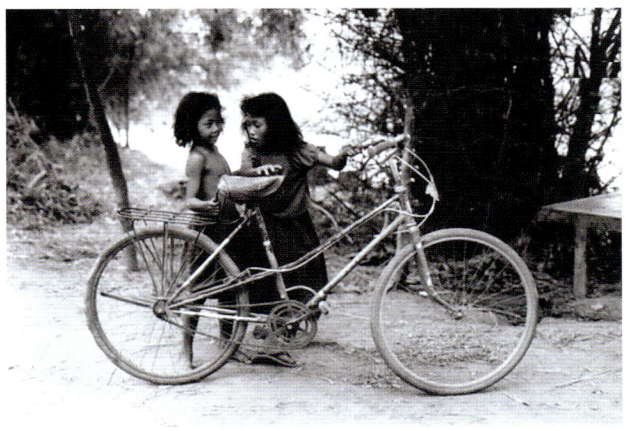
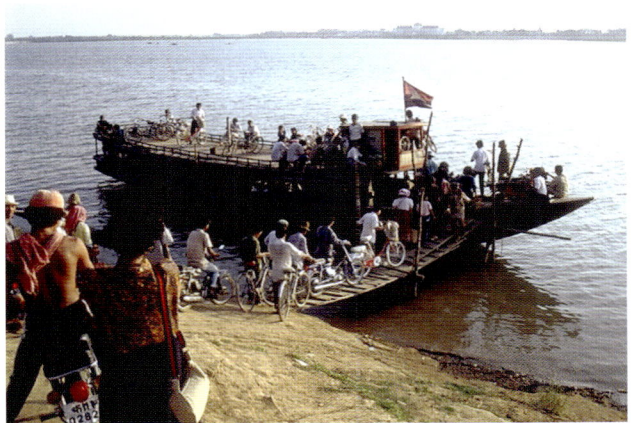

Making Do

In April and May 1991, shortly before the United Nations peacekeeping force entered the country, the writer-photographer Bruce SHARP (b. 1962) roamed the streets of Phnom Penh. These pictures demonstrate the condition of the country after decades of strife, where a sense of making do pervaded the Cambodian world as it rebuilt the shattered economy. "At the time, my cameras were a Pentax SF-1 and a Ricoh XR-10. I used to shoot with many different films depending on the situation. Kodachrome was a favorite, but I'd often shoot Ektachrome as well. For black and white, by the 1990s I used mainly T-Max 100, T-Max 400 (that's what was used for the shot of the Svay Rieng woodworkers), and Ilford HP5 Plus" (Bruce Sharp. 2020).

TOP LEFT, CLOCKWISE: **Woodworkers.** Svay Rieng. 1991.

Street scene. Phnom Penh. 1991.

Loading the ferry. Ksach Kandal. 1991.

Children contend with a too-big bicycle. Pre Ambel. 1991.

Photographs: Bruce Sharp.

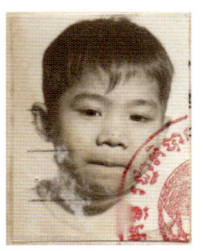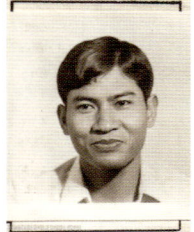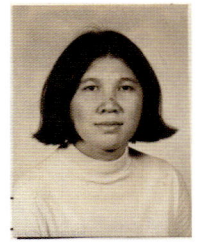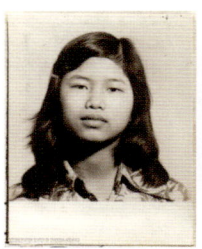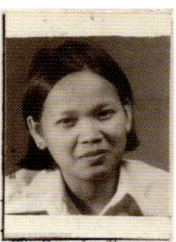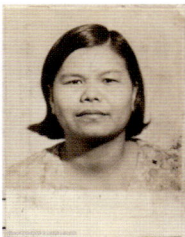
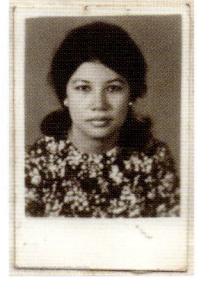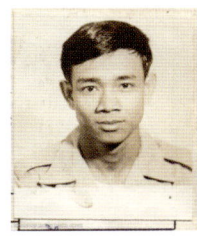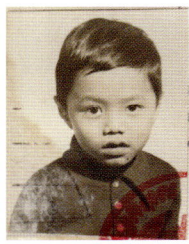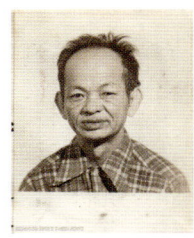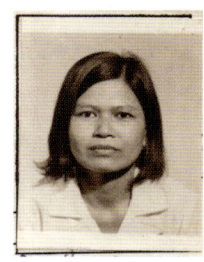

Selection of identity photographs. Pre-1975. Photographers unknown. Documentation Center of Cambodia (DC-Cam).

Recovering the Past

Established in 1995, the Documentation Center of Cambodia (DC-Cam) has collected, copied, and disseminated records of the atrocities of the Khmer Rouge. These include identity photographs taken before, during, and after the regime, confessions, diaries, maps, notebooks, and loose papers. Over one million items have been gathered to hold leaders accountable for their decisions while ensuring that "the past is not forgotten." The archives have been an invaluable resource for the Khmer Rouge Trials conducted in Phnom Penh. This material has also been used for traveling exhibitions to reconcile Cambodians with their past, and regularly mined by journalists, researchers, and historians.

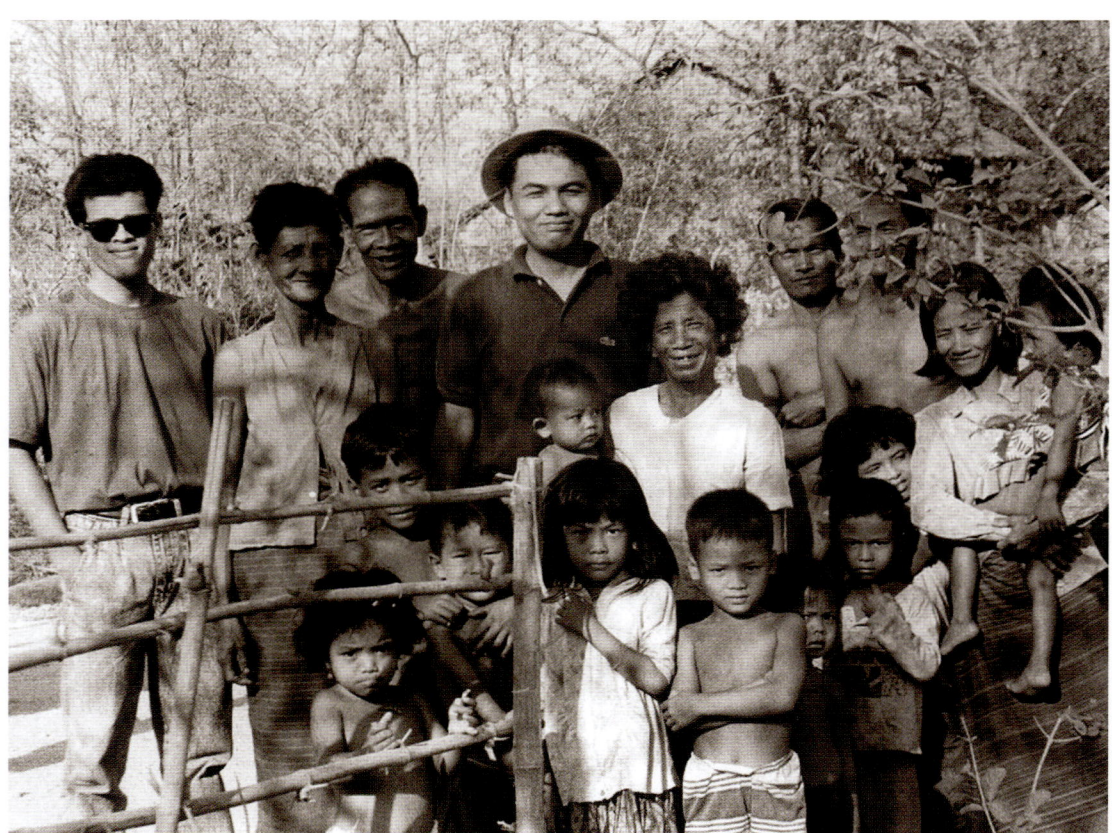

Youk Chhang and family. Khmer Leu village, Takeo Province. 1995. Photographer unknown. Documentation Center of Cambodia (DC-Cam).

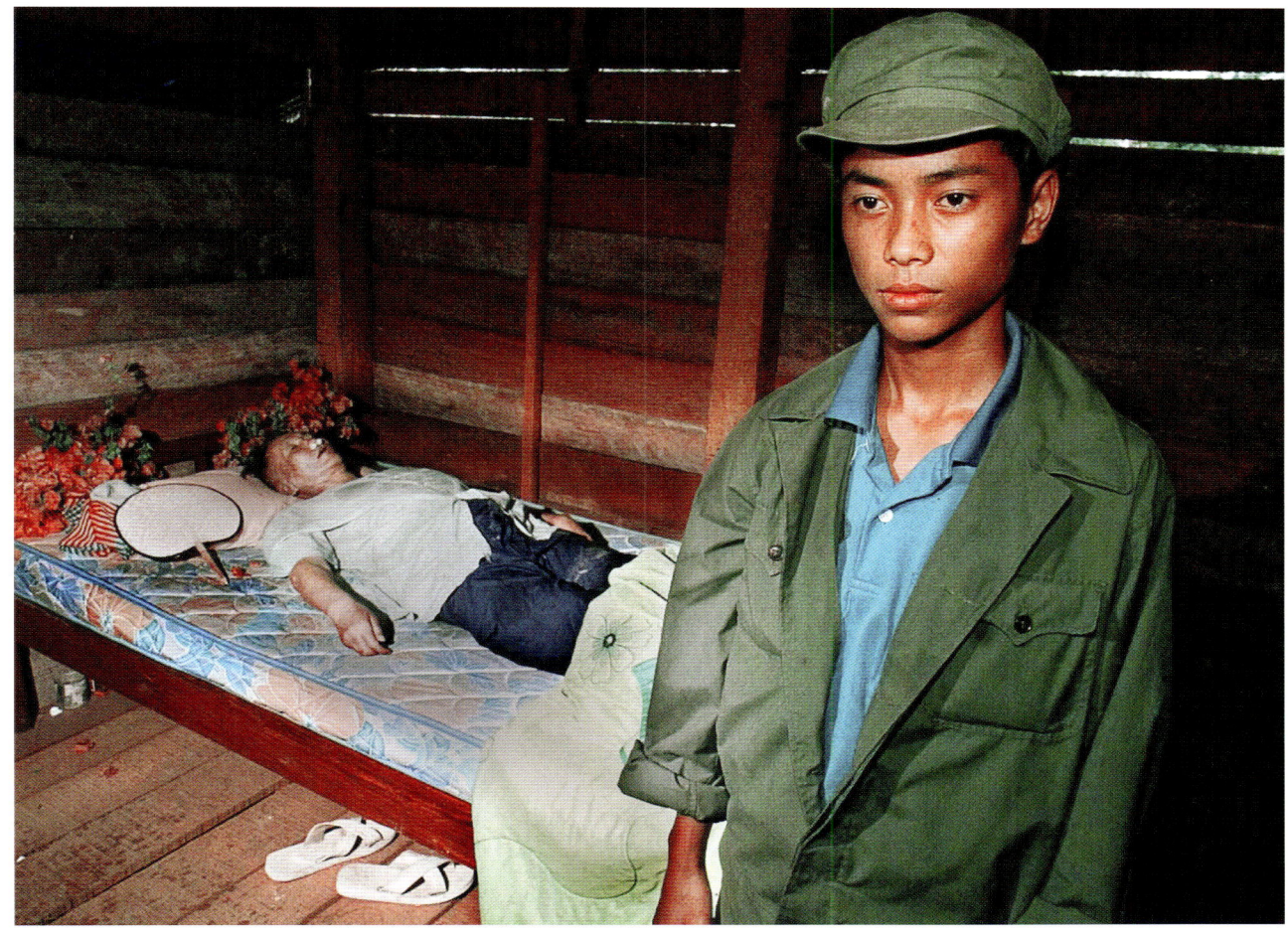

The Death of Pol Pot

In April 1998, upon hearing rumors of the death of Pol Pot, David LONGSTREATH (b. 1952) and three other journalists drove across the Thai-Cambodian border in pursuit of a groundbreaking story. They were greeted by a few Khmer Rouge soldiers, who walked them down a landmine-strewn path to a rough jungle shack. Longstreath photographed the body of Pol Pot and the young cadres milling around, who seemed disinterested in the event. Longstreath was carrying a Nikon N90 camera body adapted with a digital card reader, rather than a film roll. The NC2000, as it was called, was developed by the Associated Press. Returning across the border to Pailin, he worked the 1.6 megabyte files on his laptop into wire service photos, complete with captions. He then sent them via a temporary satellite dish to Tokyo. His witness of the ignominious death of one of Asia's great dictators signaled the symbolic end of a failed ideological experiment, while at the same time heralding the beginning of the revolution of digital photography in Southeast Asia.

A young Khmer Rouge soldier stands with the body of Pol Pot.
Pailin. 1998. David Longstreath/Associated Press.

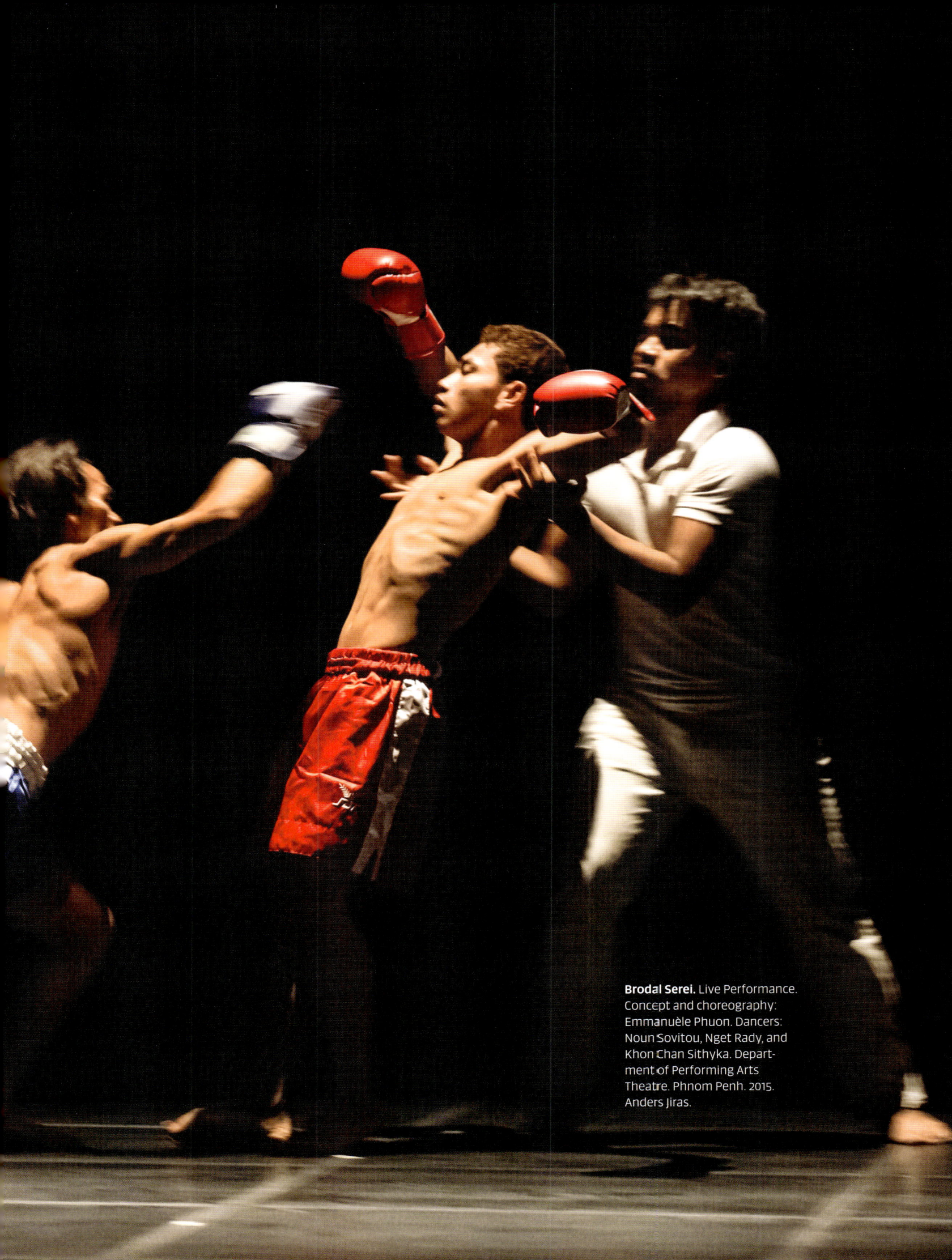

Brodal Serei. Live Performance. Concept and choreography: Emmanuèle Phuon. Dancers: Noun Sovitou, Nget Rady, and Khon Chan Sithyka. Department of Performing Arts Theatre. Phnom Penh. 2015. Anders Jiras.

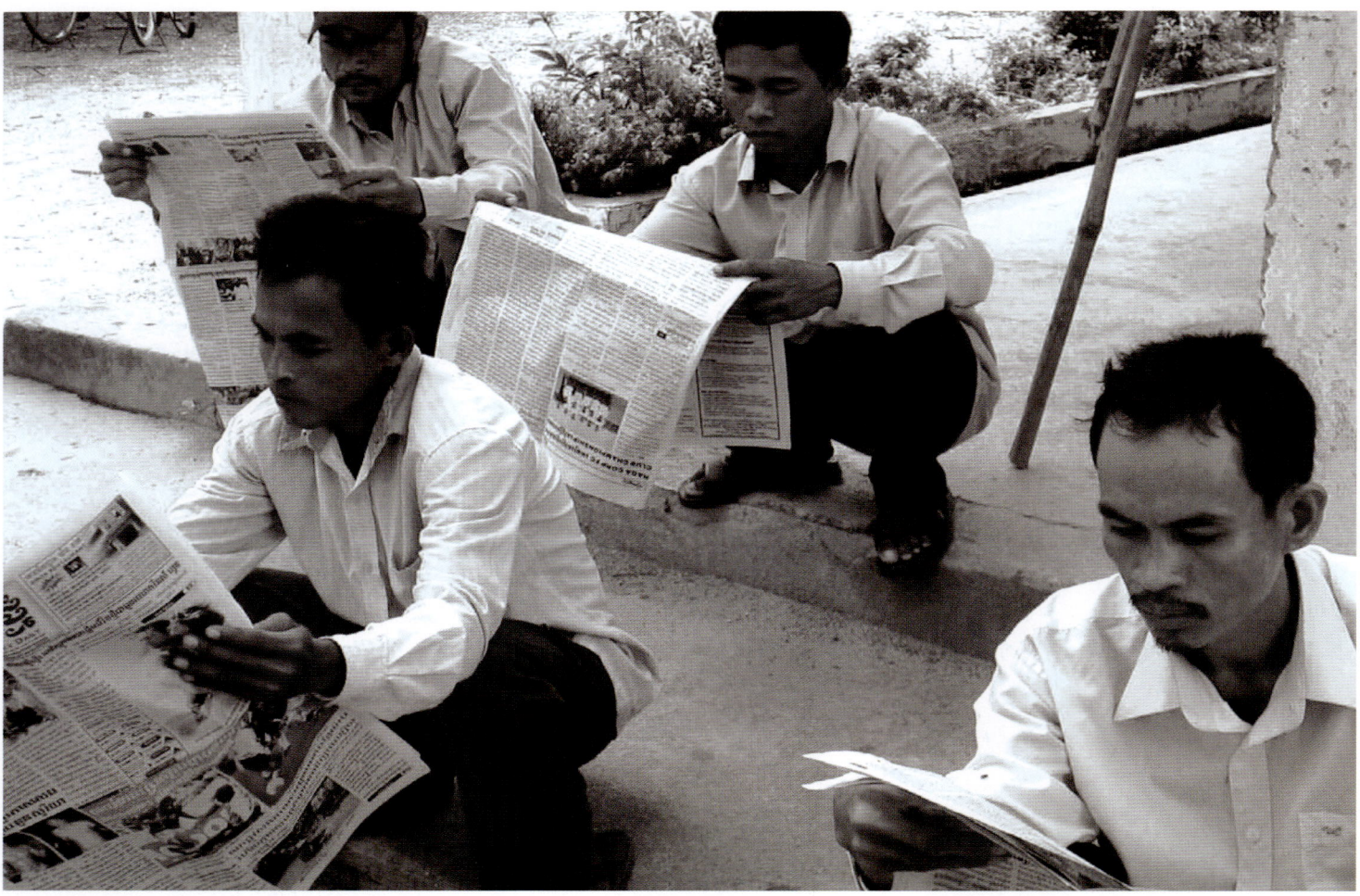

The Fourth Estate

Men reading newspapers. Kompong Speu. 2005. Liam Cochrane. First published in *Reading Between the Lines: How Politics, Money & Fear Control Cambodia's Media*. LICADHO Report. May 2008.

After the period of the United Nations Transitional Authority in Cambodia (UNTAC), there was a continual growth of media in the country. By the turn of the millennium, over 200 outlets were operating across print, radio, and television. But given the low literacy rate in the countryside and the limited reach of television, radio was probably the most influential medium. Journalism was built on weak foundations, with limited professional training and a poor understanding of ethics. The role of photography and the process of taking, editing, reproducing, and disseminating images was inextricably bound to that landscape. In the last decade, however, with Cambodia's extraordinary uptake of social media, an image of readers enjoying the morning press has become a rare event.

Riots for Social Justice

Using a telephoto lens to compress the layers of action between demonstrators, makeshift barriers, and the riot police, MENG Kimlong (b. 1991) deftly records the continual tensions between the Cambodian government and citizen's demands for social and political justice. Meng joined the Angkor Photo Workshop in 2011, and then worked as a staff photojournalist for the English-language *Phnom Penh Post*. He also specializes in drone cinematography and is an avid marine photographer. His works are credited in numerous publications, including many international broadsheets and magazines.

Riots. Borei Keila, Phnom Penh. 2012. Meng Kimlong.

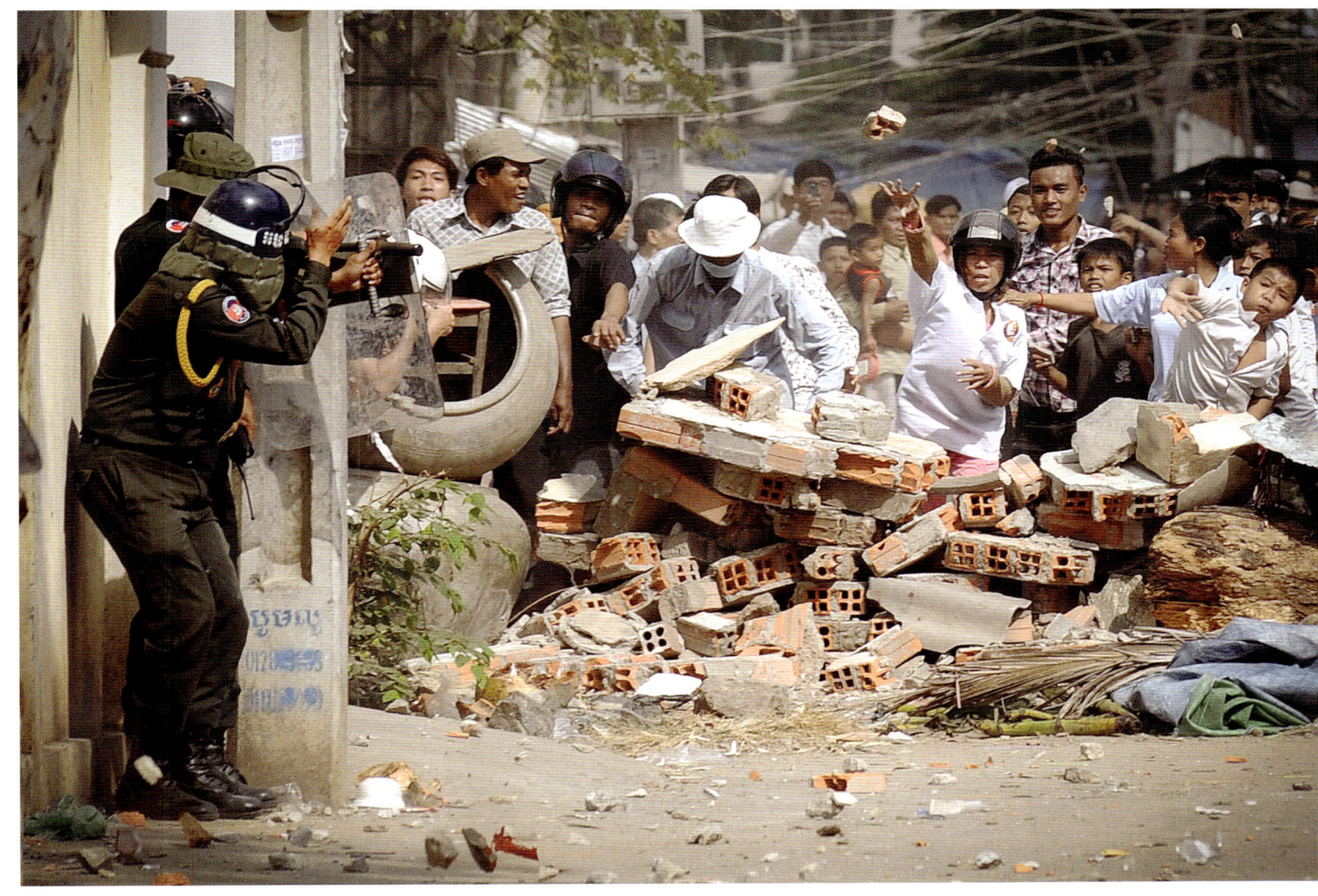

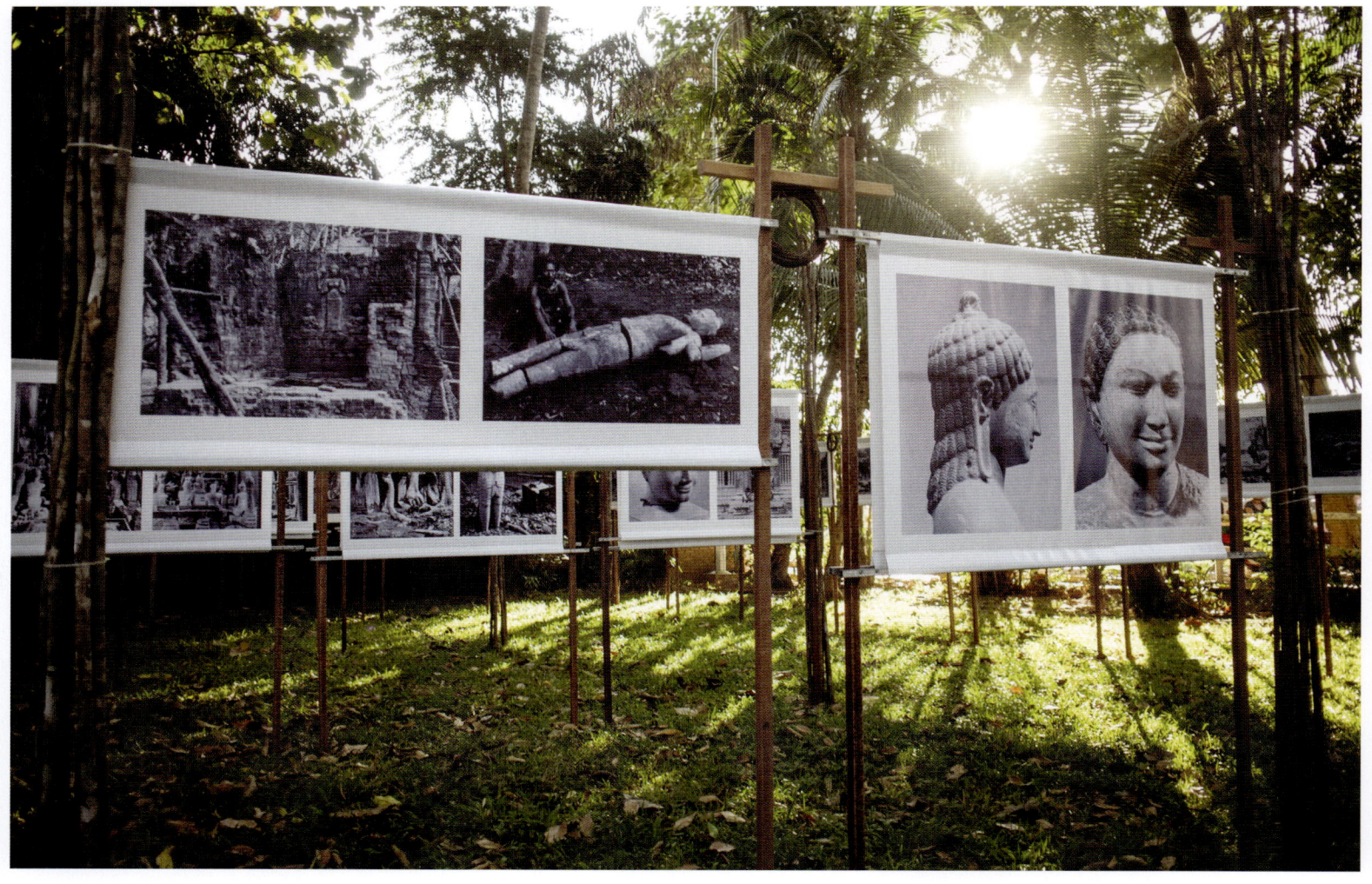

Angkor Photo Festival and Workshops

In 2004, the Angkor Photo Festival and Workshops (APFW) began in Siem Reap. The festival became influential because of its diverse content, its interactive workshops for young Asian photographers, and its free public displays dispersed across the city and along the riverfront. Françoise Callier's 2015 selection of images from the archives of the École française d'Extrême-Orient (EFEO), which included colonial photographers such as Maurice Glaize, George Groslier, Henri Marchal, and Jean Commaille, was influential for its promotion of Cambodian historical photography. Many online blogspots, including Facebook and Pinterest sites showcasing historical Cambodian photographs, particularly of the "golden years," have since flourished. Irene Yap (b. 1983), a Malaysia-based photographer, volunteered as the official photographer for APFW in 2015.

A journey into twentieth-century Cambodia through EFEO photographic archives. École française d'Extrême-Orient garden, Siem Reap. 2014. Irene Yap.

"My Motorbike and Me" Series

After lightweight, easy-to-start and maintain motorbikes were introduced into Asia in the early 1960s, they had a profound impact on personal mobility, particularly in rural communities. When Suzuki launched "Smash Revolution" in 2006, it was an instant success with Cambodian youth, symbolizing the will for change and modernity. It was also the year that LIM Sokchalina (b. 1987) said, "I begin my first training of photography … when I arouse(d) my sense of reflection, invention, observation, constructive criticism and curiosity all of which, daily take place around me. My work of photography concerns these three elements: My moped, my portrait and the environment." With a good-natured sense of humor, Lim mimics the many professions that have benefited from the economy and mobility of a motorbike.

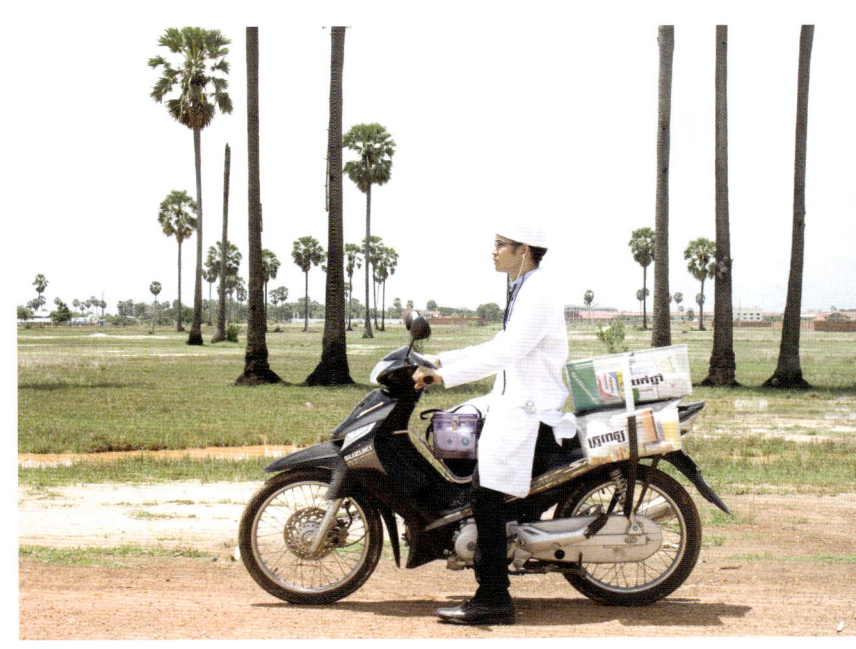

"My Motorbike and Me" series. Multiple locations, Cambodia. 2009. Lim Sokchanlina.

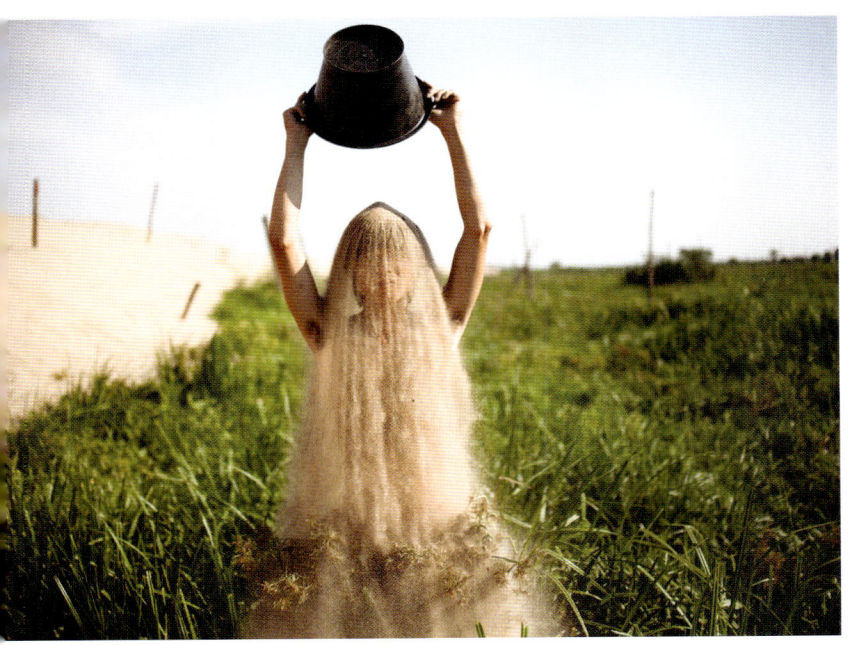

"Untitled." Phnom Penh. 2011. Khvay Samnang.

"Untitled"

In 2011, KHVAY Samnang (b. 1982) immersed himself in Phnom Penh's Boeung Kak lake and poured a bucket of sand over himself. This was in protest at the government's sale of the 247-acre (100-ha) shallow lake to private corporations for luxury development. Khvay's act was an expression of solidarity with the plight of the thousands of mostly low-income households forcibly evicted from the lake's fringes as the developers began to fill in the lake with sand. Khvay also documented his actions on video. This work was first exhibited as "Untitled" at Phnom Penh's SA SA BASSAC art gallery. Khvay is part of a new wave of contemporary Cambodian-born artists emerging from the Royal University of Fine Arts (RUFA) in Phnom Penh.

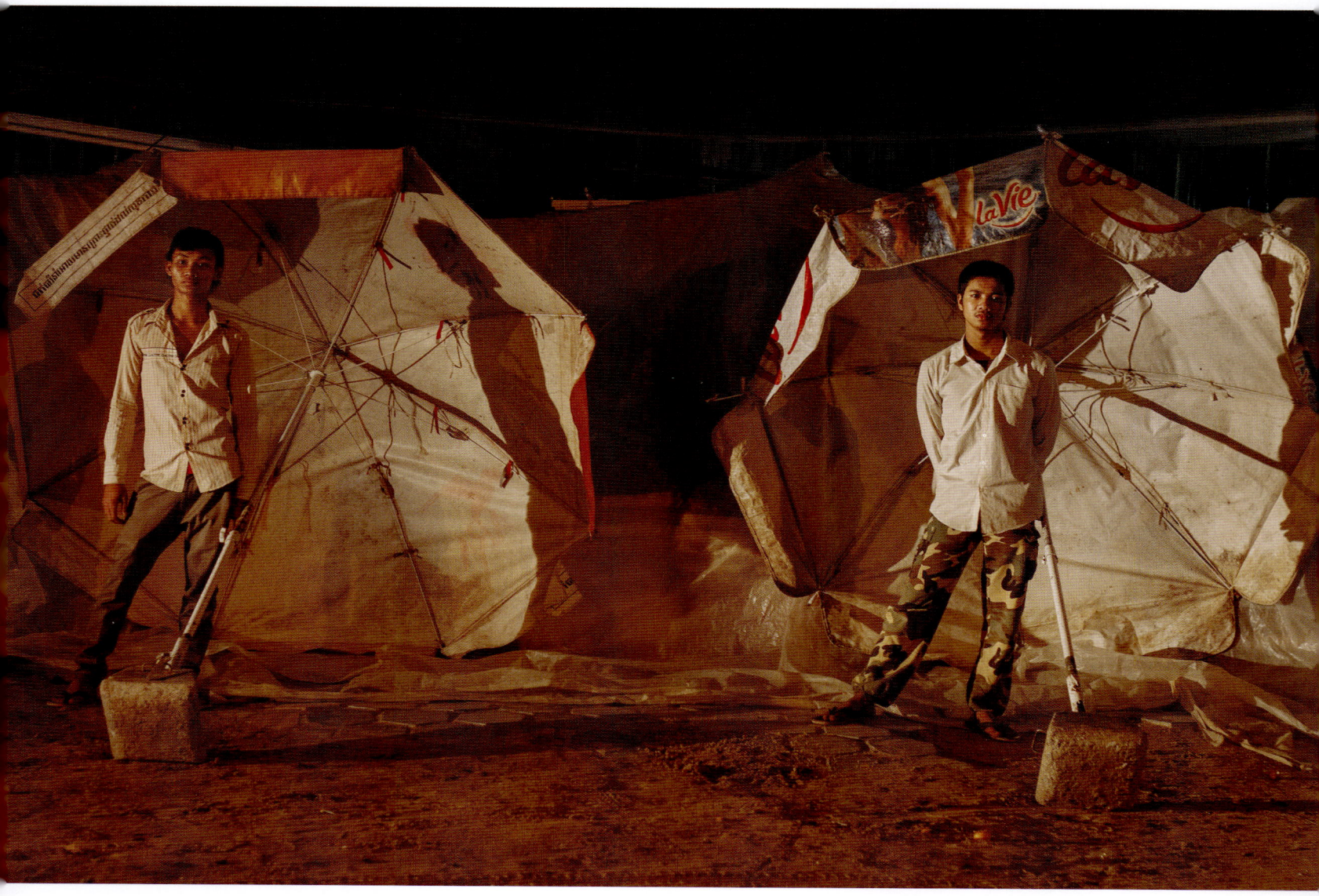

"In the City by Night" Series

"In the City by Night" series.
Multiple locations, Cambodia.
2010–15. Sovan Philong.

Like Lim Sokchanlina, SOVAN Philong (b. 1986) was also fascinated with the motorbike, not with the object itself but rather the evening scenes captured by its probing, wavering headlight. Originally a photojournalist working for the *Phnom Penh Post* and the Xinhua News Agency, he created a series of in-situ portraits over a number of years featuring people who inhabit the Cambodian night—restaurant and café workers, street-stall owners, and car park attendants. As Christian Caujolle says, "The light he adds permits a feeling of 'realistic fiction' close to a cinematic tradition." Sovan has continued the experimental line with a later series of portraits using the cold blue light of his subjects' computer screens.

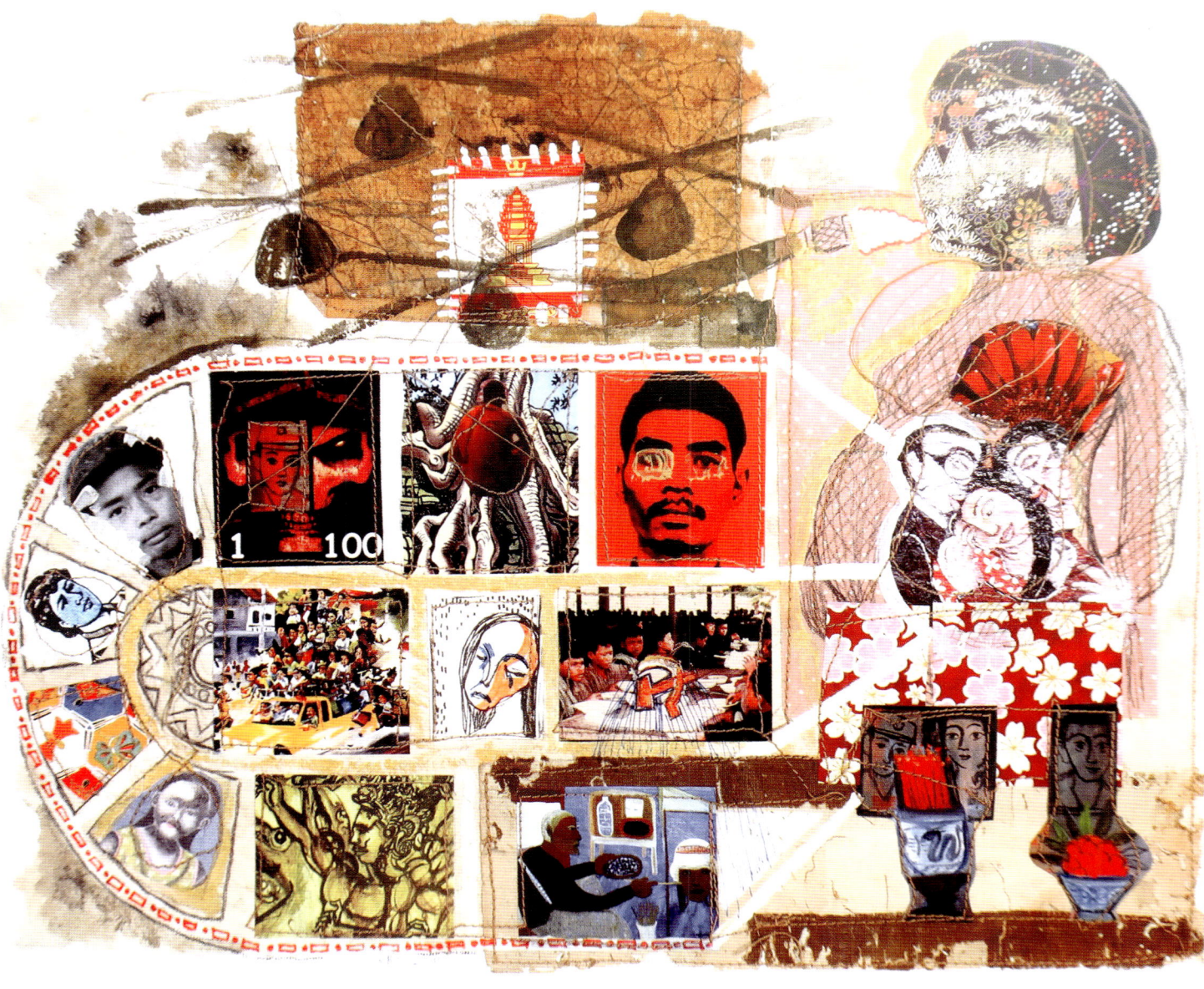

"Heavy Skirt" Series

A graduate of the Royal University of Fine Arts (RUFA) in Phnom Penh, LEANG Seckon (b. 1974) was an early leader of Cambodia's contemporary art scene. An artist who engages with collage and paint wedded with the decorative arts, Leang's "Heavy Skirt" series references his mother's quilted skirt that she wore while she was pregnant with him during the civil war of the early 1970s. This collage, "Somlaing Rom Nyor" (Whirring Rotors; Beating Hearts), includes reworked photographs and memorabilia from both Lon Nol's Khmer Republic and the revolutionary Khmer Rouge's Democratic Kampuchea that followed. Considered strongly autobiographical, the "Heavy skirt" series of large paintings and smaller collages that radiated from a large fabric installation, can be read as a metaphor for the burden of survival during these twenty years of war and turmoil.

Somlaing Rom Nyor. "Heavy Skirt" series. (Whirring Rotors; Beating Hearts). 2010. Leang Seckon.

Koh Pich Bridge Stampede

PHA Lina (b. 1986) has been a photojournalist for the French language daily *Cambodge Soir* and the *Phnom Penh Post*. On November 27, 2010, during evening celebrations for the annual Water Festival in Phnom Penh, a crowd of young, tightly packed revelers panicked as they moved along the Koh Pich suspension bridge. The structure crossed a section of the Bassac River connecting the festival grounds to the mainland. In the ensuing stampede, 347 people died and another 755 were injured. While social media was awash with unsettling images of the unfolding event, Pha Lina's photograph was taken later that evening, after the dead and injured had been taken to local hospitals. The dense litter of plastic water bottles and victims shoes, bathed in the saturated blue wash from the bridge's decorative lighting, is a compelling record of the fragility of lives. Pha continues to photograph, concentrating on social issues in the country.

Remnant of debris immediately after the stampede at Koh Pich bridge. Phnom Penh. 2010. Pha Lina. From *The Koh Pich Tragedy: One Year On, Questions Remain*. 2011. Cambodian Center for Human Rights (CCHR).

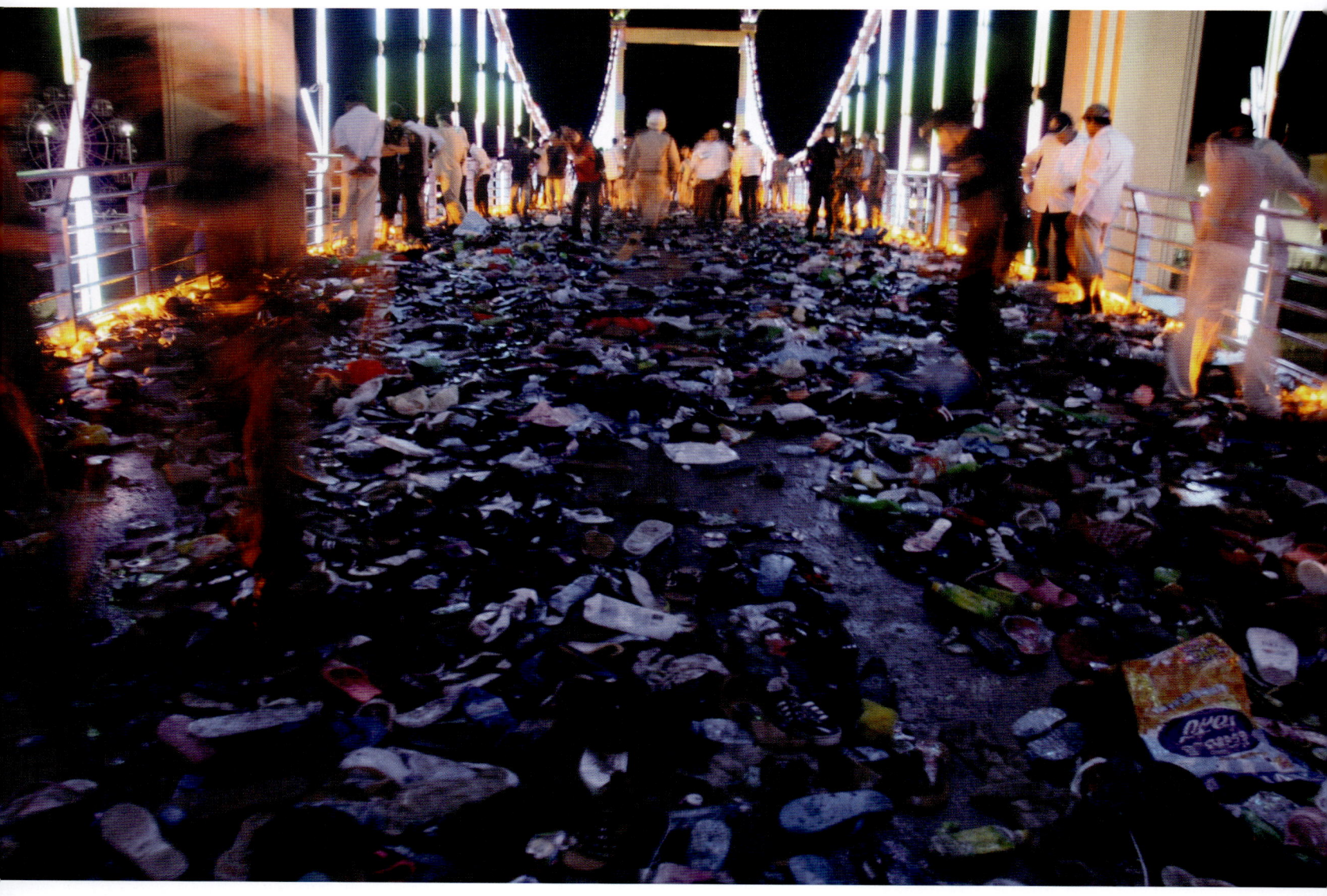

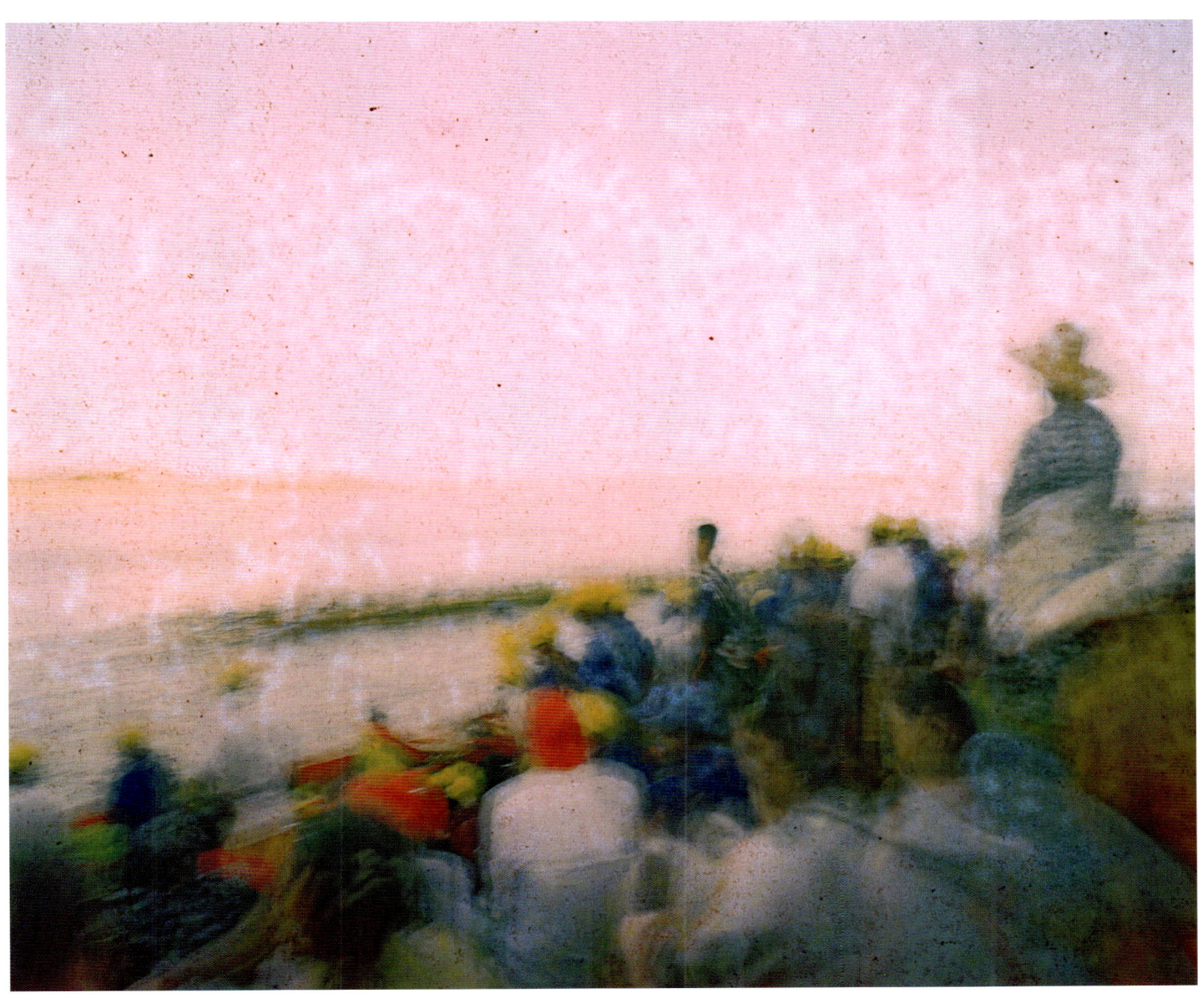

"The Stampede" Series

"The Stampede" series. Sisowath Quay, Phnom Penh. 2016. Kim Hak.

Over his successful decade-long career, KIM Hak (b. 1981) has explored a number of themes related to the cultural fabric of Cambodia, including survivor stories, the funeral of King Sihanouk, and the changing Cambodian landscape. He is a long-term participant and tutor at the Angkor Photo Festival and Workshops. After the Koh Pich bridge tragedy at the 2010 Water Festival in Phnom Penh (opposite), the event was canceled for many years. In 2016, the festival was resumed. Kim used 120 mm film to photograph the boat races, spectators, and night fireworks. It was two years before he had the chance to develop them, but in that time the intense tropical heat had a deleterious effect on the film. The results left an uncanny reference to the works of the French pointillist painter Georges Seurat, working 130 years earlier.

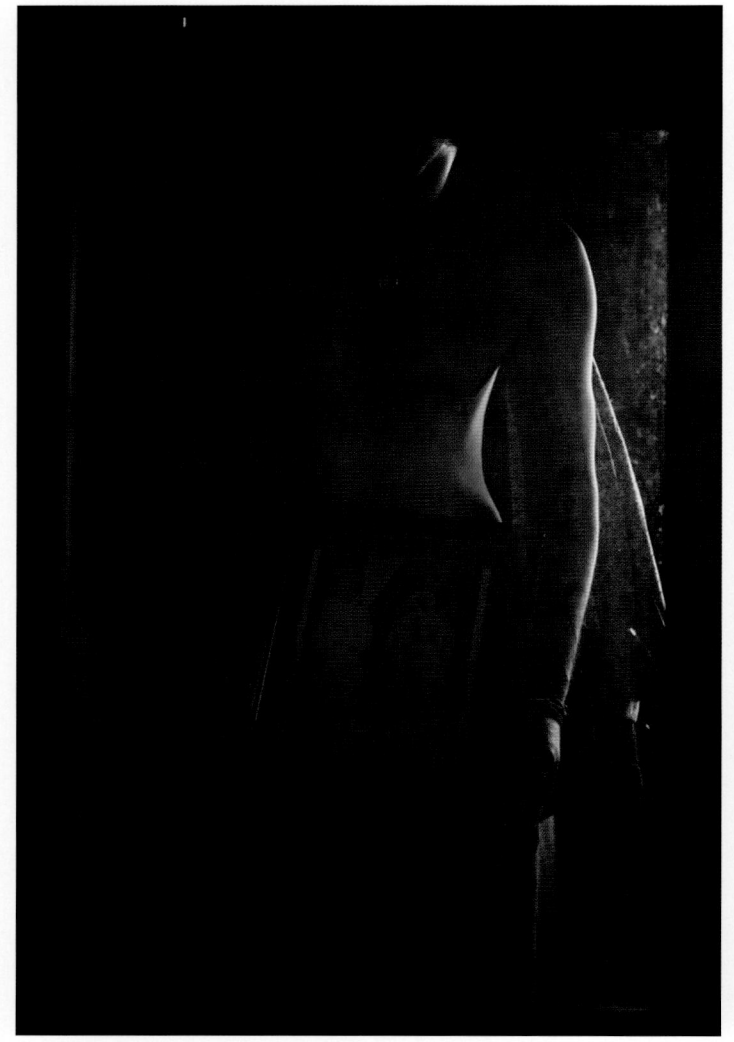
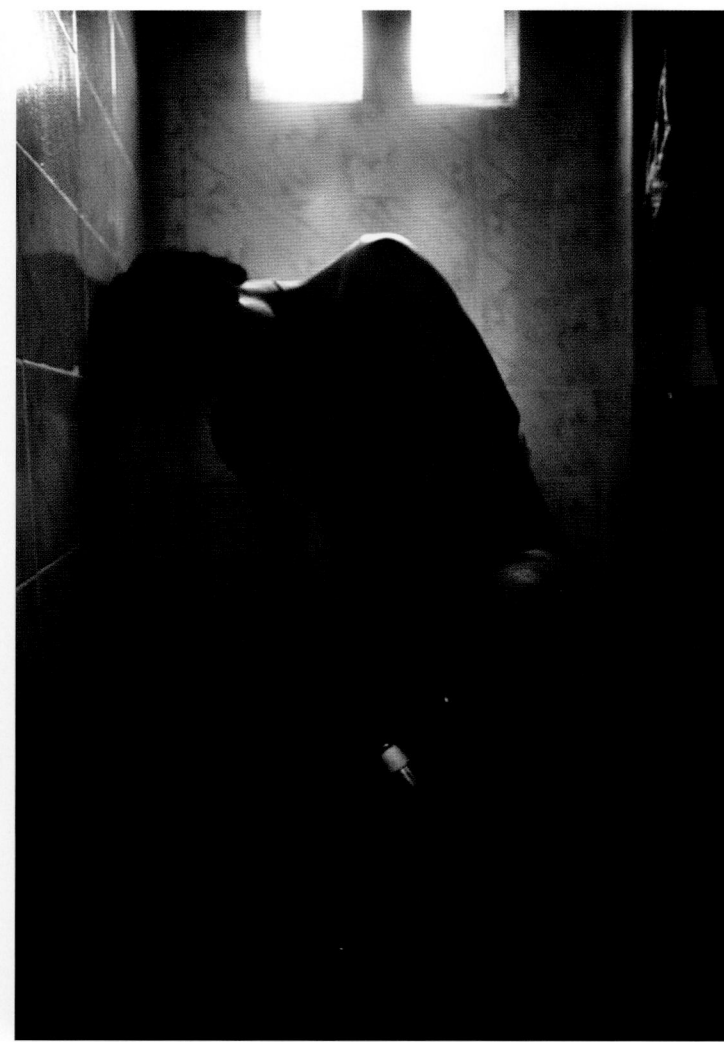

"Nude" series. 2010–11. Heng Ravuth. Darryl Collins Collection, Siem Reap.

"Nude" Series

HENG Ravuth (b. 1985) is a 2006 RUFA graduate, who received photographic mentoring from Stephane Janin. As one of the original cofounders of the Stiev Selapak artist collective, he upholds the Cambodian tradition of cooperative work environments. The intimate self-portraits that compose the "Nude" series are unusual in the genre of contemporary creative photography. To quote from the 2011 "Innermost" exhibition catalog at SA SA BASSAC, "Nudity, particularly in Cambodian culture, sounds uncomfortable and sometimes disturbing because it strongly connects to the very intimate privacy of bodies that we usually don't talk about. It also connects to shame and dignity and therefore we seem to hide it."

"Thoamada" Series

Thoamada is a Khmer colloquialism meaning "things are ok, everyday, the usual." The nine large photographic portraits were the creative outcome of a two-day professionally mentored workshop amongst Cambodian men who have sex with men (MSM). At the end of the workshop, the participants were asked to paint their faces as an act of personal identity-making. The diversity of vividly painted symbols, patterns, and colors represented the breadth of identities within the LGBTQIA+ and MSM communities. VUTH Lyno (b. 1982) is the artistic director of Sa Sa Art Projects, and a 2015 graduate in Art History from Binghamton University, New York.

'Thoamada' series. Installation at SA SA BASSAC, Phnom Penh. 2011. Vuth Lyno/SA SA BASSAC.

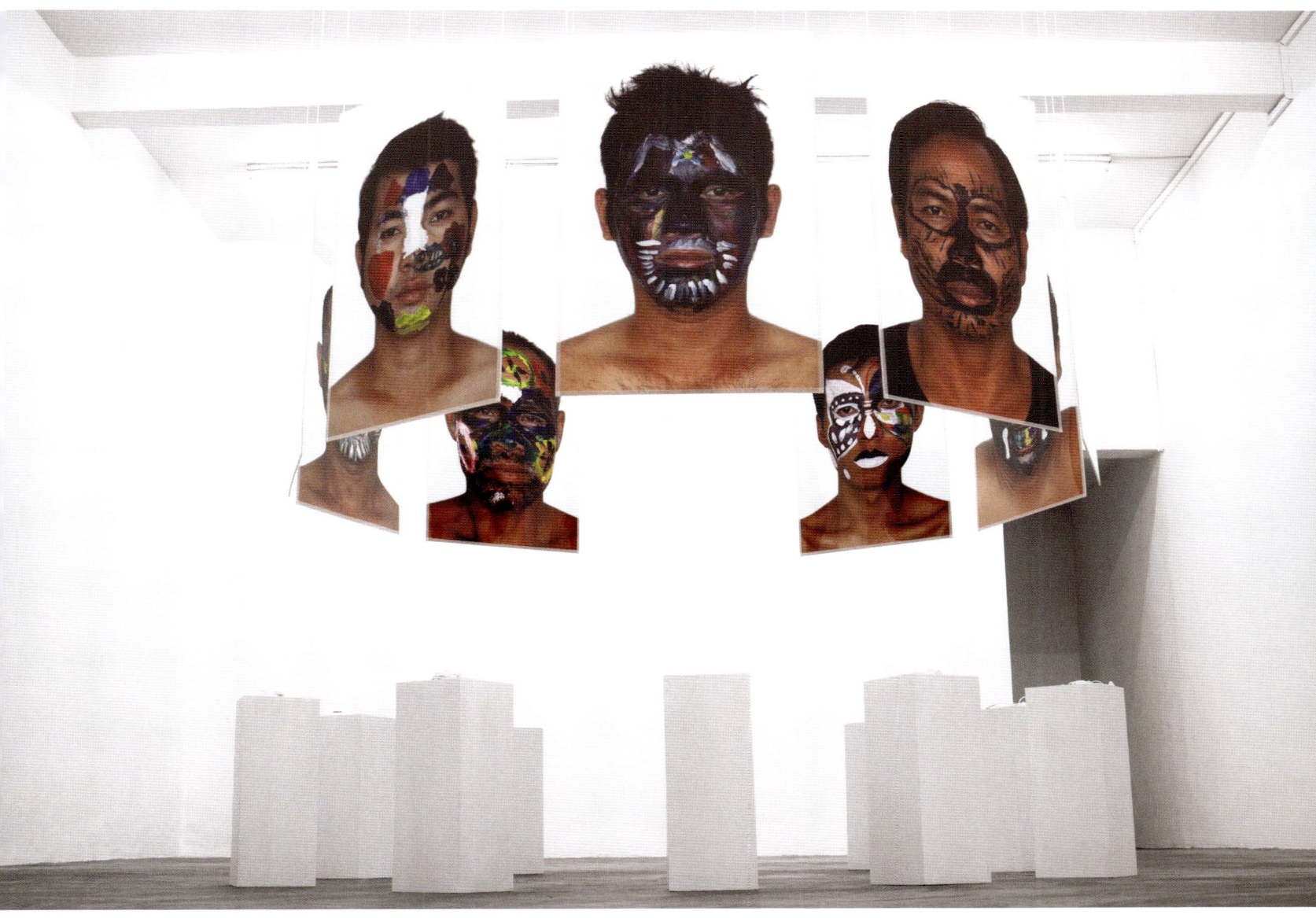

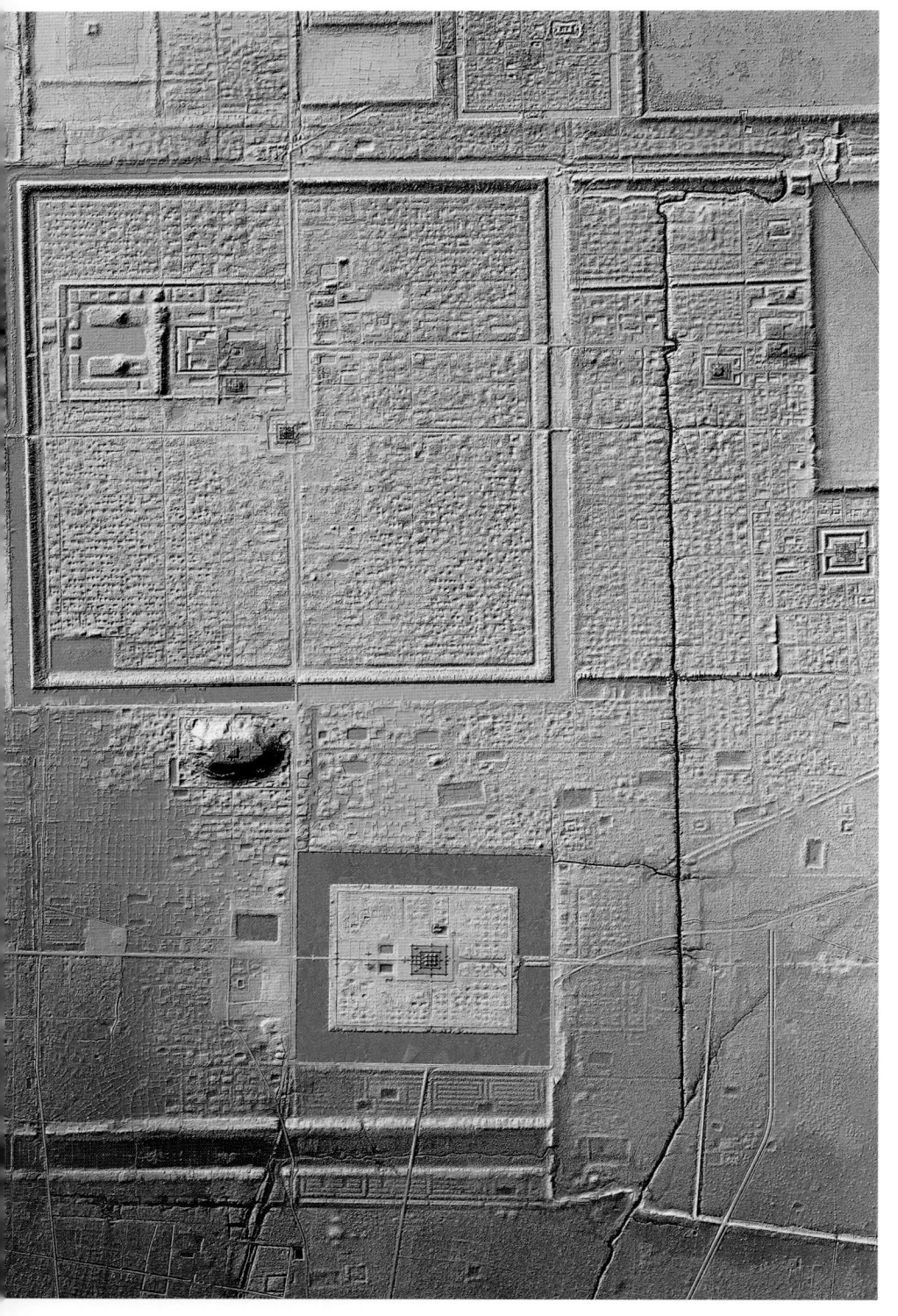

LiDAR Image, central Angkor. Showing Angkor Thom as the large walled square at the top, Phnom Bakheng as the bump in the middle, and Angkor Wat with its wide moat at the bottom. Siem Reap. 2012. Damian Evans, École française d'Extrême-Orient/Khmer Archaeology LiDAR Consortium (KALC).

Light Emitting Radar (LiDAR)

One of the most illuminating revelations about Cambodia's classical heritage was the Light Emitting Radar (LiDAR) project. Firing millions of laser beams every second from a helicopter passing overhead, some of the beams penetrated the dense jungle to the ground beneath, and then reflected back. An onboard computer processed the data, revealing medieval foundations of Angkorian temples, house mounds, roads, canals, and individual shrines previously hidden beneath the dense tropical canopy. Extrapolation of the discoveries enabled archaeologists to see that Angkor was an open city of well-organized temple communities, cluster villages, and open rice fields dotted with free-standing shrines. Cumulatively, it represents the largest medieval city in the world at that time. As far as scientific technology goes, this echoes the remarkable aerial photographs taken ninety years earlier from colonial-era biplanes.

RIGHT: **Niece with Dutch windmill.** Siem Reap. 2014. Yin Someth.

BOTTOM, FROM LEFT:
Yin's auntie at the West Baray. Siem Reap. 1985.

Yin and family visiting the West Baray. Siem Reap. 1985.

Yin Someth looking at his family archives. 2019.

Source: Yin Someth Family Archive/Siem Reap Thmey Photo.

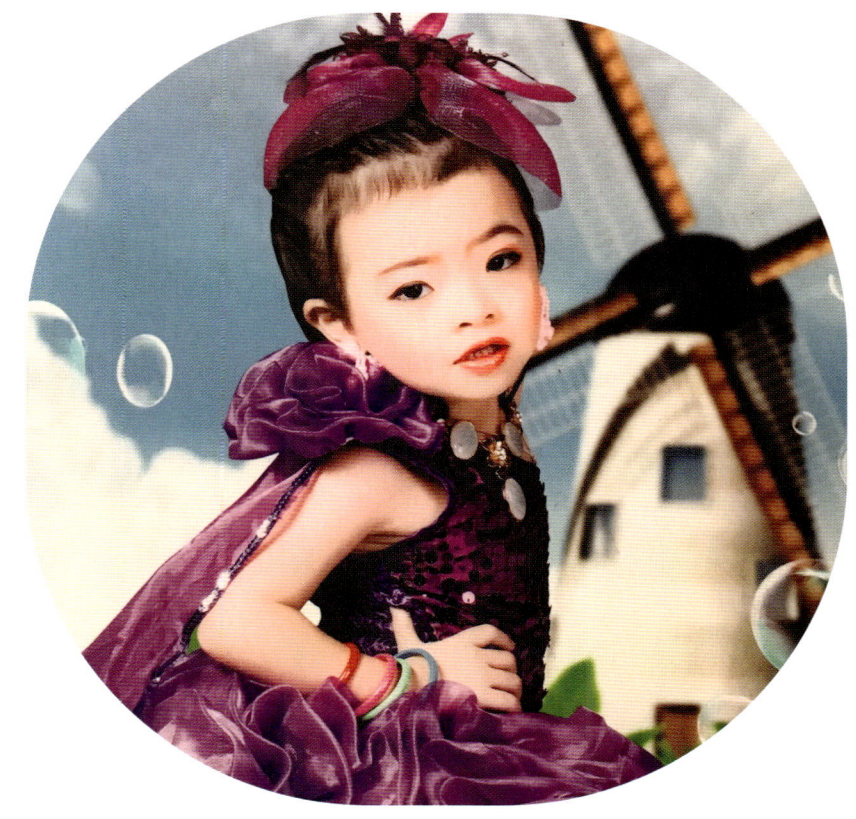

An Enduring Family Studio

When YIN Someth's (b. 1981) mother and aunties moved to Siem Reap from Phnom Penh in 1983, they brought their photo studio business with them. In 1985, as with many Cambodian families at that time, a picnic at the West Baray was regarded as a special event. As the business moved from print to digital, Yin learnt the basic skills of photography from his uncle. In 2014, he demonstrated his art by making a commemorative photograph to celebrate his gregarious young niece's birthday. He photographed her in their studio, then downloaded images of an exotic Dutch windmill and used Photoshop software to add glamor to the image. It was then printed A3 size and used as a light box advertisement at the entrance of the family's two studios. Yin has kept many of his family's old photos, digitizing and laminating them for safekeeping.

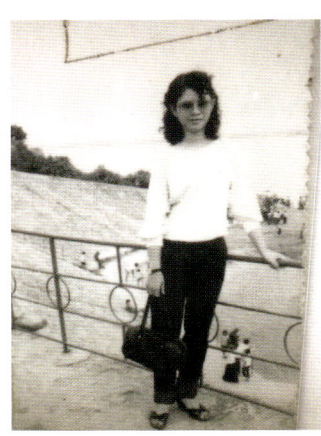
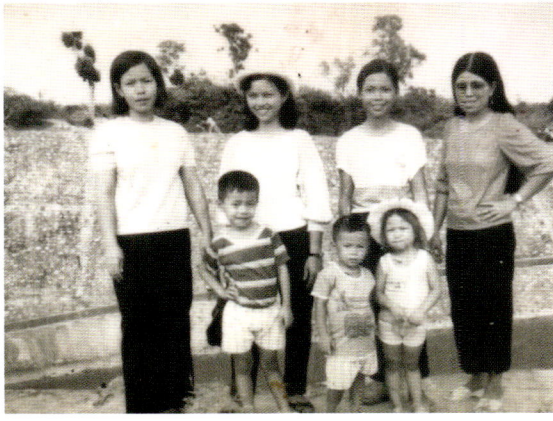
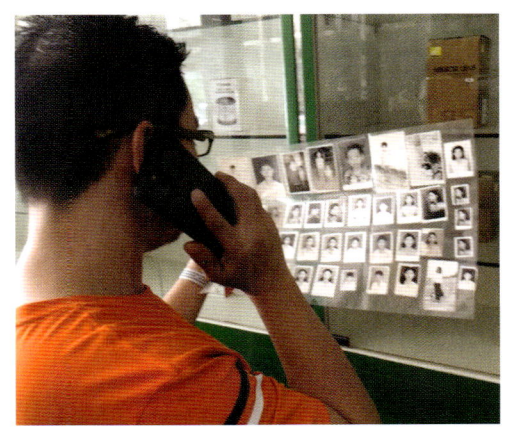

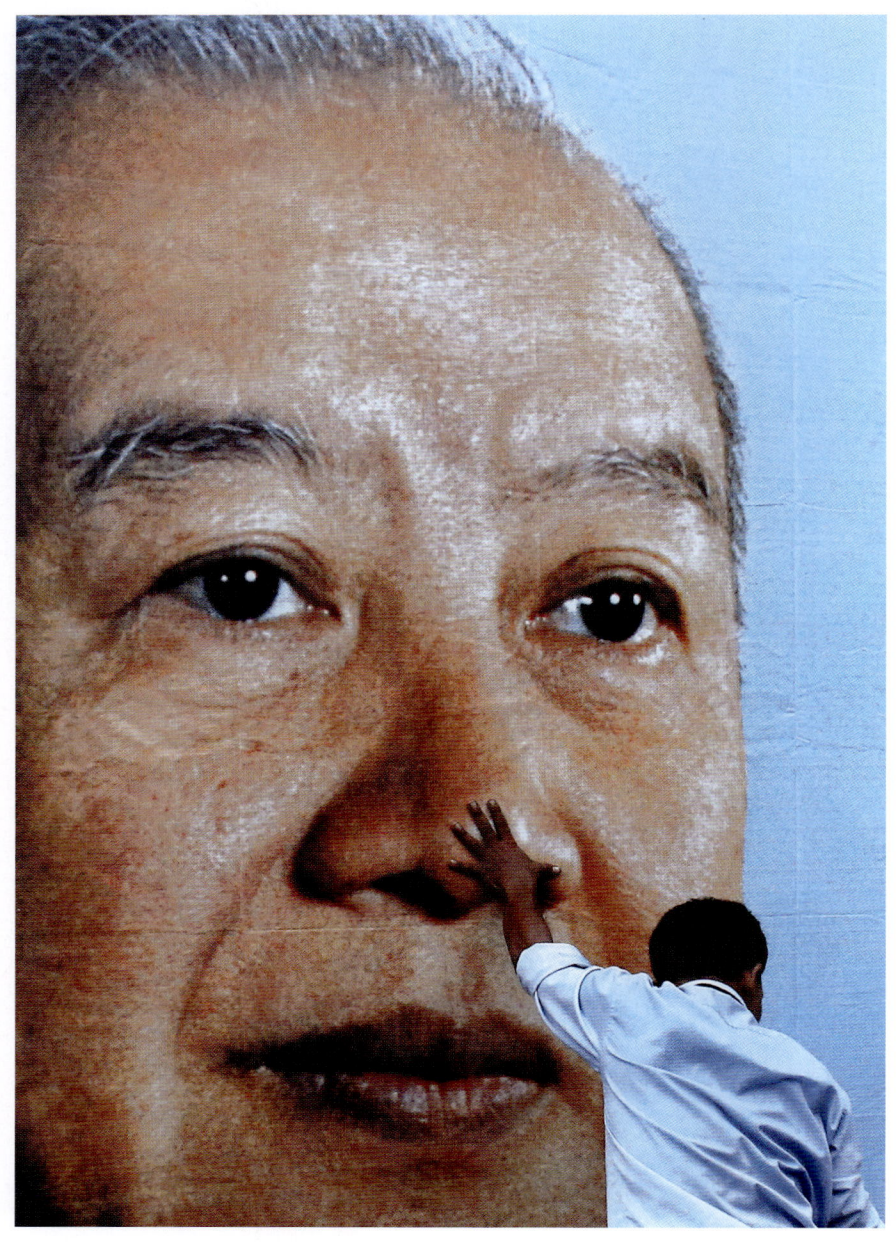

LEFT: **Sihanouk poster.** National Palace, Phnom Penh. 2012. Wong Maye-E/Associated Press.

OPPOSITE: **Sihanouk in the moon.** Screen capture from Pech Pang's mobile phone. Siem Reap. 7:56 p.m., February 4, 2013. Unknown artist.

The Death of King Sihanouk

On October 5, 2012, King-Father Norodom Sihanouk died. Cambodia went into deep mourning. Sihanouk's impact on the cultural and political landscape of the country was profound. Since being crowned in 1941, he had served for over sixty years as a charming but manipulative monarch, prime minister, figurehead of the communist revolution, head of state and, once again, monarch until he abdicated in 2004, ensuring that his son Prince Sihamoni would succeed him as king. After months of ceremonial preparation, he was cremated at the Veal Men open ground in front of the National Museum on the afternoon of February 4, 2013. That evening, as light clouds drifted across the sky, Cambodians looked heavenwards to see his face in the crescent moon. Caught on multiple smart phones, it became the fastest spreading digital photograph in the kingdom.

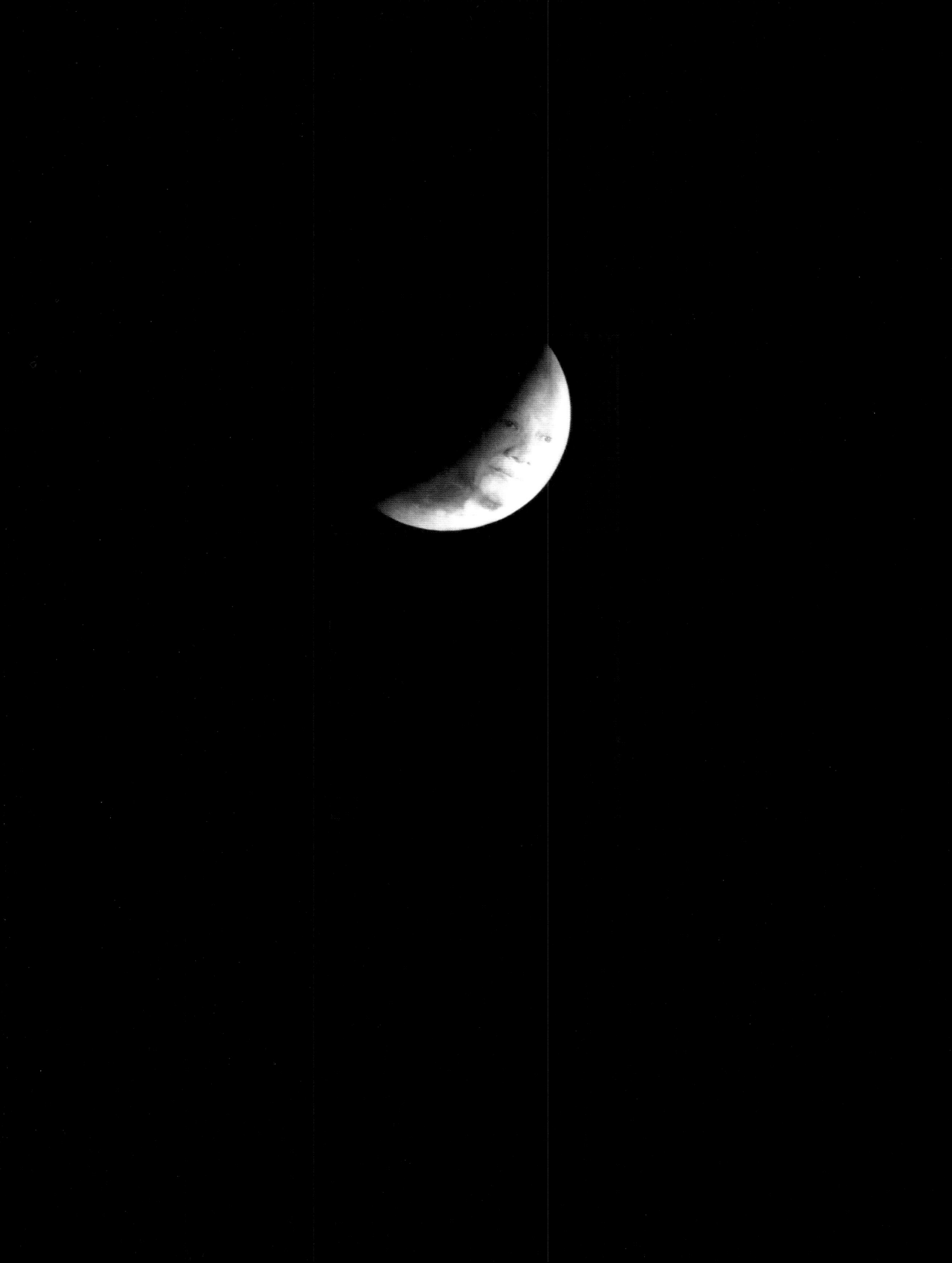

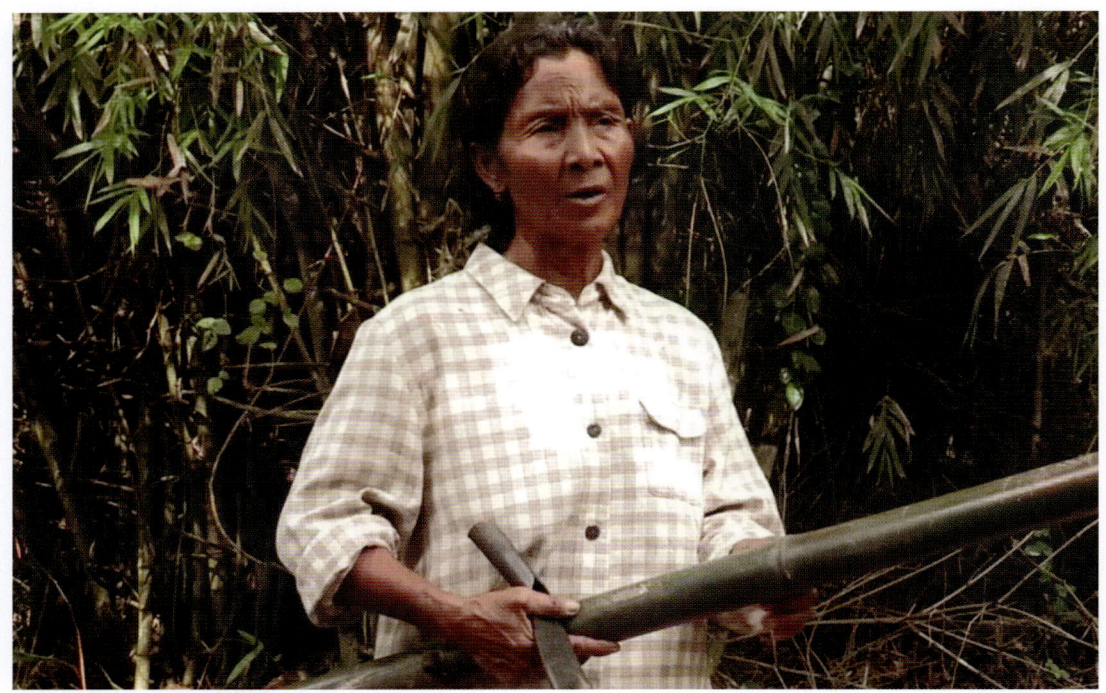

Bophana Audiovisual Resource Center

Cofounded by the French-Cambodian film-maker Panh Rithy, the Bophana Audiovisual Resource Center collects, restores, and archives the rich cinematic, photographic, and audio history of Cambodia. The center's collection includes documentaries, 1960s newsreels, and Khmer Rouge political propaganda. It also trains young film-makers in the creation of digital content, documenting issues such as artistic heritage, the environment, and social change. The eponymous Bophana was a prolific writer, eloquently composing powerful love letters to her husband Ly Sitha in the 1970s. Both were arrested by the Khmer Rouge as part of their internal purges. During the five months of torture before her death, she wrote thousands of descriptive confessional pages. They were both executed by the Khmer Rouge on March 18, 1977.

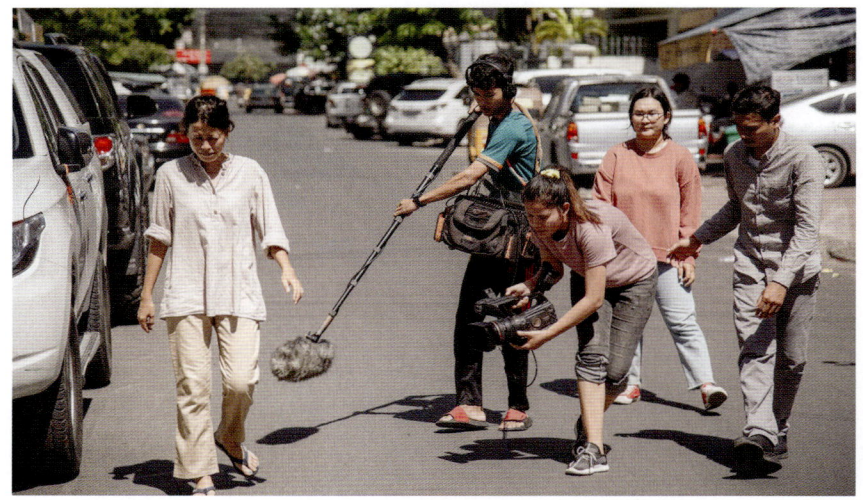

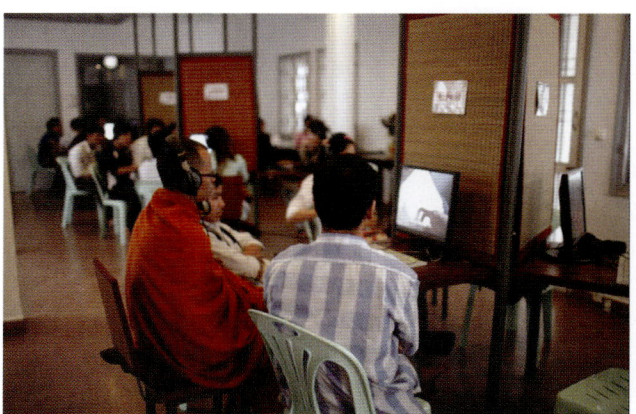

FROM TOP: **Mrs Heng speaks about her forced married life under the Khmer Rouge regime.** Still from video. Battambang. 2017.

Film crew on location. Phnom Penh.

Bophana Ausiovisial Resource Center, public research room. Phnom Penh.

Source: Bophana Audiovisual Resource Center.

Panoramic Dental X-rays

PANHAVUTH Sarpin (b. 1969) graduated from medicine in Phnom Penh during the People's Republic of Kampuchea, when Soviet medical expertise dominated the country. He opened his Siem Reap dental clinic in 1993 and first used X-ray technology imported from Germany three years later. This panoramic image, produced by the clinic's most contemporary equipment, was sent by the scanner directly to a computer screen for immediate analysis. It offers a disturbing insight into a patient's dental history.

Panoramic dental X-ray. Siem Reap. 2018. Panhavuth Sarpin.

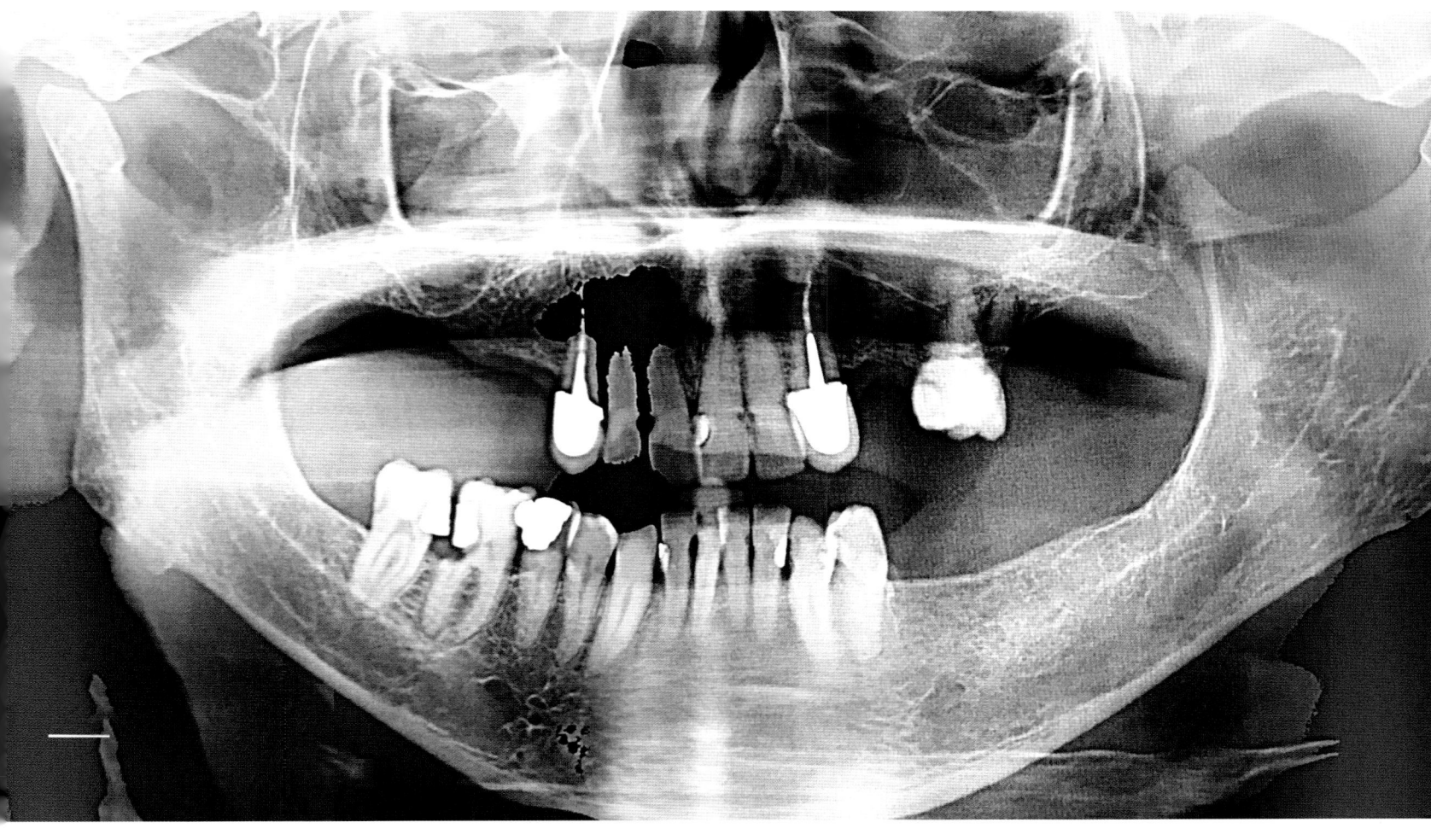

"Left Three Days" Series

Originally a photojournalist for *Cambodge Soir* and *Le Mekong* newspapers, and a stringer for Reuters and the US Environmental Protection Agency (EPA), MAK Remissa (b. 1970) commemorates the 40th anniversary of the fall of Phnom Penh in his "Left Three Days" series. When the Khmer Rouge took control of the capital in 1975, they issued an announcement to Phnom Penh residents to vacate the city within three days. Mak, who was seven at that time, remembers his father was sent to prison, his mother was sent off to a women's camp, and his elder sister was sent to work. When the regime ended in 1979, information on the whereabouts of family members was scarce. Remissa's lucky reunion with his mother and sister was largely coincidental. He never saw his father again. "We don't know what happened to him. I think he was killed, and yet I still keep some hope in my heart that he is alive because I don't know" (Mak Remissa, Phnom Penh, December 5, 2014).

"Left Three Days" series.
Phnom Penh. 2015.
Mak Remissa.

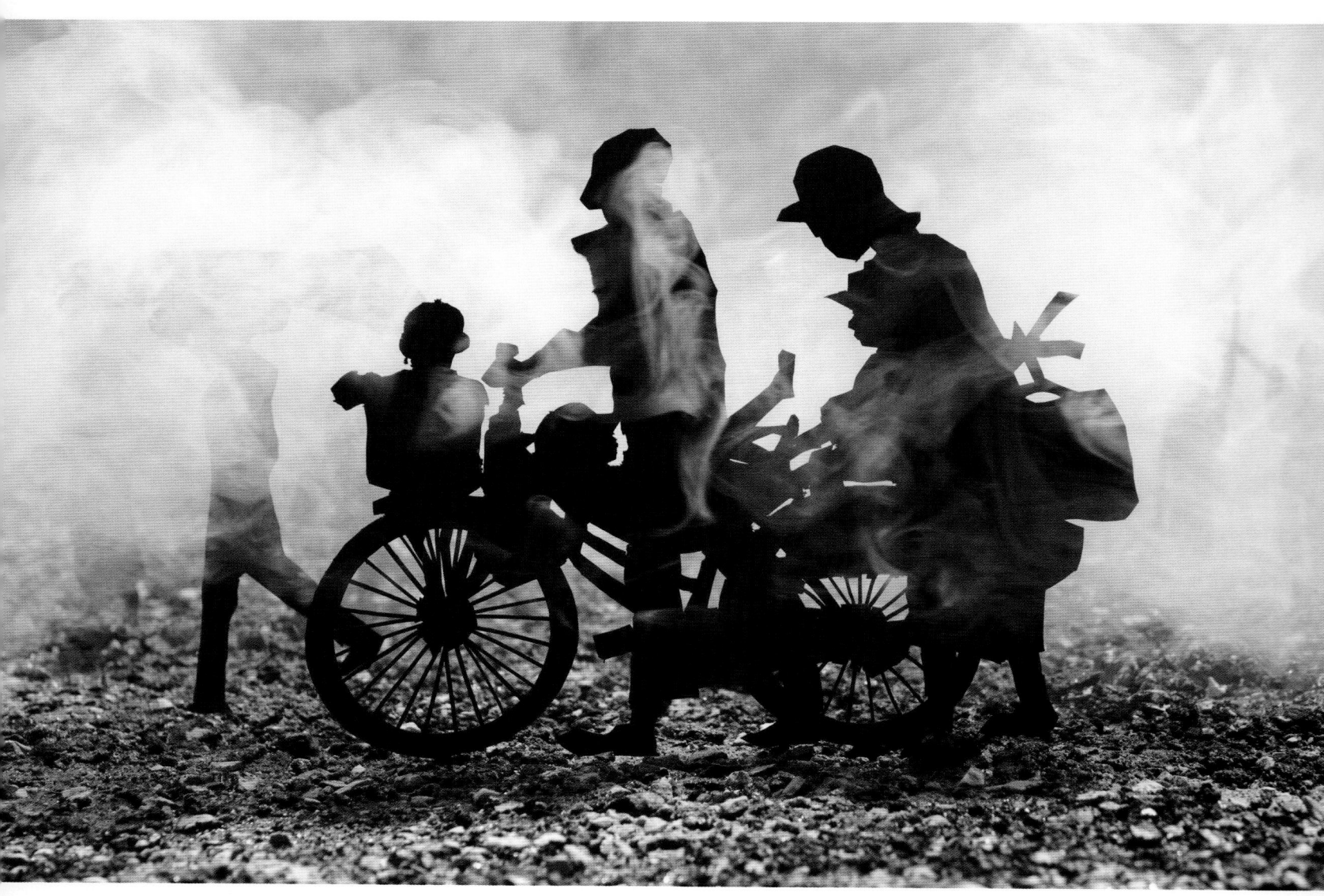

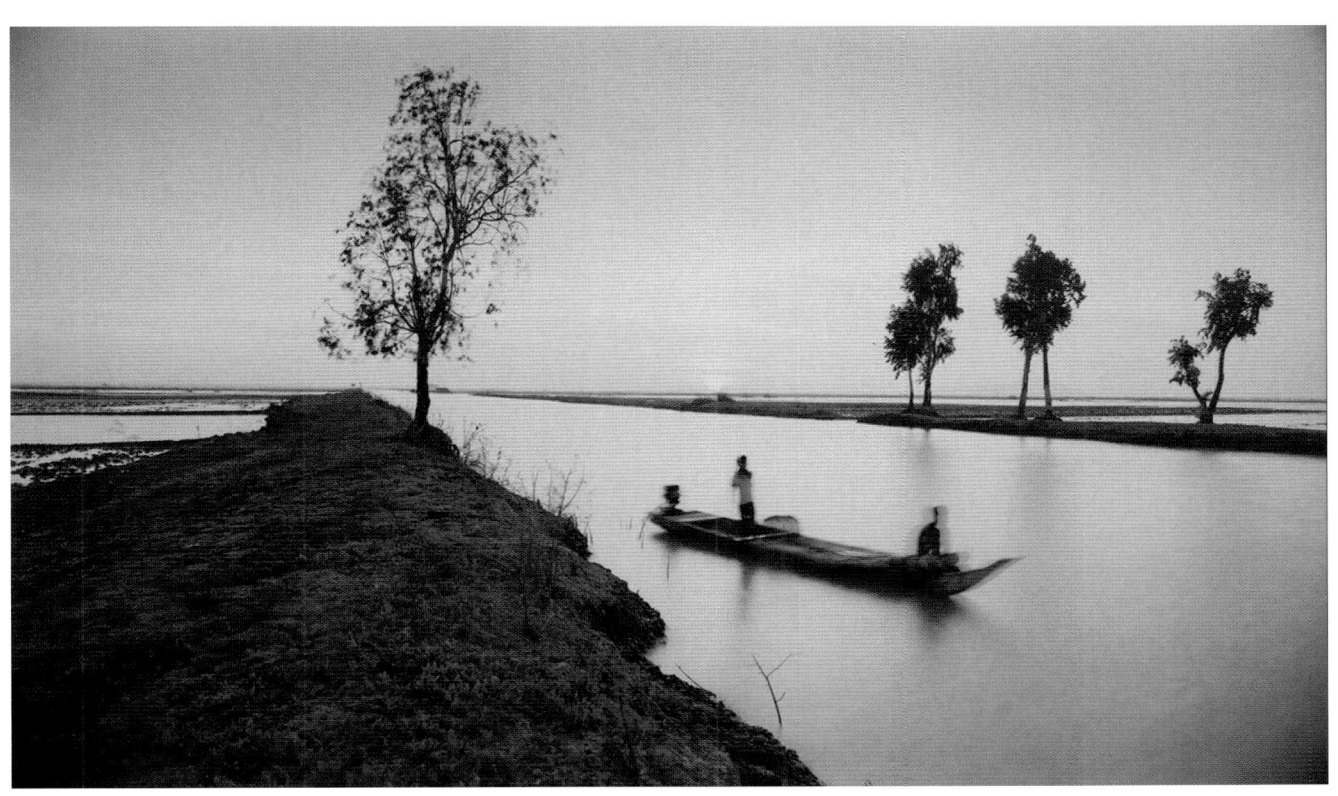

"Pre-Angkor" Series

IZU Kenro (b. 1949) studied art at Nihon University in Tokyo before moving to New York in 1970. He is well known for his lifelong project, *Sacred Places*, using a large-format 353 x 508 mm film camera to create platinum prints. A prolific self-publisher of photography books, Izu has regularly visited Cambodia. In 2012, he explored the pre-Angkorian temple site of Sambor Prei Kuk, photographing its brick and sandstone monuments while using his extra-large format camera to capture the subtle gradations of tone and light of the monsoon-flooded countryside.

Angkor 36. "Pre-Angkor" series. 2012. Izu Kenro.

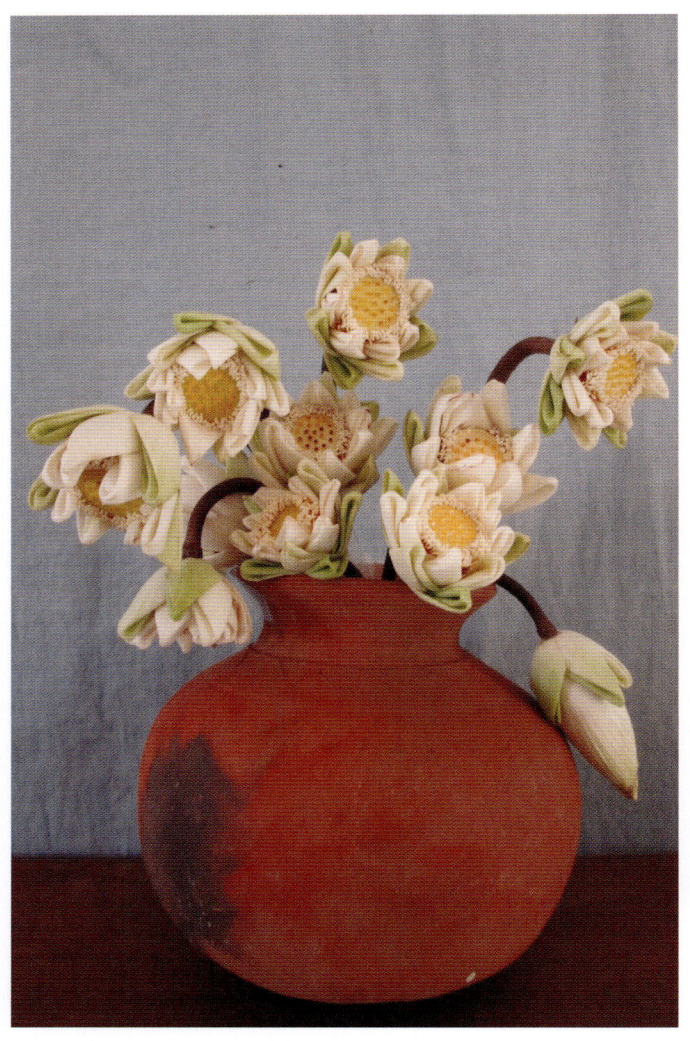

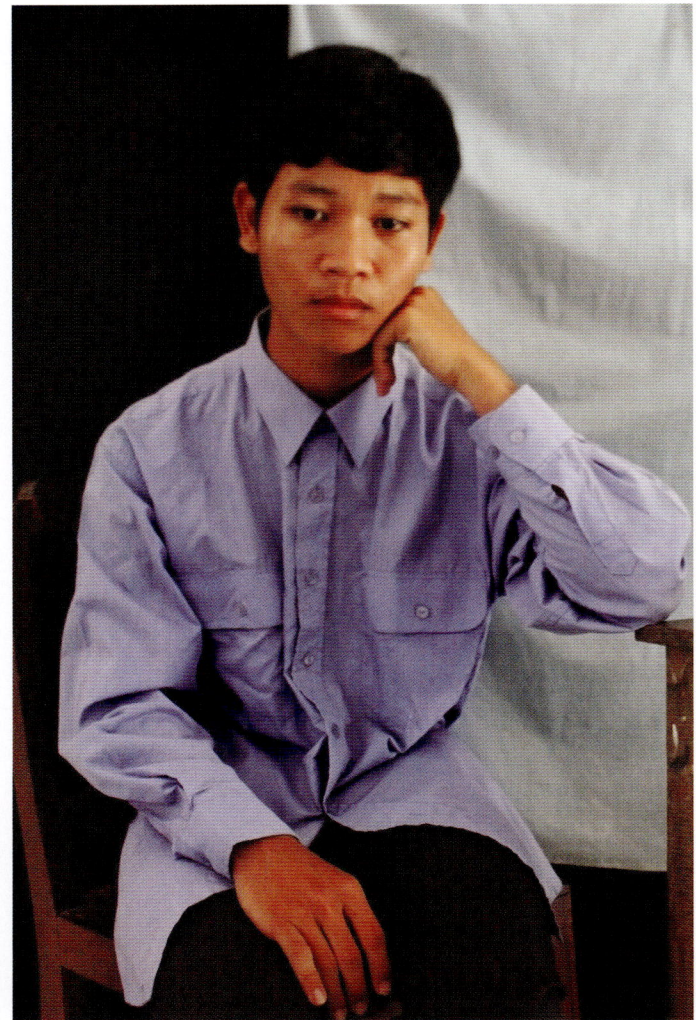

"Self-portrait." Pech Sophea. Siem Reap. 2016. (After Amendeo Modigliani's *The Boy*. 1910).

"Sunflowers" (Lotus Flowers). Pech Sophea. Siem Reap. 2016. (After Vincent van Gogh's *Sunflowers*. 1888).

Reimagining French Painting

With his excellent trilingual skills, PECH Sophea (b. 1998) was able to trump his older classmates by enrolling in a multimedia course run by the Ponleau Kampuchea Foundation at Chey Primary School near Puok, Siem Reap. After graduation, and with a youthful flourish of creativity, he carefully composed a suite of photographs of Cambodian everyday life inspired by selected late nineteeth-century European impressionist and early twentieth-century post-impressionist artists. Devoid of mockery, contempt, or conceit, his naturally lit works exude a mature dignity and calm, with "Sunflowers" (lotus flowers) a gentle meditation on mortality, and "The Boy" revealing a quiet, introspective portrait, in keeping with the facial expression of the original Modigliani painting.

The Cambodian Landmine Museum

Curated by Aki Ra, a former child soldier for the Khmer Rouge army, the Cambodia Landmine Museum and Relief Facility serves to educate the public on the dangers of landmines. It has displays of an array of destructive ordinances used across many battlefronts, interpretative panels on a thirty-year history of violence, information on landmine clearance programs, and dioramas of military personnel and their uniforms. One panel displays photographs of staff who worked at the center, one of which, a portrait of ticket seller Oeurn Kalyan, was mutilated by a woman in a nearby village who was suffering from mental illness. There is no known connection between the two women.

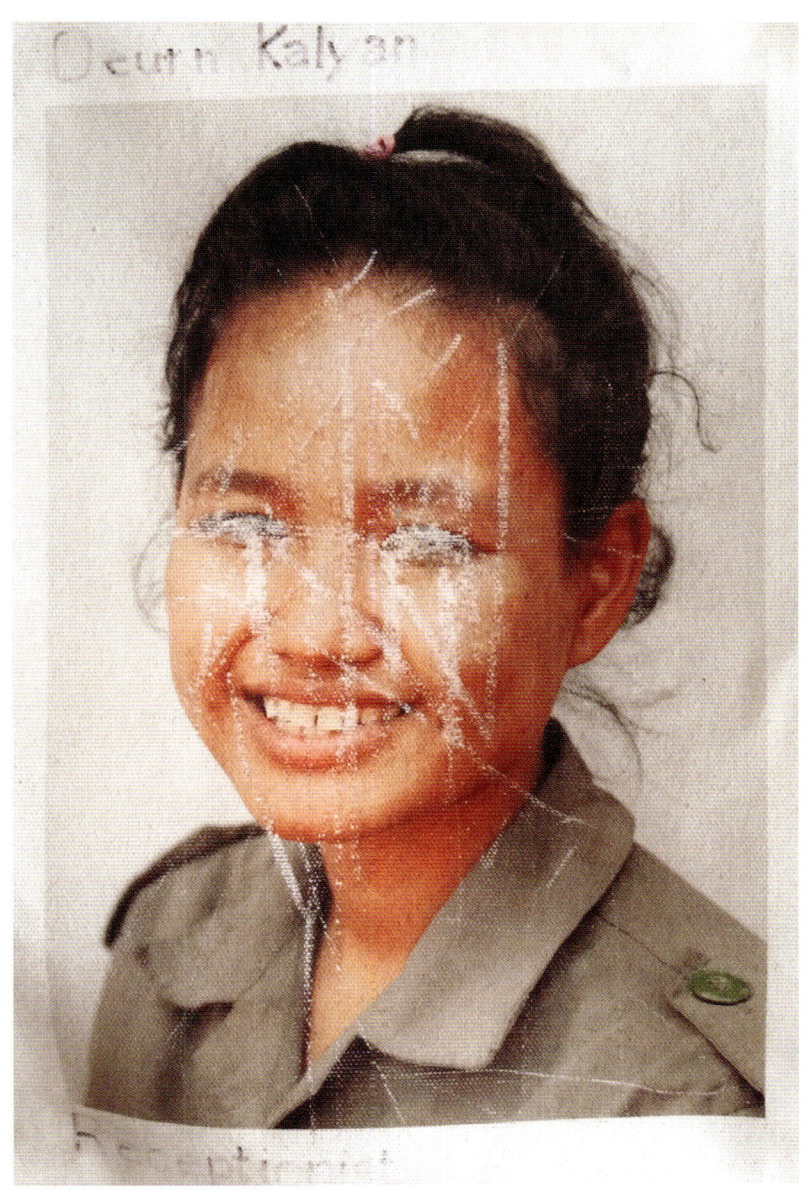

Defaced portrait of Kalyan. Siem Reap. 2014.
Original photograph by Richard Fitoussi. 2008.
Cambodian Landmine Museum, Siem Reap.

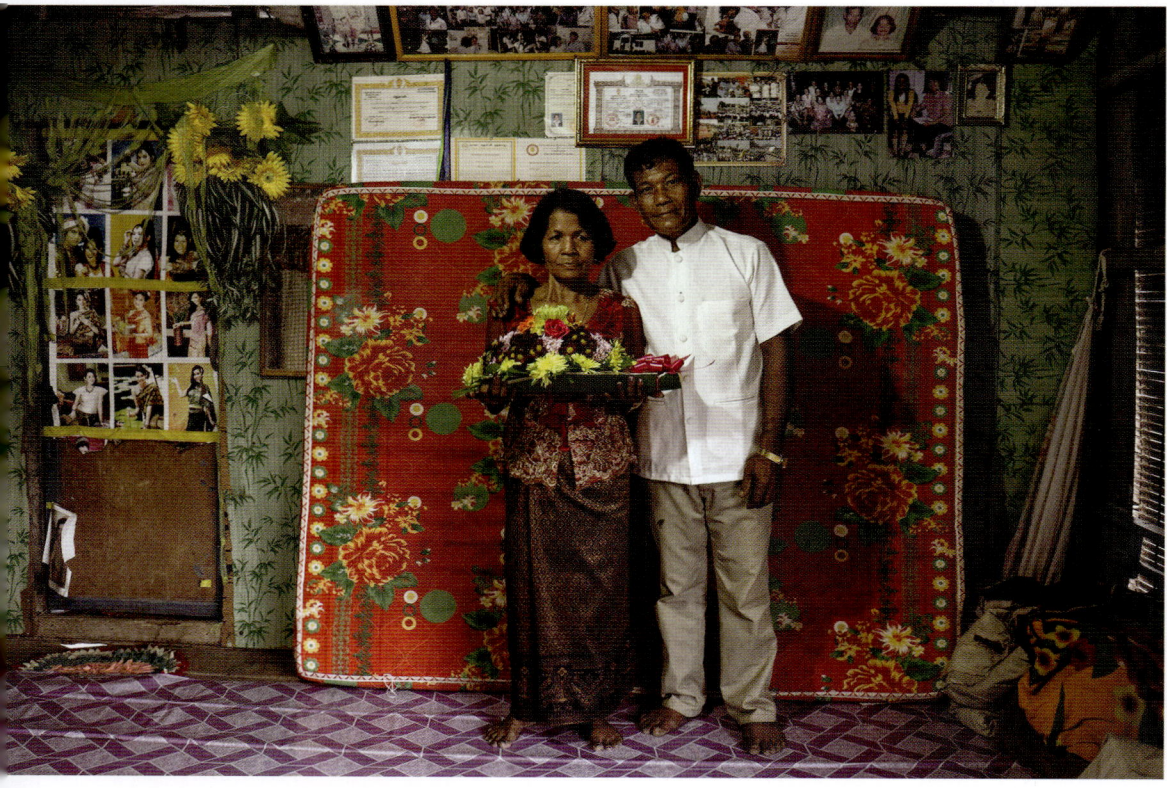

LEFT: **Portrait of groom Morb Heang and bride Nou Sout. "Remarry' Suite.** Kampong Chhnang. 2015. Hannah Reyes Morales/Al Jazzera America.

BELOW: **"Bound" series.** 2015. Vong Sopheak.

"Remarry" Suite

During the Khmer Rouge era in the latter half of the 1970s, there were many instances of forced marriage, an act considered a crime against humanity by the Khmer Rouge War Crimes Tribunal. In 2015, almost four decades after their initial forced marriage, several couples who had continued their relationship after liberation from the Khmer Rouge, decided to have a traditional wedding ceremony. It included all the trappings of a modern event—a rites-of-passage procession, a Buddhist ceremony of consecration, tears from the bride and groom, loud music, and a feast for family and friends under a gaily decorated tent. Hanna Reyes MORALES (b. 1990) was working as a freelance journalist for Al Jazzera when she took this photograph of a couple in their home on the day before the occasion.

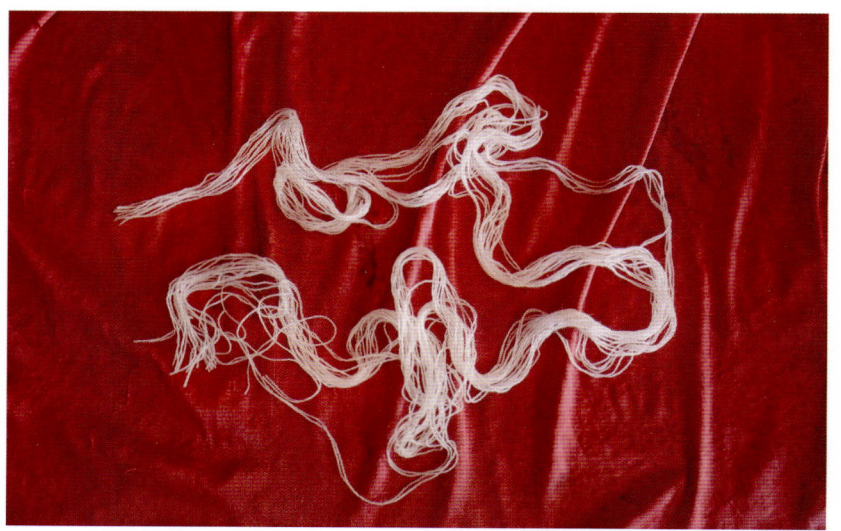

"Bound" Series

VONG Sopheak (b. 1993) is a 2013 Interior Design graduate from the Royal University of Fine Arts. In the same year, he attended his first photography class with Kim Hak at the French Institute in Phnom Penh. Two years later, he was selected for the 2015 Angkor Photo Festival Workshop, where Vong developed a body of work based around the theme of the traditional white thread used during rituals and ceremonies. The pure white thread binds the bodies of a couple being married through both happiness and misfortune.

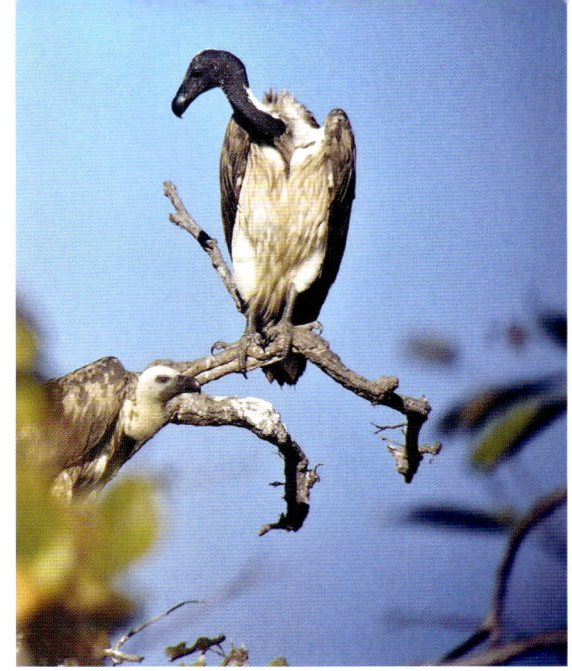
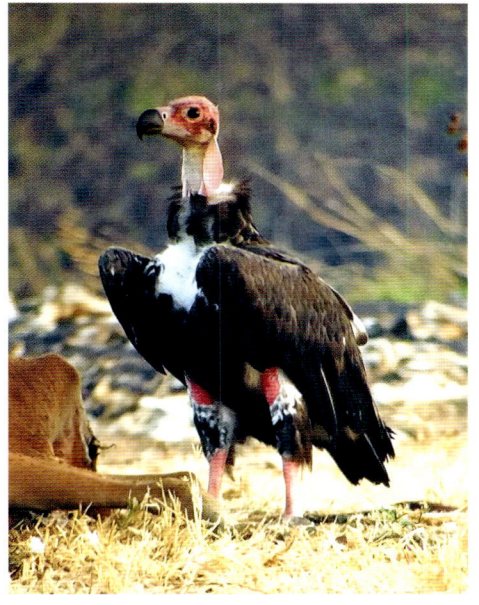

FAR LEFT: **White-rumped vulture** (*Gyps bengalensis*).

LEFT: **Red-headed vulture** (*Sarcogyps calvus*).

Photographs: Prek Toal, Tonlé Sap. 2018. Lan Nadong.

Avian Photography

LAN Nadong (b. 1990) has worked for several years as a guide for Cambodia's premier nature conservation organization, the Siem Reap-based Sam Veasna Center for Wildlife Conservation (SVC). As a keen "birder" or bird photographer, he has represented SVC in the Asian Bird Fairs in Thailand (2015) and Malaysia (2016). Tmat Boey, a wildlife refuge in northern Cambodia, is Lan's favorite place for bird-watching. It is renowned globally as a unique ecosystem for sighting Cambodia's rare giant ibis. Photography is a valuable tool for bird identification and behavioural studies. The perils of the natural world, however, can make the birds' carcasses an avian treat for ever-watching vultures.

"No Rice For Pot" Series

NEAK Sophal (b. 1989) created the "No Rice For Pot" series by collaborating with women from her home village in Takeo Province. The portraits portray women's primary role within the Cambodian family structure—cooking, childbearing, and nurturing—and the bind that this can have on their personal aspirations. A graduate of RUFA, she learned the foundations of photography at a six-month course prepared by the French Institute in collaboration with Photo Phnom Penh. She soon developed a reputation for thematic photography of people on the street, often obscuring their faces using everyday objects, creating tantalizing "erasing of identity" portraiture.

"No Rice For Pot" series. Takeo. 2012. Neak Sophal.

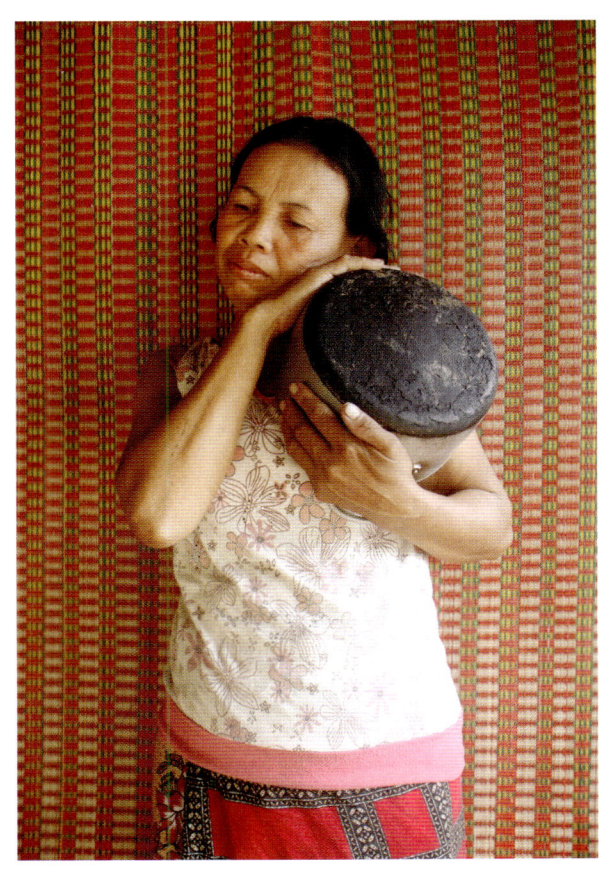

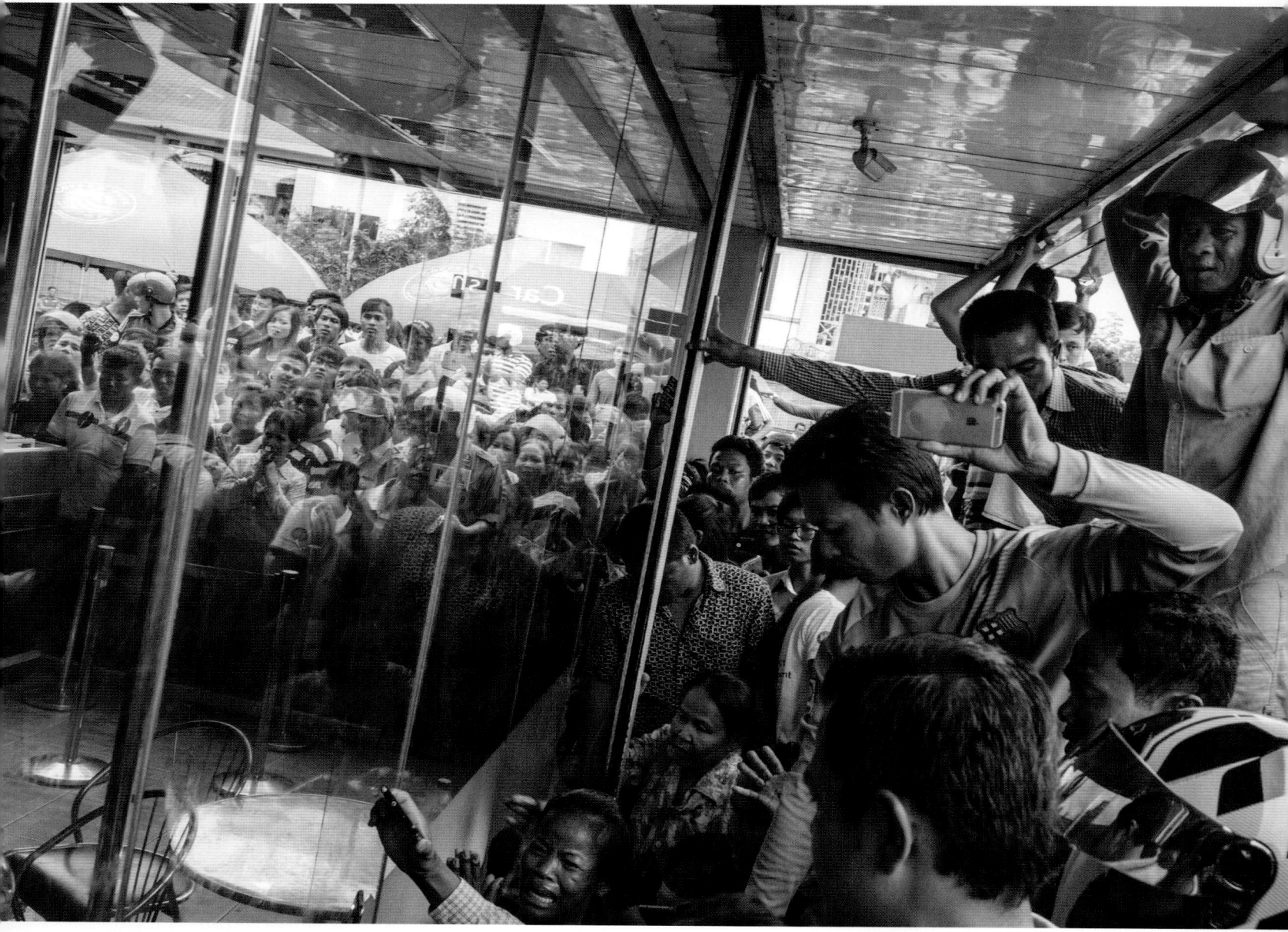

The Assassination of Kem Ley

On July 10, 2016, an angry crowd of nearly 1,000 people quickly gathered in front of the Bokor Caltex petrol station on the corner of Monivong and Mao Tse Toung boulevards, Phnom Penh. Kem Ley, a prominent Cambodian commentator and human rights activist, had been assassinated with several gunshots around 9:00 a.m. over a purported debt of $3,000. The gunman was supposedly a man called Choup Samlap ("Meeting to Kill"). The assassination occurred in a constantly deteriorating political atmosphere in the second decade of the twentieth century in Cambodia. Belgian-born John VINK (b. 1948) has worked fulltime in Cambodia since 2000. Being a Phnom Penh resident with many contacts, he was quick to record the event. Kem Ley's funeral procession two weeks later saw the largest gathering of quiet protesting mourners line the streets in Cambodia's modern history.

An angry crowd at the assassination site of Kem Ley. Bokor intersection, Phnom Penh. 2016. John Vink.

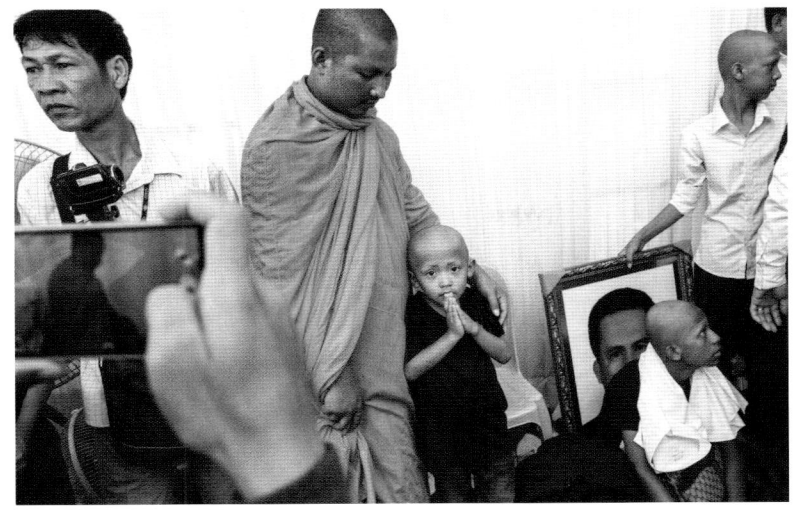

LEFT: **Three of Kem Ley's sons stand next to his body while mourners pay their respects.** Phnom Penh.

BELOW: **Mourners at Wat Chas pay their respects to Kem Ley.** Chroy Changvar Peninsula.

BOTTOM: **A monk photographs the funeral procession.** Phnom Penh.

Photographs: John Vink.

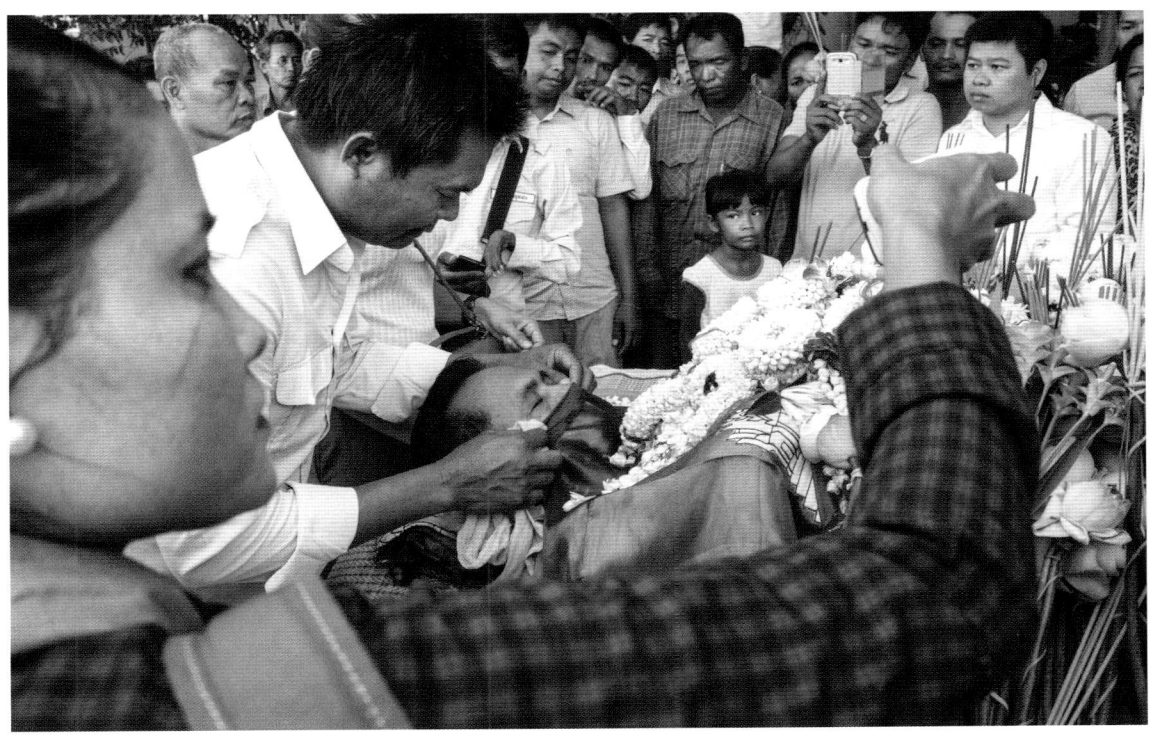

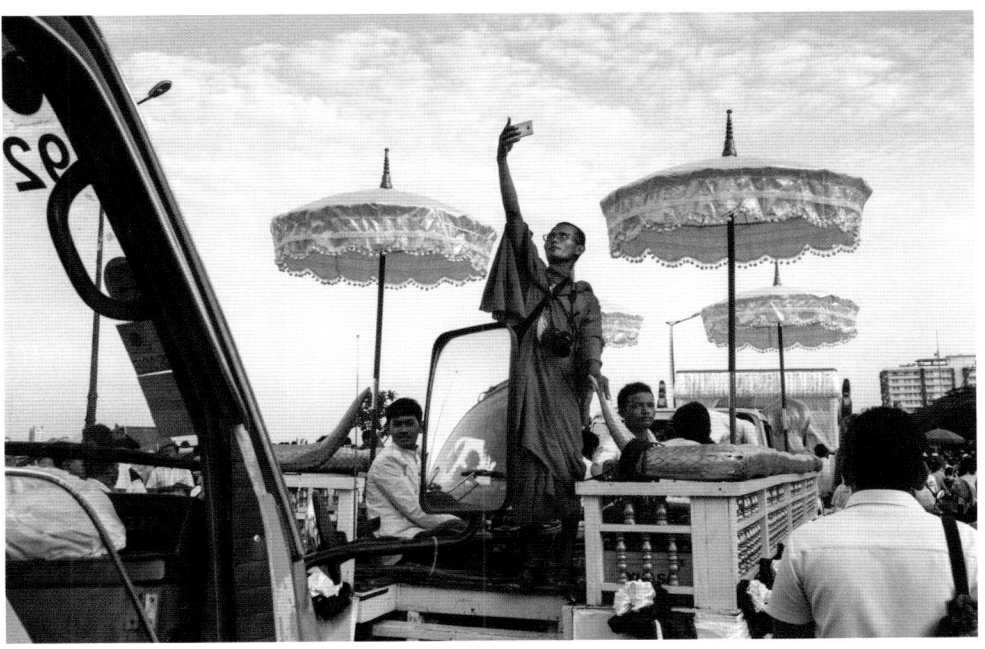

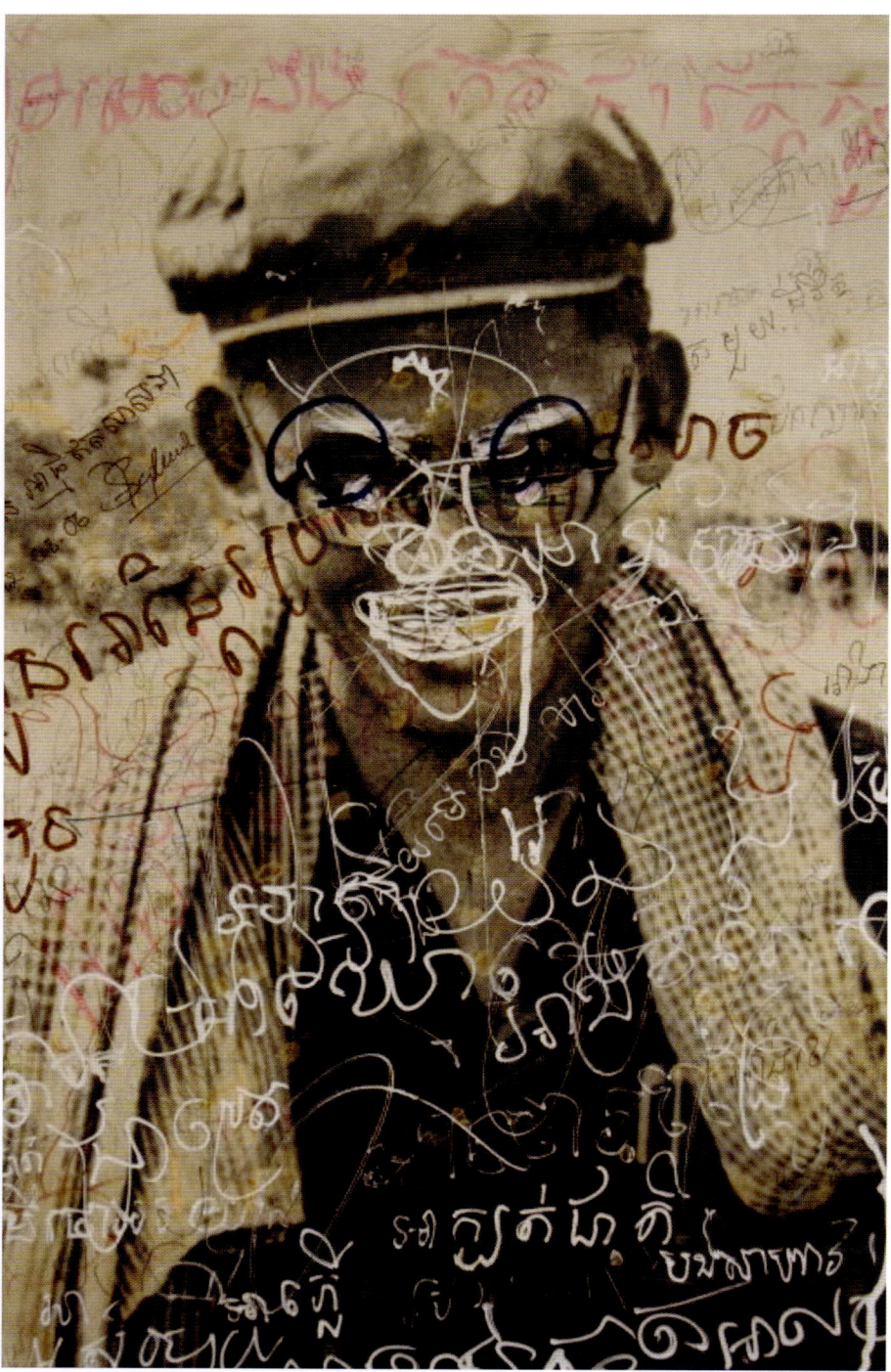

The Defacing of Son Sen's Photograph.
Toul Sleng (S-21) Genocide Museum, Phnom Penh. 2007. Dani Planas Labad.

The Defacement of Son Sen's Photograph

The Toul Sleng (S-21) Genocide Museum is renowned for its displays of disturbing photographs of prisoners' identity photographs. There are also photographs of the key leaders of Angkar, the political arm behind the more familiar Khmer Rouge army. Son Sen was the minister of defense. In the late 1970s, as the Khmer Rouge retreated to the hills surrounding Pailin, he was involved in an internal power struggle with Pol Pot, which led to both he and his family being executed. Visiting Cambodians who are familiar with the protagonists, have vented their emotions against these leaders, writing graffiti and defacing their photographs. Dani Planas LABAD (b. 1972) is a freelance documentary and travel photographer based in Barcelona, Catalunya.

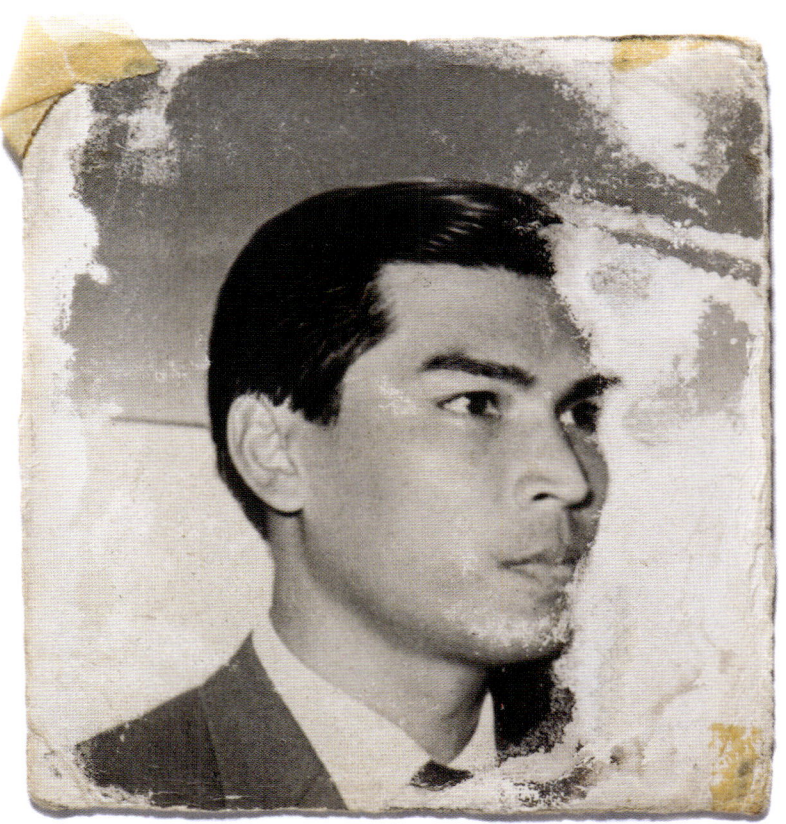
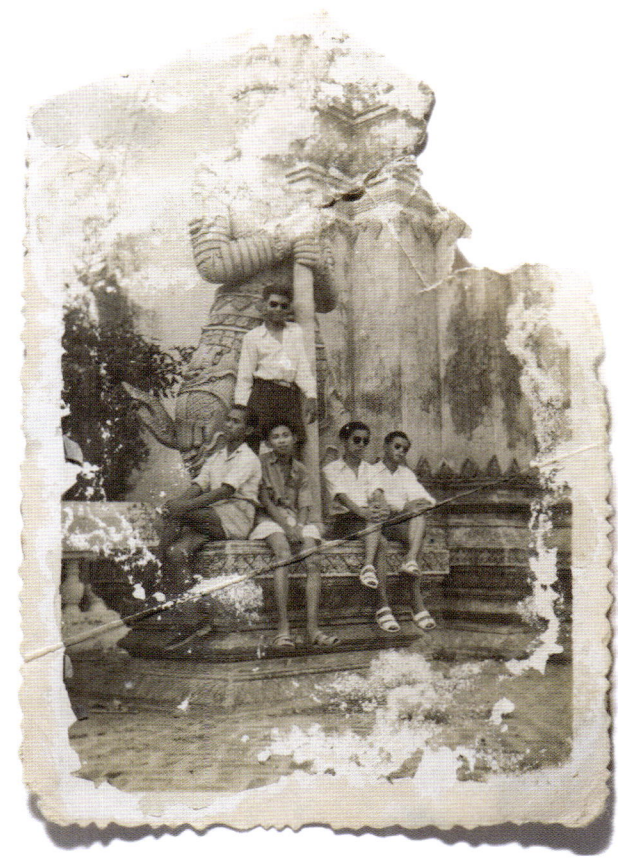
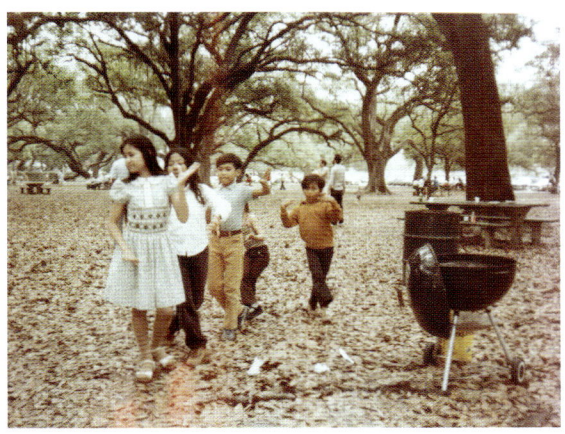
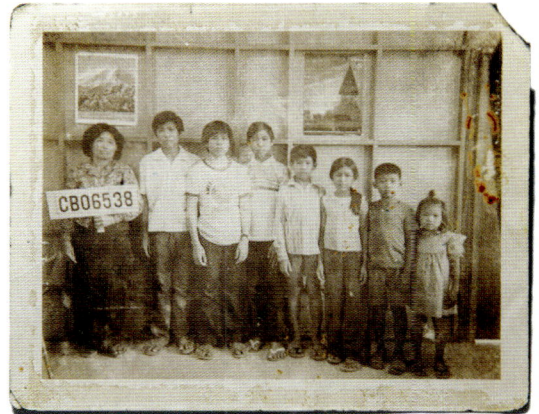
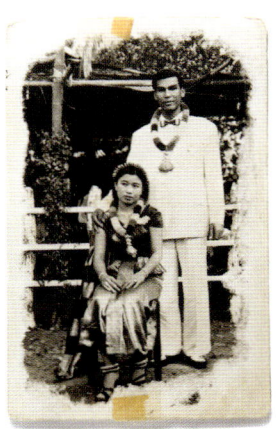

Rama Family Archive and *Buried*

Buried brings to light the extraordinary story of the Rama family and how their cache of family photographs reveals a story across multiple generations. The images recount the pleasures of family life in Battambang in the 1960s and their journey as refugees moving through Thai border camps and, finally, via the Philippines to America. During the Khmer Rouge regime, the Rama family buried their family photographs to protect their identity, only to retrieve them towards the end of the regime. *Buried* was published in 2019 by Catfish books in a collaboration between Vira Rama and Charles Fox, with a corresponding exhibition at Meta House in Phnom Penh. Importantly, *Buried* includes handwritten annotations beneath the photographs by members of the Rama family.

TOP LEFT, CLOCKWISE: **Dad receiving a medal from King Sihanouk.** Battambang. ca. 1969.

Dad with his friends at Wat Piphittharam. Battambang. Mid-1950.

Mr. and Mrs. Rama on their wedding day. Battambang. ca. 1958.

Rama family identity lineup. Refugee camp. Chonburi, Thailand. 1981.

My sister Sunday, my brother Nadirak, and other Khmer kids dance the *Romvong* around a BBQ. City Park, New Orleans, USA. ca. 1983.

Source: Rama Family Archive/Found Cambodia.

Snow Whitening Revisited

Formed in 2008 by Dutch theater director Bob Ruijzendaal, New Cambodian Artists (NCA) is co-owned by its dancers and its director, Khon Sreyneung. As an all-female contemporary dance company, it is unique in the country. While pushing the boundaries of contemporary expression and honoring their strong classical training, they have created a repertoire of work that bridges Cambodia's past and an experimental future. *Snow Whitening Revisted* is performed by Ny Lai (b. 1987), Khun Sreyneuch (b. 1996), and Kong Soengva (b. 1998). In one scene, reproductions of the infamous Tuol Sleng (S-21) identity photographs create powerful connections between the audience and memories of the victims whose characters are portrayed by the dancers.

Snow Whitening Revisited, live performance. New Cambodian Artists (NCA), Siem Reap. 2020. Anders Jiras.

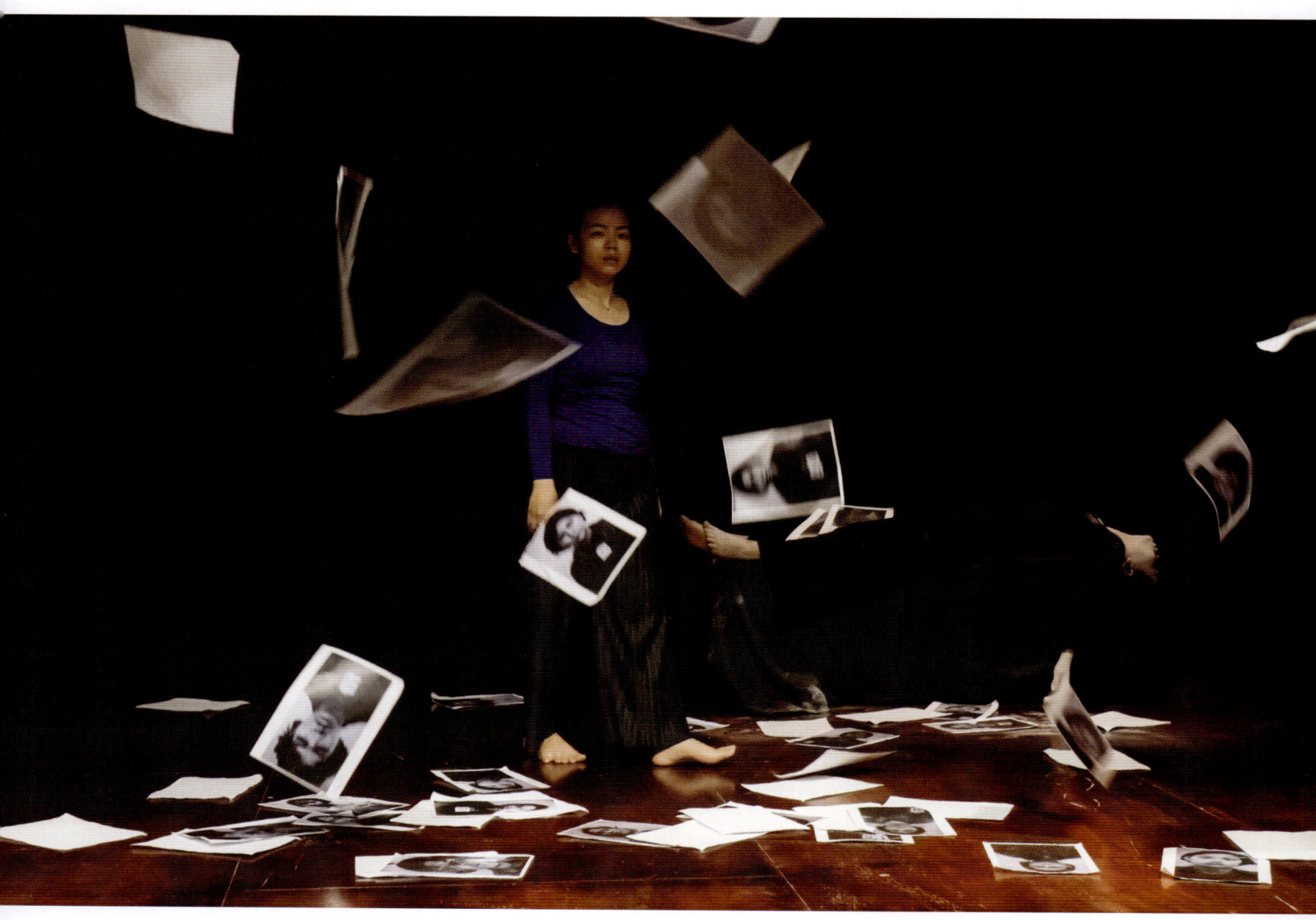

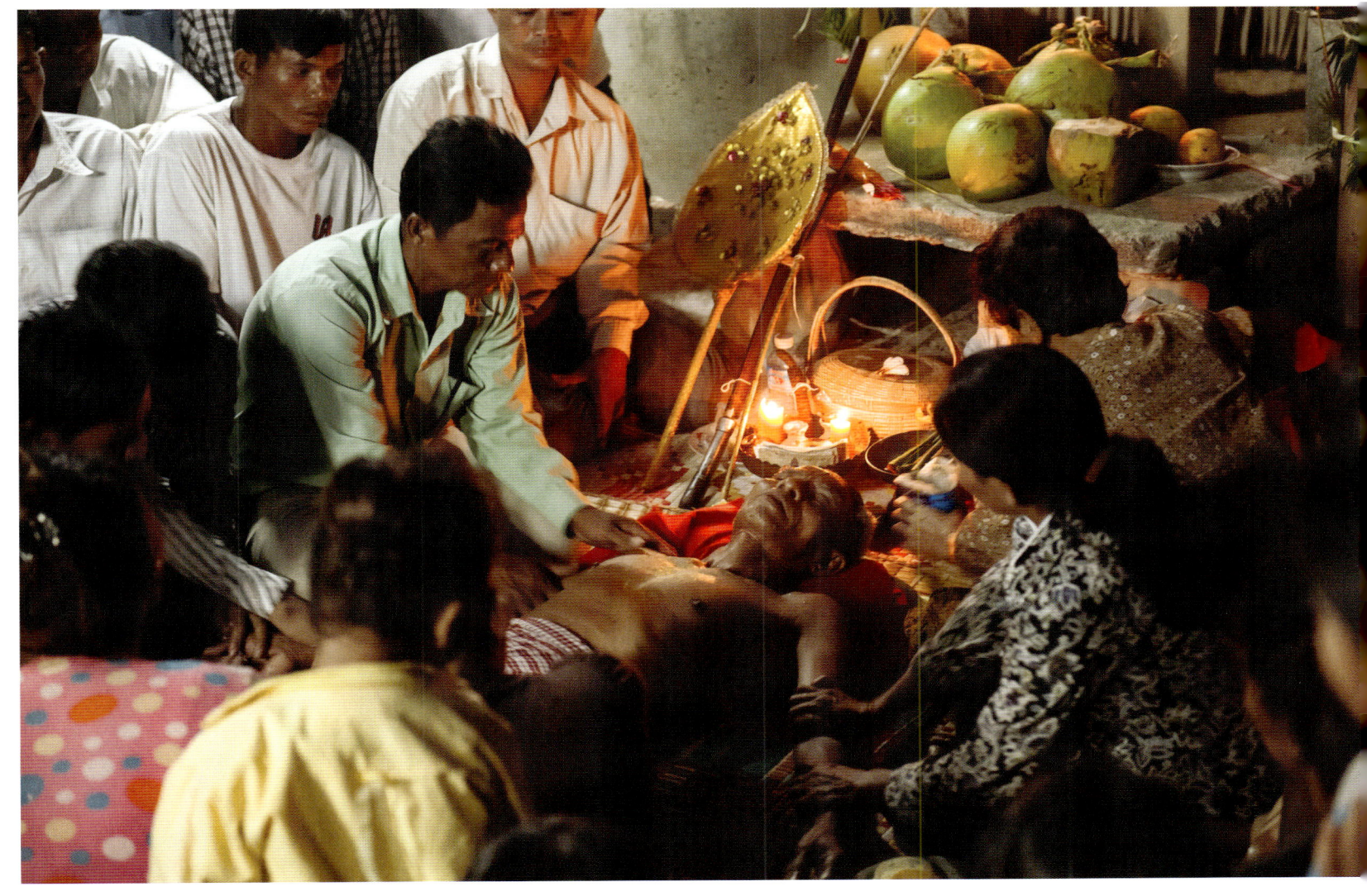

A Spirit-Healing Ceremony

A spirit-healing ceremony.
Bali, Takeo Province. 2011.
Anders Jiras.

Anders JIRAS (b. 1946) has been recording the intangible dramatic arts and dance culture of Cambodia for the past twenty years, building what is now the largest contemporary archive of this genre. His photographs include the Royal Dancers, *lakhon khol* (masked dancers), shadow theater puppeteers, and *yike* (spoken drama) performers and actors, as well as independent contemporary dance and drama troupes, both amateur and professional. In his coverage of traditional religious festivals and their practice in rural folk-healing rituals, he has expanded the boundaries of performance photography. In 2011, he went with the researcher Prum Sisaphanta to the village of Bali, Takeo Province, photographing this intimate example of a traditional spirit-healing ceremony.

Cambodian Photographers: Where Were They?

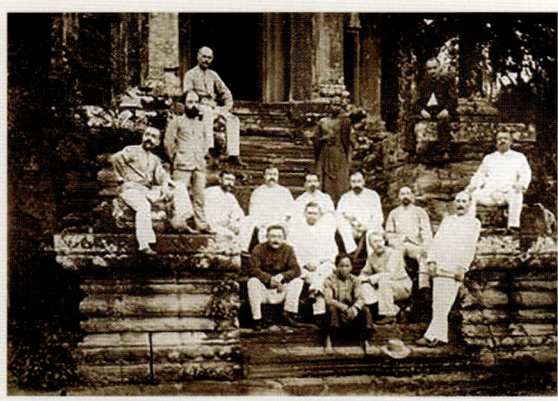

French Mekong Expedition at Angkor. 1866. Gsell may be the man wearing the dark jacket, lower left.

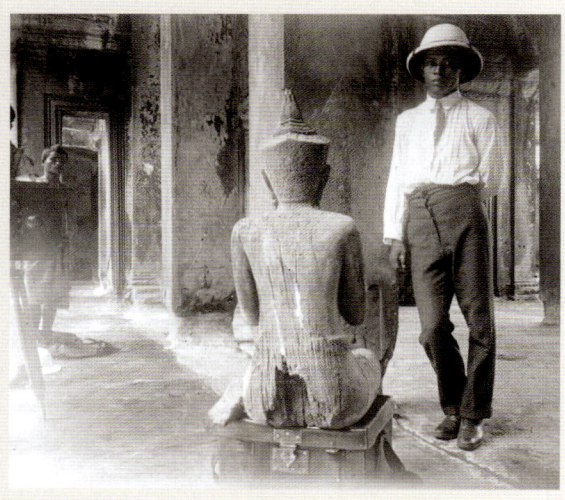

Cambodian and wooden Buddha, Angkor Wat. Siem Reap. ca. 1933. Attributed to Henri Parmentier. École française d'Extrême-Orient (EFEO).

The Cambodian Photographers

Historians researching colonial cultures often dig into their subjects' past to find kernels of indigenous self-awareness and the first expressions of an emerging national identity. With the history of photography, similar questions also arise. Who were the first Cambodian photographers? An answer is more elusive than expected.

Nineteenth-century French colonial explorers and government agencies would have employed local assistants either to carry and set up cameras and equipment or to help in developing the wet-glass plates immediately after exposure. Patrick Kersale (b. 1952), the Cambodian-based ethnomusicologist, suggests that a Cambodian might have taken one of the group portraits of the French Mekong Expedition sitting on the steps at Angkor Wat (1866; see above left), which may have included the elusive photographer Emile Gsell himself.[1] If Gsell [seated, wearing black jacket] was the expedition's official photographer and all members of the team are accounted for, then who took the photograph? To date, however, no nineteenth-century records of photography have surfaced where an explicitly Cambodian ownership can be established.

Moving forward in time, in the extensive online archives of the École française d'Extrême-Orient (EFEO), there is a stereophotograph taken by the archaeologist Henri Parmentier at Angkor Wat in 1931. It focuses on a well-dressed young Cambodian man standing in front of a wooden statue of the Buddha (ca. 1933; see left and page 92). To the extreme left of the photograph we can just make out another Cambodian standing behind a bulky wet-plate camera. Further research in the colonial archives may yet reveal names.

In neighboring Siam, King Chulalongkorn's (r. 1853–1910) love of photography is well documented, but it appears that no Cambodian monarchs or their families became interested or adept in photography until the young King Sihanouk came to the throne in 1941. Looking beyond the royal court, a perusal of archival sources such as the Documentation Center of Cambodia (DC-Cam) and the Bophana Audiovisual Resource Center, or private initiatives like the Reyum Institute, reveal the advent of studio photography in Cambodia by the early twentieth century.[2] Rare photographs from the Yok Pech and Mom Someun families collected by Reyum show relatives standing before painted canvas backdrops and posing with French colonial furniture. These are Cambodians being photographed for a Cambodian "audience." They are not the staged colonial photographs and postcards where foreigners are in control of the process, from setting the scene to taking the photograph and then the final act of reproduction and viewing by a European audience. The beginning and evolution of small studio photography in Phnom Penh, however, remains obscure, their ownership and output enigmatic. Few records remain, but those that do reveal a desire to establish a cultured urban appearance as well as a nostalgia for rural traditions—themes that have remained in circulation through to the twenty-first century. Photographic collections in the West are dominated by the work of colonial photographers and foreign travelers who were able to remove their output from Cambodia to distant archives and private collections overseas. They were able to save their collections from the ravages of twenty-five years of intermittent civil war in the 1960s and 1970s. There were some fortunate local exceptions, where families were able to hide their precious treasures and uncover them in later years of peace. The Rama family of Battambang and Chan Yoen's music collection are both examples where we are richer for their prescient actions (see '10,000 Love. *Give Me Everything*'; right and page 132).

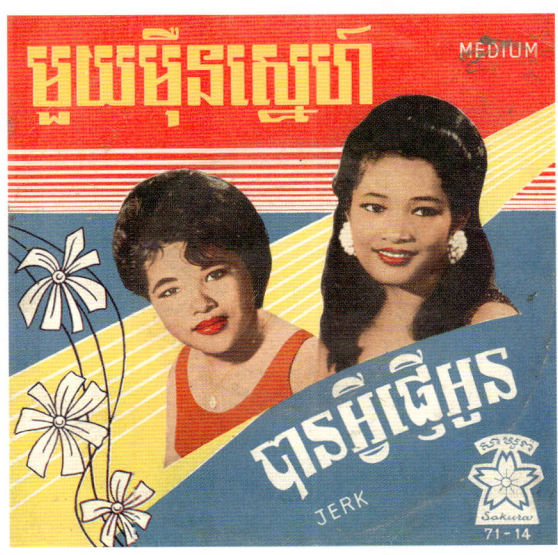

10,000 Love. *Give Me Everything.* Chan Yoen Music Collection.

With independence in 1953, Cambodians not only regained the right to govern themselves but also acquired control over the nation's printing presses. Even so, the general readership, whether in Khmer or French, would not have extended much beyond the urban periphery of Phnom Penh, Siem Reap, and a handful of other towns. This does not, however, seem to have restricted young Cambodians' engagement with photography altogether. Over the dry season of 1956–57, the United States Information Service (USIS) organized exhibitions of photography and basic courses in cinematography for students as part of American soft aid for Cambodia.[3] Apart from Ly Bun Yim, who later became a respected film director during the Sangkum years, we do not know the future trajectory of the other students who attended the exhibitions or enrolled for the courses. USIS did, however, run a full-time Communications and Media Division in Phnom Penh, employing Cambodian Nhek Dim (1934–78), who later became a successful painter, commercial artist, and art director for the *Khmer Republic Monthly Illustrated Magazine* in the 1970s. USIS also published *Free World*, a heavily illustrated magazine distributed in Cambodia, whose strong style no doubt influenced local magazine design in the following decade.

Throughout the entire Sangkum period, two lavishly illustrated pictorial magazines were published—*Le Sangkum* and *Le Cambodge*—often closely supervised by Sihanouk. While the editors and writers were acknowledged, the photographers were not accredited; perhaps their work was not regarded so highly. Whatever the reason, one wonders whether those unnamed photographers were graduates of the USIS initiative.

It is difficult to determine the precise activities and influence of smaller Chinese and Cambodian family-run studios during the twentieth century, either in the main towns or in rural communities where the depth of studio penetration is unclear. From the mid-1960s through to the late 1970s, we see photographs of intergenerational families or newly-wed couples posed

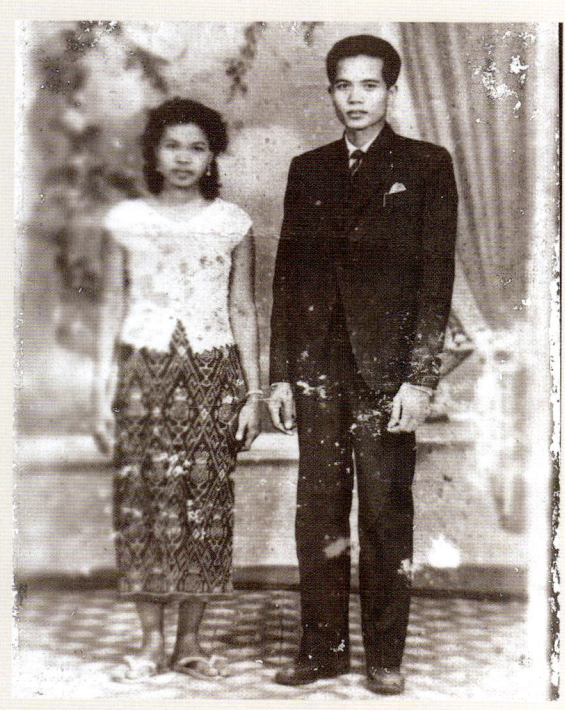

Ros Sithat and her husband Nhem Noeun's marriage photograph. Kampong Cham Province. ca. 1970. Documentation Center of Cambodia (D-Cam).

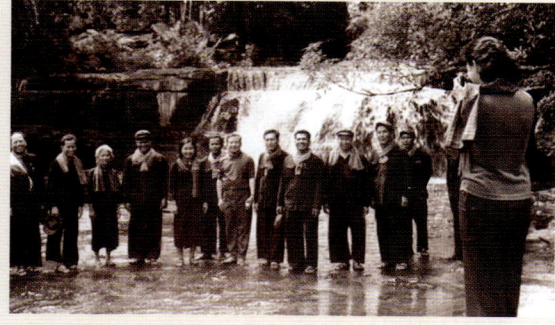

Sihanouk and senior Khmer Rouge cadres. Kulen Mountains. 1971. Norodom Monineath Sihanouk.

in rural locations, at Angkor Wat, or in stylized studio settings. The family collections of Ban Savoeun and Nhem Noeun held in the DC-Cam archives create tantalizing threads, such as "Ros Sithat and her husband Nhem Noeun's marriage photograph" (ca. 1970; see left and page 167). Many of the photographs, however, are physically damaged, either by the ravages of conflict or by the high humidity and heat of Cambodia's tropical climate, which can quite literally melt the emulsions that "fix" the image of a printed photograph.

After Sihanouk was ousted in 1970, Beijing became his base in exile. The Chinese convinced him to align with the Khmer Rouge. In 1971, he and Khmer Rouge cadres clandestinely trekked through the jungle for photo opportunities in front of sacred sites like the Kulen Mountains and various Angkorian temples (see "Sihanouk and senior Khmer Rouge cadres," 1971; below left and page 158). Although the woman standing to the right who photographed the occasion is Norodom Monineath (Monique) Sihanouk, the wife of Prince Sihanouk, who took the photograph of her as she snapped away? Was she Chinese or Khmer?

It is disconcerting that from the limited research done so far, there appear to be no instances where Cambodian photographers can be credibly named as the owner of an image until 1972. That moment comes with a flash, when the Khmer Rouge shelled the besieged capital, Phnom Penh, over the two nights of the March equinox, devastating a refugee shanty town on the edge of the city. Tea Kim Heng's sixteen black-and-white photographs, including "Injured man" (1972; see page 155), were published across an eight-page story in the *Khmer Republic Monthly Illustrated Magazine*. A year earlier, Tea, along with Sarikart, Mininformation (Ministry of Information), and Film FARK, were mentioned in the magazine's inside cover, alongside the editor and writers. Tea's prolific career continued until 1975 when he disappeared from view, presumably executed by the Khmer Rouge. During the fifteen years of the Sangkum period of government and the republican era that followed, we know from picture credits that photographers were regularly employed by Cambodia's armed forces but their identity remains enigmatic: "Picture taken by a FARK photographer" is all the anonymous credit they get.[4]

During the four-year period of the Khmer Rouge, the photographer who worked at Toul Sleng (S-21) prison, Nhem En, was sent to study photography in Shanghai in 1976, along with a host of other young cadres. His memoir, however, does not reveal the names of his fellow graduates.[5] Was Noem Oem, who also worked as a photographer for the S-24 Khmer Rouge re-education center, a fellow student?

After the Vietnamese-backed People's Republic was installed in early 1979, studio photography quickly re-emerged. The painted backdrop of an ideal urban interior returned, featuring shelves filled with homeware, television sets, and radio-cassette players, while paintings of country lifestyles and Angkor Wat adorn the walls. Ironically, though, the greatest concentration of photography during this period would have occurred in the methodical processing of identity cards in the sprawling refugee camps that straddled the Thai-Cambodian border (see "Refugee identity tag for Rama Vira," ca. 1985; right).

In 1998, veteran photographers Tim Page and Horst Faas began researching the lives and memories of fellow journalists and photographers who had died or gone missing in the adjoining Vietnamese and Cambodian warfronts. It was the first comprehensive project to include Cambodian photographers of the 1970s, who were subsequently memorialized in the landmark photography book *Requiem* (see "Cambodian soldiers carry a wounded comrade," ca. 1974; below right and page 166).[6] Hopefully, future scholarship will be able to unearth a more extensive history of local photographers who worked in Cambodia prior to the 1970s.

Taking the long view, the past 150 years of photography in Cambodia can be seen through the lens of multiple genres and different types of photography—photojournalism, family studio portraits, historical collections, frozen motion picture "stills," commercial artwork, identity photographs, photomontage, fine art photography, X-rays, and computer-generated imagery. The selection of photographers, photographs, and events in this book constitute neither a comprehensive history of photography in Cambodia nor an illustrated history of the country, but rather is situated somewhere between the two. Hopefully, though, these images and the stories they tell will provide the reader with a passport into Cambodia's rich historical past, as well as the experiences of more recent times, while taking them on a journey that both satisfies, and challenges, their expectations.

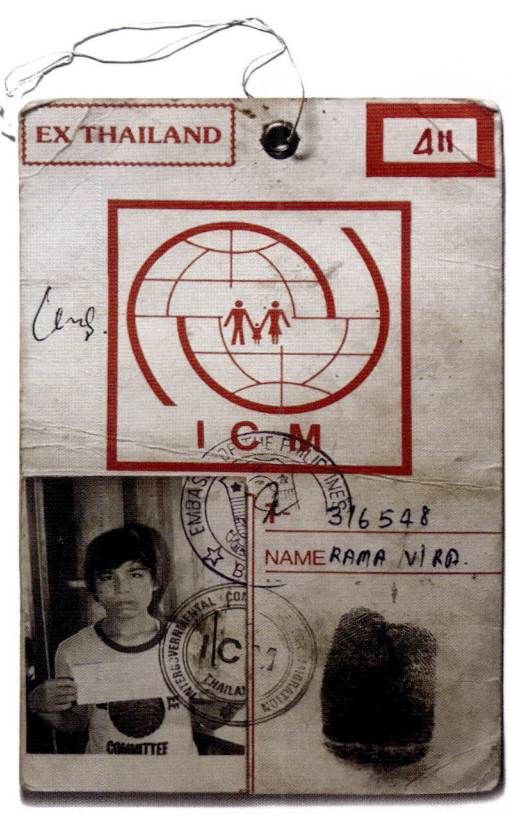

Refugee identity tag for Rama Vira. ca. 1985.
Rama Family Archive/Found Cambodia.

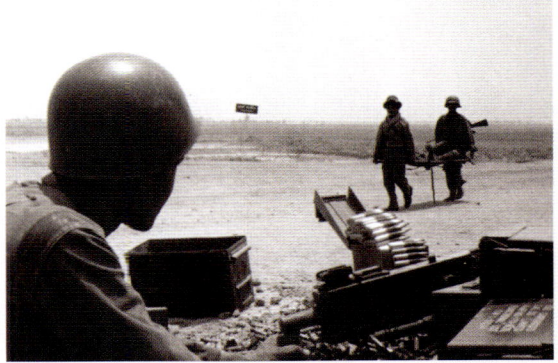

Cambodian soldiers carry a wounded comrade past a machine gunner's position on Route 5. North of Phnom Penh. ca. 1974.

1   Private conversations with Patrick Kersale. June 2019.
2   Ingrid Muan and Ly Daravuth, eds. *Seams of Change: Clothing and the Care of the Self in Late 19th and 20th Century Cambodia*. Reyum Publishing. Phnom Penh. 2003.
3   *Le Programme de L'aide Economique Americaine Au Cambodge 1955–1959*. August 1980. Administration of International Cooperation.
4   Forces armées nationales khmère (FARK) (Royal Cambodian Armed Forces).
5   Nhem En and Dara Doung, *The Khmer Rouge's Photographer at S-21 Under the Khmer Rouge Genocide*. Nhem En. Phnom Penh. 2014.
6   Horst Faas and Tim Page, eds. *Requiem: By the Photographers Who Died in Vietnam and Indochina*. Random House. 1997.

The Photographers

Agostini, Jules. (1859–1930)
Bellorget, Ghislain. Active 1970s.
Bergström, Gunnar. (b. 1951)
Bischoff, Werner. (1919–54)
Blanc. Active 1950s.
Blanchet, Fernan. (1853–1914?)
Boulbet, Jean. (1926–2007)
Buck, Craig. (b. 1952)
Burke, Bill. (b. 1943)
Candee, Helen Churchill. (1858–1949)
Caron, Gilles. (1939–70)
Carpeaux, Henri. (1825–70)
Carrard, Guy. Active 1920s.
Châtel, Marie-Françoise. (b. 1940)
Chauchetier, Raymond. (1920–2021)
Chhor Vuthi. (d. 1975?)
Cochrane, Liam. (b. 1980)
Coffin, Yves. (1924–2016)
Crespin, Ludovic. (b. 1873)
Demulder, Françoise. (1947–2008)
Dieulefils, Pierre. (1862–1937)
Dullin, Micheline. (1927–2020)
Ebihara, May Mayko. (1934–2005)
Ellis, Stefan. (1965–96)
Finot, Louis. (1864–1935)
Fitoussi, Richard. Active 2000s
Foster, Harry L. (1894–1932)
Gabelics, Antal. (b. 1987)
Gahery. Active 1950s.
Gilberte de Coral-Rémusat, Comtesse (1903–43)
Grafton, Colin. (b. 1947)
Groslier, George. (1887–1945)
Gsell, Emile. (1838–79)
Guedson, Marie-Joseph. (1852–1939)
Harvey, David Alan. (b. 1944)
Hays, Margaret Parx. (1918–2008)
Heng Ravuth. (b. 1985)
Heng Sinith (b. 1964)
Ho Van Tay. (b. 1931)
Holmes, J. Dearden. (1873–1937)

Hurlimann, Martin. (1897–1984)
Izu Kenro. (b. 1949)
Jiras, Anders. (b. 1946)
Khvay Samnang. (b. 1982)
Kim Hak. (b. 1981)
Kubeš, Antoniń
Kuoy Sarun. (d. 1977?)
Labad, Dani Planas. (b. 1972)
Lan Nadong. (b. 1990)
Leang Seckon. (b. 1974)
Leclère, Adhémard. (1853–1917)
Lim Sokchanlina. (b. 1987)
Llippincott, Hal. (1907–91)
Loke Wan Toh. (1915–64)
Longstreath, David. (b. 1952)
Mak Remissa. (b. 1970)
May, Sharon. (b. 1964)
McCullin, Don. (b. 1935)
McDermott, John. (b. 1955)
Meng Kimlong. (b. 1991)
Morales, Hanna Reyes. (b. 1990)
Moride, M. Active 1950s.
Nadal, Fernand. (b. 1900?)
Neak Sophal. (b. 1989)
Neveu, Roland. (b. 1950)
Nhem En. (b. 1961)
Nhem Noeun. (b. 1936)
Noem Oem. (1953–77?)
Nomura Naotaro. Active 1940s.
Norodom Monineath Sihanouk. (b. 1936)
Page, Tim. (b. 1944)
Paive, Auguste Jean-Marie. (1847–1925)
Palgen-Maissoneuve, Mimijac. (1918–95)
Panh Rithy. (b. 1964)
Panhavuth Sarpin. (b. 1969)
Parmentier, Henri. (1871–1949)
Pech Sophea. (b. 1998)
Pen. (d. 1975?)

Pha Lina. (b. 1986)
Ros, Ray. (b. 1993)
Salle Issa/Sales Isa. Active 1960s.
Salles, André. (1860–1929)
Samrang Pring. Active 2010s.
Sauvy-Tisseyre, Elisabeth. (1897–1966)
Sharp, Bruce. (b. 1962)
Shearer, D. L. Active 1970s.
Smith, Heide. (b. 1937)
Sou Vichith. (d. 1975?)
Sovan Philong. (b. 1986)
Spratt, "Jack" Edwin. Active 1970s.
Surel. Active 1950s.
Studio Laor Penh Chet.
Sweeny, Dan. (illustrator.) (1880–1958)
Tajasque, Albert. (1877–1959)
Tea Kim Hak. (d. 1975?)
Tea Kim Heang. (d. 1975?)
Thomson, John. (1837–1921)]
Thong Veasna. (d. 1975?)
Toutain-Dorbec, Pierre. (b. 1951)
Vareene, Alexandre. (1870–1947)
Varoqui, Raymond. Active 1950s.
Vickery, Michael. (1931–2017)
Vink, John. (b. 1948)
Vong Sopheak. (b. 1993)
Vuth Lyno. (b. 1982)
Watkins, Huw. (b. 1960)
Wertheimer, Odile. Active 1960s.
Wetterwald, Jean-Noel. (b. 1955)
Widener, Jeff. (b. 1956)
Wong Maye-E. (b. 1980)
Yap, Irene. (b. 1983)
Yin Someth. (b. 1981)

RIGHT: **Northeast view towards the rice plains of the Tonlé Sap.** Phnom Krom, Siem Reap. 1954. Margaret Parx Hays Papers, University of Wisconsin Digital Collections.

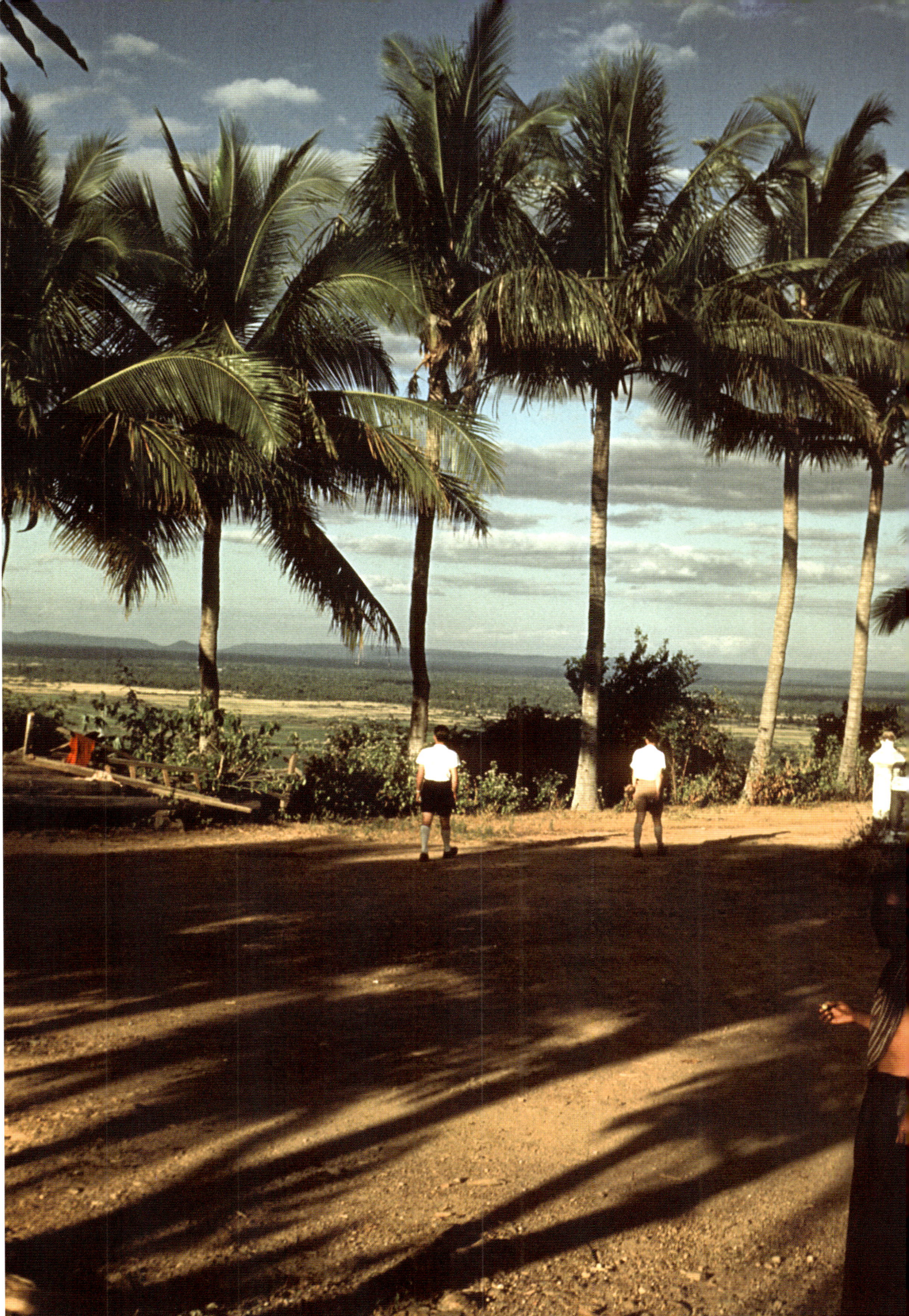

The Collections

Agence des Colonies
Agence d'images de la Défense, Paris
Agence France-Presse (AFP)
Al Jazzera America
AP Images, Associated Press photo agency
Archives nationales d'outre-mer, Paris
Archives Photographiques, Musée Guimet
Australian War Memorial
Biblothèque nationale de France
Bophana Audiovisual Resource Center, Cambodia
Cambodian Center for Human Rights (CCHR)
Cambodian Landmine Museum, Siem Reap
Center for Khmer Studies Library, Siem Reap
Chan Yoen Music Collection, Siem Reap
Charles Meyer Collection, Paris
Cindy Lippincott and Bob Berman Family Archive, Oregon
Contact Press Images, New York
Darryl Collins Collection, Siem Reap.
Dayanny So Family Archive/Found Cambodia
Delcampe International
Documentation Center of Cambodia (DC-Cam)
École française d'Extrême-Orient
H. A. C. Elmiger Archive
Indochina Media Memorial Foundation (IMMF) Project
James Hyman Gallery, London
Khmer Archaeology LiDAR Consortium
Lee Peng Heng Collection, Phnom Penh
LICADHO Report, Cambodia
Magnum Photos
Maison Chocolat Guérin-Boutron, Paris
Marie-Françoise Châtel Collection
Margaret Parx Hays Papers, Madison Library, University of Wisconsin Digital Collections
Marine Pommereau Collection, France
Masaharu Asada Collection, Tokyo

May Ebihara Digital Collection, Northern Illinois University Libraries
Meta House, Phnom Penh
Metropolitan Museum of Art, New York
Michael Vickery Collection, Chiang Mai
Micheline Dullin Archive, Paris
MimiJac Palgen Memorial Collection, Arizona State University Library
Musée des Beaux Arts et de la Dentelle d'Alençon
Musée Nicéphore-Niépce
National Archives of Cambodia
National Archives Research Center, Washington
National Gallery of Australia
National Library of Australia
National Library of Cambodia
National Museum of Cambodia
National Museum of Singapore/National Heritage Board
Old Post Office Arts Centre, London
Philippe Damas Collection, Singapore
Rama Family Archive/Found Cambodia
SA SA BASSAC, Cambodia
Singapore History Museum/National Heritage Board
Société de Géographie, Paris
State Library of New South Wales
US Defense Department Archives College Park
US National Archives
Wellcome Collection, London
Yin Someth Family Archive/Siem Reap Thmey Studio

RIGHT: Le costume traditionnel du mariage. Photographer unknown. ca. 1950. From *Mariage Cambodgien*. Mme Pich Sal. Centre de Documentation et de Recherche sur la Cvilisation Khmere. Paris/Center for Khmer Studies Library, Siem Reap.

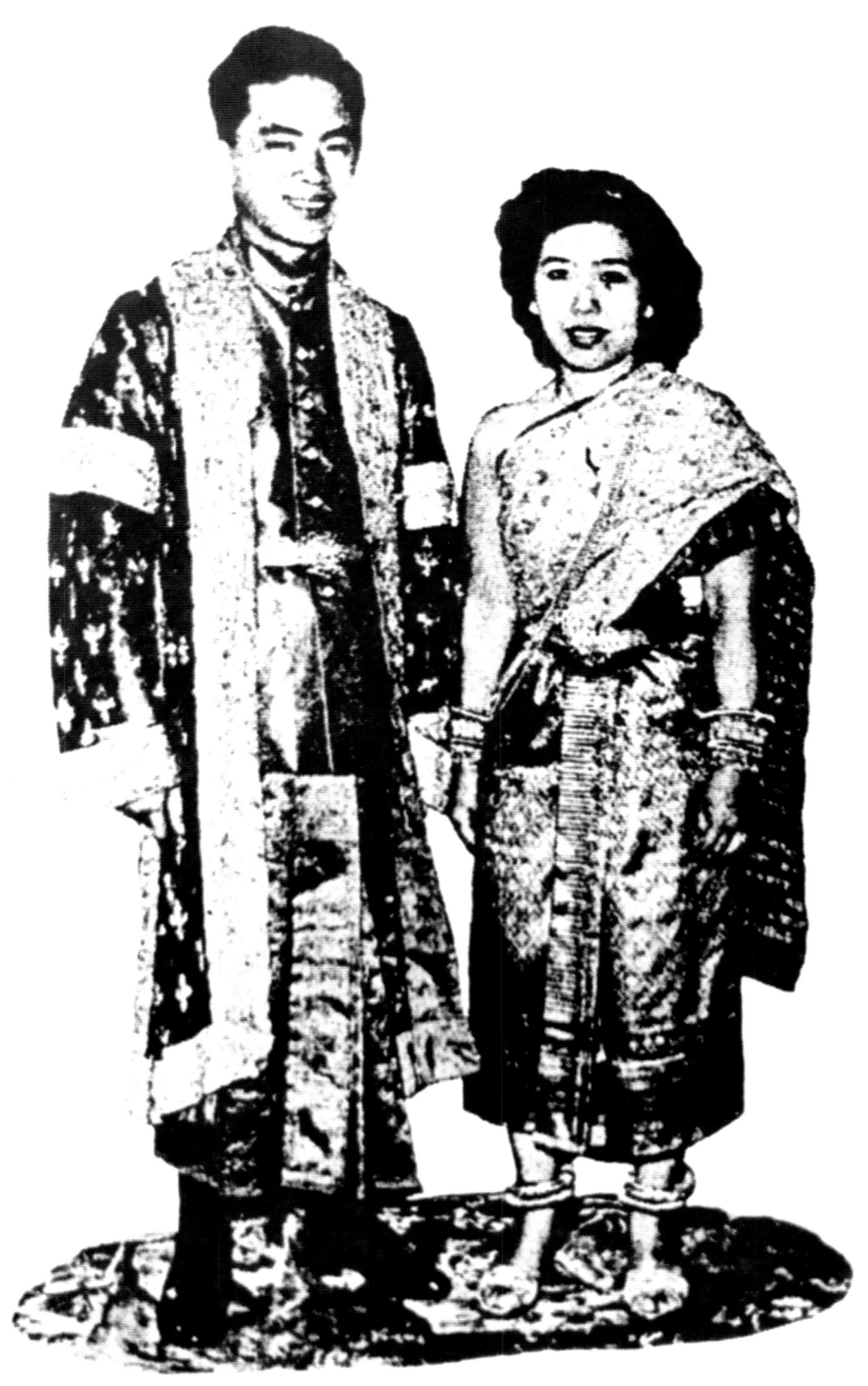

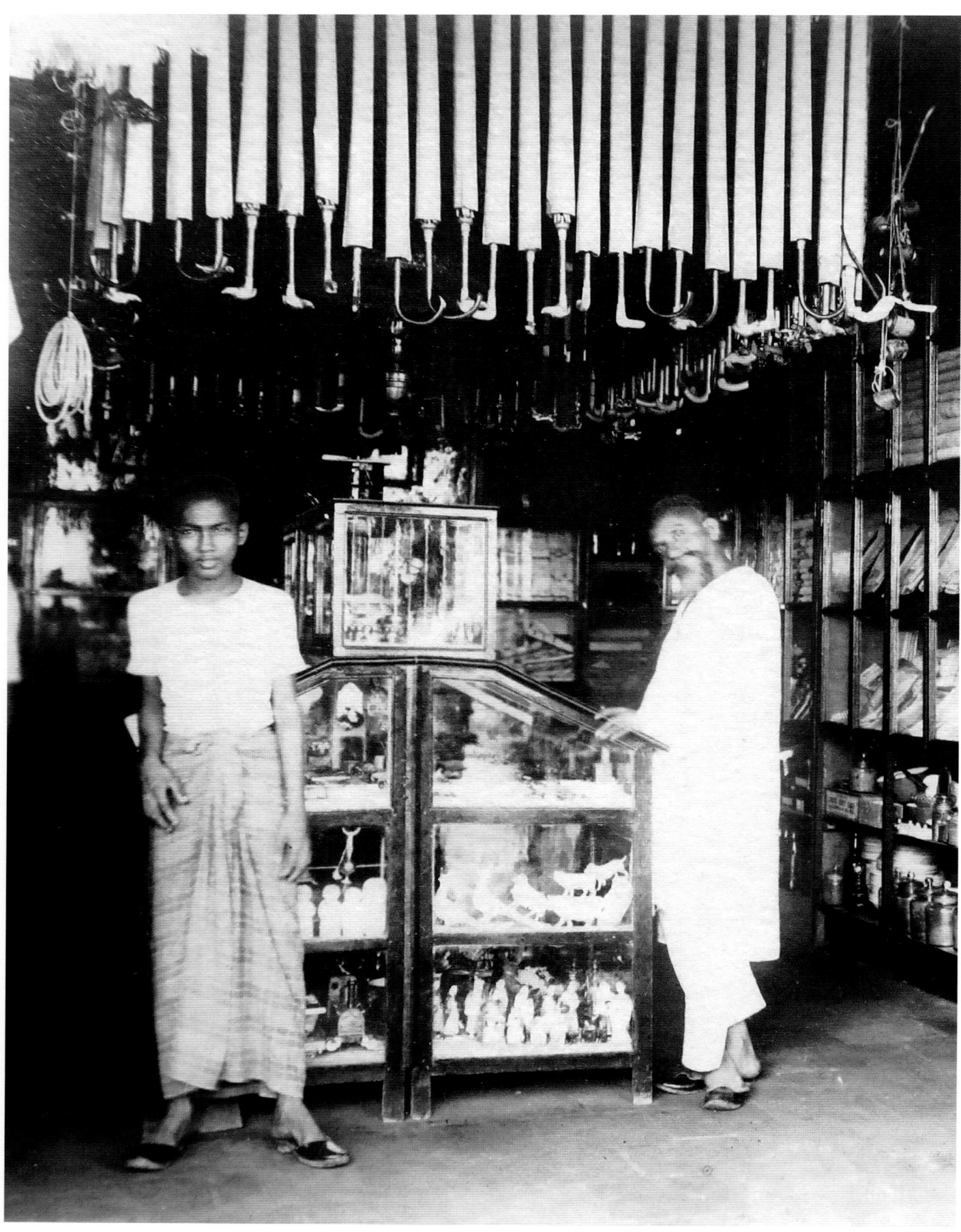

Acknowledgments

I must first thank three people whose professional efforts and fastidious oversights have guided me in creating this book: Darryl Collins, whose knowledge of Cambodia's classical and modern history has been an invaluable asset, enabling me to peer deeply into historical photographs of Cambodia and deduce dates, locations, and possible photographers of images; Dr Julian Davison, whose similar gimlet eye for detail, particularly in the structure of language and the flow of ideas, helped greatly in turning my draft into a coherent text; and Douglas Gordon, for his meticulous use of digital software to remove unwanted specks and blemishes from photographs while sensitively retaining valuable historical patina. (Douglas also created a stylish and elegant initial design for the book, prior to the publisher's final layout.)

Thanks are also due to a number of private collectors of Indochinese and Cambodian photography who have been particularly generous in giving me access to their collections: again, Darryl Collins for making available his collection of postcards and contemporary art photography; Philippe Damas for his revealing colonial collections; Marie-Françoise Châtel for opening a wonderful photographic archive taken in Kampot and Kep in the 1950s and 1960s, and her son Löic, who has been a gracious interlocutor; Chan Samnang and his father Chan Yoen for permission to reproduce his Sangkum-period record sleeves collections, and to Adam Rodwell of Little Red Fox for making the original scans; Horst Faas and Tim Page for access to their invaluable collection of images taken by Cambodian photographers who worked in very stressful environments during the five years of Lon Nol's Khmer Republic. Sadly, all but one of these pioneers in the field of Cambodian photojournalism disappeared after the Khmer Rouge came to power.

Turning to the descendants and heirs of various photographers who worked or traveled through Cambodia, I would like to thank Marine Pommereau for allowing me to reproduce the fine-du-siècle works of Albert Tajasque; Amema Saeju for giving permission to reproduce the dynamic postwar works of Michael Vickery; Nausicaa favart-Amouroux for giving me access to the collection of the superb Micheline Dullin; and Frederic Meyer for granting permission to reproduce a substantial number of photographs belonging to his father, Charles Meyer, who amassed an important collection during the period of the People's Socialist Community in the late 1950s and 1960s.

LEFT: **Bombay Indian shopkeepers.** Phnom Penh. ca. 1898. Photographer unknown. Philippe Damas Collection, Singapore.

For help in the selection of contemporary Cambodian photographers in the final chapter, I am grateful for the skilled curatorial eye of Jessica Lee, coordinator of the Angkor Photo Festival and Workshops, whose assistance has been invaluable.

Throughout the compilation of this book, I have received enthusiastic support from living photographers or their agents and galleries who hold the rights to their collections. There are too many to name here, but I have acknowledged them in the captions to the images, or in the relevant lists of Photographers and Collections on pages 244 and 246.

I have also sourced several important collections of images held in national museums, archives, and libraries, both in Cambodia and abroad, all of whom have given their fullest support to the project. As a matter of courtesy to **Cambodia**, I shall mention those first: Chea Sopheap of the Bophana Audiovisual Resource Center; Ros Sampeou of the Documentation Center of Cambodia; Mdm Y. Dari and her staff at the National Archives of Cambodia; Visoth Chhay, Samnang Hout, Sathal Khun, Mdm Lim Yi, and Bertrand Porte of the National Museum of Cambodia; Sivleng Chhor and the librarians at the Center for Khmer Studies Library, Siem Reap; and Jill and William Morse of the Cambodian Landmine Museum. I hope this book will help in some small way to promote their dedicated work in managing and protecting the country's valuable heritage.

I would like to extend my grateful thanks to the public museums and institutes beyond Cambodia, and to the staff who have helped me access their collections. In **Australia:** Ricky Phillips (Australian War Memorial); Carol Cains, Anne O'Heir, and Ellie Kate Misios (National Gallery of Australia). In **France:** Amandine Bertin (Agence d'images de la Défense); Quentin Dufour, Isabelle Andreoli, and Frédéric Gilly (Archives nationales d'outre-mer); Marta Bardaro, Pasquale Khan, and Maria-Cristina Pirvu (Bibliothèque nationale de France); Christine Hawixbrock and Isabelle Poujol (École française d'Extrême-Orient); Johanna Mauboussin (Musée des Beaux Arts et de la Dentelle d'Alençon); Dominique Reninger (Archives Photographiques, Musée Guimet); Sylvain Besson (Musée Nicéphore Niépce); Silvie Rivet (Société de Géographie). In **Japan**: Philip Gostelow, Taro Karasaki (Asahi Shimbun), Jun Takagi, and Masaharu Asada. In **Singapore:** Sheryl Koh, Ng Yew Peng, and Tan Chor Koon (Singapore History Museum/National Heritage Board). In **Spain:** Dulce Estévez López (AGEfotostock). In the **United Kingdom:** Charles Fox (Found Cambodia); the Wellcome Collection, London. And lastly, in the **USA:** Brian

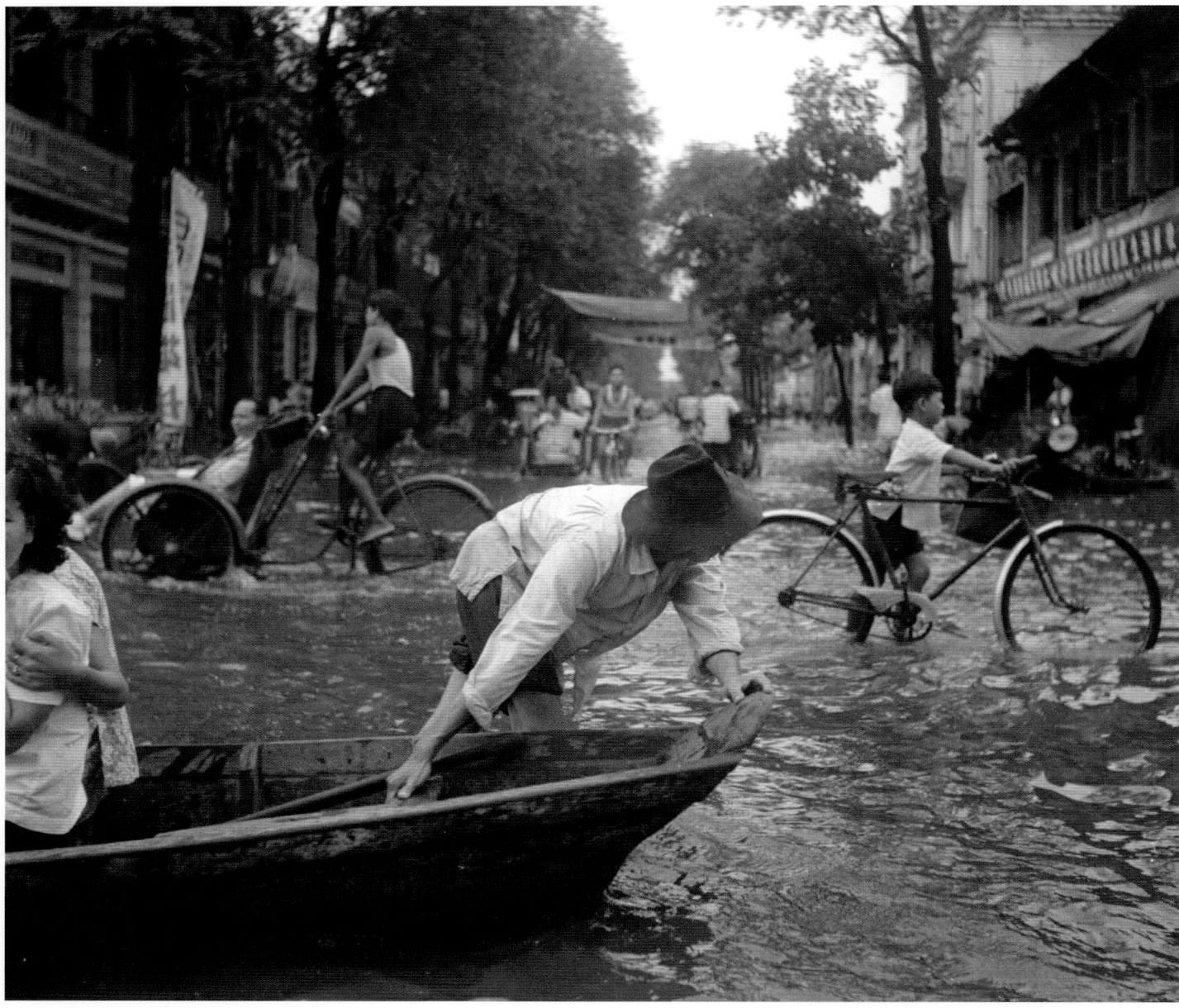

Colburn (Associated Press); Lawrence Ashmun and Steven Dast (Madison Library, University of Wisconsin Digital Collections); Professor Judy Ledgerwood and Hao Phan (May Ebihara Digital Collection, Northern Illinois University Libraries); Metropolitan Museum of Art, New York; William Bourke, Matt Messbarger, and Rob Spindler (Tufts University).

Many individuals and families have helped me with enquiries and contacts, translations and introductions, or assisted in accommodation or travel as I have roamed Australasia. They include, in **Australia:** Jane Calthorpe, Jamie Coffill, Philip Coggan, Marianne Harris, Craig Judd, Lucy MacFarlane (translations), Minh Bui Jones (*Mekong Review*), Dr Susan Osmond, Marinko Petkovich, and Rozzie Sharp, Robyn and Dr. Lindsay Sharp. In **France:** Gregory Amat, Dominic Gaessler, and Nolween Gouault (translations). In **Siem Reap:** Lori Carlson, Chan Yoen and Chan Samnang, Jon de Rule, Patrick Kersale (ethnomusicology), Malar Malararuappan, John McDermott, Narisara Murray, David George Muskett, Pan Pech, Chen Pheakdey, Julien Poulson, Ron Radford, Sreng Leang (translations), Adam Rodwell, and David Stirling (Little Red Fox). In **Phnom Penh:** Margaret Bywater, Richard Dansey, Colin Grafton, Dana Langlois (Java Creative Cafe), Nico Mesterharm (Meta House), and Larry Strange. In **Malaysia:** Law Siak Hong, Wendy Leow, Geoff Millichamp, and Tan Chor Sim. In **Singapore:** Dr Julian Davison (Topographica). And in the **USA:** Rich Remsberg and Jeffrey D. Smith.

I must also express my deepest gratitude to the initial investors in Bambu Stage, whose generous commitment enabled the theater project to bear fruit: Patrick Davenport (Cambodia), Naimah Bt Abdul Khalid (Malaysia), Jeremy King (UK), Puan Sri Dato' Sandra Lee (Malaysia), Ken Pelletier (USA), and Subramaniam Gomathy (India). Heartfelt thanks also go to Bhavna Soni Shivpuri (Hong Kong) who was, and remains, a wonderful business and strategic advisor to Jon and myself. I wish also to thank June Chong (supervising editor) and Eric Oey (publisher) of Periplus/Tuttle for steering the concept of this book through to completion, and Noor Azlina Yunus for editorial assistance.

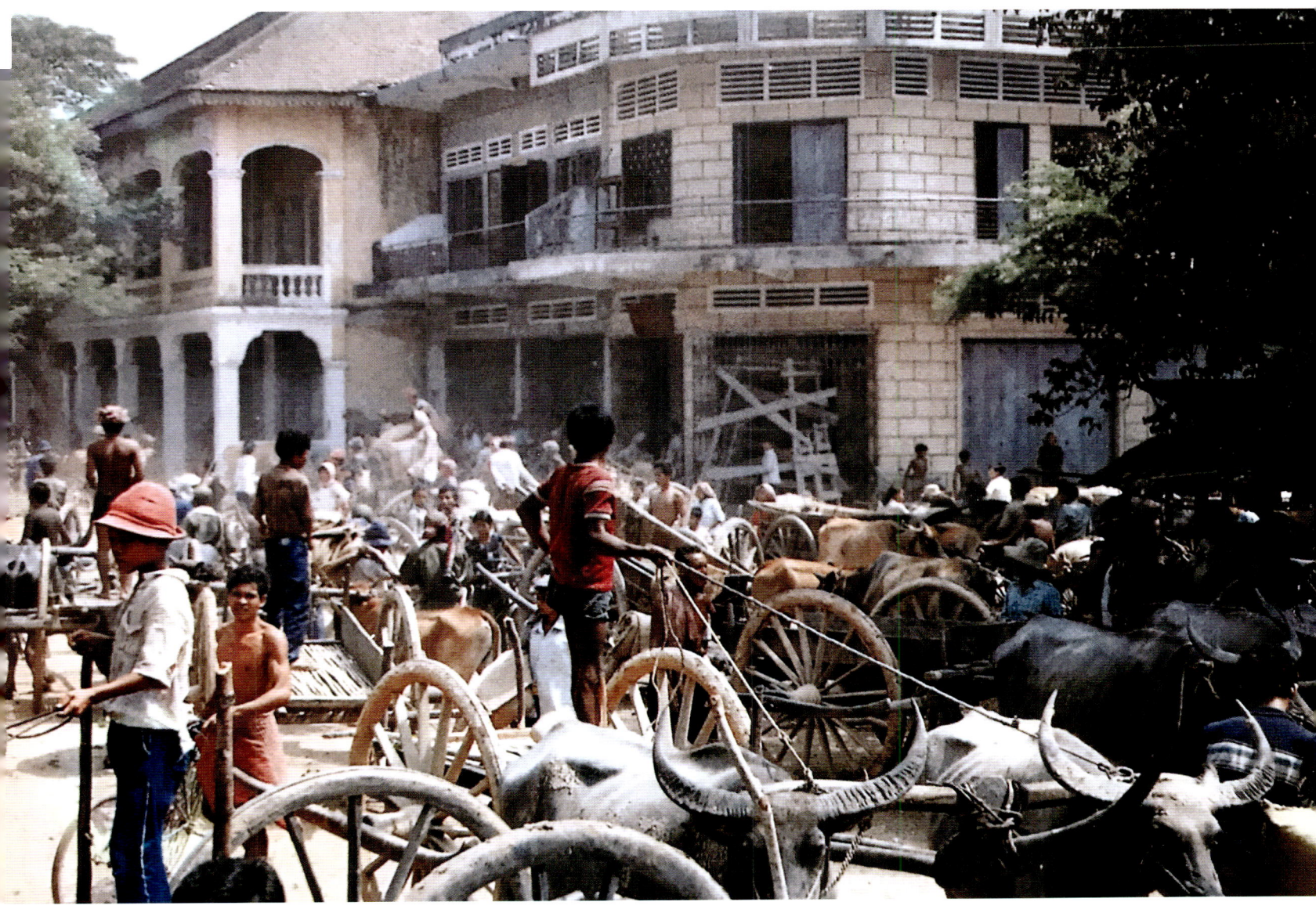

My final thanks go to two of the keenest supporters of the original *SNAP! 150 Years of Photography in Cambodia* performance, Deborah Saunders and Darryl Collins, who continued unabated for three years to applaud, correct, howl, and suggest critical improvemets to the show that enabled visitors to Bambu Stage understand with greater depth the history of Cambodia through photography.

ABOVE: **Food captured from the Vietnamese being redistributed by Khmer Rouge (NFDK) soldiers.** Straung. 1990. Photographer unknown. Front cover, NFDK Magazine, August 1990. Center for Khmer Studies Library, Siem Reap.

OPPOSITE: **Flooded streets of the Catholic quarter.** Phnom Penh. ca. 1957. MimiJac Palgen. MimiJac Palgen Memorial Collection, Arizona State University Library.

Index

A
advertising (photographic genre), 16, 21, 137
Agostini, Jules, 24, 33
Angkar Padevat (Khmer Rouge political arm), 18–20, 152, 182; focus on agriculture, 174, 176–77, 178–79; forced marriage, 184, 232; moral spirit of, 181; new society, 184; prisoners, 188, 236; propaganda, 183; purges, 174, 186
Angkor Photo Festival and Workshops, 6, 210, 214, 219, 232
Angkor Ta Prom, 90
Angkor Thom, 72, 89, 93, 101, 222
Angkor Wat, 7, 10, 17, 20–21; advertising promotion, 21; aerial view, 86; first photographer, 26–29; influence on photography, 12, 21, 22, 140; inscriptions of, 72; panoramic view, 205; replica of, 76; spiritual center, 10; symbol of national identity, 17–18, 20–21; tourist attraction, 63
Angkorian monuments, 6, 8, 22, 92, 107; archaeology of, 110; influence on tourism, 94; restoration of, 52, 110–11
Aymonier, Etienne, 55

B
Bali, Takeo Province, 239
Bambu Stage, Siem Reap, 8, 9, 22
Ban Savoeun, 152, 242
Banteay Chhmar, 65
Battambang, 29, 58, 62, 84–85, 127, 237, 241; and Khmer Rouge, 174
Baudoin, François Marius (resident-superior), 56
Bayon temple, 26, 82–83, 85, 98, 142
Bellorget, Ghislain, 150–51
Beng Trabek High School, Phnom Penh, 149
Bergström, Gunnar, 183
birding (photographic genre), 233
Bischoff, Werner, 108
Blanc, Mr., 110
Blanchet, Fernan, 39
Bophana Audiovisual Resource Center, Phnom Penh, 210, 226, 240
Boulbet, Jean, 127
Brodrick, Alan Houghton, 93
Buck, Craig, 17, 188, 192, 193
Buddha, statues of, 12, 70, 92, 93, 160, 240; hand sign of, 121; theft of, 76, 81
Burke, Bill, 203
Burma, 24, 94
Burmese, of Pailin Province, 56, 57

C
Café du Paris, Phnom Penh, 122
Callier, Françoise, 214
Cambodge Soir, 218, 228
Cambodia: books on, 6; documentation on, 9; and economy, 11–12, 144; history of, 6, 10; photography in, 6, 8, 9, 10–11, 12–22; political periods, 10–12; royalty of, 12; theater about, 8–9
Cambodian Landmine Museum and Relief Facility, 231
Cambodian People's Armed Forces (CPAF), 17
Cambodian People's Party (CPP), 206
Cambodians: colonial image of, 12; everyday/ordinary, 20–21, 55, 76, 104, 183; indigenous, 34–35; persecuted, 196–99; 208; 236; urbanized, 94, 121; working, 125, 166; wealthy, 43
Cameras: 10–11, 14, 15, 16, 24, 26, 72, 76, 104, 174, 202; and equipment, 26, 42, 52, 92, 240; types of: 16 mm movie, 94; 35 mm, 98; digital, 188, 210; glass-plate, 79; Kodak Box Brownie, 52; medium format, 112; NC2000 209; Nikon F series, 146; Nikon N90, 209; Pentax SF-1, 207; Ricoh XR-10, 207; Rolleifex, 118, 138; Sinclair Una, 91; Super-8, 192; wet-plate, 240
Camus, Marcel, 125
Candee, Helen Churchill, 63
Caron, Gilles, 148
Carpeaux, Charles, 52
Central Intelligence Agency (CIA), 19
Chan Yoen Music Collection, 132, 241
Châtel, Marie-Françoise, 11, 14, 112, 119, 162
Chau Seng, 156
Chauchetier, Raymond, 112, 138
chhay yam (band), 153
Chhor Vuthi, 16–17, 146, 157
Chim Senyint, 149
China, 146, 151, 176, 186, 198, 200
Chorn-Pond Arn, 188, 199
Claud, Monsieur, 43
Coffin, Yves, 120
Cold War, 10, 11, 16, 94, 108, 188
Collins, Darryl, 8
colonial administration, 40–41
colonialism, European, 10; French, 9
communism, rise of, 94, 151
Communist Party, 21
Crespin, Ludovic, 52, 59

D
dancers/dancing, royal, 6–7, 73, 120, 138, 153
Dayanny So Family Archive, 202
de Gaulle, Charles, 20
de Lagrée, Ernest Doudart, 29, 38
de Rule, Jon (Bambu Stage), 8, 9
decolonization, 10
Democratic Kampuchea (DK), and Khmer Rouge, 18, 20, 152, 174, 178, 195, 217
Democratic Kampuchea Is Moving Forward, 174, 178
Demulder, Françoise, 154
Dieulefils, Pierre, 55
Dinh Fong, 19
Dith Pran, 146, 163
Documentation Center of Cambodia (DC-Cam), Phnom Penh, 9, 15, 174, 188, 208, 210, 240; and identity photographs, 208; and Stilled Lives Project, 152
Duch, Brother. *See* Kaing Guek Eav
Dullin, Micheline, 112, 118, 141

E
École française d'Extrême Orient (EFEO), 15, 52, 72, 76, 92, 94, 110, 121, 127, 214, 240
Ebihara, May Mayko, 112, 123
Ellis, Stefan, 200

Eugénie, Empress, 29
Extraordinary Chambers in the Courts of Cambodia (ECCC), 20

F
family photos, 152, 167, 202, 223, 237
Fass, Hors, 164
Favart, Robert, 118
Film, types of: Ektachrome, 207; Ilford HPS Plus, 207; Kodachrome, 207; Type 55 Polaroid, 203
Finot, Louis, 52, 72
First Indochina War (1946–54), 94, 108, 138
Foster, Harry L., 52, 62
Found Cambodia (online digital archive), 15, 202
Fox, Charles, 15, 202
French Cultural Institute, 210
French Mekong Expedition (1866–68), 24, 29, 38, 240
Front uni national pour un Cambodge indépendant, neuter, pacique et coopérative (FUNCINPEC), 204, 206
Für Dich, 201

G
Gabelics, Antal, 131
Games of the New Emerging Forces (GANEFO), 130
Gilberte de Coral-Rémusat, Comtesse, 93
Grafton, Colin, 13, 162
Groslier, George, 12, 13, 14, 42, 48, 52, 65, 69, 73, 79, 214
Gsell, Emile, 8, 14, 24, 29, 38, 118, 240
Guedson, Marie-Joseph, 24, 36

H
Hannoteaux, Guy, 148
Harihara (Angkorian god), 14, 121
Harvey, David Alan, 194
Hays, Margaret Parx, 94, 106
Heng Ravuth, 210, 220
Heng Sinith, 188
Hervey, Harry, 70
Ho Van Tay, 19, 187, 188
Holmes, J. Dearden, 52, 64

Hotel Cambodiana, Phnom Penh, 16, 195, 203
Hun Sen, prime minister (1985–), 22 185, 204, 206
Hurlimann, Martin, 13, 76, 91

I
Impressionism, influence of, 12, 230
Indochina, French, 9, 29, 32, 42, 52, 55, 59, 71, 72, 74, 76, 79, 86, 96, 100, 104
Izu Kenro, 229

J
Janin, Stephane, 210, 220
Jiras, Anders, 239

K
Kaing Guek Eav (aka Brother Duch), 18, 186, 210
Kampot, 13, 32, 40, 119, 174, 249
Kem Ley, 234–35
Kennedy, Jacqueline (Jackie), 20, 112
Kep Sur Le Mer, 124
Kersale, Patrick, 240
Khieu Samphan, 188, 200
Khmer Republic (1970–75), 14, 21, 146, 154, 178, 217
Khmer Republic Monthly Illustrated Magazine, 21, 146, 153, 154, 155, 156, 161, 164, 241, 242
Khmer Rouge (1975–79), 11, 16, 17, 21, 123, 126, 132, 148, 149, 151, 152, 157, 158, 163, 167, 174, 180–81, 184, 185, 187, 232, 236, 242; child/foot soldiers, 146, 172–73, 174, 180–81, 209; daily life, 192; documentation of, 190, 192, 208, 226, 231; identity photographs, 11, 12, 18–19, 174, 186, 208, 236, 238; influence on photography, 9, 12–13, 14, 15, 18–19, 20, 21, 121, 146, 176, 183, 186, 188, 190–91, 192, 199, 200, 208, 228, 236, 237, 242
Khmer Rouge War Crimes Tribunal, 200, 210, 232
Khmer Serei, 17, 193
Khon Sreyneung, 210, 238
Khvay Samnang, 210, 215
Kim Hak, 219, 232

Ko Pich bridge, Phnom Penh, 13, 218, 219
Kompong Cham, 76, 167
Kompong Chhnang, 143
Kompong Phluk, 80
krama (cotton scarf), 66–67, 167, 174, 181
Kubeš, Antonín, 190
Kuoy Sarun, 11, 16, 166

L
Labad, Dani Planas, 15, 236
Lai Dat Huong, 21
lakhon khol (masked dance), 239
Lan Nadong, 233
landscapes (photographic genre), 12, 13, 18, 29, 36, 52, 76, 80, 91, 205, 229
Laos, 16, 34, 94
Le Cambodge, 112, 153, 156, 241
Le Fol, Aristide Eugène (resident-superior), 83
Le Mekong, 228
Le Popil Photo Gallery, 210
Le Sangkum, 112, 134, 136, 156, 241
Leang Seckon, 210, 217
Leclère, Adhémard, 15, 24, 40
Lim Sokchanlina, 210, 215, 216
Llippincott, Hal, 76, 88
Loke Wan Toh, 112
Lon Nol, prime minister (1970–75), 16, 17, 22, 146, 148, 151, 156, 158, 178, 217
Longstreath, David, 17, 188, 209
Lu Ban Hap, 195
Ly Bun Yim, 241
Ly Daravuth, 188, 199
Lycée de Kompong Thom, 116
Lycée français René Descartes, 128–29
Lycée Preah Reach Samphear, Kampot, 119
Lycée Tep Pranam, Oudong, 161

M
magazines: fan, 125; monthly illustrated/ propaganda, 81, 112, 134, 136, 146, 178–79, 198, 201, 241
Maison Chocolat Guérin-Boutron, Paris 74
Mak Remissa, 9, 188, 228

Marchal, Henri, 93, 110–11, 214
Marseille Colonial Exhibition (1922), 59
May, Sharon, 196–97
McCullin, Don, 170
McDermott, John, 22, 205
Mekong River, 24, 34, 39, 52, 64, 80, 97, 108, 126, 149, 195
Meng Kimlong, 17, 213
Meta House, 210, 237
Mizerski, Jim, 8, 38
Monivong, King Sisowath (1875–1941), 31, 76, 79, 94
montage (photo technique), 9, 21, 22, 59, 81, 87, 112, 132, 135, 161, 243
Morales, Hanna Reyes, 232
Moride, Mr., 110
Muan, Ingrid, 188
Musée Albert Sarraut. *See* National Museum of Cambodia
music/musicians, 18, 36, 45, 104, 105, 112, 123, 124, 132, 138, 144, 153, 184, 192, 196, 210, 232, 241

N
Naradipo, Prince, trial of, 151
National Army of Democratic Forces (NADK), 198
National Geographic, 142, 194
national identity, 17–18, 240; symbols of, 20–21
National Museum of Cambodia, Phnom Penh, 60, 73
National Sports Complex, Phnom Penh, 130–31
Neak Sophal, 233
Nem Sengheang, 9
Neveu, Roland, 172–73
New Cambodian Artists (NCA), 210, 238
Nhek Dim, 241
Nhem En, 18, 174, 186, 242
Nhem Noeun, 167, 242
Noem Oem, 184, 242
Nomura Naotaro, 98
Norodom, King (1834–1904), 24–25, 30
Norodom Monineath (Monique) Sihanouk, 154–55, 242

Norodom Ranariddh, Prince (b. 1944), 17, 204, 206
Norodom Sihamoni, King (b. 1953), 210, 224
Norodom Sihanouk, King (1922–2012), 10, 12, 20, 94, 112, 114, 124, 144, 188, 200; death of, 210, 224–43, 242; and public profile through photography, 10, 12, 16, 95, 112–13, 114, 134, 240; and propaganda publishing, 134–35, 138, 178–79, 241; and visits to Angkor, 20, 158–59

O
"Operation Eagle Pull" (April 17, 1975), 146, 171, 172–73

P
Page, Tim, 17, 164, 188, 204, 243
Pailin, 56, 62, 83, 162, 209, 236
Paive, Auguste Jean-Marie, 24, 32, 62
Palgen-Maissoneuve, Mimijac, 15–16, 94, 107
Panh Rithy, 9, 210, 226
Panhavuth Sarpin, 227
Paris International Exposition (1931), 76, 87
Paris Peace Agreement (1991), 11, 17, 188
Parmentier, Henri, 52, 92, 240
Pech Sophea, 15, 230
Pen, 164
peoplescapes (photographic genre), 12–13
People's Army of Vietnam (PAVN), 19, 185
People's Republic of Kampuchea, 227
People's Republic of Kampuchea, 21–22
People's Socialist Community (Sangkum Reastr Niyum), 112
Perrot, Joseph Ferdinand, 19, 52
Pha Lina, 13, 17, 218
Phnom Krom, 106, 178
Phnom Kulen, 158
Phnom Oudong, 164
Phnom Penh: bombing of (1945), 97; citizen unrest, 213; colonial administrators, 40–41; festivals, 13, 141; infrastructure, 130–31; Khmer Rouge takeover/evacuation, 11, 18, 132, 146, 155, 163, 168, 171, 172–73, 174, 187, 228, 242; museums, 13, 60, 73; palace complex, 30–31, 51, 78–79; photography/studios, 24, 43, 52, 125, 134, 202, 240; political rallies, 144–45; Sangkum period, 12, 134–35, 144–45; schools, 128–29; shops/stores, 136; Sihanouk, 12, 20, 114; streetscapes, 66–67, 207; Toul Sleng (S-21) prison, 186, 236; transport, 99, 106; urban elite, 76; Vietnamese takeover, 19
Phnom Penh Post, 213, 216, 218
photographic series (photographic genre), 216–21, 228–29, 232–33
photojournalism (photographic genre), 12, 14; 16–17, 243
photomontage. *See* montage
Photo Phnom Penh Festival, 210
Pol Pot (1925–98), Khmer Rouge leader, 17, 174, 236; death of, 17, 188, 209
Ponleau Kampuchea Foundation, 230
portraiture (photographic genre), 12, 14–15, 19, 38, 42, 52, 55, 56, 68, 75
postcards, 13, 48, 55, 59, 70, 87, 142, 240
Prasat Andeat, 121
Prasat Phnom Ba Yong, 120
Preah Khan, 70
propaganda (photographic genre), 13, 21, 94, 158, 174, 192; magazines, 198

R
Rama Family Archive, 237
refugee camps, Thai-Cambodian border, 188, 193, 196–97, 200, 243
Reyum Institute of Arts and Culture, Phnom Penh, 15, 18, 188, 240
Ros, Ray, 8–9
Royal Cambodian Armed Forces (FARK), photographers, 16, 130, 134, 156, 242
Royal Palace, Phnom Penh, 30–31, 48, 52, 70, 78–79; Chanchhaya Pavilion, 144; Phochani Pavilion, 50–51
Royal University of Fine Arts (RUFA), Phnom Penh, 215, 217, 220, 232, 233

Royal University of Phnom Penh, 210
Ruijzendaal, Bob (NCA), 238
Russia/Russians, 176, 190, 202

S

Saigon, 11, 24, 29, 55, 59, 71, 89, 97, 149, 171
Salle Issa (aka Sales Isa), 126
Salles, André, 42
Sam Veasna Center for Wildlife Conservation (SVC), 233
Sambor Prei Kuk, 229
Sanders, August, 198,
Sangkum Reastr Niyum. *See* People's Socialist Community
Sarraut, Albert (governor-general), 13
Sauvy-Tisseyre, Elisabeth, 76, 81
Second Indochina War (1955–75), 204
Service d'information française (SPI), 94, 100, 104, 108
Shanghai, 18, 89, 174, 178, 242
Sharp, Bruce, 17, 207
Shearer, D. L., 171
Siem Reap, 8, 21, 52, 76, 86, 96, 106, 121, 127, 142, 167, 174, 210, 214
Sihamoni, King. *See* Norodom Sihamoni, King
Sihanouk, King. *See* Norodom Sihanouk, King
Singapore, 26, 120, 132
Sirik Matak, Prince (1914–75), 146
Sisophon Province, 52
Sisowath, Prince, 31. *See also* Monivong, King Sisowath
Smith, Heide, 203
social media, 13, 18, 210, 212, 218
Socialism/socialist, 12, 17, 21 112, 130, 176, 188, 199, 201
sompot chong kben (traditional garment), 48, 75
Son Sen, politician, 15, 236
Sorn Samnang, 203
Sorn Soran, 8
Sou Vichith, 16, 146, 163
Sovan Philong, 216
Soviets/Soviet Union, 17, 94, 200, 203, 227
Spratt, "Jack" Edwin, 149

Srin Sokmean, 210
SS *Cambodge*, 142
State of Cambodia, 17, 188
State Palace, Chamkar Mon, 134
still life (photographic genre), 12, 15–16, 94, 107
stills photographer, 125
Studio Laor Penh Chet, 202
studio portraits (photographic genre), 6, 37, 38, 43, 48, 49, 57, 202, 223, 241–42, 243
Stung-Treng, 16, 46–47
Suravarman II, King (r. 1113–50), 20
Surel, 104
Svay Rieng, 207
Swedish-Cambodian Friendship Association, 183

T

Tajasque, Albert, 16, 24, 34, 46–47
Takeo Province, 233, 239
Tea Kim Heang, 146, 155, 160, 171, 242
Thai border, 11, 17, 192, 193, 237
Thailand, 56, 96, 127, 200, 233
Third Indochina (Vietnamese-Cambodian) War (intermittent 1975–91), 199
Thomson, John, 8, 14, 24, 26, 29
Thong Veasna, 14, 165
ting mong (puppets), 153
Tonlé Sap (lake), 13, 76, 80, 106, 108, 126, 143, 178, 203
Toul Sleng (S-21) Genocide Prison, 11, 15, 18, 19, 174, 184, 186, 188, 210, 238, 242. *See also* Khmer Rouge, identity photography
Toul Sleng (S-21) Prison Museum, 19, 236
Toutain-Dorbec, Pierre, 14, 188, 193
trade cards, 74
transport, 207: bicycle trolley (*remorque-kong*), 99, 106, 168–69; boat/canoe/punt, 40, 64, 116, 229; buffalo/bullock cart, 32, 54, 143, 154; car, 65; elephant, 26–27, 30, 39, 63, 203; motorbike, 215, 228; motorbike trolley (*remorque-moto*), 99, 194; trishaw (*cyclo-pousse*), 99

U

UNESCO Memory of the World (MOW) Register, 19
UNESCO World Heritage site, 22
United Nations: intervention, 10, 17, 22, 188; peacekeeping force, 203, 207; refugee resettlement, 10, 188; sponsored elections, 10, 188, 204, 206
United Nations Transitional Authority in Cambodia (UNTAC), 195, 204, 212
United States, 112, 171, 188, 200; aid, 115, 154
United States Information Service (USIS), 241; and *Free World*, 241

V

Van Molyvann, 20, 131
Varoqui, Raymond, 94
Vat Tep Pranam, Buddha, 93
Vickery, Michael, 112, 116, 162
Vietcong, 21, 112, 161
Vietnam/Vietnamese army/regime, 11, 16, 17, 19, 21, 112, 161, 174, 185, 187, 188, 190, 192, 194, 198, 199, 200, 201, 203, 243
Vink, John, 17, 234–35
Vishnu (Hindu god), 20, 60, 61, 120, 121
Vong Sopheak, 232
Vuth Lyno, 210, 221

W

Wat Banan, 29
Wat Phnom, 39
Wat Preah Ath Roes, 164
Watkins, Huw, 206
Wertheimer, Odile, 139
Wetterwald, Jean-Noel, 16, 195
White, Peter T., 194
Widener, Jeff, 17, 188, 199
Wong Maye-E., 224
World War I (1914–18), 12, 62, 63, 67, 76, 79, 85, 86
World War II (1939–45), 10, 14, 15, 76, 94, 96, 104, 108, 110, 112, 130

Y

Yap, Irene, 214
Yin Someth, 223

"Books to Span the East and West"

Tuttle Publishing was founded in 1832 in the small New England town of Rutland, Vermont [USA]. Our core values remain as strong today as they were then—to publish best-in-class books which bring people together one page at a time. In 1948, we established a publishing office in Japan—and Tuttle is now a leader in publishing English-language books about the arts, languages and cultures of Asia. The world has become a much smaller place today and Asia's economic and cultural influence has grown. Yet the need for meaningful dialogue and information about this diverse region has never been greater. Over the past seven decades, Tuttle has published thousands of books on subjects ranging from martial arts and paper crafts to language learning and literature—and our talented authors, illustrators, designers and photographers have won many prestigious awards. We welcome you to explore the wealth of information available on Asia at **www.tuttlepublishing.com.**

Published by Tuttle Publishing, an imprint of Periplus Editions (HK) Ltd

www.tuttlepublishing.com

Copyright © 2022 Nicholas Coffill
Cambodian history advisor: Darryl Collins
Text: Nicholas Coffill
Text advisor: Julian Davison

All rights reserved. No part of this publication may be reproduced or utilized in any form or by any means, electronic or mechanical, including photocopying, recording, or by any information storage and retrieval system, without prior written permission from the publisher.

ISBN: 978-0-8048-5440-5

Distributed by
North America, Latin America & Europe
Tuttle Publishing
364 Innovation Drive
North Clarendon, VT 05759-9436 U.S.A.
Tel: 1 (802) 773-8930; Fax: 1 (802) 773-6993
info@tuttlepublishing.com; www.tuttlepublishing.com

Asia Pacific
Berkeley Books Pte. Ltd.
3 Kallang Sector #04-01
Singapore 349278
Tel: (65) 6741-2178; Fax: (65) 6741-2179
inquiries@periplus.com.sg; www.tuttlepublishing.com

Printed in China   2201EP
25 24 23 22   10 9 8 7 6 5 4 3 2 1

TUTTLE PUBLISHING® is a registered trademark of Tuttle Publishing, a division of Periplus Editions (HK) Ltd.

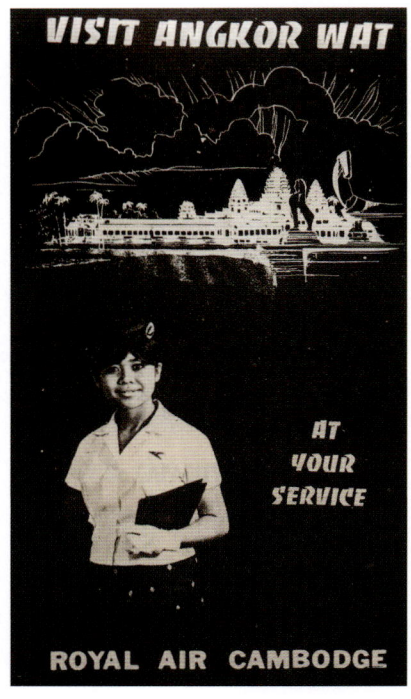

Visit Angkor Wat. Royal Air Cambodge. Advertisement. *Kambuja Illustrated Monthly Review.* May 15, 1967. Artist unknown. Center for Khmer Studies Library, Siem Reap.

"Being able to go about with a camera and seize an intimate moment of life that will never really happen again, with emotions that cannot be exactly repeated: This is what fascinates me."

Siv Serey. Conversations with Michelle Vachon. "Photographer Captures Intimacy of Daily Life in Cambodia." *Cambodian Daily*. 2017.

"In the last half of this century Indochina came to us in snapshots that lodged in our consciousness like hot metal in a wound."

Tad Bartimus. In *Requiem: By the Photographers Who Died In Vietnam and Indochina*. Horst Faas and Tim Page. Random House. New York. 1997.

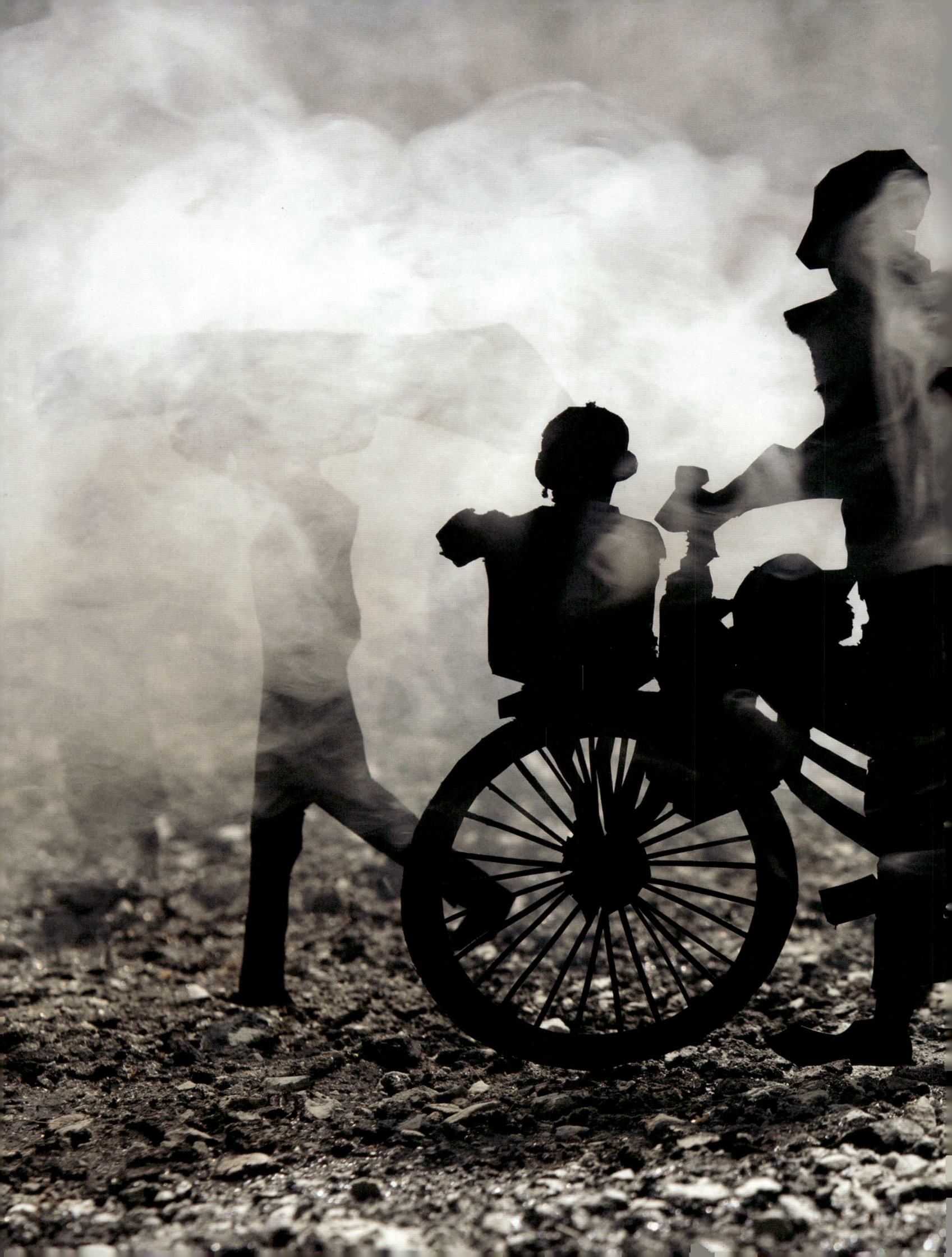